ESSAYS IN ECONOMICS

THE PAPERS OF JAMES TOBIN

Volume 1 *Essays in Economics: Macroeconomics,* revised edition, New York: North-Holland, 1976

Volume 2 *Essays in Economics: Consumption and Econometrics,* New York: North-Holland, 1975

Volume 3 *Essays in Economics: Theory and Policy,* Cambridge, MA: MIT Press, 1982

ESSAYS IN ECONOMICS
Theory and Policy

James Tobin

The MIT Press
Cambridge, Massachusetts
London, England

This book was set in VIP Times Roman by DEKR Corporation and printed and bound in the United States of America.

Library of Congress Cataloging in Publication Data

Tobin, James, 1918–
    Essays in economics, theory and policy.

    (The papers of James Tobin; v. 3)
    Includes bibliographical references.
    1. Economics—Addresses, essays, lectures.   I. Title.   II. Series: Tobin, James, 1918–
Papers of James Tobin; v. 3.
HB171.T63   330   81-20784
ISBN O-262-20042-2   AACR2

CONTENTS

PREFACE

The papers in this volume were mostly written and published since 1974, although several earlier ones, including one (chapter 24) not previously published, are included. This is the third volume of my professional papers in economics, collected under the general title *Essays in Economics*; volume 1 bore the subtitle *Macroeconomics* (Chicago: Markham, 1971; revised edition New York: North-Holland, 1974); volume 2, the subtitle *Consumption and Econometrics* (New York: North-Holland, 1975). The three volumes do not encompass less scholarly essays on economic policy intended for a popular audience. I have previously published a collection of such papers in *National Economic Policy* (New Haven: Yale University Press, 1966).

The bulk of the present volume, parts I–III, consists of papers in macroeconomics written after the preparation of volume 1. Exceptions are chapters 7, 12, and 18. These are earlier papers now included because they are substantively related to the later articles with which they are grouped.

Part IV gathers together five articles on welfare and inequality. These are related both to my interest as an economist in these subjects and my concern as a citizen with welfare and tax reforms, and with policies to diminish poverty, discrimination, and inequality. Consequently they are close to, perhaps even beyond, the line separating professional papers from popular policy-oriented pieces that these volumes were designed to respect. If any of them cross the line, I hope the reader will excuse me, and perhaps also for chapter 14 in part III, which combines economic analysis, statistical narrative, and political opinion.

Part V is of a different character altogether. The essays, either book reviews or memoirs, concern six distinguished economists.

The monetary papers of part I fall into three groups. The first four expound, and apply to the stagflationary economy of the 1970s, a framework for monetary analysis set forth in a number of the essays published in volume 1. I stress the systematic variation and unpredictable volatility of the velocity of monetary aggregates, the persistence of inflationary trends in the face of monetary contraction, the importance of equity prices in the climate for real investment, the effects of monetary policy on equity prices, and the misleading nature of simplistic real interest rate computations when, as in the case of OPEC price increases, consumer price inflation overstates the dollar returns to operational investments. Chapter 4 uses financial data for a sample of corporations to trace the changing weights of growth, cyclicality, debt, dividend payout, and other factors in security market valuations, and from these weights computes an index of the cost of capital for business investment.

"Keynesian" has become a bad word. Politicians and pundits, who probably have never read J. M. Keynes, blame his economics for all the discontents of the day. Economic theorists who have read Keynes find his influence at the root of mammoth analytic errors. As a beginner in economics in college I cut my teeth on Keynes's *General Theory*. Over the forty-odd years since, I have been a friendly critic or a critical friend. I have tried to play some part in correcting, amending, extending, and generalizing Keynes's analysis, and in constructing the "neoclassical synthesis" of Keynesian and price-theoretic traditions in macroeconomics. In part I, the message of chapters 5 and 6 is that neither recent economic history nor latter-day classical counter-revolutions in economic theory have rendered obsolete the central propositions of Keynesian macroeconomics. [This is the theme of my book *Asset Accumulation and Economic Activity* (Oxford: Basil Blackwell; and Chicago: University of Chicago Press, 1980).]

An earlier controversy in monetary theory was provoked by Milton Friedman's brand of monetarism, beginning in the mid-1960s. I entered the lists, perhaps all too often, as the eclectic Keynesian challenging the extreme theoretical and empirical claims of Friedman and other monetarists. Chapters 7–9 continue a sequence of articles republished in volume 1. Chapter 7 questions on empirical grounds Friedman's "permanent income" theory of the demand for money; he abandoned the theory about the same time—probably not because of this article! In 1970–1971 Friedman, responding to widespread and long-unsatisfied interest, published in the *Journal of Political Economy* two articles expounding the conceptual and theoretical basis of his monetarist doctrines. Chapter 8 was my contribution to the subsequent symposium. At issue is whether fiscal policies and other nonmonetary shocks can, in the absence of accommodative changes in money supplies, systematically alter aggregate demand, output, and prices. I argued against Friedman's essentially negative answer. Chapter 9 is a sequel in the same controversy, questioning a back-up monetarist position that fiscal policies have transient effects that are wiped out in time by the growth of public debt.

The first two chapters of part II continue the same subject: the effects of fiscal and monetary policies, short run and long run, on output, prices, interest rates, and capital formation. The more ambitious is chapter 11, a thorough-going exposition of the macroeconomic theory of an economy with three imperfectly substitutable kinds of assets available to savers, namely, money, bonds, and capital.

In chapter 13 Martin Baily and I considered whether public service employment or wage subsidies to private employers could be expected to increase employment in aggregate. The obvious affirmative answers are naive, and "natural rate" theories suggest that these interventions will not alter employment or unemployment, only their distribution. Our verdict was cautiously optimistic. Chapter 14 takes a nonapocalyptic view of the size and growth of the public sector in the United States and argues against freezing fiscal rules into the Constitution. I wrote chapters 15 and 16 while spending the year 1972–1973 at the University of Nairobi, Kenya; they seek to use economic analysis on matters that were in the forefront of professional and public discussions of policy at the time. Chapter 17 reprints the attempt my colleague Bill Nordhaus and I made to conceptualize and illustrate a national Measure of Economic Welfare. The approach turned out to be popular not only in this country but in Japan and elsewhere. Much more ambitious and thorough statistical efforts to construct measures of this kind are in process.

My interest in international monetary economics and policies owes a great deal to my friend and colleague Robert Triffin, and to my special responsibilities on these matters when I served on President Kennedy's Council of Economic Advisers in the early 1960s. The framework of chapter 18 is one of my reactions to the problems of balance of payments adjustment, and to the conflicts of interest these problems generate between countries. The floating exchange rate regime of the 1970s changed the game; the problems and conflicts are the same but show up in different guises. My offbeat reform proposal is set forth in chapter 20. Preceding it is a theoretical article on exchange rates, which extends to an international setting the macroeconomic modeling framework of chapter 11.

In part IV, four of the five essays were related to a crusade that engaged me in the mid-1960s. In addition to structural antipoverty strategies—measures to preserve and improve human capital and to assure equal opportunity—I favored, as I do now, some income redistribution via taxes and transfers. A national negative income tax seemed, as it does now, a very good way to accomplish humanitarian goals while minimizing perverse incentives with respect to work, family stability, and migration. Chapter 24 goes one step further by integrating welfare transfers or "negative taxes" with the regular positive income tax. Chapter 25, given as the Henry Simons Lecture at the University of Chicago

Law School in 1970, is on a different but related subject. It is interesting that public sentiment in a democracy demands egalitarian distribution of some goods and services and some obligations while also tolerating and even welcoming vast differences in total income and wealth.

As a student and practitioner of economics, I have always enjoyed reading what economists said about each other and discovering the human side of the authors whose scientific works I studied. Biographical portraits by Keynes, Schumpeter, and Samuelson are works of art, revealing of the artists as well as of their subjects. Though their examples inspire me to include part V in this collection, I do not pretend to join their league.

Alvin Hansen was for me a teacher and mentor, and then for another quarter-century a friend. Kermit Gordon, my contemporary, I knew for many years prior to an intimate working relation in Washington in 1961–1962, which cemented a close friendship for the rest of his life. Harry Johnson was also a very good friend from 1948 until his death in 1977, though mostly at a distance after our common experiences in early postwar Cambridge, England. Paul Douglas I knew less well but admired from afar. The other two are fortunately still living. The brief piece on Milton Friedman, on the occasion of his Nobel award, speaks my genuine admiration of his scientific contributions, transcending the dissents from his monetary theories and policies expressed elsewhere. A long friendship with Ken Galbraith, characterized fundamentally by mutual respect, has survived irreverent disagreements of the kind expressed in my book review (chapter 31).

Several of the essays were, as indicated in the contents, written jointly with others. I thank all my coauthors both for their pleasant and fruitful collaborations and for their consents to publish our joint work in this volume. As on many previous occasions, including the two previous collections of essays, the help of my secretary, Mrs. Laura Harrison, has been indispensable. I am grateful to the MIT Press for suggesting the assembly of another volume and for patiently putting it together. Finally, I acknowledge with thanks permissions to reprint here articles originally published in *American Economic Review*, American Enterprise Institute, American Philosophical Society, Ballinger Publishing Co., The British Academy, Brookings Institution, *Daedalus, Eastern Africa Economic Review, Economic Inquiry, The Economist*, The Industrial Conference Board, *Journal of Development Economics, Journal of Finance, Journal of Law and Economics*, Michigan State University, the MIT Press, National Bureau of Economic Research, North-Holland Publishing Co., Princeton University Press, *Quarterly Journal of Economics, Southern Economic Journal, Yale Law Journal*, and *The Yale Review*.

Part I
MONETARY THEORY AND POLICY

Reprint from *Southern Economic Journal*
Volume 44   Number 3   January 1978

Monetary Policies and the Economy: The Transmission Mechanism*

JAMES TOBIN
Yale University

I. Introduction

My subject is the process by which monetary policies are transmitted into changes in expenditures for Gross National Product. My account will be selective, and far from complete. I will concentrate on certain links between financial variables and demands for goods and services. I will say relatively little about the other part of the story, how the various instruments at the disposal of the central bank affect the financial variables. I don't have time to do both, and the proximate mechanisms of monetary control seem to me to be less important and less controversial.

As to controversy, it will be clear to you that I am presenting an account of the transmission process which is an alternative to monetarism. But I have, for the most part, resisted the temptation to point out the differences of view, preferring to let you the listeners infer them from my exposition of my own theories. It will suffice to remark at the outset that I clearly do not subscribe to the prevalent view that what the central bank does is to control the money supply, which *in turn* determines money income and prices. I would say instead that the central bank controls some short-term money-market interest rates and/or reserve aggregates and that these variables simultaneously affect other interest rates and financial quantities, GNP expenditures, *and* monetary aggregates.

Much of what I shall argue is not new but old-fashioned. I refer particularly to the attention I shall give in the second and third parts of the paper to credit, as distinct from money, i.e., to the asset, as well as the liability, accounts of commercial banks and other intermediaries. The first section concerns the link between asset valuations and capital spending. The second

*Invited address, Southern Economic Association meetings, Atlanta, Georgia, October 18, 1976. I am indebted to William Brainard and John Ciccolo for help with this paper.

Reprinted by permission from *Southern Economic Journal* 44(3) (January 1978):421–431.

3

section deals with ways in which credit availabilities affect the spending of liquidity-constrained households and firms. The final section concerns some implications of the role of commercial banks in financing the working capital requirements of business customers.

II. Asset Valuation and Capital Spending

In 1965 the bond and stock markets valued the real capital of U.S. nonfinancial corporations at almost 170% of its replacement cost. In 1974, the same ratio was 75%.[1] In 1966 fixed nonresidential investment was 10% of the capital stock, valued at replacement cost. In 1975, it was 8%. The figures are illustrative of a general positive correlation between the market value/replacement cost ratio and the rate of investment.

The correlation is scarcely surprising. As Keynes wrote in *The General Theory*,

> . . . The daily revaluations of the Stock Exchange, though they are primarily made to facilitate transfers of old investments between one individual and another, inevitably exert a decisive influence on the rate of current investment. For there is no sense in building up a new enterprise at a cost greater than that at which a similar existing enterprise can be purchased; whilst there is an inducement to spend on a new project what may seem an extravagant sum, if it can be floated off on the Stock Exchange at an immediate profit. [3, 151]

The ratio of market value to replacement cost is a summary measure of one important impact of financial markets on purchases of goods and services, in particular durable goods. I have, not very imaginatively, called the ratio q, and a couple of irreverent former students have given me a gaudy T-shirt with the legend "q is all that matters" in front and the team identification "Yale School" in back. Well, q is not *all* that matters, but it does matter. I would say the same for M.

In equilibrium q has a normal value—one in a purely competitive economy with constant returns to scale—which sustains capital replacement and expansion at the natural growth rate of the economy. In practice, even leaving aside statistical quirks, the normal value exceeds one by the capitalized value of rents or monopoly profits. In the short run, events, policies, and expectations move q up and down, creating or destroying incentives for capital investment. Among those determinants is monetary policy. It is certainly not the only factor. But whether the central bank is seeking to influence investment spending on its own, or merely to counter other disturbances, q is an indicator it should watch.

1. These are estimates made by Professor John Ciccolo of Boston College. The estimates of the Council of Economic Advisers [2] are 136% for 1965 and 84% for 1974. The two series agree in general contour, but the CEA series has smaller variance.

The theory is simple and straightforward. One way to look at q is that it represents the comparison between, on the one hand, the marginal efficiency of capital, the internal rate of return on investment at its cost in the commodity markets, and on the other, the financial cost of capital, the rate at which investors discount the future returns from such investment. In pages of the *General Theory* other than the one cited, Keynes gave the misleading impression that investment is inversely related to the level of "*the* rate of interest." His condition that the marginal efficiency of capital equal the interest rate determines the equilibrium *stock* of capital. In such a long-run equilibrium, net investment will be zero in a stationary economy, or in a growth equilibrium enough to expand the capital stock at the natural growth rate. In Keynesian short runs, marginal efficiency of capital and interest rate diverge. Investment is related to the difference or ratio of the two rates rather than to their absolute levels.

How can they ever diverge? Why doesn't arbitrage always close instantaneously any incipient gap between the present value of returns from investment projects, calculated with market discount rates, and their cost? What keeps the rate of investment within finite bounds when q exceeds one, or above zero when q falls short? Why, in other words, is the stock of capital ever out of equilibrium relative to the interest rate?

The answer surely is that investment takes time and that the acquisition and installation of capital goods costs more, both on average and on the margin, for both individual firms and the economy at large, the faster the capital stock is expanded. If these adjustment costs are added to the normal costs of the capital goods, then a q-like ratio so calculated may always be 1, but it takes variation in the speed of investment to keep it so. I trust that this explanation will satisfy purists who cannot bring themselves to believe that arbitrage opportunities can stand, even temporarily, as incompletely exploited incentives. Personally, I think that can happen, simply because it takes time for those individuals and bureaucracies in a position to exploit such opportunities to act.

An economy-wide calculation of q conceals the immense variation of the ratios for individual firms and diverse capital goods. When aggregate q is low, many firms and many kinds of capital bear q's which discourage all gross investment, even for replacement. But gross investment cannot be negative. The frequency of firms in this position is smaller when aggregate q is high. This non-linearity of aggregation reinforces the economy-wide relation of investment and q.[2]

What is "the interest rate" whose divergence from the marginal efficiency of capital regulates investment? It is the discount rate implicit in the market valuation of securities which are claims to the capital stock and its future

2. See [4] for more discussion of the relationship of q to investment and for some disaggregated estimates of q.

earnings. It is a rate appropriate for valuation of streams of future returns with the time patterns, uncertainties, and covariances of business cash flows. It is not the interest rate on long-term government bonds, or even on long-term corporate bonds, or any other interest rate on fixed-money-value contracts. Here Keynes in the *General Theory* misled readers who took literally a convenient simplifying assumption. Since businesses are at least partly financed by shareowners, the rate required to induce them to take the risks of equity capital is clearly relevant.

The true financial cost of capital is some combination of bond, equity, and other rates. It cannot be represented by any single rate. The full cost of bond finance, for example, cannot be calculated without allowing for the effects of additional indebtedness on share prices. We do not have to follow Modigliani and Miller in their contention that one financial structure for the corporation is as cheap as any other. All we need is the proposition that if the optimal allocation of finance among equity, bonded debt, and other liabilities has been attained, the cost of additional finance on the margin is the same for all financial sources in use. Since the optimal financial structure will differ from one firm to another, so will the relevant mix of market rates.

How does the central bank affect the cost of capital and q? Its influence is indirect but powerful. It operates through a chain, or network, of asset substitutions. Corporate bonds and equities are imperfect substitutes for each other and for other assets in the portfolios of many investors. The other assets include deposits in banks and other intermediaries, and short-term Treasury or commercial paper. The central bank operates in the first instance on the rates on short-term fixed-money-value instruments. Via portfolio substitutions, affected both by the current levels of these rates and by expectations of their future paths, monetary operations are transmitted to bond rates and equity yields.

The linkage is loose, and there is plenty of opportunity for slippage. Events and shocks other than monetary policies affect the cost of capital. Consider, for example, increase in generally perceived uncertainties of business earnings, or diminished willingness of investing individuals and institutions to take these risks. The cost of capital will rise, q will fall, independently of monetary policy. Of course, the ratio q will also vary, independently of monetary policy, as estimates of future earnings change. These are systematically related to other economic variables, but Keynes rightly emphasized also the subjectivity and volatility of the marginal efficiency of capital.

Business firms making investment decisions are interested in the q for specific incremental investments, not in the average q for the firm, much less for the whole economy. The relevant comparison is this: An investment costing a million dollars in the commodity markets is considered. When the prospective earnings are evaluated by the securities market, will they add at least a million dollars to the value of the firm? If so, the investment can be

undertaken—financed by some combination of security issues and retained earnings—without decreasing, but possibly increasing, the equity of the existing shareholders.

It is easy to imagine cases where marginal q's differ from average. Indeed, if capital investment were generally Schumpeterian in nature, embodying new processes or products that render existing capital, perhaps also existing firms, obsolete, this would typically be the case. Less dramatic examples are the following: Increases in energy costs or anti-pollution standards simultaneously lower the average q's of energy-using industries while raising the marginal q's for energy-saving or environmental-protecting investments. An increase in tax credit for new investments raises marginal more than average q's.

Since it is average q's that can be most easily estimated statistically, their usefulness depends on a reliable relationship of average q's to unobserved marginal q's. Confidence in such regularity will be much greater if most investments involve capital goods which are close substitutes for existing stocks. This is an empirical matter. Econometrically, there is a good relationship of investment to q's, with lags distributed over eight quarters and with an elasticity of about .8 [1].

As previous remarks already suggest, we make an even stronger abstraction of aggregation in speaking of one "q" for the economy as a whole than in speaking of "*the* rate of interest." Estimating q's for a cross section of individual companies with listed stocks, my colleague William Brainard and I found the standard deviation to be only slightly less than the mean value [4[. The concept can also be applied outside the corporate sector. Existing houses, for example, are traded and valued in a thriving market. The valuations presumably reflect a capitalization of future net rentals, actual or imputed. The incentive for new building can be measured by comparing the value of old homes with the cost of building new ones. The new ones won't be duplicates of the old, but will be close functional substitutes. We could expect residential investment to be sensitive to the housing q. Probably, as Keynes suggested, the valuation of houses depends on expected rentals and the mortgage rate; but other factors—rationing of mortgage credit, taxes, expected inflation in real estate prices—are also relevant. A similar mechanism applies for automobiles and other consumer durables.

I turn now to the effects of inflationary expectations on q. The first approximation is that there are none. This answer applies for a change in expected inflation which applies to the future prices of all commodities, does not alter expectations of relative prices or other real magnitudes, and is fully reflected in nominal interest rates and discount factors. After all, the goods value of claims to goods should be independent of the money price of goods. But there are several other factors leading to somewhat contradictory modifications of the first answer. Given the real quantity of money or of the

monetary base, an increase of expected inflation lowers the real interest rate on money, pulls other real interest rates down in sympathy, and raises q. The neutrality of the conventional story—which says that nominal interest rates rise point-for-point with expected inflation—requires restrictive monetary intervention by the central bank. There are other reasons why a change in the inflation rate will not be neutral, given the overlap of debts, tax valuations, and other dollar magnitudes geared to the old inflation rate. One reason for non-neutrality of great current relevance in the United States is the following: If the public believes that inflation will induce strong deflationary counter-measures by the central bank, it is understandable why inflationary news is bad for the stock market and for q.

One warning I would like to emphasize: Naive calculations of Fisherian real rates of interest are very unreliable indicators of financial incentives for real investment. It is easy to subtract moving averages of inflation rates from nominal interest rates on bonds, bills, and loans and obtain zero or negative real rates. The fallacy is the implicit assumption that at those nominal rates actual live borrowers have, or perceive themselves as having, operational opportunities to earn without risk dollar returns equalling or exceeding those rates of inflation. If such opportunities had been available during recent double-digit inflation, there would not have been a stock market collapse which took q down to .7 or a collapse of residential construction. It is not in fact possible to invest in the GNP Deflator or to hoard the basket of goods, services, and taxes valued by the Consumer Price Index. Moreover, I repeat my earlier point that the absolute level of interest rates is of no particular consequence by itself. It is important only in comparison with the marginal efficiency of capital. Although this is in the long run governed by such funda-mental factors as technology and capital/labor ratios, in the short run it is, as Keynes emphasized, a highly variable and psychological magnitude. It is hard to imagine any proposition more divorced from experience than the cur-rently fashionable proposition that marginal efficiency of capital and real interest rates are always equal to each other and constant.

III. Liquidity Constraints and Credit Policy

In the theory I have just outlined, I have spoken as if savers and investors choose freely among alternative financial and real assets, taking long or short positions constrained only by their net worth and the balance sheet identities. I also assumed implicitly that asset markets are cleared by adjustments of asset prices and yields. While I do not think the story I told is misleading, it does miss important features of the transmission of monetary impulses to demands for GNP. The features I have in mind fall under the general heading of liquidity constraints.

An individual is potentially liquidity-constrained if he possesses wealth which he can spend only at certain dates in the future, or if he can substitute current for future spending only at an interest cost in excess of what he can earn by postponing spending. Effective liquidity constraints are the combined effects of two things: (1) the nature of certain forms of wealth and of the markets, if any, in which they are traded, and (2) the time and risk preferences of the wealth-owner. For example, human capital is an illiquid asset; for good reasons, the opportunities for borrowing against, or selling shares in, future labor incomes are extremely limited. Most workers, nonetheless, are not liquidity-constrained; they would not choose to mortgage future wages even if they could do so at prevailing interest rates; they voluntarily choose a lifetime consumption pattern which implies positive net worth in non-human capital. But many households, mainly the young and the poor, are at corners of maximum current consumption; they would borrow more and spend more today if they could. Prospective social security benefits and other retirement pensions are another illiquid asset; many workers can consume such wealth now by restricting other kinds of saving, but for many others payroll taxes and pension contributions fall fully on consumption.

Over the past thirty years, some structural trends in our financial system have increased the likelihood of liquidity constraints, and others have reduced it. In the first category is the vast increase in compulsory or semi-compulsory provision for retirement. In the second is the increased availability of mortgage credit and consumer credit, both of which by making homes and consumer durables more liquid assets serve to increase the intertemporal fungibility of wages and salaries. Home mortgage debt has risen from 20% to more than 40% of the value of the housing stock, and in a number of recent years mortgage indebtedness has risen by more than the increment in value of the stock. Outstanding consumer credit has risen from 15% to 60% of the value of the stock of consumer durables, and the fraction of new purchases covered by new debt is now ⅔ instead of ⅓.

Liquidity-constrained consumers behave as if they have short horizons, measured in weeks or months or years rather than decades or lifetimes. They will spend any increment of liquid resources within those short horizons, rather than diluting the impact by spreading the resources thinly over many years. That is why tax reductions, even if temporary, are more powerful than is implied by a model which relates consumption solely to fully fungible lifetime wealth. That is why the distribution of tax cuts, rebates, and other windfalls has an important bearing on the strength of the consumption response.

More to our present point, that is why monetary policies and events which relax or tighten liquidity constraints are especially powerful, beyond what would be expected by considering marginal responses to changes in interest rates and asset prices. Liquidity-constrained borrowers spend every cent they are permitted to borrow, or every cent they can raise by asset sales; they do

9

not require the inducement of lower interest rates, and they are not borrowing just to reshuffle their portfolios of financial assets and liabilities. There are several mechanisms at work here. I give three examples. (1) Lending institutions adjust down payments, collateral requirements, amortization speeds, and credit standards as their own costs of funds vary. (2) The terms of trade credit, and their enforcement, vary in the same way. (3) There are always some individuals who by circumstances or choice are spending the proceeds of liquidity or borrowing against variable-price assets; the amount of their spending depends directly on the value of those assets, which in turn depends on monetary policy.

Many businesses, like many households, are liquidity-constrained. The pace of their real investment, whether in working capital or fixed capital, is limited by their cash flow and the credit they can obtain. Their own estimate of the marginal efficiency of such capital exceeds the interest rate on such loans. Perhaps they are unobjectively optimistic; perhaps they are risk-lovers instead of risk-averters. In any case their borrowing is limited by collateral and margin requirements rather than by rates. Credit rationing is not necessarily a market imperfection. It is intrinsic to the difference of perspective between lender and borrower. As the lender cannot really control the borrower's use of the funds, there is no way the lender can make an actuarially sound loan simply by setting interest rates and letting the borrower decide how much to take. The implication is that there is almost always an "unsatisfied fringe of borrowers" at existing rates, and these borrowers are sure spenders. When easy money conditions diminish the cost of funds to banks and other lenders, extra lending to venturesome entrepreneurs is a powerful effect. An indirect mechanism by which risk-loving and liquidity-constrained businesses obtain finance, in amounts which likewise vary with general monetary conditions, is through trade credit extended by suppliers or customers who have credit ratings more acceptable to banks and other institutional lenders.

These mechanisms illuminate some phenomena of credit markets which participants in those markets understand much better than monetary theorists. A "credit crunch" is not just a time of high and rising interest rates. It is a time when some business customers of commercial banks find that they cannot fully use the credit lines they thought they had, that they cannot obtain the timely accommodation they presumably had paid for by good deposit behavior in the past. They are liquidity-constrained all of a sudden, in the sense that they need credit to carry out their investment and financial budgets. Of course many priority loan customers are partially or fully accommodated. They then displace mortgage and consumer credit applicants, many of whom are also liquidity-constrained. The upshot is that reductions in spending are exceptionally large for the interest rates nominally quoted.

The futility of "pushing on a string" is a refrain regularly heard from cen-

tral bankers around cyclical troughs. It's not a very good excuse for inaction if possible futility is the worst that can be said of an aggressive easy credit policy. But the refrain does make some sense. Just as the prevalence of liquidity-constrained unsatisfied borrowers in booms augments the power of tight money and credit crunches, so the relative absence of such borrowers in depressions and deep recessions weakens expansionary monetary policy. There is some merit to the view that in those times few credit-worthy households or firms are limiting spending for lack of liquidity. Once the system is thrown back on the marginal responses of unconstrained agents to reductions of interest rates, the gains from monetary actions are much less dramatic.

IV. Commercial Banks as Financial Intermediaries

These observations lead me to a general point about commercial banks, which are after all the institutions through which monetary policies are transmitted in the first instance and the institutions whose liabilities are the major component of money stock. Like other intermediaries, their business is to borrow from one set of people and lend to another. Their liabilities are tailored to the needs and preferences of their depositors, for safe, liquid, convenient, divisible, negotiable, fixed-money-value assets. Their assets are tailored to the needs and preferences of their borrowers, longer in maturity and often risky, lumpy, and illiquid. The function which banks and other intermediaries perform is to accommodate the borrowers at lower cost and easier terms than they could get by direct loans from the ultimate lenders, the depositors. Via the fractional reserve system, the central bank controls the availability and cost of credit to bank borrowers. It also controls the aggregate scale of banks' assets, and given the balance sheet identity, their monetary liabilities. The two sides of the T account rise and fall together, and it seems to me gratuitously one-sided to say that the importance of the banks' intermediary operations lies solely in the scale of their monetary liabilities. It is equally unfortunate to ignore the similar magic of transformation accomplished by intermediaries whose liabilities are arbitrarily defined as near-money rather than money.

Let me remind you of the tremendous change in the nature of commercial banking that has occurred since the second world war, a change which is really a return to the historic role of commercial banks. In 1950, loans to private borrowers were only a third of deposits, business loans less than a fifth, and half of deposits were invested in Treasury securities. In 1970, loans to private borrowers were almost ¾ of deposits, business loans about 30%, and Treasury securities had dwindled to ⅛. At the earlier date the banks were, in effect, custodians, simply sparing depositors the trouble of holding government debt directly. Now the banks are monetizing, if you like, the

11

debts of many private businesses and households who would otherwise be accommodated, if at all, at much higher rates. The real effects, both average and marginal, on GNP spending are certainly much more substantial.

The distinctive business of commercial banks is to finance the working capital of business, specifically their inventories of materials, goods in process, and finished products, the wages they must disburse prior to selling the produce of their labor, and their accounts receivable. To the extent that working capital is financed by bank loans, businesses can use their open-market sources of debt and equity capital to finance long-term capital accumulation. The working capital positions of individual businesses fluctuate seasonally and cyclically in many diverse patterns. In considerable degree, banks are the vehicle through which the temporary surpluses of some businesses, deposited in banks, finance the temporary deficits of others. In addition, of course, banks mobilize in deposits the fluctuating working balances of households.

The reciprocal relationship of business customers to banks, sometimes as depositors, sometimes as borrowers, is a central fact which exclusive emphasis on monetary aggregates obscures. The size of business deposits is payment for credit lines and credit accommodation when needed. The compensatory arrangements vary considerably in formality and tightness, but no one can doubt that they are there. It follows that holdings of deposits will be related, not just to the variables conventionally included in money demand relations, but also to past, present, and prospective use of bank credit by business depositor-customers, to the size of compensating balance requirements, and to the difference between the prime rate and the open-market commercial paper rate. I suspect that this relationship is a major part of the explanation of recent increases in the velocity of M_1 which are otherwise surprising. Over the past two years, until just recently, commercial lending by banks has declined, even in dollar value, partly because of the severity of the recession, partly because both business and banks have been shifting to more cautious and liquid balance sheets. The banks have allowed the differential of prime above the commercial paper rate to widen drastically. If this is correct, and if the process has run its course, the pleasant surprise which kept the Federal Reserve's conservative monetary growth targets from raising interest rates during the recovery to date may not recur in future years.

Let me conclude with some possibly controversial propositions that summarize my message. The institutional fact that our monetary supplies are predominantly "inside" rather than "outside" money is far from trivial. The system behaves quite differently from one in which monetary liabilities are subject to 100% reserves. When banks and other intermediaries monetize private debts, and indirectly the real capital asset holdings those debts finance, their economic impact is quite different from monetization of federal debt. Indeed inside money is, in this sense, more powerful stuff than outside money.

Attention to the process of financial intermediation has other implications, derived from the inevitable realization that borrowers and lender-depositors are different in economic behavior. The celebrated Pigou effect concerns the impact on spending of changes in the purchasing power of fixed-money-value assets. When the public is treated as homogeneous, and inside debts and credits are washed out, the base for the Pigou effect is reduced to the high-powered monetary base, the non-interest-bearing demand debt of the central government. But the neutrality assumed in the washing out of inside debts and credits is very implausible. Debtors are intrinsically bigger marginal spenders than creditors, and in this degree the effects of price level changes run counter to, and may dwarf, the conventional effect on the real value of the monetary base. In this observation I follow my great Yale precursor Irving Fisher, who emphasized the effect of price deflation on debt burdens as a factor intensifying, not cushioning, the depression.

A second implication of the approach I have sketched is that the effects of an expansion of monetary aggregates depends on how it is brought about. Here is another and final example. A common feature of various definitions of money is that the included assets have legally controlled interest rates. It is possible, therefore, to increase their supply by raising these rates, e.g., by allowing interest on demand deposits and lifting ceiling rates on savings deposits. Anyone who thinks an expansion thus induced has the same effects as one stimulated by open market purchases is mistaking appearance for substance. There really is no substitute for analysis which does justice to the significant institutional complexities of our monetary and financial institutions and markets.

References

1. Ciccolo, John. *Four Essays on Monetary Policy*, unpublished Ph.D. dissertation. Yale University, 1975, Essay III.

2. *Economic Report of the President 1977*. Washington: Government Printing Office, 1977, pp. 27–31.

3. Keynes, J. M. *The General Theory of Employment, Interest, and Money*. London and New York: Macmillan, 1936.

4. Tobin, James and William C. Brainard, "Asset Markets and the Cost of Capital," in *Economic Progress: Private Values and Public Policy* (Essays in Honor of William Fellner), edited by R. Nelson and B. Balassa. Amsterdam: North-Holland, 1977, 235–262.

13

MONETARY POLICY, INFLATION, AND UNEMPLOYMENT

WHAT DETERMINES THE rate of price inflation in an economy like ours? How is it related to unemployment? In particular, what is the role of monetary policy in controlling inflation and unemployment?

Economists differ among themselves on these questions, and recent history contains unpleasant surprises for all theories and forecasting models. But even more striking than differences within our profession is the gulf between economists and the informed lay public — businessmen, financiers, journalists, politicans — in their views of the inflationary process and the mechanisms by which "money" and Federal Reserve policy affect the economy. In the hope of bridging this gulf, I seek here to set forth economists' approaches to these questions.

I shall try in the course of the paper to outline the major disagreements among economists, between monetarists and neo-Keynesians. But I cannot pretend to be a neutral rapporteur. I am not a monetarist. I am, if I must be labeled, a neo-Keynesian. Truth in packaging requires this advance disclosure. Nevertheless, I shall hope to show that some reconciliation of the two approaches is possible, and that differences in policy recommendations arise more from differences of objectives than from disagreements about mechanisms.

"Inflation is at all times and everywhere a monetary phenomenon." This famous aphorism of Milton Friedman is a good place to begin. The message is two-fold: On the one hand, look to central banks — in this country the Federal Reserve System — both for the source of inflation and for the remedy. On the other hand, do not try to understand inflation by looking at trade unions, monopolies, unemployment rates, oil cartels, and food shortages. In the monetarist view, these phenomena may explain *relative* prices — the cost of oil in terms of construction labor, the cost of beef in terms of television sets. But, the monetarists argue, they are only superficially and transiently related to the *average economywide absolute price level* — the cost of a representative bundle of goods and services in terms of *money.*

"Inflation" is the increase in that cost from day to day, month to month, year to year, and the very definition supports the claim that "money," in some sense, plays some role. For that reason, few economists would quarrel with Friedman's aphorism. But large issues of diagnosis and policy remain. Monetarists are inclined to blame most of our recent double-digit inflation on erroneous policies of the Federal Reserve and other central banks. They argue that, given the will to avoid similar errors in the future, the monetary authorities can cure this inflation and even achieve price stability.

Nonmonetarists assign both less blame and less future control to the central banks. They observe that monetary policies aimed at offsetting the impacts on price indexes of large and rapid increases of individual prices, like petroleum and food, are bound to cause recession and unemployment, as happened in

1974-1975. They fear a stubborn anti-inflationary monetary policy will hold the economy well below its potential for production and employment for many years. I shall return to this basic disagreement in detail below.

Wage and Price Inflation in a Modern Industrial Economy

I shall begin by a description of the inflationary process which will seem to violate Friedman's aphorism and to ignore "money." But the omission is only superficial and temporary. In succeeding sections I will put money and central-bank policy into the picture I now start to sketch.

The sketch itself is intended to be a distilled exposition of the framework — economists would call it the "model" — which many economists use in thinking about the problems and issues with which this paper and this conference are concerned. Time and space do not permit, however, an extended theoretical and empirical defense of the framework.

To predict the rate of inflation next quarter or next year, the most valuable single piece of information is the rate of inflation in the period immediately preceding. If prices have been increasing at 5 percent per annum, continuation at 5 percent is a better bet than a sudden change to 0 percent, 10 percent or even 3 percent or 8 percent. The trend of prices is solidly built into the economy, with a powerful and persistent momentum.

Obviously this does not mean that the speed of inflation never changes. Inflation accelerates or decelerates in response to economic events, random shocks, and government policies. But it takes large stimuli to alter significantly and quickly the entrenched inflationary pattern.

It takes particularly strong stimuli to *diminish* whatever rate of inflation has been built into the economy's habits and expectations. This asymmetry, this "ratchet effect" — the difficulty of reversing increases in speed of inflation — has been especially evident in the last decade.

The self-sustaining momentum of inflation is distinctive to that part of the economy Galbraith calls the "planning system" — in the United States, the bulk of the private nonfarm economy. The relevant features of this sector are: (1) the predominance of *hired* labor, in contrast to self-employed labor; and (2) the prevalence of *administered* wage rates and prices, in contrast to wages and prices determined jointly by buyers' and sellers' bids in market transactions. In this context, "administered" means simply that someone consciously, deliberately sets the price — the seller, or the buyer, as in the case of labor, or the two sides together in explicit agreement.

"Administered" does *not* necessarily imply monopoly or oligopoly. The prices of gasoline at service stations are administered, but the industry is often highly competitive. In contrast, the soybean farmer does not decide and announce a price for his crop and wait for potential takers. He sells, if he wishes, at impersonal prices determined continuously by supply and demand in an organized market.

Competition affects administered prices, too, but indirectly and often slowly. Disappointing sales may eventually induce the sellers to set lower prices, as we

3

have recently observed in the automobile industry. Labor shortages may induce employers to offer higher wage rates or to consent to them in collective bargaining. But since policy decisions at discrete intervals are involved, the adjustment of prices and wages to imbalances of supply and demand is imperfect and slow.

Wage setting is especially crucial in the private nonfarm economy. Wage scales are reviewed and announced periodically, usually annually. In organized sectors, they are set contractually in periodic collective bargaining. Both for employer and employee, the pattern of wage increases observed and experienced in relevant geographical areas, industries and occupations is an important reference point. If competing employers are giving 10 percent increases, an employer knows that he will not be at a competitive disadvantage in either product or labor markets if he follows suit. If he follows the reference pattern, he does not damage the morale of his existing work force or invite higher turnover. Likewise, union leaders who keep up with the pattern do not risk unfavorable comparison with rivals.

For these and other reasons, the "wage-wage" spiral is usually stubborn. Patterns of wage increases in one market are followed in others. For the same reasons, however, an irrational competitive escalation, such as occurred in the construction trades a few years ago, is hard to stop once it gets started.

Nonetheless wages and unit labor costs rise faster in markets of labor shortage, as employers bid above the previous pattern for needed workers, or are forced to upgrade workers beyond their skill and experience. For similar reasons, wages rise more slowly in markets of labor surplus. But there is considerable asymmetry in these two responses. Not only unions, but employers too, are slow to recognize the availability of unemployed replacements for employed workers as a reason for retarding the accustomed and expected advance of wages. A stingier wage policy risks costs in lower morale and higher turnover. However, when employers have compelling financial reasons for reducing their work forces, by layoffs and short hours rather than by gradual attrition, we can observe significant responses of wages to job shortages.

There is a two-way relation between wage inflation and price inflation. The price-wage direction is often discussed. Obviously workers like to be compensated for increases in the cost of living. This is a frequent debating point in wage complaints and negotiations, and some employees have obtained formulas for partial escalation.

But in thinking about the feedback from cost-of-living inflation to wage rates, it is important to distinguish among three components of the cost-of-living index: (1) prices received by the workers' employers themselves; (2) prices paid for goods and services imported from elsewhere; and (3) taxes. Employers enjoying normal sales volume can compensate their workers for inflation in the first component. But they cannot do so for cost-of-living inflation from the other two sources except at the expense of their profits. Employers will resist wage demands inspired by increases in the prices of Arabian oil or Iowa corn, especially when their own sales and prices are threatened by recession. That is why wage increases in 1974 were more moderate than might have been feared in view of the double-digit inflation in consumer prices.

4

The other direction is from wages to prices. In the administered-price sector, prices are commonly set to mark up unit labor costs estimated at normal rates of operating capacity. Because of labor-saving technological advance and capital accumulation, unit labor costs rise less than wages. Thanks to the trend of labor productivity, annual inflation in the prices of the nonfarm economy is normally 2.5 to 3 percent points below the rate of wage inflation.

This relation applies strictly to the pricing of the *net* "value added" by industry to materials imported from U.S. agriculture and resource industries and from overseas. As recent events have reminded us, sharp increase in materials costs may cause *gross* prices to rise faster than wages. This is a manifestation of the second type of cost-of-living inflation listed above. A similar qualification is in order for increases in indirect business taxes, excises and payroll taxes.

At the beginning of 1973, the permanent inflation rate internal to the U.S. nonfarm economy was around 5 percent. To this was added the spectacular bulge in prices as the economy absorbed the price increases stemming from the fourfold increase in OPEC prices, the world shortages of food and other materials, the depreciation of the dollar in the foreign exchanges, and the abolition of price controls. The result was a temporary spell of double-digit inflation — temporary because these were one-shot events. They could not continue to contribute to inflation statistics unless they recurred regularly.

The danger was that the internal inflation rate would be permanently raised to double digits if labor successfully obtained wage increases to match the painful boosts of external prices. Events have largely vindicated the argument above that there was no reason to expect wage increases of such magnitude. "Wage-wage" momentum is a more accurate description of the process than "price-wage" feedbacks.

In this event, if we judge from current wage increases of the order of 9 to 10 percent, the permanent inflation rate is now 6 to 7.5 percent. Transient phenomena — now that external prices are level or declining — are likely to make for even lower inflation statistics toward the end of 1975. Those numbers will be as misleading as the double-digit bulge from which they are the rebound. They will not be a cause for celebration or self-congratulation.

Aggregate Demand, Macroeconomic Policy, and the Rate of Inflation

I have argued in the previous section that at any time the economy inherits from the past an internal rate of inflation which is firmly and stubbornly built into its habits, expectations and wage patterns. Cost-of-living statistics and other price indexes will reflect, in addition or subtraction, divergent movements in the prices of materials and consumer goods imported from American agriculture and from other countries.

The internal rate of inflation itself will change up or down as a result of (1) random, unsystematic and unpredictable developments in particular product and labor markets, and (2) the overall balance between the demand for goods and services and the capacity of American industry to produce, and between the demand for labor and the supply. It is the second source of acceleration or deceleration in inflation which can be influenced by the overall fiscal and mone-

5

tary policies of the Federal Government, and it is that to which I turn now.

The unemployment rate is a good, but imperfect, barometer of the pressure of aggregate demand on the productive resources of the economy. In terms of this barometer, we can distinguish roughly three zones: (1) *Accelerating inflation*. How unemployment rates signal shortages of labor. Pressures to exceed existing norms of wage increase are very strong, both for employers and for unions. A large proportion of recorded unemployment represents voluntary movement between jobs, or selective job-seeking by workers who quit previous positions or are new entrants to the labor force. A large proportion represents workers of low skill and experience. Moreover, low unemployment is generally associated with low margins of excess capacity; in consequence, markups may accelerate at the same time as labor costs. (2) *Stable inflation*. At moderate unemployment rates, associated with normal rates of utilization of industrial capacity, inflation rates will be roughly stable. There will still be unsystematic and structural sources of change up or down, as suggested above. But the overall balance of demand and productive capacity will not be contributing systematically either to acceleration or deceleration of inflation.[1]

(3) *Decelerating inflation*. At high unemployment rates, associated with high margins of excess capacity, inflation rates will gradually decline. The mechanisms of zone 1 work in reverse. But the process is asymmetrically slow. It takes prolonged periods of substantial unemployment to melt the inflation previously frozen into the economy.

It is a hazardous empirical task to give numerical boundaries to these zones. Today, perhaps the boundary between zone 1 and zone 2 is somewhere between 4.8 percent and 5.3 percent unemployment, and the boundary between zone 2 and zone 3 between 5.5 percent and 6.0 percent.

The boundaries shift over time. It is estimated that changes in the demographic composition of the labor force, in favor of types of workers with less permanent attachment to the labor force and to particular jobs, has moved boundaries of this kind up by about .8 of a percentage point since 1960. This means that if the Kennedy target of 4 percent unemployment was a reasonable noninflationary target in 1961-1965 — and we did virtually reach it in 1965 with negligible inflation consequences — 4.8 percent would be the corresponding figure now. Yet in the early 1950's, the economy operated at about 3 percent unemployment without serious inflationary effect.

The major recent trip of the economy into zone 1 began in 1966 when the Johnson Administration, ignoring the advice of its own economists as well as outside economists, escalated the Vietnam war without increasing taxes to pay

---

[1] A controversial issue, which we need not discuss in this paper, is whether this zone of unemployment rates — some economists would collapse the zone to a single "natural rate" — has any further normative significance. Does it signify the absence of *involuntary* unemployment? Is it the *optimal* amount of unemployment? I have argued to the contrary elsewhere. ("Inflation and Unemployment," *American Economic Review*, March 1972, Vol. LXII, No. 1, pp. 1-18.) My basic point is that, because wages and prices adjust more slowly to excess supply than to excess demand, the economy has a bias toward either accelerating inflation or involuntary unemployment.

6

for sharply increased military procurement. This fiscal escalation occurred when the economy was already close to the "full employment" goal of 4 percent. The result was a classic case of excess-demand inflation. A subsequent dose of over-stimulation occurred in 1968-1969. Comparing 1970 and 1965, the rate of ongoing wage inflation was raised from 3.6 percent per year to 7.2 percent. The stubborn internal wage and price inflation which we still have with us is largely an inheritance from this period.

That in itself is a strong indication of the persistence of built-in inflation, and of its powerful and asymmetrical resistance to deflationary stimuli. The 1970-1971 recession was a deliberate, policy-engineered attempt to bring down the internal inflation rate. Two and a half years of unemployment in excess of 5 percent, assisted by wage and price controls, succeeded in reducing wage inflation by at most one percentage point. Price inflation abated by two points, but some of this improvement was a transient mark-up squeeze due to controls and it vanished when controls were relaxed and lifted.

Now comes the important analytical point: To a very close first approximation, *the path of inflation – accelerating, stable, decelerating – depends on the overall state of the economy*, i.e., *on which zone it is in, and not on the combination of policies and events that put it there.* Monetary and fiscal policies are important, indeed crucially important. But they do not affect prices, wages and the course of inflation directly. They do so indirectly, by helping to determine the overall pressure of aggregate demand on the economy's resources of labor and productive capacity, i.e., by helping to determine which of the three zones describes the state of the economy.

Let me be both more precise and more topical. Suppose we assume a particular path of recovery of production and unemployment for 1976, 1977, and 1978. Suppose, for example, we imagine moving from 8.5 percent unemployment in the final quarter of 1975 to 6.5 percent unemployment at the beginning of 1977, and to 5.5 percent unemployment a year later. This would involve growth in production averaging 9 to 10 percent per year through 1976, slowing down to 7 percent in 1977. Imagine three ways of accomplishing this recovery:

(1) Without changes of fiscal and monetary policy, private consumption and investment spending miraculously revives.

(2) Without new fiscal stimulus, aggressively expansionary monetary policy achieves the necessary expansion of residential construction, business investment, and consumer credit.

(3) With a passively neutral monetary policy, massive tax reductions and budget expenditures provide the necessary stimulus.

To our first approximation, the path of internal price and wage inflation would be the same under all three scenarios. Specifically, the state of the economy would be zone 3 throughout the assumed recovery, and the inflation rate would be slowly decelerating. Only if the economy were pushed into zone 1 would the outcome be to accelerate inflation, and this would be the case whether the culprit was excessive fiscal stimulus, excessive monetary stimulus, or unexpected buoyancy in private spending.

7

The example of the previous paragraph utilized two important and well-documented empirical rules of thumb. One is that it takes about a 4 percent annual growth in real production, at constant prices, to hold the unemployment rate constant. The 4 percent growth is needed to absorb the trend increase in labor force (about 1 to 1.25 percent per year) and the normal growth of productivity per worker (about 2.75 percent per year). The second, commonly called Okun's Law, is that it takes an additional 3 percent per year growth of output in the short run to diminish cyclical unemployment by one percentage point. This rule of thumb reflects a combination of effects: the short-run response of labor force participation to the availability of jobs; the pro-cyclical variation of hours to work; the pro-cyclical variation of productivity per hour of work.

Two qualifications of the "first approximation" just advanced are in order. One concerns speed limits. The rate of inflation may depend in some degree not only on the state of aggregate demand, the zone, but also on how rapidly demand is increasing, how rapidly production and employment are increasing. Even within zone 3, a rocket-like recovery could be inflationary. Temporary bottlenecks and shortages would be encountered in a sharp recovery, but anticipated and avoided in a more gradual expansion. That is why it is not prudent to attempt to make up in one year the ground we have lost in one year. The same recovery would not be inflationary if stretched out over a longer period. I do not believe my example violates any speed limits.

The second qualification has to do with the exchange rate of the dollar with foreign currencies, and thus with the dollar prices of internationally traded goods. A money-fueled expansion, (2) of our three alternatives, would involve lower U.S. interest rates and, therefore, possibly more outflow of short-term funds than the other scenarios. For this reason, it might lead to further depreciation of the dollar relative to other currencies. However, this consequence might be reversed once a strong recovery was under way and improved profit prospects in the U.S. attracted equity purchases and direct investment. In any case, it is wrong to regard foreign monetary policies and interest rates as independent of our own. European countries and Japan are enjoying even sharper recessions than ours; they can be expected to follow our lead and to use any room we give them for easier monetary policies.

Finally, I would emphasize that monetary policy is extremely flexible. It is not locked into any particular targets, whether in terms of interest rates or of growth of monetary aggregates. The Federal Open Market Committee meets monthly and consults by telephone in between regular meetings. When, as now, there are so many months and so many percentage points of unemployment between the present state of the economy and the zone of inflationary danger, the Fed has ample time to "lean against the wind" and to apply the brakes.

The Stock of "Money," Monetary Policy, and Inflation

The foregoing account may seem to have paid little explicit attention to Friedman's aphorism that inflation is a monetary phenomenon, and the time has

8

come to remedy the apparent omission. To do so, I shall use monetarist language, the age-old equation of exchange:

(1)
$$MV = PQ$$

Here M is the stock of money. Since there are many assets denominated in the monetary unit of account, the dollar, there are vast conceptual and empirical problems in even defining a money stock. But let us finesse them for the time being and adopt M_1, the quantity of currency and demand deposits owned by the public, i.e., not including these assets if they are held by commercial banks or by the Federal Reserve or by the Federal Government itself. Note that M is a *stock*, a balance sheet entry, not a *flow* per year of newly created money or of spending.

To convert it into a flow, the rate of spending on goods and services per year, we must multiply M by V, velocity, the average number of times per year that a unit of "money" is involved in a purchase of the goods and services counted in the Gross National Product. This velocity is not a mechanical constant. The same money stock can be used with widely varying speeds to make such final purchases. These are by no means the only transactions in which money thus defined is used, and many goods-and-services transactions are accomplished without transfer to currency or demand deposits. More important, velocity varies with the behavior of the households and business firms who hold the stock of money. Sometimes they have strong incentive to use it intensively, to minimize their cash holdings; at other times they have stronger reasons for holding large liquid balances, including cash.

Q is the rate of production, per year, in real terms, e.g., in practice, GNP in constant 1958 prices. P is then the "GNP deflator," an overall index of prices of the goods and services counted in GNP. PQ is the nominal or current-dollar value of GNP, which it will be convenient to denote as Y.

The two sides of the equation of exchange are equal by definition. That is, the only way to measure velocity is to calculate PQ/M.

From equation (1) we can derive a similar identity in rates of change. Let the corresponding lower case letter, in each case, stand for the annual rate at which the variable is increasing (or if negative, decreasing). Thus m is $\frac{\Delta M}{M}$, the annualized rate of growth of M, p is $\frac{\Delta p}{p}$, the annualized rate of inflation, and so on. Then:

(2)
$$m + v = p + q = y$$

Chart 1 presents quarterly series for these four rates of change, 1968-1974. The summary data are reported in Table 1. Note that v has not been constant at zero or any other number, but has varied a great deal. On average, V has an upward trend at a rate of about 2 percent per year. This means that an average y of about 8 percent has been associated with a lower average m, about 6 percent.

The "quantity theory of money" is an ancient proposition — not a tautology like the Equation of Exchange. It says that the price level P (the inverse of the

9

Chart 1: End of Quarter Planning

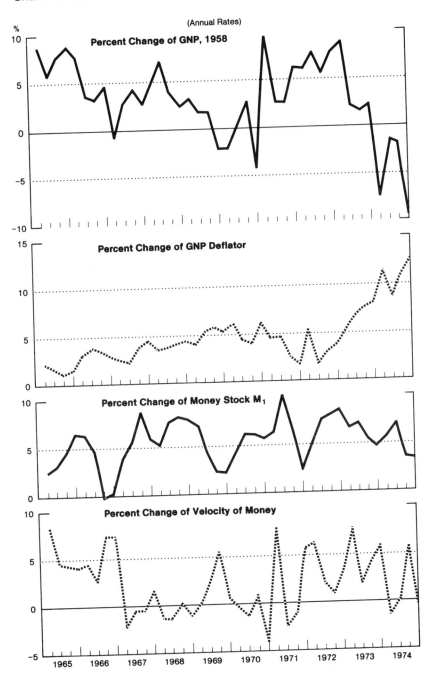

(Annual Rates)

Percent Change of GNP, 1958

Percent Change of GNP Deflator

Percent Change of Money Stock M$_1$

Percent Change of Velocity of Money

10

Table 1: Equation of Exchange: Statistics of Annualized Percentage Rates of Change, 1965-1 to 1974-4

	Mean	Standard Deviation		
GNP	3.08083	4.39206		
P	4.79348	2.68202		
M_1	5.44604	2.3075		
V	2.42828	3.26667		
Correlation Matrix:	*GNP*	*M_1*	*P*	*V*
GNP	1			
M_1	0.186	1		
P	−0.752	−0.028	1	
V	0.596	−0.479	−0.170	1
Covariance Matrix:				
GNP				
M_1	1.88505			
P	−8.85825	−0.173285		
V	8.55113	−3.61066	−1.48943	

value of a unit of money in terms of goods and services) is proportional to the stock of money M. Like most pieces of time-honored wisdom, it contains some grains of truth. Its logic is simple and appealing. The most elementary common-sense economics suggests the generalization that the value of any commodity is, other things equal, inversely related to its supply. Why should this not apply to money?

The trouble is with the proviso *"other things equal."* The quantity theory proposition requires that V and Q remain constant when M is changed.

Modern quantity theorists prefer equation (2). The proposition then would be that p has a one-to-one dependence on m. Thus if q stays constant at its long-term trend of 4 percent, and v at its trend value of 2.5 percent, raising m from 4 percent to 8 percent would lift p from 3.5 to 6.5 percent. Thus we have a modern version of the quantity theory proposition: other things equal, an increase in the rate of growth of the money supply will lead to an equal increase in the rate of price inflation. Again, however, we must examine the proviso that q and v are constants.

Consider first the constancy of q. Suppose for the time being we assume the constancy of v and thus assume that the rate of growth, y, of nominal GNP, Y, depends one-to-one on the rate of growth, m, of the money stock M. Even monetarists who believe this do not assert that in the short run the rate of inflation, p, depends in a one-to-one way on the rate of expansion, y, of nominal income. They do not assert that q, the rate of growth of output, is fixed independently of what is happening to total spending. They agree, I believe, that the decomposition of y between p and q depends on the state of the economy.

11

In slack economic times like the present, with idle men and machines in ample supply, an increase in y would go mainly into q, i.e., into a faster increase, or slower decline, in production. In times like 1966, with the economy already producing close to capacity, most of an increase in y would go into an increase in p, i.e., into acceleration of inflation.

Indeed the formulation of equation (2) is by no means inconsistent with the "zone" analysis of inflation on pages 6 to 8 above. What that analysis suggests is that *in the short run,* p has a life of its own, a value predetermined by past history. Thus suppose that the economy starts 1976 with an inflation rate of 7 percent, predetermined by past history and by contemporaneous external developments. Then to achieve a rate of growth of output q, of 9 percent, as in the illustrative recovery scenario advanced above, requires a y of 16 percent. If v stays at 2.5 percent, the required level of m is 13.5 percent. Under these assumptions, a lower rate of growth of M_1 would cut down q correspondingly.

In similar vein, consider the dilemma of the Federal Reserve in 1973 and early 1974. Because of the exceptional external contributions to our prices, the rate of inflation had reached double digits, let's say 11 percent per year. Allowing for the upward trend of velocity, the Fed would have had to let M grow at 12.5 percent in order to sustain the normal 4 percent growth of production. Failing to do so did not mean that the inflation rate would immediately fall. It meant that spending on goods and services would be insufficient to purchase the increasing output the economy was capable of producing. It meant that unemployment was bound to rise. It meant recession. Given the inflation attributable to petroleum, food and other external influences, there was no way in the short or medium run to keep inflation statistics down. That would have required sharp reduction in the rates of inflation in American industry, and probably actual reductions in many prices and wages. In the circumstances, it was foolish to blame Fed policy for the double-digit inflation, or to expect the Fed to have any remedy for it except the lengthy, circuitous, painful route they have, in fact, followed.

In less dramatic form this dilemma has repeatedly faced the Federal Reserve and other central banks, as well as the executive and legislative officials who make budget policy. Shall they provide the money to support normal economic growth at inherited inflation rates over which they have precious little immediate control? Or shall they deny the economy that money, provoke additional unemployment, slowdown and recession, and count hopefully on stagflation gradually to bring inflation down to more tolerable levels? Whenever they chose the first alternative, they could be accused of causing, or at least ratifying, the inflation. But they are not responsible for the features of democratic capitalist societies that bias non-Communist economies toward inflation and produce the recurrent dilemma. Their critics, monetarists and others, are unfair and misleading when they imply that the continuation of inflation is simply a reflection of obtuse stupidity by policymakers, of conceptual and operational errors which could be corrected at no cost to the economy.

It is true, of course, that policy does affect p in the longer run. According to the analysis above, p itself rises, stays constant, or falls depending on the un-

12

employment zone in which the economy is operating. To return to our 1976 recovery example, suppose that monetary expansion is, in fact, sufficient to increase nominal income at 16 percent per year, real income at 9 percent. Since the economy is in a high unemployment zone, p will in fact be falling from its assumed initial value of 7 percent per year. (We are always abstracting from random events and new external shocks which may change p for reasons unconnected with the current balance between aggregate demand and capacity.) But if policy continues to promote or allow a 16 percent per year growth of nominal income, the economy will move to lower and lower unemployment, into zone 2 and then into zone 1, causing a renewed acceleration of inflation. Indeed in the very long run, given that q cannot average better than the 4 percent compatible with labor force and productivity growth, 16 percent per year expansion of nominal income means 12 percent per year inflation.

In this sense, and for this long horizon, the monetarists are right. But does this mean that the money stock should never, even for short periods of time, be allowed to grow at the rate (12.5 percent in the example) associated with the 16 percent value of y? Or does it mean that the monetary authorities should promote a recovery when it is needed and slow down the expansion in time to keep the economy from overshooting?

An alternative policy for 1976-1978, which has received much vocal support, is a steady 6 percent growth in money stock. In the very long run this might be associated with 4.5 percent inflation (p = m + v - q = 6 + 2.5 - 4). But suppose we begin 1976 with 7 percent inflation. Then q(= m + v - p = 6 + 2.5 - 7) will be confined to 1.5 percent. Unemployment will rise from the initial 8.5 percent rate previously assumed. The rate of price inflation will fall, and no doubt it will fall faster than in the recovery scenario previously discussed. Only when the inflation rate has fallen to 4.5 percent will unemployment cease to rise — remember that it takes a q of 4 percent just to keep the unemployment rate constant. In a previous paper, I estimated that it would take at least 3 years of increasing unemployment to diminish the inflation rate by 3 points, but I admit I was not contemplating the deflationary pressures that might build up at unemployment rates of 8 to 11 percent, unprecedented since the Great Depression.[2]

Up to now we took for granted the constancy of v, the upward trend of velocity. Velocity and its rate of increase are, however, subject both to random and to systematic variability. Random changes occur when the public becomes more or less liquidity-conscious, when the distribution of M_1 among households and firms changes, when banks' compensating balance requirements vary, when the availability and popularity of the manifold money-substitutes change, and for many other reasons. Systematic variability of velocity requires closer attention.

Variation in nominal rates of interest on close substitutes for money — time deposits, certificates of deposit, savings accounts in commercial banks and thrift

---

[2] "Monetary Policy in 1974 and Beyond," *Brookings Papers on Economic Acitivity*, 1:1974, pp. 219-232.

13

institutions, Treasury bills, open-market commercial paper, accounts with mutual liquid asset funds — is the most important systematic source of variability of velocity. The common sense of this relationship is straightforward. High rates of interest are an incentive to firms, even to households, to use sharp pencils and to make frequent financial transactions in order to hold down the average size of cash balances on which they earn no interest. When those interest rates are low, the management effort and transactions costs involved in economizing cash balances are less rewarding. Repeated empirical studies substantiate the reality of this effect. One manifestation of it is that velocity rises in cyclical booms, when interest rates are high, and falls in recessions along with interest rates. Note the positive correlation of q and v in Table 1.

What are the implications of this relationship? There are important implications both for monetary policy itself and for fiscal policy. I shall discuss them in turn.

Monetary policy itself affects velocity. In the short run, at least, an expansionary monetary policy means a reduction of interest rates and a fall in velocity. Note the negative correlation of m and v in Table 1. Thus an increase in m engineered by the Federal Reserve is *partially and temporarily* offset by a fall in v. (I emphasize "partially" because it is only in deep depression situations like the 1930's, with short-term interest rates virtually zero and the economy in Keynes's "liquidity trap," that monetary policy becomes completely impotent.)

The reason for the offset is that expansionary monetary policy works by lowering interest rates (or, in any event, by making them lower than they would otherwise be).

It is important to remember that the Federal Reserve does not directly control M_1 or its rate of growth, m. There is no control dial in the Chairman's office which he can set, like a thermostat, to some desired target for a monetary aggregate. The Fed works indirectly, mainly by buying and selling Treasury securities in the open market. By these operations the Fed provides additional reserves for the banks or takes reserves away. There are other forces determining the supply of bank reserves, and the banks themselves can borrow more reserves at the Fed's own discount window. The main point is that operations, chiefly open market purchases, which increase reserves do so by lowering interest rates in the short-term credit markets. With additional reserves, the banks themselves become buyers of securities and more willing lenders. Interest rate reductions and increases in asset prices spread throughout the financial markets to long-term bonds, mortgages, common stocks, and also to real assets — houses, factories, producers' and consumers' durable goods. It is by this chain of transmission, ultimately encouraging business and consumer investment spending, that monetary policy affects the real economy. In this process interest-rate reduction is both an essential link and a by-product.

The same process yields an increase of M_1. It is better to regard that as another by-product of the process and as a barometer, rather than as a link in a linear chain of causation. As banks buy securities and make additional loans, they also expand their deposits. Why does the public hold additional deposits? It is the reductions of interest rates and increases in asset prices that induce the

14

public to sell assets and to hold additional deposits instead. Moreover, as economic activity increases, the public has greater need for currency and deposits. But demand deposits are just one of several kinds of deposits into which the public may choose to put its new funds.

The lesson is that expansionary monetary policy aimed at recovery must allow for a decline in velocity, associated with the interest-rate reductions essential for the recovery itself. Calculations which assume that velocity continues to rise at its trend rate will understate the need for monetary expansion. But once interest rates are down to levels that promote recovery, this need for extra monetary growth ceases. And once recovery is well under way, the Fed will wish to allow rates to rise as it "leans against the wind." In those circumstances the Fed can expect velocity to rise above its normal trend.

Fiscal policy does not *per se* affect the rate of monetary growth, but it does affect velocity. An expansionary fiscal policy involes an increased rate of government expenditure, or lower taxes, or some combination. The resulting deficits are financed by sale of Treasury securities. With unchanged monetary policy, the Federal Reserve neither absorbs these securities nor adds to the capacity of commercial banks to absorb them without displacing other assets.

Nevertheless velocity increases for two reasons. One is simply that government expenditures for goods and services are transactions which do not require advance accumulation of any *private* cash balances — only private holdings are counted in M_2. The other is that interest rates rise and induce greater economy in the use of private cash balances. The rise in velocity is a one-shot consequence of a one-shot shift of fiscal policy; the rate of increase of velocity, v, goes up only temporarily, during the transition from one fiscal policy to the other. Nominal GNP is increased by the government expenditures themselves, by the private spending induced directly by tax reduction, and by the secondary "multiplier" waves of private spending. To say that these increases in spending occur without any new money creation is just another, but probably more illuminating, way of saying that monetary velocity increases.

In discussions of expansionary fiscal policy in the current recession, the Secretary of the Treasury and other observers of the financial scene have expressed doubts that private saving would be adequate to finance federal deficits without "crowding out" business investment, residential construction, and other private uses of saving. This question cannot be answered without some assumption about monetary policy.

Let us first continue the assumption that monetary policy is unchanged — the same path of M_1 is followed whatever fiscal policy is adopted. Purely for illustration, suppose that government expenditures for fiscal year 1976 are raised by $50 billion, with no change in tax laws. How will the extra $50 billion be financed? There are four sources: (1) additional taxes generated from the extra incomes resulting from the fiscal stimulus; (2) additional saving generated from those incomes; (3) additional borrowing from abroad because of response of U.S. imports to higher incomes; and (4) "crowding out" — reduction in domestic private investment because of higher interest rates. Suppose that the multiplier — taking into account all these effects — is 1.6, implying an $80 billion increase of

15

GNP. The four sources of finance might then look as follows: (1) taxes — $20 billion, .25 of the extra GNP; (2) saving — $16 billion, .20 of the extra GNP; (3) foreign borrowing — $6 billion, .075 of the extra GNP; and (4) "crowding out" — $8 billion. Total — $50 billion.

Precise empirical estimates of this kind depend on the structure of the economy — tax laws; "marginal propensities" to consume, save and import; the sensitivity of demand for cash balances, or of velocity, to interest rates; and the sensivity of private investment demands to interest rates. Conceivably there could be no crowding out at all; more private investment might be induced by the increase in income than deterred by the rise in interest rates. The multiplier would then be larger; the increase in income would have to be enough to finance the extra government expenditure from the other three sources.

The same analysis applies if the fiscal stimulus takes the form of tax reduction, say $50 billion calculated as the reduced yield of taxes on the incomes projected before taking account of the fiscal stimulus itself. However, the multiplier for tax reduction is smaller than the expenditure multiplier by the fraction of the tax cut which is initially saved rather than spent. In any case, the realized tax reduction will be smaller than the advertised amount, $50 billion in the example, by the tax revenues generated from the expansion of income.

Official worries about "crowding out," and official calculations of budget deficits, apparently ignore the elementary central point that both taxes and saving rise as incomes expand in response to fiscal stimulus. It is easy to be alarmist about expansionary fiscal measures if one assumes from the outset that they won't work, or that monetary policy will deliberately cancel out their potential multiplier effects.

The real issue raised by a fiscal proposal of the type illustrated is not the imaginary difficulty of financing the deficit. Nor is it the prospect of "crowding out" private investment expenditures which the recession itself has already so disastrously crowded out. One real issue is whether the income growth implied by the proposal — $80 billion in the example — is a good idea. This depends on what it would do to unemployment and inflation, as discussed in preceding sections of this paper. If the answer is affirmative, a second issue is whether fiscal expansion is the best way to achieve it. A partial, or possibly even complete, alternative is expansionary monetary policy.

A logical way to make policy would be to decide first on the most desirable feasible path for the economy. At present, this means deciding how fast and how far recovery should proceed in 1976-1978. In general, there will be many combinations of fiscal and monetary policy which could produce the desired path. The second decision, therefore, is to choose the preferred mixture.

If the objective path remains constant, and if we confine ourselves to policy mixtures which are realistically adequate to the objective, then every expansion in fiscal measures means an offsetting contraction of monetary stimuli. In calculations of this kind, there is indeed 100 percent crowding out. If the same GNP is going to be realized and more is taken for government expenditure or taxpayers' consumption, then obviously other expenditures must give way. Monetary policy will have to be sufficiently tighter, interest rates sufficiently

16

higher, to bring private investment spending down to make room for the fiscal expansion.

A fiscally generated expansion will in general be accompanied by higher interest rates, more public and private consumption, and less private investment than the same recovery engineered by monetary policy. (This generalization must be qualified to the extent that the fiscal measures are, like the investment tax credit, substitutes for low interest rates as investment incentives.) A fiscally generated expansion may also — since higher interest rates attract capital from abroad — be characterized by a stronger dollar exchange rate, less exports, and more imports, than the same expansion generated by monetary stimulus. These are the comparisons which policymakers should consider in deciding on the desirable mix of fiscal and monetary policy.

In much discussion of current policy, the fear is expressed that a strong fiscal policy involving large deficits will drag monetary policy into an over-expansionary posture. The truth is the opposite. The easier fiscal policy is, the tighter monetary policy can and should be. In the absence of expansionary fiscal policy, the whole burden of starting and supporting the recovery falls on the Federal Reserve. It is a fallacy that the desirable and safe amount of monetary expansion can be determined, or fixed at any numerical constant, without reference to the state of the economy and the stance of the federal budget.

The primary and urgent desideratum, of course, is that the total fiscal-monetary package be adequate to the task of ending recession and promoting recovery. The package is far from adequate now. Both monetary and fiscal policy need to be much more stimulative. The questions of mixture just discussed are questions of relative emphasis in designing a generally more expansionary strategy.

How Fast and How Complete a Recovery?

This is the real issue. It is dramatized in Chart 2, which shows: the hypothetical path of potential GNP (in constant 1974 prices) at 5 percent unemployment, together with parallel paths indicative of 6 percent, 7 percent, and 8 percent unemployment rates; the actual course of output since 1973-IV, with a guess for the current quarter; the Administration's program for 1976-1980 as stated in the Budget Message; the alternative recovery program discussed earlier in this paper.

The cumulative difference in production between the two programs is $350 billion in 1974 prices. A large fraction of this difference would be in capital accumulation. Under the Administration's program the capital capacity of the economy in 1980 would be significantly impaired.

What is the justification for so massive a waste of productive resources for so long a period, for recovering incompletely in five years the ground lost in one year of recession?

The Administration's program is a continuation of the determined attack on inflation which inspired the policies that deliberately brought on the current recession. As advertised, the program is to bring the inflation rate gradually

17

Chart 2:

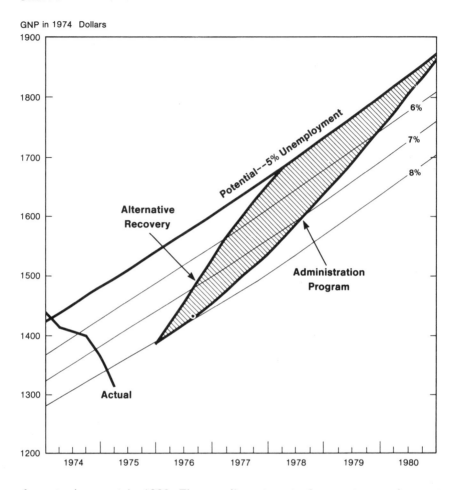

GNP in 1974 Dollars

down to 4 percent in 1980. The speedier return to 5 percent unemployment contemplated in the alternative program would not do as well on the inflation front. Perhaps we would end the decade with 6 or 6.5 percent inflation instead.

Are the gains in abating inflation worth the losses of output and employment? Both unemployment and inflation involve redistributions of income and wealth, in which some citizens gain relative to others. It is hard to say that one of these redistributions is more unfair than the other. What about losses to the nation as a whole, losses to individuals with no counterpart gains elsewhere in the society? The $350 billion already mentioned is the loss due to the extra unemployment involved in the Administration's program. Is there a national loss from extra inflation which can be set against this?

The only national loss from extra inflation arises from the fact that nominal

18

interest rates will be correspondingly higher. With the incentive of higher interest rates, more resources will be used in economizing cash holdings. This is a waste of resources which might otherwise be producing goods and services, or of labor which might otherwise be enjoying leisure. How big is this waste? Over the period in question M_1 would average about $300 billion in 1974 prices, and the difference in inflation rates and interest rates would not on average exceed 2 percent. The loss is then $6 billion a year for five years.

It is true that this loss will continue after 1980, assuming that both programs would have stable inflation rates thereafter. But against this must be weighed the loss of social income from the capital stock with which the speedier recovery would endow the economy.

I can see no possible cost-benefit justification for the prolonged, single-minded attack on inflation which the Administration proposes.

19

JAMES TOBIN

Yale University

Monetary Policy in 1974 and Beyond

WHAT SHOULD BE THE AIM of monetary policy in 1974? One answer is the fulfillment of the administration's forecast for the year. As explained in the President's *Economic Report*, the forecast is also the target; according to the Council of Economic Advisers, it is the best feasible path for the economy. I personally do not agree with this policy, nor do I believe it carries out the mandate of the Employment Act of 1946. But accepting it, one can ask what kind of monetary policy is likely to fulfill the forecast.

The expected and approved path appears to be quarter-to-quarter rates of growth of real gross national product in 1974 of roughly −0.5, 0, 1, and 1 percent, with unemployment rising to about 5.6 percent in the second quarter and remaining there the rest of the year. The rate of price inflation would fall sharply in the second quarter, but rise slightly toward the end of the year.

The target forecast of January does not differ radically from more recent forecasts made by private economists. Table 1 reports George Perry's latest guesses. (A difference of semantic and political significance, but of no economic import, is that Perry's trajectory qualifies as a "recession.")

What monetary policy will achieve this outcome in 1974? The council suggests a year-over-year increase of 8 percent in M_2, about the same as the projected gain of nominal GNP. A unitary income elasticity of demand for M_2 is historically consistent with one of about 0.7 for M_1. On this basis, the 1973–74 increase in M_1 would be 5.6 percent. The *Economic Report* provides few clues to interest rates in 1974. But the council's monetary tar-

Reprinted by permission from *Brookings Papers on Economic Activity* 1 (1974):219–232. Copyright © 1974 by the Brookings Institution.

Table 1. Alternative Forecasts for Selected Economic Indicators, 1974, by Quarter

Dollar amounts in billions, seasonally adjusted annual rates; annual rates of change from previous period in percent

Year and quarter	Perry							CEA	
	Real GNP		GNP deflator		Nominal GNP		Unemployment rate (percent)	Real GNP	
	Amount (1958 dollars)	Growth rate	Index (1958 = 100)	Growth rate	Amount	Growth rate		Amount (1958 dollars)	Growth rate
Actual									
1973:4	844.6	1.6	158.4	8.8	1,337.5	10.5	4.7	...	...
Projection									
1974:1	838.6	−2.8	161.9	9.1	1,358.0	6.2	5.3	840	−2.0
2	833.5	−2.4	165.0	7.7	1,375.3	5.3	5.9	840	0.0
3	841.8	4.0	166.8	4.4	1,404.1	8.4	6.0	848	4.0
4	853.0	5.3	169.0	5.3	1,441.3	10.8	6.0	857	4.0
Actual									
1973	837.4	...	153.9	...	1,289.1	...	4.9	...	...
1974 Projection									
Perry	841.7	0.5	165.7	7.6	1,394.7	8.2	5.8	...	...
CEA	846	1.0	164.5	6.8	1,390	7.8	5.5	...	...

Sources: Actual, *Survey of Current Business*, Vol. 54 (March 1974), pp. 12, 13, 15, S13. CEA data are from, or are based on data from, *Economic Report of the President together with the Annual Report of the Council of Economic Advisers, February 1974*; Perry forecasts are from George L. Perry, "The Economic Outlook for 1974," tabulation (Brookings Institution, March 1974; processed).

Table 2. Required Annual Rates of Increase of M_1 and Time Deposits to Effect Various Movements in Interest Rates, 1973:4 Actual and Projections for 1974, by Quarter

Percent

Interest rate and monetary variable	1973:4 Actual	1974 projection, by quarters			
		First	Second	Third	Fourth
		Slow decline in interest rates			
Rate on commercial paper	9.0	8.3	8.0	7.7	7.4
Growth rate					
Currency plus demand deposits, M_1	3.9	8.5	7.2	5.1	7.2
Time deposits	5.3	7.4	6.7	5.2	8.2
		Moderate decline in interest rates			
Rate on commercial paper	9.0	8.2	7.7	7.2	6.7
Growth rate					
M_1	3.9	8.6	7.5	5.5	7.8
Time deposits	5.3	7.6	7.4	6.4	9.8
		Substantial decline in interest rates			
Rate on commercial paper	9.0	8.1	7.4	6.7	6.0
Growth rate					
M_1	3.9	8.7	7.8	5.9	8.4
Time deposits	5.3	8.1	8.2	7.7	11.6

Sources: Based on Stephen M. Goldfeld, "The Demand for Money Revisited," *Brookings Papers on Economic Activity* (3:1973), pp. 577–638; and Perry, "Economic Outlook for 1974."

get and its judicious balancing of factors raising and lowering rates both suggest that no significant changes are expected or desired. If interest rates remain stable or rise during the current (growth) recession and recovery, this will be a unique episode in business cycle annals.

Stephen Goldfeld recently reported some carefully estimated econometric equations of demand for money.[1] Table 2 shows rates of increase of M_1 needed, according to his preferred equation, for three alternative paths of interest rates in 1974. In each case Perry's forecasts for real GNP and prices from Table 1 were used. These estimates take off from 1973:4, when demand for money was unusually high, in the sense that there was a large positive residual from the systematic part of Goldfeld's equation.[2] The

1. Stephen M. Goldfeld, "The Demand for Money Revisited," *Brookings Papers on Economic Activity* (3:1973), pp. 577–638. Hereafter, this document will be referred to as *BPEA*, followed by the date.

2. I am grateful to Professor Goldfeld for these estimates, which are based on the specification in equation (4), ibid., p. 582.

1974 projections carry this residual with gradually diminishing weight. The residual for 1973:4, reflecting a shift of asset preferences toward money, is scarcely surprising. The same uncertainty and failure of confidence have been painfully evident in the stock market.

Goldfeld also has an equation for the time deposits component of M_2, but it is not as successful over the sample period as his M_1 equation. Using this equation, I calculated annual rates of increase in demand for time deposits for the four quarters of 1974, for the same three hypothetical paths of interest rates. These are also shown in Table 2.

I conclude that the standard forecast—the administration target—will not be met without rates of monetary growth that will (a) exceed the recommendation of the council, and (b) draw screams from monetarists.

I am very skeptical that the standard GNP scenario can be staged without declines in interest rates at least as sharp as those shown in the third panel of Table 2. My skepticism has three sources.

First, one act of the play is a revival of residential construction in the second half of the year. Indeed, February figures suggest that the worst may already be over. But the current interest rate structure does not induce large flows of savings into thrift institutions. Such flows will not occur, the record suggests, until open market rates dip below 7 percent. Meanwhile, during the current slump, mortgage rates have continued a steady rise that has scarcely been interrupted since mid-1971. Although nonmonetary measures—advances from the Federal Home Loan Banks and purchases by the Federal and Government National Mortgage Associations—are billed as remedies to ease the mortgage market, they have not yet lowered rates. Tight credit conditions continue in a housing market weakened by the energy crisis. Prospective home buyers are doubtful about suburban or exurban locations and uncertain about house size and design.

Second, consumer demand looks weaker than the standard forecast assumes. Perry's forecast puts personal saving rates in 1974 below the 7.3 percent of 1973:4—at 6.5, 6.0, 6.1, and 6.4 percent in successive quarters. The most recent University of Michigan survey of consumer attitudes is the most pessimistic ever, by far. Independently of this information, Tom Juster has tried to estimate the influence of expectations and uncertainties about inflation, jobs, and incomes on the personal saving rate.[3] For 1974

3. F. Thomas Juster, "Savings Behavior, Uncertainty and Price Expectations," in *The Economic Outlook for 1974*, Papers presented to the Twenty-first Conference on the Economic Outlook, 1973 (University of Michigan, Research Seminar in Quantitative Economics, 1974), pp. 49–70.

his equations predict rates in excess of 8 percent of disposable income. A third factor lowering the propensity to consume is the transfer of income to sellers of food and fuel at home, as well as abroad. A fourth is the decline in auto sales because of the gasoline scare. Given the heavy use of installment finance in auto purchases, most of the money that would normally be spent for cars will be saved rather than spent on other goods.

Finally, optimism about the prospects for recovery later this year depends principally on the strength of nonresidential investment in 1974, as registered in surveys of anticipations. The survey reported in March by the Commerce Department indicates that business anticipates spending 13 percent more for investment in plant and equipment in 1974 than was spent in 1973. Yet there is an underlying weakness in the financial climate for corporate investment, the high cost of capital relative to expected earnings. If this is not corrected, it may retard investment later in 1974 or in 1975. In the plans for this year, three types of investment play an unusually large part: increases in energy-producing capacity; capacity additions in materials and other bottleneck sectors; and defensive investments to adapt to new scarcities and higher costs. These kinds of investment are probably relatively insensitive to interest rates and capital costs, but a sustained and broadly based investment boom will depend upon an improvement in expected earnings relative to costs of finance. I turn to this topic in the next section.

Is the Real Rate of Interest Really Low?

Figure 1 shows the quarterly time series of Q, the ratio of the valuation of corporate physical capital in the stock and bond markets to its estimated cost of reproduction at current prices of goods. The ratio is now below 1, for the first time since 1970:3 and only the third time since 1958. A high value of Q is favorable to investment, since a corporation can sell paper claims to physical capital for more than the capital costs. A low value of Q, on the other hand, means that the rate of return required in the market by current and potential share- and bondholders is high relative to the marginal productivity of capital. As Keynes has said,

[The] daily revaluations of the Stock Exchange, though they are primarily made to facilitate transfers of old investments between one individual and another, inevitably exert a decisive influence on the rate of current investment. For there is no sense in building up a new enterprise at a cost greater than that at which a similar existing enterprise can be purchased; whilst there is an inducement to spend on a

Figure 1. Estimated Ratio of Market Valuation to Replacement Cost of Corporate Capital Stock, 1951:2 to 1973:4

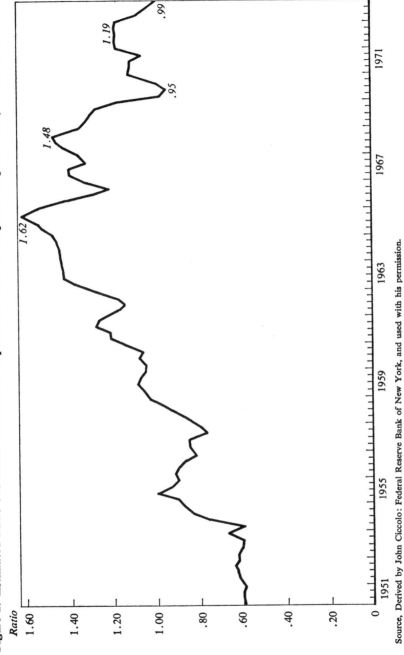

Source, Derived by John Ciccolo: Federal Reserve Bank of New York, and used with his permission.

new project what may seem an extravagant sum, if it can be floated off on the Stock Exchange at an immediate profit.[4]

Figure 2 shows I/K_{-1}, gross investment as a percentage of the lagged capital stock (both in 1958 dollars), over the same time period.[5] John Ciccolo has also computed a regression of I/K_{-1} on K_{-1} and eight lagged values of Q. From this regression can be calculated projections of 1974 nonresidential fixed investment, in 1958 dollars, assuming that Q remains at its 1973:4 value of 0.995.

As I stated above, I have no doubt that special factors will be favorable for investment in 1974, and, of course, it is possible that the stock market will pick up. Table 3 is meant to show that in the absence of special factors or a stock market recovery, investment demand might be weak.

Table 3. Alternative Forecasts of Nonresidential Fixed Investment, 1974, by Quarter

	"Q" forecast (billions of 1958 dollars)	Perry forecast	
Year and quarter		Billions of current dollars	Billions of 1958 dollars[a]
Actual			
1973:4	94.5	141.8	94.5
Projection			
1974:1	93.7	145.8	96.0
2	92.6	147.0	95.6
3	91.7	153.5	98.6
4	91.4	158.0	100.2

Sources: The "Q" forecast (explained in the text) was calculated by John Ciccolo. Other data are from Perry, "Economic Outlook for 1974."

a. Assumes investment deflator rises at 5 percent per year.

Further evidence is provided by William Nordhaus' calculations, in his article in this issue, of the internal after-tax rate of return on corporate capital. This rate reached its post-1950 high of 10.0 percent in 1965 and fell to 5.4 percent in 1973. Standardized cyclically to an average unemployment rate of 4.5 percent, the rate was 10.0 percent in 1965 and 5.6 percent in 1973. The profit squeeze is not a myth. In these circumstances, real rates of interest as high as those that prevailed in the 1960s are not an appropriate target for the Federal Reserve.

4. John Maynard Keynes, *The General Theory of Employment, Interest and Money* (Macmillan, 1973 ed.), p. 151.

5. I am indebted to a former student, John Ciccolo, now of the New York Federal Reserve Bank, for the calculations of Q and I/K_{-1}.

Figure 2. Ratio of Real Gross Investment to Gross Capital Stock, 1951:2 to 1973:4[a]

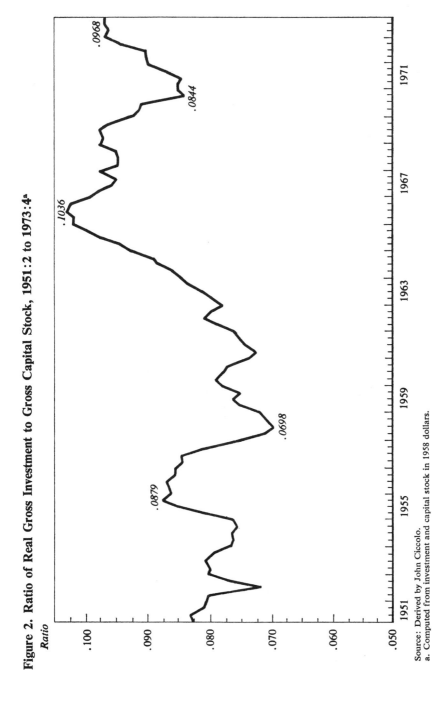

Source: Derived by John Ciccolo.
a. Computed from investment and capital stock in 1958 dollars.

In my opinion, it is a fallacy to conclude that real rates of interest are low simply because current rates of inflation are high compared with nominal market interest rates on dollar-denominated assets. The important thing, as I have argued above, is the comparison of earnings prospects and interest rates. This is the comparison the stock market makes, and it is hard to argue that real rates have declined in any meaningful sense after price-earnings ratios have declined by a third over the year.

The rates of increase of price indexes do *not* represent operational investment opportunities; it is not possible to acquire and hold for future sale the consumer price index's market basket or a share of gross national product. Anyway, recent increases in price indexes have large one-shot components; rational savers and investors would not extrapolate those rates into the future. Inflation premiums are not immaculately added to interest rates. They are put there by market forces and monetary policy. Inflationary expectations do not force bond rates up unless they induce borrowers to float bonds and investors to shift into other assets. One would expect equities to rise in value. When inflationary news makes *both* bonds and stocks fall in price, the explanation, I think, is that these markets know that the Federal Open Market Committee reads the papers too and will react by making policy more restrictive.

I have lately been reading how money markets react adversely to news of high rates of growth of the stock of money. Perhaps the market is full of convinced monetarists. More likely, the market, knowing that the Fed sets targets and limits for growth in the money stock and is sensitive to monetarist criticism, anticipates that the FOMC will act restrictively to reverse "excessive" growth of monetary aggregates. This game is an unfortunate consequence of the Fed's adoption of money-stock criteria in making policy and of the market's use of these criteria in interpreting policy. But it does not mean that the Fed is impotent to reduce interest rates if it really aims to do so. Expectational markups of interest rates will not be sustained unless real live borrowers appear to take all the funds available, and this will not happen unless the Fed confirms the expectations by contracting bank reserves and supplies of loanable funds.

The Recommendations of the "Shadow Open Market Committee"

The press recently reported that the "Shadow Open Market Committee" advises the Fed to set the growth of M_1 at a constant rate of 5 to 5½ percent per year.[6] Just as Milton Friedman did in his letter of February 20, 1974, to Senator William Proxmire, the shadow committee blamed the Fed for the major part of current inflation. Friedman likewise urged the Fed to slow down monetary growth. Advocates of this position rarely tell the public the costs of the policy they espouse. Friedman does say ". . . there is literally no way to end inflation that will not involve a temporary, though perhaps fairly protracted, period of low economic growth and relatively high unemployment."[7]

In one sense the Fed can be held responsible for all inflation that occurs. If the Fed were willing to starve the economy for liquidity, regardless of the consequences for real output and employment, presumably price indexes could be held down even when unit labor costs are rising or even when special factors raise the prices of internationally traded goods like oil and grain. But the Fed is not responsible for the structural features of modern industrial economies that give them an inflationary bias even at reasonable rates of utilization. Nor can the Fed be blamed for unwillingness to accept the "temporary, though perhaps fairly protracted" costs of trying to cure structural inflationary bias by deflation of aggregate demand.

We already know that these temporary costs *can* be fairly protracted. In 1970 Andersen and Carlson simulated their St. Louis monetarist model for steady rates of monetary growth in the period 1970–80.[8] With 6 percent monetary growth, unemployment stayed above 5 percent until 1976 and above its natural rate of 4 percent until 1978. With 4 percent monetary growth, consistent with long-run price stability, unemployment was above 6 percent in 1971–75 and above 5 percent until 1978, and it had not reached 4 percent by 1980.

In a monetarist spirit I have made some similar calculations for the present context. I assume that the shadow committee's proposal for M_1 means an 8 percent annual rate of growth of nominal GNP. I also assume that the normal rate of growth of potential output is 4 percent per year and, for the sake of argument, that the natural rate of unemployment is 5 percent.

6. The Shadow Open Market Committee is a private group of economists who meet occasionally to recommend monetary policies to the Federal Reserve.
7. "Letter on Monetary Policy," *Federal Reserve Bank of St. Louis Review,* Vol. 56 (March 1974), p. 23.
8. Leonall C. Andersen and Keith M. Carlson, "An Econometric Analysis of the Relation of Monetary Variables to the Behavior of Prices and Unemployment," in *The Econometrics of Price Determination,* Conference Sponsored by Board of Governors of the Federal Reserve System and Social Science Research Council, 1970 (FRB, 1972), pp. 177–81.

The rate of increase of the GNP deflator each quarter is the sum of two components. One is a weighted average of the eight preceding quarterly increases, the weights summing to one. The other is a correction depending on U_{-1}, the unemployment rate for the previous quarter: the correction is positive if U_{-1} is less than 5 percent; negative if it exceeds 5 percent.

The specific form of the second component is $(b/U_{-1}) - (b/5)$. I have used two vastly different values for b. The first is 13.32, which comes from the Phillips curve of the old Fed-MIT-Penn model as reported by de Menil and Enzler in 1970.[9] This is an optimistic view of the efficacy of unemployment in slowing down inflation, for it implies that the difference between 6 percent and 5 percent unemployment is a reduction of 0.4 percentage point each quarter in the annual percentage rate of inflation. This is surely overoptimistic for the purpose, since the de Menil-Enzler Phillips curve has no natural rate and attributes variations in wage inflation predominantly to variations of unemployment. The second value of b is 4.0, from an Eckstein-Brinner wage equation (reestimated by Gordon),[10] in which full feedback of past price changes accounts for the lion's share of explained variance of wage inflation. On this basis, unemployment of 6 percent cuts down the annual rate of inflation only by 0.13 percentage point each quarter.

The simulations, displayed in Figure 3, assume that the Perry forecasts are realized in 1974 and that the monetarist recommendation takes hold in 1975:1. From then on, nominal GNP grows at an annual rate of 8 percent. In the optimistic version, unemployment rises to 6.9 percent in 1978:2 and finally gets down to 5 percent in 1982:4. In 1978:2 the rate of price inflation crosses its long-run equilibrium value of 4 percent. That is why unemployment begins to decline. But by 1982:4 the rate of price inflation is only 2 percent, so unemployment overshoots and continues to decline. Eventually the rate of inflation accelerates again, and so on. I stopped the cycle at the end of 1985, assuming that the Shadow Open Market Committee might have had another meeting by that time.

The second version is even worse, as might be expected in view of the weak effect of high unemployment on wage inflation. Unemployment rises steadily for eight years.

9. George de Menil and Jared J. Enzler, "Prices and Wages in the FR-MIT-Penn Econometric Model," in ibid., pp. 277–308.

10. Robert J. Gordon, "Wage-Price Controls and the Shifting Phillips Curve," *BPEA* (2:1972), pp. 385–421.

Figure 3. Simulations of Inflation and Unemployment with Constant 8 Percent per Year Growth of Nominal GNP, Alternative Wage Responses to Unemployment, 1975:1 to 1985:4

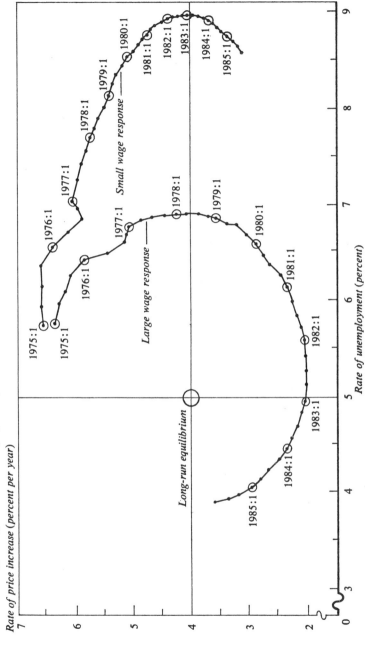

Source: Derived by author. See text discussion.

The Old Dilemma Once More

The recommendations of the shadow committee and of Friedman raise once again the big and terribly uncomfortable issues of macroeconomic policy. So, for that matter, does the CEA at the beginning of its 1974 Report:

... while continued rapid inflation is not inevitable, the course of unwinding it will be long and difficult ... to hope that we can "wring the inflation out of the system" by the end of some short period is to assure disappointment. Whoever undertakes now to fight inflation must be prepared to stay the long course. We think it is necessary to do this, and also to recognize why we must do it. Experience extending over almost a decade teaches us that if we do not fight inflation effectively it will accelerate. ...

[The facts of our prosperity over the past eight years] do not relieve us of the need to bring inflation under control, and to accept the cost of doing so for the sake of avoiding the greater costs of an accelerating inflation.[11]

This statement makes me wonder what macroeconomic scenario the administration has in mind for 1975 and subsequent years.

In the fight against inflation, the urgent matter in 1974 is to keep the fuel-food bulge in prices from escalating the rate of wage inflation. From the record so far, one can be moderately hopeful, and there are reasons why one would not expect rising commodity prices to pull wages all the way up after them. These price increases do not improve the bargaining power of most employees. They do not inflate the profits of employers or the value of labor to them; in many instances the opposite is true. They do not distort the pattern of relative wages and provoke another round of wage-wage spiral. Still, with George Meany talking 12 percent, no one would underrate the problem.

But I doubt that the wage outcome this year will depend appreciably on whether the unemployment rate is 6 percent or 5.5 percent or 5 percent. As I have already noted, wage equations that assign high coefficients to past price experience do not assign a strong influence to unemployment. The short-run Phillips curve is flat at high rates of unemployment. Since it is steep at low rates, a much longer time is required to unwind an inflation than to generate one.

In the circumstances, neither monetary policy nor aggregate-demand

11. *Economic Report, February 1974*, p. 21.

policy in general is a useful tool. As Arthur Okun has observed, if there really is a danger that a one-shot bulge in particular prices will be permanently incorporated in general wage and price inflation, and if the damage of such acceleration is as great as the CEA suggests, then all kinds of preventive measures—controls, subsidies, rollbacks—would be justified, in spite of their temporary allocational costs.

Should not a real effort to negotiate a social treaty with George Meany and other labor representatives be the first order of business? I suspect that American consumers, wage earners, union leaders, and businessmen are quite capable of understanding that scarcities of food and fuel make it impossible for their real incomes to grow at the accustomed pace. Workers might accept wage guideposts for 1974 and 1975 that recognize this fact of life. But they would have to regain confidence that the sacrifices will be equitably shared. Indeed, wage guideposts might be more acceptable if workers were assured that the burdens of layoffs and short time were not piled on top of the inescapable burdens of commodity scarcities.

The abiding problem will be with us whatever happens in 1974. My views and values respecting unemployment and inflation are not shared by all economists. I do not agree that inflation, or even acceleration of inflation, is *ipso facto* evidence of excess aggregate demand. I do not agree that all unemployment up to the "natural" rate compatible with zero or steady inflation is *ipso facto* voluntary. Anyone who does agree to those propositions would have no qualms in aiming monetary and fiscal policy at the single target of zero inflation.

For the rest of us, the tormenting difficulty is that the economy shows inflationary bias even when there is significant *in*voluntary unemployment. The bias is in some sense a structural defect of the economy and society, perhaps a failure to find and to respect orderly political and social mechanisms for reconciling inconsistent claims to real income. Chronic and accelerating inflation is then a symptom of a deeper social disorder, of which involuntary unemployment is an alternative symptom. Political economists may differ about whether it is better to face the social conflicts squarely or to let inflation obscure them and muddle through. I can understand why anyone who prefers the first alternative would be working for structural reform, for a new social contract. I cannot understand why he would believe that the job can be done by monetary policy. Within limits, the Federal Reserve can shift from one symptom to the other. But it cannot cure the disease.

Asset Markets and the Cost of Capital

James TOBIN and William C. BRAINARD*

A central theme of macro-economic theory throughout the twentieth century has been the sensitivity of capital formation to interest rates in financial markets. Theories of business fluctuations attribute great significance to variation in the pace of real investment, and attribute much of this variation to changes in the relative attractions for wealth-owners of physical capital, on the one hand, and money or obligations to pay money, on the other hand. Moreover, some of these changes are engineered by the monetary operations of governments and central banks; they represent a principal channel by which the authorities stabilize or destabilize the economy.

William Fellner's writings on these subjects place him in a tradition which includes, among others, Wicksell, Keynes, Schumpeter, Robertson, and Hayek. In addition to his many contributions to general macroeconomics and cycle theory, Fellner has advanced our understanding of the relation between technological change and capital formation and of business decisions with respect to risk. Our own approach to macroeconomics and its behavioral foundations has profited from our many years of contact with "Willy" at Yale.

Our paper concerns a concept which we have elsewhere baptized "q", the ratio between two valuations of the same physical asset. One, the numerator, is the market valuation: the going price in the market for exchanging existing assets. The other, the denominator, is the replacement or reproduction cost: the price in the market for newly produced commodities. We believe that this ratio has considerable macroeconomic significance and usefulness, as the nexus between financial markets and markets for goods and services.

Section 1 of the paper explains the rationale for "q", and its role in macroeconomic theory and policy. We consider also the determinants of

*Research for this paper was in part supported by grants from the National Science Foundation and the Ford Foundation. We are also grateful for expert help in computation from Roger Grawe, Jeremy Bulow, and David Hsieh.

Reprinted by permission from *Economic Progress, Private Values and Public Policy: Essays in Honor of William Fellner*, eds. Richard Nelson and Bela Balassa, Amsterdam: North-Holland, 1977, pp. 235–262.

q, both for the economy in aggregate and for specific assets and business firms.

Section 2 reports an empirical investigation of the factors determining differences in *q*'s among non-financial corporations in the United States in each of the fifteen years 1960–1974. Although this study relies on microeconomic data, its motivation is, like that of Section 1, macroeconomic. We seek to estimate the changing market valuations of various characteristics of firms – growth, cyclical sensitivity, risk, leverage, earnings rate on replacement value of capital. From these estimates we construct measures of the cost of capital to American corporations, which we regard as better indicators of the impact of monetary policy and financial events on corporate investment than the nominal or real interest rates commonly used.

1. Valuation of Capital Stocks and their Earnings Streams

1.1. Used and New Goods

Markets for used durable producers' and consumers' goods are a central feature of capitalist economies. These may be – direct or indirect – markets for the goods themselves or for claims to the goods and to their fruits. Direct used goods markets provide everchanging market valuations both of non-reproducible real assets, like land and mineral deposits, and of reproducible assets, like buildings and equipment. In the case of reproducible assets, the current cost of producing identical or competitive goods is obviously an important factor in the valuation of an existing asset. Thus a rise in residential construction costs can be expected to raise the value of existing homes, and a rise in the price of new cars is "good" for the price of previous years' models. The reverse is also true. High valuations of existing stocks will lead both to increased production and higher prices of newly produced substitutes.

New and used prices can diverge significantly for extended periods of time, and the valuations of existing assets are more volatile than the costs or prices of their newly produced counterparts. An increase in the market valuation of houses relative to current cost of building will encourage residential construction. The incentive is the gain to be made by the excess of market price over replacement cost.

This profit is not wiped out immediately because construction takes time, and rapid construction is especially expensive, both for the individual builder and for the economy as a whole. In the longer run, however, the increase in stock brings market value into line with replacement cost, lowering the former and/or raising the latter. In equilibrium the volume of construction will meet demands for replacement and normal growth, and the size of the stock will be such that market value is the same as marginal production cost for the equilibrium volume of construction.

1.2. Business and Corporate Capital

The same mechanism applies to non-residential structures and producers' equipment. But there is an important difference. The various physical assets of a business enterprise are often designed, installed, and used in complex combinations specific to the technology. It is costly or impossible to detach and move individual assets or to apply them to alternative purposes. The valuation of the business as a whole as a going concern is generally much more relevant than the separate valuations of the assets on used goods markets.

Markets for businesses take several forms. Small unincorporated businesses are bought and sold directly or through brokers; see, for example, the advertisements in any Sunday *New York Times* or in trade journals. Corporations acquire other companies either by buying their assets or by acquiring their stock.

The most important markets, however, are those for corporate securities. In these markets ownership of corporate businesses, and other claims upon the assets, change hands daily. The securities markets provide, therefore, a continuing market valuation of the enterprise, and thus indirectly of the productive assets of the company. These markets are well organized and efficient. Their valuations are sensitive and volatile. Here, even more than in used goods markets, discrepancies arise and persist between the market valuations and the replacement costs of the assets which the market is indirectly and implicitly valuing. But here too we can expect the formation of new businesses and the expansion of existing ones to respond to such discrepancies.

As is so often the case, the point was expressed succinctly by Keynes, *General Theory* (p. 151):

> "[The] daily revaluations of the Stock Exchange, though they are primarily made to facilitate transfers of old investments between one individual and another, inevitably exert a decisive influence on the rate of current investment. For there is no sense in building up a new enterprise at a cost greater than that at which a similar existing enterprise can be purchased; whilst there is an inducement to spend

on a new project what may seem an extravagant sum, if it can be floated off on the Stock Exchange at an immediate profit."

This is the common sense justification for paying attention, as we have previously advocated,[1] to the ratio "q" of the market valuation of reproducible real capital assets to the current replacement cost of those assets. In the illustrative case of houses discussed above, q would be the ratio of market value to replacement cost, for an individual house, or for an aggregate stock. The same concept applies to a business or to corporate business in aggregate, though "replacement cost" must be interpreted to cover not only physical assets but other items on the firm's balance sheet.

Economic logic indicates that a normal equilibrium value for q is 1 for reproducible assets which are in fact being reproduced, and less than 1 for others. Values of q above 1 should stimulate investment, in excess of requirements for replacement and normal growth, and values of q below 1 discourage investment. We shall discuss below why the normal value for statistical representations of q may be different from 1.

1.3. Discounting Future Earnings

The simplest model of valuation of an earning asset says that its present value is the sum of discounted earnings at all future dates. For a house, the earnings are rents – cash or imputed, net of costs of operation and maintenance, taxes, etc. For the durable productive assets of a business, earnings are the net cash flows over their lifetimes. For a share of stock, the earnings stream includes all future dividends and other distributions.

The discount rates applied to expected earnings represent, in principle, interest costs: rates of return which the investor must pay to borrow funds to hold the asset or must sacrifice by holding smaller amounts of other assets.

The securities – debt, preferred stock, common stock – of a corporation are essentially claims to the earnings thrown off by the real productive capital assets of the business. The securities will rise in value when "the market" revises upward its expectations of future earnings, or revises downward its discount rates. Those discount rates are related to open market interest rates, which are powerfully influenced by monetary polices. The market may also take Federal Reserve actions into account

---

[1]See Tobin–Brainard (1968) and Tobin (1969); these are respectively Chapters 20 and 18 in Tobin (1971).

in judging future earnings. In any event it is a fact of common observation, especially in recent years, that the stock market, as well as the bond market, is highly sensitive to movements in short-term interest rates under the control of the monetary authority.

1.4. Valuations and Risks

As we stated at the outset, the margin of asset substitution between obligations to pay specified amounts of money and ownership of physical capital is an important one in macroeconomic models. Theorists have differed in the degree of substitutability assumed between bonds and capital. While Keynes' investment theory takes them as close or even perfect substitutes, we have emphasized that they are imperfect substitutes, with a margin of differential yield as important and as variable as liquidity preference theory finds between bonds and bills or bills and cash.[2] A principal reason for distinguishing, at an aggregate level, between bonds and capital is their difference in risk. The major risks on capital relate to real events – changes in technology, utilization, relative scarcities, and labor costs. The major risks on financial assets arise from uncertainties about future rates of inflation and interest.

Risk is also crucial at a disaggregated level. Differences in the magnitude and nature of risk are probably the most important factors leading to differences of required rates of return on investment in various firms and types of capital.

How would one expect valuations of assets to depend on the nature of their risks? Portfolio theory has provided some insights, which can be given precision under special assumptions [Lintner (1965), Sharpe (1964)]. The standard assumptions are that there exists a riskless asset, that investors may borrow as well as lend at the riskless rate, that they are concerned only about the mean and variance of the total return to their portfolio, and that they all agree on a joint probability distribution of asset returns. Then it can be shown that the relevant risk on any one asset is not the total variance of its return but only the "undiversifiable" part. This undiversifiable risk (which may be negative) reflects the covariation of the asset's rate of return with an overall market index of rates of return, in which assets are weighted by their relative supplies. If, for example, the asset's returns are independent of those on other assets, its "undiversifiable" risk reflects only its own weight in the index. Such an asset's own risk matters, but a single firm or particular investment in a large economy will

---

[2]See, for example, Tobin (1961); also Chapter 13 of Tobin (1971).

have a weight close to zero. On average, covariation of returns on business assets tends to be positive. Most assets have some undiversifiable risk.

The risk premium on a particular asset – the excess of its expected return over the riskless rate – depends on the amount of its undiversifiable risk and on a market-wide "price of risk". This common "price of risk", reflecting the aggregate supplies of the riskless and risky assets and the risk preferences of investors, provides all the information required to value the undiversifiable risk associated with any particular asset.

The simplicity of these results obviously reflects the very special nature of the underlying assumptions. Although relaxation of even one of these assumptions greatly complicates the problem of valuation, some of the qualitative characteristics of this valuation model probably survive.

For example, suppose that transactions costs limit the number of assets a typical investor can hold in his portfolio. The "undiversifiable" risk of a particular asset to him then depends on its covariation not with the entire market but with his own portfolio. Obviously an asset will be a higher proportion of the portfolios in which it is held than in the aggregate market "portfolio". Hence its own variance will be more important. In the extreme and unrealistic case where only one risky asset is held in each portfolio, its own variance is a complete and accurate measure of "undiversifiable" risk. In principle, it would be possible to relate risk premia to covariations with individualized portfolios, but as a practical matter, these are unobservable. The conclusion is that restrictions or economic limitations on the number of assets typically held in a portfolio make the estimation of undiversifiable risk difficult and increase the importance of own variance. But it is still possible to describe asset return throughout the market in terms of a riskless rate and a single "price of risk".

Relaxing other assumptions, e.g., the existence of a riskless asset, the possibility of borrowing and lending at the same rate, the homogeneity of expectations, further complicates matters. These complications not only make it difficult, both conceptually and empirically, to measure the relavant risks on particular assets. They also make it impossible to speak of, let alone estimate, a single price of risk.

In recent years there has been considerable empirical investigation of the effect of risk on the valuation of assets using the general analytic framework discussed above. Almost all of this work has focused on the market for equities. There are several conceptual difficulties with attempting to estimate the required rate of return on physical assets from equities markets alone. These have led us to look at the valuation of firms, not simply the valuation of their common stock issues.

First, even under the restrictive assumptions necessary for the simple valuation model, the list of assets should include corporate and government bonds as well as equities. Relaxation of those assumptions seems likely to make their omission even more important. In principle, even the risks on less marketable assets, such as houses, consumer durables, and human capital, are relevant to the valuation of stocks and bonds.

Second, the valuation of a firm's productive business assets may depend importantly on the firm's financial structure. It is true that the celebrated Modigliani–Miller theorem says that a firm's valuation should be independent of its financial structure, implying that a firm could theoretically estimate the required rate on a new investment just by looking in the stock market and observing the market's valuation of equities whose distribution of returns were proportional to those on the contemplated investment. But there are important reasons for believing that the valuation of a firm's physical assets and their returns cannot be divorced from its financial structure. These include corporate income taxation, which is not neutral as between debt interest and dividends; the implications of leverage for probability of bankruptcy and loss of control; economies of scale in borrowing which enable stockholders to borrow more cheaply through the corporation than individually. Looking directly at the market valuation of firms' total earnings, interest as well as common stock earnings, requires less restrictive assumptions than looking separately at the firm's various securities.

1.5. Effects of Inflation

What is the effect of inflation on the value of q? As usual, it is important to distinguish between anticipated and unanticipated inflation.

For anticipated inflation, a first approximation is (1) that q is independent of the inflation rate and (2) that q will not change over time as a result of the realization of anticipated inflation. The denominator of q moves, of course, with the prices of new capital goods in the commodity markets. The numerator will do likewise if both expected real earnings and the real interest rate used to discount them are independent of the expected rate of inflation. Stated in nominal terms, these sufficient conditions are that the dollar earnings anticipated at any future date are proportional to the price level expected at that date, and that the interest rate for that date varies point for point with the expected rate of inflation from now until then.

However, this first approximation, neutrality of inflation, fails in practice for several reasons:

Taxes are not neutral. In particular, nominal "earnings" which simply maintain the real value of an asset are taxed. Profits are overstated and over-taxed when depreciation is based on original cost.[3] This tends to lower q, but working in the other direction is the reduction of aftertax real interest rates due to the taxation of nominal interest.

Nominal interest rates do not accurately incorporate inflation premiums. Certain nominal rates are frozen or controlled – the zero rate on currency and demand deposits, the ceiling rates on savings and time deposits. Inflation expectations necessarily reduce the real rates on these assets and tend, therefore, to lower real rates in general.[4] But this q-raising effect can be offset by deliberate monetary policy.

Unanticipated inflation, or more generally upward revisions in expectations of future prices, will have additional non-neutral effects. The windfall gains of borrowers, including levered corporations, will be reflected in higher market valuations, but since similar gains cannot be expected to recur, marginal q's will not benefit. In the past, inflationary news was frequently considered a favorable sign for real business activity. Firming of prices was a symptom of strength in aggregate demand. Nowadays, however, inflationary news is more likely to be considered the harbinger of anti-inflationary policies – bringing recession, stagflation, or price controls, all damaging to the stream of earnings. Recent experience has firmly implanted this view in the market.

1.6. Market Valuation and Investment

The neoclassical theory of corporate investment is based on the assumption that the management seeks to maximize the present net worth of the company, the market value of the outstanding common shares. An investment project should be undertaken if and only if it increases the value of the shares. The securities markets appraise the project, its expected contributions to the future earnings of the company and its risks. If the value of the project as appraised by investors exceeds the cost, then the company's shares will appreciate to the benefit of existing stockholders. That is, the market will value the project more than the cash used to pay for it. If new debt or equity securities are issued to raise the cash, the prospectus leads to an increase of share prices. To state the point another way round, suppose the firm sells additional shares at the going market

---

[3]For empirical estimates of this and other non-neutral effects, see Shoven and Bulow (1975/6).

[4]For explanation, see Tobin (1969).

price. Will the proceeds suffice to purchase the earnings that justify that price? If they will do so, with margin to spare, then the joint operation – share issue and investment – benefits the original shareholders.

Clearly it is the q ratio *on the margin* that matters for investment: the ratio of the increment of market valuation to the cost of the associated investment. The crucial value for marginal q is 1, but this is consistent with average q values quite different from 1. A firm with monopoly power, or other sources of diminishing returns to scale, will have an average q ratio higher than its marginal q. The difference is the market's valuation of its rents or monopoly profits or "good will".

A similar but conceptually distinct problem arises from the heterogeneity of capital goods and from technological progress. The average q ratio for existing capital stocks may be a serious understatement of q for new capital goods of quite different nature. This occurs spectacularly when the new have rendered the old obsolete. The Schumpeterian phenomenon may occur within a single firm, but it is more likely to characterize whole industries or economies during periods of rapid innovation. It is at least conceivable to observe investment booms during periods when observed average q ratios are low and even declining.

Changes in factor prices make profitable new investments which promise to economize scarce factors at the same time that they lower the value of old capital goods adapted to previous prices. For example, the drastic increase in oil prices in 1973 lowered the q's for firms committed to high energy-using technologies, while making attractively profitable on the margin investments embodying energy-saving technologies.

Another dimension of heterogeneity is risk. This too can make q on the margin exceed average q. The new investments of a firm may be in a different "risk class" from the old, with different connections with the rest of the economy. They will make the firm's securities more attractive to investors by reducing the amount of undiversifiable risk they carry. Transactions costs and other limits on the sizes of individual portfolios make diversification within firms an efficient alternative to portfolio diversification across firms. This has been one of the incentives for conglomeration.

Nevertheless, the forces of continuity in the economy are strong. Especially for short-run variations of aggregate demand, we can expect that the same factors which raise or lower q on the margin likewise raise or lower q on average. This is confirmed by John Ciccolo's regressions of aggregate business fixed investment on eight quarters distributed lag values of q [Ciccolo (1975)]. These alone explain 40% of the 1953–73 quarterly variation of the ratio of gross investment to the capital stock, I/K. The eventual full effect of a 0.10 increase in q is to raise I/K by 0.08.

Investment would not be related to q if instantaneous arbitrage could produce such floods of new capital goods as to keep market values and replacement costs continuously in line. For reasons given above, such arbitrage does not occur. Discrepancies between q and its normal value do arise. The speed with which investment eliminates such discrepancies depends on the costs of adjustment and growth for individual enterprises, and for the economy as a whole on the short-run marginal costs of producing investment goods.

This is a different investment theory from what appears to be the Keynesian investment function of the *General Theory*, Keynes' condition that the marginal efficiency of capital equal the rate of interest determines not the flow of investment but the stock of capital. Specifically, it determines the capital/labor and capital/output ratios. In a stationary economy, satisfaction of the condition – at whatever level of the interest rate – means zero investment. In a growing economy, it means capital accumulation at the natural growth rate of the economy. (Since the capital stock will be larger the lower the interest rate, investment will also be larger the lower the interest rate. But this long-run steady state relationship is clearly not what Keynes had in mind in postulating an inverse relation between investment and interest rate.)

Since Keynes discusses at length independent variations in the marginal efficiency of capital and the rate of interest, he does not really imagine that investment adjusts the capital stock fast enough to keep them continuously equal. Indeed the true message is that investment is related to discrepancies between the marginal efficiency and the interest rate. This is the tradition of Wicksell and of Keynes' earlier work *The Treatise on Money*. The q ratio theory of investment follows this same tradition. Indeed under special conditions q could be equivalently defined as the ratio of the marginal efficiency of capital R to the interest rate r_k used to discount future earnings streams.[5]

---

[5]The marginal efficiency R is defined by the equation

$$V = \int_0^\infty E(t)\, e^{-Rt}\, dt,$$

where V is the cost of capital goods at time 0 and $E(t)$ their expected earnings.

$$\overline{MV} = \int_0^\infty E(t)\, e^{-r_k t}\, dt,$$

where $\overline{MV}$ is the market valuation of the capital goods and r_k the discount rate. If E is constant then

$$V = E/R, \qquad \overline{MV} = E/r_k, \qquad MV/V = R/r_k.$$

Several points deserve emphasis. First, the statistic q is observable as a ratio of market valuation and replacement cost, whereas R and r_k are not observable. Second, the discount rate r_k is not any observed interest rate on long-term bonds or other fixed-money-value obligations. Those interest rates are the discount factors for streams of payments with the risks and other characteristics of those instruments, while r_k is the discount rate for streams of return with the characteristics of earnings on business capital. The rates are related but not identical. Third, the rates r_k and R are in the same interest-rate numéraire. As discount for a stream of dollar earnings, they both would be nominal rates. As discount for a stream of earnings in constant dollars, they both would be real rates. The ratio q is the same either way.

The hypothesis that investment is related to the difference between R and r_k, or to the value of q, bears some resemblance to the "flexible accelerator" idea that investment is a function of the difference between a desired and actual capital stock. The desired stock appropriate to r_k is larger than the actual stock which yields R, when r_k is lower than R. Indeed the market value of the existing stock is a sort of estimate of the desired stock at replacement cost.[6]

1.7. A "q" Formulation of IS/LM Equilibrium

The investment function for a macroeconomic model could take the form $\Delta K/K = \varphi(q - \bar{q}) + g$, where $\bar{q}$ is the normal value of q, perhaps 1, $\varphi(+) = +$, $\varphi(0) = 0$, $\varphi(-) = -$, and g is the natural growth rate. Growth equilibrium occurs at that value of net output $\bar{Y}$ at which saving supports net investment gK, with $q = \bar{q}$. An "IS" locus in (q, Y) space will normally have $\partial q/\partial Y > 0$. As Y increases, saving increases at given value of q. Thus a higher value of q is required to induce additional investment, or to discourage saving. Consumer wealth rises with q, and consumption spending is stimulated by additional wealth.

An "LM" locus can also be constructed in (q, Y) space, for given *real* quantities of high-powered money and other government debts, and for a given expected rate of inflation. The financial system may contain any number of assets and determine any number of interest rates, as well as q. These outcomes will depend on Y, for the usual reason that Y affects the demands for money and for other assets. If long-run expectations of earnings, summarized in the marginal efficiency of capital, are insensitive

---

[6]This is exact if the elasticity of the marginal productivity of capital with respect to the stock is unity, so that $K^* r_k = KR$, where K^* is the desired stock corresponding to r_k.

to current Y, the LM locus will have $\partial q / \partial Y < 0$. Increasing transactions requirements for cash raise interest rates in general, and in particular raise the rate of discount of future earnings. But if the marginal efficiency of capital is sensitive to current Y, the sign of $\partial q / \partial Y$ may be positive: an increase in Y raises R faster than r_k. (In conventional IS/LM frameworks, this same phenomenon is usually modelled as an upward-sloping IS curve because marginal propensities to invest and to consume sum to more than one.)

Figure 1 shows these IS and LM curves. To preserve familiarity, q is measured downward on the vertical axis. Two alternative LM curves are drawn, the first on the assumption that the marginal efficiency R used in calculation of q is always $R(\bar{Y})$, based on earnings along the growth equilibrium path. The second LM curve, upward sloping, assumes R to be an increasing function of Y, $R(Y)$. Exogenous increases in R will shift the LM curve down, even though they generally raise interest rates. Expansionary monetary policy will also move the LM curve down, while lowering interest rates. Autonomous increases in consumer or government spending will, as usual, move the IS locus up.

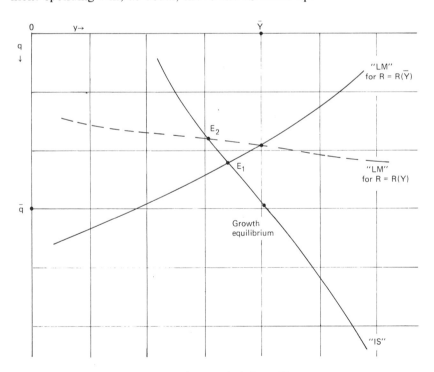

FIGURE 1. IS/LM analysis in (q, Y) space.

The above exposition embodies all the simplicities of aggregation of textbook macroeconomic models. To avoid misunderstanding, we reiterate our recognition that in fact there are many kinds of capital and accordingly many q's coexisting with different values. Moreover, there are channels other than "q's" by which monetary policies and events are transmitted to demands for goods and services. The most important of these are liquidity constraints of various kinds – credit limits, credit rationing, illiquidity of human capital and many other assets, rate ceilings, governmental restrictions on financial portfolios, etc. As these constraints are made to bind less or more tightly, spending effects occur which are inadequately modelled if related simply to prices of assets and commodities.

For these reasons, among others, it would be foolish to advocate any estimate of "q" as the sole indicator for monetary policy. But estimates of "q" are useful indicators. The fact that the indicator is in part policy-determined and in part endogenous is in this case a virtue. If "q" is low, we cannot tell whether the cause is pessimism about future profits or high discounts of future earnings, or whether, if it is the latter, the source is tight central bank policy or public asset preference. The indicated response for monetary policy is the same whichever the cause. Whether pessimistic earnings expectations, conservative asset preferences, or stingy supply of high-powered money is the reason for low q, the appropriate remedial action – and the only remedial action available to the monetary authority – is to expand the supply of bank reserves. The exceptions to the rule are the cases, discussed above, where marginal and average q's are moving in opposite directions.[7]

2. Empirical Study of Determinants of "q" 1960–74

2.1. The "Fundamental" Approach

The remainder of the paper reports a statistical investigation of stock market determinations of q's for individual industrial corporations listed on the New York Stock Exchange 1960–74. The data used were read from the Standard and Poor "Compustat" tape.

The approach is, in stock market parlance, "fundamental". That is, differences among firms in stock market prices are attributed to earnings,

---

[7]But the relevance of this caveat should not be exaggerated. In early 1974 the q model threw off pessimistic predictions of fixed investment. Yet it was easy to think that, given the embargo and OPEC price increase of 1973, energy-related projects would make total investment much stronger than the model predicted. This proved not to be the case.

dividends, and observable characteristics of the firms and not to previous histories of stock prices themselves.

In most studies the market value of equities is made to depend upon the characteristics of the distribution of market yields (dividends and capital gains) rather than on the more fundamental characteristics of the firm. The distribution of market yields reflects fluctuation of market discount rates as well as fluctuation in the firm's earnings. It is difficult to construct a "bootstrap" model of asset markets in which the risk characteristics of market yields used in the valuation of assets are consistent with the fluctuations in value generated by the market itself. Further, it is difficult to know how firms in making investment, and financing decisions, should react to changes in the market's valuation of risk which reflect speculative movements, or to changes in capitalization rates in response to investor preferences. For these reasons, we have taken the direct and simple expedient of asking how the market values that which the firm has to sell, the claims on prospective earnings associated with the firm's investment in physical assets.

2.2. The Variables

For each of the fifteen years 1960–74 a cross-section regression is calculated for a sample of firms. The dependent variable is q for the firm. The explanatory variables are characteristics of the firm which, theory suggests, should affect its market valuation. These characteristics, which will be defined precisely below, are as follows:

"Beta"   *Growth Rate.*   The prior trend of the logarithm of earnings.

"Gamma"   *Cyclical Sensitivity.*   Past relationship of earnings to the national unemployment rate.

"X"   *Covariance.*   Observed relationship of firm's earnings to aggregate earnings, both relative to growth trends. This is calculated for the mean unemployment rate previously observed.

"Sigma"   *Earnings Volatility.*   Variability of firm's earnings around trend, whether due to business cycle (as indicated by unemployment rate) or to unexplained factors.

"PB"   *Default Probability.*   Estimated probability that earnings will fall short of fixed debt service charges.

"PD" *Vulnerability of Dividend.* Estimated probability that earnings will fall short of fixed charges plus preferred and common dividends.

"D/V" *Dividend Rate.* Common dividends per dollar of capital.

"E/V" *Earnings Rate.* Earnings per dollar of capital.

The firm's q is measured as the ratio of market value $\overline{MV}$ to invested capital at replacement cost, V. The numerator $\overline{MV}$ includes three aggregates; common stock, preferred stock, and long-term debt. The firm's outstanding common stock is valued at its end-of-year prices. However, the tape does not provide data on market values of preferred stock and long-term debt, only book values. We were therefore not able to take account of inter-firm variations in these valuations. But we have tried to improve on the book values, by eliminating year-to-year economy-wide sources of divergence between book and market value.

We have estimated the market value of the firm's preferred stock from its reported preferred dividends for the year, dividing this quantity by the published Standard and Poor index of preferred stock yield for December. This index varies from year to year but is, for any one year, the same for all firms. A similar expedient was used to convert book value of long-term debt to market value. An economy-wide annual index of the ratio of market value of corporate debt securities to their principal value was estimated. The index was estimated from the series on gross issues from 1941 to 1974, assuming that all bonds have 20-year maturity, are issued at par with a common equal to the average Baa yield in the year of issue, and in each subsequent year are valued to yield until maturity the average Baa yield of that year.

The denominator V, invested capital at replacement cost, is the sum of the book values of common stock, preferred stock, and long-term debt, corrected by a common annual index of the ratio of replacement cost to book value. The book value of securities is not identical to the book value of physical capital assets; there are various short-term financial assets and liabilities on the balance sheet. Ignoring these items, we have corrected the book value by estimating an economy-wide index of the ratio of current replacement cost of fixed capital assets (non-residential plant and equipment) to original cost. Our index assumes exponential depreciation at 5% per year, and uses the deflator for the fixed investment component of GNP. Multiplicative correction of book values by the index is the same for all firms in any given year. But by avoiding increasing understatement of replacement value during recent years of high inflation, the correction helps to preserve comparability of results from year to year.

The "earnings" of a firm in a year include debt service and preferred stock dividends as well as the earnings attributable to common stock. Our reasons for inclusive definition both of earnings and of the capital base of earnings were explained in Section 1.

In the fifteen annual cross-section regressions, the ratio of earnings to replacement value (E/V) is, of course, the most important variable explaining q, the ratio of market value to replacement value $(\overline{MV}/V)$. Dividends paid on common stock, also measured relative to V, (D/V), may also influence q.

The other six characteristics used as regressors in the cross-section regression for year T are based on a time series regression specific to the firm using observations for the years 1955 through $1955 + T - 1$. This regression for firm i for year T takes the form

$$\ln E_{it} = \alpha_{iT} + \beta_{iT}t + \gamma_{iT}U_t + \epsilon_{it}, \qquad t = 1, 2, \ldots, T - 1. \tag{1}$$

U_t is the standard series for national unemployment rate, in percent of labor force, average for the year. Regression (1) is estimated by ordinary least squares, but with recent observations weighted more heavily. Specifically, the weights are proportional to $\exp(-0.12(T - t))$. Regression (1) attempts to simulate what market investors in year T can infer from the simple statistical history of the earnings of the firm. Clearly it does not allow for many other sources of firm-specific information.

The firm characteristics "beta" and "gamma" are the estimates of β_{iT} and γ_{iT}. These characteristics vary across firms every year, and for each firm they are re-estimated every year. To define the remaining characteristics we must consider for each firm, for each year T, expected earnings

$$\ln \hat{E}_{it} = \alpha_{iT} + \beta_{iT}t + \gamma_{iT}\bar{U}_T, \tag{2}$$

where the coefficients α, β, γ are the estimates from the weighted OLS regression (1) already described and $\bar{U}_T$ is the simple arithmetic mean value of U for the years 1 through $T - 1$. Thus $\hat{E}_{it}$ is an estimate of earnings at what an investor might regard as a cyclically normal unemployment rate. Let σ_{iT} be the standard deviation of $E_{it} - \hat{E}_{it}$ over the years of the regression, each deviation weighted in the same manner as the observations for the regression itself. The characteristic "sigma" is then σ_{it}/V_T. Dividing by the capital value V eliminates scale differences between firms. Sigma is a measure of the historical volatility of the firm's earnings, whether the variability was due to the business cycle, via U, or the factors other than trend and cycle represented by ϵ in equation (1).

PB is the estimated probability that earnings E_T will not exceed fixed debt charges I_T. Let s_{iT} be the standard deviation of $\ln E_{it} - \ln \hat{E}_{it}$, computed with the same decaying exponential weights used before. *PB* is then calculated on the assumption that $\ln E_{iT}$ is normally distributed with mean $\ln \hat{E}_{iT}$ and standard deviation s_{iT}. *PD* is similarly calculated as the probability that E_T will not exceed I_T plus preferred and common dividends. Note that these probabilities, like "sigma", allow for uncertainties about business cycle developments as well as other variability in firm earnings. Since these probability measures are used in regression along with "sigma", *PB* is really a measure of leverage. For given "sigma", a larger *PB* means a higher level of fixed charges, only measured in "probits" rather than dollars. Likewise, given "sigma" and *PB*, a high *PD* means a high dividend policy, again measured in "probits".

The remaining characteristic *X* requires further explanation. Consider the sample of firms used in year *T*, and let E_t be ΣE_{it} for that sample. A weighted regression of $\ln E_t$ on t and U_t, of the same form as (1), is computed on observations $(1, 2, \ldots, T - 1)$. Likewise, $\ln \hat{E}_t$ is calculated according to equation (2). Then

$$X_{iT} = \frac{\text{cov}(\ln E_{it} - \ln \hat{E}_{it}, \ln E_t - \ln \hat{E}_t)}{\text{var}(\ln E_t - \ln \hat{E}_t)}, \tag{3}$$

where the covariance and variance are computed with the usual weights through year $T - 1$.

The characteristic *X* is analogous to the β commonly calculated in portfolio analysis as a measure of the relationship of the yield, including appreciation, of an individual stock to the yield of an overall market index. It is this which is multiplied by the "price of risk" to get the risk premium for an individual stock. Here, however, in keeping with our "fundamentalist" approach, the elasticity *X* relates the earnings of an individual firm to aggregate earnings. It is a partial elasticity to the extent that growth trends are eliminated. Theory suggests that the market will downgrade firms whose earnings move with economy-wide earnings and prize firms whose earnings move counter to the aggregate. That is, *q* should be negatively related to *X*.

2.3. The Results

The cross-section regression computed for each year *T*, (1960–1974 inclusive), is simply linear and has been fit by ordinary least squares,

$$q_{iT} = a_{0T} + a_{1T}\beta_{iT} + a_{2T} + a_{3T}X_{iT} + a_{4T}(\sigma_{iT}/V_{iT}) + a_{5T}\overline{PB}_{iT}$$
$$+ a_{6T}\overline{PD}_{iT} + a_{7T}(D_{iT}/V_{iT}) + a_{8T}(E_{iT}/V_{iT}) + u_{iT}. \tag{4}$$

For each year *T*, as many firms were included as met the following conditions:[8] Earnings were positive in all years through T, and all the data necessary to compute regression (1), E_{iT}, D_{iT}, V_{iT}, and q_{iT} were available.

Table 1 summarizes the regressions, showing the sizes of the samples in each year and the values of R^2. Table 2 reports the mean values and standard deviations of q and the eight independent variables for each year. Tables 3–10, one table for each independent variable, give the coefficients of the fifteen cross-section regressions. Tables 11 and 12, and Figures 2 and 3, record some summary measures, and it is these results we shall discuss first.

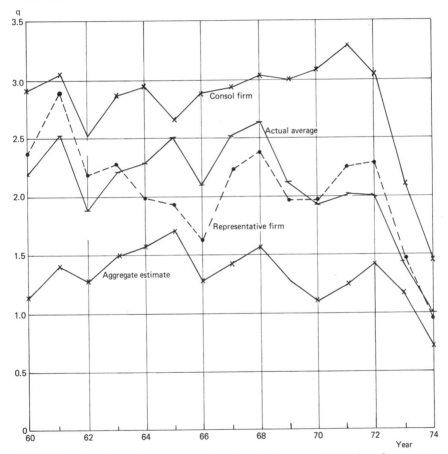

FIGURE 2. Alternative estimates of q, ratio of market to replacement value of corporate capital, 1960–74.

[8]Actually, two samples were assembled and two cross-section regressions computed for each year, one for all eligible companies, and one for dividend-paying companies only. Since the results were negligibly different, they will be presented only for the "all companies" samples.

TABLE 1
SUMMARY OF CROSS-SECTION REGRESSIONS, 1960–74.

Year	All companies		Div.-paying companies		Year	All companies		Div.-paying companies	
	No.	R^2	No.	R^2		No.	R^2	No.	R^2
1960	424	0.40	405	0.42	1968	409	0.48	399	0.50
1961	419	0.50	398	0.52	1969	406	0.46	394	0.48
1962	419	0.48	398	0.49	1970	397	0.44	383	0.47
1963	419	0.45	399	0.46	1971	395	0.49	373	0.54
1964	418	0.47	400	0.50	1972	392	0.49	370	0.54
1965	415	0.49	405	0.50	1973	392	0.36	376	0.38
1966	415	0.40	408	0.40	1974	384	0.24	371	0.30
1967	414	0.46	405	0.47					

TABLE
MEANS (STANDARD DEVIATIONS) OF

Year	q	Beta	Gamma	X
1960	2.21 (1.85)	0.104 (0.127)	−0.0925 (0.159)	1.145 (1.92)
1961	2.51 (2.10)	0.083 (0.128)	−0.0737 (0.156)	0.965 (1.92)
1962	1.88 (1.41)	0.081 (0.122)	−0.0754 (0.154)	0.983 (1.96)
1963	2.21 (1.83)	0.068 (0.105)	−0.0566 (0.146)	0.743 (1.91)
1964	2.29 (1.81)	0.069 (0.092)	−0.0574 (0.156)	0.672 (1.89)
1965	2.50 (2.25)	0.078 (0.079)	−0.0784 (0.153)	0.864 (1.67)
1966	2.11 (2.20)	0.083 (0.074)	−0.0954 (0.152)	0.990 (1.58)
1967	2.51 (2.37)	0.086 (0.072)	−0.1055 (0.150)	1.129 (1.63)
1968	2.54 (2.22)	0.084 (0.070)	−0.1007 (0.152)	1.148 (1.67)
1969	2.12 (1.88)	0.084 (0.068)	−0.0966 (0.150)	1.123 (1.68)
1970	1.92 (1.61)	0.084 (0.065)	−0.0954 (0.150)	1.130 (1.69)
1971	2.00 (1.70)	0.084 (0.066)	−0.0949 (0.132)	1.124 (1.53)
1972	1.99 (1.83)	0.087 (0.062)	−0.0840 (0.119)	1.188 (1.57)
1973	1.43 (1.84)	0.089 (0.058)	−0.0768 (0.116)	1.153 (1.54)
1974	0.97 (0.70)	0.094 (0.053)	−0.0736 (0.116)	0.965 (1.28)
Avg.[b]	2.08	0.084 (0.083)	−0.0838 (0.144)	1.021 (1.70)

[a] q = Ratio market to replacement value.
Beta   = Past growth rate of earnings.
Gamma = Past relation to unemployment rate.
X = Relation firm earnings to economy earnings.
Sigma   = Earnings variability.

By a "representative firm" we mean a hypothetical firm with characteristics fixed at the overall means (the simple average of the fifteen yearly means) for the period 1960–74. These are the figures in the bottom row of Table 2. By applying to these fixed characteristics the varying regression coefficients, we compute a time series of hypothetical q's for a representative American non-industrial corporation (column 1 of Table 11). This is not the same as the series of mean q's from Table 2 (also column 2 of Table 11), which apply to firms of changing characteristics. The two series generally conform, but diverge appreciably in several years. They are both plotted in Figure 2, together with Ciccolo's aggregate estimates of q. Given the differences of data base and statistical method, the *level* difference between our q's and Ciccolo's are not alarming. As should be expected, his aggregate estimate conforms better to our series of mean q than to our fixed-weight index.

To compare with the representative firm, we consider a non-existent "consol firm", with zero levels of all characteristics except the last two, D/V and E/V. They are put equal to each other and fixed at the overall mean of E/V for the period 1960–74. This theoretical consol firm is riskless, trendless, and cycle-free; it has no debt or preferred stock and pays out all its earnings at dividends. Its q series (column 3 of Table 11) is

2

REGRESSION VARIABLES, 1960–74.[a]

Sigma	PB	PD	D/V	E/V
0.0186 (0.017)	0.0106 (0.068)	0.0765 (0.155)	0.0415 (0.0301)	0.0906 (0.0456)
0.0169 (0.014)	0.0149 (0.096)	0.0726 (0.156)	0.0411 (0.0296)	0.0886 (0.0461)
0.0155 (0.014)	0.0176 (0.097)	0.0765 (0.155)	0.0380 (0.0287)	0.0846 (0.0439)
0.0144 (0.012)	0.0109 (0.068)	0.0770 (0.165)	0.0412 (0.0312)	0.0945 (0.0473)
0.0131 (0.010)	0.0106 (0.071)	0.0822 (0.168)	0.0422 (0.0324)	0.1047 (0.0496)
0.0121 (0.008)	0.0071 (0.044)	0.0730 (0.0145)	0.0428 (0.0317)	0.1107 (0.0483)
0.0122 (0.008)	0.0135 (0.072)	0.0971 (0.180)	0.0418 (0.0307)	0.1132 (0.0463)
0.0130 (0.008)	0.0218 (0.099)	0.1163 (0.200)	0.0392 (0.0285)	0.1003 (0.0449)
0.0129 (0.008)	0.0297 (0.123)	0.1433 (0.223)	0.0374 (0.0270)	0.0971 (0.0420)
0.0128 (0.007)	0.0398 (0.142)	0.1689 (0.246)	0.0353 (0.0259)	0.0944 (0.0400)
0.0127 (0.007)	0.0466 (0.151)	0.1671 (0.235)	0.0326 (0.0246)	0.0857 (0.0407)
0.0117 (0.007)	0.0355 (0.129)	0.1061 (0.176)	0.0296 (0.0236)	0.0815 (0.0388)
0.0112 (0.007)	0.0298 (0.112)	0.0763 (0.150)	0.0275 (0.0214)	0.0849 (0.0355)
0.0107 (0.007)	0.0375 (0.122)	0.1001 (0.178)	0.0262 (0.0197)	0.0949 (0.0337)
0.0103 (0.007)	0.0450 (0.131)	0.1276 (0.208)	0.0251 (0.0185)	0.0971 (0.0338)
0.0132 (0.009)	0.0247 (0.102)	0.1040 (0.183)	0.0361 (0.0269)	0.0949 (0.0424)

PB   = Probability fixed charges not earned.
PD   = Probability dividend not earned.
D/V = Ratio current div. to replacement value.
E/V = Ratio earnings to replacement value.
[b]Simple average of column.

also plotted in Figure 2. The consol series generally follows the contours of the other series. But the market has generally prized greater security and dividend pay-out.

Another summary form of the calculations is to compute the ratio of earnings to market value for our two hypothetical firms. These are estimates of the cost of capital to the firms. They are reported in Table 12 and Figure 3. For comparison, the Baa corporate bond rate is also plotted. Since our estimates of cost of capital are in principle *real* rates of return, the relevant comparison is with a Baa real rate, which has been computed by subtracting the geometric average inflation rate of the preceding five years.

Figure 3 makes two important points. First, the cost of capital relevant for investment decisions bears little relationship to the "real rate of interest" calculated by subtracting inflation rates from nominal interest rates. The tightness or ease of monetary policy and financial markets cannot be gauged by such naive calculations. Second, the effective real rate of interest is far from constant, contrary to a viewpoint of increasing currency.

The regression coefficients of Tables 3–10 provide some confirmations of theoretical expectations and some surprises and puzzles.

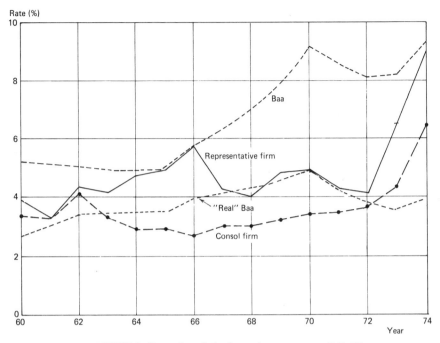

FIGURE 3. Cost of capital, alternative measures, 1960–74.

TABLE 3

EFFECT OF GROWTH RATE ON VALUATION, 1960–74;
REGRESSION COEFFICIENTS OF BETA.[a]

Year	Coefficient	t-ratio	Variable mean (std.dev.)
1960	2.1379	2.8	0.10398 (0.127)
1961	1.0601	1.4	0.08264 (0.128)
1962	1.1837	2.1	0.08072 (0.122)
1963	1.7500	2.0	0.06778 (0.105)
1964	1.5843	1.8	0.06858 (0.092)
1965	2.1020	1.7	0.07810 (0.079)
1966	4.3793	3.0	0.08335 (0.074)
1967	6.1046	4.1	0.08576 (0.072)
1968	8.2898	5.9	0.08440 (0.070)
1969	8.6692	6.8	0.08402 (0.068)
1970	7.3217	6.3	0.08404 (0.065)
1971	7.9576	6.9	0.08400 (0.066)
1972	7.1643	5.2	0.08718 (0.062)
1973	5.2383	4.9	0.08946 (0.058)
1974	3.4282	5.0	0.09400 (0.053)

[a]In 1960 addition of one percentage point (0.01) to growth rate
raises q by 0.214.

TABLE 4

EFFECT OF SENSITIVITY TO UNEMPLOYMENT ON
VALUATION, 1960–74; REGRESSION COEFFICIENTS OF
GAMMA.[a]

Year	Coefficient	t-ratio	Variable mean (std.dev.)
1960	−3.0713	1.5	−0.09251 (0.159)
1961	−1.5451	0.7	−0.07367 (0.156)
1962	−4.2588	2.8	−0.07540 (0.154)
1963	−4.6730	2.3	−0.05657 (0.146)
1964	−6.4126	3.2	−0.05744 (0.156)
1965	−4.9808	2.1	−0.07842 (0.153)
1966	0.4668	0.1	−0.09545 (0.152)
1967	−1.9421	0.4	−0.10548 (0.150)
1968	−8.9670	3.3	−0.10067 (0.152)
1969	−11.6678	4.1	−0.09658 (0.150)
1970	−9.3314	3.5	−0.09544 (0.150)
1971	−8.1916	2.9	−0.09489 (0.132)
1972	−4.4452	3.4	−0.08401 (0.119)
1973	−1.7786	2.5	−0.07680 (0.116)
1974	−0.2273	0.7	−0.07364 (0.116)

[a]Gamma is proportionate increase of firm earnings per
percentage point unemployment. Gamma equal to −0.10 means
that one more point of u reduces earnings 10%. In 1960 a firm with
gamma = −0.10 has a 0.307 higher q than with gamma equal to
zero.

The importance of E/V is, of course, to be expected. The striking fact
in Table 10 is the sharp recent decline in the marginal value of earnings,
which actually accounts for more than the observed drop in mean q from
1972 to 1974. In general, the mean value of the earning rate E/V has been
quite stable compared to the regression coefficient of this variable. In
terms of our discussion of section 1, r_k has moved around more than R.

As Table 9 indicates, payment of common dividends has been valued
positively throughout the period, especially during the last ten years.
Interpretation of this result is complicated by the fact that the alternative
to common dividends may be either earnings retention or payment of debt
interest and preferred dividends. According to Table 8, the market does
not like dividend protection, given the dividend rate D/V. Likewise,
Table 7 says that the market is indifferent or negative regarding protection
of fixed debt service obligations. In combination with the expected
negative coefficients on "sigma", these three results could be interpreted
to mean that the stock market likes leverage (contradicting Modigliani–
Miller), and for given leverage prefers pay-out of common stock earnings
to their retention.

Turning now to the other three characteristics, we find significant
coefficients of expected sign for "beta" and X. The market likes growth
and dislikes undiversifiable risk. On the other hand, cyclical sensitivity of

TABLE 5

EFFECT OF EARNINGS COVARIANCE ON VALUATION,
1960–74; REGRESSION COEFFICIENTS OF X.[a]

Year	Coefficient	t-ratio	Variable mean (std.dev.)
1960	−0.3000	1.8	1.14480 (1.92)
1961	−0.1592	0.9	0.96503 (1.92)
1962	−0.3518	3.0	0.98342 (1.96)
1963	−0.3936	2.5	0.74344 (1.91)
1964	−0.5766	3.5	0.67228 (1.89)
1965	−0.5673	2.6	0.86427 (1.67)
1966	−0.0709	0.2	0.98973 (1.58)
1967	−0.2333	0.6	1.12853 (1.63)
1968	−0.7738	3.2	1.14776 (1.67)
1969	−0.9244	3.7	1.12272 (1.68)
1970	−0.7076	3.0	1.12995 (1.69)
1971	−0.5690	2.4	1.12376 (1.53)
1972	−0.1955	2.1	1.18810 (1.57)
1973	−0.0973	1.9	1.15283 (1.54)
1974	−0.0474	1.5	0.96502 (1.28)

[a]X is a measure of elasticity of firm earnings with respect to aggregate earnings. In 1960 a firm with an elasticity of one has a 0.3 lower q than a firm with zero elasticity.

TABLE 6

EFFECT OF EARNINGS VARIABILITY ON VALUATION,
1960–74; REGRESSION COEFFICIENTS OF SIGMA.[a]

Year	Coefficient	t-ratio	Variable mean (std.dev.)
1960	−30.3908	5.3	0.01861 (0.017)
1961	−26.3363	4.2	0.01637 (0.014)
1962	−21.3649	4.7	0.01549 (0.014)
1963	−31.1917	4.7	0.01441 (0.012)
1964	−43.1204	5.7	0.01307 (0.010)
1965	−53.2205	4.5	0.01213 (0.008)
1966	−37.3147	2.9	0.01225 (0.008)
1967	−48.0175	3.8	0.01297 (0.008)
1968	−42.4623	3.7	0.01292 (0.008)
1969	−43.8442	4.2	0.01282 (0.007)
1970	−35.2073	3.9	0.01274 (0.007)
1971	−34.7516	3.3	0.01170 (0.007)
1972	−42.0332	3.5	0.01123 (0.007)
1973	−30.0797	3.7	0.01070 (0.007)
1974	−6.6970	1.4	0.01026 (0.007)

[a]Sigma is standard deviation of firm earnings unexplained by growth trend and normal unemployment, relative to replacement value. In 1960 a firm with sigma = 0.01 would have a 0.304 lower q than a firm with sigma equal to zero.

TABLE 7

EFFECT OF DEFAULT PROBABILITY OR LEVERAGE ON
VALUATION, 1960–74; REGRESSION COEFFICIENTS OF
PB.[a]

Year	Coefficient	t-ratio	Variable mean (std.dev.)
1960	−0.0637	0.1	0.01056 (0.068)
1961	0.6858	0.6	0.01493 (0.096)
1962	0.9225	1.2	0.01761 (0.097)
1963	3.1154	2.8	0.01092 (0.068)
1964	3.3678	3.3	0.01062 (0.071)
1965	3.0404	1.5	0.00707 (0.044)
1966	1.7787	1.3	0.01351 (0.072)
1967	1.6707	1.5	0.02183 (0.099)
1968	0.0470	0.1	0.02966 (0.123)
1969	0.6882	1.1	0.03978 (0.142)
1970	0.1818	0.3	0.04660 (0.151)
1971	0.5602	0.8	0.03547 (0.129)
1972	1.8649	1.8	0.02981 (0.112)
1973	0.8353	1.3	0.03751 (0.122)
1974	−0.0526	0.1	0.04502 (0.131)

[a]*PB* is probability that firm's earnings fall short of fixed
charges. In 1960 a firm with 0.01 probability has a 0.006 lower q
than one with zero probability.

TABLE 8

EFFECT OF DIVIDEND VULNERABILITY ON VALUA-
TION, 1960–74; REGRESSION COEFFICIENTS OF *PD*.[a]

Year	Coefficient	t-ratio	Variable mean (std.dev.)
1960	1.8148	3.1	0.07654 (0.155)
1961	0.8375	1.2	0.07259 (0.156)
1962	1.3898	2.8	0.07647 (0.155)
1963	1.0604	2.0	0.07704 (0.165)
1964	1.6715	3.3	0.08216 (0.168)
1965	2.9236	4.1	0.07299 (0.145)
1966	2.0829	3.3	0.09711 (0.180)
1967	3.0965	5.1	0.11628 (0.200)
1968	2.8680	5.5	0.14331 (0.223)
1969	0.9346	2.3	0.16890 (0.246)
1970	0.8780	2.2	0.16712 (0.235)
1971	1.3137	2.4	0.10612 (0.176)
1972	0.7092	0.9	0.07633 (0.150)
1973	0.3249	0.7	0.10013 (0.178)
1974	0.3420	1.4	0.12762 (0.208)

[a]*PD* is probability that earnings fall short of fixed charges plus
preferred and common dividends. In 1960 a firm with 0.10
probability has a 0.18 lower q than one with zero probability.

James Tobin and William C. Brainard

TABLE 9

EFFECT OF DIVIDEND RATE ON VALUATION, 1960–74;
REGRESSION COEFFICIENTS OF D/V.[a]

Year	Coefficient	t-ratio	Variable mean (std.dev.)
1960	6.5427	1.6	0.04148 (0.0301)
1961	0.3603	0.1	0.04109 (0.0296)
1962	5.5370	1.7	0.03797 (0.0287)
1963	7.1936	1.7	0.04120 (0.0312)
1964	10.4610	2.6	0.04225 (0.0324)
1965	5.4126	1.1	0.04282 (0.0317)
1966	21.2520	4.7	0.04177 (0.0307)
1967	14.5751	2.9	0.03923 (0.0285)
1968	17.8827	3.6	0.03741 (0.0270)
1969	21.6240	5.2	0.03532 (0.0259)
1970	23.8244	6.3	0.03261 (0.0246)
1971	25.2621	6.4	0.02959 (0.0236)
1972	17.6494	3.2	0.02754 (0.0214)
1973	14.4957	3.8	0.02625 (0.0197)
1974	10.6793	5.0	0.02513 (0.0185)

[a]In 1960 increasing D/V, rate of common dividend on replacement value, from 0 to 0.01 raises q by 0.065.

TABLE 10

EFFECT OF EARNINGS RATE ON VALUATION, 1960–74;
REGRESSION COEFFICIENTS OF E/V.[a]

Year	Coefficient	t-ratio	Variable mean (std.dev.)
1960	21.5197	7.5	0.09061 (0.0456)
1961	31.7088	10.0	0.08857 (0.0461)
1962	20.1404	8.8	0.08459 (0.0439)
1963	22.3690	7.2	0.09454 (0.0473)
1964	20.3923	7.0	0.10467 (0.0496)
1965	30.2356	9.0	0.11072 (0.0483)
1966	17.6837	5.2	0.11320 (0.0463)
1967	27.1118	7.9	0.10032 (0.0449)
1968	22.6401	6.7	0.09710 (0.0420)
1969	15.6372	5.5	0.09442 (0.0400)
1970	10.3069	4.3	0.08571 (0.0407)
1971	13.8440	5.4	0.08152 (0.0388)
1972	24.1437	6.6	0.08492 (0.0355)
1973	10.9175	4.7	0.09488 (0.0337)
1974	3.9861	3.4	0.09711 (0.0338)

[a]E/V is ratio of earnings to replacement value. In 1960 increasing earnings rate from 0 to 0.10 raises q by 2.152.

TABLE 11

ESTIMATES OF q, RATIO OF MARKET TO REPLACEMENT VALUE OF CORPORATE CAPITAL, 1960–74.

Year	Actual average for year	Representative firm	Consol firm	Aggregate estimate[a]
1960	2.21	2.40	2.92	1.15
1961	2.51	2.85	3.04	1.40
1962	1.88	2.18	2.54	1.27
1963	2.21	2.27	2.85	1.48
1964	2.29	2.00	2.94	1.56
1965	2.50	1.93	2.65	1.70
1966	2.11	1.64	2.89	1.28
1967	2.51	2.23	2.93	1.41
1968	2.64	2.36	3.04	1.56
1969	2.12	1.97	2.97	1.26
1970	1.92	1.95	3.08	1.08
1971	2.00	2.24	3.27	1.21
1972	1.99	2.29	3.01	1.42
1973	1.43	1.45	2.19	1.18
1974	0.97	0.96	1.44	0.72

[a]Computed for economy as a whole by John Ciccolo, fourth quarter estimates.

TABLE 12

MEASURES OF COST OF CAPITAL, 1960–74.

Year	Representative firm	Consol firm	Corporate Baa yield[a] (Moody's)	"Real" Baa rate[a]
1960	3.96	3.39	5.19	2.63
1961	3.32	3.34	5.08	3.00
1962	4.35	4.17	5.02	3.39
1963	4.17	3.34	4.86	3.47
1964	4.75	2.93	4.83	3.46
1965	4.91	2.95	4.87	3.46
1966	5.79	2.63	5.67	3.96
1967	4.25	3.00	6.23	4.11
1968	4.02	3.03	6.94	4.29
1969	4.81	3.21	7.81	4.54
1970	4.86	3.43	9.11	5.13
1971	4.23	3.45	8.56	4.24
1972	4.14	3.66	8.16	3.82
1973	6.54	4.32	8.24	3.59
1974	9.93	6.45	9.50	3.84

[a]Corporate Baa yield less geometrical value of increase of GNP deflator (in series) over previous five years.

earnings appears – ceteris paribus – to increase q. In interpreting this result, we must remember that cyclical variability of earnings also enters "sigma" and X, and contributes there to penalizing q. The coefficients of "gamma" in Table 4 means that the market prefers that whatever covariance a firm has with the aggregate earnings of other firms be due to their common dependence on the unemployment cycle rather than to other common influences.

We conclude that the theory of asset valuation sketched in section 1 is fairly well confirmed. However, the weights the market places on the different characteristics change from year to year. The most striking empirical result is the sharp fall in q, sharp rise in cost of capital, in 1973 and 1974. This is not due to a decline in earnings but to a spectacular rise in the discount applied to earnings. Tight anti-inflationary monetary policies were undoubtedly responsible.

3. References

Ciccolo, J., 1975, A linkage between product and financial markets – Investment and q, Essay III of unpublished Ph.D. dissertation (Yale University, New Haven, CT).

Lintner, J. H., 1965, The evaluation of risk assets and the selection of risky investments in stock portfolios and capital budgets, Review of Economics and Statistics 47, Feb., pp. 13–37.

Sharpe, W. F., 1964, Capital asset prices: A series of market equilibrium under conditions of risk, Journal of Finance 19, Sept., pp. 425–442.

Shoven, J. B. and J. I. Bulow, 1975/6, Inflation accounting and non-financial corporate profits, Brookings Papers on Economic Activity 1975:3 and 1976:1.

Tobin, J., 1961, Money, capital, and other stores of value, American Economic Review 51, May, pp. 26–37.

Tobin, J., 1969, A general equilibrium approach to monetary theory, Journal of Money, Credit and Banking 1, Feb., pp. 15–29.

Tobin, J., 1971, Essays in economics, vol. 1 – Macroeconomics (North-Holland, Amsterdam).

Tobin, J. and W. C. Brainard, 1968, Pitfalls in financial model building, American Economic Review 58, May, pp. 99–122.

Keynesian Models of Recession and Depression

By James Tobin*

Keynes's *General Theory* attempted to prove the existence of equilibrium with involuntary unemployment, and this pretension touched off a long theoretical controversy. A. C. Pigou, in particular, argued effectively that there could not be a long-run equilibrium with excess supply of labor. The predominant verdict of history is that, as a matter of pure theory, Keynes failed to prove his case.

Very likely Keynes chose the wrong battleground. Equilibrium analysis and comparative statics were the tools to which he naturally turned to express his ideas, but they were probably not the best tools for his purpose. For one thing, he explicitly confined the *General Theory* to a time period in which are given "the existing skill and quantity of available labor, quality and quantity of available equipment, the existing technique" and other factors. As he said (p. 245), "in this place and context, we are not considering or taking into account the effects and consequences of changes in them." But his model produces a solution in which, in general, the stock of capital, and other stocks, are not constant. Changes in these stocks will in turn alter investment, saving, and other behavior. For this reason alone, the solution of Keynes's model cannot be stationary, even in its own endogenous variables; and on this ground alone, it fails to qualify as an equilibrium. The evolution of Keynesian equilibrium as stocks change is receiving a great deal of attention these

days and I shall not dwell on this point here. (See, however, A. S. Blinder and R. M. Solow and J. Tobin and W. Buiter.)

The second important point, the one on which Pigou insisted, is that excess supply of labor must cause money wages to decline. Even if this did not succeed in eliminating unemployment, one might not call a situation in which money wages and prices are persistently falling an equilibrium. But of course Pigou went further in contesting Keynes's claim that a "trap" might exist from which the economy could not be rescued, however low the wage and price level.

Keynes tried to make a double argument about wage reduction and employment. One was that wage rates were very slow to decline in the face of excess supply. The other was that, even if they declined faster, employment would not—in depression circumstances—increase. As to the second point, he was well aware of the dynamic argument that *declining* money wage rates are unfavorable to aggregate demand.[1] But perhaps he did not insist upon it strongly enough, for the subsequent theoretical argument focused on the statics of alternative stable wage levels.

The real issue is not the existence of a

* Sterling Professor of Economics, Yale University. The research described in this paper was undertaken by grants from the National Science Foundation and the Ford Foundation.

[1] "... it would be much better that wages should be rigidly fixed and deemed incapable of material changes, than that depression should be accompanied by a gradual downward tendency of money-wages, a further moderate wage reduction being expected to signalise each increase of, say, 1 percent in the amount of unemployment. For example, the effect of an expectation that wages are going to sag by, say, 2 percent in the coming year will be roughly equivalent to the effect of a rise of 2 percent in the amount of interest payable for the same period. The same observations apply *mutatis mutandis* to the case of a boom." (See Keynes, p. 265.)

Reprinted by permission from *American Economic Review, Papers and Proceedings* 65(2) (May 1975):195–202.

74

long-run static *equilibrium* with unemployment, but the possibility of protracted unemployment which the natural adjustments of a market economy remedy very slowly if at all. So what if, within the recherché rules of the contest, Keynes failed to establish an "underemployment equilibrium"? The phenomena he described are better regarded as disequilibrium dynamics. Keynes's comparative statics were an awkward analytical language unequal to the shrewd observations and intuitions he was trying to embody. If the purity of neoclassical equilibrium is preserved, this verdict is no real blow to Keynes or solace for Pigou. The Great Depression is the Great Depression, the notorious "Treasury View" is still ridiculous, whether mass unemployment is a feature of an equilibrium or of a prolonged disequilibrium.

The issue is by no means dead. Today "full employment" has become the "natural rate," and "equilibrium" often allows for any steady rate of deflation or inflation, not just zero. But the proposition which Keynes was questioning is once again strongly argued in the profession and in public debate. Once again it is alleged that the private market economy can and will, without aid from government policy, steer itself to full employment equilibrium. This is the basis for advocacy of fixed rules of monetary growth and fiscal policy, as against active discretionary policy responding to information fed back from the private economy. At this very moment it is the basis for a policy of letting the recession run its course, in confidence that in a relatively short run—two or three years—equilibrium will be restored at full employment with reduced or even zero inflation.

I. Keynesian and Marshallian Price Dynamics

Milton Friedman (p. 18) has pointed out that Keynes was a "Marshallian in method" and translated the supply-demand framework of Alfred Marshall from individual markets to the whole economy. "Where he deviated from Marshall, and it was a momentous deviation, was in reversing the roles assigned to price and quantity. He assumed that, at least for changes in aggregate demand, quantity was the variable that adjusted rapidly, while price was the variable that adjusted slowly, at least in a downward direction." Friedman is correct that this was a momentous deviation, and one way to appreciate the point is to look explicitly at the dynamic stability implications of Walrasian vs. Marshallian assumptions about quantity adjustment.

Marshallian adjustment in a particular market is that quantity adjusts to the difference between demand price and supply price for existing quantity. Walrasian adjustment is that quantity adjusts to the difference between demand and supply at existing price.

Let us now apply these two adjustment assumptions to a simple macroeconomic model. Let Y be aggregate real output, and Y^* its value at full employment, i.e., at the "natural rate" level of unemployment. Let E be aggregate real effective demand, which can differ in short-run disequilibrium both from Y and from Y^*. Given the nominal stock of outside money M and other exogenous or policy-set variables, effective demand E is a function $E(p, x, Y)$ of three variables: p the price level, x its expected rate of change, and Y the level of output and real income.

In finer detail, E is the sum of consumption C, private investment I, and government purchases G:

$$(1) \quad E = C\left(Y, Y^*, -T, -R, x\frac{M}{p}, W\right)$$
$$+ I(Y, Y^*, -K, -R) + G$$

Here the C and I functions have positive derivatives in all their arguments. T represents taxes, a function of Y and Y^*. W is private wealth, equal to

$$\frac{M}{p} + qK,$$

where the coefficient q is the ratio of market valuation of capital equity to replacement cost. An increase in the real interest rate R relative to the marginal efficiency of capital makes q fall, and makes investment fall. The marginal efficiency of capital depends positively on Y and Y^*, negatively on K. The real interest rate R depends inversely on both M/p and x, and rises with Y and W.

The *price level effect* E_p on demand is negative, for the following familiar combination of reasons. First is the Keynes effect. A given nominal quantity of money will be a larger real quantity at a lower price level. Consequently the interest rate may be lower, and investment demand higher. The Keynes effect is expected to be weaker the larger the real supply of money relative to output Y, and to vanish altogether in the "liquidity trap." This will tend to make E_p smaller in absolute value at low levels of Yp/M.

Second is the Pigou effect, the wealth effect on consumption. The lower the price level, the higher the real value of those components of net private wealth fixed in nominal value. The relevant components are outside money (and some part of any nonmonetary public debt in existence). Consumption demand is expected, *ceteris paribus*, to respond positively to increases of wealth.

The short-run Pigou effect is very likely weaker than the long-run effect and may not even have the same negative sign. And it is the short-run effect which is relevant for Keynesian theory and for the dynamics of this paper. The difference arises as follows: among the stocks fixed in the short

run are private debts in the unit of account. These are a heavier burden to debtors the lower the price level, and there are good reasons why transfer of real income and wealth to creditors spells a net deficit of aggregate demand. Debtors are debtors because they have high propensities to spend. Many of them are liquidity-constrained, and as their debt/equity ratios increase their credit lines dwindle or, in case of bankruptcies, disappear. Although these are "only" distributional effects, they may be more important than the real value of outside money and debt.

The long-run comparative-static Pigou effect, in contrast, assumes that each alternative price level has prevailed for a sufficiently long time so that inside debts are scaled to that price level—although strangely enough exogenous outside money is not. In this counterhistorical "as if" mental experiment, debtors are no more burdened at one price level than at another.

As for *the price change effect* E_x, there are several effects. A decrease in the expected inflation rate raises the real rate of interest. This increase discourages investment, and it also deters consumption both directly and by lowering the market value of equity capital, one component of wealth. On the other hand, expected capital gains on money holdings xM/p are favorable to consumption. This is a "flow Pigou effect," to be distinguished from the stock effect. The question here involves the size of the marginal propensity to spend from expected real capital gains. Econometric evidence has been that this marginal propensity is small, although capital gains eventually affect consumption via the wealth effect. I have assumed that the other effects of expected inflation dominate the flow Pigou effect.

The *marginal propensity to spend* E_y is taken to lie between 0 and 1 on usual Keynesian grounds. As is well-known, a high response of investment demand to contemporaneous income could easily make E_y exceed one. But Keynes typically regarded investment as determined more by long-run sales and profit expectations than by current business activity. The likelihood that, in prolonged departures from full employment, investment will come to be governed more by contemporaneous than by full employment sales and profits is a source of possible instability and of prolonged disequilibrium to which I shall return later in the paper.

In equilibrium, the following three conditions hold:

(2.1) $E(p, x, Y) - Y = 0$

(2.2) $Y - Y^* = 0$

(2.3) $x = \dot{p}/p = 0.$

(I shall also denote $\dot{p}/p$ as π.)

I shall call the first dynamic version of this model the *WKP* model (Walras-Keynes-Phillips). All the adjustment functions which follow will conform to the notation $A_y z$, where y is the variable adjusting, z the variable on which the adjustment depends, and A_y a positive constant. The *WKP* model is as follows:

The WKP Model

(2.1.1) $\dot{Y} = A_y(E - Y)$

(2.2.1) $\pi = A_p(Y - Y^*) + x$

(2.3.1) $\dot{x} = A_x(\pi - x)$

Equation (2.1.1) says that production Y moves in response to discrepancies of E and Y. This implements the Keynesian view that in the very short run money wages and prices are set and output responds to variations of demand.

How can E and Y diverge even for an instant? Many words have been spilled, both by Keynes himself and by others, on this question, usually posed in terms of the possibility of inequality of Saving and Investment. In our present context, let D be

the demand which must always equal Y to preserve the national income identities. Let D be a function of $\dot{Y}$ as well as of x, p, and Y. Then $D(\dot{Y}, x, p, Y) = Y$, $E(x, p, Y) = D(0, x, p, Y)$. Equation (2.1.1) follows from a negative value of $\partial D/\partial \dot{Y}$, which means that demand is lower, at given Y, when Y is increasing. Lags in consumption spending lead to this sign and so does *unintended* inventory decumulation. The investment accelerator works in the other direction, but for the reason already given it is not a Keynesian idea.

Equation (2.2.1) is a natural-rate version of the Phillips curve. The short-run Phillips curve is the obvious Keynesian version of price dynamics. Throughout this paper I am condensing product and labor markets into one sector and assuming with Keynes that prices are determined by marginal variable costs, i.e., by labor costs. Excess labor supply and $Y - Y^*$, the "Okun gap," are linked,—when one is zero so is the other. So it is the gap which causes wage rates to fall. But to "fall" does not mean to decline absolutely; it means to decline relative to x, the accustomed and expected rate of inflation of both labor costs and prices. This is the more modern wrinkle. By here assuming (2.2.1) I do not mean necessarily to associate myself— much less Keynes!—with the natural-rate hypothesis in all its power and glory.

The third equation (2.3.1) is the well-known model of adaptive expectations. There is nothing particularly Keynesian about this equation, and the same formulation will carry over to the non-Keynesian dynamic model. Keynes himself would scorn it and stress instead the stochastic and historical sources of expectations. But like so many of his observations, these do not lend themselves to simple formal analysis.

As two extremes of interest I shall wish to consider:

(2.3.2) $x = \pi$

(extrapolation of current rates of price *change*)

(2.3.3) $x = 0$

(extrapolation of current price *level*)

The alternative dynamic version may be called the M model (Marshall). The equations are:

The M Model

(2.1.2) $\pi = B_p(E - Y) + x$

(2.2.2) $\dot{Y} = B_Y(Y^* - Y)$

(2.3.2) $\dot{x} = A_x(\pi - x)$ (or 2.3.1 or 2.3.3)

As compared with the WKP model, the adjustment roles of the first two equations are interchanged. The first equation now says that the immediate impact of excess demand for goods and services is to raise prices, or more strictly to raise them faster than they had been expected to rise. (It is not entirely accurate to regard (2.1.2) as non-Keynesian. When there is an inflationary gap $(E > Y^*, Y = Y^*)$, this looks very much like the Keynesian model of inflation. But in Keynes's inflation theory, Y^* is considered an absolute short-run constraint on production, as in wartime. In normal conditions, Keynes would, I think, regard Y^* as a medium-run labor market equilibrium with normal margins of excess capacity and of frictional unemployment, a level of output which could be at least temporarily exceeded.)[2] In any event, equation (2.1.2) is one way to inject into the model the view that prices respond quite flexibly to changes in excess demand for goods, whether or not the economy is close to full employment.

The non-Keynesian partner of this price adjustment equation is (2.2.2), where the gap between potential and actual output

inspires adjustments of production and employment. This is because they are associated with gaps of the same sign between the demand price for labor (the value of its marginal product) and its supply price.[3] The idea is that when Y^* exceeds Y the real wage is less than marginal productivity. Competitive employers therefore add to their work forces and their production. In Keynesian theory, on the other hand, production increases only when demand at existing prices expands.

II. Local Stability of the Two Models

Let us now consider the local stability of the WKP and M models, around their equilibrium values $Y = Y^*$, $p = p^*$, $x = 0$. For this purpose it is convenient to substitute in the third equation the value of $\pi - x$ drawn from the second or first equation. Thus the third equations in the WKP and M models become respectively:

(3.1) $\dot{x} = A_x A_p(Y - Y^*)$

(3.2) $\dot{x} = A_x B_p(E - Y)$

For the WKP model, the linearized equations are:

$$(3.3) \begin{bmatrix} \dot{Y} \\ \dot{p} \\ \dot{x} \end{bmatrix} = \begin{bmatrix} A_Y(E_y - 1) & A_Y E_p & A_Y E_x \\ A_p p^* & 0 & p^* \\ A_x A_p & 0 & 0 \end{bmatrix} \cdot \begin{bmatrix} Y - Y^* \\ p - p^* \\ x \end{bmatrix}$$

The critical necessary condition for stability is:

(3.4) $p^* E_p + A_x E_x < 0$

The first term of (3.4) is negative and the second term positive. As would be expected, a strong negative price-level effect on aggregate demand, a weak price-

---

[2] In the *General Theory*, Keynes discusses frictional and involuntary unemployment on p. 6 and, in defining involuntary unemployment on p. 15, says, "Clearly we do not mean by 'involuntary' unemployment the mere existence of an unexhausted capacity to work."

[3] This is true even if the labor supply curve is downward sloping, provided it is closer to vertical than the schedule of marginal productivity of labor.

expectation effect, and a slow response of price expectations to experience are conducive to stability. In one extreme case (2.3.3), where $x = \dot{x} = 0$, the system is of course stable. In the other extreme case (2.3.2), where $x = \pi$, the first term of (3.4) drops out and the system is necessarily unstable.

The M model is quite different. It is separable into output and price equations. Equation (2.2.2) is a stable differential equation in the single variable Y. The stability of the price system depends on (3.4), in the same way as the stability of the WKP model. The formal system is:

$$(3.5) \quad \begin{bmatrix} \dot{Y} \\ \dot{p} \\ \dot{x} \end{bmatrix} =$$

$$\begin{bmatrix} -B_Y & 0 & 0 \\ B_p(E_Y-1)p^* & B_p p^* E_p & B_p p^* E_x + p^* \\ A_x B_p(E_y-1) & A_x B_p E_p & A_x B_p E_x \end{bmatrix}$$

$$\cdot \begin{bmatrix} Y - Y^* \\ p - p^* \\ x \end{bmatrix}$$

As Friedman surmised, Keynes's choice of adjustment mechanisms is a crucial element of his theory. In particular, the Walras-Keynes-Phillips adjustment model allows the distinct possibility that lapses from full employment will not be automatically remedied by market forces. Keynes could also be interpreted to hold the view that price-level effects E_p are weak relative to speculative effects E_x. I shall discuss this interpretation further in the next section.

III. Irreversible Recessions and Deep Depressions

Let us take a more global look at the equilibrium condition $E = Y$ (2.1). In Figure 1 are shown in (p, x) space several loci

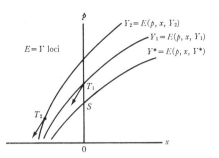

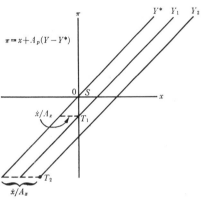

FIGURE 1

along which the condition is met. The slope of such a locus, $-E_x/E_p$, is positive. Each locus is for a given value of Y; a reduction in Y shifts the locus to the left. In the Figure, the right-most locus is for full employment output Y^*. The weakening or vanishing of the "Keynes effect" at low values of Y and p tends to reduce E_p in absolute value. This is reflected in the curvature of the loci.

Consider an initial position T_1 at levels of E and Y short of Y^*. Prices begin to decline because Y_1 is less than Y^*. To a degree that depends on the speed of adaptation, expectations of price change become negative. The arrow indicates the direction of movement. As drawn, the movement is stabilizing, taking the economy to higher E and Y, toward Y^* and the equilibrium S.

The lower panel of Figure 1 concerns the direction of the arrow, the relationship of π and x. The horizontal axis matches in origin and scale that of the upper panel. The lines are parallel 45 degree lines, for Y^*, Y_1, and Y_2, the same output levels as in the upper diagram. The points S, T_1, T_2 correspond to the similarly labeled points above. At S, $\pi = 0$. At T_1, π is negative. So is $\dot{x}$, by an amount proportional to the difference between π and x, shown horizontally as $\dot{x}/A_x$.

Consider instead an initial position T_2 in the two panels. At T_2 both the slope of the $E = Y$ locus and that of the arrow are steeper. The reason that the arrow is steeper can be seen in the lower panel: $\dot{x}/A_x$ has doubled, but π has more than doubled. The net outcome could go either way. The possibility illustrated is that at T_2 the locus $E = Y$ is so steep that the movement is destabilizing. The system might be stable for small deviations from its equilibrium but unstable for large shocks.[4] The failure of automatic market processes to restore full employment would be reinforced if large and prolonged recession caused investors to gear their estimates of the marginal efficiency of capital more to current than to equilibrium demand and profitability.

Under these adverse circumstances, and in the absence of countercyclical policy, the economy could slip into a deep depression.

In nonlinear nonmonetary business cycle models like those of M. Kalecki, R. Goodwin, and Sir John Hicks, a long depression phase occurs with the economy at a floor. At this floor the capital stock is excessive

and gross investment is zero; production is solely to meet minimal private and social consumption requirements, which are independent of income and wealth. The depression phase lasts a long time, while depreciation slowly whittles the capital stock down to the amount needed for floor level production.

It is not part of this paper to provide a model of such a floor. The relevant question is whether deflation will by itself lift the economy from the floor. Will deflation so augment private wealth that consumption rises above its floor level? Clearly this will not happen unless condition (3.4) is met at the depression income level.

But at the floor, E_z is higher than in the normal regime. An increase in the deflation rate $-x$ lowers the value of the capital stock. The physical capital stock declines slowly. But its value—its *real* value—can decline rapidly; when no gross investment is taking place, the existing stock will be valued well below replacement cost. At the liquidity trap, the real interest rate is the irreducible nominal rate $\bar{r}$ plus the expected rate of deflation $-x$. The value of a unit of capital is $(\rho - \delta/(r - x))$ where $\rho - \delta$ is the marginal productivity of capital net of depreciation. Although the attrition of the stock slowly raises ρ, deflation rapidly raises $\bar{r} - x$.

IV. Concluding Remarks

God may have made the world so that full employment equilibrium exists and is stable. Perhaps the divine design guarantees that capitalist market economies will never be trapped in depressions with involuntary unemployment and will never need to depart from fixed no-feedback rules of fiscal and monetary policy. But Keynes had good empirical and theoretical reason to suspect otherwise. He did not establish an underemployment equilibrium. But he did not really need to. Even with stable monetary and fiscal policy,

---

[4] Robert Solow has pointed out to me that the possibility illustrated by T_2 is only suggestive of a global instability. The global properties of the system require further investigation.

combined with price and wage flexibility, the adjustment mechanisms of the economy may be too weak to eliminate persistent unemployment.

REFERENCES

A. S. Blinder and R. M. Solow, "Does Fiscal Policy Matter?," in *J. of Pub. Econ.*, 1973, *2*, 319–37, and *Econ. of Pub. Fin.*, Brookings Institution, 1974, 452–58.

M. **Friedman,** *A Theoretical Framework for Monetary Analysis*, Nat. Bur. of Econ. Res. occas. pap. 112, New York 1971.

J. M. **Keynes,** *The General Theory of Employment, Interest, and Money*, 1st ed., London 1936, 245.

J. **Tobin and W. Buiter,** "Long-Run Effects of Fiscal and Monetary Policy on Aggregate Demand," Cowles Foundation disc. pap. no. 384, Dec. 1974.

HOW DEAD IS KEYNES?*

JAMES TOBIN

The man J. M. Keynes died in 1946. But today there are frequent reports that Keynes is dead. The *Wall Street Journal* publishes them regularly. *Newsweek* has confirmed the event. Economists write books and articles in explanation. Washington, under Administrations of both colors, acts as if it believes these reports. Who or what did it? Some say other economists, with rapier logic. Some say high time. A few mourn.

Maybe the reports are true. Maybe they are wishful thinking. Maybe they are exaggerated. There is a counter-rumor that Keynes is alive and well and living in New England. The whole matter seems worth investigation. Unlike Tom Sawyer, Keynes cannot attend his own funeral. It's just as well, considering what is being said. Tom wept in grief; Keynes might laugh. I make no pretense of being his stand-in. But the cliché, only a few years ago went "We're all Keynesians now." It was reportedly endorsed even by R. Nixon and M. Friedman. So the bell is tolling for all of us.

Have events refuted Keynes? Let's recall the central propositions of the *General Theory* and ask how they stand up to current history.

First proposition: In modern industrial capitalist societies, prices and wages respond slowly to excess demand or supply, especially slowly to excess supply. Over a long short run, ups and downs of demand register in output; they are far from completely absorbed in prices.

For evidence, Keynes needed to look no further than Britain in the 1920s and the world in depression. Churchill's return to gold in 1925 made British wages and internal costs uncompetitive, but massive unemployment failed to bring them in line. During the slump of 1929-32, American wages fell sluggishly — and real wages rose thanks to the collapse of food prices — while unemployment rose from 4% to 25%. In the 1930s recovery, output and employment responded to demand.

And now? After three years of recession and slow recovery, high unemployment and excess capacity persist, while domestic price and wage inflation proceeds with little abatement. On the other hand, output and employment have responded to increased demand, while inflation has not accelerated.

Is the first proposition patently irrelevant and inapplicable today?

Second proposition, a corollary of the first, is the vulnerability of economies like ours to lengthy bouts of involuntary unemployment. People willing to work at or below prevailing real wages cannot find jobs.

*Yale University. Invited address, Western Economic Association, June 23, 1977, Anaheim, California.

Reprinted by permission of Western Economic Association from *Economic Inquiry* 15(4) (October 1977):459–468.

They have no effective way to signal their availability.

Was this an improper extrapolation from an aberrant episode, the Great Depression? Maybe such an objection was credible before 1974. Today, is involuntary unemployment a clearly foolish concept or an obviously misplaced concern?

Third proposition. Capital formation depends on long run appraisals of profit expectations and risks and on business attitudes toward bearing the risks. These are not simple predictable functions of current and recent economic events. Variations of the marginal efficiency of capital contain, for all practical purposes, important elements of autonomy and exogeneity. But business expectation of steady prosperity is an important stabilizer of investment and of the economy, limiting cyclical instability. Likewise destruction of such expectation can turn mild cyclical recessions into periods of protracted stagnation.

This is why the recession of 1920-30 slipped into depression and became, in kind as in degree, different from preceding downturns. How about the recession of 1974-75 compared to its post-war predecessors? Even now real fixed non-residential investment remains in the doldrums, 7% below 1973.

Does this Keynesian proposition self-evidently deserve interment?

Fourth proposition. Even if money wages and prices were responsive to market excess demands and supplies, their flexibility would not necessarily stabilize monetary economies subject to demand and supply shocks. This was Keynes's challenge to accepted doctrine that market mechanisms are inherently self-correcting and stabilizing. He found the alleged demonstrations for particular markets especially unconvincing for the economy as a whole. He suggested, therefore, that it was easier to stabilize real economic variables by moving aggregate monetary demand relative to a given path of money wage rates than by moving wages relative to given monetary demand — even if the latter were a realistic option.

Experience provides little evidence on this issue. The theory of price adjustments in interrelated competitive markets is a lot more sophisticated than the hand wavings that evoked Keynes's skepticism four decades ago. But can his doubts be firmly dismissed as unjustified?

I submit that none of these four central Keynesian propositions is inconsistent with the contemporary economic scene here or in other advanced democratic capitalist countries. At least the first three fit the facts extremely well. Indeed the middle 70s follow the Keynesian script better than any post-war period except the early 60s. It hardly seems the time for a funeral.

Yet there is certainly great resistance, among economists, men of affairs, and policy-makers, to a Keynesian diagnosis of the present economic situation. Perhaps deficient aggregate demand is too simple, too old-hat, too boring. Perhaps people are afraid of the prescriptions that might accompany the diagnosis. Some of the arguments against the diagnosis are theoretical; some are empirical.

They are all inspired by faith that the economy can never be very far from equilibrium. Markets work, excess supplies and demands are eliminated, expectations embody the best available information, people always make any and all deals which would move all parties to preferred positions. With such faith the orthodox economists of the early 1930s could shut their eyes to events they knew *a priori* could not be happening. With such faith their successors of the 1970s can tell us that the very persistence of high unemployment and excess capacity reveal them to be the voluntarily preferred state of affairs. Keynes might say this is where he came in.

It is indeed difficult to give a rationale for the observed persistence of rising wages and prices coexistent with excess supply. It is difficult to give a convincing rationale within the paradigm of utility and profit-maximizing behavior in competitive markets. Keynes's own observations on money wage stickiness have not satisfied the canons of proof of subsequent theorists. Increasingly their reaction has been, "If we can't explain this phenomenon to our satisfaction within the paradigm, then it doesn't happen."

One currently popular explanation of variations in employment is temporary confusion of relative and absolute prices. Employers and workers are fooled into too many jobs by unexpected inflation, but only until they learn it affects other prices, not just the prices of what they sell. The reverse happens temporarily when inflation falls short of expectation. This model can scarcely explain more than transient disequilibrium in labor markets.

So how can the faithful explain the slow cycles of unemployment we actually observe? Only by arguing that the natural rate itself fluctuates, that variations in unemployment rates are substantially changes in voluntary, frictional, or structural unemployment rather than in involuntary joblessness due to generally deficient demand. Search theory is an important contribution. Applied to labor markets, it helps us to understand the level and trend of aggregate unemployment in prosperous times, and the differences in unemployment rates among labor markets and types of workers. However, as an explanation of cyclical fluctuations, search models are contradicted by a number of statistical regularities: voluntary quit rates move procyclically, counter to overall unemployment; the help wanted index, our closest approach to a job vacancy series, also moves procyclically; recession unemployment contains a large component of layoffs subject to recall; most job searches and changes by adult workers involve no interruption of employment at all.

You are all familiar with evidence commonly advanced to minimize the involuntary deficient-demand component of post-1973 unemployment: the concentration of unemployment on demographic groups prone to high turnover, the extraordinary growth of the labor force, the flood of women job-seekers, the minimum wage, the advantages of living on unemployment insurance and other doles. They simply do not fit the facts.

Demographic shift may explain an increase in the overall unemployment rate of as much as a point since 1965. Teenagers and young adults, now larger proportions of the labor force, experience higher than average unemployment rates. These can be attributed in part to turnover and search, and if not to voluntary choice then at least to structural mismatch between available jobs and workers rather than to generally deficient demand. (It's strange, however, that the structure of labor demand has not better adjusted in all this time to the actual composition of the labor force.) But the *increase* in unemployment since 1973 cannot be explained by demographic shift. The increase was concentrated on prime workers. Unemployment rates for prime age adults, for married males, for experienced workers — for every demographic classification associated with low voluntary turnover and with employer preferences — rose relative to rates for the high-turnover and structurally disadvantaged groups. Moreover, job losers rose strikingly as a proportion of the unemployed relative to job leavers and to persons entering or re-entering the labor force.

Another excuse for the persistence of high unemployment since 1973 is rapid growth of the labor force — job creation just can't keep pace. Look at the doughnut, we are told, not at the hole, look at the ratio of employment to working age population, not the unemployment rate. But the upward trend in labor force participation is nothing new, and neither is procyclical response of participation to employment prospects. In fact the growth of the labor force during 1975 and 1976 was smaller than in each of the three preceding years. And as previously noted, labor force entrants and re-entrants have not been an unusually high fraction of the unemployed.

Special attention, indeed special consternation, has been focused on the growth of the female labor force. This too is nothing new, only the continuation of a long term trend toward convergence of female and male participation rates. Women's labor force participation has risen from 38% in 1960 to nearly 50% now. No wonder Geoffrey Moore's employment ratio can be at an all-time high at the same time as unemployment rates also set post-war records. Incidentally, the use of his doughnut ratio as the criterion of labor market performance should evoke protests from both women's lib and men's lib. It implies that women who choose careers can get jobs only if they displace men.

The minimum wage, I agree, contributes to teenage unemployment. But during a period when it fell relative to average wages and to product prices, it can hardly be blamed for dramatic increases in unemployment. Likewise unemployment compensation, together with other assistance available to the unemployed, no doubt increases the amount of voluntary and recorded unemployment. There are plenty of anecdotes and some econometrics to support the charge. But even now only half the unemployed are covered. Anyway the liberalization of benefits in amount and duration was a legislative response to the massive unemployment created by the recession; it can scarcely have caused the unemployment, and most of the emergency improvements are scheduled to vanish when unemployment rates fall.

No, the rise in unemployment was not a sudden shift in the natural rate, but a decline in the number of jobs relative to the supply of labor. Excess supply, involuntary unemployment, persist.

Along with excess supply of labor we have had, we still have, an excess supply of capital services. I have yet to hear a convincing story how the unemployment of machines and factories reflects either voluntary search — are they waiting for those lush quasirents in the upper tails of the distribution? — or revealed preferences for idleness unsubsidized by unemployment insurance or food stamps. Maybe it could be argued — Keynes himself made such an argument in his "user cost" appendix — that use of capital now sacrifices future capacity in stronger markets. The technological premise seems shaky; more likely capital services foregone today are lost forever, thanks to time depreciation and obsolescence. Anyway the argument, for what it is worth, is a reason for price stickiness in the face of temporarily low demand. It may help to explain why capacity is idle when demand is deficient. It is not a reason to attribute reduced utilization of existing capacity to an increase in the reservation price of its services. Machines are ready to work at existing quasi-rents, like labor at existing wages.

I have labored the obvious, but only because the obvious is so often denied or ignored. Failure to accept or understand the Keynesian diagnosis — demand deficiency — is especially apparent in discussion of remedies. Fiscal and monetary measures to expand aggregate demand are dismissed on grounds that would make sense only if the economy were already in full employment or natural rate equilibrium or indeed suffering from demand-pull inflation. I do not say that these are the only grounds on which expansionary measures can be or are opposed. I will discuss other grounds shortly. Right now I wish to call to your attention some examples of misplaced equilibrium arguments.

Recall the excitement, not to say panic, generated by federal deficits in 1975 and 1976. Selling all those Treasury securities would crowd business out of the financial markets and capital formation out of the economy. The argument was applied even to the passive deficits resulting from recession, but its main debating thrust was against actively expansionary fiscal policy, new spending or tax reduction. Again Keynes might say, "This is where I came in": the famous or notorious Treasury View of Winston Churchill's Exchequer in 1929 was reborn in William

Simon's Treasury. Now one does not have to be a monetarist to agree that a determined central bank can find and follow a monetary policy which cancels out fiscal expansion and makes the crowding out story true. But why should they? In an economy with under-employment of labor and capital, resources to satisfy the demands of government and its transferees do not have to be taken from other users.

But, it was said and will be said, monetary expansion is per se inflationary. Catch 22! Fiscal policy can't work without monetary accommodation. Monetary expansion can't work because it is dissipated in price inflation. At full employment, at the natural rate, this would make sense. In an economy suffering from insufficiency of demand, the Keynesian disease, it does not. More labor and capital services will be supplied, if demanded, along the on-going path of wages and prices, without accelerating their increase. Indeed for this very reason many of the opponents of expansionary *policy* have been and remain willing to accept expansions spontaneously generated. Somehow growth of M x V is innocuous and effective when it is due to V but dangerous and ineffective, both, when it is due to M. We should be grateful for small favors. Such recovery as we have enjoyed was consistent with Federal Reserve money stock targets only because of fortuitous bulges of velocity, i.e., demand for money was unexpectedly low for prevailing incomes and interest rates.

The taboo on actively expansionary monetary policy remains. Its rationale is that the public's interpretation of such policy deprives it of effectiveness. Rational, or at least reasonable, people will expect more inflation to follow from more rapid monetary growth. Interest rates and actual prices will follow the expectations upward, but there will be no gains in real variables. Is this scenario self-consistent, as the canons of rational expectations require, in an under-employed economy? The answer is negative. Nominal interest rates cannot increase by as much as the assumed escalation of expected inflation. If they did, the demand for real money balances would have declined, while the supply has risen or at worst remained constant in real terms. So real interest rates must decline, expanding real demand, output, and employment, and accelerating inflation less than the speed-up of monetary growth. Naive association of inflation expectation and monetary growth rates is not rational. Rational expectations would support a Keynes-Phillips path so long as the economy is on the high side of the natural rate. This is not to deny that if the public has been strongly and wrongly indoctrinated, irrational expectations may be an obstacle to expansionary policy.

Neither is it to deny that the public may rationally believe that more inflation leads to recession, although I think the connection is usually not well understood. Policy, particularly monetary policy, is an indispensable link in the chain. The 1974-75 recession was the result not of double-digit inflation but of the quixotic measures taken by the Fed to oppose an externally generated bulge of specific prices. It was not the first recession generated by anti-inflationary policy. Consequently expansionary monetary policy during recovery — indeed recovery itself however fueled — may be regarded as a portent of contractionary policy to come.

Let me return to the question of the efficacy of fiscal policy. Another crowding out argument, more subtle than displacement of private investment via higher interest rates, is what is sometimes called *ex ante* crowding out. The argument is that bond-financed government expenditures cannot absorb saving, any more than tax-financed expenditures do. The ever-rational far-sighted public, it is alleged, knows that tax bills will be rendered later. Their new saving in anticipation of future tax liabilities will match the deficit. There will be no increase in aggregate demand — except, I guess, the old balanced budget multiplier effect of government purchases. It's some consolation that this time investment is not crowded out, just consumption; but financial crowding out may be piled on top since the bonds are a part of portfolio wealth if not of true net wealth. I have some problems with this doctrine even for full employment and the very long run. These concern the distributional, incentive, and risk effects of the future non-lump-sum taxes actually expected. Debt finance would, I think, crowd out capital in long-run steady states. For the same reasons it would absorb saving in Keynesian short runs.

In a Keynesian short run with under-employment, the public, even if they fully discount future taxes, can correctly calculate improvement in the present value of future real after-tax incomes. They are raised by the near term employment of otherwise idle resources. Expecting that, households will increase their spending and make the scenario come true. Failing that, they will not have to pay additional taxes anyway, in a tax system which relates tax liabilities directly or indirectly to economic activity.

Exponents of *ex ante* crowding out ignore a feature of real world economies that significantly reduces the equivalence of future and current taxes. This is the fact that capital markets are imperfect, notably in limiting the capacity of individuals to borrow against future labor income or retirement pensions. Consequently many households are at any moment liquidity-constrained. Their spending will be increased if the government allows them to defer tax payments.

In short, Keynesian diagnosis still applies to situations like the present, and latter-day macroeconomic theory has not rendered Keynesian remedies obsolete.

I said earlier that there are other reasons for opposing such remedies. The over-riding motive is to keep the economy under-employed while the hard-core built-in inflation melts. In Keynes's day the stubborn wage price pattern was one of wage stability with moderately declining prices — what Hicks would call the flexprice sector was relatively much larger. Today our mutually reinforcing wage-price pattern, inherited

from the past decade, is roughly 8% wage inflation and 6% price inflation. As in the past, shocks can move it up or down, and those who regard
the present inflation rates as intolerable don't want to take any outside
risks. These are the substantial reasons for the go-slow recovery policy
of our government since 1974.

The go-slow policy is terribly expensive in irretrievably lost output.
Fifty billion dollars for every excess point of unemployment — that ain't
peanuts. Suppose that the policy succeeds in restoring 5% unemployment
in 1981, while, thanks to its gradualism, inflation falls by a couple of
points in the process. We will have taken six years to recover from a 15-
month recession, with output losses I would find impossible to justify on
any pragmatic cost/benefit calculus. But I will not argue that case this
afternoon. More germane to my topic is the unlikelihood of achieving
those modest goals.

Sustained and complete recovery depends on business investment. But
the long delayed revival of investment depends on confidence in sustained
and complete recovery. Prospective capacity bottlenecks and sectoral
price pressures scare the inflation-conscious authorities and their watch-
ful constituents. But without confidence in future sales and profits and
without receptive markets for corporate debt and equity, investment to
avert the putative bottlenecks is not undertaken. The Fed announces
lower monetary targets and promises to lower them further until they
accord with zero (not 4%) inflation. The specter of collision between
those targets and the economy's inflationary momentum hangs over the
recovery. When and if they collide, everyone knows in his bones, it is
output not prices which will give way.

Many economists and policy-makers hoped, some even expected, that
wage and price inflation would adapt to well advertised monetary
targets. Let labor and industry know their monetary rations and choose
how they wish to divide them between real growth of output and
employment and inflation of wages and prices. One current academic
theory is that labor markets will clear as rapidly as contracts expire
and are renegotiated, or whenever non-union employers reconsider
administered wage scales. Disequilibrium lasts only as long as the parties
are frozen into past errors of expectation. With faith in both market efficiency and rational expectations, these theorists may declare confirma-
tion by tautology. But the evidence suggests to me that the momentum
of wage patterns carries beyond the duration of formal contracts or
budgets from contract to contract, from this year's administered wage
increase to next year's.

Other inflation hawks, like my respected friend and former colleague
William Fellner, regard the control of inflation as a war game. On one
side are the forces of altruistic discipline, the monetary authorities; on the
other is the shortsighted unruly economy. What is needed, they say, is a
clear and resolute declaration that inflationary wage and price behavior

will not be ratified by accommodative monetary policy — lock in the money supply and throw away the key. This, they argue, will yield more dramatic and prompt disinflation than anyone's econometric equations, estimated from past observations, would forecast. Isn't this what Arthur Burns has done, without spectacular results? Fellner and others would answer, I paraphrase, that the threat has not been credible enough precisely because Keynesian economists and politicians undermine it by advocating accommodation. In similar vein, two Presidents complained that they could win the war in Southeast Asia if only political opposition at home would cease to impair their credibility to the enemy. The analogy underscores the difficulty of the threat approach in a democracy. In any case, I do not see how, in our decentralized system of wage- and price-setting, there is any incentive for a firm or union or individual worker to be the first to de-escalate. I note also that when Dr. Burns disciplines his class for inflationary offenses, the innocent are punished more than the guilty. Even after the punitive recession OPEC is ahead of the game.

Is there no alternative? Must we *either* hold the real performance of the economy hostage to disinflation *or* accommodate monetary demand to the inflation that history happens to have bequeathed us? Our quandary today is a vivid example of the general dilemma I mentioned at the beginning: Hew to a noninflationary line of monetary demand and rely on market forces to produce a compatible and stabilizing path of wages and prices? Or, as Keynes was advocating in the 1920s and 1930s, adapt the course of monetary demand to the wage-price trend. The first, experience suggests, often gives poor performance in the real payoffs of economic activity. The second leaves prices unanchored, their path the cumulative history of random shocks.

The way out, the only way out, is incomes policy. In 1961 the same dilemma, on what seems in retrospect an incredibly less provocative scale, inspired the "guideposts for noninflationary price and wage behavior." In the same retrospect they may even deserve some credit for the inflation-free recovery to 4% unemployment completed prior to the fiscal disaster of 1966. Those guideposts were advisory. But similar standards could be given, if not teeth, at least some carrots and sticks. Use corporate, personal income, and payroll taxes to reward and insure compliant employers and workers, and possibly — as Wallich and Weintraub independently proposed — to penalize violators.

Proposals of this kind, avoiding the straitjackets of full-blown controls and the futilities of unassisted open mouth operations, deserve much more professional and public attention than they have received. Unfortunately, thanks to Nixon's ventures into wage-price control, incomes policy of any kind is unpopular today. It is especially unpopular with the same economists and opinion leaders who place the highest priority on the conquest of inflation. Any economics student can expatiate on the inequities, distortions, and allocational inefficiencies of controls or guideposts or tax rewards and penalties. But just consider the alternative. The microeconomic distortions of incomes policies would be trivial compared to the macroeconomic costs of prolonged under-employment of labor and capital. It takes a heap of Harberger Triangles to fill an Okun Gap.

A final footnote will bring us back to Keynes. As I reminded you earlier, he was appalled by Britain's return to gold in 1925. He was further appalled by the government's failure to take any direct action to bring internal wages and prices into line with the new exchange rate. Later, after the *General Theory*, he recognized that some direct wage/price policy would be needed if the economy were stabilized near full employment.

MONEY AND PERMANENT INCOME: SOME EMPIRICAL TESTS*

By James Tobin *and* Craig Swan
Yale University

According to an increasingly influential school of thought, centered in this city, variation in the money supply is the principal determinant—indeed virtually the exclusive determinant—of variation in money income. The supporting arguments have been more empirical than theoretical. The empirical evidence has included careful historical narrative [6], systematic investigation of cyclical leads and lags among relevant time series [7], and single-equation regression analyses [4]. Less attention has been given to the task of providing a theoretical rationale of the empirical findings, a monetary theory of income determination to set against the neo-Keynesian models of many macro-economics textbooks. However, Friedman and Schwartz (FS) have presented an explicit model in [7]. Their "permanent income" theory of money demand has testable implications, and in this paper we test some of them.

The Friedman-Schwartz Model

First, a brief outline of the permanent income theory: FS hypothesize that per capita demand for real money balances is related to permanent real income as follows:

$$(1) \qquad M/P_p = \gamma y_p^{\delta}$$

where

M = nominal money stock (Currency + Demand Deposits + Time Deposits), per capita

P_p = permanent price index of consumer goods

y_p = permanent real income, per capita

* The research described in this paper was carried out under grants from the National Science Foundation and from the Ford Foundation.

The money stock M is taken to be exogenous; demand must adapt to the supply. Equation (1) is, as a first approximation, always satisfied; the economy is always on its money demand curve.

The permanent value of a variable—price or income—is a weighted average of its current and past actual values, with account taken of trend. For a variable, $X(t)$, permanent $X_p(t)$ is defined as follows:

$$(2) \qquad X_p(t) = (1 + \alpha_X)^t$$
$$\prod_{i=0}^{\infty} [X(t-i)/(1+\alpha_X)^{t-i}]^{w_i}$$

where

α_X is the trend rate of growth of X

w_i is the exponential weight of actual X_{t-i};

$$\sum_{i=0}^{\infty} w_i = 1.$$

With several substitutions and simplifications, (2) can be expressed in a more manageable form. First, taking the logarithms of (2) yields

$$\log X_p(t) = t \log [1 + \alpha_X]$$
$$+ \sum_{i=0}^{\infty} w_i \{ \log X(t-i)$$
$$- (t-i) \log (1 + \alpha_X) \}$$

which can be rewritten as:

$$\log X_p(t) - t \log (1 + \alpha_X)$$
$$(3) \qquad = \sum_{i=0}^{\infty} w_i \{ \log X(t-i)$$
$$- (t-i) \log (1 + \alpha_X) \}$$

Second, FS assume that the w_i can be characterized as a simple geometrically

Reprinted by permission from *American Economic Review, Papers and Proceedings* 59 (May 1969):285–295.

declining series of weights which sum to unity; i.e., $w_i = w_o(1 - w_o)^i$. It is convenient to note that

$$
\text{(4)} \quad
\begin{aligned}
&\sum_{i=1}^{\infty} w_o(1 - w_o)^i \\
&= (1 - w_o) \sum_{j=0}^{\infty} w_o(1 - w_o)^j
\end{aligned}
$$

This property of the lag structure makes possible the following substitution in (3):

$$
\begin{aligned}
\log X_p(t) &- t \log (1 + \alpha_X) \\
&= w_o[\log X(t) - t \log (1 + \alpha_X)] \\
&+ (1 - w_o)[\log X_p(t - 1) \\
&- (t - 1) \log (1 + \alpha_X)]
\end{aligned}
$$

or

$$
\text{(5)} \quad
\begin{aligned}
\log X_p(t) &= w_o \log X(t) \\
&+ (1 - w_o) \log X_p(t - 1) \\
&+ (1 - w_o) \log (1 + \alpha_X)
\end{aligned}
$$

Taking logarithms of equation (1), the equality of supply and demand for real money balances, gives

$$
\text{(6)} \quad
\begin{aligned}
\log M(t) &= \log \gamma + \delta \log y_p(t) \\
&+ \log P_p(t).
\end{aligned}
$$

FS assume that the w_i associated with y_p and P_p are identical. Using (5) to calculate y_p and P_p gives:

$$
\text{(7)} \quad
\begin{aligned}
\log M(t) &= \log \gamma + \delta w_o \log y(t) \\
&+ w_o \log P(t) \\
&+ (1 - w_o)[\log (1 + \alpha_P) \\
&+ \delta \log (1 + \alpha_y)] \\
&+ (1 - w_o)[\delta \log y_p(t - 1) \\
&+ \log P_p(t - 1)]
\end{aligned}
$$

Since FS assume that the economy is always on its demand curve for money, they can use (6) for period $t-1$ to eliminate the unobserved permanent variables in (7) and get

$$
\text{(8)} \quad
\begin{aligned}
\log M(t) &= w_o \log \gamma + (1 - w_o) \\
&[\log (1 + \alpha_P) + \delta \log (1 + \alpha_y)] \\
&+ \delta w_o \log y(t) + w_o \log P(t) \\
&+ (1 - w_o) \log M(t - 1)
\end{aligned}
$$

Equation (8) can then be solved for $\log y(t)$:

$$
\text{(9)} \quad
\begin{aligned}
\log &y(t) \\
&= -\frac{1}{\delta} \log \gamma - \frac{(1 - w_o)}{\delta w_o} \\
&[\log (1 + \alpha_P) + \delta \log (1 + \alpha_y)] \\
&+ \frac{1}{\delta w_o}[\log M(t) - \log P(t)] \\
&- \frac{1 - w_o}{\delta w_o}[\log M(t - 1) - \log P(t)].
\end{aligned}
$$

Equation (9) is an expression for real per capita income. It could be converted into an expression for money per capita income by adding $\log P(t)$ to both sides.[1] This would leave $\log P(t)$ on the right with a coefficient of $1 - 1/\delta$. For purposes of estimation, equation (9) has the advantage of being identified. It can be used to derive estimates of δ, the elasticity of money demand with respect to permanent income, and w_o, the weight of current information in estimating permanent values. An equation for money income would be over-

---

[1] However, there are problems in using equation (9). First, as indicated below the price level is not really exogenous; there is another structural relationship concerning the division of increases in aggregate demand between real income and prices. Single equation treatment of equation (9) ignores this other relationship. Second, it is by no means obvious that the stochastic elements in the model produce a well-behaved additive error term in equation (9). Suppose that (1) were $M/P_p = \gamma y_p{}^\delta \cdot \exp^\epsilon$ where ϵ is a normally distributed error. The error in (9), call it $\eta(t)$, will then be $\epsilon(t) - (1 - w_o)\epsilon(t-1)$. For $\eta(t)$ to be serially independent, $\epsilon(t)$ would have to be positively serially correlated in a specific manner. If $\epsilon(t)$ is serially independent, then $\eta(t)$ will show negative serial correlation (not the high positive serial correlation shown in the residuals from the level regression).

TABLE 1

ANNUAL AND QUARTERLY REGRESSIONS OF INCOME ON MONEY 1951–66

| Equation | Intercept | Coefficient of:* | | R^2 | DW | n | w_o | δ |
		$\log \dfrac{M(t)}{P(t)}$	$\log \dfrac{M(t-1)}{P(t)}$					
Annual								
Levels.........	.74	1.43 (.530)	−.61 (.709)	.76	.74	16	.57	1.23
First differences..		.27 (.320)	.62 (.364)	.32	2.44	15	3.30	1.12
Quarterly								
Levels.........	.73	1.31 (.707)	−.35 (.743)	.74	.11	64	.73	1.04
First differences..		.12 (.239)	.61 (.238)	.25	1.18	63	6.08	1.37

* Standard errors of the coefficients are reported in parentheses.
R^2 = Coefficient of determination
DW = Durbin-Watson statistic
n = number of observations
For data sources see Data Appendix.

identified. Although equation (9) concerns real income, there is no implication that the effects of an increase in the money supply will affect real income to the exclusion of prices. Actually FS, like other economists, expect short-run changes in money income to be divided between output and prices.

Estimates from Annual and Quarterly Regressions 1951–66

Equation (9) was fitted to annual and quarterly data from 1951 through 1966. Results of level and first difference forms of the regression are reported in Table 1.

On the basis of his study of the consumption function and other work, Friedman estimates the weight of current year income in permanent income at $\frac{1}{3}$. (This would imply a value of w_o of .096 in the quarterly regressions.) Friedman also estimates δ, the elasticity of money demand with respect to permanent income, to be 1.8 (see [7]).

Our estimates of w_o are higher than the estimates Friedman has reported and our estimates of δ are considerably lower than Friedman's own in [1]. Friedman's estimates referred to a longer time period. Virtue does not necessarily lie with long time periods; structural changes have occurred. Commercial banks have in recent decades faced much stronger competition for savings from other financial intermediaries than they did in the late nineteenth and early twentieth century. (See [8, p. 105].) It is not surprising, therefore, that Friedman's estimates of δ, the long-run income elasticity of money demand, are higher than ours. Furthermore, the major financial reforms of the 1930's might well have changed these parameters.

The Durbin-Watson statistics suggest that the level regressions show high positive serial correlation of the residuals. Use of first differences meets this problem, but the explanatory power of the model then becomes very low, and in terms of the theory the estimates of w_o become absurd. (Indeed, they suggest an opposite model, in which permanent money holdings are related to current income.) A tempting interpretation is that the correlation exhibited in the level regressions reflects common trends in income and money rather than a causal relationship between the variables, and that there are important, serially persistent nonmonetary determinants of income.

A low value of w_o plays an important part in FS's explanation of the observation that short-run fluctuations in income are larger in amplitude than the monetary fluctuations that cause them. The income velocity of money moves pro-cyclically, and the permanent income model is supposed to explain this fact, among others. When money supply increases exogenously, faster than the permanent price level, permanent income must increase sufficiently to absorb the new money. If δ is 1.8, as FS estimate, then permanent income must rise .55 percent to create demand for an addition of 1 percent to the real stock of money. But the only component of permanent income that can rise is current income; the past incomes that enter the weighted average are irrevocably fixed. With $w_o = \frac{1}{3}$ for annual incomes, current year's income must rise 3 percent to raise permanent income 1 percent, or 1.65 percent to raise permanent income the necessary .55 percent. The calculation illustrates how the model reconciles FS's finding that velocity declines in the long run ($\delta > 1$) with their finding that short-run changes in money stock cause more than proportionate changes in income.

FS recognize in [7] that the model proves too much if it is applied literally to quarterly data. As already noted, the $\frac{1}{3}$ estimate for w_o for annual data implies a weight of .096 for the income of the current quarter. If the entire income adjustment to a change in money stock must occur within a quarter, then it will be more than three times as large as indicated in the previous paragraph. It will take a 5.7 percent rise in current income for the quarter to raise permanent income .55 percent. As Table 1 indicates, our quarterly regressions indicate much larger values of w_o than the FS model, literally applied, would imply. As FS themselves suggest, perhaps we should relax the assumption that money demand adjusts so rapidly as to keep the community on its demand curve every quarter.

In this spirit we introduce the following modification: Assume people do not adjust their current money balances to income and prices but rather adjust a weighted average of the current and preceding quarters' money balances. Consequently we define $M^*(t)$ as $(1-\beta)M(t) + \beta M(t-1)$ and recompute the quarterly regressions with $M^*(t)$ substituted for $M(t)$. Results for $\beta = .25, .5, .75$ and 1.0 are reported in Table 2. The quarterly results in Table 1 are equivalent to $\beta = 0$. While estimates of w_o decline as β rises, they are still large. They imply a much larger response of the demand for money to changes in current income than the FS model.

Interest Rate Effects?

An alternative explanation of observed pro-cyclical movements of velocity is sensitivity of money demand to interest rates. Given such sensitivity, short-run fluctuations in income can have nonmonetary as well as monetary causes. If the monetary authorities "lean against the wind," then money supply, interest rates, and velocity will all increase in booms and decline in recessions. This would be a Keynesian interpretation of the same observations that the FS model is designed to explain. It would of course have very different policy implications, leaving room for fiscal policy and exogenous changes in

95

TABLE 2
QUARTERLY REGRESSIONS OF INCOME ON CURRENT AND LAGGED MONEY STOCKS
1951.1–1966.4

| Equation | Intercept | Coefficient of: | | R^2 | DW | w_0 | δ |
		$\log\left(\dfrac{M^*(t)}{P(t)}\right)$	$\log\left(\dfrac{M^*(t-1)}{P(t)}\right)$				
Levels							
$\beta = .25$	.73	1.69 (.778)	− .74 (.821)	.74	.11	.56	1.05
$\beta = .5$	.73	2.03 (.817)	−1.09 (.865)	.74	.11	.46	1.06
$\beta = .75$	.73	2.20 (.806)	−1.26 (.856)	.74	.12	.43	1.06
$\beta = 1.0$	.73	2.14	−1.20	.74	.15	.44	1.06
First differences							
$\beta = .25$		.01 (.313)	.76 (.311)	.28	1.21	77.0	1.30
$\beta = .5$		− .01 (.365)	.82 (.364)	.29	1.21	−81.0	1.23
$\beta = .75$		.20 (.311)	.62 (.310)	.29	1.20	4.10	1.21
$\beta = 1.0$		.34 (.233)	.47 (.233)	.29	1.21	2.38	1.23

private spending, as well as monetary events, to affect income.

While Friedman has doubted the empirical significance of interest rates, other than expected changes in the value of money, on the demand for money [1], other researchers have found evidence of such influence. (See, for example, [9] [10].) Certainly there is ample theoretical reason to suppose that the holding of money is influenced by its own real yield—which for the FS definition of money depends both on the rate paid by commercial banks on time deposits and on the expected rate of price change—and by the real yields on substitute assets such as Treasury bills.

These effects can be built into the FS equation (1) as follows:

$$(10) \quad \frac{\dfrac{M(t)}{P_p(t)}}{} = \gamma y_p(t)^\delta \left(\frac{P_p(t)}{P_p(t-1)}\right)^v R_{TD}(t)^s R_T(t)^c$$

where

R_{TD} = rate paid by commercial banks on time deposits,

R_T = market yield on new issue Treasury bills.

$$\left(\frac{P_p(t)}{P_p(t-1)}\right)$$

is a measure of the change in the permanent price level; it is also, as can be shown by application of equation (5) letting X

TABLE 3

ANNUAL AND QUARTERLY REGRESSIONS OF INCOME ON MONEY AND RATES OF RETURN

	Intercept	Coefficient of:				
		$\log \dfrac{M(t)}{P^{(t)}} - \log \dfrac{M(t-1)}{P^{(t)}}$	$\log P(t) - \log P(t-1)$	$\log R_{TD}(t) - \log R_{TD}(t-1)$	$\log R_T(t)$ $-\log R_T(t-1)$
Annual	.70	.66	−.18	.05	.05
		(.050)	(.230)	(.012)	(.013)
Quarterly	.70	.66	−.29	.05	.05
		(.025)	(.339)	(.005)	(.005)

	R^2	DW	w_0	δ	ν	η	ϵ
Annual	.98	1.62	.99	1.52	.27	−.08	−.08
Quarterly	.98	.68	.97	1.52	.44	−.08	−.08

ν Elasticity of demand for real money balances with respect to permanent price increase.
η Elasticity of demand for real money balances with respect to the rate paid on time deposits.
ϵ Elasticity of demand for real money balances with respect to the yield on new issue Treasury bills.

equal $P(t)/P(t-1)$, the permanent value of price change. Substitutions similar to those previously made in equation (1) yield the following formulation:

$$
\begin{aligned}
(11) \quad \log y(t) = & -\frac{1}{\delta}\log \gamma - \frac{1-w_0}{\delta w_0} \\
& \cdot [\log \alpha_P + \delta \log \alpha_\nu] \\
& -\frac{\nu}{\delta}[\log P(t) - \log P(t-1)] \\
& +\frac{1}{\delta w_0}\big\{[\log M(t) - \log P(t)] \\
& - (1-w_0)[\log M(t-1) \\
& - \log P(t)]\big\} \\
& -\frac{\eta}{\delta w_0}\big\{\log R_{TD}(t) \\
& - (1-w_0)\log R_{TD}(t-1)\big\} \\
& -\frac{\epsilon}{\delta w_0}\big\{\log R_t(t) \\
& - (1-w_0)\log R_t(t-1)\big\}
\end{aligned}
$$

It is easily seen that equation (11) is over-identified; aside from constants, there are seven coefficients to determine five parameters. But by fixing w_0 it is possible to combine terms for $M(t)$ and $M(t-1)$, $R_{TD}(t)$ and $R_{TD}(t-1)$, and $R_T(t)$ and $R_T(t-1)$ and to regard (11) as an equation involving four coefficients to determine four parameters other than w_0. Equation (11) was then estimated by varying w_0 in steps between 0 and 1.0 and choosing that value of w_0 which maximized the R^2.[2] Results are presented in Table 3.

The estimates of δ in this more general version, equation (10), are larger than before. Perhaps the exclusion of relevant interest rate terms biased downward the earlier estimates of δ. High income may have served as a proxy for high market interest rates, which have a predominantly negative effect on money holdings. More surprising is the positive coefficient on the R_{TD} term. This result may be in part explained by the strong correlation between the time deposit rate and the Treasury bill rate and by shifts within M

[2] In fact w_0 was first varied from .1 to .9 in increments of .1. w_0 was then varied by .01 in the region of the previous maximum.

between demand and time deposits. Most surprising, however, is the apparent positive elasticity of money holdings with respect to price changes. Perhaps people do not in fact extrapolate current and past price trends. Finally, these results do not confirm the hypothesis that behavior will be better explained by relating it to permanent values of income, price, and price change. The estimates of w_o are so close to one as to eliminate almost all difference of permanent from current values.

Prediction Tests

Another test of the basic structure of equation (1) is to see how good a predictor it is. Friedman has expressed the view that "the only relevant test of the *validity* of a hypothesis is comparison of its predictions with experience" [2, pp. 8–9]. Correspondingly, a variant of (9) was used to predict annual and quarterly changes in money income from 1959 through 1968. Expressing $\log y(t)$ as $\log Y(t) - \log P(t)$ and taking first difference of (9) yields:

$$(12) \quad \begin{aligned} \Delta \log Y(t) &= \frac{1}{\delta w_o} \Delta \log M(t) \\ &\quad - \frac{1 - w_o}{\delta w_\bullet} \Delta \log M(t - 1) \\ &\quad - \frac{w_o(1 - \delta)}{\delta w_\bullet} \Delta \log P(t) \end{aligned}$$

Let each first difference be expressed as a deviation from its average value; if X is subject to a geometric trend $X(0)(1+\alpha_X)^t$, this contributes a constant, $\log(1+\alpha_X)$, to growth of $\log X$ each period. Thus, let

$$\bar{Y}(t) = \Delta \log Y(t) - \log(1 + \alpha_Y)$$
$$\bar{P}(t) = \Delta \log P(t) - \log(1 + \alpha_P)$$
$$\bar{M}(t) = \Delta \log M(t)$$
$$\quad - \log[1 + \delta(\alpha_Y - \alpha_P) + \alpha_P]$$

For the present tests, α_Y and α_P were measured as the actual average compound rates of change of money income and prices from 1950 to 1960. Substituting these definitions into (12) yields

TABLE 4

PREDICTIONS OF ANNUAL PERCENTAGE CHANGES IN MONEY INCOME
1959–67

Year	Actual	FS13	FS14	Naïve*	Trend†	Adjusted Trend‡
59	8.3	3.2	3.6	1.1	5.6	5.5
60	4.1	−2.9	−3.1	8.3	5.6	5.8
61	3.2	10.8	11.8	4.1	5.6	5.6
62	7.5	6.8	7.6	3.2	5.6	5.4
63	4.4	7.0	7.6	7.5	5.6	5.6
64	7.0	5.2	5.7	5.4	5.6	5.6
65	8.0	6.1	6.6	7.0	5.6	5.7
66	8.8	8.1	8.2	8.0	5.6	5.8
67	6.6	5.4	4.7	8.8	5.6	6.0
Average absolute change...	8.7					
Average absolute error.....		3.1	3.2	2.7	1.9	1.8

* Actual change last period taken as forecast.
† Average annual rate of change, 1950–60.
‡ Predicted change for year t is found by solving for r
$$Y(t - 1) = (1 + r)^{(t-1-1950)} Y(1950).$$

TABLE 5

PREDICTIONS OF QUARTERLY PERCENTAGE CHANGE IN MONEY INCOME
1959.1–1968.2

Quarter	Actual	FS13	FS14	Naïve*	Trend†	Adjusted Trend‡
59.1	2.1	1.1	1.1	3.1	1.6	1.6
2	2.7	−.7	−.7	2.1	1.6	1.6
3	−.8	−1.1	−1.2	2.7	1.6	1.6
4	1.2	−5.4	−5.8	−.8	1.6	1.5
60.1	2.6	−.6	−.7	1.2	1.6	1.5
2	.4	3.1	3.4	2.6	1.6	1.5
3	−.1	8.2	9.1	.4	1.6	1.5
4	−.2	1.4	1.5	−.1	1.6	1.5
61.1	−.1	2.5	2.7	−.2	1.6	1.4
2	2.3	1.9	2.2	−.1	1.6	1.4
3	1.8	.8	1.0	2.3	1.6	1.4
4	2.7	1.9	2.0	1.8	1.6	1.4
62.1	1.5	3.6	4.0	2.7	1.6	1.5
2	1.8	.1	.3	1.5	1.6	1.5
3	1.3	−5.7	−6.1	1.8	1.6	1.5
4	1.4	12.0	13.0	1.3	1.6	1.5
63.1	.9	.1	.1	1.4	1.6	1.5
2	1.1	1.0	1.1	.9	1.6	1.5
3	1.9	.4	.5	1.1	1.6	1.5
4	1.9	2.4	2.5	1.9	1.6	1.5
64.1	1.8	−.5	−.6	1.9	1.6	1.5
2	1.8	−1.5	−1.6	1.8	1.6	1.5
3	1.6	8.5	9.4	1.8	1.6	1.5
4	.9	−.6	−.7	1.6	1.6	1.5
65.1	2.7	2.9	3.1	.9	1.6	1.5
2	1.8	−.6	−.8	2.7	1.6	1.5
3	2.0	−.7	−.7	1.8	1.6	1.5
4	2.8	13.9	15.3	2.0	1.6	1.5
66.1	2.5	−7.2	−8.0	2.8	1.6	1.5
2	1.5	2.6	2.6	2.5	1.6	1.5
3	1.8	−4.8	−5.4	1.5	1.6	1.5
4	1.9	−2.9	−3.3	1.8	1.6	1.5
67.1	.4	12.4	13.5	1.9	1.6	1.5
2	.9	5.7	6.1	.4	1.6	1.5
3	1.9	3.8	3.9	.9	1.6	1.5
4	2.0	−3.1	−3.7	1.9	1.6	1.5
68.1	2.6	−3.0	−3.5	2.0	1.6	1.5
2	2.4	2.0	1.8	2.6	1.6	1.5
Average absolute change...	1.6					
Average absolute error.....		3.7	3.9	.8	.7	.7

* Actual change last period taken as forecast.
† Average annual rate of change, 1950–60.
‡ Predicted change for year t is found by solving for r
$$Y(t-1) = (1+r)^{(t-1-1950)} Y(1950).$$

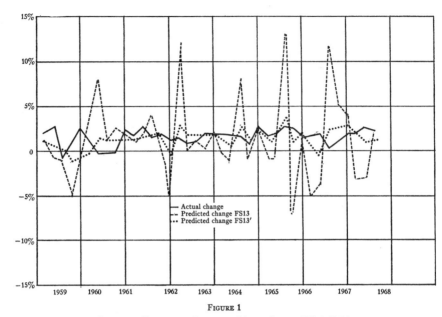

FIGURE 1

QUARTERLY PERCENTAGE CHANGES IN MONEY INCOME 1959.1-1968.2

$$\tilde{Y}(t) = \frac{1}{\delta w_o} \tilde{M}(t) - \frac{1-w_o}{\delta w_o} \tilde{M}(t-1)$$

(13)
$$- \frac{w_o(1-\delta)}{\delta w_o} \tilde{P}(t)$$

Use of (13) yields predictions of deviations of money income per capita from its trend. Predictions of actual percentage changes in aggregate money income can then be obtained by adding population change and trend change in income. FS estimates of w_o and δ, .33 and 1.81, respectively, were used. For quarterly predictions w_o was set equal to .096.

In [7] FS indicate that one might expect prices and money income to move together systematically. They consider the elasticity of the measured price level with respect to measured income and assign it a value of .2. Substituting $.2\Delta$

$\log Y(t)$ for $\Delta \log P(t)$ in (12) yields another predictor of changes in money income,

$$\tilde{Y}(t) = \frac{1}{(.2+.8\delta)w_o} \tilde{M}(t)$$

(14)
$$- \frac{1-w_o}{(.2+.8\delta)w_o} \tilde{M}(t-1)$$

Results of these predictions are presented in Tables 4 and 5. FS13 indicates predictions based on equation (13) and FS14 indicates predictions based on equation (14). Three simpleminded modes of prediction are presented for comparison, in the last three columns of Tables 4 and 5. Figure 1 illustrates actual quarterly percentage changes in money income and the predictions of those changes based on equation (13). The dashed line, FS13 is a graph of the figures reported in Table 5.

The dotted line FS13' uses estimates of w_0 and δ—.73 and 1.04—from our original quarterly regression (see Table 1).

A theory that leads to worse error than the naïve hypothesis that last year repeats itself is of questionable reliability. The quarterly predictions are even worse than the annual; see Table 5 and Figure 1. This may be partly due to the problems of lag structure discussed above. As our own experiment indicated, quarterly results can be somewhat improved by relaxing the requirement that current income adjust enough to create demand for all the new money, requiring instead that only a fraction of the new money supply be immediately matched by permanent new demand. This can be done, but only at some expense to the power of the FS hypothesis to produce a large money multiplier and to explain how short-run varia-

tions in money creation induce reinforcing changes in velocity.

The moral of the exercises of estimation and prediction that we have presented here is simple. Contrary, perhaps, to much popular belief, the evidence does not support the view that there is a simple, direct relationship of income to money. Policymakers and forecasters would not have much luck in trying to infer movements of money income from changes in money stock. The permanent income hypothesis is an interesting theoretical rationale for certain qualitative features of observed fluctuation of income and money. But it does not fit postwar data very well, and our results certainly provide no reason to prefer the FS model to a Keynesian interest rate interpretation of short-run fluctuations in the demand for money.

DATA APPENDIX

M Demand deposits+time deposits+currency per capita (thousands)
       From: *Fed. Res. Bul.*, June, 1964; Sept., 1966,
           and *Survey of Current Business*, Jan., 1967.

Y Net National Product per capita (thousands of current dollars)
       From: *National Income and Product Accounts of the U.S. 1929–1965*, Table 1.9,
           pp. 12–13
           and *Survey of Current Business*, Jan., 1967.

P GNP deflator (1958=100)
       From: *National Income and Product Accounts of the U.S. 1929–1965*, Table 8.1,
           pp. 158–59
           and *Survey of Current Business*, Jan., 1967.

POP Total Population (millions)
       From: *Current Population Reports, Population Estimates*, Census Series P-25
           No. 331 Mar. 22, 1966
           No. 357 Jan. 18, 1967
           Population for year defined as population on July 1.
           Population for quarter defined as average of population for first day of
             second and third month of quarter.

y Net National Product per capita (constant 1958 dollars)
       Y/P

R_{TD} Rate paid by commercial banks on time deposits.
       From: U.S. Savings and Loan League *Fact Book*, 1968.
           Published figures assumed to represent rate paid on June 30.
           Quarterly figures from linear interpolation to mid-quarter.

R_T Market yield on new issue 3-month Treasury bills
From: *Business Statistics*, 1967 (pp. 90 and 237)
Data for predictions through 1968.2 came from the *Survey of Current Business*, July, 1968, or from more recent sources as listed above. In order to eliminate the problem of data revisions, values for 66.4 were altered in proportion to the more recent data.

REFERENCES

1. M. FRIEDMAN, "The Demand for Money: Some Theoretical and Empirical Results," *J.P.E.*, Aug., 1959, pp. 327–51.

2. ———, *Essays in Positive Economics* (Univ. of Chicago Press, 1953).

3. ———, *Studies in the Quantity Theory of Money* (Univ. of Chicago Press, 1956).

4. ———, *A Theory of the Consumption Function* (N.B.E.R., Princeton Univ. Press, 1957).

5. M. FRIEDMAN AND D. MEISELMAN, "The Relative Stability of Monetary Velocity and the Investment Multiplier in the United States, 1897–1958," in CMC *Stabilization Policies* (Prentice-Hall, Inc., 1963).

6. M. FRIEDMAN AND A. SCHWARTZ, *A Monetary History of the United States* (Princeton Univ. Press, 1963).

7. M. FRIEDMAN, "Money and Business Cycles," *Rev. of Econ. and Statis.*, Feb., 1963, Sup., pp. 32–64.

8. M. J. HAMBURGER, "Household Demand for Financial Assets," *Econometrica*, Jan., 1968, pp. 97–118.

9. H. R. HELLER, "The Demand for Money: The Evidence from Short Run Data," *Q. J. E.*, May, 1965, pp. 291–303.

10. H. A. LATANÉ, "Cash Balances and the Interest Rate: A Pragmatic Approach," *Rev. of Econ. and Statis.*, Nov., 1954, pp. 456–60.

Friedman's Theoretical Framework

James Tobin

Milton Friedman has earned our gratitude by setting forth his theoretical framework. He has certainly facilitated communication by his willingness to express his argument in a language widely used in macroeconomics, the Hicksian *IS-LM* apparatus. He undoubtedly hoped that use of a common theoretical apparatus would reduce the controversy about the roles of monetary and fiscal policies to an econometric debate about empirical magnitudes. If the monetarists and the neo-Keynesians[1] could agree as to which values of which parameters in which behavior relations imply which policy conclusions, then they could concentrate on the evidence regarding the values of those parameters. I wish that this contribution had brought us closer to this goal, but I am afraid it has not. I have been very surprised to learn what Professor Friedman regards as his crucial theoretical differences from the neo-Keynesians.

Money, Income, and Prices in Short-Run Equilibrium

First, let me explain what *I* thought the main issue was. In terms of the Hicksian language of Friedman's article, I thought (and I still think) it was the shape of the *LM* locus. This locus is for given stock of money M and price level p, the combinations of real income Y and interest rate r that satisfy $M/p=L(Y, r)$.[2] It will be vertical if the demand for money is

[1] I do not know what to call those of us who take an eclectic nonmonetarist view. "Neo-Keynesian" will do, I guess, but so would "neoclassical." The synthesis of the last twenty-five years certainly contains many elements not in the *General Theory* (Keynes 1936). Perhaps it should be called Hicksian, since it derives not only from his *IS-LM* article but, more importantly, from his classic paper on money (Hicks 1935). One thing the nonmonetarists should *not* be called is "fiscalists." The debate is not symmetrical. Whereas neo-Keynesians believe that *both* monetary and fiscal policies affect nominal income, monetarists believe that only monetary policies do so. At least, I *think* that is the distinctive and characteristic message that monetarists have been conveying to the profession and the public. Friedman agrees that this gives "the right flavor of our conclusions."

[2] To minimize misunderstanding, I should point out that imagining an *LM* curve in (Y, r) space for a given price level p does *not* mean that p is taken to be an exogenous variable in

Reprinted by permission of The University of Chicago Press from *Milton Friedman's Monetary Framework: A Debate with His Critics*, ed. Robert J. Gordon, Chicago: University of Chicago Press, 1974, pp. 77–89. Copyright © 1974 by The University of Chicago Press. (Without postscript this appeared in *Journal of Political Economy* 80(5) (September/October 1972):852–863.)

wholly insensitive to interest rates. This assumption leads to the following characteristic monetarist propositions:

a) Y can be changed only if M/p is changed. Or, if one prefers a relation between nominal magnitudes, pY can be changed only if M is changed. The link may or may not be one of proportionality, and it may of course involve lags and leads and stochastic terms.

b) In particular, a shift of the IS locus, whether due to fiscal policy or to exogenous change in consumption and investment behavior, cannot alter Y.

c) If Y is supply-determined, then M/p is determined and both the price level p and money income pY are proportionate to M.

The neo-Keynesian view is that the LM locus is upward sloping, because $L/\partial Y$ is positive and $\partial L/\partial r$ is not zero but negative. Assuming that there is also some interest sensitivity of investment and/or consumption, we have the following characteristic neo-Keynesian propositions:

d) If Y is not uniquely determined by the supply equations of the system, it can be changed *either* by shifts in the IS curve, whether they stem from policy or other exogenous shocks, *or* by shifts in the LM locus, whether due to monetary policy or exogenous shocks.

e) In particular, an increase in the nominal stock of money M will be absorbed partly in an increase in Y, partly in an increase in p, and partly in a reduction in velocity due to a decline in the interest rate r.

f) Even with Y supply-determined, price level and money income are not uniquely related to the nominal money supply M. They also depend on the interest rate and thus on fiscal policy. For example, an expansionary fiscal policy or any other upward shift in the IS locus will raise r, lower the stock of real balances demanded, and raise the price level corresponding to any nominal money stock.[3]

---

the complete system of which the LM relation is only a part. Even if M is exogenously given, there is a whole family of LM curves, one for each possible value of p. (Indeed, there may be other endogenous variables, including actual or expected rate of change of p, which help to determine the position of the LM curve.) In system-wide equilibrium, the economy must be on that LM curve which corresponds to a value of p that satisfies the other relations of the system, notably including those that describe the labor market. The crucial issue is the shape of a typical member of the LM family. Because of the way in which p enters the equation $M/p=L$, all members of the family have essentially the same shape, which depends on the partial derivatives of the demand for money function L. The monetarist-Keynesian differences listed in the text depend on whether $\partial L/\partial r$ is zero, so that a typical LM curve is vertical, or negative, so that a typical LM curve has positive slope.

[3] None of these propositions depends on absolute liquidity preference (the trap) or, Friedman to the contrary, on any "tendency to regard k or velocity as passively adjusting to changes in the quantity of money" (p. 26).

All this is the stuff of macroeconomics courses all over the country. Friedman, however, explicitly disavows belief that the demand for money is independent of interest rates and denies that his propositions depend on any such assumption. May we, therefore, assume that he accepts propositions *d, e,* and *f* and rejects *a, b,* and *c*?

Friedman shifts attention to the supply side of the model, the short-run relation of *Y* and *p*. I was certainly amazed to find this relationship—which he calls the "missing equation"—identified as the crux of the controversy. I had thought that both monetarists and neo-Keynesians agreed that short-run variations of money income (*pY* or *MV*), however caused, were generally divided between changes in output and changes in price. The common view, I thought, was that the proportions in which an increment in aggregate nominal demand go into output increase and price increase depend on the degree of pressure on existing labor and capital resources. There is plenty of qualitative empirical evidence for such a proposition, though plenty of theoretical and statistical doubt about its precise specification.

Anyway, it is a caricature of the monetarist position to identify it with the notion that *Y* is wholly supply-determined in the short run. We know that Friedman himself has not assumed that. He summarizes his own view as follows: "I regard the description of our position as 'money is all that matters for changes in *nominal* income and for *short-run* changes in real income' as an exaggeration but one that gives the right flavor of our conclusions."[4]

It is equally a caricature of the neo-Keynesian view to say that *p* is an "institutional datum" in the short run. Keynes certainly did not make this assumption, nor did Hansen—and neither has any careful version of a complete neo-Keynesian macroeconomic model.[5] Nor is it at all necessary

---

[4] Friedman goes on to say that " 'money is all that matters, period' is a basic misrepresentation of our conclusions." When I tried to clarify the debate by distinguishing among the three propositions "money does not matter," "it does too matter," and "money is all that matters," the context was perfectly clear. It was what matters in the determination of money income. In the same paragraph, "money is all that matters" is translated into "the stock of money [is] the necessary and sufficient determinant of money income" (Tobin 1965*a*). There has been no basic misrepresentation. No one has accused Friedman and his colleagues of claiming that money is all that matters for the determination of *real* income in the long or short run, to the neglect of supply factors—or all that matters for the cold war, or for the rotation of the planets. They have been represented as claiming exactly what he now agrees "gives the right flavor of our conclusions."

[5] At some stage during the various discussions of the papers here combined, Friedman learned that Keynes could at worst be charged with assuming a constant value of the money wage rate (p. 32, n. 20). Since Keynes also assumed increasing marginal labor and user cost, a constant money wage implies a price level that rises with nominal income. But Keynes did not even assume a constant money wage; see his discussion (Keynes 1936, p. 285) of "the

for proposition *d*. As long as *Y* is not wholly supply-determined, as long as prices are not completely flexible in the short run, the monetary authorities can change the *real* supply of money, not just the nominal stock. As long as *Y* is not wholly supply-determined, any analysis of the consequences of changes in the real supplies of monetary assets is relevant and legitimate.[6] Once again, just as in the debate over the shape of the money demand function, Friedman has tried to saddle his opponents and critics with an extreme assumption and to claim the entire middle ground for himself. In both cases, the truth is that it is his propositions, not theirs, which depend on a special polar case.

His "third approach" model in section 8 is, if possible, even more surprising than the preceding parts of the paper. The "missing equation" —apportioning changes in money income between price and output—is

------

elasticity of money-wages in response to changes in effective demand in terms of money." See also Hansen (1949, p. 136), where fig. 18 shows both prices and wages as increasing (and concave upward) functions of nominal effective demand. Keynesian theory does not require money wage rate rigidity, only stickiness in the sense that, in the short run, labor supply varies directly with the money wage rate for any given real wage.

[6] Friedman (p. 21, n. 11) attacks papers by me and my colleague William Brainard on the ground that "the entire analysis is valid only on the implicit assumption that nominal prices of goods and services are completely rigid." This is not true, as Friedman's own footnote of explanation makes clear. An example of our crime, it turns out, is to "assume that central banks can determine the ratio of currency (or high-powered money) to total wealth including real assets. . . . If prices are flexible, the central bank can determine only nominal magnitudes, not such a real ratio." To believe that the central bank can affect real magnitudes as well as nominal quantities, it is not necessary to assume that prices are rigid. What assumption is necessary depends on whether there is only one or more than one exogenous asset denominated in the monetary unit of account. In some of our models, there is more than one exogenous asset denominated in the monetary unit of account. In addition to having a monetary debt, the government has obligations not payable on demand. Unless the government is constrained always to change the nominal quantities of its *n* types of monetary obligations in the same proportion, it must be capable of altering the real quantities of at least *n*—1 of them. Far from requiring an assumption of price rigidity, this proposition is obviously true even if prices are completely flexible. Open market operations, as observed in the final section of this paper, will have real consequences. In particular, they will alter interest rates and the demand for money. If there is only one exogenous monetary asset, currency or high-powered money, it is still not necessary to assume rigid prices. It is necessary only to assume that prices are not perfectly flexible, that output is not perfectly rigid. Some further observations on Friedman's attack are in order: (*a*) The papers he is criticizing did not pretend to provide complete macroeconomic models. Their objective was to refine and generalize the "*LM*" sector. Given this limited focus, we did not feel obligated to elaborate all other macrorelations, including those connecting *p* and *Y*. We did not think it would be controversial to attribute to the monetary authorities some real effects in the short run. After all, that is what Friedman believes, too. (*b*) Even if *Y* were supply-determined and prices were completely flexible, the structure of the demand sectors of the macroeconomy (*IS* and *LM*) is still of interest. Our system of "*LM*" equations could be solved for the commodity price level and the structure of interest rates, given the level of real income, the real rate of return on capital, and the nominal values of exogenous monetary quantities.

no longer the crux of the matter. Instead, we are asked to assume that in the short run both the real interest rate and the nominal interest rate are fixed. The real rate, which is relevant to real investment and saving decisions, is identified with the net marginal productivity of capital along a normal growth path.[7] This yield changes very slowly, if at all. The nominal rate is simply the real rate plus the anticipated rate of inflation, which is taken to be firmly predetermined by past experience and other considerations.

Friedman invokes the memory of Keynes, as well as that of Fisher, as inspiration for this construction. The Keynesian touch is that speculators keep the actual nominal rate at its proper value. But it is important to note that these are not Keynesian "liquidity preference" speculators between money and bonds. They are Fisherian speculators between goods, or equities in goods, and bonds. The nominal interest rate is not in a liquidity trap. There is indeed, for every M/p, a normally shaped LM curve in the nominal interest rate and real income. But the only point on it that matters is the one that corresponds to the exogenously determined interest rate.

The level of real income is determined wholly by the IS (or multiplier) equations, once the real rate of interest is given. Given $M/p = L(r, Y)$, the fixing of both r and Y determines M/p and leads to a short-run quantity theory of both price level and money income.

The system is illustrated in figure 1. Given the $(IS)_0$ locus and the real rate ρ^*, the equilibrium E_0 is determined with real income Y_0. The nominal rate is measured on the right-hand vertical axis, displaced from the left-hand, real rate, axis by the expected rate of inflation. There is a family of LM curves, connecting real income and the nominal rate, of which two are shown: $(LM)_1$ corresponds to a greater real stock of money M/p than $(LM)_0$. The only LM locus that can coexist with $(IS)_0$ is $(LM)_0$. If the authorities try to shift $(LM)_0$ to the right by increasing M, their efforts will be frustrated by an offsetting rise in p.

Fiscal policy, however, can control real income. Indeed, an increase in real government purchases will have the full multiplier effect—for example, shifting the IS locus to $(IS)_1$ and real income to Y_1. The LM curve will follow along, shifting to $(LM)_1$; this will require a reduction of p if the

---

[7] The real interest rate is constant, ρ^*, in a neoclassical golden age. So also, of course, is its difference from the long-run rate of growth, g^*, as indicated in eq. (29). But Friedman's eq. (30), which implies $\rho^* = g^*/s^*$, is puzzling to those of us who would have expected $\rho^* = (\alpha^* g^*)/s^*$. Here s^* and α^* are the equilibrium proportions of saving and of capital income, respectively, in net national product. Friedman is assuming that $\alpha^* = 1$, that all productive resources are reproducible capital endogenously supplied.

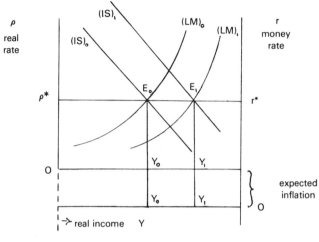

Fig. 1

nominal stock of money is kept constant or increased insufficiently.[8] So deficit spending increases output and employment and lowers prices and money wages. Prices are completely flexible, not because output is supply-determined but because it is multiplier-determined.

As this result suggests, the model is bizarre, and it is hard to imagine that it is seriously intended. Critics have complained that the constant-velocity assumption of monetarism ignores interest-rate effects on the demand for money. It is indeed difficult to persist in maintaining that they are negligible while simultaneously stressing the importance of the rate of price inflation both for nominal interest rates and for velocity. So here is a model that acknowledges the interest sensitivity of the demand for money but preserves the quantity theory by the simple expedient of fixing interest rates. But the cost of this expedient is to concede fiscal policy more control over output and employment than virtually any Keynesian would claim.

The author himself offers this model as tentative and expresses serious doubts. He doubts that the real rate should really be regarded as a constant in the short run, and he is surely justified. The rate of investment depends, on the one hand, on estimates of the future stream of quasi-rents from the ownership of capital and, on the other, on the discount rate at

[8] The model is reminiscent of Mundell's *IS-LM* analysis of fiscal and monetary policy in a small open economy with complete international mobility of capital and fixed exchange rate. There, too, the interest rate is externally given and the *LM* curve floats to whatever equilibrium the *IS* equations determine.

which this stream is converted to present value for comparison with the cost of capital goods. Both of these determinants are subject to short-run changes connected with departures from the long-run growth path of the economy. Securities markets provide a somewhat exaggerated index of these fluctuations, in the ratio of the market value of claims on business income to the reproduction cost of business assets. The sensitivity of this ratio to short-run changes in business activity and the sensitivity of investment to this ratio are important determinants of the short-run stability or instability of the economy.

Friedman finds it easy to accept the assumption of his model that the only short-run fluctuations of nominal interest rates relevant to the demand for money are those associated with the inflation premium. This is not consistent with his acknowledgment that real rates relevant for investment and saving decisions vary in the short run. Nor is it consistent with the ample empirical evidence of rapid interest-rate gyrations. When the Treasury bill rate falls 350 basis points and the corporate bond rate 150 basis points in seven months, as happened July 1970–February 1971, it strains credulity to attribute the decline to a change in inflationary expectations, the more so when inflation continued unabated and when in any case Friedman has taught us that these expectations are a slowly changing derivative of past experience.

The Dynamics of Price and Income

Friedman's ostentatious discovery of the problem of "the missing equation" may give innocent readers the idea that macroeconomics has neglected or fudged an important relationship, without which its models are logically and empirically incomplete. This is not true. Keynes certainly included in his system a relationship between real output and the price level, derived from a theory of labor demand and supply. All careful expositions, mathematical or verbal, of the Keynesian model have done likewise. In postwar macroeconomics, the price variable has slipped one derivative, and the "missing equation" is the complex of price-wage-employment-output relations summarized partially in "Okun's law" and partially in "Phillips curves" for wages and prices. A large fraction of the profession is preoccupied with theoretical and empirical investigations of these matters.

Friedman's particular proposal is simply a Phillips trade-off which vanishes in the long run. Characteristically, his long-run equilibrium relations connect expected or normal values of output, nominal income, wage, and price—both levels and rates of change. These normal values are moving averages of past actual values. Disequilibrium relations apply to surprises, that is, to deviations of the actual values of these variables from expected values. In particular, surprises in the growth rate of nominal income are divided, for unexplained reasons, between deviations in the growth rates of price and real output. Moreover, deviations in the level of real output contribute to positive deviations in the rate of price inflation. Friedman's equation for the rate of inflation, as derived from equations (44)–(46), is:

$$\frac{\dot{p}}{p} = \frac{\dot{p}^*}{p^*} + \frac{a}{1-a}\left(\frac{\dot{y}}{y} - \frac{\dot{y}^*}{y^*}\right) + \frac{\gamma}{1-a}\ (\log y - \log y^*),$$

where p is price level, y is real income, and the starred symbols represent expected values; a, $1-a$, and γ are all positive. The parameter a measures the price proportion of a deviation in the growth rate of nominal income; $1-a$ is the output share. The equation will be recognized as a standard price Phillips curve. The variable

$$\frac{\dot{y}}{y} - \frac{\dot{y}^*}{y^*}$$

is related to the change in unemployment, and the variable $\log y/y^*$ to its level. That the long-run Phillips curve is vertical is ensured by entering expected price change $\dot{p}^*/p^*$ with a coefficient of 1; y^* corresponds to the natural rate of unemployment.

This is not the place to discuss the natural rate hypothesis. I will merely record my view that there is a great deal more to the short-run interrelations of wages, prices, employment, and output than can be captured by a model of universally agreed expectations and deviations from them. Aggregation is always risky, but it seems particularly inappropriate to pretend that aggregate variables obey the relationships that would be expected in a single homogeneous product and labor market.

In the architecture of Friedman's theoretical framework, nominal income is the keystone. The "missing equation" dynamics just reviewed are designed to explain the division of changes of nominal income between price and output. The other side of the arch is the dynamic dependence of nominal income on money supply. Apparently, it is now doctrine that the link of these two variables is the same regardless of the split of changes in nominal income between price and output. It was not always so: in Friedman's earlier permanent income model of the demand for money, both price and income histories were determinants of velocity.

The dynamic link of nominal income to money is only suggestively sketched. The basic idea is that, in moving equilibrium, the growth rate of the money supply and the expected growth rate of money income are equal. As usual, the expected growth rate of money income is a slowly changing moving average of actual growth rates in the past. When money supply grows faster than the equilibrium rate, money income does likewise. This is the dynamic proposition.

However, Friedman is interested in establishing a stronger proposition, namely, that the income velocity of money rises when the growth rate of the money stock exceeds the expected growth rate of money income. In the past, he offered his permanent income theory of money demand as an explanation of this phenomenon.[9] He now offers an alternative or complementary explanation (pp. 41-42). This relates the procyclical movement of velocity to the procyclical movement of interest rates— superficially, at least, the orthodox Keynesian interpretation which Friedman has so stubbornly resisted for so long. In Friedman's version, it is true, interest rates rise during a money-generated boom in nominal income only because the boom in actual income raises expectations of income and price inflation.[10] But the camel's nose is in the tent.

The Long-Run Quantity Theory

Friedman begins with an exposition of the "quantity theory." The phrase has, it turns out, a number of different meanings: (1) emphasis on the distinction between the real and the nominal quantity of money, and on the fact that what matters to rational individuals is the real quantity; (2) use of the quantity identity, $MV = PQ$ or some variant, as an organizing framework for macroeconomic analysis; (3) belief that the central equation of macroeconomics is that of the demand for money to a largely exogenous supply; (4) interest in the determinants of the demand for money, and the size and direction of their effects; (5) assertion that in the short run, nominal income is proportional to the supply of money, although changes in nominal income may affect output as well as prices; (6) assertion that real magnitudes are in long-run equilibrium independent of the nominal quantity of money, so that nominal magnitudes— prices, money incomes—are simply proportional to the nominal quantity of money.

---

[9] See Tobin (1970) for criticism of this explanation. Although it is consistent with observed procyclical fluctuations of velocity, it is not consistent with Friedman's own evidence on the cyclical timing of money and income peaks and troughs.

[10] Incidentally, Friedman's Phillips curve does not justify his assumption that price and money income expectations always move together. Nor does his "monetary theory of nominal income" imply that all changes in money income, inflation expectations, and interest rates are induced by changes of money supply. Within his own framework, the determination of velocity is a good deal more complex than he suggests.

Version 1 is not in dispute and does not imply any other quantity theory proposition. Versions 2 and 3 concern the language in which substantive arguments are expressed, not the substance of the arguments. Keynes could have cast his arguments in the language of the quantity equation, just as Friedman could convey his message in *IS-LM* diagrams. In monetarist language, all influences on nominal income other than the stock of money are dumped into velocity (or its Cambridge reciprocal). This may be awkward, but it is not impossible. Of course, the roster of determinants of velocity may include more than one endogenous variable. If so, the demand-supply equation for money cannot constitute a complete model of nominal income in Chicago or anywhere else. This brings us to version 4 and to the observation that nonmonetarists as well as monetarists fill the journals with studies of the demand for money in its several definitions. The fifth assertion has been the subject of the first part of my comment.

The sixth proposition is the neutrality of money in long-run equilibrium: absolute prices and other nominal quantities are proportional to the stock of money; real magnitudes and ratios of prices (including interest rates) are independent of the stock of money.

It is important to stress that this quantity theorem—which should be called the "quantity of money" theory of prices rather than the quantity theory of money—is not in general implied by rationality, by the absence-of-money illusion. True, no self-respecting theorist believes that de Gaulle made any real economic difference when he cut two zeros off the franc, thus reducing the supply of money in the unit of account to one-hundredth its former amount.

The fallacy of misplaced concreteness is the tacit identification of every change in the supply of money, as engineered by government, central bank, and private banks, with a monetary change of the nature, if not the magnitude, of the change from old to new francs. There is a true quantity theorem, to be sure, but it is a more general proposition than the quantity-of-money theory of prices, and an emptier one.

The true quantity theorem is as follows. Consider a system of supply and demand equations for goods and services and for stocks of assets and debts denominated in the monetary unit of account. Given tastes, technologies, and certain exogenous variables, these supplies and demands will be functions of nominal prices. Among the exogenous data will be some quantities defined in the monetary unit of account, including the monetary base of currency and bank reserves, and the outstanding stocks of government debts of other kinds and maturities. Now suppose that, with a given vector of these exogenous monetary quantities, the system is solved for equilibrium commodity prices p_e. If every exogenous monetary variable is then multiplied by the same positive scalar λ, then the price vector λp_e will solve the system, with every physical quantity unchanged and every endogenous variable measured in the unit of account scaled up or down by λ. This theorem, if it should be so dignified, is a simple consequence of the "homogeneity postulate" or the absence-of-money illusion. A corollary is that the prices of various monetary assets in terms of the unit of account will be unchanged; interest rates do not depend on the quantities of these assets when they all change in the same proportion.

It should take only a moment's reflection to convince anyone that the usual operations that alter the quantity of money, in any of its usual definitions, fail to meet the conditions of the theorem. First, open market operations typically consist in changing some exogenous monetary variables in the opposite direction from others, not in moving them all in the same direction and same proportion. Second, except in the longest of runs, the list of exogenous monetary variables is very long, including individual as well as aggregate stocks and unmatured private debts contracted in the past. While a Gaullist monetary reform scales all these up or down in proportion, ordinary monetary operations do not.

The strict quantity theory applies only if there is a single exogenous monetary variable which *is* "money" except for a factor of proportionality, for example, reserve requirements. Much monetary theory, modern as well as ancient, has developed from a model in which government debt and the monetary base are one and the same. But in a model with various kinds of government liabilities, time as well as demand obligations, it is easy to show that the real equilibrium—for example, capital intensity and marginal productivity of capital—depends on the proportions in which these liabilities are supplied. Even in the long run, the real quantity of money depends on monetary policy, and accordingly monetary policy has other real consequences.

The crucial issue is whether government interest-bearing time debt is of any significance. If not, then an increase in the quantity of money has the same effect whether it is issued to purchase goods or to purchase bonds. If all kinds of debt matter, then the genesis of new money makes a difference. To borrow an overworked metaphor, is a "rain" of Treasury bills—promises to pay currency in three months or less—of no consequence for the price level, while a "rain" of currency inflates prices proportionately?

It may be true that the debt involves an expected stream of taxes equivalent to the stream of interest. But the two streams do not wash out. Bills and bonds share some of the attributes, and perform some of the functions, of the currency they promise to pay. The government has a monopoly of their issue, as it does of currency. As long as the government does not expand the supply of these assets to the point where the public no longer pays an interest premium for their advantages, they will be valued more highly than the corresponding stream of taxes. The tax liabilities forced into public balance sheets are not the same in maturity, risk, convenience, etc., as the government obligations of which they are the counterpart. The tax liabilities will be discounted at the rate appropriate for the incomes on which the taxes are levied.

Interest-bearing debt will also, in general, have important distributional effects. Some of the taxes to pay the interest may be levied on wage income. If such levies were just proportional to property income, one could argue that—risk and portfolio considerations aside—government debt is neutral. It changes neither the demand of the population for a given stream of after-tax income from nonhuman wealth nor the capacity of any given capital stock to generate such a stream. But if wage incomes are taxed to pay bond interest, after-tax human wealth is reduced while nonhuman wealth is increased. Now human wealth and nonhuman wealth are not in general perfect substitutes for each other; indeed, they are complements—the larger households' permanent labor incomes are, the greater will be their demand for nonhuman wealth. Government debt displaces some capital investment from the saving of the labor force; taxation of wages to pay bond interest also diminishes the total supply of saving. Monetization of the debt eliminates the second effect.

Friedman's "theoretical framework" does not provide monetarism, either its short-run or its long-run propositions, with strong theoretical support.

*　　*　　*

Postscript

My paper was written originally as a comment on two separate papers by Friedman, one published in the *Journal of Political Economy* in 1970 (Friedman 1970*a*), the other in the same *Journal* a year later (Friedman 1971). In the present version these two articles have been combined, with considerable reordering of sections, rephrasing of transitional material, and revision and rearrangement of footnotes. Most important, the four paragraphs which here conclude Friedman's section 5 were not present in the original versions. The editor has therefore invited me to comment on this new material, and my comment follows.

The new material—a return, as Patinkin observes in footnote 25 of his comment, to a previous Friedman theme—argues that monetary shocks affect demands for goods and services by setting in motion complex, interrelated chains of asset substitutions and revaluations. If portfolios are to absorb greater quantities of money, prices of other assets—not just Treasury bills and corporate bonds but equities and used cars—must change, mostly rise. Increases in the values of existing stocks of physical assets, or titles to physical assets, encourage the production of new goods of the same type or of close substitutes.

Now this scenario is quite standard. It is one which "neo-Keynesian" monetary economists have been teaching and expounding for years. It is, for example, the principal point of my own "portfolio" approach to monetary theory. Neo-Keynesian econometric models, notably the Federal Reserve-M.I.T.-Penn model, link monetary policies via financial markets and intermediaries to the markets for producer capital, houses, and durable goods.

The puzzle is how Friedman could think that his account of the transmission mechanism supports monetarist conclusions. On the contrary, emphasis on portfolio substitutions suggests, for example, (1) that there is no unique relation between any monetary aggregate and nominal income, (2) that nonmonetary events—fiscal policies, shifts in asset preferences, revisions of expectations—will also affect the attractiveness of accumulating physical assets, and (3) that the market does not automatically put full changes in inflation expectations into nominal interest rates.

Friedman stresses that he is more catholic than nonmonetarists in the list of assets he includes in portfolios—in particular his inclusion of durable goods for which there are not good organized markets. Specific asset lists are not usually presented in theoretical models, but my own conception of "capital" has always included consumer durables. I doubt that anyone disagrees with the principle that portfolio adjustments and interest rate changes will affect asset demands across a broad spectrum. But Friedman has never offered any argument, theoretical or empirical, to support the implicit claim that the existence of untraded physical assets implies strong, direct effects of the *quantity* of money, effects which bypass credit and securities markets and leave no imprint on interest rates and prices of traded assets.

It is true that the formal structure of Keynes's *General Theory* focuses on "*the* rate of interest" and concentrates on its role in substitution between money and bonds. The assumption is that capital and bonds are nearly perfect substitutes, so that *the* rate of interest is also the cost of equity capital, to which the marginal efficiency of capital is equated by investment. This could be regarded as an elliptic version of the now standard transmission scenario, not an alternative approach. In pointing out that financial and real assets are not perfect substitutes, more modern theory actually weakens the link of monetary policy to aggregate demand.

LONG-RUN EFFECTS OF FISCAL AND MONETARY POLICY ON AGGREGATE DEMAND

James TOBIN and Willem BUITER

1. Introduction: The Setting of the Problem

This paper is a theoretical exercise addressed to a rather esoteric and artificial question in the logic of aggregate demand. Does expansionary fiscal policy raise aggregate demand permanently or at best only temporarily? The controversy is reminiscent of the Pigou–Keynes–Lerner controversy on the efficacy of reduction of money wages and prices in expanding aggregate demand, where also much was made of the distinction between short-run impacts and ultimate cumulative effects. The trouble with such discussions, including this one, is that a long run constructed to track the ultimate consequences of anything is a never-never land. For that abstraction we apologize in advance.

A characteristic monetarist proposition is that pure fiscal policy does not matter for aggregate real demand, nominal income, and the price level. The course of aggregate nominal demand, stochastic influences aside, depends solely on the path of the quantity of money somehow defined. Although increases in this monetary aggregate may frequently in practice be associated with budget deficits, the central bank always can break this link and very often does. The fiscal policies alleged not to matter are variations of government expenditure, transfer payments, and taxes while the quantity of money or its path over time remain unchanged.

We have stated this monetarist proposition baldly for the purpose of theoretical discussion. We realize that monetarists, Professor Friedman in particular, usually soften their assertions with qualifying adjectives and adverbs "minor", "almost", etc. After all, no one would wish to have his salvation depend on the literally complete independence of any two variables in a complex interdependent economy. Hedges of this order really do not alter the monetarist message for theory and policy, and they are not intended to. Therefore, let us hope that we can discuss the strong proposition without semantic and textual quarrel about the strength and purity with which it has been asserted.

Reprinted by permission from *Monetarism: Studies in Monetary Economics,* vol. 1, ed. Jerome L. Stein, Amsterdam: North-Holland, 1976, pp. 274–336.

Non-monetarists have argued on numerous occasions that a necessary condition for the proposition is zero elasticity of demand for money with respect to interest rates, and we have offered against the proposition the theoretical reasons and empirical evidence for believing this elasticity is not zero. In the comparative statics of short-run macro-equilibrium this condition appears as a vertical *LM* curve. When the condition is not met, the analysis indicates that a shift in the *IS* curve, – which could be brought about by an increase in the rate of government expenditures or transfers or by reduction in the flow of tax revenues – will raise aggregate real demand.

The extent to which this expansion evokes an increase in supply depends on how close the economy is to its productive capacity. Perhaps we should stress the point that no one is contending that fiscal policy can increase output when production is supply-constrained. Neither can monetary policy. Moreover, this particular debate is not about the existence or size of the natural rate of unemployment. Logically the natural rate proposition is distinct from the monetarist propositions about fiscal policy; one could accept either one without the other.

Even when output is supply-constrained issues concerning aggregate demand remain. The monetarist proposition then is that expansionary fiscal policy – purged of incidental and extrinsic monetary expansion – does not affect the price level. Basically the assertion is that government cannot change, by its own spending behavior or by measures designed to affect that of taxpayers and other citizens, the income velocity of money.

On its face this is a very surprising assertion. If those present at the conference were to decide to lower our average cash holdings while maintaining our spending, we would all agree that national income velocity would rise, though the change would hardly be detectable by our measuring devices. If the Fortune 100 did likewise, it would be detectable. Why not when the federal government does so– especially considering that the measure of velocity includes its spending in the numerator but excludes its cash from the denominator?

Monetarists argue that their proposition holds whether or not the *LM* curve is vertical. Friedman (1972, pp. 915–917) reaffirmed this view in his rejoinder to Tobin's comments on his "theoretical framework" articles. He says that fiscal effects are "certain to be temporary and likely to be minor", and that our difference of opinion is "mostly, whether one considers only the impact effect of a change or the cumulative effect". He agrees that the impact effect of a rise in government expenditure or reduction in taxes is expansionary; there is a once-for-all shift of "*IS*" and this pulls up income and interest rate along a non-vertical *LM* locus. By labelling this effect on income not only "minor" but "temporary" he seems to be saying that non-monetary financing of the accompanying budget deficits moves *LM* to the left, cancelling the expansionary shift of *IS*. But he does not say this explicitly, stressing instead that monetary financing of the same fiscal program would be more and longer expansionary than the issue of interest-bearing debt.

Anyway, the issue we wish to discuss is whether and when the impact effects typified by *IS–LM* statics are reversed, modified, or amplified by shifts in those curves. But we have a few more general observations in prelude.

First, how relevant is this issue to the policy controversy which generated the theoretical debate in the first place? The policy controversy concerns such practical matters as the effects of the 1964 tax cut, the anti-inflationary content of the 1968 tax surcharge, the role of the escalation of war spending in escalating inflation in 1966, the importance of budget economy in fighting inflation or accentuating recession in 1974. In cases like these, advocates of fiscal measures were looking for short-term effects on aggregate demand, without committing themselves to changes of expenditures and taxes never to be repeated or reversed. They were certainly not contemplating that the stock of money should remain forever constant while the stocks of other assets grow. When Walter Heller argued that the tax cut of 1964 would increase demand and reduce unemployment he was talking about what would happen in 1965. He was not talking about what would happen in 1970 or 1980 if the tax cut were even then the only change from pre-1964 monetary and fiscal policies. In this context it was no answer to say that years of accumulation of debt in exclusively non-monetary form would be contractionary. It *was* an answer, right or wrong, to say that demand for money is interest-inelastic.

Second, the claim that growth of non-monetary government debt has the same qualitative effects as reduction of money supply depends on a particular view about asset preferences – roughly that non-monetary debt is a closer substitute in portfolios for capital than for money. This is the traditional view, shared by Keynes. In his "Essay on the Principles of Debt Management" Tobin (1971) distinguished between fiscal or flow effects of government budgets and deficits and the monetary or stock effects of the accumulated debt. He pointed out that, for a one-time change of budgetary program, the flow effect is one-shot while the stock effect cumulates. A corollary is that the flow effect is reversed when the budgetary change is reversed, while the stock effect persists. But at the same time Tobin entertained the possibility that the stock effect of non-monetary debt may be expansionary, that such assets are in investors' eyes closer to money than to capital. If so the growth of non-monetary debt would shift the *LM* curve to the right rather than to the left. (The relevant interest rate on the Hicks diagram would be in this case the true Modigliani–Miller cost of equity capital, which would diverge from the rates on government securities.) We mention this here because we shall not pursue the matter in this paper, where we shall acquiesce in an extreme version of the traditional assumption, namely that government securities and capital are perfect substitutes in portfolios.

Third, there is some tendency to couple the monetarist proposition with a general attack on the use of equilibrium analysis and comparative statics, particularly the *IS–LM* apparatus, in short-run macro-economics. The attack has some justification, because it is generally true that the *incomplete* stock–flow equilibrium determined in such models implies changes in some stocks whose assumed constancy was a condition of the flow equilibrium itself. What is not true is that recognition of the temporary nature of the "equilibrium" invalidates all the propositions of such analysis or validates contrary propositions.

Keynes explicitly restricted his *General Theory* to a time period in which the stock of capital is for practical purposes constant. Yet a Keynesian equilibrium generally involves non-zero net investment, implying changes in capital stock and thus quite possibly in the investment function and other behavioral equations of his model. The same short-run assumption applies to other stocks and flows, including government debt and deficit: the analysis does not apply to a "run" long enough for the flow to make a significant change in the stock. Careful teachers of *IS–LM* and all that have never allowed their students to use the apparatus on questions like "the effects of an increase in government spending financed by printing money" because they knew that the change in money stock was indeterminate and time-dependent. Unfortunately they seldom get around to dynamic models in which the question makes sense.

2. The Plan and Notation of the Paper

In a pioneering paper, Blinder and Solow, inspired by the same questions which concern us, have presented a model of long-run equilibrium similar to the one we shall discuss below.[1] Our reasons for offering another version are two. First, we wish to consider some additional ways of modelling fiscal and monetary policy. Second, we wish to structure the long-run demands for wealth, capital, and money somewhat more definitely and explicitly than Blinder and Solow did, especially in their original article. We shall discuss the differences in some detail in section 3.

[1] Blinder and Solow (1973). A summary, with an important amendment, is given by the same authors in Blinder and Solow (1974, pp. 45–58). The amendment is to include income Y in the investment function; we discuss its significance below in section 3. Blinder and Solow appear to have contributed the first systematic treatment of long-run effects of fiscal policy in an economy without binding labor constraints on output. Of course, growth theory has treated the long-run effects of fiscal and monetary policies in economies with full employment and flexible prices. Even there, fiscal and monetary measures are generally so intertwined that "money-growth" models shed little light on the issues concerning "pure" fiscal and monetary effects.

Like Blinder and Solow, we shall consider a Pigovian stationary state. The advantage of this abstraction is that it allows in a simple manner for adjustments of stocks of capital and other assets. It avoids the possible flow–stock inconsistencies of the short-run equilibrium models. It therefore permits us to consider the monetarist claim that the apparent power of fiscal policy in those models depends wholly on such inconsistencies. Yet the model is artificial in several respects. To be relevant to the issue at hand, the model must permit unemployment even in long-run stationary equilibrium; and this requires the implausible indefinite persistence of wage and price rigidities. We shall also, however, consider the effects of fiscal policy on the price level in a long-run equilibrium with full employment and flexible prices.

The plan of the rest of the paper is as follows: Section 3 discusses briefly the Blinder–Solow contributions. Section 4 discusses the long-run comparative statics and stability properties of pure fiscal measures in economies with unemployed labor. In Model I the instrument of fiscal policy is G', government purchases of goods and services plus debt interest net of taxes on such interest. We trace the effects of once-for-all changes of G', while both the money stock and the proportional tax rate remain constant. As net debt interest changes, government purchases are adjusted dollar for dollar in the opposite direction to hold G' at its policy-determined level.

In Model II, the parameter of fiscal policy is G, government purchases, as it is in Blinder–Solow. This means that the fiscal stimulus varies endogenously as the volume of debt and the interest rate change.

Finally, section 4 analyzes briefly the use of the tax rate θ as an instrument of fiscal policy.

Section 5 takes up, still in the context of long-run unemployment, the effects of changing the quantity of money. Two kinds of monetary change are considered. One is a change in the quantity of money via open market operations, while fiscal instruments, θ and G or G' are held constant. The second is monetary change linked to fiscal policy: budget deficits consequent to a change in G or G' are financed by printing money while the non-monetary public debt is fixed.

Section 6 shifts from the Keynesian world of long-run unemployment to the neo-classical long run of full employment and flexible prices. Once again the questions are how variation of G' affects the long-run equilibrium and whether the equilibrium is stable.

The variables of our models are as follows:

Y = real net national product,
K = capital stock,
N = employment of labor,
$\overline{N}$ = labor force,

D = nominal government interest-bearing debt,
R = nominal rate of return on debt,
$r = R(1 - \theta)$, after-tax rate of return,
G = real government expenditure, not including debt interest,
G' = real government expenditure, including net debt interest,
M = nominal monetary debt of government,
θ = tax rate,
W = real private wealth, $K + \{(D + M)/p\}$,
α = capital share in income,
p = price level,
x = expected rate of inflation.

In the unemployment models of sections 4 and 5, employment N is always less than labor force $\overline{N}$, the price level p is assumed constant, and expected inflation x is zero. In the full employment model of section 6, N is equal to $\overline{N}$, and both p and x are endogenous.

Non-monetary debt is modelled like bills of short maturity, indeed strictly like interest-bearing deposits. It is always valued at par although its yield is market-determined and varies. The only convenient alternative, the one adopted by Blinder and Solow, is to go to the opposite extreme and to assume that all government debts are perpetuities with constant coupons but variable prices. The difference is not consequential for the questions of interest. More realistic specifications, with debts of finite maturity, enmesh dynamic analysis in a morass of complex bookkeeping which is not worth the trouble.

It is assumed throughout that production of Y obeys a constant-returns-to-scale function of capital K and labor N, with the usual neo-classical properties. In equilibrium the marginal product of capital derived from the production function, is equal to the real before-tax rate of return on debt (R in sections 4 and 5, $R - x$ in section 6). As previously stated, we follow – without endorsing – the Keynesian assumption that debt and capital are perfect substitutes in portfolios. At times of disequilibrium the marginal product of capital may differ from the return on debt. Their divergence is the signal and incentive for net investment or disinvestment in capital.

3. The Blinder–Solow Models of Fiscal Effects

Blinder and Solow present first a "long-run" model with a fixed capital stock but variable government debt, and then a model in which both stocks are endogenous. The first has at best expository relevance, since it is unrealistic and potentially misleading to assume that over a horizon in which wealth and government debt change no capital accumulation can occur. For that reason, we will confine our comments and comparison to their variable-capital model. B will denote the number of bonds and the money value of current debt service. (Bonds are consols with a coupon of one unit of money.) Using our own notation where possible, we can write their model as follows:

$$Y = C\big[Y + B - T(Y + B), M + (B/R) + K\big]$$
$$+ I(R, K) + G; \qquad\qquad 0 < C_Y < 1, \quad C_W > 0, \qquad (1)$$

$$M = L\big[R, Y, M + (B/R) + K\big]; \qquad 0 < T' < 1, \qquad\qquad\quad (2)$$

$$\dot{K} = I(R, K); \qquad\qquad\qquad\qquad I_R < 0, \quad I_K < 0, \qquad\quad (3)$$

$$\dot{B} = \big[G + B - T(Y + B)\big]R; \qquad L_R < 0, \quad L_Y > 0,$$
$$0 < L_W < 1. \qquad\qquad\quad (4)$$

C and T are, respectively, consumption and tax functions. $Y = F(B, K)$ and $R = H(B, K)$ are the *IS–LM* solutions for income and interest rate, respectively.

The main differences between this model and ours are in the specification and in policy options considered:[2]

(a) We have opted to put more explicit structure on the stationary state demand functions for stocks of wealth and capital. Our short-run saving and investment functions are derived from these demand functions via mechanisms of adjusting actual to desired stocks. In the Blinder–Solow model, in contrast, the long-run desired stocks are implicit in the consumption and investment equations [by setting $C + G = Y$ and $I = 0$ in (1) and (3)].

(b) The investment function (3), in the original Blinder–Solow, is poorly motivated. They argue that the function "is in line with modern investment theory, which envisions an equilibrium demand for capital stock and a disequilibrium demand for investment" [Blinder–Solow (1973, p. 330)]. Yet the omission of Y from the function vitiates this rationalization for a model in which Y is endogenous. The omission is corrected in their second exposition [Blinder–Solow (1974, p. 55)]. The investment function here is $\dot{K} = I(R, Y, K)$, presumably with $I_Y > 0$. However, the stability conditions repeated in the second version are those derived for the model with the misspecified investment equation.

---

[2] An inessential difference, the modelling of government debt as perpetuities, has already been mentioned.

In their original model, sufficient conditions for stability are

$$F_B > (1 - T')/T' \quad \text{and} \quad I_K + C_W < 0,$$

(F_B is the reduced form impact multiplier of an increase in the number of bonds held by the private sector). It can be shown that in this model stability implies $dB/dG > 0$ and vice versa [if $F_B > (1 - T')/T'$]–the new equilibrium number of bonds after an increase in government spending on goods and services is larger than the old equilibrium number of bonds if, and only if, the equilibrium is stable.

In the model with the amended investment function, two things happen:

First, the stability conditions become very much more stringent – the linearized system is now

$$\begin{bmatrix} \dot{B} \\ \dot{K} \end{bmatrix} = \begin{bmatrix} R(1 - T' - T'F_B) & R(-T'F_K) \\ I_R H_B + I_Y F_B & I_K + H_K I_R + F_K I_Y \end{bmatrix} \begin{bmatrix} (B - B^*) \\ (K - K^*) \end{bmatrix}.$$

$(1 - T')/T' < F_B$ and $F_K < 0$ $[C_W + I_K < 0]$ are no longer sufficient for stability, since the determinant condition is no longer necessarily satisfied.

Second, stability of the system now isn't sufficient to guarantee $dB/dG > 0$, or vice versa. If $dB/dG < 0$, the long-run multiplier for bond-financed deficit spending no longer exceeds that for money-financed deficit spending [Blinder–Solow (1973, p. 327)]. It is even possible that dB/dG is negative and so large numerically that it causes

$$\frac{dY}{dG} = \left(1 + (1 - T')\frac{dB}{dG}\right)\Big/T'$$

to become negative. This comparative-static result can obtain whether or not the equilibrium is stable.

In the stable case, this intuitively implausible result would require the government to run more surpluses than deficits along the adjustment path, even though the initial impact of higher government spending may be to create deficits. This problem arises because Blinder and Solow do not restrict, by their consumption function, the long-run equilibrium relationship of wealth to income. It may turn out that, when the public is content with the fixed money stock and has adjusted both capital and wealth to desired magnitudes, there is less, not more, room in portfolios for debt. This possibility is evaded by their original investment function, which implies an equilibrium capital stock independent of Y, but it can occur wh :. desired K rises with Y.

(c) As regards the fiscal policy options considered, Blinder and Solow deal exclusively with our Model II. The possibility that the long-run government spending multiplier is negative under bond-financed deficits arises only in that regime. In our Model I the multiplier for G' is always positive.

4. Analysis of Effects of Debt-Financed Government Expenditures

Variations of fiscal policy are characterized by changes in government outlays, with the tax rate θ and the money stock M held constant. In Model I the parameter of policy is G'; in Model II, it is G. The former is simpler analytically and in a sense more plausible in examining the long-run consequences of a one-step change of the parameter. Model I assumes that if debt interest increases purchases are curtailed correspondingly.[3] Model II, as in Solow–Blinder, credits a given fiscal policy with expansionary effect just because interest rate increases or deficits raise outlays for debt interest. Some might regard this procedure not as a constant fiscal policy but as an ever more expansionary policy.

4.1. Comparative Statics in the Two Models

Here are the long-run equilibrium equations for Models I and II:

$$W = \mu(Y - RK)(1 - \theta) = \mu(1 - \theta)(1 - \alpha)Y = \hat{\mu}Y. \tag{5}$$

This is the condition for zero private saving. On life cycle principles, wealth is a multiple of disposable labor income. For simplicity, μ and α and thus $\hat{\mu}$, are taken to be constants, but they could made functions of R.

$$\text{(I)} \qquad G' - \theta Y = 0,$$

$$\text{(II)} \qquad G + R(1 - \theta)D - \theta Y = 0. \tag{6}$$

This is the condition for zero government saving, a balanced budget. The tax rate θ applies to wages, capital income, and debt interest.

$$M = L(r, Y/W)W = L(r, 1/\hat{\mu})\hat{\mu}Y; \qquad L_1 < 0, \quad \hat{\mu}L > L_2 > 0. \tag{7}$$

The fraction of wealth held in money is inversely related to the after-tax return on alternative assets and positively related to the income/wealth ratio, which is

---

[3] An alternative which would be more plausible would to be aim fiscal policy for budget balance at a target income level Y^*, fixing the level of government exhaustive expenditures at G, and letting θ vary with debt interest so as to maintain budget balance at Y^*. We investigated such a model, but the analysis is too messy to report.

constant in equilibrium. Since debt and capital are perfect substitutes, (7) is a complete description of portfolio allocation.

$$K = F(R)Y, \qquad K = (\alpha/R)Y. \tag{8}$$

Technologically, the capital/output ratio is inversely related to the rate of return on capital.

$$W = K + D + M. \tag{9}$$

This is the definition of private wealth given above.

The stationary-state equilibrium of this model has the following properties. At the equilibrium Y the public has the desired amount of wealth W. Some of it is in money, the amount of which is the constant M. The interest rate r is such that the public is willing to hold the fraction M/W of its wealth in monetary form. Some of the public's wealth is in capital K, namely an amount such that the return on capital is R. The rest of the public's wealth is in non-monetary government debt D. These conditions can be met for any Y. But the budget-balance equation for the government is necessary to keep D fixed, and the addition of this requirement determines the equilibrium Y.

The models can be condensed into two relations of Y and R, taking as given G' or G, M, and θ.

$$L(r,1/\hat{\mu})\hat{\mu}Y = M. \tag{10}$$

This is the long-run "*LM*" curve, which we shall denote *LLM*.

(I) $G' - \theta Y = \dot{D} = 0,$

(II) $r(\hat{\mu}Y - M - F(R)Y) + G - \theta Y = \dot{D} = 0.$ (11)

This is the long-run budget-balance equation, to be denoted as *GT*. It also takes into account full adjustment of W and K to Y and R, which with M given implies a value for D. But this D does not meet portfolio preferences unless (10) is also satisfied.

The slope of *LLM* is given by

$$\left(\frac{\partial R}{\partial Y}\right)_{LLM} = -\frac{M/Y}{L_1\hat{\mu}Y(1-\theta)} > 0. \tag{12}$$

The slope of *GT* is

(I) $\left(\dfrac{\partial R}{\partial Y}\right)_{GT} = \infty,$

(II) $\left(\dfrac{\partial R}{\partial Y}\right)_{GT} = \dfrac{(G - rM)/Y}{(1-\theta)(D - RF'(R)Y)}.$ (13)

For non-negative D, the denominator of the slope for Model II is certainly positive. The numerator is also positive if G exceeds the hypothetical after-tax interest on the money stock, negative otherwise. $(G - rM)/Y$ is equal to $\theta - \hat{\mu}r + \alpha(1 - \theta)$, and is the rate at which an increase of Y raises the budget surplus with R constant, starting from a position of budget balance.

We are interested in the shift of GT for an increase of G' or G.

$$\text{(I)} \quad \left(\frac{\partial Y}{\partial G'}\right)_{GT} = \frac{1}{\theta},$$

$$\text{(II)} \quad \left(\frac{\partial Y}{\partial G}\right)_{GT} = \frac{1}{(G - rM)/Y}. \tag{14}$$

In Model I the long-run "multiplier" is simply the reciprocal of the tax rate. In Model II the multiplier is positive if GT is upward sloping, but GT shifts left if it is downward sloping. With non-negative D, GT always shifts downward;

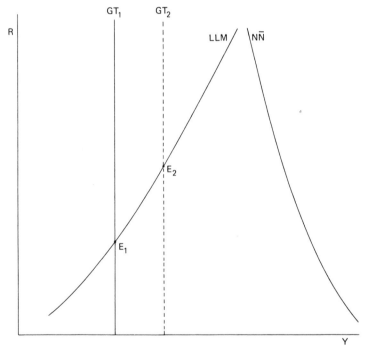

FIGURE 1. Long-run equilibria for Model I.

when G increases, R must decrease in order to lower debt interest and keep the budget balanced.

Model I is pictured in figure 1. To the right of GT, the budget deficit $\dot{D}$ is negative; to the left, it is positive. Above LLM – given M and assuming that W and K are fully adjusted to R and Y – the stock of debt D is too small; the public would like to exchange money for debt. Below LLM, D is too large. As the shift of GT illustrates, an increase of G' leads to higher equilibrium values for both Y and R.

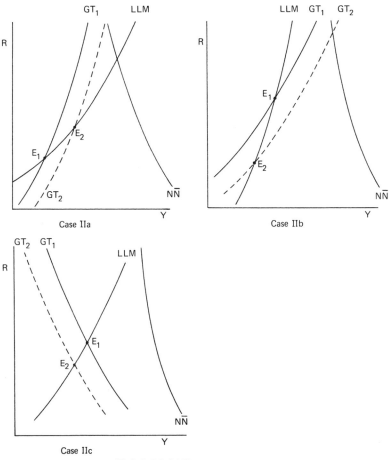

FIGURE 2. Long-run equilibria in Model II.

Model II is pictured in the three panels of figure 2. Case IIa is little different from Model I. In case IIb, the *LLM* curve is the steeper. The comparative statics suggests that fiscal expansion diminishes *Y* and *R*, but perverse results of this type make one doubt the stability of the equilibria. In case IIc, *GT* is negatively sloped, the comparative static result is again "perverse" and there is reason to doubt stability.

These comparative statics apply, of course, only for $N \leq \overline{N}$. Equilibrium demand for labor depends directly not only on *Y* but also on *R*, because higher *R* means use of labor-intensive technique. The full employment ceiling to *Y* is shown in figures 1 and 2, as $N\overline{N}$. A demand equilibrium on the far side of $N\overline{N}$ means an inflationary gap. One way it can be eliminated is reduction of the real stock of money by inflation; we discuss this case in section 6.

4.2 Temporary Solutions and Dynamics: Stability in Model I

Our dynamic story is the familiar *IS–LM* tale. We postulate conventional *IS* and *LM* loci for the Keynesian short run, i.e., for given stocks of wealth, debt, capital, and money. The solution of this system determines the momentary values of *Y* and *R*. As the stocks change, the solution changes. The question is whether this process leads to the stationary equilibrium.

The short-run *LM* relation is implicit in the equation $L(r, Y/W)W = M$, holding *W* constant. Its short-run slope, $-L_2/\{L_1(1 - \theta)W\}$, is less steep than its long-run slope, $\{-L(r, 1/\hat{\mu})\hat{\mu}\}/\{L_1(r, 1/\hat{\mu})(1 - \theta)W\}$, on the usual assumption, empirically supported, that the short-run income elasticity of demand for money, $L_2 Y/LW$ is less than unity. It is convenient to put the *LM* curve in explicit form (suppressing θ so long as it is being held constant),

$$R = R(Y, W, M); \qquad R_1, R_2, > 0; \quad R_3 < 0. \tag{15}$$

The short-run slope is R_1; the long-run slope is $R_1 + \hat{\mu}R_2$.

The short-run *IS* locus is derived from the usual identity that capital accumulation equals the sum of private and public saving. Since asset revaluations have been assumed away, private saving is equal to $\dot{W}$. The identity differs between Models,

(I) $\dot{K} + G' = \dot{W} + \theta Y$,

(II) $\dot{K} + G = \dot{W} + \theta Y - rD$. $\qquad\qquad$ (16)

We assume investment and saving functions of the stock-adjustment type,

$$\dot{K} = i(F(R)Y - K),$$
$$\dot{W} = s(\hat{\mu}Y - W). \tag{17}$$

The *IS* curves are combinations of (16) and (17),

(I) $Y(s\hat{\mu} + \theta - iF(R)) = G' + sW - iK,$

(II) $Y(s\hat{\mu} + \theta - iF(R)) - Dr = G + sW - iK.$

$$(18)$$

The coefficient of Y in (18) is the reciprocal of the conventional multiplier m. We assume throughout that $\hat{\mu}$ exceeds $F(R)$ in the range of relevant values: the desired wealth/income ratio exceeds the desired capital/output ratio. Indeed we shall assume that $1/m$ is positive even if $i > s$. We wish to bypass questions of short-short-run dynamics and instability. Nevertheless, in Model II the *IS* curve may become upward sloping for high stocks of debt. This can be seen from

(I) $\left(\dfrac{\partial R}{\partial Y}\right)_{IS} = \dfrac{1/m}{YiF'(r)} < 0,$

(II) $\left(\dfrac{\partial R}{\partial Y}\right)_{IS} = \dfrac{1/m}{YiF'(R) + D(1 - \theta)}.$

$$(19)$$

Consider first the dynamics of Model I. Figure 3 duplicates figure 1 for *LLM* and *GT* curves, and in addition shows the short-run LM_1 and IS_1 curves corresponding to the initial equilibrium at E_1, i.e., corresponding to the equilibrium stocks W, K, D, M at E_1 and to the initial value of G'. The short-run loci naturally intersect at E_1. Now suppose that G' is increased in one step, shifting the GT locus and indicating a new long-run equilibrium E_2.

The immediate impact is to shift the *IS* curve to IS_{12}, producing a short-run solution S_{12}. This is evanescent, of course, because stocks do not remain at their initial E_1 values. The question now is whether the configuration of figure 1 is stable.

At the new equilibrium E_2, with higher Y and R, the public will hold more wealth, but smaller fractions of wealth in money and in capital ($\partial L/\partial R$ and dF/dR are both negative). Consequently the volume of debt will be higher, both absolutely and as a proportion of wealth and income. A dynamic path from E_1 to S_{12} to E_2 must involve deficits which achieve this accumulation of debt.

As figure 3 is drawn, IS_{12} is shifted horizontally from E_1 by less than the shift of *GT*. This means that the short-run multiplier m is less than the long-run multiplier $1/\theta$, and it guarantees that at S_{12} the budget is in deficit. It is conceivable that m exceeds $1/\theta$, if the short-run marginal propensity to invest $iF(R)$ is high. But m would have to exceed $1/\theta$ by some margin to place S_{12} in the budget surplus region to the right of GT_2.

Taking $m < 1/\theta$ as pictured, at S_{12} both W and D are increasing. *LM* will be shifting up. The growth of wealth also tends to shift *IS* up (via the sW term). We

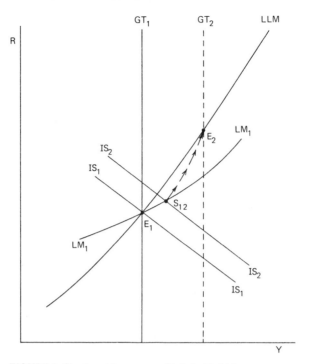

FIGURE 3. Short- and long-run equilibria in Model I.

cannot be sure whether $\dot{K}$ is positive or negative at S_{12}. Compared with E_1, the increase in Y raises the demand for capital but the increase in R lowers it.

A path from S_{12} to E_2 in figure 3 seems plausible. On such a path stocks of assets other than M are increasing and shifting upward both IS and LM. But the dynamics are not easy to display graphically, and the pictured path is not the only possibility. We turn to formal stability analysis.

The system consists of four equations in (K, D, Y, R):

$$\left. \begin{aligned} \dot{K} &= i(F(R)Y - K) \\ \dot{D} &= G' - \theta Y \\ 0 &= Y(s\hat{\mu} + \theta - iF(R)) - sM - sD - (s - i)K - G' \\ 0 &= R - R(Y, M + D + K, M) \end{aligned} \right\} \tag{20}$$

The local stability of the system can be analyzed from the following characteristic quadratic equation in λ:

$$
\begin{vmatrix}
-i - \lambda & 0 & iF(R) & iYF'(R) \\
0 & -\lambda & -\theta & 0 \\
-(s - i) & -s & 1/m & -iYF'(R) \\
-R_2 & -R_2 & -R_1 & 1
\end{vmatrix}
\tag{21}
$$

Here $1/m$ is as before shorthand for the coefficient of Y in the third equation of (20).

Considering (21) as $(a\lambda^2 + b\lambda + c = 0)$, sufficient and necessary conditions for local stability – the real parts of both roots negative – are that both b/a and c/a exceed zero. Both conditions are met on assumptions already made, that the multiplier m is positive, that $\hat{\mu} > F(R)$ (so that there is room in portfolios for assets other than capital), that $F'(R) \leqq 0$, and that R_1 and R_2 are both positive. It turns out that

$$
\begin{aligned}
a &= (1/m) - R_1 iYF'(R) > 0, \\
c &= \theta is > 0, \\
b &= \theta s + \theta i + is(\hat{\mu} - F(R)) - isF'(R)Y(R_1 + \hat{\mu}R_2).
\end{aligned}
\tag{22}
$$

All the terms of b are positive under the assumptions. Note that, in contrast to the Blinder–Solow conditions, no restriction on the relative sizes of s and i, other than the one required to keep the multiplier positive, is part of the sufficient conditions for stability.

4.3. Stability in Model II

The system of four equations is

$$
\left.
\begin{aligned}
\dot{K} &= i(F(R)Y - K) \\
\dot{D} &= G + rD - \theta Y \\
0 &= Y(1/m) - sM - (s + r)D - (s - i)K - G \\
0 &= R - R(Y, M + K + D, M)
\end{aligned}
\right\}
\tag{23}
$$

The characteristic equation is

$$
\begin{vmatrix}
-i - \lambda & 0 & iF(R) & iYF'(R) \\
0 & r - \lambda & -\theta & D(1 - \theta) \\
-(s - i) & -(s + r) & 1/m & -iYF'(R) - D(1 - \theta) \\
-R_2 & -R_2 & -R_1 & 1
\end{vmatrix}
= 0.
\tag{24}
$$

Calling this equation $a'\lambda^2 + b'\lambda + c'$,

$$a' = a - R_1 D(1 - \theta) = (1/m) - R_1(iYF'(R) + D(1 - \theta)), \qquad (25)$$

$$b' = b + r(s\hat{\mu} - iF(R)) + rR_1 iYF'(R) - D(1 - \theta)(s\hat{\mu}R_2 + (s + i)R_1),$$

$$c' = is(\theta - r\hat{\mu} + rF(R)) - is(R_1 + \hat{\mu}R_2)(D(1 - \theta) - rYF'(R)).$$

For interpretation, we recall the slopes of *GT* and *LLM* given above in (12) and (13) and restate them in the symbols of this section of the paper,

$$\left(\frac{\partial R}{\partial Y}\right)_{LLM} = R_1 + R_2\hat{\mu}, \qquad (12')$$

$$\left(\frac{\partial R}{\partial Y}\right)_{GT} = \frac{\theta - \hat{\mu}r + rF(R)}{D(1 - \theta) - rF'(R)Y}. \qquad (13')$$

Given the non-negativity of the denominator in (13') and the expression for c' in (25),

$$\left(\frac{\partial R}{\partial Y}\right)_{GT} \gtreqless \left(\frac{\partial R}{\partial Y}\right)_{LLM}$$

as

$$(\theta - \hat{\mu}r + F(R)) - (R_1 + \hat{\mu}R_2)(D(1 - \theta) - rF'(R)Y) \gtreqless 0,$$

i.e., as $c' \gtreqless 0$. Hence in case IIa, c' is positive, while in cases IIb and IIc, c' is negative.

The value of a' is the effect of G on the short-run solution Y, specifically $\partial Y/\partial G$ calculated from the third equation of (23). The normal expectation is that it is positive; indeed the issue under discussion is whether this positive effect is temporary or not. With positive a', we know that in cases IIb and IIc one of the roots λ is positive. With normal short-run effects, therefore, the stationary equilibrium is unstable in those cases, as previously conjectured.

As for case IIa, with a' positive the equilibrium will be stable if b' is positive, unstable otherwise. Now even with D low enough to make a' positive, b' may be negative. Thus IIa may be either stable or unstable.

A negative value of a' seems at first glance to reverse these stability findings, making IIb and IIc possibly stable. Then one might conclude that fiscal expansion is contractionary both in short run and long run! But this conclusion is illusory. The *IS–LM* solution itself is unstable under usual assumptions about short-run dynamics. This may be seen as follows:

Let the *IS* slope [equation (19), Model II] be $(1/m)/z$. Then $a' = 1/m - R_1 z$. R_1 is the *LM* slope. Here are the possibilities:

	$m > 0$	$m < 0$
$z < 0$	(i) $a' > 0$	(iii) if $a' < 0$ $(1/m)/z > R_1 > 0$
$z > 0$	(ii) if $a' < 0$ $0 < (1/m)/z < R_1$	(iv) $a' < 0$ $(1/m)/z < 0 < R_1$

(i) is the normal case already discussed. In case (ii) an increase in G shifts the *IS* curve right; it is upward sloping but flatter than *LM*. In cases (iii) and (iv) an increase in G shifts the *IS* curve left. In (iii) it is upward sloping but steeper than *LM*. In (iv) it is downward sloping. The four cases are pictured in figure 4. The short-run dynamics indicated by the arrows follow the usual assumption that R always moves towards *LM*, while Y moves towards *IS* if $m > 0$ and away from it if $m < 0$. On this assumption, case (i) is the only stable configuration. (Cases not shown, which are also stable, involve $a' > 0$, $z < 0$.)

4.4. Variation in Tax Rate

We briefly consider the long-run effects in Model I of a third type of pure fiscal policy: changing the tax rate θ, keeping G' constant and financing temporary deficits by debt issue.

A reduction in θ shifts the vertical *GT* line of Model I to the right. The long-run multiplier $\partial Y/\partial \theta$ is $-Y/\theta$. But the *LLM* curve is not invariant to this type of fiscal action. It may shift either way. On the one hand, a tax reduction increases, for given R and Y, the opportunity cost of holding money; this effect moves *LLM* right. On the other hand, tax reduction increases after-tax human wealth and therefore, other things equal, raises $\hat{\mu}$. This effect moves *LLM* left. The net effect is uncertain, and so we cannot exclude the possibility that equilibrium R will be lower with lower θ. The stability analysis is the same as in section 4.2.

5. Monetary Policy in the Long Run

Of the several possible meanings of monetary policy in this framework, we shall consider two. The first is a one-shot open market purchase. The second is a combination of fiscal and monetary expansion, a once-for-all increase in government expenditure with deficits financed by printing money instead of issuing interest-bearing debt.

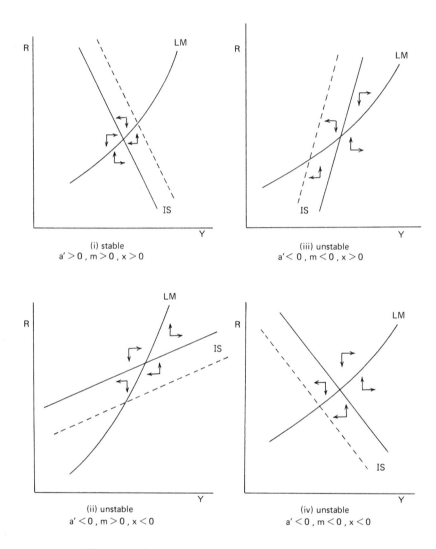

FIGURE 4. Stability or instability of short-run *IS–LM* solution.

5.1. Open Market Purchase of Bonds

The story of the open market purchase is pictured in figure 5. The framework is Model I, in which $G' = G + rD$ is the parameter of budget policy. The economy starts in long-run equilibrium E_1, with the associated short-run curves LM_1 and IS_1. The new long-run curve LLM_2 implies a new equilibrium E_2, with unchanged Y and lower R. The new stock equilibrium involves the same wealth $W = \hat{\mu}Y$, but a different portfolio. At E_2 the public will hold more money, and less debt-cum-capital, than at E_1. But they will also hold more capital, because the

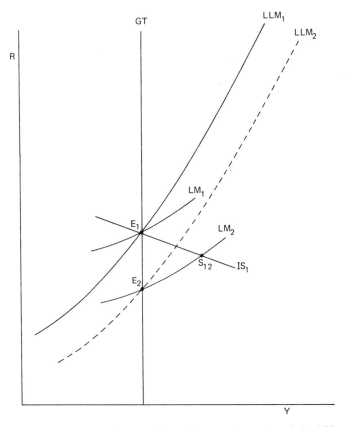

FIGURE 5. Short- and long-run effects of open market purchase in Model I.

desired capital/output ratio $F(R)$ is increased by the reduction in R. Thus ultimately there are two substitutions against debt, one of money in the initial open market operation and one of capital during the process of adjustment.

The shift of short-run LM accomplished by the open market purchase reflects only a money-for-debt substitution. The subsequent capital-for-debt substitution does not affect the LM curves. That is why LM_2 and LLM_2 cross the vertical GT line at the same point. The IS curve is unaffected by the initial operation. (If capital gains on bonds were taken into account, as in Blinder–Solow, IS would shift up because of the increase in wealth.) The first impact of the monetary expansion is the short-run solution S_{12}. But the increase in income is temporary. The government is now running a surplus, and, as we have already seen, the contraction of debt brings income down. Meanwhile the public is also saving more (wealth is below $\hat{\mu}Y$) and investing more [capital is less than $F(R)Y$]. The temporary increase in wealth retards the decline of R, and is reversed once capital and wealth catch up with income, which is on its way down.

In Model II, higher interest rates and debt accumulation have an expansionary fiscal effect because they enlarge the budget deficit. The story for case IIa is essentially the same as for Model I, except that the open market purchase shifts the initial IS curve down. E_2 represents a *smaller* output than E_1. It may seem paradoxical that monetary expansion is, in the long run, contractionary. We do not think the result should be taken seriously, given that it depends on the assumption that monetary expansion entails a fiscal contraction via reduction of debt interest transfers.

In case IIb, E_2 is at higher levels of Y and R than E_1. But there is no way to get there. The open market purchase shifts down the short-run LM curve, increases Y, and decreases R. But from this point the dynamic previously described moves the temporary solution down and to the left.

In case IIc it is quite possible that the dynamics lead to the new equilibrium E_2 with higher Y and lower R.

5.2. Fiscal Expansion with Money-Financed Deficits

We turn briefly to the monetary financing of deficits combined with expansionary fiscal policy. The previous discussion of fiscal policy is now altered by holding D constant instead of M. In Model I, the long-run GT locus is unchanged, still vertical. But the LM locus becomes

$$\hat{\mu}Y - L(r,1/\hat{\mu})\hat{\mu}Y - F(R)Y = D, \tag{26}$$

$$\left(\frac{\partial R}{\partial Y}\right)_{LLM} = \frac{D/Y}{L_1(1 - \theta)\hat{\mu}Y + F'(R)Y} < 0. \tag{27}$$

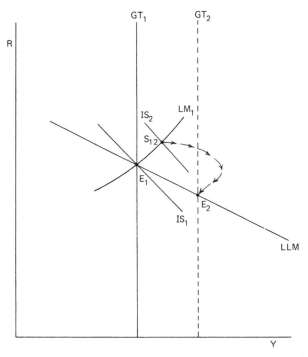

FIGURE 6. Short- and long-run effects of monetized deficit spending in Model I.

Thus we see that the long-run *LLM* locus is negatively sloped. A rightward shift of $\overline{GT}$, as shown in figure 6 is bound to raise equilibrium income Y and lower equilibrium R. The conclusion is not altered in Model II. There the *GT* locus has an upward slope due the term rD in the budget-balance equation, even though D is constant. But it is still true that a rightward shift in *GT* raises equilibrium Y and lowers R.

The dynamics are as follows: the short-run *LM* locus is

$$W - L(R(1 - \theta), Y/W)W - K = D. \tag{28}$$

It is upward sloping, because M does not increase until a budget deficit actually appears,

$$\left(\frac{\partial R}{\partial Y}\right)_{LM} = -\frac{L_2}{L_1(1 - \theta)\, W} > 0. \tag{29}$$

The short-run *IS* curve, defined as before, shifts to the right with the increase of G', but on usual assumptions not as far as the *GT* line. The temporary solution is at S_{12}. But now there is a budget deficit: M increases, W increases, *IS* moves up, *LM* moves down. When the solution crosses GT_2 budget surpluses appear and arrest the expansion.

For formal analysis of the dynamics of this case, it is convenient to express the short-run model in terms of the four variables K, W, Y, and R,

$$\left. \begin{aligned} \dot{K} &= i(F(R)Y - K) \\ \dot{W} &= s(\hat{\mu}Y - W) \\ 0 &= Y(s\hat{\mu} + \theta - iF(R)) - sW + iK - G' \\ 0 &= R - R(K,W,Y) \end{aligned} \right\} . \tag{30}$$

Here the function $R(K,W,Y)$ is implicit in (28), and its partial derivatives are

$$\left. \begin{aligned} R_1 &= \frac{-1}{L_1(1 - \theta)W} > 0 \\ R_2 &= \frac{1 - L + L_2(Y/W)}{L_1(1 - \theta)W} < 0 \\ R_3 &= \frac{-L_2}{L_1(1 - \theta)W} > 0 \end{aligned} \right\} . \tag{31}$$

The characteristic equation is

$$\begin{vmatrix} -i - \lambda & 0 & iF(R) & iF'(R)Y \\ 0 & -s - \lambda & s & 0 \\ i & -s & 1/m & -iF'(R)Y \\ -R_1 & -R_2 & -R_3 & 1 \end{vmatrix} = 0. \tag{32}$$

In the quadratic equation $a\lambda^2 + b\lambda + c$ all three coefficients a, b, c are unambiguously positive, confirming that the comparative static story of figure 6 makes sense.

6. Effects of Fiscal Policy with Full Employment and Flexible Prices

The standard short-run *IS–LM* analysis applies to situations of full employment as well as unemployment, and in this section we extend our long-run analysis to conditions of full employment and flexible prices and wages. In the short run, output is fixed by the full employment labor supply. The standard short-run comparative statics is familiar: Expansionary fiscal policy, with constant nominal money stock, always raises the interest rate. Unless the demand for money is interest-inelastic and the LM curve vertical, it also raises the velocity of money and the price level. Increased real government expenditure "crowds out" private investment, and possibly also private consumption, to the extent necessary to equate total real demand to fixed real supply. But the short-run analysis does not trace the further effects of these changes in the rates of growth of capital and government debt.

Our long-run full employment model resembles as closely as possible both the long-run models of the previous sections and the standard short-run full employment version of IS–LM analysis. But differences necessarily arise. Once the price level is made endogenous in a long-run model, we must explicitly consider price expectations and distinguish real and nominal rates of return. Moreover, in a long-run full employment model the capital stock is endogenous. Output is not fixed, as it is in the short run, by labor supply; output per worker varies with the capital/output ratio and the real interest rate, as illustrated by the $N\overline{N}$ curves of figures 1 and 2.

Capital and bonds are, as before, perfect substitutes in portfolios. The portfolio choice of money vs. bonds-and-capital depends on the real after-tax rate of return differential between money and bonds. The nominal rate of return on money balances is institutionally fixed at zero. If x is the expected instantaneous proportional rate of change of the price level p, and R the nominal rate of return on bonds, the real rate of return on bonds is $R - x$, and the real after-tax rate of return differential is $R(1 - \theta)$.

Portfolio balance is therefore given by

$$L\left(R(1 - \theta), \, Y \middle/ \frac{M + D}{P} + K\right) \left(\frac{M + D}{p} + K\right) = \frac{M}{p}. \tag{33}$$

The production function is, as throughout the paper, a well-behaved constant returns to scale neoclassical production function in capital and labor, N,

$$Y = Nf(K/N); \qquad f' > 0, \qquad f'' < 0. \tag{34}$$

Labor is supplied inelastically and is always fully employed. Since we are only considering stationary states we choose units such that $N = 1$.

Rather than specifying the investment function as $I = i[F(R - x)f(K) - K]$, we shall now find it convenient to write it as

$$I = I(f'(K) - (R - x)), \qquad I(0) = 0, \qquad I' > 0. \tag{35}$$

This function makes the rate of investment an increasing function of the difference between the rate of return obtainable from investing a dollar in the production of new capital goods and the rate of return on existing assets.

We shall consider 3 simple mechanisms for generating price expectations:

Static expectations: $\qquad x(t) = 0,$ (36a)

Myopic perfect foresight: $\qquad x(t) = \dot{p}(t)/p(t),$ (36b)

Adaptive expectations: $\qquad \dot{x}(t) = \beta[(\dot{p}/p) - x(t)]; \qquad \beta > 0.$ (36c)

Government consumption expenditure is fixed in real terms. With bond-financed deficits, the government budget restraint is therefore given by

$\quad$ (I) $\qquad \dot{D}/p = G' - \theta f(K),$ (37a)

$\quad$ (II) $\qquad \dot{D}/p = G + (1 - \theta)R\,(D/p) - \theta f(K).$ (37b)

For reasons of space we shall consider only Model I.

6.1. The Long-Run Equilibrium

The complete dynamic model is

$$(IS) \quad I\big[f'(K) - R + x\big] + G' - \theta f(K) - s\left[\hat{u}f(K) - \left(\frac{M + D}{p}\right) - K\right]$$

$$- x\left(\frac{M + D}{p}\right) = 0. \quad (38)$$

The last term in (38) represents expected additions, positive or negative, to wealth, due to changes in the real values of nominal stocks of money and debt. It is assumed that current saving from income is adjusted correspondingly.

$$(LM) \quad L\left[R(1 - \theta), \frac{pf(K)}{M + D + pK}\right]\left[\frac{M + D}{p} + K\right] = \frac{M}{p}, \quad (39)$$

$$\left(\frac{D}{p}\right) = G' - \theta f(K) - \frac{\dot{p}}{p}\frac{D}{p}, \quad (40)$$

$$\left(\frac{\dot{M}}{p}\right) = -\frac{\dot{p}}{p}\frac{M}{p}, \quad (41)$$

$$\dot{K} = I\big[f'(K) - R + x\big], \quad (42)$$

$$x = 0, \quad (43a)$$

$$x = \frac{\dot{p}}{p}, \quad (43b)$$

$$\dot{x} = \beta\left[\frac{\dot{p}}{p} - x\right]. \quad (43c)$$

In a stationary long-run equilibrium, expectations are realized, momentary equilibrium holds at each point of time, and real stocks and flows remain constant. Since we are considering only fiscal policies with a constant nominal quantity of money, actual and expected rates of inflation must be zero in long-run equilibrium. In summary,

$$\dot{p}/p = x = \dot{x} = \dot{D} = \dot{K} = 0.$$

The choice of expectations function is irrelevant for the comparative static results of the model, although it crucially affects the dynamics. The stationary state equilibrium is completely described by the following four equations, which as it happens are recursive, in K, R, p and D,

$$(GT) \qquad G' = \theta f(K), \tag{44}$$

$$R = f'(K), \tag{45}$$

$$(LLM) \quad L\left[R(1 - \theta), \frac{1}{\hat{\mu}}\right]\hat{\mu}f(K) = \frac{M}{p}, \tag{46}$$

$$\hat{\mu}f(K) = \frac{M + D}{p} + K. \tag{47}$$

Equation (45) gives a stationary state relationship between K and R,

$$K = g(R), \qquad g'(R) = 1/f'' < 0.$$

We can therefore represent the long-run equilibrium in $R - p$ space by the GT and LLM curves,

$$G' = \theta f(g(R)),$$

$$L\left[R(1 - \theta), \frac{1}{\hat{\mu}}\right]\hat{\mu}f(g(R)) = \frac{M}{p}.$$

These are illustrated in figure 7.
The slope of the LLM curve is

$$\left(\frac{dR}{dp}\right)_{LLM} = \frac{-Mf''(K)}{[\hat{\mu}f(K)L_1(1 - \theta)f''(K) + L\hat{\mu}f'(K)]p^2} > 0.$$

The slope of the GT curve is

$$\left(\frac{dR}{dp}\right)_{GT} = 0.$$

An increase in G' from G'_1 to G'_2 shifts the GT curve down along the LLM curve

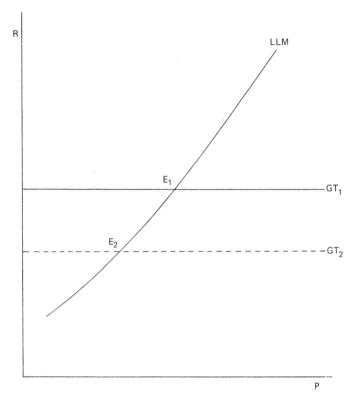

FIGURE 7. Long-run equilibria in the full employment model.

in figure 7, lowering equilibrium R and p. Algebraically,

(a) $\dfrac{\partial R}{\partial G'} = \dfrac{f''}{\theta f'} < 0,$

(b) $\dfrac{\partial p}{\partial G'} = -\dfrac{L_1 \hat{\mu} f f''(1 - \theta) + L \hat{\mu} f'}{\theta f'(K)\,(M/p^2)} < 0.$

$$(48)$$

Note that even in the full employment model $\partial Y/\partial G' > 0$; the reason here, however, is capital deepening rather than the elimination of unemployment of labor.

Note also that the effectiveness of fiscal policy here is not at all dependent on the fact that government interest-bearing debt has been counted as part of private sector net worth. Even if the capitalized value of future taxes "required" to service the debt were exactly equal to the value of these bonds – and there are many sound economic reasons for arguing against such a complete offset – the balanced budget condition: $G' = \theta f(K)$ will guarantee the long-run effectiveness of fiscal policy, in a comparative-static sense.

The intuitive story behind equations (16) is simple: An increase in G' requires, given θ, a higher level of income to balance the budget. With full employment and a fixed labor force, this means a larger capital stock. This in turn requires a lower R and a higher stationary state level of wealth. The *LLM* curve shows that both these effects will increase the demand for real money balances. Since the nominal stock of money is fixed, the price level must be lower to increase the real value of the fixed nominal quantity of money. Prima facie these results would seem to be unstable. As we observed at the outset of this section, the impact effect of an increase in G' is to shift the short-run *IS* curve to the right and to raise R and p. For the long-run equilibrium to be stable, these impact effects have to be reversed, implying that the economy "overshoots" in the short run. Nevertheless, under certain conditions, which depend crucially on the expectations mechanism and on the precise numerical values of certain coefficients, the model may be stable.

6.2. The Impact Effects

Figure 8 shows the impact effect of an increase in government expenditure G'. The slope of the *IS* curve is

$$\left(\frac{dR}{dp}\right)_{IS} = -\frac{(s - x)(M + D)}{I'p^2}.$$

When we are considering the *IS* curve that goes through the long-run equilibrium, $x = 0$ and

$$\left(\frac{dR}{dp}\right)_{IS} = -\frac{s(M + D)}{I'p^2} < 0.$$

The impact effect of an increase in G' will be to shift the *IS* curve to the right,

$$\left(\frac{\partial R}{\partial G'}\right)_{IS} = \frac{1}{I'} > 0.$$

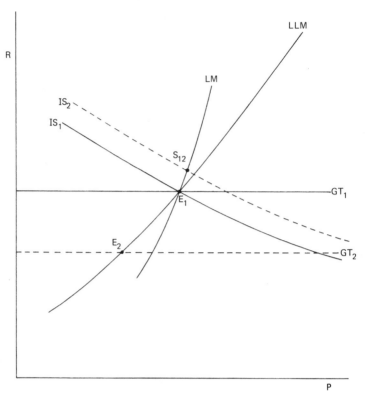

FIGURE 8. Short- and long-run effects of expansionary fiscal policy in the full employment model.

The slope of the *LM* curve is

$$\left(\frac{\mathrm{d}R}{\mathrm{d}p}\right)_{LM} = \left(-L_2\frac{f(K)}{p}\left[1 - \frac{K}{W}\right] - \frac{MK}{Wp^2}\right)\Big/WL_1(1 - \theta) > 0.$$

The impact effect of an increase in G' – given M, D, K, x, θ and the new higher level of G' – is a new temporary equilibrium, as shown in figure 8, (before stocks and expectations have had time to change) at S_{12} with higher p and R. At S_{12}, D will be increasing and K will be decreasing. Except in the case of static expectations, $\dot{x}$ will be positive. The new long-run equilibrium, however, is at E_2, with lower R and p than at E_1.

6.3. Stability

The tedious mathematics of the local stability conditions for the full employment model are relegated to the appendix. To summarize, the long-run equilibrium is unstable in case of static expectations [(43a)] (6.11a) and potentially but not necessarily stable in cases of myopic perfect foresight [(43b)]. In the intermediate case of adaptive expectations [(43c)], stability requires but is not guaranteed by a finite minimum speed of adaptation.

These results may seem paradoxical. Usually static expectations are considered stabilizing, while quick translation of actual price experience into expectations is considered destabilizing. The opposite conclusion here is related to the difference in direction between short- and long-run effects, as exhibited in figure 8. This means that some over-shooting is necessary for the long-run equilibrium to be stable.

The apparent paradox arises from the endogeneity of K and Y, and the related endogeneity of $\dot{D}$ and D. At a position like S_{12} in figure 8, the Pigou effect is pulling consumption down, and the increase in $R - x$ is unfavorable to investment. On the other hand, the real deficit is positive and D is growing, an effect accentuated as real tax revenues decline along with the capital stock K and real income Y. The latter effect, which is the source of instability, is absent from the short-run story. The expected rate of inflation itself has two effects on short-run aggregate demand along the adjustment path. One is to raise investment by lowering the real rate of interest, and the other is to increase saving to make up for expected real capital losses on money and debt. A necessary, but not sufficient, condition for stability is that the investment effect is the stronger. This means that if the rate of inflation slows down and if the slowdown is translated fairly promptly into expectations, aggregate demand and the income-related demand for money will weaken. A weakening of aggregate demand leads, in an economy with flexible prices, to a reduction in the price level and the real interest rate and to an increase in capital stock and real income. Unfortunately, the issue of stability turns on relatively minor details of specification and on small differences in values of coefficients. It is possible that fiscal expansion sets off an unstable spiral of inflation, deficits, rising interest rates, and dwindling capital stock and output. It is also possible that is the start of an oscillation that converges to an equilibrium with lower price level, lower interest rate, higher capital stock and income.

7. Conclusion

Nothing in the analysis of this paper supports the claim that expansionary fiscal effects on aggregate demand are only transitory. To investigate the question, the main section of this paper focussed on the pure logic of aggregate demand. Supply constraints were assumed away – there is always labor available to produce the output demanded. In this situation, an increase in government expenditure either leads to a new long-run equilibrium with higher real income or, in unstable cases, to an explosive increase in income and interest rate. We do not stress the latter possibility, since it depends on built-in fiscal expansion via debt interest payments and since the economy would sooner or later hit a full employment ceiling.

Interest-inelasticity of demand for money seems to be crucial for the strong monetarist proposition after all. A fiscally driven expansion could, of course, occur but vanish if the short-run *LM* curve is not vertical while the long-run *LLM* curve is vertical. We are not aware that this argument has been made.

In future work on this subject, not motivated by any particular propositions, monetarist or otherwise, we would embed the moving short-run equilibria in a growth model rather than a stationary state. (The growth model is more confining. A stationary-state equilibrium just requires zero changes of stocks, and there are lots of configurations of stocks consistent with that condition. An equilibrium growth path requires that flows stand in the same relation to each other as the corresponding stocks.) Moreover, we would find more congenial a model which allows debt and capital to be imperfect substitutes with distinct rates of return. Clearly a more satisfactory model would also recognize that even when the economy is not at full employment nominally denominated stocks change in real value from price movements as well as from fiscal and monetary policies.

In section 6 we considered the long-run effects of fiscal expansion in an economy with full employment and flexible prices. Here there is a striking difference between impact and ultimate effects. The new long-run equilibrium, after a permanent increase of government expenditure, has larger real income and capital stock but lower price level and interest rate. But such equilibria are stable, if at all, only if price expectations adapt fairly quickly to price experience.

Finally, we observe again that it is disturbing that the qualitative properties of models – the signs of important system-wide multipliers, the stability of equilibria – can turn on relatively small changes of specification or on small differences in values of coefficients. We do not feel entitled to use the "correspondence principle" assumption of stability to derive restrictions on structural equations and parameters. There is no divine guarantee that the economic system is stable.

Appendix: Stability in the Full Employment Model

We solve the short-run *LM* and *IS* equations for R and P as functions of D, K and x, given M, G' and θ and evaluate these solutions at the long-run equilibrium $(D^*, K^*, 0)$,

$$R = h^1(D, K, x; M, G', \theta), \tag{A-1a}$$

$$P = h^2(D, K, x; M, G', \theta). \tag{A-1b}$$

The reduced-form impact multipliers are solved for from

$$
\begin{bmatrix}
-I' & \dfrac{-s(M + D)}{p^2} \\[3ex]
WL_1(1 - \theta) & \dfrac{L_2 f(K)}{p}\left(1 - \dfrac{K}{W}\right) + \dfrac{MK}{Wp^2}
\end{bmatrix}
\begin{bmatrix}
dR \\[3ex]
dP
\end{bmatrix}
$$

$$
=
\begin{bmatrix}
\dfrac{-s}{p}\,dD + ((\theta + s\hat{u})f'(K) - I'f''(K) - s)dK - \left(I' - \dfrac{(M + D)}{p}\right)dx \\[3ex]
\left(\dfrac{L_2 f(K)}{pW} - \dfrac{L}{p}\right)dD + \left(-L_2 f'(K) + \dfrac{L_2 f(K)}{W} - L\right)dK
\end{bmatrix}
$$

The signs of these derivatives are not all determined, given the a priori restrictions we have imposed so far,

$h_D^1 > 0$,
h_K^1 is undetermined; if $(\theta + s\hat{u})f' - I'f'' - s < 0, h_K^1 > 0$,
h_D^2 is undetermined,
h_K^2 is undetermined; if $(\theta + s\hat{u})f' - I'f'' - s > 0, h_K^2 < 0$,
h_x^1 is undetermined; $h_x^1 > 0$ if and only if $I' - (M + D)/p > 0$,
h_x^2 is undetermined; $h_x^2 > 0$ if and only if $I' - (M + D)/p > 0$.

We now consider stability for the three mechanisms for generating expectations:

Static expectations: $x = 0$

The dynamic equations are

$$\dot{D} = p[G' - \theta f(K)], \tag{A-2a}$$

$$\dot{K} = I[f'(K) - R]. \tag{A-2b}$$

Substituting (A-1a) and (A-1b) into these equations, and taking the linear approximation at the long-run equilibrium (D^*, K^*) we get

$$
\begin{bmatrix}
\dot{D} \\
\dot{K}
\end{bmatrix}
=
\begin{bmatrix}
0 & -p\theta f' \\
-I'h_D^1 & I'[f'' - h_K^1]
\end{bmatrix}
\begin{bmatrix}
D - D^* \\
K - K^*
\end{bmatrix}. \tag{A-3}
$$

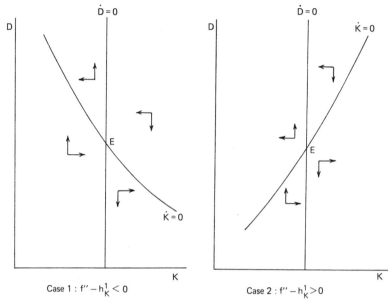

FIGURE 9. Stability in the full employment model under static expectations

Necessary and sufficient conditions for stability are

$$I'(f'' - h_K^1) < 0, \tag{A-4a}$$

$$-I'h_D^1 p\theta f' > 0. \tag{A-4b}$$

(A-4a) may be satisfied, (A-4b) never is; the long-run equilibrium is unstable under static expectations. Figure 9 illustrates this instability with the familiar phase diagram in D, K space.

Myopic perfect foresight: $\dot{p}/p = x$

The complete dynamic system can in this case be written as

$$I\left[f'(K) - R + \frac{\dot{p}}{p}\right] + G' - \theta f(K)$$

$$- s\left[\hat{\mu}f(K) - \frac{M+D}{p} - K\right] - \frac{\dot{p}}{p}\frac{M+D}{p} = 0, \tag{A-5a}$$

$$L\left[R(1 - \theta), \frac{pf(K)}{M + D + pK}\right]\left[\frac{M + D}{p} + K\right] = \frac{M}{p}, \tag{A-5b}$$

$$\dot{D} = p[G' - \theta f(K)], \tag{A-5c}$$

$$\dot{K} = I\left[f'(K) - R + \frac{\dot{p}}{p}\right]. \tag{A-5d}$$

We solve (A-5b) for R as a function of p, K and D, given M and θ,

$$R = R(p, D, K), \tag{A-5b'}$$

$$R_P = \left(\frac{-L_2 f(K)}{p}\left[1 - \frac{K}{W}\right] - \frac{MK}{Wp^2}\right)\bigg/ WL_1(1 - \theta) > 0, \tag{A-6a}$$

$$R_D = \left(\frac{L_2 f(K)}{pW} - \frac{L}{p}\right)\bigg/ WL_1(1 - \theta) > 0, \tag{A-6b}$$

$$R_K = \left(-L_2 f'(K) + \frac{L_2 f(K)}{W} - L\right)\bigg/ WL_1(1 - \theta) > 0. \tag{A-6c}$$

Substituting (A-5b) into (A-5a), (A-5c) and (A-5d) and linearizing at the equilibrium (K^*, D^*, p^*) gives

$$\begin{bmatrix} \dot{p} \\ \dot{D} \\ \dot{K} \end{bmatrix} = \begin{bmatrix} \dfrac{\left[I'R_P + s\dfrac{(M + D)}{p^2}\right]p}{I' - \dfrac{M + D}{p}} & \dfrac{\left[-\dfrac{s}{p} + I'R_D\right]p}{I' - \dfrac{M + D}{p}} \\[3em] 0 & 0 \\[1em] \dfrac{I'\dfrac{M + D}{p}\left[R_P + \dfrac{s}{p}\right]}{I' - \dfrac{M + D}{p}} & \dfrac{\dfrac{I'}{p}[R_D(M + D) - s]}{I' - \dfrac{M + D}{p}} \end{bmatrix}$$

$$\begin{bmatrix} \dfrac{[-I'f''(K) + I'R_K + \theta f'(K) + s\hat{\mu}f'(K) - s]p}{I' - \dfrac{M + D}{p}} \\[3em] -p\theta f'(K) \\[1em] \dfrac{I'\left[-f''(K)\dfrac{M + D}{p} + R_K\dfrac{M + D}{p} + \theta f'(K) + s\hat{\mu}f'(K) - s\right]}{I' - \dfrac{M + D}{p}} \end{bmatrix} \begin{bmatrix} p - p^* \\[3em] D - D^* \\[3em] K - K^* \end{bmatrix} \tag{A-7}$$

The characteristic equation of the coefficient matrix can be written as

$$a_0 \lambda^3 + a_1 \lambda^2 + a_2 \lambda + a_3 = 0; \quad a_0 > 0.$$

Necessary and sufficient for all characteristic roots to have negative real parts are

$$
\begin{aligned}
a_1 &> 0, \\
a_2 &> 0, \\
a_3 &> 0, \\
a_1 a_2 - a_0 a_3 &> 0,
\end{aligned}
$$

One of the first two inequalities can be eliminated since it is implied by the remaining three.

The characteristic equation of the system is

$$
\lambda^3 + \left(\frac{-I'\left[\frac{(M+D)}{p}(R_K - f'') + f'(\theta + s\hat{\mu}) - s \right] - \left[I'R_P + s\frac{(M+D)}{p^2} \right]p}{I' - \frac{M+D}{p}} \right) \lambda^2
$$

$$
+ I' \left(\frac{\theta f'\left[R_D(M+D) - s \right] + R_P\left[f'(\theta + s\hat{\mu}) - s \right]p + \frac{s}{p}(M+D)(f'' - R_K)}{I' - \frac{M+D}{p}} \right) \lambda
$$

$$
+ \frac{s\theta I'f'\left[pR_P + (M+D)R_D \right]}{I' - \frac{M+D}{p}} = 0.
$$

A detailed analysis of the necessary and sufficient conditions for stability would require a lot of space for rather little additional insight; some brief remarks will suffice:

$a_3 > 0,$ requires $I' - (M+D)/p > 0$: the effect of an increase in the expected rate of inflation is to create excess demand in the goods market. As we shall see this condition is also necessary for stability in the adaptive expectations case.

$a_1, a_2 > 0,$ these two conditions set rather strict bounds on the permissible values of s; it has to be large enough to make the numerator of a_1 positive, but small enough to make the numerator of a_2 positive.

$a_1 a_2 - a_0 a_3 > 0,$ no great intuitive insight can be obtained from this condition; it does not contradict any a priori sign restrictions on the coefficients; stability however becomes a rather detailed empirical question.

150

Adaptive expectations: $\dot{x} = \beta\left(\dfrac{\dot{p}}{p} - x\right)$

This case too, will turn out to be at least potentially stable. Substituting (A-la) and (A-lb) into the dynamic equations, we get

$$\dot{D} = p[G' - \theta f(K)],$$
$$\dot{K} = I[f'(K) - h^1(D, K, x) + x],$$
$$\dot{x} = \left(\beta\,\dfrac{h^2(D, K, x)}{h^2(D, K, x)} - x\right).$$

A linear approximation at the equilibrium $(D^*, K^*, 0)$ gives

$$
\begin{bmatrix} \dot{D} \\ \dot{K} \\ \dot{x} \end{bmatrix} =
\begin{bmatrix}
0 & -p\theta f' & 0 \\
-I'h_D^1 & I'(f'' - h_K^1) & I'(1 - h_x^1) \\
\dfrac{-\beta h_K^2 I'h_D^1}{p - \beta h_x^2} & \dfrac{p\beta}{p - \beta h_x^2}\left[-h_D^2\theta f' + \dfrac{h_K^2}{p}I'(f'' - h_K^1)\right] & \dfrac{p\beta}{p - \beta h_x^2}\left[\dfrac{h_K^2}{p}I'(1 - h_x^1) - 1\right]
\end{bmatrix}
\begin{bmatrix} D - D^* \\ K - K^* \\ x - 0 \end{bmatrix}
$$

$$(A\text{-}8)$$

The characteristic equation is

$$\lambda^3 - \left\{I'(f'' - h_K^1) + \dfrac{p\beta}{p - \beta h_x^2}\left[\dfrac{h_K^2}{p}I'(1 - h_x^1) - 1\right]\right\}\lambda^2$$
$$- \left\{I'(f'' - h_K^1)\dfrac{p\beta}{p - \beta h_x^2} - I'(1 - h_x^1)\dfrac{p\beta}{p - \beta h_x^2}h_D^2\theta f' + I'h_D^1 p\theta f'\right\}\lambda$$
$$- I'h_D^1 p\theta f'\dfrac{p\beta}{p - \beta h_x^2} = 0.$$

The linearized version of the static expectations model (A-3) is found back as the UPPER LEFT 2 × 2 submatrix in the linearized version of the adaptive expectations model (A-8). The static expectations model can therefore be regarded as a limiting case of the adaptive expectations model, when $\beta = 0$ [and terms like h_x^1 and h_x^2 are irrelevant because $x \equiv 0$],

$$a_3 = -I'h_D^1 p\theta f' \frac{p\beta}{p - \beta h_x^2} > 0$$

is necessary for stability. Since $h_D^1 > 0$, $a_3 > 0$ iff $p = \beta h_x^2 < 0$, i.e., only if $h_x^2 > 0$; the impact effect of a rise in inflationary expectations is to increase the price level. $h_x^2 > 0$ iff $I' - \left[(M + D)/p\right] > 0$ which is the condition we derived for myopic perfect foresight. It is clear that with $\beta = 0$ [the static expectations case] $a_3 = 0$ and the system won't be stable.

Bibliography

Blinder, A. S. and R. M. Solow, 1973, Does fiscal policy matter?, Journal of Public Economics 2, pp. 319–337.

Blinder, A. S. and R. M. Solow, 1974, The economics of public finance (Brookings Institution, Washington, D.C.)

Friedman, M., 1972, Comments on the critics, Journal of Political Economy, Sept.

Tobin, J., 1971, Essays in economics, vol. I: Macroeconomics (North-Holland, Amsterdam) pp. 378–455.

REPLY

Is Friedman a Monetarist?

James TOBIN

I alone am responsible for section 1 of our joint paper and for any misinterpretation of Milton Friedman's monetarism which it contains. If there is guilt, none of it falls on Willem Buiter.

On a previous occasion I wrote:

Milton Friedman's work on money is important and influential: it commands the attention of economists, policy-makers, journalists, and men of affairs throughout the world. That is why it deserves and receives serious critical discussion. I am continually perplexed by Friedman's propensity in professional debate to evade by verbal quibbling the responsibility and the credit for the characteristic propositions of 'monetarism' associated with his name. [Tobin (1970a, p. 329)]

This time I have the following specific comments:

(1) Friedman is quite right that a horizontal *IS* locus, derived from infinite elasticity of investment or consumption with respect to the real interest rate, will sustain what I termed the "characteristic monetarist proposition". I should have recognized this alternative to the vertical *LM* locus. But I could not take it very seriously for short-run macro-economic analysis, even if I were to agree to Frank Knight's view that the demand for capital stock is infinitely elastic in the long run. Real interest rates, whether on fixed-nominal-value obligations or on equities, do vary in the short run.

(2) Our main differences may be empirical, not theoretical, as Friedman says. But the purpose of this discussion, as of the "Theoretical Framework" exchange, was to focus on theoretical differences. This focus also has an empirical purpose. Jerry Stein wanted to carry out my hope that we might "agree on which values

of which parameters in which behavior relations imply which policy conclusions, then . . . concentrate on the evidence regarding the values of those parameters" [Tobin (1972, p. 852)]. This approach is a needed supplement to the empiricism of quasi-reduced-forms and of large macro-models, which have not been conclusive. It is regrettable that Friedman will not state his theory in a way which makes Stein's approach possible.

(3) Friedman chides me for implying that his words "certain to be temporary and likely to be minor" refer to *all* fiscal effects. He says that the words refer only to the two sources enumerated earlier in the same paragraph of his *Newsweek* column. But the full paragraph begins with a sentence that makes clear that these are the *only* sources of "any *net* effect on private spending". Of course the lower velocity is a fiscal effect, as he says. But it is not a new source; he had already listed it as the first of the sources of "temporary" and "minor" effects, additions to idle balances.

I must say that it did not occur to me that "temporary" could mean "once-for-all". No one has argued – except for unstable situations inviting "pump-priming" – that a one-time permanent reduction in government spending or increase in taxes causes velocity to decline continuously and indefinitely.

(4) In the same *Newsweek* (January 30, 1967) article, Friedman said:

To have a significant impact on the economy, a tax increase must somehow affect monetary policy – the quantity of money and its rate of growth. It clearly need not have any such effect. The Federal Reserve can increase the quantity of money by precisely the same amount with or without a tax rise. However, a tax rise may embolden the Fed politically to hold down the quantity of money, because such a policy would then be more consistent with lower interest rates than if taxes were kept unchanged.

The tax reduction of 1964 had this effect – in the opposite direction. It encouraged the Fed to follow a more expansionary policy. This monetary expansion explains the long-continued economic expansion. And it is the turnabout in monetary policy since April 1966 that explains the growing signs of recession.

The level of taxes is important – because it affects how much of our resources we use through government and how much we use as individuals. It is not important as a sensitive and powerful device to control the short-run course of income and prices.

Indeed he quoted the first sentence of this passage in his J.P.E. comment [Friedman (1972, p. 915)].

In a previous exchange I quoted the first part of this passage in support of the following sentences:

Milton Friedman asserts that changes in the supply of money M are the principal cause of changes in money income Y. In his less guarded and more popular expositions, he comes close to asserting that they are the unique cause. [Tobin (1970b, p. 301)]

Friedman objected strongly to the first sentence but said (1970, p. 319) that the second "does give the right flavor of my views, and I have no wish to quibble over wording." Speaking of the *Newsweek* passage cited above, he said also (1970, pp. 318–319), "The excerpt . . . says that a *tax increase* will not have a significant impact on normal income unless it somehow affects the quantity of money and its rate of growth. *This does say that taxes by themselves are unimportant for the course of nominal income* (my italics), it does not say that variables other than taxes and money may not have important effects on money income."

(5) I am at fault for some misunderstandings because I took for granted but did not explicitly state that there are, in addition to the systematic effects on velocity attributable to changes in the exogenous – policy or non-policy – variables of a macro-model, unsystematic or random variations in velocity. Friedman says that "about 50% of the variance of nominal income. . . can be attributed to fluctuations of velocity", although he notes that this exaggerates the fraction attributable to non-monetary forces. He includes fiscal policies in the same category as relative price changes, technological developments, and other events which are from a macro-economic vantage point the sources of unsystematic noise in the time series of velocity.

For me this is enough to justify the amazing claim of section 1 of our paper: Friedman is a monetarist. The Pope is a Catholic.

(6) Whether fiscal policy has a significant systematic effect on monetary velocity or is a source of minor noise is important in evaluating fiscal policy. But it is important for the conduct of monetary policy too. If fluctuations in velocity – other than those related to current and past money stock – are unsystematic and unpredictable, the Federal Reserve might as well follow a fixed monetary rule. But if there are important systematic effects attributable to fiscal policies, export surpluses, or other causes, the "Fed" should try to measure them, predict them, and to modify its policies accordingly.

(7) I believe that my language made clear my uncertainty about Friedman's views on the longer-run demand effects of accumulation of stocks of money or government debt. His J.P.E. comment does claim that growth of monetary debt is

much more expansionary than growth of non-monetary debt, but beyond that it is not explicit.

I pointed out a possible rationalization of the assertion that fiscal impacts are temporary. The absorption of non-monetary debt into portfolios might raise interest rates, enough eventually to cancel out the one-time fiscal impact. This sequence of events would also be consistent with Friedman's statement that growth of government debt occurs "largely" at the expense of growth of private debt. Otherwise, it is hard to understand such "crowding out" in an economy *not* fully employed. At any rate the possibility that debt accumulation shifts *LM* to the left seemed worth investigating, as a route by which the monetarist conclusion could be reached without a vertical *LM* curve.

(8) I recognize that an even more fundamental question is the effect of growth of government debt on saving. I discussed this briefly in my J.P.E. comment, but it is not the subject of our paper. Is the public satisfying any part of its desire for wealth when it purchases Treasry bonds? If not, its consumption spending will be the same whether a given budget of government expenditure is financed by taxes or by non-monetary borrowing. This is a central argument in a very recent *Newsweek* article (January 27, 1975), where Friedman is once again a monetarist, opposing proposals to stimulate recovery by tax reduction without equivalent expenditure cuts. Note that the argument that government debt issues, like taxes, crowd out consumption, is not consistent with the claim that it crowds private borrowers and investors out of the capital markets.

(9) While strong monetarism survives in *Newsweek* and in the pronouncements of the Shadow Open Market Committee, the monetarism of professional conferences is pretty tame. Monetarists certainly give different policy recommendations from other economists, but they have a hard time grounding those recommendations in their theories or even differentiating their theories from other models. I see nothing particularly monetarist, as I used to understand the word, in the Brunner–Meltzer paper. I certainly cannot accept their imperialist claim that concern for long-run equilibrium and for stock and balance sheet equilibrium is an invention and exclusive possession of "monetarists".

Friedman's own litmus paper test, "What is the price of money?" is fun at cocktail parties. But some of my friends are good enough capital theorists to question the question. They can recognize *both* the purchasing power value of a dollar bill and the per annum opportunity cost of holding a dollar bill rather than some other asset. Others are good enough Marshallians or Walrasians to reject Friedman's favorite money–credit dichotomy. They suspect that "monetary policy and monetary change" operate *both* through credit markets and through "actual and desired cash balances".

(10) Distinctively monetarist policy recommendations stem less from theoretical or even empirical findings than from distinctive value judgments. The preferences revealed consistently in those recommendations are for minimizing the public sector and for paying a high cost in unemployment to stabilize prices. Maybe at the next conference we should discuss those basic issues.

Bibliography

Friedman, M., 1970, Comment on Tobin, Quarterly Journal of Economics, May.
Friedman, M., 1972, Comments on the critics, Journal of Political Economy, Sept.–Oct.
Tobin, J., 1970a, Rejoinder, Quarterly Journal of Economics, May.
Tobin, J., 1970b, Money and income: Post hoc ergo hoc?, Quarterly Journal of Economics, May.
Tobin, J., 1972, Friedman's theoretical framework, Journal of Political Economy, Sept.–Oct.

Part II
MACROECONOMIC FISCAL POLICIES AND ECONOMIC GROWTH

Deficit Spending and Crowding Out in Shorter and Longer Runs

James Tobin

Does expansionary fiscal policy fail because of the restrictive effects of the accumulation of nonmonetary debt? Are the direct effects of government spending on aggregate demand canceled or reversed with the passage of time as the public debt grows? Does explicit recognition of the government budget identity overturn standard Keynesian doctrine regarding fiscal policy? These questions have been much discussed in recent years.[1]

The main point I wish to make here is the following: Suppose it is agreed that the public's demand for money, given their total wealth, is negatively related to interest rates. Then it will also be agreed that the very short-run impact effect of increasing the rate of government expenditure is expansionary. Although the money supply is unchanged, its velocity will rise along with interest rates. This impact effect will be canceled or reversed only if the passage of time turns the negative response of money demand to interest rates into a zero or positive response. This in turn will happen only if wealth effects on demand for money come to dominate the substitution effect. Specifically the condition is that the public's demand for wealth, and their saving, are positively related to interest rates, and that part of the accumulation induced by higher interest rates on assets other than money is held in money.

Stock-Flow Problems in Interpretation of Keynesian Equilibrium

According to Keynes, his *General Theory* refers to a short run in which "the existing quality and quantity of available equipment," among other "elements in the economic system," are taken as given.[2] Yet the solution of the model determines a rate of net investment in capital equipment that

The research reported in this paper was in part assisted by a grant from the National Science Foundation. I am grateful to William Brainard, Willem Buiter, and Gary Smith for helpful discussions of the problems and issues under study, but I absolve them of responsibility for what I say.

Reprinted by permission from *Theory for Economic Efficiency: Essays in Honor of Abba P. Lerner,* eds. Harry I. Greenfield, Albert M. Levenson, William Hamovitch, and Eugene Rotwein, Cambridge, MA: MIT Press, 1979, pp. 217–236.

is in no way constrained to be zero. In general it will not be zero, and with the passage of time, the stock of capital—one of the given or independent variables of the system—will change. But "the schedule of the marginal efficiency of capital depends partly on the existing quantity of equipment."[3] Therefore the investment function, one of the crucial equations, will shift as capital accumulates or decumulates. This is an obvious reason, though not the only one, why the Keynesian solution cannot be a steady state in time.[4] The solution contains the seeds of its own destruction.

Abba Lerner long ago recognized the confusion of stock and flow in the treatment of capital investment in the *General Theory*.[5] He proposed a model in which the marginal efficiency of *investment* depends, inversely, on both the stock of capital and the flow of investment. If equation of this marginal efficiency to the interest rate requires positive net investment, the capital stock will gradually increase, lowering the rate of investment induced by the same interest rate. Ultimately net investment will dwindle to zero, and the capital stock will be stationary. In this equilibrium the marginal efficiency of investment can be identified with the marginal productivity of capital, and both will be equal to the interest rate. This was one of Lerner's many brilliant clarifications of macroeconomic theory.

The investment-capital dynamic is not the only flow-stock relationship that makes the Keynesian "equilibrium" temporary. Saving adds to wealth; wealth affects the propensity to consume and possibly the demand for money. Government deficits add to public debt and thus to the outstanding stocks of nonmonetary and monetary government liabilities; changes in the supplies of these assets may change interest rates. It is this latter observation that has attracted so much attention in the literature of macroeconomic theory in recent years. Some authors claim to have discovered a fatal flaw in the Keynesian macro model as exemplified in the common IS/LM apparatus. The flaw is described as ignoring the government budget identity.

It is more accurate, however, to regard the failure to track the cumulation of deficits into debt as just one aspect of the model's temporary and short-run character. Investment is not cumulated into capital or saving into wealth. Keynes's excuse was that he was concerned with so short a time period that, whatever the rate of investment, its effects on the capital stock would be negligible. He refers to "factors in which the changes seem to be so slow. . . as to have only a small and comparatively negligible short-term influence on our question. Our present object is to discover what determines at any time the national income of a given economic system."[6] Even though he was not explicit about other assets, the spirit of the approach is that there is not enough time for the flows to alter the stocks significantly. Deficits do add to public debt, but even a $50 billion per year federal deficit adds only $5 billion a month to a $500 billion stock. Curiously the latter-day discoverers of the government budget equation have confined to government debt their objection to the constant-stock assumption. Indeed they have generally been content to acquiesce in Keynes's assumption that the physical capital stock is constant. But if the time span of the model is to be extended enough to allow flows to affect stocks, all stocks should be tracked, not just government debts.

The only precise way to justify the Keynesian procedure is to regard the IS/LM model as determining the values of variables at a point in time. Then this model must be regarded as a slice, in time of measure zero, of a continuous-time dynamic model. Asset stocks are among the state variables of the model at that time; they are constant (independent of the solution of the model) insofar as they are completely inherited from the past. They change as time passes, moving the instantaneous IS and LM curves. The short-run model has a new solution each microsecond; whether and where it settles down requires dynamic analysis.

It is still possible to answer certain questions by comparative static analysis of the temporary solution: How will the solution at that moment be different if, for given values of stocks and other state variables, government expenditure is different? How will the solution be different if the government, by open-market transactions with the public that take zero time, instantaneously alters the supplies of its several liabilities? How would the solution be different if past history had been different and had bequeathed to the present different stocks of assets? But the relevance of these exercises is limited because the same changes in exogenous variables will affect subsequent temporary solutions as well.

Certainly, it must be admitted, the Keynesian model, particularly the IS/LM version, has not usually been acknowledged to be so evanescent. The equilibrium language of Keynes suggests that he had a more durable solution in mind. Moreover, since the *General Theory* and even before, the dynamics and stability of Keynesian equilibrium have been discussed on the tacit presumption that it is the steady state of a dynamic system rather than itself a momentary stage of a dynamic process. Examples of such discussion include the theory of the multiplier as an infinite series, Samuelson's application of his correspondence principle to the Keynesian model, and the analysis, pioneered by Hicks himself, of the stability of IS/LM "equilibrium."[7] Presumably such dynamic analysis would be unnecessary and irrelevant if the model itself determined the values of its variables at every moment of time. If it did so, its structural equations would allow for the adjustment lags that are considered in the stability analyses cited. To make the point another way, it is somewhat inconsistent to assume that the Keynesian "equilibrium" is the asymptotic result of a long process of behavioral adjustment while ignoring the changes in stocks that are bound to occur during the period of convergence.

Interpreting the Keynesian equilibrium as the momentary solution of a dynamic continuous-time process is subject to another class of objections. The model is, after all, a set of simultaneous equations. To be sure, looking at the economic interdependence in this way is one of the most useful and insightful abstractions of economic science. But it is perhaps an unusual strain on credulity to imagine that a new set of simultaneous equations, finding the prices and quantities that clear several markets at once, is solved every instant. The weight on that much burdened *deus ex machina*, Walrasian auctioneer, would be extremely heavy.

An alternative to the continuous-time abstraction is a discrete-time model. Time is broken into periods of finite duration, during which each of the simultaneously determined endogenous variables assumes one and only one value. Flows add finite amounts to stocks: saving during the period makes wealth larger at the end of the period, investment adds to the capital stock, government deficits add to public debt, and so forth. In deciding their consumption, investment, and asset demands, economic agents are determining their end-of-period stocks; their behavior takes this into account.[8] Thus the government budget identity, for example, is explicitly respected. Bonds issued to finance a government deficit must be absorbed into savers' portfolios. The same is true of bonds or equities issued to finance private capital formation.

In this way the solution of a discrete-time Keynesian IS/LM model accounts for some phenomena that the instantaneous model does not. The discrete-time IS and LM curves include effects that in the continuous-time approach are displayed by shifting the curves as stocks change and tracking the moving solutions. The discrete-time solution also is only a temporary equilibrium; the new stocks will generally lead to different solutions in the next period.

Taken literally, both approaches are implausible. If it strains credulity to imagine simultaneous market clearings repeated every instant, it is certainly arbitrary to require the famous Auctioneer to clear every market on the same periodic schedule. Both treatments of time are imperfect and unrealistic representations of simultaneous and intertemporal interdependence. Theorists had better avoid dogmatism in favor of either method.

Deficit Financing and Crowding Out

The previous section is a prelude to my main subject, reconsidering the issue of financial crowding out, the effectiveness of expansionary fiscal policy unaccompanied by monetary expansion. *Financial* crowding out refers to an underemployment situation, in which displacement is not necessary to release resources for the use of the government or its transferees.

The standard IS/LM analysis says that complete crowding out will not occur unless (1) investment is perfectly interest-elastic (IS "curve" horizontal) or (2) demand for money is perfectly interest-inelastic (LM "curve" vertical). Condition (1) may be dismissed on the ground that adjustment costs and lags prevent investment from responding instantaneously or quickly to small deviations of the interest rate from the marginal efficiency of capital. Condition (2) may be dismissed, at least in principle, on the theoretical logic and empirical evidence of substitution between money and interest-bearing assets. Consequently the standard conclusion is that the impact of fiscal expansion will be expansionary, and crowding out will be only partial.

However, the force of the dismissal of condition (2) is weakened as longer time periods are considered. At the instant when government outlays are increased, wealth and its component asset stocks are given. The public can be reconciled to the existing money stock, even if its income-related transactions needs are greater, by higher interest rates. But wealth increases with the passage of time; the supply of government bonds is greater than it would have been less expansionary fiscal policy, while the money supply is unchanged. This is an additional source of upward pressure on interest rates. In continuous-time models, it would be represented by upward and leftward shifts of the LM curve. In a discrete-time model, part of this wealth effect would be included in the LM curve, which would for that reason be steeper than in the momentary model.

Do these wealth effects overcome the initial impact of expansionary fiscal policy? The monetarist answer is affirmative. This is, I believe, the rationale for Milton Friedman's assertion that no important proposition of monetary theory requires zero interest elasticity of the demand for money[9] (with respect to crowding out, I interpret him to mean that the instantaneous LM curve may be positively sloped but shifts backwards as deficits enlarge the stock of bonds relative to money); claims that Keynesian analysis of fiscal effects does not survive explicit recognition of the government budget identity;[10] and empirical findings, as in the St. Louis monetarist econometric model, that positive fiscal effects last only a few quarters.[11]

Figures 15.1 and 15.2 illustrate this monetarist scenario, carried to the extreme of more than 100 percent crowding out. In figure 15.1 the process is one of moving monetary equilibrium. In figure 15.2 it is telescoped into a single solution for a discrete time period, in which the increment of wealth is enough to make the LM locus negatively sloped. In figure 15.1, E_1 is the initial equilibrium at t_1, and, let us assume, one that would persist until t_2 in the absence of policy change. E_2 is the equilibrium at t_2 as a result of the new fiscal policy begun at t_1. In figure 15.2, E_1 and E_2 are alternative solutions for the period $t_2 - t_1$, E_2 with the more expansionary fiscal policy.

Within either of these frameworks, there are two necessary (but not sufficient) conditions for this scenario, or more precisely for output Y_2 at E_2 to be less than or equal to the output Y_1 at E_1. One is that the demand for money is positively related to wealth. The second is that the demand for wealth is positively related to the interest rate.

The argument is simple enough. At E_2 the demand for money must be the same as at E_1. But the interest rate is higher, and income is no higher. What keeps the demand for money up? It can only be that wealth is higher.

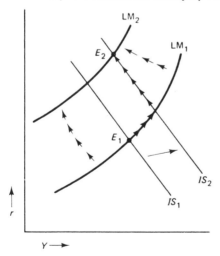

Figure 15.1 Crowding out more than 100 percent: continuous time version

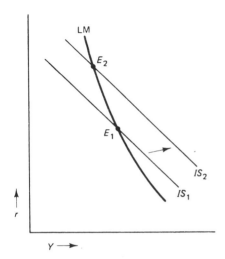

Figure 15.2 Crowding out more than 100 percent: discrete time version

Why do people want more wealth when their income is no higher? It can only be because the interest rate is higher.

Let the LM locus of figure 15.2 be defined by $M = L(r, Y, W)$ and suppose that $W = W(r, Y)$. The slope of the locus $\partial r / \partial Y$ is $-L_Y + L_W W_Y / L_r + L_W W_r$. Given that $L_Y, W_Y, L_W > 0$ and $L_r < 0$, this slope will be negative only if $L_W W_r > -L_r > 0$.

Is it plausible to expect this condition to be met? Money, in this context, is an asset on which the nominal interest rate is institutionally or legally fixed at zero or some other ceiling. As a constituent of public wealth, it is outside money, printed by the government to finance government deficits, an alternative to the issue for the same purpose of nonmonetary liabilities bearing market-determined interest rates. The real world counterpart in the United States is the stock of high-powered money, defined as currency outside banks plus unborrowed bank reserves. The demand for this stock is derivative, via banks' reserve requirements and reserve behavior, from the public's demand for fixed-rate deposits.

In the scenario sketched above, interest rates on nonmonetary assets rise while those on monetary assets are unchanged; under this inducement, the public saves more and their wealth increases. Certainly they will hold more of the assets whose yields have risen. Will they also hold more money? On portfolio-theoretic grounds this seems unlikely; after all the motivation for the additional saving is the higher yield, which is lost to the extent that saving is diverted to money. The allocation of wealth accumulated in response to interest rate incentive will not be the same as of wealth accumulated at unchanged interest rates.

One possible rationalization is the transactions requirement for cash associated with portfolio management. Let α be the fraction of additional yield-induced wealth that goes into high-powered money to meet this transactions requirement. Let m be the ratio of high-powered money to wealth. Then the condition that $\partial L/\partial r$ be positive is $(Wr/W)/(-Lr/M) > m/\alpha$. Now m is very much larger than α, given the many purposes for which money is held other than portfolio transactions. So the elasticity of wealth with respect to the interest rate would have to be much larger than the substitution elasticity of demand for money.

Crowding Out in a Short-Run Discrete Time Model

I propose now to explore the issues raised in the previous section in two simple formal models. They are discrete-time models, and the government budget identity is explicitly respected. They are short-run models not in the sense that stocks are fixed but in the sense that stocks and other state variables are not stationary. I shall consider first an economy without capital and show that a positive total interest elasticity of money demand, derived from a positive interest-elasticity of saving, is necessary (but not sufficient) for the monetarist result. I shall turn then to an economy with an endogenous capital stock and show the same proposition. A comparison of the two models will indicate that the condition is both less likely to be fulfilled and less likely to be sufficient when capital accumulation is recognized.

A Model without Capital

The national product identities are:

$$Y = C + G = C + S + T - B_{-1}. \tag{15.1}$$

Here Y is national product, C private expenditure on goods and services. G government purchases, S saving, T tax payments, and B_{-1} government interest payments (equal to bonds outstanding at the beginning of the period). All variables refer to a time period of finite duration. Within the period the price level is taken as fixed. determined by events in previous periods. It may be different next period because of events in this one, but within the one-period model it is not endogenous. The same is true of price expectations. Thus the variables can be considered both real and nominal.

Taxes, net of transfers other than interest, will be taken throughout as a function of income $T(Y)$, with $T_Y > 0$. The points about fiscal policy can be made by regarding G as the policy variable. Accordingly S may be taken as a function of two endogenous variables. Y and the interest rate r, and of lagged variables like B_{-1}. The implications of the sign of S_r is a matter of central interest; the previous discussion suggests that $S_r > 0$ is necessary, though not sufficient, for complete or more than complete crowding out. Of course C can be derived from S. Thus $C_Y = 1 - T_Y - S_Y$ and $C_r = -S_r$. Although C connotes consumption, it could be interpreted to include investment expenditure in hybrid models of this genre, which allow investment but hold the capital stock constant. Indeed one way in which the important assumption $S_r > 0$ slips into such models is the natural assumption that investment is inversely related to the interest rate, $C_r < 0$.

The government deficit for the period is

$$D = G + B_{-1} - T. \tag{15.2}$$

The deficit is financed in proportion γ_B by selling bonds and in proportion $\gamma_M = 1 - \gamma_B$ by printing high-powered money. Unless otherwise noted, I consider only nonnegative values of both γ_B and γ_M. The fraction γ_B is a policy parameter; I shall be particularly interested in the case $\gamma_B = 1$. Bonds are assumed to be consols paying \$1 net of tax per period. Their quantity B is measured by the coupon liability. During the period the increase in quantity of bonds is $\Delta B = B - B_{-1}$. The price of bonds is q_B.

Similarly the increase in the stock of money is $\Delta M = M - M_{-1}$. Thus:

$$q_B \Delta B = \gamma_B D$$
$$\Delta M = \gamma_M D. \tag{15.3}$$

In this model all private saving is absorbed by the government deficit, as implied in (15.1):

$$S = D = q_B \Delta B + \Delta M. \tag{15.4}$$

The public's wealth changes not only by saving but by capital gain or loss on their initial bond holdings B_{-1}. The capital gain, positive or negative, is $(q_B - q_{B,-1})B_{-1} = \Delta q_B B_{-1}$. The relevant interest rate is the one period rate on bonds r_B, which depends on the expected price of bonds next period q_B^e. A bond costing q_B held until next period will yield the holder $(1 + q_B^e)/q_B - 1 = r_B$. Thus $q_B = (1 + q_B^e)/(1 + r_B)$. Now q_B^e may depend on q_B, but I assume some regressivity in this dependence, so that $\partial q_B^e/\partial q_B < 1 + r_B$. This insures that $\partial q_B/\partial r_B$, which is equal to $-q_B/(1 + r_B) - \partial q_B^e/\partial q_B$, is negative. This derivative also describes the relation of Δq_B to r_B. I shall represent it as q_B' below.

Wealth owners decide the values of the two assets they will hold at the end of the period, or equivalently the increments in these values during the period. $F^B(\ )$ and $F^M(\ )$ represent these increments for bonds and money respectively. The targets F^B and F^M are achieved by saving and, in the case of bonds, by capital gain. They are both functions of within-period endogenous variables, r_B and Y, of predetermined initial stocks $q_B, {}_{-1}B_{-1}$ and M_{-1}, and of other lagged or exogenous variables. Their relation to saving is

$$S(\ ) = F^B(\ ) - \Delta q_B B_{-1} + F^M(\ ). \tag{15.5}$$

This identity may be regarded as a definition of saving in terms of asset accumulations, and I will dispense with the saving function in the formal model below. The marginal propensity to save S_Y is the sum $F^B_Y + F^M_Y$, which will be assumed, as is traditional, to be positive but less than $1 - T_Y$. Note that the capital gains term in (15.5) may make $S_{r_s} > 0$ even if $F^B_{r_s} + F^M_{r_s} \leq 0$, because the public will save to recoup the capital losses due to an increase in the bond interest rate. In order to concentrate on the monetarist issue, I shall assume that $S_{r_s} > 0$.

Here is the model, relating three within-period endogenous variables (r_B, Y, D) to the policy parameters (G, γ_B):

$$\begin{cases} F^B(\ ) - \Delta q_B B_{-1} - \gamma_B D = 0 \\ F^H(\ ) \qquad\qquad - \gamma_M D = 0 \\ \qquad T(Y) + D \quad = G + B_{-1}. \end{cases} \tag{15.6}$$

The principal interest is in the effects of variation of G on the solution of (15.6).

$$\begin{bmatrix} F^B_{r_s} - q_s' B_{-1} & F^B_Y & -\gamma_B \\ F^M_{r_s} & F^M_Y & -\gamma_M \\ 0 & T_Y & 1 \end{bmatrix} \begin{bmatrix} \partial_r/\partial G \\ \partial Y/\partial G \\ \partial D/\partial G \end{bmatrix} = \begin{bmatrix} 0 \\ 0 \\ 1 \end{bmatrix}. \tag{15.7}$$

Let Δ be the determinant of the Jacobian and Δ_{ij} its minor with respect to the element in row$_i$, column$_j$. Then:

$$\varDelta = \varDelta_{33} - T_Y \varDelta_{32}$$
$$\frac{\partial r_B}{\partial G} = \frac{\varDelta_{31}}{\varDelta}, \quad \frac{\partial Y}{\partial G} = -\frac{\varDelta_{32}}{\varDelta}, \quad \frac{\partial D}{\partial G} = \frac{\varDelta_{33}}{\varDelta} \qquad (15.8)$$

The two principal cases to consider are $F_{r_s}^M < 0$ and $F_{r_s}^M \geq 0$. In the first case, the substitution effect is dominant, as in conventional short-run Keynesian analysis. In the second case, the wealth effect dominates the substitution effect; an increase in interest rate induces additional saving, and some of it goes into money.

Case 1

The sign pattern of the determinant is

$$\begin{bmatrix} + & ? & -\gamma_B \\ - & + & -\gamma_M \\ 0 & +T_Y & +1 \end{bmatrix}. \qquad (15.9)$$

$\varDelta_{33}$ is positive, even if F_Y^B, the ? in (15.9), is negative. (If the second row of $\varDelta_{33}$ is added to the first, $\varDelta_{33}$ becomes $[\pm \ \pm]$ on the assumption that $S_Y = F_Y^B + F_Y^M > 0$.)

$\varDelta_{32}$ is negative. Hence $\varDelta$, $\partial Y/\partial G$, and $\partial D/\partial G$ are all positive. $\varDelta_{31}$ is $F_Y^B(\gamma_B - 1) + F_Y^M \gamma_B$. If F_Y^B is negative, $\partial r_B/\partial G$ is certainly positive, however the deficit is financed. (It would be possible to reduce the interest rate while increasing G if not only the deficit but part of the preexisting debt were monetized, that is, if γ_B were sufficiently negative. This is true because $F_Y^B + F_Y^M$ is positive.) If F_Y^B is positive, $\partial r_B/\partial G$ will be positive for high values of γ_B, notably 1, but negative for low values, notably 0.

These are standard Keynesian results and here serve only to show that they are altered neither by explicit respect for the government budget equation nor by the assumption that saving responds positively to interest rate.

Case 2

The sign pattern of the Jacobian is

$$\begin{bmatrix} + & ? & -\gamma_B \\ + & + & -\gamma_M \\ 0 & +T_Y & +1 \end{bmatrix}. \qquad (15.10)$$

The sign of $F_{r_s}^M$ in the second row, first column, is positive instead of negative. Here it is convenient to consider first $\gamma_B = 1$, and $F_Y^B < 0$. Then $\varDelta_{33}$ is positive, but $\varDelta_{32}$ is also positive. So $\varDelta$ may have either sign. It will be positive if and only if $F_{r_s}^B/F_{r_s}^M > (F_Y^B + T_Y)/F_Y^M$. Roughly and allegorically speaking, the condition is that a rise in interest rate has a comparative advantage in absorbing bonds, a rise in income in absorbing money. (Taxes generated by income increases are a way of absorbing bonds when the deficit is bond financed, hence the term T_Y on the right-hand side of the inequality.)

If this condition is met, then the monetarist configuration of figure 15.2 results: $\partial r_B/\partial G > 0, \partial Y/\partial G < 0, \partial D/\partial G > 0$. Letting F_Y^B, the ? in (15.10), become positive does not change this outcome as long as the condition for positive Δ is fulfilled. However a rise in F_Y^B relative to F_Y^M makes the condition less likely. A priori portfolio substitution effects justify the assumption that $F_{r_*}^B$ exceeds $F_{r_*}^M$, and transactions balances the assumption that F_Y^M exceeds F_Y^B. This is enough to make Δ_{33} positive but guarantees positive Δ only if T_Y is zero.

If the condition is not met and Δ is negative, then the counterintuitive conclusions are: $\partial r_B/\partial G < 0, \partial Y/\partial G > 0, \partial D/\partial G < 0$. Figure 15.3 shows this outcome in IS/LM terms. Both IS and IM are negatively sloped, but IS is steeper. It is tempting to dismiss this solution as unstable. But if system (15.6) really describes the equations that the economy somehow solves simultaneously within the period, we have no right to do so. There is no shorter run, no dynamic process in real time of which this solution is an equilibrium. To say any solution is unstable is just to impugn gratuitously the iterative computer program of the Walrasian auctioneer who simultaneously clears the markets.

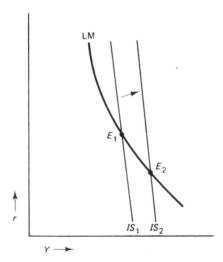

Figure 15.3 Fiscal expansion lowers interest and raises income?

In any event, there is always a positive value of γ_B, less than or equal to 1, below which $\partial Y/\partial G$ is positive. $\partial r_B/\partial G$ will also be positive if F_Y^B is negative. But if F_Y^B is positive, $\partial r_B/\partial G$ will be negative. Still excluding the possibility that Δ_{33} is negative, $\partial D/\partial G$ will always be positive.

A Model with Capital

In this model, part of each period's production is added to the capital stock available for use in subsequent periods. A unit of capital stock in use earns an aftertax return of R per period. The public owns equity titles to the whole stock, and the market value of equity per unit of capital is q_K. The yield to the equity holder for the period is r_K. This depends, of course, on q_K^e. Analogously to the relation between the valuation and one-period yield of bonds, $q_K = (R + q_K^e)/(1 + r_K)$. I assume, as in the bond case, sufficient regressivity of expectations so that q_K is negatively related to r_K. However equity valuation is also a function of another within-period endogenous variable, Y, for two reasons. One is that the contemporary earnings rate R varies directly with Y. The other is that expected future earnings R and interest rates r_K, summarized in q_K^e, are affected by current business activity. This calculation may go either way. As daily stock market reports remind us, we cannot generalize about the effect of current economic news on equity values, the relation between q_K and Y. Taking $q_K = q(r_K, Y)$, I will denote the partial derivatives as q_{r_K}, q_Y.

As previously assumed for other assets, savers have a demand for accretion of the value of their holdings of equity during the period $F^K(\ )$. This demand is met in two ways. One is the capital gain $\Delta q_K K_{-1}$ on the stock of capital at the beginning of the period. This capital gain depends indirectly on r_K and Y via the valuation function $q(r_K, Y)$ The other source of supply is by new net investment $q_K \Delta K$. This is taken to be $I = \varphi(q_K)K_{-1}$ where φ is an increasing function of q_K and thus related to r_K (negatively) and to Y. The quantity I serves the same role for capital as $\gamma_B D$ and $\gamma_M D$ serve for bonds and money.

The accounting identities (15.1), (15.4), and (15.5) are extended in obvious ways:

$$Y = C + I + G = C + S + T - B_{-1}. \tag{15.11}$$

$$S = D + I = q_B \Delta B + \Delta M + q_K \Delta K. \tag{15.12}$$

$$S(\ ) = F^B(\ ) - \Delta q_B B_{-1} + F^M(\ ) + F^K(\ ) - \Delta q_K Y_{-1}. \tag{15.13}$$

The model, relating four within-period endogenous variables (r_K, r_B, Y, D) to the policy parameters (G, γ_B), is the following:

$$\begin{cases} F^K(\;\;) - \varDelta q_K K_{-1} - \varphi(q_K)K_{-1} = 0 \\ F_B(\;\;) - \varDelta q_B B_{-1} - \gamma_B D \quad = 0 \\ F_M(\;\;) \qquad\qquad - \partial_M D \quad = 0 \\ \qquad\quad T(y) + D \qquad = G + B_{-1}, \end{cases} \tag{15.14}$$

$$\begin{vmatrix} F^K_{r_K} - q_{r_K}K_{-1} & F^K_{r_B} & F^K_Y - q_Y K_{-1} & 0 \\ -\varphi'q_{r_K}K_{-1} & & -\varphi'q_Y K_{-1} & \\ F^B_{r_K} & F^B_{r_B} - q'_B B_{-1} & F^B_Y & -\gamma_B \\ F^M_{r_K} & F^M_{r_B} & F^M_Y & -\gamma_M \\ 0 & 0 & T_Y & 1 \end{vmatrix} \begin{vmatrix} \frac{\partial r_K}{\partial G} \\ \frac{\partial r_B}{\partial G} \\ \frac{\partial K}{\partial G} \\ \frac{\partial D}{\partial G} \end{vmatrix} = \begin{vmatrix} 0 \\ 0 \\ 0 \\ 1 \end{vmatrix},$$

$$\tag{15.15}$$

$$\begin{cases} \varDelta = \varDelta_{44} - T_Y \varDelta_{43} \\ \frac{\partial r_K}{\partial G} = -\frac{\varDelta_{41}}{\varDelta}, \; \frac{\partial r_B}{\partial G} = \frac{\varDelta_{42}}{\varDelta}, \; \frac{\partial y}{\partial G} = \frac{-\varDelta_{43}}{\varDelta}, \; \frac{\partial D}{\partial G} = \frac{\varDelta_{44}}{\varDelta}. \end{cases} \tag{15.16}$$

Like the previous model, there are two principal cases to consider: $F^M_{r_K}, F^M_{r_B} < 0$ and $F^M_{r_K}, F^M_{r_B} > 0$.

Case 1

The sign pattern of the determinant of the Jacobian is

$$\begin{vmatrix} + & - & ? & 0 \\ - & + & ? & -\gamma_B \\ - & - & + & -\gamma_M \\ 0 & 0 & +T_Y & +1 \end{vmatrix} \tag{15.17}$$

The standard Keynesian results apply once again. For 100 percent bond finance, ($\gamma_B = 1$), Y, D, and r_B all rise with G. (As in the first model, these conclusions do not depend on the signs of the ? terms, provided every column in $\varDelta_{44}$ has a positive sum.) But r_K might possibly fall if the top ? is positive (for example, if prosperity tends to lower expected equity values).

Case 2

The sign pattern is

$$\begin{bmatrix} + & - & ? & 0 \\ - & + & ? & -\gamma_B \\ + & + & + & -\gamma_M \\ 0 & 0 & T_Y & 1 \end{bmatrix}. \tag{15.18}$$

To avoid a tedious catalog, I consider solely $\gamma_B = 1$ and confine myself to the plausible assumption that $\varDelta_{44}$ is positive. As in the first model, positive interest responses in the money row make $\varDelta_{43}$ positive. The monetarist configuration then arises when $\varDelta = \varDelta_{44} - T_Y\varDelta_{43}$ is also positive.

However, a high T_Y can make $\varDelta$ negative, particularly if the ? entries in (15.18) are strongly positive. This gives rise to the same type of counter-intuitive results as in the simpler model: $\partial r_K/\partial G < 0, \partial Y/\partial G > 0, \partial D/\partial G < 0$. However the bond interest rate may go either way.

Finally consider a case intermediate between cases 1 and 2, with $F^M_{r_K}$ positive, and $F^M_{r_B}$ negative. An increase in wealth induced by higher equity yields raises the demand for money. But bonds and money are strong substitutes. With positive entries in the third (Y) column, and with a pattern of signs indicating that bonds are a closer substitute for money than for capital, $\partial Y/\partial G$ will be positive.

Long-Run Stationary Equilibrium

The long-run equilibria of models of this type, and the comparative statics of these stationary states, have been examined in the Blinder-Solow and Tobin-Buiter studies cited in note 1. The latter looks at the stability of those states, using a continuous-time model, but does not consider the implications of interest-responsive demand for wealth.

Here I shall confine myself to a cursory look at the long-run equilibrium of the second model of the previous section. The purpose is not realism. It is not realistic to imagine that policy never changes or that output is demand-determined over so long a run. The purpose is rather to pursue the pure logic of the issue. For example the persistence of the "Keynesian" conclusions cited earlier would be called into question if under the same behavioral assumptions the stationary state value of Y turned out to be inversely related to G.

In the long run, there are steady-state stock demands K^D, B^D, M^D, summing to desired wealth. These are functions of Y and of the interest rate r_B and r_K. Actual and expected q's are equal: $r_K = R$ and $q_K = 1$;

$q_B = 1/r_B$. The supply of capital is endogenous, $K(Y, r_K)$, with $K_Y > 0$, $K_{r_\kappa} < 0$. This relationship is technological. For example, a Cobb-Douglas CRS production function implies $K = \alpha Y/r_K$. Taking the supply of money M as exogenous, then the outstanding stock of bonds B is endogenous. (Alternatively one could specify the fractions of money and bonds in the total value of debt and let that total be the endogenous variable.) The budget is balanced in long-run equilibrium. The equations, in the four endogenous variables (r_K, r_B, Y, B) are:

$$\begin{cases} K^D(\ ) - K(Y, r_K) & = 0 \\ B^D(\ ) - B/r_B & = 0 \\ M^D(\ ) & = M \\ T(Y) - B & = G, \end{cases} \tag{15.19}$$

$$\begin{bmatrix} K^D_{r_\kappa} - K_{r_\kappa} & K^D_{r_\kappa} & K^D_Y - K_Y & 0 \\[2ex] B^D_{r_\kappa} & B^D_{r_s} + \dfrac{B}{r_B^2} & B^D_Y & -\dfrac{1}{r_B} \\[2ex] M^D_{r_\kappa} & M^D_{r_s} & M^D_Y & 0 \\[2ex] 0 & 0 & T_Y & -1 \end{bmatrix} \begin{bmatrix} \dfrac{\partial r_K}{\partial G} \\[2ex] \dfrac{\partial_B}{\partial G} \\[2ex] \dfrac{\partial Y}{\partial G} \\[2ex] \dfrac{\partial B}{\partial G} \end{bmatrix} = \begin{bmatrix} 0 \\[2ex] 0 \\[2ex] 0 \\[2ex] 1 \end{bmatrix} \tag{15.20}$$

The Jacobian has the same structure as (15.15), except that the bottom diagonal element is -1 instead of $+1$. Thus $\Delta = -\Delta_{44} - T_Y \Delta_{43}$. A Keynesian sign pattern insures $\Delta_{43} < \Delta_{44} > 0$, $0 < T_Y < 1$. So Δ may have either sign. Positive Δ implies positive $\partial Y/\partial G$, $\partial B/\partial G$, and $\partial r_B/\partial G$ and ambiguous $\partial r_K/\partial G$. Note that because of the increase in bond interest B, $\partial Y/\partial G$ exceeds $1/T_Y$, the amount necessary to collect taxes enough to cover the increase in G. Figure 15.4 is illustrative. LLM is the long-run balance of money demand and supply, and GT is the balanced budget locus. Both curves carry with each point the value of B that maintains portfolio balance. The rightward shift in GT represents an increase in G.

It is also possible that Δ is negative—if T_Y is low, for example. This means that the LLM curve is steeper than GT, and the comparative statics give perverse results. In the Tobin-Buiter paper, it is shown—though for a continuous-time model of somewhat different structure—that this equilibrium is unstable. An increase in government purchases starts the economy off on a track of increasing income and interest rates, which, left to itself, never converges to a balanced budget equilibrium.

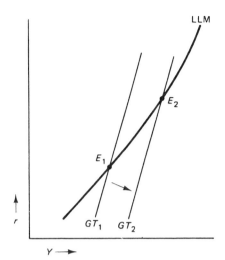

Figure 15.4 Long run fiscal effect: Keynesian case

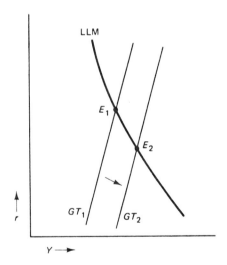

Figure 15.5 Long run fiscal effect: monetarist case 1

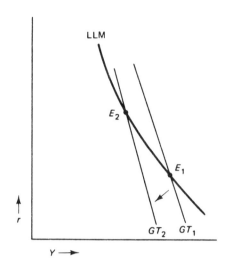

Figure 15.6 Long run fiscal effect: monetarist case 2

With the monetarist sign pattern, the two possibilities are illustrated by figures 15.5 and 15.6. In formal terms Δ_{43} is now positive. If Δ_{44} is positive, then Δ is negative and $\partial Y/\partial G = -\Delta_{43}/\Delta$ is positive, while $\partial r_B/\partial G$ and $\partial B/\partial G$ are negative. Figure 15.5 (monetarist case 1) applies. But in the analogous short-run case, Y is moving in the other direction. This suggests that the equilibria displayed in figure 15.5 are unstable and irrelevant. A monetarist nightmare comes true. Deficit spending feeds on itself in an ever weaker economy afflicted with high and rising interest rates. Figure 15.6 (monetarist case 2) represents a Δ_{44} so negative that Δ becomes positive. The budget balance line GT slopes the wrong way; moving northeast along it, the demand for bonds declines, and taxes fall to match. Expansionary fiscal policy is represented by a downward shift of GT. This long-run configuration is possibly a stable version of the monetarist scenario.

Concluding Remarks

I have tried to rationalize the monetarist claim that fiscal policy is ineffective or worse in its effects on aggregate demand, even though the instantaneous demand for money is inversely sensitive to interest rates. I found a rationalization in interest-induced saving, provided greater wealth, whatever motivated its accumulation, entails greater transactions balances. I doubt the empirical importance of such behavior, but that is another question.

At the same time, I have shown that the standard Keynesian results can, in theory, apply for long periods of time. They do not violate the government budget constraint.

What difference does it make? After all no one need advocate or practice the use of fiscal stabilization policies without the active help of monetary policies. Yet if money is not all that matters, monetary policy itself must take account of the macroeconomic effects of fiscal measures. With two major tools we can aim not only at domestic stabilization but at some other target too—growth or external balance. The moral is embarrassingly obvious, but it is frequently denied or ignored.

Notes

1. See Alan S. Blinder and Robert M. Solow, *The Economics of Public Finance* (Washington, D.C.: Brookings Institution, 1974), pp. 48–57 and literature there cited. See also their article "Does Fiscal Policy Matter?" *Journal of Public Economics* (November 1973): 318–37. My own contribution, with Willem Buiter, is "Long-run Effects of Fiscal and Monetary Policy on Aggregate Demand," in J. Stein, ed., *Monetarism: Studies in Monetary Economics* (Amsterdam: North-Holland, 1976), 1: 273–336.

2. J. M. Keynes, *General Theory of Employment, Interest, and Money* (New York: Harcourt Brace, 1936), p. 245. He goes on to say, "This does not mean that we assume these factors to be constant; but merely that, in this place and context, we are not considering or taking into account the effects and consequences of changes in them."

3. Ibid., p. 246.

4. Writing before Harrod inaugurated modern growth macroeconomics, Keynes embedded his model in a stationary setting: constant labor force, technology, and so forth. Thus the only steady state would be one with constant capital stock. But it is easy to embed it instead in a setting with a nonzero natural rate of growth. The same problem of interpretation arises when solution of the Keynesian equations gives a rate of net investment relative to the capital stock different from the natural growth rate.

5. A. Lerner, *Economics of Control* (New York: Macmillan, 1944), pp. 330–345. Lerner had previously presented the ideas in a 1937 paper of which a summary was published in Manchester Statistical Society *Report of Group Meetings*, 1936–1937.

6. Keynes, *General Theory*, p. 247.

7. P. A. Samuelson, *Foundations of Economic Analysis* (Cambridge: Harvard University Press, 1945), pp. 276–283. J. R. Hicks, *The Trade Cycle* (New York: Oxford University Press, 1950), pp. 136–154.

8. Some authors consider a beginning-of-period stock equilibrium, in which existing asset supplies are priced, followed by a within-period "flow equilibrium" in which asset accumulations, among other variables, are determined. This construction makes no sense to me.

9. M. Friedman, "Interest Rates and the Demand for Money," *Journal of Law and Economics* (October 1966), 71–85.

10. W. L. Silber, "Fiscal Policy in IS-LM Analysis: A correction *Journal of Money, Credit and Banking* 2 (November 1970), 461–72.

11. L. C. Anderson and K. M. Carlson, "A Monetarist Model of Economic Stabilization," *Federal Reserve Bank of St. Louis Review* 54 (April 1970).

Fiscal and Monetary Policies, Capital Formation, and Economic Activity

James Tobin and
Willem Buiter

Large econometric models assign to fiscal and monetary policies considerable influence on the paths of output, employment, investment, and other real economic variables and through them on wages, prices, and inflation. These models are generally Keynesian in structure. They attribute short-run fluctuations in economic activity primarily to variation of aggregate demand. They explain aggregate demand for goods and services from its components—consumption, domestic investment, government purchases, foreign investment. Among the determinants of these expenditures and their subcomponents are macroeconomic policies, or variables more or less directly dependent on these policies. Empirical models of this genre are widely used for forecasting and for comparing alternative policies.

Yet their theoretical foundations are under strenuous attack. The attacks differ, but they converge on a single point: fiscal and monetary policies have little or no influence on real economic outcomes, short or long run. Active use of these instruments to stabilize and steer the economy will not succeed and may have adverse side effects. These views have gained a substantial following among economists, policymakers, and influential laymen. If they are correct, most econometric models are wrong, and so are similar but less elaborate and less formal accounts of the way macroeconomic policies work.

This chapter will review major theoretical issues concerning the effects of fiscal and monetary policies, with particular stress on their effects on capital formation. We will consider challenges to the modern Keynesian paradigm. The lively theoretical controversies of

Reprinted by permission from *The Government and Capital Formation*, ed. George M. von Furstenberg, vol. II in the Series on Capital Investment sponsored by the American Council of Life Insurance, Cambridge, MA: Ballinger, 1980, pp. 73–151. Copyright © 1980 by Ballinger Publishing Co.

recent years have sharpened understanding of macroeconomic structure and of the complexities of policymaking. We conclude that the essential messages of the paradigm remain relevant: macroeconomic policies have important and durable real effects, for better or worse.

Readers who wish to avoid the technicalities of formal analysis of theoretical models will be able to find our central message in the text. However, the appendix sets forth a model of asset and commodity markets in which the effects of government fiscal and financial policies are rigorously analyzed.

I. CROWDING OUT AND NEUTRALITY: THEORETICAL ISSUES

The government policies to be discussed are of three main types: (1) purchases of goods and services, (2) financing of purchases by taxation, debt issue, and monetary issue, (3) other monetary and financial policies. The first refers principally to variations in the aggregate real amount of goods and services purchased for government use. The content of these purchases—for example, the mix of public investment, collective consumption, and "regrettable necessities" like defense and internal security—is also relevant to some issues. The second refers to the mixture of sources of financing of a given expenditure program. Taxation is to be reckoned net of transfer payments or "negative taxes," government payments to economic agents for which no goods or services are currently rendered in return. The kinds of taxes and transfers used—whether lump-sum, direct, or indirect—are important for some issues. Debt issue means sale of interest-bearing obligations to nongovernmental buyers, typically at market-determined prices. Public debt obligations are predominantly promises to pay the national currency at specified dates in the future. Price-indexed bonds are seldom issued, and we shall not consider them in this chapter.

A national government can also finance outlays by issuing its own currency, which bears no interest at all. With modern banking institutions, the printing press is largely supplanted by a more sophisticated process. Central bank purchases of its government's securities augment, directly or indirectly, the government's demand deposit account in the central bank. As the Treasury draws on the account to pay its bills, this convenient equivalent of currency is transferred to private ownership. In the U.S. deposits in Federal Reserve Banks are reserves for member commercial banks. The supply of base money, or what we call "high-powered" money, is also augmented when the central bank buys foreign currency assets, gold, or other international reserves. Monetary financing of current government expenditure is operationally the same as monetization of preexisting debt by central bank open market purchases. But it is useful to maintain a conceptual distinction between monetary issue for financing the current budget deficit and other open market operations. The third category of policies could include central bank manipulation of other instruments including its lending rate, reserve requirements, and ceiling rates on bank deposits. But we shall not discuss them in this chapter.

The effects of these policies are likely to depend on the economic environment in which they are applied and to differ with the length of time during which the economy adapts to them. With respect to economic environment, the important distinction is between situations with unemployed resources which can be productively employed by expansion of aggregate demand and situations in which output is limited by supplies of productive resources. By supply limits we do not mean the technological and physical maxima applicable to wartime mobilizations. We refer rather to market-clearing equilibria in which product and factor prices have successfully balanced supplies and demands throughout the economy. Output is not supply-constrained in disequilibria in which excess supplies of labor, capital services, and other resources persist at prevailing prices, disequilibria to which price and wage levels and trends adjust slowly and sluggishly. Some theorists—the protagonists of the "new classical macroeconomics"—contend that underemployment disequilibria are infrequent and transient. They describe the economy as a sequence of market-clearing equilibria. This viewpoint naturally colors their view of macroeconomic policy interventions.[a] We shall not debate this empirical proposition here, but simply record our belief that underemployment of labor and capital is sufficiently frequent and persistent to justify analysis of policy interventions in both environments.

[a]The view that the economic system is always at the natural rate of unemployment or the natural level of capacity utilization, except for transient disturbances due to errors in private economic agents' price or wage forecasts, was first formalized by Milton Friedman [20, 1968] and Edmund Phelps [24, 1970]. The proposition that the only source of departures from the natural rate are expectational errors has recently been combined with the "rational expectations" assumption that forecast errors are completely random and cannot be affected by deterministic policy behavior. Jointly, the two hypotheses of the short-run natural rate and rational expectations formation imply that stabilization policy, or at any rate monetary policy, will be powerless. (Robert Lucas [23, 1976], Thomas Sargent and Neil Wallace [27, 1976], Robert Barro [3, 1976]. For an opposing view see James Tobin [31, 1972], Stanley Fischer [16, 1977], Phelps and John Taylor [26, 1977], and Martin Bailey [1, 1978].) The separate roles of the rational expectations assumption and the market clearing assumption can

As for time horizons, we shall consider short runs of both environments, and long runs with full utilization, meaning by "short run" a period in which the economy has not reached a stationary or steady growth equilibrium, and, in particular, has not adapted completely to prevailing policies. Full adaptation has several dimensions. One is that expectations about policy and other variables are realized: agents have no reason in experience to revise the expectations on which they act. Another is that stocks of assets and debts are stationary or growing at a common steady rate; otherwise behavior will change as a result of uneven stock accumulation. But unlike Keynes's short run, ours are not so short that asset accumulation is altogether ignored. We wish to allow current saving and financial flows to affect supplies and demands in asset markets, saving to augment wealth, investment to increase the capital stock, government deficits to raise the public debt. The model specified in the appendix enables us to examine both stock and flow effects of government financial policies.

We shall also analyze the effects of policies in long-run stationary or steady-growth equilibrium, where expectations are fulfilled and

---

be brought out with a simple example: p_t denotes the actual price level in period t, p_t^* the equilibrium price level, and $\hat{p}_{t-1,t}$ the price level anticipated, in period $t-1$, for period t (all in logs), Y_t is actual output, $\overline{Y}_t$ full capacity output. Consider the "Lucas supply function"

$$p_t^* = \alpha(Y_t - \overline{Y}_t) + \hat{p}_{t-1,t} \qquad \alpha > 0.$$

The actual price level adjusts sluggishly toward the equilibrium price level, according to

$$\Delta p_t \equiv p_t - p_{t-1} = \beta(p_t^* - p_{t-1}) \qquad 0 \leq \beta \leq 1.$$

Such a partial adjustment function is not implausible for an economic system with no underlying inflationary or deflationary trend. If such trends occurred, the disequilibrium price adjustment mechanism would be likely to involve first or higher differences of p_t and p_t^*. Note that instantaneous equilibrium is the special case of our lagged price adjustment equation when $\beta = 1$. In that case $p_t^* \equiv p_t$. Combining the equilibrium price equation and the disequilibrium price adjustment equation, we obtain

$$\Delta p_t = \alpha\beta(Y_t - \overline{Y}_t) + \beta(\hat{p}_{t-1,t} - p_{t-1}).$$

Rational expectations, or perfect foresight in this deterministic model, imply $\hat{p}_{t-1,t} = p_t$. Thus rational expectations rule out systematic deviations of actual from capacity output if and only if $\beta = 1$. If we are not always in temporary Walrasian equilibrium, policy can affect price behavior through the market disequilibrium channel even if price forecasts are rational.

asset supplies have adjusted to permanent long-run demands. In both "runs," one of our interests is the effect of policy on capital formation. In the short run the variable of interest is real investment; in the long run it is the stock of capital per worker or per unit of output.

Government Purchases of Goods and Services

The proposition that government purchases have macroeconomic effects is scarcely controversial. In buying goods and services for public use, the government is clearly doing something real, which will almost inevitably have real consequences. Neutrality has been claimed for government financial policies, but rarely for exhaustive (resource-using) public expenditures. Indeed those who argue that finance doesn't matter stress that the true measure of fiscal burden is always the share of national product used by government.

In a fully employed economy, government purchases necessarily displace other uses of resources. The only question is which ones. The answer may depend partly on the nature of public expenditures. Perhaps they provide goods or services which are close substitutes for current private consumption. Perhaps they are capital projects which will yield future consumption or augment the productivity of the nation's resources, whether employed privately or publicly. Perhaps they are expenditures for war or defense or internal security, which substitute for neither present nor future consumption. Rarely are government purchases perceived to provide citizens with such close duplicates of what they are already doing for themselves that citizens cut their private purchases and automatically cede the economic room. As a rule, less direct mechanisms of "crowding out" are needed: increases in prices or interest rates.[b]

In underemployment situations, "crowding out" is not arithmetically inevitable. The question is then the degree to which government purchases increase aggregate demand. If the government provides goods that are by nature substitutes for private consumption or investment, direct "crowding out" may occur. Otherwise, government purchases add to aggregate demand at prevailing prices and interest rates. Private agents have no incentive to make offsetting reductions in their spending, and no tightening of their budget constraints forces them to do so. According to the famous "balanced budget multiplier theorem," this is true even if the incremental government expenditures are matched by taxes: the multiplier is 1. It is *at least* equally true if they are financed by borrowing or by printing money. Keynesians would expect the multiplier to exceed one in those cases; pre-

[b] For a discussion of the distinction between direct and indirect crowding out, see Willem Buiter [6, 1977].

sumably the "neo-Ricardians" who argue that finance doesn't matter would keep it at one.

Monetary Crowding-Out versus Monetary Accommodation

However, monetary policy may not *accommodate* an increase in national product as large as the increase in government purchases. In this case, the multiplier will be less than 1, perhaps zero. Private expenditures for goods and services will decline, perhaps by as much as government purchases rise. Monetary crowding-out is a third mechanism, to be distinguished from crowding-out forced by supply constraints and from displacement by individual agents' substitution of public for private goods.

Accommodation means that the central bank provides an additional supply of money equal to the additional demand for money generated by the new government purchases, enough to keep constant the interest rates relevant for private spending decisions. The additional demand for money arises from the extra private transactions involved; agents receive incomes from selling goods and services to government, and return the funds to government in taxes or purchases of securities. To manage the extra transactions, they may need on average somewhat higher cash balances. (The government does, too, but its cash balances are not conventionally counted in the money stock under any definition. For this reason, the extra transactions demand for money is smaller when GNP rises from government purchases than when it rises by the same amount from private purchases.) If the central bank does not provide the extra money, the attempts of households and businesses to obtain it by borrowing or selling securities will raise interest rates; monetary crowding-out will occur.

The most common scenario is that interest rates rise, inducing some economy in cash management and reduction in money demand but also inducing some reduction in investment, and possibly in consumption. Complete crowding out would occur if the money stock were maintained unchanged and if the rise in interest rates induced no economy of money demand.[c]

---

[c]This is the vertical *LM* "curve" of textbook fame. A less plausible extreme scenario is that private real spending is perfectly elastic with respect to the prevailing interest rate; national product is limited by the volume of transactions the money supply will finance at that rate. This means that the *IS* "curve" is a horizontal line. It is not the only case that can be so described in the Hicksian diagram. Another case applies to an open economy with perfect international capital mobility, facing a fixed foreign interest rate. If the foreign exchange rate is market-determined without official interventions, the economy's foreign in-

Analyses of this kind assume a monetary policy, expressed in terms of money stock or interest rates or some combination, which remains the same regardless of the government budget and its consequences for aggregate demand. Normally, though not invariably, the monetary authority has discretion. The central bank can accommodate or not, as it chooses. Thus the central bank can oppose and offset a fiscal stimulus by restricting the money stock and its growth as necessary. Or the central bank can accommodate the fiscal stimulus by whatever money supply is needed to validate its multiplier. In this sense, whatever crowding out occurs is either accidental and unintentional or is the deliberate consequence of monetary policy.[d] Leaving aside transient errors of policy, it is possible to attribute decline in investment to an increase in government purchases if, and only if, one takes for granted the path of total national product the central bank is willing to accommodate. The monetary constraint on output then has the same effect as a resource or supply constraint.

In interpreting and appraising monetary crowding-out, several possible cases should be distinguished.

1. The central bank and the fiscal authorities—Congress and president in the United States—agree on the desirable path of GNP. The increase in government purchases is not intended to stimulate the economy but only to carry out the government's substantive programs. Here it is quite appropriate that the needed resources be obtained from other uses of GNP. Individual economists and citizens may, of course, disagree either with the macroeconomic policy or with the allocation of resources. But the policies are consistent. The policymakers may regard a GNP path with unemployed resources as desirable because the government desires to diminish the prevailing

---

vestment, equal to its current account surplus, is perfectly elastic at the fixed interest rate. Given that rate and the domestic money stock, additional government purchases crowd out foreign investment 100 percent, simply by appreciating the home currency and reducing net exports. Another case of horizontal *IS* can occur when expenditure on national product is less than infinitely elastic with respect to interest rate. Suppose the marginal propensity to spend with respect to national product itself, including investment as well as consumption, happens to be exactly unity. The *IS* curve is horizontal, but the interest rate level at which it is horizontal will be raised by government purchases or by any other increase in autonomous expenditure. Here complete crowding out will not occur if the higher interest rate will reduce money demand or increase money supply. If the *IS* locus is given by $Y = E(Y, r) + G$, its slope is $(1 - E_Y)/E_r$, and is zero if $E_Y = 1$, $E_r < 0$. However, at any given Y, $dr/dg = -1/E_r$. It is important not to confuse this case with either of the first two.

[d]In a recent paper Ray Fair [15, 1978] demonstrates, via simulation experiments with his econometric model, that fiscal policy effects are very sensitive to the behavior of the Federal Reserve.

inflation rate or to avoid risks of accelerating inflation by a more rapid growth in aggregate demand. Or the government may be unwilling to accept the external consequences, current account deficit, loss of international reserves or exchange depreciation, of a higher GNP path.

2. The central bank and the fiscal authorities differ in their GNP targets, and the central bank has independent power. The government would welcome a higher GNP path, but cannot persuade the central bank to bring it about. The government tries to reach its objective by fiscal stimulus, or at least welcomes the expansionary byproducts of budget expenditures adopted on their own merits. The central bank's refusal to accommodate thwarts the fiscal stimulus, and crowding out is a symptom and consequence of this unresolved conflict over macroeconomic policy. Here it is almost inevitable that the composition of output, along whatever aggregate path results from the policy tug-of-war, is less than optimal from the viewpoint of either side. For example, the path will contain less private investment and more government purchases than either would have desired had they compromised in advance on the actually realized GNP path. Even though the central bank has the last word, the realized path is not necessarily its original target. Apart from the inevitable errors of monetary marksmanship, the central bank probably modifies its GNP target in the government's direction, for obvious political reasons but also for economic reasons. One reason to give a little on GNP is to avoid large increases in interest rates and to limit the crowding-out of investment.

3. The central bank and the fiscal authority agree that more rapid expansion of aggregate demand is desirable. But the monetary managers are, or feel they are, unable to bring it about. Consequently fiscal stimulus is welcomed by both sets of policymakers, and the central bank is happy to accommodate. Why is monetary stimulus impossible? One case is the "liquidity trap," the nominal interest rate floor Keynes detected in the Great Depression. The floor is no problem today, but the economy may be highly liquid even when nominal interest rates are well above zero. In such circumstances expansionary monetary policy may work but only weakly and slowly; as the central bankers say, "You can't push on a string." Another case is that external financial objectives establish a floor for interest rates. In the early 1960s, for example, exchange rates were pegged and U.S. payments deficits threatened losses of gold reserves and of foreign confidence in the dollar. The Federal Reserve and Treasury were committed to hold short-term interest rates competitive with

those abroad. Fiscal stimulus was the only tool available for the 1961–1965 recovery.

4. The central bank is making policy by reference to its instruments or to intermediate targets, as well as or instead of macroeconomic results. The result of fiscal stimulus then depends on what this policy is. During most of the 1950s and 1960s Federal Reserve policy was "leaning against the wind." The Treasury-Federal Reserve Accord of 1951 released the "Fed" from its wartime commitment to peg interest rates on government securities. Thereafter the central bank supplied only partially the bank reserves required to meet the demands for credit and deposits generated by cyclical expansion of economic activity, and withdrew only partially the reserves released in cyclical contractions. As a result, interest rates moved procyclically. In effect, the policy introduced a short-run positive interest elasticity to money supply, reinforcing whatever negative interest elasticity there is in money demand. In this monetary environment, expansionary fiscal policy—like any other autonomous increase in demand—has a positive multiplier but crowds out some interest-sensitive private expenditure. In the 1970s the Fed has shifted toward money stock targets, specifically to ranges of growth rates for monetary aggregates. They have not gone so far in this direction as to adopt the strict monetarist rule advocated by Milton Friedman, namely growth of money stock at a constant rate invariant to interest rates and other economic events. The result of this policy shift is to increase the procyclical variability of interest rates, to make the short-run "*LM*" curve steeper, to diminish fiscal policy multipliers, and to increase the degree of crowding out attributable to government expenditures.

The Financing of Government Expenditure

We turn now to the financing of government expenditures for goods and services. *Given* the volume and composition of government expenditures, does it matter whether they are financed by taxes, debt issues, or printing money? Does it make any difference to aggregate demand? Do tax reductions or increased transfer payments stimulate business activity? Do they increase employment and output when there is slack in the economy? Are they inflationary when resources are fully employed? Do government deficits absorb saving that would otherwise either disappear in unemployment or finance private capital formation?

"Yes" is the traditional Keynesian answer to all these questions. "No" is the new classical answer: only government purchases are a burden or stimulus, and their effect is independent of their financing.

189

The issue is whether or not households internalize government saving or dissaving and adjust private saving dollar for dollar to realize a desired amount of total national saving. Keynes argues that they do not. In his discussion of the national propensity to save he included the government budget as an independent determinant [21, 1936, Chapter 8, especially pp. 94–95, 98]. In subsequent theoretical and empirical work, this view was rationalized and simplified by relating personal consumption and saving to *disposable income*, income after taxes and transfer payments (and excluding retained corporate profits). This specification implies that a dollar of tax reduction, for example, increases personal saving from a given pretax income only by a fraction of a dollar, the marginal propensity to save.

Real disposable income "explained" extraordinarily well both variations of annual real consumption in the United States between the two world wars and variations across households in cross-section surveys. Consequently many theorists, statistical model-builders, and textbook writers embraced this simple consumption function too uncritically. Abba Lerner's doctrine of *functional finance* [22, 1946, Chapter 24], for example, relied on the premise that consumer spending could be closely controlled by adjusting taxes and transfers.

This position emphasized, if only tacitly, consumers' dependence on income receipts for the cash needed to make purchases. This emphasis is suggested by the very word "disposable." It surely exaggerates the dependence of consumers on contemporaneous receipts as a source of liquid cash. Moreover, disposable income as computed omits some cash inflows and contains some illiquid accruals, for example, deductions and employer contributions for pensions and other fringe benefits which appear as "other labor income" in U.S. national income accounts. Keynes himself, in expounding the consumption function as a "psychological law," did not regard it as a liquidity-constrained relation between cash inflow and cash outflow.

Over the postwar years the theory and statistical practice of consumption and saving relations have moved toward a longer-run perspective on household behavior. Most households do not live hand-to-mouth, but consciously or unconsciously base consumption outlays on calculation of the standard of living they can afford over a horizon of months or years or decades. They are able to free consumption from slavish conformity to receipts by reducing their current saving, by borrowing, or by drawing down liquid assets. Their budget constraints allow considerable choice between consumption now and at various future dates. From this perspective, wealth—the sum over the horizon of current net worth and the present value of future after-tax earnings from household labor and of future transfers—becomes the effective constraint. This modification increases the estimated marginal propensity to save from current disposable income and lowers the tax-cut or transfer multiplier.

According to the *permanent income hypothesis* of Milton Friedman [19, 1957] current consumption is related to average expected disposable income, *permanent income*, rather than to contemporaneous disposable income alone. His theoretical development of the hypothesis refers to horizons of expectation varying from infinite to two periods. In empirical applications he seems to have in mind horizons of only three to five years. The claim that the marginal propensity to consume from transient deviations of current from permanent income is zero does not apply strictly to finite horizons. But the hypothesis explains why consumption is less variable than income and why saving is more volatile than either consumption or income. And it predicts that temporary tax reductions or transfers will have much less effect on consumption than permanent changes of equal annual amount.

In similar spirit the *life cycle* model assumes a lifetime horizon and relates consumption and saving to the present value of lifetime consumable resources. This model also downgrades the effect of temporary tax cuts or transfers. Current consumption and saving are simply one decision variable in a household's multi-period plan designed to spread existing and expected resources over a lifetime in a pattern that maximizes expected utility.

Household horizons can be extended to allow for utility enjoyed by descendants and for intergenerational bequests and gifts. In the extreme, these linkages make the household's horizon infinite. Just as utility allows directly or indirectly for the consumption of descendants, so the effective budget constraint includes their expected earnings discounted to the present. Individuals' concern for the well-being of their parents and grandparents, and gifts from younger to older contemporaries, can also be modeled. The longer the horizon the weaker the connection between consumption and contemporary income, and the greater the influence of remote events on current behavior.

In application of these models to government financial policy, a great deal depends on what expectations current policies generate about future real incomes after taxes. For example, conventional analysis of the effects of temporary tax cuts or transfers assigns them some stimulative power, though less than permanent changes, on the assumption that taxes and transfers will revert to the levels previously anticipated. The multi-period budget constraint faced by a typical household is relaxed; the present value of current and future tax liabilities net of transfers is diminished.

A stronger assumption is that the current fiscal stimulus will be offset by subsequent increases in taxes above the reference path, to pay the interest and/or principal of the currently incurred government debt. Assuming households perceive those liabilities and discount them at the interest rate at which the government borrows, their multi-period budget constraint has not changed, and neither will their behavior. Current fiscal deficits are perceived simply as deferred tax levies, as certain as death and taxes are proverbially reputed to be. This is the new classical or "Ricardian" theory of public debt, supporting the proposition that government finance has no effect on either aggregate demand or its composition.[e]

The proposition, in its strongest form, is applied both to debt finance and to money finance. When the government shifts from taxes to interest-bearing debt, expectations of additional future taxes of equal present value offset the current tax reduction. When the shift is to money, free of nominal interest, there is no implication that taxes will be higher in the future. What losses, currently incurred or expected, offset the public's increased holdings of money? The losses are losses of purchasing power because of changes in commodity prices, current or expected. To assimilate those losses to explicit taxes, they are metaphorically described as inflation taxes.

These strong assertions of neutrality deserve serious consideration. We shall discuss first the case of debt finance, examining critically the Ricardian theory. This is followed by discussion of monetary finance and by critique of monetarist propositions that real economic outcomes are invariant to changes in the stock of money or its rate of growth. The fourth section of the paper reports the implications of our model, formally described in the Appendix, concerning the effects of government fiscal and financial policies. The final section offers some concluding remarks.

---

[e]In our chapter "Debt Neutrality: A Brief Review of Doctrine and Evidence," in the companion volume *Social Security versus Private Saving*, we point out that while Ricardo clearly stated the proposition that taxation and government borrowing are equivalent in their economic effects, he also refuted this "equivalence theorem." In spite of the injustice to Ricardo, we shall for convenience conform to prevalent usage and refer to the modern revival of neutrality doctrine as Ricardian.

II. DEBT NEUTRALITY: CRITIQUE OF RICARDIAN THEORY

The Ricardian doctrine has strong implications for the short-run effects of government finance, both in unemployment and full employment situations, and for its long-run effects: In short-run underemployment disequilibrium, a shift from tax finance to debt finance is not expansionary. It does not increase consumption demand, or aggregate demand, at prevailing prices; therefore it will not increase realized output, real income, and employment. In short-run full employment equilibrium, debt finance is not inflationary. Since it leaves aggregate demand unchanged, supply and demand will still balance without any increase in prices or any rise of interest rates. In long-run steady states, debt finance does not reduce the capital intensity of the economy.

The common thread of these propositions is that substitution of government debt for taxation absorbs no saving. That is why it is not expansionary or inflationary. That is why it does not crowd out investment in the short run or displace capital in the long run. That is why the present generation cannot shift the burden of its public expenditures to future generations. If as voters they try to do so by lowering their own taxes and issuing bonds, they will as individuals buy the bonds to enable their heirs to pay the deferred taxes.

As expounded by Robert Barro [2, 1974], the modern Ricardian theory relies on a number of simplifying assumptions: (1) households so linked to subsequent and past generations by bequests and gifts that their horizons are effectively infinite, (2) correct beliefs that current deficits imply future taxes of equal present value, (3) lump-sum taxes, (4) no liquidity constraints, and (5) homogeneity of households, allowing their behavior in aggregate to be represented as that of a single representative household.

Elsewhere in this series one of us presents a model of overlapping generations which shows that decentralized competitive behavior will not necessarily produce outcomes invariant to government financial policy, even when intergenerational bequests and gifts are taken into account [9, Buiter, 1979]. Here we consider plausible ways in which Barro's assumptions may be violated and argue that realistic departures from his assumptions support modern Keynesian views of the short-run and long-run effects of debt finance.

The Endless Chain of Intergenerational Gifts and Bequests

Clearly voters always have some incentive to shift the burden of public expenditure to other taxpayers whose welfare is of no concern. Any citizen with no heirs, or none he cares about, would be glad to defer taxes beyond his own lifetime; and he would consume his gains today. Ricardian theory depends on complete effective intergenerational chains of bequests and gifts. How plausible are they? A chain is broken in any lineal family if any generation is childless or indifferent to the utility of its successor. Though parents may care about their own children, their bequests will be smaller if they know that their great-grandchildren will have no children they care about. In particular, they will not adjust their bequests to provide for any increase in taxes to be levied after the break in the chain.

For the neutrality theorem to be valid, bequest and gift motives have to be operative for each and every economic agent affected by the public-sector financing policies. Some households in each generation are childless or do not care about their children's well-being. They consume more as their taxes are shifted to future generations. The remaining households, who have children and care about them, cannot maintain both their own lifetime consumption and that of their children, because the latter will also be liable for the taxes shifted from the childless members of the older generation. The net result for the households who care will be an increase in bequests, to be sure, but not enough to pay their children's taxes. Aggregating both kinds of households, the substitution of debt finance for tax finance increases current consumption.

Parents' utility may well depend in some degree on the size of their bequests to their children, independently of the utility or earning potential of the children. The convention of equal division among children, who may differ widely in wealth from other sources, suggests this motivation. To the extent that giving is for the gratification of the giver rather than the welfare of the receiver, bequests are related to the wealth of the parents rather than to the well-being of the child. There is then no presumption that bequests will be increased enough to keep children at the same utility level when taxes are shifted on to the children.

Utility optima at zero bequest "corners" can occur even for households that are concerned with their children's utility. The parents would choose negative bequests if these were an available option. Accordingly, they will not bequeath more but consume more if taxes are shifted to their heirs. Corner solutions are more likely if households' utility functions place small weight on the future utility of their heirs, if they place large probability weights on the possibilities that the chain will somehow be broken, and if the economy is experiencing productivity growth leading parents to expect their descendants to be much better off than they are.

Dependence of Future Taxes on Current Deficits, and Expectations About Their Relationship

It is an empirical question how individuals' expectations of future real incomes are altered by their perceptions of current fiscal policy. What inferences do taxpayers draw from reading about large budget deficits? These probably differ from time to time and from one individual to another. Future tax policy is rarely announced in advance; and even when tax surcharges or tax credits have been legislated as temporary, everyone knows that expiration dates can be changed and frequently are. It is not obvious that citizens will always assume that a current deficit carries with it future tax liabilities of equal present value. Nor is it necessarily irrational "public debt illusion" if they assume and behave otherwise.

The government's net worth may be considered the present value of its stream of net revenues less its stream of purchases of goods and services. Suppose that to every dollar of currently outstanding public debt corresponds a dollar of discounted value—at the government's interest rate—of future tax receipts to pay coupons and principal. Then the dollar of debt subtracts nothing from the government's net worth. And if purchases are also balanced, in present value, with taxes the net worth of government is zero. But there is no reason that this should always be so or that taxpayers should always believe it to be so. Perhaps the debt will grow with the interest rate, new debt always being issued to service existing debt. Then the net worth of the government is negative, and private citizens would be correct so to estimate it. They could also be correct to expect that current government deficits do not foreshadow future taxes of equivalent present value. It is very likely, and very fortunate, that Americans did not scale their tax expectations up to the debt inherited from World War II.

The sole condition on collective rationality is that basic economy-wide constraints on current and future capacities to produce be respected. The combined present values of government and private consumption cannot exceed the existing capital stock and the present value of future resource endowments. It would be irrational for society to behave, as voters, taxpayers, and private consumers and investors, on expectations which violate these constraints. But it is quite possible for the government to have negative net worth, and the private sector to have correspondingly a net worth exceeding the national wealth, without their joint consumption plans exceeding productive capacity. A well-known example occurs in long-run growth models, where some private saving is diverted from capital formation into acquisition of public debt. In certain circumstances, such diversion is not only feasible but optimal.

Consider, as another example, a deficit incurred in recession either as passive result of revenue shortfall or as active countercyclical policy. It is not "public debt illusion" to observe that the economy is operating inside its production possibilities, long-run as well as short-run. If so, taxpayers can rationally believe that the deficits represent a permanent increase in public debt with no implications of higher taxes later—that is, a downward adjustment of government's net worth. The public can rationally believe that the adjustment will yield for them higher real incomes, produced by resources otherwise underutilized. Acting on that belief, they can consume more today and help to confirm their own expectations. It is hard to see how this self-consistent scenario can be ruled out, except by those who deny a priori, indeed tautologically, the possibility that the economy can ever be operating short of capacity. In the present context, they would be saying that prices always adjust to clear markets so that the public buys all the potential output the government does not take, regardless of present and expected taxes, or however large or small the government's net worth.

Lump-sum and Conditional Taxes

Ricardian doctrine assumes that all taxes are lump-sum. Our vast array of non-lump-sum indirect and direct taxes, transfers and subsidies, will alter the shapes of private opportunity sets. Such sources of nonneutrality are no less important for being so obvious. The nature of real world tax systems creates a presumption that debt finance of government spending increases current consumption.

First, taxes induce tax-reducing behavior. Consider, for example, current lump-sum transfer payments financed by debt issues to be serviced by future taxes on wealth or on income from wealth. The combination will surely encourage substitution against saving and capital formation. Wage taxes will have qualitatively similar effects to the extent that they tax the proceeds of human capital investments. They will also induce substitution in favor of leisure and other untaxed uses of time. Anticipating this kind of behavior by his heirs, a Ricardian parent will know that in order to maintain his heirs' utilities it is unnecessary to maintain their real incomes against an expected increase in wage taxes. Labor and leisure substitution will do part of the job, and the parent can consume some of his tax reduction without reducing his heirs' utility.

Second, the positive correlation of tax liability with wealth and income means that higher future tax rates reduce the variance of the present value of future consumable resources. At the same time, the current tax cut or transfer maintains the mean. Household saving is in some degree motivated by risk aversion, designed to limit losses of future consumption if earnings are disappointing. To the extent that the tax and transfer system insures this risk, current consumption can be increased at the expense of future consumption without loss of utility.

An individual's expectation of his future tax liabilities depends on his expectations of his tax base, and the taxes are at least as uncertain as the base. If there is no uncertainty about tax incidence, he will discount the future taxes at the same rate at which he discounts the base. For many reasons, some of which will be discussed below, this rate is higher than the interest rate applicable to government securities.

Liquidity Constraints

The crude Keynesian function relating consumption to disposable income exaggerated the importance of liquidity constraints, but that is no license for ignoring them altogether. Financial markets do not in fact provide unlimited opportunities for consuming future incomes today; they certainly do not provide these opportunities for intertemporal substitution at the interest rates at which governments borrow. Consequently many households may be at "corners." They cannot dissave, or dissave on attractive terms, when the government taxes them even if they perceive the current taxes as substitutes for future taxes on themselves or their heirs. By the same token, they will not save more on their own when tax cuts or transfers increase their current disposable income; they will take advantage of an opportunity, which capital markets do not provide them, for consuming now resources that they or their descendants will have at their disposition later. The government is in effect lending to them at its borrowing rate of interest, an option not available to these households in the private credit markets.

The liquidity effects of deficit finance have considerable importance for countercyclical stabilization policy. Consider a stochastic economy subject to regular cycles in real economic activity. Capital markets are imperfect and the fraction of economic agents that are constrained in their current spending by current cash flow varies countercyclically. The government does not have enough information to single out the cash flow-constrained agents from those that are constrained only by net worth. A lump-sum transfer payment to everyone during the slump, financed by borrowing, will expand real demand during the slump, even if the government announces that it will use tax revenues to service and redeem the bonds during the next boom. During the slump the bonds are bought by those economic agents that are not cash-flow constrained. The transfers go at least in part to economic agents with marginal spending propensities of unity because of binding cash flow constraints. The future taxes required to service the debt will be levied during the boom on a population that is, on average, less cash-flow constrained than it was during the slump. To a liquidity-constrained individual, the value of the transfer payments in the slump exceeds the value of the future tax payment of equal actuarial value. The implicit discount rate is higher than the market rate of interest.

Heterogeneity of Households, Portfolio, and Distributional Effects

A number of important dimensions in which households differ in circumstances, tastes, and behavior have been discussed under the preceding four points. A further point concerns the role of government securities in private portfolios, in combination with private securities and expected future tax liabilities. The neutrality proposition assumes that government securities are a perfect hedge against tax liabilities, so that the introduction of both into a portfolio would change neither its expected return nor its risk. Given the uncertainties about when, how, and on whom future taxes will be levied, and about future issues of debt to refund maturing issues or finance new deficits, it is hard to see how so perfect a hedge against all contingencies could be constructed. In any case we observe some holders of government securities with little or no taxes to pay in future, and some future taxpayers with no government securities.

The Ricardian theory, however, also assumes that government interest-bearing debt and private debt are perfect substitutes. On this assumption private debt can also be used to hedge tax liabilities. Thus any private economic agent can, by borrowing or lending on personal account (via home-made leverage) construct a portfolio that is equivalent to a portfolio containing any amount of public debt. The menu of assets from which the individual can choose has not been enlarged by the introduction of government debt.

The assumption that households can lend and borrow on the same terms as governments is strictly for classroom use only. The Modigliani-Miller theorem is an unrealistically simplistic description of the relationship between households and corporations, and it is unlikely to apply any better to households vis-à-vis government. The power of the government to tax and to declare its liabilities legal tender is unique. The risk and liquidity properties of central government debt cannot be duplicated by private debtors.

Barro [2, 1974] correctly points out that the effect of government borrowing on the risk composition of private portfolios requires an analysis of both the asset and the liability side of these portfolios. Future tax liabilities, whether they are associated with current public debt or not, should be included in the risk-return analysis of the entire private portfolio. To argue that the effect of public sector borrowing and associated tax expectations on the "total risk" contained in private portfolios might go either way does not warrant an appeal to the principle of insufficient reason to support his neutrality conclusion.

An interesting area for future research is to investigate to what extent or under what circumstances it is possible to represent the effects of uncertainty by applying different subjective discount rates to anticipated future streams of interest income and tax payments. The traditional Keynesian position, as already noted, has been to argue that the discount rate for future taxes is the one appropriate for the streams of income on which the taxes are levied. Given the uncertainties in those streams (but ignoring additional uncertainty caused by uncertain incidence), that rate is higher than the discount rate for government obligations. The differential means that government bond issue does indeed raise effective net wealth even if taxpayers correctly expect that higher future taxes will match the increased income from the debt.

III. MONETARY FINANCE: NEUTRALITY AND SUPERNEUTRALITY

Monetary finance, unlike debt finance, entails no explicit obligations to pay interest or principal. Consequently, it induces no expectations of future explicit taxes to meet such obligations. The argument that substitution of deficit spending for taxation, in the finance of a given government expenditure program, has no real effect, takes different shapes for money and for debt. One difference concerns the role of commodity prices and inflation. The new Ricardian argument for debt neutrality implies that at prevailing prices of commodities and assets, current and expected, aggregate demand for goods and services is unchanged by shifting from tax to debt finance. In short, bond-financed deficits are neither expansionary nor inflationary. This argument does not apply to money finance.

Rather the alleged neutrality depends on the argument that price increases, current or expected, deprive monetary issue of any real effects. Unlike bonds, money is inflationary.

Open Market Operations

The two neutrality arguments, for debt and for money, are logically bound together. The Ricardian story of interest-bearing debt is a necessary premise of monetarism. To see their connection, it is convenient and instructive to analyze open-market operations by which the central bank buys publicly held government debt with money. The reverse operation, selling debt for money, would be symmetrical. Substitution of money financing for taxation can be viewed in two steps: substitution of debt issue for taxes, and open market purchases of the debt issue. This is in fact how it occurs in the United States.

Here is the Ricardian-monetarist description of an open market purchase. Replacing interest-bearing public debt in the public's hands with non-interest-bearing money, the central bank wipes the corresponding tax expectations from the minds of taxpayers. The public's net worth is increased by the amount of the operation, just as if the same amount of currency had been dropped by helicopter. At existing prices, households will wish to consume some of these gains. But if the economy was already in equilibrium, additional demand cannot be accommodated by supply. To maintain supply/demand equilibrium, both current and expected prices rise in proportion to the increase in the quantity of money. Real (and nominal) interest rates and other relative prices are unchanged. Portfolios contain the same asset mixtures as before. True, the real stock of bonds is smaller, but equally so is the real stock of future tax liabilities. These are equivalent but opposite in sign in wealth-owners' portfolios; together they constitute a composite asset whose supply is zero both before and after the open market purchase.

If the initial situation were one of deficient aggregate demand, with excess supplies of labor and other productive resources, the open market purchase would not necessarily be neutral even if the Ricardian theory of public debt holds. Additional demand at prevailing prices could result in additional output and employment, with sticky current prices rising less than the proportionate increase of money stock and possibly less than expected future prices. The monetarist story is still a consistent one: a full price increase would leave the economy in the same real situation—with the same excess supplies—as before. The actual outcome depends on the mechanism by which product and factor prices are determined in disequilibrium.

Appeal to market-clearing cannot provide the answer; by assumption, the disequilibrium signifies that markets are not clearing.

Here is another critical split in contemporary macroeconomics. Keynesians, econometric model-builders, and students of wage and price determination in imperfectly competitive markets would not expect money wages and prices to jump on the news of central bank open market purchases. They rely on Phillips curves and full cost pricing equations which give great weight to historical trends in wages and prices and some weight to the tightness of labor and product markets. Monetarists tend to think of the commodity price level as the reciprocal of the price of the asset money and as being determined, both in short run and in long run, in the money "market," along with other assets, rather than in the markets for the commodities being priced. That is, they think of the price level, rather than other arguments in the demand-for-money function, as the variable that immediately adjusts to equate demand for and supply of money.

More fundamental objections to the monetarist scenario apply if for any or all of the reasons advanced above the Ricardian propositions on neutrality of debt fail. It will not be true that tax expectations match debt holdings in aggregate, or that government securities are found in portfolios just as hedges against future tax liabilities. It will not be true that open market purchases annihilate an equal amount of present value of tax obligation. It will not be true that the open market purchase is the equivalent of a helicopter drop of money; the purchase will increase private wealth but by less than 100 percent of the amount. A proportionate increase in prices will not by itself restore portfolio equilibrium, keep interest rates constant, and avoid changes in real variables. Should a proportionate rise in prices occur and interest rates remain constant, real money balances would be unchanged, but the real value of outstanding government bonds would be smaller relative both to money and to involuntarily held tax debt. Therefore, private net wealth would be less than before the operation, and aggregate real demand would be smaller, too. Hence that scenario is inconsistent. To sustain a full employment equilibrium takes a lesser price increase; thus the real stock of money increases while that of bonds falls. To sustain portfolio balance then requires that the yields on bonds and on real capital fall relative to that on money. The open market purchase alters the composition of output in favor of investment. With full employment, consumption must decline; this requires a net reduction of wealth, engineered by the combination of higher price level and lower nominal bond supply. If there are unemployed resources, part of the adjustment will occur by increase in output and real income. These short-run fiscal and monetary effects are formally analyzed below with the help of the model of our Appendix.

Money, Government Debt, and Other Assets as Imperfect Substitutes

Some insight as to why open market operations work can be obtained by reflecting on the nature of money, government debt, and other portfolio assets and on the reasons money is held at a lower explicit yield than competing assets. The characteristics of government-issued money are imparted in some degree to the government's debt issues, time obligations to pay its own money. The same reflections, therefore, explain also why government debts provide services which enable them to be held at lower explicit yields than private debts, and accordingly why increasing their supply adds to private wealth and liquidity.

Why do wealth-owners hold money at zero nominal interest when they can earn a positive rate on government bonds? The answer, of course, is that money yields services worth the difference. Large average cash balances mean that people wait a long time, as cash receipts build up, before converting cash into interest-earning assets, and convert those assets into cash long in advance of the payments for which the cash is needed. Conversions cost resources, if only the time and trouble of the investor. Given the volume and pattern of cash transactions, the larger are average money holdings the lower are conversion costs. Marginal saving of conversion costs is one of the services of money that compensates for loss of interest, and it declines with the size of real money holdings. Another service is avoidance of risk: as cash receipts and desired cash outlays are uncertain, holding money lowers the probability of making costly conversions, conversions at unfavorable asset prices, or costly postponements of outlays. The marginal gain from precautionary balances also declines with the size of real money holdings.

The government has a monopoly of issue of legal tender currency generally acceptable throughout its jurisdiction. Additions to the stock of currency, measured in purchasing power equivalent, provide the social gains—economizing resources and reducing risk—just mentioned. Holders of currency pay for those gains by accepting a lower interest rate than they would get on government debt or other assets. Taxpayers escape taxes to pay debt interest; their government earns "seignorage" as currency monopolist. This situation prevails so long as the real supply of money falls short of the amount that would drive to zero the *net* marginal value of its services, that is, the difference between the nonpecuniary return from holding an additional dollar of currency and that from holding an extra dollar's worth of an alternative asset. If this implicit advantage of money were zero, the explicit yield of money would have to be equal to that of other assets. In particular, nominal interest rates on the government's time obligations would have to be zero if the nominal zero rate on its demand obligations, money, were maintained.

From this standpoint the bite of monetary policy may be seen to depend on two related facts. First, the public is generally not, save in the exceptional circumstances of the Great Depression described by Keynes as "liquidity trap," saturated with money. Second, other portfolio assets are substitutes, albeit imperfect ones, for money; central bank operations that lower the net marginal advantage of money will lower the explicit yield differentials of substitute assets, including real capital as well as government securities. By open market purchases of securities with money the central bank can, at least in the first instance, lower interest rates on securities and increase the public's wealth. At unchanged commodity prices, this operation increases consumption demand, by increasing wealth and possibly by lowering interest rates. It also increases investment demand; wealth-owners shift from money and bonds, with lower yields but increased joint supply, to real capital. If goods and labor markets are already in equilibrium, these new demands are excess and generate price increases that in part nullify the central bank's attempt to augment the real value of the public's money holdings. But only in part—as we have seen above in the previous subsection, the open market operation is not (except in a Ricardian world) neutral in its effects even in full employment environments. It alters the total real wealth of the public, the real supplies of assets available to wealth-owners, the structure of asset yields, and the composition of output.

Why not saturate the economy with cash balances, providing the public the extra services and wealth? It is not easy to do unless the economy is also saturated with capital. So long as capital investment offers a marginal return above the explicit real return on money (its nominal yield of zero less the expected inflation rate), the real stock of money must be consistent with a positive net marginal service value. Open market purchases increasing the nominal money stock can hardly go so far as to saturate the economy with real cash balances; the demand-increasing and price-increasing consequences of such purchases make this an unrealistic option.

A possible way to bring the public closer to saturation would be to move in the opposite direction, progressively diminishing the nominal money stock relative to GNP and generating deflation. But practical consequences, given the slowness of downward price adjustments in modern industrial economies, would be unfavorable to output, employment, and capital formation. The important institutional fact is that the nominal interest rate on money is fixed—not that it is fixed at zero, although it would take awkward practical arrangements to set it at any other level on circulating currency. The way to increase the public's holdings of nominal and real cash balances simultaneously is to raise the nominal yield of money at the same time that the nominal stock of money balances is increased.

The explanation of the expansionary and inflationary content of monetary finance applies also—with less force, to be sure—to debt finance of government purchases. An analogous argument can be made for government securities which are close substitutes for money, even though the interest on them may burden future government budgets. The government's securities are promises to pay its own currency at specified future dates—tomorrow, next month, next year, ten or twenty years from now. The government's currency monopoly extends to these future currency contracts as well; no private debtor can print the wherewithal to pay his own debts. Within the class of nominal assets, all of which share risks of changes in commodity prices and market interest rates, government time obligations have advantages in liquidity, marketability, and security against default. Individual citizens choose voluntarily how much, if any, and what kinds of the government's monetary and nonmonetary debts to hold. Like holders of money, citizens holding government obligations are willing to pay in interest foregone for liquidity and for risk reduction. Others are as taxpayers in effect borrowing through the government more cheaply than they lend or invest. The government is an efficient financial intermediary connecting the two groups. As in the case of money, the government is gaining seignorage on its debt obligations and increasing the outstanding stock adds to public wealth. This is the basic logic underlying the model described below, which shows that debt-financed increases in government purchases and tax reductions expand aggregate demand, raising output in situations of underemployment and raising prices in situations of full employment.

Inflation Expectations and Monetary
Financing: Short-Run Effects

So far we have argued, contrary to the Ricardian-monetarist position, that government finance is not neutral in its macroeconomic effects. In particular: (1) substitution of debt finance for taxation raises aggregate demand, and increases output or prices depending on the state of the economy; (2) substitution of money finance for taxes or debt finance is likewise expansionary or inflationary, and changes the composition of output in favor of investment; and (3) the consequences of a one-shot increase in money stock, by open market purchase of outstanding debt, are not confined to price increases; the real state of the economy is altered.

We have not yet considered the effects of fiscal and monetary policies that alter expected and realized rates of price inflation. Those who argue that the financing of public expenditure does not matter have cited inflation as an anticipated cost of money holding which will induce saving in advance.[f] Anticipation of the "inflation tax," it is argued, deprives money finance of demand effects in the same way that anticipation of explicit taxes neutralizes debt finance. We turn to this question now.

The analogy is faulty in several respects. (1) The inflation tax falls on those who hold the money the government has printed to finance deficits. Explicit taxes fall on bondholders only to the extent that those who expect to pay additional taxes voluntarily hold bonds. (2) Any individual can diminish his inflation tax· by holding less money. It is clearly not a lump-sum tax. Neither are the explicit taxes that might be levied to service interest-bearing debt, but these are harder and costlier to dodge. (3) A one-shot increase in debt carries with it, in the Ricardian scenario, expectations of future taxes. A one-shot increase in money carries with it, in a classical world, the expectation of an immediate equal proportional increase in the general price level. This is analogous to a capital levy, reducing the value of previously acquired money. It is not per se a source of expectations of higher inflation. Those expectations, as monetarists usually tell us, are aroused by anticipations of a *sustained* increase in growth rates of money stock.

Expectation of higher inflation, however generated, is certainly not neutral in its short-run macroeconomic effects. The basic source of non-neutrality is the institutional fact that the nominal interest rate on currency and other government-issued money (reserve balances in the central bank) is fixed. In the U.S. system, bank deposits and other inside monies also have legally or conventionally fixed nominal rates. The expected real return on these dollar-denominated assets declines whenever the expected inflation rate rises. This is a real effect, lowering the demand for real money balances in favor of other stores of value. Other real rates will move to balance asset demands and supplies. In general an increase in the expected rate of

---

[f]For a discussion of inflation effects, see the chapter by Paul Wachtel in the present volume.

inflation will lower real rates of interest and encourage capital investment.[g] While an inflation premium will be added to nominal interest rates, it is less than a point per point of expected inflation.

For this reason, a financial policy that involves more rapid increase of money stock is not neutral. In an underemployment environment, where wage and price trends are dominated by historical inertia, the policy will clearly be expansionary. Its wealth and interest rate effects increase aggregate demand even without any revision of inflationary expectations. If the expectation of higher monetary growth also raises inflationary expectations, the expansionary effect is reinforced. For the reasons given above, real interest rates decline with inflationary expectations, even though nominal rates rise. However, a one-for-one translation of monetary growth rates into expected inflation will not be confirmed by events if actual wage and price trends are sticky and output responds to increased demand. Of course if an easier monetary policy breeds expectations of its own reversal, fears of future recession may deprive the policy of its normal expansionary effects. But in that case it can scarcely be inflationary, either.

In a short-run full employment environment, expectation of more rapid monetary growth will raise both inflationary expectations and the current price level. A one-shot jump in the price level is necessary to restrain aggregate demand, to offset the increase in demand due to higher expected inflation. This does not mean that the policy is neutral. The composition of output will be altered; it is not possible to generalize about the nature of the change. Substitution of money for taxes in financing government deficits has, on impact, consumption effects in both directions. The reduction of taxes increases consumption, as does any accompanying increase in the expected rate of inflation, but the rise in the price level works the other way.

Long-Run Effects of Monetary Growth and Steady Inflation: Superneutrality?

"Superneutrality" is the monetarist proposition that long-run equilibria are the same in the magnitudes of real variables, whatever

---

[g] If this theoretical proposition seems surprisingly unrealistic in the light of the economic history of the 1970s, there are several explanations. The inflation that erupted in 1973–74 was associated with several events and policies discouraging to investment. This definitely does not mean that inflation per se is bad for investment. A dramatic increase in the price of energy relative to product prices reduced estimates of profitability in many industries. It also brought about a severe though temporary inflationary bulge. Anti-inflationary monetary policy engineered a sharp rise in the cost of financial capital and a severe recession. Extrapolating from this history, businessmen and other economic agents now believe that increases of inflation rates will induce similar restrictive policies in future.

the inflation rate. This means that they are invariant with respect to the *rate of growth* of the nominal money stock. Whether government financial policies engineer a monetary growth trend of 10 percent per year, or 0 percent, or −10 percent, steady-state capital stock, real output, real wage, consumption, and real interest rates will all be the same. (This is a stronger proposition than simple neutrality, which says merely that one-shot variation of the *level* of the nominal money stock will not alter real economic outcomes. We discussed simple neutrality in the previous section.)

Superneutrality seems dubious on its face. As we already observed, a change in the expected rate of inflation alters the real interest rate on monetary assets with fixed nominal rates. This is a real variable, and in general one would not expect the long-run equilibrium values of other real variables to be unaffected [29, Tobin, 1965].

However, one theoretical recipe for long-run superneutrality which appears in various guises in the literature merits comment.[h] The argument is essentially that asset stocks are not direct substitutes for each other in the long run. Rather, each asset will be independently accumulated until its marginal advantage to the representative consumer just compensates him for postponing consumption. Consumer-savers will hold each asset in whatever quantity provides acceptable payoff in future consumption for refraining from additional consumption today. Capital, in particular, will be held in whatever amount yields a return that compensates consumers for their subjective discount of future consumption. If another asset, money, for example, is also available and can also yield such a return, households will simply expand their total wealth holdings to include it. Money, too, will be held in such quantity, in real terms, that its marginal return compensates consumers for their discount of future consumption. The marginal return on money includes the subjective value of its implicit services in facilitating transactions, providing liquidity, and limiting risk, as well as its objective or explicit yield, positive or negative, from price deflation or inflation. The same argument applies to government debt and other financial assets, except that their explicit returns include nominal interest. The implication is that variations in explicit returns on financial assets, including the rate of inflation, will be absorbed wholly by changes in the real quantities of these assets held, changes that alter their implicit returns just enough to keep their total returns intact. Consequently the equilibrium capital stock is independent of the stocks of other assets and their explicit returns.

[h]See, for example, Miguel Sidrauski [28, 1967] and Stanley Fischer [17, 1978].

To state the argument more precisely, suppose that the total return to each asset j can be decomposed into an explicit return r_j and an implicit service return s_j. In long-run equilibrium assets are held in such amounts that the total returns $r_j + s_j$ are all equal, and equal to ρ, the consumers' rate of discount of future consumption. Differences in the s_j make up for the commonly observed differences in r_j. Now suppose (1) that each s_j depends only on its own real stock X_j relative to income or consumption, and not on any other stock; and (2) that the common intertemporal consumption discount ρ does not vary with total wealth or its composition. These assumptions are necessary and sufficient for the independence and additivity of asset demands described in the previous paragraph. Their necessity makes clear how special and restrictive is the case for superneutrality. We consider the two assumptions in turn.

1. Implicit service returns s_j are to be viewed relative to one another; they are just interest rate differentials by another name. The marginal implicit advantage of bonds over equity, for example, can be expected to decline when the stock of bonds rises; but the same reasons apply when the equity stock falls. If cross effects are allowed, the demand for capital will not be independent of alternative asset supplies and of the explicit returns on them.

One source of interdependence is that financial stocks—money, in particular—may be substitutes for capital and labor in the handling of transactions. The larger the real money stock the less resources are diverted to managing conversions between money and other assets, thus the higher may be the consumption path corresponding to a given capital intensity. However, the corresponding rate of return to capital is not altered if transactions technology uses capital and labor in the same proportions as commodity production. We do not pursue this line of analysis here. A complete story would require not only specification of transactions technology but also consideration of the fiscal alternatives to the "inflation tax" and the deadweight losses they entail.

2. The second assumption implies that savers' long-run demands for wealth in aggregate and for individual assets are infinitely elastic at the constant rate of return ρ. Savers will hold whatever quantities of assets yield them that total return, implicit plus explicit. Suppose instead that wealth demand is finite at any rate of return, possibly inelastic or possibly following a schedule along which the required return is greater as wealth is larger. Then imagine, for example, a variation of policy, or some other exogenous change, that lowers the in-

flation rate and adds to the demand for real money balances. It may thus add to the total demand for wealth. But if the public will hold more wealth only when its general intertemporal consumption return is higher, other assets—including capital—will have to clear a higher hurdle. Therefore their stocks will be cut back to make room for at least some of the additional money desired.

The difference between perfectly and imperfectly elastic wealth demand can be associated with the difference between infinite and finite horizons in household saving behavior. We noted above that infinite horizons are essential for the Ricardian equivalence theorem, and it is not surprising they are also crucial for superneutrality. Consider steady growth equilibrium of a money-capital model with immortal consumers. Along every possible path the rate of growth of per capita consumption is the same, namely the exogenous rate of labor-augmenting technological progress. There will be some intertemporal discount rate, some terms on which present consumption can be exchanged for future, that will make the typical consumer content with the path, content not to make any intertemporal exchanges that deviate from it. This discount rate ρ is formally $\delta + \lambda \epsilon$, where δ is the pure rate of time preference, λ the rate of growth of per capita consumption, and $-\epsilon$ the elasticity of the marginal utility of consumption with respect to consumption.[i] The term δ allows for

[i]If real money balances are added as an argument in the direct utility function—a very questionable practice—as in Sidrauski [28, 1967] and Fischer [17, 1978], the expression for ϵ is somewhat different. c denotes real per capita consumption, m the stock of real per capita money balances, a real per capita household wealth, k the stock of capital per unit of efficiency labor, L the size of the natural labor force, $\tilde{L}$ the size of the labor force in efficiency units, p the price level, T lump-sum transfers, and M the nominal stock of money. $\dot{L}/L = n$ and $\dot{\tilde{L}}/\tilde{L} = n + \lambda$. The model can be written as

$$\text{maximize} \quad \int_0^\infty u(c,m)e^{-\delta t}dt$$

$$\text{subject to} \quad m + \frac{\tilde{L}}{L}\, \tilde{k} = a$$

$$\dot{a} = \frac{\tilde{L}}{L}\, f(\tilde{k}) + \frac{T}{pL} - c - \frac{\dot{p}}{p}\, m - na$$

$$\dot{\tilde{k}} = f(\tilde{k}) - \frac{L}{\tilde{L}}\, c - (n + \lambda)\tilde{k}$$

$$\dot{M} = T.$$

the postponement of consumption and the term $\lambda \epsilon$ for its declining marginal utility. Both time preference δ and the elasticity $-\epsilon$ must be constants, independent of time and consumption level, for a steady state to be possible at all. This condition also implies that ρ is the same in every steady state, for the steady states differ in level of consumption path and not in λ. The equilibrium steady state is the one for which the marginal productivity of capital, *net of the rate of population growth n*, is equal to ρ. Immortal consumers, in the form of households who anticipate the number of their descendants and the utilities of each, internalize the capital requirements of population growth.

On the other hand, a life cycle or finite horizon model of saving and wealth demand is also consistent with steady state growth equilibrium. We argued above that for many reasons it is the more realistic model. The life cycle model implies that the aggregate desired wealth-to-consumption ratio is a finite constant along any path of steady growth. Its value depends on the age distribution of the population and thus on its rate of growth; the typical age-earnings profile, which depends in turn on the rate of technological progress; and the age-consumption profile chosen by the typical household, which will in general vary with the returns to saving. There is a definite age sequence of wealth holdings for each household, and by summation over households of various ages a finite aggregate wealth demand at each date. The desired ratio of wealth to labor income or to con-

---

The first two constraints are individual balance sheet and budget constraints; the last two are economy-wide constraints. An interior solution to this problem is given by the four constraints and by

$$u_c \left(f' + \frac{\dot{p}}{p} \right) - u_m = 0$$

$$u_c (f' - n - \delta) + u_{cc} \dot{c} + u_{cm} \dot{m} = 0.$$

In long-run equilibrium the last equation becomes $f' = n + \delta + \epsilon\lambda$,

where $-\epsilon = c \dfrac{u_{cc}}{u_c} + m \dfrac{u_{cm}}{u_c}$, the sum of the elasticities of the marginal util-

ity of consumption with respect to consumption and to real money balances. For a steady state to exist if $\lambda > 0$ we require not only that ϵ be constant but

that $\dfrac{u_m}{u_c}$ be constant, that is, that

$$c \frac{u_{mc}}{u_m} + m \frac{u_{mm}}{u_m} + \epsilon \quad \text{be constant.}$$

sumption may be greater when returns to capital and other assets are higher. In any case capital must compete with other assets in the portfolios of life cycle savers. If they decide to hold more money, it will be at least partly at the expense of capital.

Asset interdependence and finite interest-sensitive wealth demand are assumed in our formal model of the Appendix, discussed in Section IV. We impose some further restrictions on asset and wealth demand functions. The demand for each asset, in relation to income, depends on the entire list of explicit rates of return. So also does the demand for wealth in total. Assets are assumed to be gross substitutes: an increase in the return on any asset, other things equal, raises the demand for that asset and diminishes, or anyway does not increase, the demand for any other. The net effect on demand for wealth is assumed to be positive or zero. Thus expectation of higher inflation may be, as often warned, a disincentive to saving. But it is mainly a disincentive to saving in the form of money and actually a positive incentive to save in other assets, particularly goods and equities in goods. The net effect on total saving might well be negative, but—other things equal—it seems likely that a reduction in the real rate of return on money will make savers wish to accumulate more of those assets which have become relatively more attractive. This is why our model implies that higher steady inflation rates, expected and realized, are generally associated with greater capital formation.

It may seem paradoxical that the long-run capital intensity of the economy can be greater under policies that diminish the total private propensity to save. Total saving is (in a closed economy) necessarily equal to capital investment plus the government deficit, all in real terms. Likewise, total private real wealth is equal to the sum of the capital stock and the real value of government debt, bonds plus money. Investment and capital stock can be larger, while private saving and wealth are smaller, if and only if the government's deficit and debt are even smaller in real terms. Now in long-run steady states the real magnitudes of the deficit and debt are not determined by the government alone, but also by the willingness of savers to acquire and hold government liabilities. These liabilities are expressed in nominal terms, that is, in dollars, and the price *level* is free to adjust the real values of the stocks to the amounts desired by savers and wealth-holders. Policies that lead to more inflation diminish those desired holdings, and by our assumptions about asset choice diminish them by more than they reduce total private saving. This is why those policies allow more room for capital formation.

Things are not always what they seem, and policy variations sometimes have consequences the reverse of normal intuition and the reverse of their short-run effects. The rate of growth of government liabilities, of money or of promises to pay money, is not itself a policy parameter. It is the endogenous outcome of basic policy parameters: government expenditure, taxation, the composition of deficits and debt. An increase in spending or reduction in taxation appears to be a deficit-increasing policy. But such a policy does not necessarily increase the steady-state *real* deficit or debt relative to national output. By leading to more inflation it may make government liabilities less attractive, and the price level will then be enough higher to diminish the real quantities of those liabilities to the amounts that savers desire. Thus a fiscal or financial policy that looks expansionary, and is inflationary, may in the final analysis absorb less saving rather than more, and divert saving into capital formation.

To illustrate the mechanism we compare tax finance and money finance in a steadily growing economy with only two assets, money and capital. In this example interest-bearing public debt is ignored for simplicity. The natural growth rate is g, and a constant fraction z of real national output Y is purchased by government. Taxes, net of transfers, are a proportion t of Y. Let H/p be the real stock of government-issued high-powered money held by the public. Let i be the actual and expected rate of inflation $\dot{p}/p$, and h be the rate of growth of the nominal money stock $\dot{H}/H$. In a steady state we know that $h = g + i$. The government's budget equation is

$$\dot{H}/p = h(H/p) = (z-t)Y = (g+i)(H/p) \quad \text{or} \quad z = (g+i)(H/pY) + t.$$

Now if $h = g$ and $i = 0$, t must be $z - gH/pY$. Compare a more inflationary policy: $h' > g$, yielding $i' > 0$. Now t' must be $z - h'H/pY$, equal to $t - i'H/pY$ if H/pY is the same. The inflation tax $i'H/pY$ is substituted for part of the explicit tax t. But it doesn't make sense to assume that H/pY remains the same. Presumably it will be smaller, because reduction in the real return on money—possibly also increase in the after-tax return on capital—shifts saving and wealth from money to capital. Capital stock is higher relative to labor force and output, and its before-tax return is accordingly lower.

If the asset substitution elasticity is very high, an inflation tax cannot be substituted for explicit taxation. Indeed a more inflationary policy might be associated with a *higher* tax rate t. To state the matter the other way round, the only way to have a low real deficit might be to have such a high inflation rate that people are reconciled to the small quantity of money the tight fiscal policy supplies. It would require a value exceeding unity for the total (that is, not holding other rates of return constant but allowing them to adjust as necessary to restore equilibrium) elasticity of demand for high-powered money with respect to the sum of the inflation rate and the growth rate (E_h). Note that this condition could be met, for positive inflation rates, even if the absolute value of the elasticity of money demand with respect to the inflation rate, E_i, is smaller than unity, as conventionally believed, since $E_h = [1 + (g/i)]E_i$.

Notice that we are here comparing two steady states, one with a higher tax take t than the other, and asking which has the higher inflation rate. In theory the answer can go either way. It depends on the relationship of the product $h(H/pY)$ to h. The higher the tax rate the lower this product must be. If a reduction in the inflation rate i lowers the product—as will be the case if the H/pY desired by the public is not very sensitive to i—then i will be lower in a steady state with a higher t. If an increase in the inflation rate i lowers the product—the H/pY desired by the public is very sensitive to i—then i will be higher in a steady state with higher t. These comparisons say nothing about the stability of steady state equilibria. We may well suspect that the second possibility—higher t associated with higher i—is unstable. After all, in the short run we expect an increase in tax rate, a tightening of fiscal policy, to slow down inflation. The range of possible outcomes becomes even wider when government interest-bearing debt is included as a third asset.

IV. A MODEL OF ASSET MARKETS AND MACROECONOMIC POLICIES

Here we summarize the results of a formal analysis of short-run and long-run effects of government fiscal and financial policies. The mathematical model and analysis are presented in the Appendix.

Structure of the Model

The model focuses on the balance of supply and demand in three asset markets: high-powered money, government bonds, and claims to productive capital. In an extension of the model to apply to an open economy, a fourth asset—securities of foreign issue denominated in foreign currency—is added.

In the short run, the public begins with initial holdings of the several assets and decides how much to accumulate of each one during a period of time. These decisions are saving and portfolio choices combined. They depend on the rates of return expected of the assets, on income and taxes, and on the initial holdings. On the supply side, the increments of money and government debt depend on the government's budget deficit and on how it is financed. Also, the central bank can, during any period, engage in open market transactions in money and government securities, and in foreign assets in the open-economy model. The incremental supply of capital during the period results from real investment decisions, which are taken to depend on the difference between the expected rate of profit on the commodity cost of capital goods and the market yield on equity claims. The increment to the nation's stock of foreign assets is the surplus in international current-account transactions.

In the long-run steady state, asset stocks are stationary in real terms, or are growing at a common constant rate, the natural rate of growth of the economy, that is, the sum of the rate of growth of the labor force and the rate of labor-augmenting technical progress. The asset demand/supply equations of the model then refer to stocks that meet the steady-state condition. Stocks are adjustable to savers' preferences in the long run, unconstrained by initial holdings. The parameters of fiscal and financial policy determine the available supplies of money and government debt per unit of output or per efficiency unit of labor. For capital the long-run supply function is the technological relation between capital intensity—the capital/output ratio or ratio of capital to efficiency labor—and the rate of return to capital. In an open economy the current account payments surplus must keep the stock of foreign assets, measured in purchasing power over domestic goods, constant relative to output. Long-run asset demands depend on real rates of return including the real return on money, the negative of the inflation rate.

Note that balance of the government budget is not a requirement of long-run equilibrium, even if the natural rate of growth is zero.[j] A constant real steady-state deficit per unit of output provides for the required growth in the nominal stocks of money and government bonds. The inflation rate is endogenous and can adjust to reconcile a large variety of deficit outcomes to the steady-state conditions of the previous paragraph. In long-run equilibrium the nominal stocks of money and government bonds must grow at the natural rate of

---

[j] Some earlier contributions [11, Carl Christ, 1968; 4, Alan Blinder and Robert Solow, 1973; 32, Tobin and Buiter, 1976] may have fostered the opposite view. See, however [25, Edmund S. Phelps and Karl Shell, 1969] and [7, Buiter, 1977; 12, Christ, 1978; and 13, David Currie, 1978; 14, 1978]. It is true that budget balance is an equilibrium condition for stationary economies with fixed price level, as discussed in [4, Blinder and Solow, 1973] and [32, Tobin and Buiter, 1976]. But in general this is not true, and therefore one cannot derive long-run effects of policy measures from a balanced budget equation. All steady-state relations, including long-run portfolio balance equations, enter into determination of the long-run policy multipliers.

growth plus the rate of inflation. Of course, if the deficit is endogenous its equilibrium value might happen to be zero. Or a balanced budget might be a deliberate policy choice. In these cases the stocks of government-issued assets would be constant in nominal amounts in long-run equilibrium, and their real growth at the natural rate would be accomplished by steady deflation. Steady-state budget surpluses would mean dwindling nominal stocks accompanied by price deflation faster than the natural rate.

Applied to the short run, the three asset equations of the closed economy model determine three variables in each period. Two of these within-period endogenous variables are rates of return, on government bonds and capital equity. The third real rate of return, that on money, is not endogenously determined within a period. The expected rate of inflation is taken to be predetermined from past history; it varies, but only as periods go by and history accumulates. Thus the system of three equations is free to determine a third variable each period. Two obvious choices are real income and price level. These correspond to the two short-run environments discussed throughout the chapter: an underemployment case, in which output is demand-determined at historically predetermined prices, and a full employment situation in which output is supply-constrained and the price level adjusts flexibly within the period. An intermediate case would involve adding a within-period price adjustment equation and solving for both price and output. The open economy model adds one equation. The corresponding endogenous variable is either the foreign exchange rate or, for a regime of fixed parities, the quantity of foreign assets purchased or sold by the central bank and government.

In the long run the inflation rate is endogenous, along with the real rates of return on capital and government bonds. The inflation rate, moreover, affects both asset demands and asset supplies, in ways discussed in Section III. No equation is needed for output or the price level. The capital/output ratio follows immediately from the solution value of the return on capital; given this ratio and an initial condition the path of real income is determined. Likewise, once the solution of the system gives the permanent inflation rate, an initial value for any nominal variable suffices to pin down the path of prices.

The short-run system can be viewed as a generalized Keynesian "*IS−LM*" model. (The *IS* equation is actually the sum of the asset demand/supply equations, and we do not use it explicitly in our analysis in the Appendix. The same results could be obtained by dropping one of the asset equations instead and keeping the *IS* relation.) The major generalization is on the portfolio side. Keynes's assumption of perfect substitutability between long-term bonds and equity is dropped. Instead all the three or four assets are assumed to be gross substitutes, both in short-run saving decisions and in long-run portfolio choice. For the purposes of this chapter we retained the simplifying assumption of aggregation, that the economy produces one homogeneous commodity, usable either in consumption or in investment or as exports. It is not, however, the same as the commodity imported from abroad. Conversion of current output into capital is subject to diminishing returns; rapid additions to the capital stock entail adjustment costs. This is why the rate of investment is a finite increasing function of the difference between the marginal efficiency of capital at normal replacement cost and the market yield of equity. Finally, for the purposes of this chapter it was not necessary to model the labor market separately.

We deliberately chose to model time in discrete periods, within which variables assume one value and one value only. At each hypothetical set of values of endogenous variables the agents in asset markets formulate demands and supplies related to positions desired at the end of the period. The clearing of the markets determines an "end-of-period" equilibrium (Duncan Foley [18, 1975], Buiter [5, 1975]). This means that the saving decision and the portfolio allocation decision cannot be separated.[k] In addition, government deficits have time within the period to add to supplies of money or bonds or both, business investment increases the supply of equities in the same period, and current account surpluses immediately augment the supply of foreign assets. The continuous-time $IS-LM$ snap-shot has been charged with failure to take account of the stock-increasing effects of the flows its solution generates. These could be handled by dynamic analysis that tracks stocks. Otherwise the $IS-LM$ account of the effects of a deficit-increasing fiscal policy omits the financial consequences of the additions to stocks of money or debt that will occur with the passage of time. Some critics have contended that such neglect of the "government budget constraint" is responsible for misleading conclusions about the effects of fiscal policy. The short run of our model, which does not neglect the government budget identity or any other mechanical flow-stock relationships, does not substantiate this complaint. It shows that stan-

---

[k]This approach is therefore different from the continuous time portfolio balance approach. The latter permits separate treatment of the saving decision—adding to existing wealth—and the portfolio allocation decision—the reshuffling of existing net worth [30, Tobin, 1969].

dard Keynesian conclusions survive explicit recognition of these phenomena.

Short-Run Policy Effects

In the short run an increase in public spending or a cut in taxes will stimulate output in the unemployment model or raise the price level in the full employment model. Investment varies positively with current profits per unit of capital and negatively with the rate of return on equity, the required rate of return on capital. In the short run, profits per unit of capital increase with the level of output. The positive effect on output of expansionary fiscal policy in the unemployment model will therefore encourage investment. There will be "crowding in."

In the full employment model this effect is absent. The effect of changes in public spending and taxation on the required rate of return on capital depends crucially on the manner in which the government finances its budget deficits or surpluses. If money financing is chosen, the required rate of return on capital is lowered by an increase in public spending or a tax cut, both in the full employment model and in the unemployment model. In both cases expansionary fiscal policy combined with accommodative monetary policy "crowds in" investment. If mixed financing or bond financing is chosen, the effect on the required rate of return on capital, r_K, is ambiguous. With bond financed deficits, r_K is more likely to increase if bonds and equity are close substitutes. If r_K increases, expansionary fiscal policy definitely "crowds out" private investment in the full employment model. In the unemployment model the negative effect on investment of a higher r_K will be offset at least partly by higher output and profits.

An open market sale of bonds raises the real rate of return on bonds. It lowers output in the unemployment model and the price level in the full employment model. The rate of return on equity is likely to be increased if government bonds and equity are close substitutes, lowered if bonds and money are close substitutes.

There is a widely held view that the combination of contractionary fiscal policy and expansionary monetary policy favors investment. We evaluate this proposition by considering the effect on investment of different combinations of fiscal and financial policy parameters that keep constant real output or the price level. For example, raise taxes or reduce public spending and compensate for the contractionary effect by raising the share of money in financing the deficit. The traditional view is confirmed for a reduction in public spending combined with an increase in the share of money. A tax increase, however, may by its direct effect on disposable income, have such a strong negative effect on the demand for equity, that r_K increases, discouraging investment.

It is sometimes argued that an increase in public spending, or a tax cut, raises inflation expectations, especially if financed by printing money. The model shows that a rise in inflation expectations will give a boost to investment by encouraging a portfolio shift toward real assets. This conclusion might not hold if the higher expected rate of inflation were systematically accompanied by increased uncertainty about the future. It would not hold if households and businesses have learned to expect severely restrictive monetary and fiscal measures whenever the expected rate of inflation increases.

Long-Run Policy Effects

Analysis of the long-run effects of fiscal and financial policies proceeds by comparison of balanced growth paths. All real stocks and flows grow at the natural rate of growth, the sum of the rate of growth of the labor force and the rate of labor-augmenting technical change. Expectations are realized. The economy is fully adjusted to the values assumed by the policy instruments.

In Section III above a number of long-run policy issues have already been discussed, especially those concerned with superneutrality. The propositions advanced there are formally substantiated in the Appendix. In the three-asset model, the long-run effects of fiscal policy changes on variables like the capital-output ratio and the rate of inflation are complicated and frequently ambiguous without further quantitative information. A number of propositions emerge clearly, however.

Long-run crowding out of private capital by public spending or by a shift from tax financing to bond or money financing is a possibility, but not a necessity. The proximate effect of an increase in public spending or a cut in taxes—for a given rate of inflation and given values of the real rates of return on bonds and capital—is to increase the steady-state stocks of bonds and money. *Ceteris paribus* this will stimulate the demand for capital without affecting the supply. There will therefore be a tendency for the required rate of return on capital to go down and for the capital-output ratio to increase. Of course, this is not the complete story. The proximate effect of these same policy changes on the bond market and the money market is to create excess supply. If bonds and equity are close substitutes, this will create upward pressure on r_K. When we allow for these further substitution and wealth effects, the final outcome can go either way.

Neither "crowding out" nor "crowding in" can be ruled out on a priori grounds.

Implications of the Analysis for Open Economies

The analysis is extended to an economy that is open to international commodity trade and financial transactions. The home country is large in the market for its exports and small in the market for its imports. The terms of trade are therefore endogenous. The asset menu is enlarged by adding an internationally traded financial claim, denominated in foreign currency. Domestic government bonds, money, and equity are not internationally traded, and the internationally traded asset is a gross substitute, but not a perfect substitute, for the domestic assets. Therefore, both the quantity of money and either the exchange rate or the official settlements deficit in international payments can be controlled by domestic policy.

In both fixed and floating exchange rate regimes, the short-run effects of fiscal and financial policy on output, the required rate of return on capital and the rate of investment are very similar to those in the closed economy. The open economy model, of course, explains a wider set of endogenous variables, including the current account, the capital account, and either the official settlements balance or the exchange rate, depending on the regime. It also includes an additional instrument of financial policy: either the exchange rate or the volume of open market transactions in the internationally traded asset by the monetary authority.

The possibility of long-run "crowding in" of capital by expansionary fiscal policy, discussed above for the closed economy model, also applies to the open economy. Perhaps more important than the sign of these long-run multipliers is the conclusion that changes in fiscal, monetary and financial instruments will have real effects, short run and long run. Properly specified econometric models will not be policy-neutral. In general, *both* fiscal and monetary instruments have domestic macroeconomic consequences in the expected directions in both exchange rate regimes, fixed and floating. It is also true that floating exchange rates will not insulate the economy from foreign shocks, for example changes in export demand.

V. CONCLUDING REMARKS

The economic performance of the United States and other capitalist democracies in the 1970s has been disappointing in many respects. The non-Communist world has suffered the deepest recession, the highest general inflation, and the most unemployment of the three decades since the Second World War. Until the late 1960s the postwar record had been remarkably good, twenty years of unparalleled stability, prosperity, and growth. Many observers, economists and others, assigned much credit to the active use of government fiscal and financial policies for management of aggregate demand. But with the reverses of the 1970s, disillusion and reaction have replaced earlier euphoria, and the same government policies receive much of the blame. Within the economics profession and beyond, intellectual challenges to the neo-Keynesian foundations of macroeconomic policy are increasingly influential.

One dimension of recent economic performance that has evoked widespread concern, particularly in the United States, is the low rate of private nonresidential capital formation. The share of potential GNP devoted to this purpose, always low in this country compared to other more rapidly growing economies, has fallen in this decade. A future capital shortage, inhibiting growth in output and employment, is predicted and feared. One aspect of the disenchantment with government policies is the charge that they inhibit capital formation, overtaxing the earnings of capital, channeling an excessive share of the nation's resources to the public sector, diverting into finance of budget deficits private saving that would otherwise finance private investment. The growth of the federal budget in the last decade and the large deficits realized in recent years of recession and slow recovery have accentuated the charges of "crowding out." At the same time, the inflation of the 1970s has been attributed to government financial policies.

In the economics profession the reaction against neo-Keynesian macroeconomic theory and policy has taken two distinct shapes. Both find the theory mistaken and the policies unsuccessful. One school, following traditional conservative lines, also finds the policies harmful and dangerous, distorting the allocation of resources, crowding out private investment, and causing debilitating inflation. The other school, the *new* classical macroeconomics, finds the policies ineffectual, harmless except that the public has to go to the trouble of figuring them out and bypassing them.

In this setting, our chapter has reexamined the theory of the macroeconomic effects of fiscal and financial policies. Our conclusions are intellectually conservative, in the sense that we confirm the general thrust of the neo-Keynesian paradigm. But we hope that our analysis contains some novel features. We reject the neutrality propositions of the new Ricardian theorists who contend that the financing of government expenditure—whether by taxation, bond issue, or printing money—makes no difference to real economic outcomes. The conditions required for these neutrality propositions are so special and so unrealistic that it would be foolish and foolhardy to base policy upon them. Thus we agree with the more traditional critics of demand management policies that they are capable of doing harm as well as good. We do not agree that they have done nothing but harm, or all the harm attributed to them.

We share the concerns about the inadequacy of capital formation in the United States in recent years. The federal government should be concerned about it, too. The neutrality doctrines that we have criticized in this chapter imply that the government need not worry about the nation's economic future because citizens as individuals will take care of it on their own. This is bad advice, whether applied to the conservation of natural resources or to the overall management of the economy. Government is an essential part of the mechanism by which societies provide for their continuity and survival; one big reason for its institution is to make collective provisions for future generations supplementing the provisions individuals make for their own descendants.

It is important to be clear when and how government finance crowds out capital investment and when and how it encourages it, crowds it *in*. One of the more misguided episodes of recent public economic discussion was the flurry of anxiety about "crowding out" when the government was running large deficits in 1975 and 1976. The economy had barely begun to recover from the severe recession of 1974—75. The deficits were largely the result of the depressed level of business activity, which lowered taxable income and raised entitlements to unemployment insurance and other transfers. They were partly the result of modest tax rebates and reductions voted by the Congress to stimulate recovery. High unemployment and excess capacity indicated that the economy was operating nowhere near its productive potential. Capital investment was low, not because saving and finance were in short supply, but because excess capacity, low equity prices, and dim prospects of future sales made it unattractive. In these circumstances it was absurd to complain that federal deficits were displacing private investment. Additional government spending or tax reduction probably would have stimulated—crowded in— investment. Resources were adequate to increase consumption, government purchases, and investment all at the same time. Certainly the opposite policies, had they been adopted in an effort to trim the deficit, would have slowed the recovery or prolonged the recession and made investment even weaker. As we stressed in previous sections, it is important to distinguish situations in which output is limited by resources and investment is limited by potentially available saving from cases in which output and investment are both limited by demand.

In underemployment situations any crowding out that occurs through financial stringency is the work of the central bank. If the monetary authority refuses to accommodate increases in output in response to fiscal stimulus, then rising interest rates and declining share prices will indeed deter some investment. Only if the central bank's view of the desirable path of total output is accepted can fiscal policy be blamed for substituting consumption, private and public, for investment. In Section I we discussed the importance of coordinating fiscal and monetary policy. Unfortunately, the repeated use of fiscal measures for stimulus and of monetary measures for restraint results in a policy mix unfavorable to capital formation in the long run. A mix favorable to investment would involve an easier monetary stance offset by taxes bearing particularly on consumption.

Economists have long debated the optimal trend of prices—rising, stable, or falling. An advantage of a steadily rising price level is the incentive it gives for investment in real productive capital, by making the holding of wealth in liquid form unrewarding. We examine and formalize this idea in the body of the chapter, and we investigate the fiscal and financial implications of policies aimed at high long-run capital/labor ratios. Deficit finance provides the growing nominal stocks of money and debt that sustain steady inflation and, somewhat paradoxically, reduce the *real* stocks desired by savers. So it is quite possible that deficit finance, especially if an adequate share of it takes monetary form, "crowds in" capital formation. If so, this effect is purchased at the cost of depriving the society of the services that larger stocks of money and debt, with higher explicit returns, could provide.

A theoretical finding that steady inflation is favorable to capital investment no doubt seems bizarre in the 1970s, when the opposite view has become an unquestioned article of faith in business and financial circles. The reason is that the central bank, government, and public are committed to bring down a rate of inflation generally regarded as intolerable. The only weapons at their command are restrictive financial policies that slow the economy down, causing recessions, or interventions in private price decisions and wage bargains. These weapons all seem to threaten profitability, and that is why inflation news is discouraging to investors. By the same token disinflation would be a good sign, but only if the authorities took advantage of it to aim for higher aggregate output and faster growth.

Is there a long-run investment-oriented strategy that does not rely on deficits and inflation to diminish savers' preferences for liquid forms of wealth? The government could serve more directly and explicitly as a financial intermediary, investing in private sector financial claims the proceeds of issuing its unique monetary and non-monetary obligations. Then the public could enjoy the services these assets provide without tying up in them any net saving at the expense of capital formation. There is no reason that the assets of Federal Reserve Banks cannot include private debts and even equities, as well as Treasury obligations.

The economic malaise of the 1970s relates at bottom to the intractable inflation/unemployment dilemma, a problem outside the scope of our paper. Government financial policy is the scapegoat for the frustrations bred by stubborn stagflation. No doubt some policy errors, notably the deficit financing of the Vietnam war, contributed to our present plight. But inflationary bias seems to be endemic in the political and economic institutions of modern capitalist democracies. It is naive whistling in the dark to think that the problem will disappear if only central banks and legislatures follow different monetary and fiscal rules. The combinations of inflation and unemployment feasible with existing policy instruments are just not acceptable to the society. Unless we find new instruments to make acceptable combinations feasible, or until we wearily decide that some feasible combination is acceptable, macroeconomic performance will continue to be disappointing and frustrating, and capital formation and other provisions for the future will continue to be inadequate.

Appendix

A FORMAL MODEL OF SHORT- AND LONG-RUN EFFECTS OF FISCAL AND FINANCIAL POLICIES

Notation

r_K : real one-period after-tax return on capital.

r_B : real one-period rate of return on government bonds.

r_H : real one-period rate of return on money balances.

r_A : real one-period rate of return on foreign assets.

r_A^*	:rate of return on foreign assets in terms of foreign currency.
p	:price of domestic output.
p_f^*	:price of imports in terms of foreign currency.
w	:unit labor cost.
q_K	:price of installed capital in terms of current output.
q_B	:price of government bonds in dollars.
e	:foreign exchange rate (number of dollars per unit of foreign exchange).
b	:coupon on the government bond in dollars per period.
$x(p)$	:expected one-period proportional rate of change in p.
$x(q_K)$	:expected one-period proportional rate of change in q_K.
$x(q_B)$	:expected one-period proportional rate of change in q_B.
$x(e)$	:expected one-period proportional rate of change in e.
H	:nominal stock of money balances per unit of efficiency labor.
B	:number of government bonds per unit of efficiency labor.
K	:capital per unit of efficiency labor.
A	:value, in foreign exchange, of foreign bonds held by the private sector, per unit of efficiency labor.
$\hat{A}$	:value, in foreign exchange, of foreign bonds held by the public sector, per unit of efficiency labor.
Y	:real output per unit of efficiency labor.
I	:resources devoted to investment per unit of efficiency labor.
G	:government spending on goods and services per unit of efficiency labor.
X	:trade balance surplus per unit of efficiency labor.
R	:real profits before taxes per unit of capital.
D	:real value of public sector deficit per unit of efficiency labor.
T	:real taxes net of transfers per unit of efficiency labor.
t	:proportional tax rate on factor income.
γ_B	:share of the public sector deficit or surplus financed by bonds.

γ_H :share of the public sector deficit or surplus financed by money.

Z_B :dollar value of total net government bond sales, per unit of efficiency labor, minus the value of bond sales associated with the financing of the public sector deficit through the deficit financing rule of our model. A negative value of Z_B means government purchases of bonds.

Z_H :dollar value of total net money issues by the government, per unit of efficiency labor, minus the value of money issues associated with the financing of the public sector deficit through the deficit financing rule of our model. A negative value of Z_H means government purchases of money.

Z_A :dollar value of total net sales of foreign bonds by the government, per unit of efficiency labor. A negative value of Z_A means government purchases of foreign bonds.

n :proportional rate of growth of the labor force.

λ :proportional rate of labor augmenting technical change.

$g = n + \lambda$

$i = \Delta p/p$

Δ :forward difference operator $\Delta Z(\tau) \equiv Z(\tau+1) - Z(\tau)$, where τ designates period.

$\bar{Q}$:Q per unit of output.

I. THE CLOSED ECONOMY MODEL

The model is essentially a representation of asset demands and supplies, both stocks and flows. Three assets are available to wealthowners: government fiat money, perpetual government bonds paying a coupon of b dollars per period, and equity claims to real capital.

One share of equity represents ownership of one unit of physical capital. One good is produced and can either be used as a private or public consumption good or can be converted, at some cost, into durable productive capital. The real price of a unit of installed capital and the real value of a share of equity, q_K, is equal to the marginal cost of producing goods and converting them into capital. This cost depends each period on the amount of new investment relative to the existing stock.

"Equity" in our model stands for all claims on the productive capital assets of business enterprises and on the earnings from those assets. In actuality, of course, such claims take a variety of forms, including debts denominated in dollars as well as shares. We do not model those business financial decisions that determine the supplies of the several types of claims or the separate demands of savers for them. Our "equity" stands for the whole package of shares and debts of business. The reader should not identify it with shares alone. Thus the q_K to which real investment is related below would be empirically approximated by summing the market values of all financial claims on business firms, debts as well as shares, netting out financial assets of firms, and comparing the resulting net market value to the replacement cost of the real capital stock at commodity prices. Likewise the real world counterpart of the return to "equity," r_K, would not be the one-period yield of shares alone but a properly weighted average of the yields of the several claims on capital stock and earnings. Interest and appreciation on bonds would enter this calculation, along with dividends and appreciation on stocks.

While our framework could easily handle a larger menu of assets, for example, splitting "equity" into shares and business debts, the simpler three-asset model is capable of handling the issues addressed in this paper. The Modigliani-Miller theorem justifies aggregation of financial claims on a business firm into a single asset by showing that, under certain conditions, the value and yield of the aggregate are independent of its composition. The conditions are unrealistically restrictive, and disaggregation would be important and interesting for a number of problems. But for our present purposes, all we need is that the package of claims we call "equity" be a gross substitute for the two government-issued assets in our model. Our treatment implies that corporate bonds and government bonds are not perfect substitutes for each other. If they were, corporations could finance virtually all their capital investment at the government bond rate. Our three-asset model respects the essential distinction between interest-bearing claims on government and claims, of whatever financial form, on private business. But most of our results would stand even if we adopted the frequent convention of macroeconomic models of requiring government bonds to bear the same real return as "equity."

Asset demands are for end-of-period stocks to be carried over to the next period. Market supplies consist of stocks carried over from the previous period and new "production" of assets during the period. Thus current period flows of financial claims—generated by public sector deficits or private sector investment—have immediate effects in asset markets. Equations (A.1), (A.2), and (A.3) represent demand/supply equilibrium for one period for the three assets:

$$F^K - q_K K = I(q_K, K) \tag{A.1}$$

$$F^B - q_B \frac{B}{p} = \gamma_B (G + \frac{b}{p} B - T) + \frac{Z_B}{p} \tag{A.2}$$

$$F^H - \frac{H}{p} = \gamma_H (G + \frac{b}{p} B - T) + \frac{Z_H}{p} . \tag{A.3}$$

The left-hand sides represent savers' demand for acquisition of the several assets during the period. They are in each case the difference between the market value of the stock desired at the end of the period (F^K, F^B, F^H), each expressed in real terms, and the real value of the beginning-of-period stock (K, B, H). The end-of-period stock demands F^K, F^B, F^H are all functions of the same list of variables: the three rates of return r_K, r_B, r_H; the values of the initial stocks $q_K K, q_B B/p, H/p$; real output Y and taxes T. We impose the following restrictions on these demand functions. With respect to rates of return, the assets are gross-substitutes. An increase in any rate of return increases total asset demand $F^K + F^B + F^H$. An increase in the value of beginning-of-period asset holdings or current income is allocated over all three assets. An increase in the aggregate value of any initial holding increases total asset demand but by less than the increment in the initial holding; it increases consumption too.

A fourth equilibrium condition, the *IS* curve, is implied by the other three. Let S denote real saving:

$$S \equiv F^K + F^B + F^H - (q_K K + q_B \frac{B}{p} + \frac{H}{p}) = I + G + \frac{bB}{p} - T. \tag{A.4}$$

The investment function is given by

$$I = I(q_K, K) \quad (I(1,K) = (n+\lambda)K; \ I_{q_K} > 0; \ I_K < 0). \tag{A.5}$$

Taxes, net of transfers, are simply proportional to output:

$$T = tY \ (0 < t < 1). \tag{A.6}$$

Coupons on government bonds are free of tax. Capital gains are not taxed. Earnings of capital are taxed before distribution to shareowners.

The government deficit $G + (bB)/p - T$ is financed either by printing money or by issuing bonds, in proportions γ_H and γ_B, respectively. Open market operations are swaps of money for bonds of equal value. Thus

$$\gamma_B + \gamma_H = 1 \qquad (\gamma_B, \gamma_H \geq 0) \tag{A.7a}$$

$$Z_B + Z_H = 0. \tag{A.7b}$$

Real one-period rates of return are related to current and expected asset prices as follows:

$$r_B \approx \frac{b}{q_B} + x(q_B) - x(p) \tag{A.8a}$$

$$r_K \approx \frac{R(1-t)}{q_K} + x(q_K) \tag{A.8b}$$

$$r_H \approx -x(p). \tag{A.8c}$$

Profits per unit of capital vary positively with real output and inversely with the capital stock:

$$R = R(K/Y) \qquad R' < 0. \tag{A.9}$$

For the short-run analysis of the model, we consider two versions: one with price p predetermined for the period and, thanks to unemployment of labor and capital, with output in infinitely elastic supply at the prevailing price; the other with full employment and a price level completely flexible. In the full employment version the capacity constraint is

$$Y = f(K) \qquad (f' > 0; \; f'' < 0). \tag{A.10a}$$

In the unemployment version price is set for the period by past history. But events of the period determine the next period price, via an augmented price Phillips curve:

$$\frac{\Delta p}{p} = \psi(Y - f(K)) + x(p) \qquad \psi' > 0; \; \psi(0) = 0. \tag{A.10b}$$

$x(p)$ could be interpreted as the expectation of inflation. If so, (A.10b) implies that actual output can differ from full capacity output if and only if there are errors in the inflation forecast. Another interpretation is that $x(p)$ depends on the past history of prices and stands for all the factors in the economy that give inertia to built-in trends in wages and prices. In either case the first term of (A.10b) could differ systematically and for many periods from zero. With the first interpretation this will be the case if there is gradual adjustment of inflation expectations, as exemplified, for example, by an adaptive expectation mechanism. With the second interpretation, anticipated stabilization policy can have systematic effects on real output even if rational expectations or perfect foresight prevail. (See note a.) The dynamics of the model are provided by changes of assets stocks and of expectations, and by the Phillips curve in the unemployment version.

For most of the analysis, we assume that the expected rates of change of q_B, q_K, and p are predetermined each period. As time passes, they are revised in response to forecast errors.

$$\Delta x(q_B) = \alpha_1 \left(\Delta q_B / q_B - x(q_B) \right) \tag{A.11a}$$

$$\Delta x(q_K) = \alpha_2 \left(\Delta q_K / q_K - x(q_K) \right) \qquad (\alpha_1, \alpha_2, \alpha_3 \geq 0) \tag{A.11b}$$

$$\Delta x(p) = \alpha_3 \left(\Delta p / p - x(p) \right) = \alpha_3 \left(i - x(p) \right). \tag{A.11c}$$

The changes of real asset stocks (per unit of efficiency labor) are given by

$$\Delta K = \frac{I}{q_K} - gK \tag{A.12}$$

$$\Delta \frac{q_B B}{p} \approx \gamma_B \left(G + \frac{bB}{p} - T \right) + \frac{Z_B}{p} - \left(i + g - \frac{\Delta q_B}{q_B} \right) \frac{q_B B}{p} \tag{A.13}$$

$$\Delta \frac{H}{p} \approx (1 - \gamma_B) \left(G + \frac{bB}{p} - T \right) - \frac{Z_B}{p} - (i + g) \frac{H}{p}. \tag{A.14}$$

The only approximation in (A.13) and (A.14) involves our ignoring capital gains or losses on current-period additions to stocks of money and bonds.

Short-Run Effects of Fiscal and Financial
Policies in the Unemployment Model

The basic equations (A.1), (A.2), and (A.3) can be solved for (r_K, r_B, Y) after using (A.6), (A.8), and (A.9) to eliminate q_K, q_B, and T. The system expresses the three endogenous variables as implicit functions of predetermined variables (stocks, expectations, price level) and of policies. There are four parameters of policy. Fiscal policy is described by G and t, financial policy by γ_B ($\gamma_H = 1 - \gamma_B$), and monetary policy by Z_B ($Z_H = -Z_B$).

The equations for the twelve multipliers with respect to policy parameters are tedious to print and read but, along with other mathematical details not presented here, are available from the authors on request. The structure of these equations is as follows:

$$(A.15)$$

$$
\begin{bmatrix}
+ & - & +(?) \\
- & + & + \\
- & - & \mp \\
+ & + & +
\end{bmatrix}
\begin{bmatrix}
dr_K \\
dr_B \\
dY
\end{bmatrix}
=
\begin{bmatrix}
0 & 0 & 0 & -(?) \\
\gamma_B & D & \frac{1}{p} & -(?) \\
1-\gamma_B & -D & -\frac{1}{p} & -(?) \\
1 & 0 & 0 & -
\end{bmatrix}
\begin{bmatrix}
dG \\
d\gamma_B \\
dZ_B \\
dt
\end{bmatrix}
$$

$$D \equiv G + \frac{bB}{p} - tY.$$

Our a priori restrictions on the sum of the elements of each column are given below the columns. An increase in the required rate of return on capital stimulates saving and reduces investment. An increase in the rate of return on bonds stimulates saving. Expansion of real output is assumed to have a stronger effect on saving than on investment (the analogy of the assumption that the *IS* curve is downward sloping in the simple *IS−LM* model). If an increase in output creates excess demand in the market for equity, the last column of the Jacobian on the l.h.s. of (A.15) is positive and its determinant is also positive. Even if an increase in output were to create excess supply in the equity market, the determinant of the Jacobian will be positive if the excess demand created in the money market by an increase in Y is larger.

Another ambiguity is the effect of an increase in the tax rate t on excess demand in the three asset markets. In aggregate, increasing t creates excess demand for assets. The deficit declines, and the new government supply of money-cum-bonds is diminished more than the reduction in private saving induced by the decline of disposable income. This is indicated by the negative sign for the sum of the last r.h.s. column in (A.15). But this effect may not prevail for every asset individually. For example, if γ_B is close or equal to zero, the deficit reduction does little or nothing to the supply of bonds, and the general saving-reducing effect of the decline of disposable income may dominate. In the case of equity, the tax effects on demand and supply are somewhat different. Lowering the deficit does not directly diminish the new supply of equity; however, the higher tax rate deters private investment. On the asset flow demand side, the decline in disposable income and the reduction in after-tax returns have negative effects, offset only by the capital loss on equity inflicted by the tax increase.

Table 3—A1 shows the results for the twelve multipliers, so far as definite signs follow from our assumptions. The final t column assumes that the excess demand effects dominate in all three assets (negative signs throughout the dt column of (A.15)). The signs shown in the Table 3—A1 for γ_B, the share of the deficit that is bond-financed, assume a positive deficit. If the budget is initially in surplus, an increase in γ_B would have the opposite effects. Of course a change in γ_B would have no effect if the budget was balanced. An increase in Z_B, like an increase in γ_B with an initial deficit, involves the sale of bonds for money by the central bank. They both raise the real rate of return on bonds and reduce aggregate demand and output. The after-tax rate of return on equity r_K is likely to be higher if bonds and equity are close substitutes, lower if bonds and money are close substitutes. If r_K increases, q_K will be lower because Y also declines. Private capital formation is "crowded out." If r_K declines, the net effect on q_K is ambiguous.

An increase in public spending G will raise output. Its effect on r_K is uncertain. If deficits are exclusively money-financed, $\gamma_B = 0$, an increase in G will lower r_K and stimulate investment. In that case the

Table 3—A1. Signs of One-Period Policy Multipliers, Unemployment Model

Policy Variable	G			γ_B	Z_B	t
	$\gamma_B = 0$	$0 < \gamma_B < 1$	$\gamma_B = 1$			
r_K	—	?	?	?	?	?
r_B	—	?	+	+	+	?
Y	+	+	+	—	—	—

stimulating effect on investment of higher current profits is reinforced by a lower required rate of return. Both raise q_K. With money-financed budget deficits and surpluses, an increase in G will also lower r_B. Thus, given idle resources, an increase in public spending coupled with accommodating monetary policy will "crowd in" private investment. This may happen even if γ_B exceeds zero. The monetary share of deficit finance does not have to be 100 percent to prevent r_B from rising. Furthermore, r_B can rise—as will certainly happen if $\gamma_B = 1$—while r_K falls. This would occur if bonds are in some sense closer to money than to capital in the chain of asset substitution.

Short-Run Effects of Fiscal and Financial Policies in the Full Employment Model

The solution for the full employment version is obtained by reversing the roles of Y and p. Output Y is predetermined by the capital stock previously accumulated, given of course the exogenous supply of efficiency labor. The price level p is endogenous within the period. As in the previous section, the system consists of the three basic equations (A.1), (A.2), and (A.3) with extra variables eliminated by use of subsequent equations. In our comparative static analysis of this version of the model we add a fifth exogenous variable $x(p)$ to the four policy parameters. The structure of the equations for the fifteen multipliers is given in (A.16), and the results are summarized in Table 3—A2.

$$(A.16)$$

$$
\begin{bmatrix} + & - & ? \\ - & + & + \\ - & - & + \end{bmatrix}
\begin{bmatrix} dr_K \\ dr_B \\ dp \end{bmatrix}
=
\begin{bmatrix} 0 & 0 & 0 & -(?) & - \\ \gamma_B & D & \frac{1}{p} & -(?) & - \\ 1-\gamma_B & -D & -\frac{1}{p} & -(?) & + \end{bmatrix}
\begin{bmatrix} dG \\ d\gamma_B \\ dZ \\ dt \\ dx(p) \end{bmatrix}
$$

$$
\begin{matrix} + & + & + \end{matrix} \qquad\qquad \begin{matrix} +1 & 0 & 0 & - & + \end{matrix}
$$

The Jacobian matrix, on the left-hand side of (A.16), differs from that of (A.15) for the unemployment case only by having a question mark in the third column. In general, an increase in the price level stimulates saving via the "real balance effect." This is the only effect at work; our assumption that $x(p)$ is given eliminates any possible substitution effect from a rise in the current price level relative to the future price level. The reduction in the real value of existing holdings of bonds and money is the reason for the plus signs in the second and third entries of the column and in the sum for total saving at the bottom. Does this loss of wealth spill over into more saving in the form of equity, too? This is the uncertainty indicated in the first row. But even if the answer is negative, it is likely that the positive effect on saving in the form of money is absolutely larger than the negative effect on equity saving. This is sufficient, but not necessary, to insure that the Jacobian still has a positive determinant, as is assumed in Table 3—A2. The other assumptions of Table 3—A2 are the same as for Table 3—A1.

The policy effects on p are straightforward. An increase in public spending, G, raises the price level and a substitution of bonds for money lowers it. As in the unemployment version, the effect of an increase in the income tax rate is complicated by the non-lump-sum nature of the tax which directly affects the rate of return on investment and the required rate of return on equity. The tax column of Table 3—A2 assumes again that an increase in t causes excess demand for all three assets. To obtain the result that a substitution of bonds for money raises r_B, it is sufficient (but not necessary) that the effect of an increase in the price level on the bond market is larger, in absolute value, than the effect in the equity market. With that assumption, we can determine the signs of a few more multipliers. First, the substitution of bonds for money will raise r_K when bonds and equity are close substitutes, lower r_K if money and bonds are close substitutes. Second, with money financing ($\gamma_B = 0$) an increase in G lowers r_K and r_B.

Note that whenever real output increases in the unemployment model, the price level rises in the full employment model. In the latter version, private spending is crowded out by public spending dollar for dollar. Resources appropriated by the government may

Table 3—A2. Signs of One-Period Multipliers, Full Employment Model

Policy Variable	$\gamma_B = 0$	$0 < \gamma_B < 1$	$\gamma_B = 1$	γ_B	Z_B	t	$x(p)$
		G					
r_K	—	?	?	?	?	?	—
r_B	—	?	+	+	+	?	—
p	+	+	+	—	—	—	+

come partially or wholly from private consumption rather than private investment, however. With sufficient money-financing, investment may even be "crowded in" by deficit finance. This is particularly likely if the source of increased deficit is tax reduction rather than exhaustive government purchases.

An autonomous rise in expected inflation is a decline in the real return on money, and by our standard assumption will generate excess supply of money and excess demand for the other two assets. This is reflected in the last column of the r.h.s. matrix of (A.16). The last column of Table 3–A2 shows the implications: an increase in p and declines in the other real rates of return r_K and r_B. Along with the decline in r_K goes an increase in capital investment. Room in the economy is made by a decrease in consumption, in response to the wealth losses arising from the price level increase which more than offsets the stimulating effect on consumption of the general reduction in rates of return.

The Fiscal-Monetary Policy Mix and Capital Formation

The analysis can be simplified in a number of ways by assuming that the tax is a lump-sum tax, T_o, rather than a proportional tax on labor and capital income. This simplification will be used to consider the validity of a common proposition about the monetary-fiscal policy mix most likely to favor investment. It is widely held that a combination of expansionary monetary policy and restrictive fiscal policy favors capital formation by keeping interest rates low while taxes discourage private consumption.

In the unemployment version of the model, we shall evaluate this proposition for the short run by investigating what combinations of the tax, T_o, and of the share of money in the deficit, $\gamma_H = 1 - \gamma_B$, keep Y constant. The analysis is repeated for combinations of G and γ_H. We then consider the effect of such changes in policy mix on r_K, and thus on q_K and I. In the full employment version of the model we shall consider, by analogy, which combinations of T_o or G and γ_H sustain a given price level, and how capital formation varies when the policy mix is altered in a way that preserves the price level. We continue to assume the government budget to be in deficit initially.

We summarize the results verbally. Mathematical details of the analysis are available from the authors.

An increase in G, with an offsetting change in γ_H that just keeps Y at its original level, raises r_K. With Y constant by assumption, q_K will fall and investment is crowded out. As one would expect, a downward compensating change in γ_H is needed to keep Y constant when G increases. This result supports the view that a combination of expansionary fiscal policy and restrictive financial policy deters investment. The reverse policy, a fall in G and a rise in γ_H, will favor capital formation.

The case of tax increases and monetary expansion is not completely straightforward, however. Granted that an increase in taxes raises the sum of private and public saving, this policy can, and in our model will, initially reduce saving in the specific form of equity. If this effect is very strong, the excess supply pressure in the equity market could raise r_K, and thus lower q_K and investment when taxes increase. This is less likely to happen the smaller is the income effect on the demand for equity. If this effect is zero, an increase in T_o, with a compensating change in γ_H to keep Y constant, unambiguously lowers r_K and stimulates investment; r_B is also lower. The direction of the compensating change in γ_H is unambiguously positive when there is no income effect on the demand for equity because we assume throughout that the mix of bond and money financing is such that *ceteris paribus* an increase in taxes would create excess demand in both the bond market and the "money market." With both r_K and r_B lowered, the demand for money will increase further. To preserve equilibrium, γ_H will have to increase.

The counterintuitive phenomenon—an increase in taxes reduces the demand for equity to such an extent that the required rate of return on capital is increased—cannot occur in the traditional Keynesian $IS-LM$ model. The reason is that bonds and claims to real reproducible capital are in that model perfect substitutes in private portfolios. The more general portfolio-theoretic structure of our model includes the Keynesian model as a special case but can also generate the nontraditional results just mentioned.

In the full employment version, the relevant fiscal-monetary policy trade-offs are those that keep the price level constant. The analysis is exactly the same as for the unemployment model. In both cases both p and Y are formally exogenous, one by policy manipulation and one by assumption regarding the economic environment. The financial parameter γ_B, or γ_H, is formally endogenous. The results just presented apply to either environment.

Tax Cuts, Deficits, Inflation Expectations, and Investment

In the short-run analysis of our model, we have so far treated expectations as parametric. The expected proportional rates of change of the price of capital, the price of bonds and the general price level are given for any single period. In the long-run steady state of the model, expectations are always realized. To extend this perfect fore-sight assumption to the short run is fashionable but probably not very useful in many cases. Instead we shall analyze the impact of a specific combination of tax and financing policies under the assumption that economic agents (or at any rate the portfolio holders whose behavior is modeled in our asset-demand functions) have "crude monetarist" expectations. A cut in taxes will, when deficits are financed mainly or entirely by increased money creation, lead to an increase in the expected rate of inflation. The full employment version of the model will be used to analyze the impact of a tax cut on capital formation under these circumstances. Taxes are again taken to be lump sum.

An increase in the expected rate of inflation will induce substitution out of money balances. With the nominal interest rate on money fixed, the real rate of return declines by the full amount of the increase in the expected rate of inflation. Bonds too are nominally denominated. We would therefore expect substitution out of bonds as well. The portfolio reshuffling consequent on an increase in the expected rate of inflation, however, results in changes in the nominal interest rate on bonds which compensate, although in all likelihood only partly, for the increase in expected inflation. The higher expected rate of inflation will correspondingly lower q_B, the nominal price of the bonds.

As we have seen above, an increase in the expected rate of inflation will by itself reduce both r_K and r_B. (The positive effect on investment implied by this analysis needs to be qualified in real-world application, as we suggested in the text, by allowing for the increased uncertainty, and increased likelihood of subsequent restrictive policy, possibly engendered by higher inflation.) As we also observed above, a tax reduction by itself normally will "crowd in" investment, especially if the resulting deficit is financed by money; the only reservation is that the resulting rise in the price *level* and decrease in wealth might tend to diminish saving in equity. Thus if inflationary expectations are enhanced by tax reduction, there is a double reason for expecting favorable effects on capital formation. It is not inflation per se, but rather the future policy responses associated with inflation (monetary contraction, tax increases, and so on) that might discourage investment.

II. STEADY-STATE EQUILIBRIUM

We now describe the steady-state characteristics of the model. In long-run equilibrium, all real stocks and flows grow at the natural rate of growth, $g = n + \lambda$, and expectations are realized. The open market operations parameter, Z_B, is set equal to zero. Unless we state otherwise, the government is assumed to pursue mixed deficit financing policies ($0 < \gamma_B < 1$). Certain steady-state conditions are set out in equation (A.17).

$$x(q_B) = \frac{\Delta q_B}{q_B} = 0; \quad x(q_K) = \frac{\Delta q_K}{q_K} = 0; \quad x(p) = i \qquad \text{(A.17a)}$$

$$q_K = 1 \qquad \text{(A.17b)}$$

$$Y = f(K) \qquad \text{(A.17c)}$$

$$\frac{H}{p} = \frac{(1 - \gamma_B)}{\gamma_B} \frac{q_B B}{p} \qquad \text{(A.17d)}$$

$$\frac{H}{p} + \frac{q_B B}{p} = (G + \frac{bB}{p} - tY)/(g + i) \qquad \text{(A.17e)}$$

$$r_K = R(K/Y)(1 - t) \qquad \text{(A.17f)}$$

$$r_B = \frac{b}{q_B} - i \qquad \text{(A.17g)}$$

$$r_H = -i. \qquad \text{(A.17h)}$$

Equation (A.17a) states that expectations are realized. Since the nominal coupon on government bonds, b, is constant, the nominal price of bonds, q_B, is constant even in an inflationary or deflationary steady state. There are no real capital gains on equity. Equation (A.17b) implies that net investment is at its steady-state value: $I = gK$. From (A.17c) we see that output is at the full employment level. The ratio of the value of the money stock to the value of the bond stock is given by $(1 - \gamma_B)/\gamma_B$, the ratio of the shares of money and bonds in the financing of budget deficits or surpluses (A.17d). The real value of the public sector deficit has to be sufficient to maintain the real value of total government debt per unit of efficiency labor, in the face of price level changes, labor force growth and technical change (A.17e). Equations (A.17f-h) define real rates of return, all constant in a steady state.

Steady states cannot exist at all unless the behavioral and technological relations of the economy satisfy certain homogeneity properties. The production function must be homogeneous in capital and efficiency labor, as already assumed in (A.17e and f). Thus each possible steady state is characterized by a capital/output ratio constant over time. Policies also must be consistent with growth of all real variables at the common natural growth rate of the economy. Thus both G and T must be proportional to output Y. Finally, asset portfolio demands must allow all real stocks to grow at the same rate, g, as Y and other aggregate real variables. We exploit these homogeneity properties by expressing the steady-state equations in terms of stocks and flows per unit of output, as follows (stocks and flows per unit of output are distinguishable by bars):

$$\bar{K} = \bar{K}(R) \qquad \bar{K}' < 0. \tag{A.18a}$$

This is just the inverse of the R function in (A.17f).

Likewise, the steady state supplies $\bar{H}$ and $\bar{B}$ depend on fiscal and financial policies and on rates of return. Using (A.17d, e, g) we obtain

$$\frac{q_B \bar{B}}{p} = \frac{\gamma_B (\bar{G} - t)}{g - (\gamma_B r_B - (1 - \gamma_B) i)} \tag{A.18b}$$

$$\frac{\bar{H}}{p} = \frac{(1 - \gamma_B)(\bar{G} - t)}{g - (\gamma_B r_B - (1 - \gamma_B) i)} \tag{A.18c}$$

Note that the denominator in these two expressions could be written as $g - r_D$ where r_D is the weighted average of the real rates r_B and r_H on government debt, with the weights corresponding to the shares of the two kinds of debt in the total.

We write steady state demands for asset stocks proportional to output Y as $F^{\bar{K}}$, $F^{\bar{B}}$, and $F^{\bar{H}}$. Each is a function of the three rates of return and of the tax rate ($R(1-t)$, r_B, $-i$, t). Thus the basic equations are

$$F^{\bar{K}} = \bar{K} \tag{A.19a}$$

$$F^{\bar{B}} = \frac{q_B \bar{B}}{p} \tag{A.19b}$$

$$F^{\bar{H}} = \frac{\bar{H}}{p} \tag{A.19c}$$

where the r.h.s. variables can be eliminated by use of (A.18). The three equations (A.19) determine the three rates of return (R, r_B, $-i$) as functions of the policy parameters ($\overline{G}$, t, γ_B). Once the rates of return are determined, (A.18) can be used to find the steady state stocks. In particular (A.18a) gives steady-state capital intensity.

Before looking at some special cases, we make some general observations about the steady-state solutions and the long-run policy multipliers.

Budget Balance, Asset Growth, and Steady-State Inflation

First, the steady state is not in general characterized by a balanced public sector budget (Currie [14, 1978] and Christ [12, 1978]). The long-run balanced budget emerges only under very special circumstances. One trivial circumstance, related to the algebra of steady states, occurs when both nominally denominated debt instruments of the government are demanded by the private sector in nonzero amounts, while the government finances by only a single instrument (γ_B = 0 or γ_B = 1). If the nominal quantity of one government-issued asset is kept constant at a nonzero level, the nominal quantity of the other liability must be constant in the steady state, so that *all* real stocks and flows may grow at the common natural rate of growth. In that case the growth of real holdings of nominal public debt is generated exclusively by a steady proportional rate of price level deflation equal to g (Tobin and Buiter [32, 1976], Buiter [7, 1977]). A second circumstance occurs when the government pursues mixed financing policies ($0 < \gamma_B < 1$). Either by design—the policy authority fixes the common steady-state rate of growth of H and B at zero by appropriately adjusting one or both of its fiscal controls ($\overline{G}$, t)— or by coincidence, the endogenous steady-state budget deficit assumes the value zero. Finally, the steady-state budget will have to be balanced if the price level is fixed even in the long run in a model without growth (Blinder and Solow [4, 1974] and Tobin and Buiter [32, 1976]).

Second, it is easily seen from equations (A.17d) and (A.17e) that the steady-state rate of inflation equals the excess of the common steady-state rate of growth of the two nominally denominated public sector debt instruments over the natural rate of growth.

$$\frac{\Delta H}{H} - g = \frac{\Delta B}{B} - g = i \qquad (A.20)$$

Third, we stress that the role of money is quite different in the long run from the short run. The reason is that its real rate of return is in the long run endogenous. In our short runs, it was exogenous: we took the nominal return on money as constant at zero and the expected rate of inflation as temporarily predetermined. In the long run the nominal rate on money is still fixed, but the assumed flexibilities of prices and their rates of change plus the requirement that expected and actual inflation rates coincide make the real return endogenous. This removes money from it special position and makes it like other assets. If its real supply is to be increased, one way the public can be persuaded to accept it is by an increase in its real rate of return, a decline in inflation. This means that some of the effects customarily associated with money, as compared to government bonds, need not show up in comparison of long-run steady states. For example, steady states with larger deficits or larger monetary shares of deficits need not be more inflationary; wealth-owners may instead be led to accept the larger monetary issues because inflation rates are lower.

Crowding Out and Crowding In

In analyzing the long-run effects of government fiscal and financial policies, we will be comparing the steady-state equilibria associated with different values of policy parameters. "Crowding out" in this context means that the steady state associated with a changed value of a policy parameter, say a higher value of $\bar{G}$, has a smaller capital intensity $\bar{K}$ than a reference steady-state path associated with another parameter value, say a lower value of $\bar{G}$. "Crowding in" means that the variation of the policy parameter is associated with an increase in capital intensity.

Clearly crowding out means that steady-state private saving, relative to national product Y, in the specific form of equity capital is decreased, while crowding in means that it is increased. There are several ways in which the private rate of equity saving may vary. One mechanism is that total private saving is higher relative to output in one steady state than in another and that at least part of the increment goes into equity. Another mechanism is that private saving is diverted from government liabilities into equity even though total private saving is not increased. A policy variation may tend to crowd in via the first mechanism if it generally fosters private saving; this is in our model, for example, one effect of tax reduction. A policy variation may tend to crowd in via the second mechanism if it lowers the real return on government bonds and money and induces savers to shift to equity, even though total private saving is deterred; this is also a possible effect of tax reduction, though as we shall see it could work the other way.

Things are not always what they seem, and policy variations sometimes have long-run consequences that are the reverse of normal intuition and the reverse of their short-run effects. In our model the nominal rate of growth of government liabilities is not itself a policy parameter. It is the endogenous outcome of more basic policy parameters $\overline{G}$, t, γ_B. Another way to state the point is that the rate of inflation i is an endogenous outcome of the whole system, and the nominal growth of both government bonds and money is necessarily $g + i$. It is important to remember also that there is a presumption of generally negative relationship between the nominal growth of these government liabilities and their real stocks. This arises because a high rate of inflation means a low real return on money, and usually on the substitute asset, government bonds, as well. This shifts savers to capital, as discussed in the previous paragraph. The level of prices adjusts to make the high nominal stocks of debt and money the low real stocks that savers wish to hold.

An increase in $\overline{G} - t$ appears to be a deficit-increasing policy. But it does not necessarily increase the steady-state real deficit or debt as a percentage of national product. As shown by (A.18b and A.18c), the debt-income ratio is $(\overline{G} - t)/(g - r_D)$. An increase in $\overline{G} - t$ may or may not increase this ratio. It may so lower r_D, by raising the rate of inflation, that the ratio actually declines. Then the fiscal policy looks expansionary, and is inflationary, but it absorbs less rather than more saving. Private saving and wealth are shifted into the more attractive asset, equity, whose rate declines too. Thus there can be "crowding in" by asset substitution and reduction—*ex post*—of the real public sector deficit per unit of output, even though total private saving is smaller. The opposite is also possible: an increase in $\overline{G} - t$ may crowd out capital and be counterinflationary. The outcomes depend on the system as a whole. That is the reason why the analysis is sometimes complex and why the results sometimes cannot be determined, even in sign, without empirical knowledge of the asset demand and supply functions.

Neutrality, Superneutrality, and Other
Long-Run Policy Neutrality

From the short-run equilibrium equations of the full employment model, we can conclude that money is not neutral, but that money and bonds together are neutral. A once-and-for-all increase in H accompanied by an equal proportional increase in p—and, as $x(p)$ is assumed constant, an equal proportional increase in the future expected price level—will not restore the original real equilibrium. The real quantity of bonds would be reduced, necessitating further real adjustments. A hypothetical once-for-all equal proportional increase in H, B, and p will, however, leave the real equilibrium unchanged.

Shifting from *level* changes to *rate of growth* changes, we notice from the long-run model that a given percentage point increase in the rate of growth of H alone will not be consistent with an equal percentage point increase in the steady-state rate of inflation. *Both nominally denominated assets* must grow at the same rate in a steady state, and then the rate of inflation will be associated point-for-point with their common growth rate. However, the consequences of changing the common steady-state rate of change of H and B are not limited to an equal change in the steady-state rate of inflation. Money and bonds are in general not "superneutral." Changes in the steady-state rate of inflation alter the steady-state real rate of return on money balances. The reason for this is the fact that the nominal interest rate on the monetary base is institutionally fixed (realistically at zero as assumed in this model). A higher rate of inflation will *ceteris paribus* induce portfolio holders to shift out of money into other assets. These other assets can be real-valued financial claims such as equity, or nominally denominated claims with market-determined rates of return. The portfolio shift out of money into capital and bonds will tend to reduce their real rates of return. This rather informal argument suggests that a steady state characterized by a higher rate of inflation will also have higher capital-labor and capital-output ratios. The formal analysis below demonstrates that this is indeed a possible configuration, but not the only one.

As explained in the text, *superneutrality* means formally that real long-run outcomes are independent of the rate of growth of the money supply. We can generalize this to general, long-run *policy neutrality*, the property that real long-run outcomes are independent of any government fiscal and financial policies. In the context of our model, it means specifically that R and $\overline{K}$ are unaffected by the government policies. System (A.18—A.19) and, in particular, the combination of equations (A.18a) and (A.19a) $F^{\overline{K}} = K(R)$ reveals what policy-neutrality necessitates. This equation of equity demand and capital supply must give the same steady-state solution for R, the pretax return on capital, whatever the settings of policy instruments.

Now the only policy parameter directly involved in the equation is t, the tax rate. So one requirement of superneutrality is that these direct tax effects on demand for equity be zero. There are two such effects. One is the wedge that taxation of profit income enters between the marginal productivity of capital R and the after-tax return to savers r_K. We observed in the text that neutrality propositions evidently assume lump-sum taxation. The other direct tax effect on equity saving, which would apply even to lump-sum taxes, is the disposable income effect on saving and demand for wealth. Assuming it to be zero means that savers will aim at the same ratio of wealth to consumption regardless of the level of consumption. In the text, a rationalization of this assumption is sketched: consumers with infinite horizons make intertemporal choices in accordance with time discounts invariant across steady states.

The other requirement of policy-neutrality, in terms of our model, is that there be no cross-effects of r_B and r_H ($=-i$), the rates of return on bonds and money, on demand for capital equity $F^{\overline{K}}$. This makes the equity-capital equation by itself sufficient to determine R and thus $\overline{K}$. Policy parameters ($\overline{G}$, t, γ_B) obviously affect r_B and $-i$ in the two other equations, and would indirectly affect R if the values of the other rates of return make a difference to $F^{\overline{K}}$. Assuming those cross-effects to be zero says that any additional demands for bonds and money induced by increases in their yields do not come even partially by diversion of saving from equity but represent wholly additional saving. The special assumptions involved in this zero-substitution theory of saving are examined in the text.

A Money-Capital Model: Balanced Budget

We now turn to formal analysis of the effect of changes in the policy instruments on the steady-state endogenous variables, with special emphasis on R. It is instructive to consider first a simplified version of the model that includes only money and capital as assets. The steady-state equations of this simplified model are obtained by setting $\gamma_B = 0$ in the full model and omitting r_B, B, and the bond market equation. The condensed model is as follows:

$$F^{\overline{K}} = \overline{K}(R) \qquad \text{(A.21a)}$$

$$F^{\overline{H}} = \overline{H}/p. \qquad \text{(A.21b)}$$

Equation (A.18c) becomes, with $\gamma_B = 0$,

$$\frac{\overline{H}}{p} = \frac{\overline{G}-t}{g+i}. \qquad \text{(A.18c$'$)}$$

It is instructive to consider first a balanced budget policy: $\overline{G} = t$. Imagine, to begin, that no stock of government-issued money is available to the public; capital is the only vehicle for saving and for holding wealth. The equity market equation (A.21a) says that an increase in t—to finance an increase in $\overline{G}$—will increase R and diminish $\overline{K}$. The reasons are straightforward and familiar. The reduction in disposable income diminishes savers' desired wealth relative to pretax income Y. In addition to this income effect, higher taxation of earnings from capital deters equity saving and favors present consumption. This is a very orthodox story. Increasing government consumption and taxation crowds out capital.

An economy without government-issued money is hard to imagine. Suppose there is a fixed nominal stock of such money, inherited from the distant past, the same throughout every possible steady-state path. Suppose that the government budget is balanced as above, and consider how steady states vary with the size of the budget. All steady states must have the same real rate of return on money, namely g; this is accomplished by price deflation at the natural growth rate. Given g, the two equations (A.21a, b) determine the two variables R and $\overline{H}/p$. The latter is the ratio $\widetilde{H}/pY$, where $\widetilde{H}$ is the fixed nominal stock. The price level p is in any steady-state falling at rate g, but the *level* of this path can adjust to reconcile $\widetilde{H}$ to any $\overline{H}/p$ that wealth-owners desire. Clearly the outcome is the same as in the previous paragraph. With the deflation rate invariant at g; the capital equation is independent of the second equation, and for the reasons already given, an increase in t raises R and lowers $\overline{K}$. Formally, the structure of this system is

$$\begin{bmatrix} + & 0 \\ & \\ - & -1 \end{bmatrix} \begin{bmatrix} dR \\ \\ d(\dfrac{\overline{H}}{p}) \end{bmatrix} = \begin{bmatrix} + & + \\ & \\ ? & - \end{bmatrix} \begin{bmatrix} dt \\ \\ dg \end{bmatrix} \tag{A.22}$$

$$+ \quad - \qquad\qquad + \quad -$$

The *?* in (A.22) indicates ambiguity about the tax effect on demand for money. The disposable income effect is in the same direction as for capital, but the substitution effect goes the other way, encouraging accumulation of the asset whose yield is untaxed. However, our assumption that the cross-effects of a rate of return will never exceed the own-effect means, in this case, that the overall effect of a tax increase on wealth demand is negative (so that the dt column on the r.h.s. has a positive sum). Consequently the increase in t (and $\bar{G}$) will lower $\bar{H}/p$ as well as $\bar{K}$; in other words, a larger budget spells a generally higher price path.

The natural growth rate g is not a policy variable, at least within the spectrum of fiscal and financial policies here examined. But it is of some interest to note that, because g here is also the real rate of return on money, an increase in it will raise R and $\bar{H}/p$, lower p and $\bar{K}$. This conclusion abstracts from any direct effects an increase in the economy's real growth rate might have on desired wealth relative to income.

There is another way in which a long-run balanced budget policy could be reconciled with the need of the economy for governmental money. This is for the government to serve as an intermediary, issuing money and buying private sector assets with the proceeds. In our primitive two-asset model, the government can only buy equities; a more likely mechanism would involve government loans to private borrowers, negative public debt. In the two-asset model this simply means that the supply of capital, relative to Y, available for private ownership is reduced from $\bar{K}(R)$ to $\bar{K}(R) - \bar{H}/p$, where $\bar{H}/p$ is now a parameter of government policy, the volume of its equity holdings relative to national product. Equity purchases are not counted in $\bar{G}$, purchases for government consumption. The rate of inflation is now endogenous. The formal structure is as follows:

$$
\begin{bmatrix} + & - \\ \\ - & + \end{bmatrix} \begin{bmatrix} dR \\ \\ d(-i) \end{bmatrix} = \begin{bmatrix} + & -1 \\ \\ ? & +1 \end{bmatrix} \begin{bmatrix} dt \\ \\ d\bar{H}/p \end{bmatrix} \qquad \text{(A.23)}
$$
$$
\begin{array}{cc} + \quad\quad + & \quad\quad + \quad\quad 0 \end{array}
$$

Analysis easily shows that a balanced-budget increase in t once again raises R and lowers $\bar{K}$. The effect on the inflation rate is definitely negative if the disposable income effect on demand for money dominates ($?$ in (A.23) is $+$), and may be negative in the other case. An increase in $\bar{H}/p$, providing private portfolio owners with more real money balances and less capital, naturally lowers the real return on capital R and raises that of money $(-i)$. Such a policy is both counterinflationary and favorable to capital formation.

However, practical implementation of the intermediary strategy just described would be difficult. The steady-state equilibria of the system (A.23) may well be unstable. The short-run impact of purchases of equities—or, in general, other privately owned assets—with new money is to raise the price level. Only if this leads to a reduction in inflationary expectations can the public be induced to hold larger real money balances. A more reliable way to increase the real return on money, while channeling the public's money holdings into the equity market, would be to raise the nominal yield on money.

A Money-Capital Model: Deficit Budget

The government's normal method of providing its money to the economy is to issue money to finance budget deficits. We now consider cases where $\bar{G}$ exceeds t, and $\bar{H}/p$ is determined by (A.18c'). Since $\bar{H}/p$ is by nature nonnegative, we are also assuming that $g + i$ is positive, that is, that the real rate of return on money is smaller than the economy's growth rate g. This does not mean that either R or r_K, before- and after-tax returns to capital are less than the growth rate. In general, we expect r_K, and, a fortiori, R, to exceed the return on money for familiar reasons of risk and liquidity.

The equations for the multipliers now have the following structure:

$$
\begin{bmatrix} + & - \\ & \\ - & ? \\ & \\ + & ? \end{bmatrix}
\begin{bmatrix} dr \\ \\ d(-i) \end{bmatrix}
=
\begin{bmatrix} 0 & + \\ & \\ \dfrac{1}{g+i} & - \\ & \\ \dfrac{1}{g+i} & - \end{bmatrix}
\begin{bmatrix} d\bar{G} \\ \\ dt \end{bmatrix}
\tag{A.24}
$$

The ambiguity in the Jacobian arises from the double role of the inflation rate. A lowering of i increases the demand for money, but it also—as inspection of the r.h.s. of (A.21b) shows—increases the supply. We assume that an increase in the tax rate lowers the sum of $F^{\bar{K}}$ and $F^{\bar{H}}$ for given rates of return, but lowers the deficit even more. The previous ambiguity about the effect of a tax increase on the excess demand for money is thus removed; the decline in supply of money reinforces the increase in demand due to substitution of money for capital.

The ambiguity in the Jacobian leaves us with two cases to consider. In what we shall call the standard case, the Jacobian determinant is negative. Demand for money is relatively insensitive to its own real rate of return. The implications of (A.24) are then (1) an increase in $\overline{G}$ lowers R and raises $\overline{K}$, "crowding in" capital. It also raises the rate of inflation i. Although an increase in government purchases takes resources that might be used for capital formation, its financial consequence is to increase the deficit and thus to accelerate the growth of the nominal money supply. The inflationary result makes money a less attractive asset and induces wealth-owners to place savings in equity instead. (2) An increase in t lowers the rate of inflation and increases R. Capital intensity is diminished. As might be expected, these results are just the opposite of those for an increase in $\overline{G}$. The after-tax return on capital, r_K, may move either way. It would rise if taxes were lump-sum and did not alter the marginal return on capital. But if the tax is a disincentive to equity investment, r_K may decline. This does not, however, mean that capital intensity is increased; it will be diminished because the before-tax return R is higher. (3) An equal increase in $\overline{G}$ and t, keeping the real deficit unchanged, can be analyzed by adding the two columns in the r.h.s, matrix of (A.24), so that both entries are positive. The result of the marginally balanced budget operation is to raise the rate of inflation. It may or may not crowd out capital. The decline in both after-tax rates of return is discouraging to accumulation of wealth and capital, but if the direct tax effects on equity investment are weak, the inflation effect—substitution of equity for money—may prevail.

The nonstandard case arises if the Jacobian determinant is positive. This means that the elasticity of demand for money with respect to its own real return is high. Or it could occur if the deficit was small. As discussed in the text, the implications reverse the standard case. Higher $\overline{G}$ is associated with lower i, higher R, lower $\overline{K}$. Higher t is associated with higher i; the effects on R, r_K, and $\overline{K}$ are not clear. As for a balanced increase in $\overline{G}$ and t, both i and $\overline{K}$ are reduced.

Figure 3–A1 illustrates the money-capital model. The horizontal axis measures the real rate of return on money, the negative of the inflation rate. Reading right to left from the vertical line at g, the horizontal axis shows $g + i$, positive values only. The vertical axis measures $\overline{H}/p$, the amount of money held relative to income. The hyperbola $S_o S_o'$ gives $(\overline{G}_o - t)/(g + i.)$. Clearly an increase in $\overline{G}$ from $\overline{G}_o$ to $\overline{G}_1$ (or a reduction of t) shifts this, the money supply curve, upwards to $S_1 S_1'$. Now for each value of i—and for given t—solve the capital equation (A.21a) for R, and add to $S_o S_o'$ the corresponding

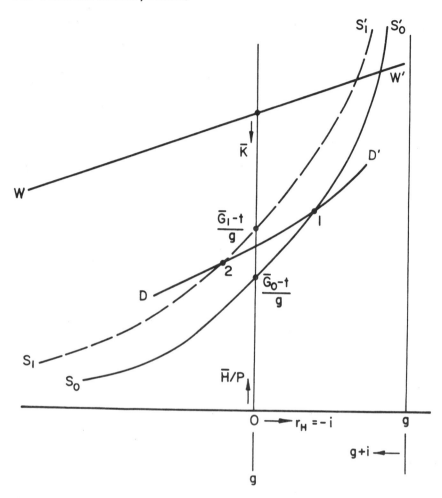

Figure 3–A1. Money-Capital Model; Illustration of Effect of Fiscal Expansion on Steady-State Inflation (i) and Capital Stock (K)

amount $\bar{K}(R)$. This operation yields the locus WW'. Along it as r_H increases from left to right R is rising, too, and $\bar{K}$ is falling. The curve DD' shows the demand for money for each value of r_H and the associated value of R. DD' must be steeper than WW', but it can be either steeper or flatter than $S_o S'_o$. In the standard case, depicted in Figure 3–A1, it is flatter. As the figure shows, an increase in $\bar{G}$ leads to higher inflation and larger $\bar{K}$. The reverse would be true if DD' crossed $S_o S'_o$ from below. Graphical analysis of a tax cut is more difficult, because DD' and WW' are shifted upward, too.

Policy Effects in the Three-Asset Model

The reintroduction of government bonds as a third asset, providing the government with a third instrument γ_B, widens the range of possible steady-state effects of policy variations. Adding (A.18b) and (A.18c), and recalling the definition of r_D as the weighted average rate of return on total debt, we note that total debt may be written as $(\bar{G} - t)/(g - r_D)$. The analogy to (A.18c') suggests that it might be possible to apply the above analysis of the money-capital model to the three-asset model, making it in effect a two-asset, debt-capital, economy. This could be misleading, however. The composition of the portfolio as between capital and total debt is not independent of the composition of debt between bonds and money.

Analysis of the three-asset model disclosed ambiguities of the same nature as those of the money-capital model but greater in number. Once again, a standard case implies that expansionary fiscal policies will be inflationary and "crowd in" capital investment. But there are also "perverse" cases in which restrictive policies and lower deficits are associated with more inflationary steady states and with "crowding in." Numerical information about behavioral parameters is required to obtain unambiguous answers.

It is not possible to generalize about the effects of altering the financing parameter γ_B. Under some circumstances increasing the share of bond-financing will lead to a higher inflation rate and/or to a lower return on capital and greater capital intensity. This is not really as counter-intuitive as it sounds, or as it would be in the short run. When all rates of return are flexible, it may be that wealth-owners are induced to absorb a larger supply of bonds by reductions in competing rates as well as an increase in the own-rate.

We should emphasize that these are exercises in comparative statics, showing how the characteristics of steady-state paths differ if different policies are steadily pursued. They say nothing about paths of adjustment if policies are changed sequentially. We have not attempted a stability analysis of the nonstandard or perverse cases, where the policy variations push the long-run equilibria in different directions from their initial one-period impacts.

III. OPEN ECONOMY EXTENSION

To study the effects of fiscal and financial policy in an open economy, we extend the model of this Appendix in a number of directions. The major additions and modifications are the following:

A fourth asset market equilibrium condition is added for an internationally traded private bond. This bond has a fixed market value and a fixed rate of return r_A^* in terms of foreign currency. Domestic supply of the foreign bond consists of private domestic holdings at the end of the previous period, A, eA in home currency value, plus the private capital account deficit of the current period. The private capital account deficit is the sum of the current account surplus and the net sales of foreign assets by the government (the official settlements deficit on the balance of payments). The current account surplus is the trade surplus, X, plus net interest income (private and public) from abroad. Official holdings of foreign bonds are denoted A.

The exchange rate e is the domestic currency price of foreign currency. A rise in e is depreciation, a fall is appreciation, of the home currency. There are two channels connecting the exchange rate and the domestic economy: capital account and current account. In the capital account, exchange rate depreciation increases, appreciation decreases, the domestic currency value of net holdings of foreign bonds, the only internationally traded financial claim. Expectations of depreciation increase the return on foreign bonds to domestic holders, and expectations of appreciation lower the return. Domestic money, government bonds and equity are not held by foreigners. To the home country, small in the international financial market, r_A^* is given; any amount of foreign bonds can be traded at that interest rate. But domestic and foreign bonds are not assumed to be perfect substitutes in private portfolios. Instead the gross substitutes assumption is extended to all four assets.

In the current account, the trade surplus is assumed to vary positively with the ratio of the price of imports to the price of domestic output—the Marshall-Lerner conditions are satisfied—and negatively with domestic output Y. To the home country, the foreign price of imports p_f^* is parametric. Likewise, to foreign export markets the price of domestic output p is parametric.

$$X = X(ep_f^*/p, Y) \qquad X_{ep_f^*/p} > 0 \qquad X_Y < 0. \qquad (A.25)$$

The domestic price level, p, is influenced directly by the cost of imports. We use the simple specification (Buiter [8, 1978])

$$p = w^\beta (ep_f^*)^{1-\beta} \qquad 0 < \beta < 1. \qquad (A.26)$$

Here w is the domestic component of unit costs of production. It consists mainly of labor costs. In the unemployment version of the model, w is treated as parametric in the short run. Its behavior over time can then be determined by the expectations-augmented Phillips curve $\frac{\Delta w}{w} = \psi(Y - f(K)) + x(w)$, or $\frac{\Delta w}{w} = \psi(Y - f(K))$ $+ x(p)$. In the full employment version, w is modeled as a short-run endogenous variable and actual and capacity output are assumed equal: $Y = f(K)$. Interest on private and official foreign asset holdings is, in real terms, $er_f^*(A + \hat{A})/p$. Government budget receipts now include the interest income on official holdings of foreign bonds. Open market operations now include sales of foreign assets Z_A as well as domestic bonds and money:

$$Z_H + Z_B + Z_A = 0. \qquad \text{(A.27)}$$

The real rate of return on foreign assets equals the foreign interest return plus the expected rate of depreciation of the domestic currency minus the expected rate of change of the domestic general price level.

$$r_A = r_A^* + x(e) - x(p). \qquad \text{(A.28)}$$

**Short-Run Effects of Fiscal
and Financial Policy**

The short-run equilibrium conditions are summarized in equations (A.29).

$$F^K - q_K K = I \qquad \text{(A.29a)}$$

$$F^B - q_B \frac{B}{p} = \gamma_B D + \frac{Z_B}{p} \qquad \text{(A.29b)}$$

$$F^A - \frac{eA}{p} = X\left(\frac{ep_f^*}{p}, Y\right) + er_A^*\left(\frac{A}{p} + \frac{\hat{A}}{p}\right) + \frac{Z_A}{p} \qquad \text{(A.29c)}$$

$$F^H - \frac{H}{p} = (1 - \gamma_B)D - \left(\frac{Z_B + Z_A}{p}\right). \qquad \text{(A.29d)}$$

The list of variables in the asset demand functions includes those in the closed economy model, and in addition r_A and eA/p. The real deficit D is $G + \frac{bB}{p} - tY - \frac{eR_A^* \hat{A}}{p}$.

These four-asset market equations can be summed to yield the open economy *IS* curve.

$$S = I + G + \frac{bB}{p} - tY + X + er_A^* \frac{A}{p} \; . \tag{A.29e}$$

In the unemployment version of the model, the four market-clearing conditions determine the temporary equilibrium values of Y, r_B, r_K and one foreign exchange variable. This could be the exchange rate e if policy fixes Z_A, or Z_A if policy holds e at a predetermined rate. Intermediate regimes could be modeled, but we shall concentrate on the freely floating exchange rate ($Z_A = 0$) and the fixed exchange rate. Under both exchange rate regimes H, B, A, $\hat{A}$, K, $x(q_K)$, $x(q_B)$, $x(p)$, and $x(e)$ are short-run predetermined variables. The unemployment model has w as an additional predetermined variable, while the full-employment model has Y instead.

In addition to extending the gross substitutes assumption to all four assets, we also extend two other assumptions: An increase in the rate of return on any asset increases total saving. An increase in the value of existing holdings of any asset increases the values demanded for all assets and for current consumption.

To save space we present only the analysis of the unemployment model. Subject to minor qualifications, the results again carry over to the full-employment model, with the price level taking qualitatively the place of real output. A few of the short-run effects of changes in (G, t, γ_B, Z_B) on (r_K, r_B, Y) are considered both for fixed and floating exchange rate regimes. When considering a fixed exchange rate we shall in addition derive the impact effect of a devaluation. With a market-determined exchange rate the effect of open market sales of foreign bonds by the government can also be considered.

Policy Effects with a Fixed Exchange Rate

The impact multipliers for the unemployment model under a fixed exchange rate can be found from equations with the structure shown in (A.30). The rows correspond to the asset demand/supply equations for equity, domestic bonds, foreign bonds, and money in that order. It is assumed that the domestic counterpart of official sales or purchases of foreign bonds is always money, that is, that there is no "sterilization." It is also assumed that the government budget is initially in deficit and that private holdings of foreign bonds are positive.

$$(A.30)$$

$$
\begin{bmatrix}
+ & - & 0 & +(?) \\
- & + & 0 & + \\
- & - & + & + \\
- & - & - & + \\
+ & + & 0 & +
\end{bmatrix}
\begin{bmatrix}
dr_K \\ dr_B \\ d(-Z_A) \\ dY
\end{bmatrix}
=
\begin{bmatrix}
0 & ? & 0 & 0 & +(?) \\
+ & -(?) & D & \dfrac{1}{p} & -(?) \\
0 & + & 0 & 0 & +(?) \\
+ & -(?) & -D & -\dfrac{1}{p} & -(?) \\
1 & -(?) & 0 & 0 & ?
\end{bmatrix}
\begin{bmatrix}
dG \\ dt \\ d\gamma_B \\ dZ_B \\ de
\end{bmatrix}
$$

The Jacobian matrix of (A.30) has a dominant diagonal and positive determinant. We shall consider the effects of changes in G, γ_B, and e on the short-run endogenous variables. A cut in t will, subject to the qualifications mentioned for the closed economy, have effects of the same signs as those of an increase in G. An increase in Z_B has the same impact effects as an increase in γ_B.

An increase in G will raise Y however it is financed. It will lower the returns on capital and bonds r_K and r_B if public sector deficits are wholly money-financed. With mixed financing or exclusively bond-financing, the effect on r_K is ambiguous. The trade balance and the current account deteriorate as Y increases, the relative price of imports and exports remaining unchanged. If budget deficits are exclusively money-financed, the official settlements deficit Z_A on the balance of payments increases. The lowering of r_K and r_B induces portfolio substitution toward domestic money and foreign assets. The deterioration in the trade balance is therefore compounded by an increased deficit on the private capital account. If budget deficits are not exclusively money-financed, either r_K or r_B or both may be higher when G is increased. In that case improvement in the private capital account may accompany and even overcome the deterioration in the current account.

An increase in γ_B or in Z_B lowers Y and raises r_B, as in the closed economy model. Since the rate of return on the foreign asset is fixed, the effect on r_K depends only on the relative degrees of substitutability among money, domestic bonds and capital. The closer substitutes are bonds and equity, compared to bonds and money, the more likely is r_K to increase. The decline in Y improves the trade account. Lower Y and higher r_B both reduce demand for foreign bonds. If r_K also increases, this shift out of foreign assets will be reinforced and the capital account will definitely improve. The official settlements balance will then reflect improvements in both current and capital accounts.

Devaluation will operate through a number of channels. With the foreign currency price of imports determined exogenously and with w predetermined in the short run, devaluation shifts the terms of trade against the home country. By assumption this will improve the trade balance and thereby stimulate domestic output. This "elasticities effect" will be countered by a "monetary effect," however. Exchange rate depreciation increases the domestic general price level, p, and reduces the real value of given nominal stocks of money and domestic bonds. This will tend to depress domestic consumption demand for domestic output. As the country is assumed to be a net creditor to the rest of the world, devaluation will increase the domestic currency value and the real value of foreign currency-denominated assets. This will generate a positive wealth effect on domestic consumption demand. (If the country were a net foreign debtor, the opposite outcome prevails.) If the column sum corresponding to de in (A.30) is negative, devaluation is on balance contractionary as regards aggregate demand for domestic goods and services, a result consistent with the monetary approach to the balance of payments. A positive column sum favors the elasticities approach. The general scenario suggested by the monetary approach pictures a devaluation increasing r_K and r_B, reducing Y, and improving the official settlements balance. In our model that is a possible scenario, but not the only possible one.

Policy Effects with a Floating Exchange Rate

The structure of the matrix equation from which impact multipliers can be derived for the floating exchange rate regime is in (A.11). We shall make the Keynesian, "elasticities approach," assumption that, *ceteris paribus*, exchange rate depreciation is expansionary in the domestic output market. The column sum of the third column of the Jacobian of (A.31) is therefore negative. The de column of (A.30) for the fixed rate regime had a positive sum under the same assumption, but now that column is on the l.h.s. We also assume that exchange rate depreciation, augmenting the value of existing holdings of foreign bonds, creates excess supply in that market. This spills over into excess demands for domestic assets, reinforced in the case of bonds and money by the reduction in the real value of existing stocks because of the import component of the domestic price level. We assume the net wealth effect to be non-negative for equity demand as well. A small negative effect on equity demand would not alter our conclusions.

$$(A.31)$$

$$
\begin{bmatrix}
+ & - & + & +(?) \\
- & + & + & + \\
- & - & - & + \\
- & - & + & + \\
+ & + & - & +
\end{bmatrix}
\begin{bmatrix}
dr_K \\
dr_B \\
de \\
dY
\end{bmatrix}
\begin{bmatrix}
0 & (?) & 0 & 0 & 0 \\
+ & -(?) & D & \frac{1}{p} & 0 \\
0 & + & 0 & 0 & \frac{1}{p} \\
+ & -(?) & -D & -\frac{1}{p} & -\frac{1}{p} \\
1 & -(?) & 0 & 0 & 0
\end{bmatrix}
\begin{bmatrix}
dG \\
dt \\
d\gamma_B \\
dZ_B \\
dZ_A
\end{bmatrix}
$$

The determinant of the Jacobian matrix of (A.30) is negative. (If the signs of the *de* column were reversed, the matrix would have the familiar standard sign pattern.) We have seen that most of the results derived for the closed economy remain valid in the open economy when the exchange rate was fixed. With a floating exchange rate, there is one new complication: the general price level, p, becomes a short-run endogenous variable even in the unemployment model. Domestic costs are sticky; import prices in domestic currency are not.

As in all other cases, an increase in public spending will boost real income. If the public sector deficit is financed by money creation ($\gamma_B = 0$), the rate of return on capital equity and the real rate of return on domestic bonds will fall and the exchange rate will depreciate. Domestic capital formation will be stimulated. With mixed public sector deficit financing policies, real rates of return on domestic bonds and/or equity may rise and the exchange rate may appreciate.

An open market sale of foreign assets by the government ($dZ_A >$ 0) will cause the exchange rate to appreciate and will depress real output. Remember that domestic bonds and foreign bonds are not perfect substitutes in private portfolios and that the rate of return on domestic bonds is not determined in international markets.

Steady-State Equilibrium

As in the closed economy case, a long-run steady-state equilibrium requires that all asset stocks grow in real value at the natural growth rate of the economy. For foreign assets, this means that some combination of exchange depreciation, current account surplus and inflation must keep the real stock in constant ratio to national output. This ratio, like those for other asset stocks, will be endogenously determined, partly by portfolio and saving demands that are functions of the several real rates of return.

In a fixed exchange rate regime, two of the four rates of return are exogenously determined. The domestic inflation rate must equal the foreign inflation rate, uninfluenced by events in the small open economy. Otherwise the terms of trade will be continuously changing. The real rate on foreign assets is likewise exogenous. What, then, are the two endogenous variables besides R and r_B? One is the ratio of domestic price to foreign price. This must be such that the trade surplus X is consistent with growth of foreign assets at the natural rate. The other is one of the policy parameters; the government must adjust one endogenously in order to make the nominal stocks of its bonds and money grow at the predetermined rate $g + i$ while meeting savers' demands. Among the policy instruments which might be endogenous in this sense is the ratio of official reserves of foreign assets, in real value, to national output. Alternatively, the government might set a target for its foreign exchange reserves, and let one of its domestic fiscal or financial instruments adjust as necessary to achieve this target.

Under a floating exchange rate regime, domestic inflation can differ from the world inflation rate, with steady exchange depreciation or appreciation equal to the difference. The real rate of return on foreign assets is still exogenous, equal to the real rate on such assets abroad. The four basic equations determine the other three rates of return, among them the domestic rate of inflation. As in the fixed exchange rate regime, the terms of trade provide another endogenous variable. Choice of exchange rate regimes is much less momentous in the long run than in the short run. By assumption prices are flexible in the long run, unlike the short run. Price flexibility can accomplish the same adjustments in terms of trade as exchange rate flexibility. The government has no more free policy instruments in one regime than the other; under floating rates official reserve stocks and interventions are constrained to be zero. The opportunity to have a divergent inflation rate may nonetheless be useful. Conceivably some objectives—regarding the composition of output and the capital intensity of the economy—might be unattainable if domestic rate of inflation and thus the real return on money were constrained to equal the international rate of inflation.

We have already seen that, even with three assets and a closed economy, it is impossible to generalize about the effects of steady-state policies on equilibrium capital intensity and inflation rates. Naturally the number of possible cases is multiplied by opening the economy and enlarging the asset menu. For example, whether the nation is creditor or debtor to the rest of the world will make an important difference. The relevance of steady-state exercises is in any event, more doubtful for open than closed economies. The trade surplus, for instance, will not have the homogeneity property needed for steady growth equilibrium unless foreign export demand is, for given terms of trade, expanding at the natural rate of growth of the domestic economy. It would also be desirable, of course, to model two or more interacting economies rather than a small economy in a big world. The United States is not powerless to influence inflation rates and interest rates overseas.

We can conclude, anyway, that the major policy issues cannot be solved by theoretical analysis alone but require empirical estimates of economic structure and behavior. No shortcuts are available in sweeping a priori claims of neutrality.

REFERENCES

1. BAILY, MARTIN N. "Stabilization Policy and Private Economic Behavior," *Brookings Papers on Economic Activity*, 1978(1), pp. 11-50.

2. BARRO, ROBERT J. "Are Government Bonds Net Wealth?" *Journal of Political Economy*, Nov./Dec. 1974, *82*(6), pp. 1095-1117.

3. ____. "Rational Expectations and the Role of Monetary Policy," *Journal of Monetary Economics*, Jan. 1976, *2*(1), pp. 1-32.

4. BLINDER, ALAN S., and SOLOW, ROBERT M. "Does Fiscal Policy Matter?" *Journal of Public Economics*, Nov. 1973, *2*(4), pp. 319-37.

5. BUITER, WILLEM H. *Temporary Equilibrium and Long-Run Equilibrium*, Yale Ph.D. Thesis, December 1975. Published New York: Garland Publishing, Inc., 1979.

6. ____. "Crowding Out and the Effectiveness of Fiscal Policy," *Journal of Public Economics*, June 1977, *7*(3), pp. 309-28.

7. ____. "An Integration of Short Run Neo-Keynesian Analysis and Growth Theory," *De Economist*, 1977, *125*(3), pp. 340-59.

8. ____. "Short-run and Long-run Effects of External Disturbances under a Floating Exchange Rate," *Economica*, August 1978, *45*, pp. 251-72.

9. ____. "Government Finance in an Overlapping Generations Model with Gifts and Bequests," in *Social Security Versus Private Saving in Post-Industrial Democracies.* Edited by GEORGE M. VON FURSTENBERG. Cambridge, Mass.: Ballinger Publishing Company, 1979.

10. ____, and TOBIN, JAMES. "Debt Neutrality: A Brief Review of Doctrine and Evidence," in *Social Security versus Private Saving.* Edited by GEORGE M. von FURSTENBERG. Cambridge, Mass.: Ballinger Publishing Co., 1979.

11. CHRIST, CARL F. "A Simple Macroeconomic Model with a Government Budget Restraint," *Journal of Political Economy*, Jan. 1968, *76*(1), pp. 53-67.

12. _____. "Some Dynamic Theory of Macroeconomic Policy Effects on Income and Prices under the Government Budget Restraint," *Journal of Monetary Economics* Jan 1978. *4*(1), pp. 45-70.

13. CURRIE, DAVID. "Macroeconomic Policy and the Government Financing Requirement: A Survey of Recent Developments," in *Studies in Contemporary Economic Analysis, Vol. I.* Edited by MICHAEL ARTIS and R. NOBAY. London: Croom-Helm, 1978.

14. _____. "Monetary and Fiscal Policy and the Crowding-Out Issue," mimeographed, January 1978.

15. FAIR, RAY C., "The Sensitivity of Fiscal-Policy Effects to Assumptions about the Behavior of the Federal Reserve," *Econometrica*, September 1978, *46*(5), pp. 1165-78.

16. FISCHER, STANLEY. "Long-Term Contracts, Rational Expectations, and the Optimal Money Supply Rule," *Journal of Political Economy*, Feb. 1977, *85*(1), pp. 191-206.

17. _____. "Capital Accumulation and the Transition Path in a Monetary Optimizing Model," mimeograph, February 1978.

18. FOLEY, DUNCAN K. "On Two Specifications of Asset Equilibrium in Macroeconomic Models," *Journal of Political Economy*, April 1975, *83*(2), pp. 303-24.

19. FRIEDMAN, MILTON. *A Theory of the Consumption Function.* Princeton, N.J.: Princeton University Press, 1957.

20. _____. "The Role of Monetary Policy," *American Economic Review*, March 1968, *58*(1), pp. 1-17.

21. KEYNES, JOHN MAYNARD. *The General Theory of Employment, Interest, and Money.* London: Macmillan, 1936.

22. LERNER, ABBA P. *The Economics of Control.* New York: Macmillan, 1946.

23. LUCAS, ROBERT E. "Econometric Policy Evaluation: A Critique," in *The Phillips Curve and Labor Markets.* Edited by KARL BRUNNER and ALLAN H. MELTZER. Amsterdam: North-Holland, 1976.

24. PHELPS, EDMUND S., et al. *Microeconomic Foundations of Employment and Inflation Theory.* New York: W.W. Norton, 1970.

25. PHELPS, EDMUND S., and SHELL, KARL. "Public Debt, Taxation, and Capital Intensiveness," *Journal of Economic Theory*, Oct. 1969, *1*(3), pp. 330-46.

26. PHELPS, EDMUND S., and TAYLOR, JOHN B. "Stabilizing Powers of Monetary Policy under Rational Expectations," *Journal of Political Economy*, Feb. 1977, *85*(1), pp. 163-90.

27. SARGENT, THOMAS J., and WALLACE, N. "Rational Expectations and the Theory of Economic Policy," *Journal of Monetary Economics*, April 1976, *84*(2), pp. 207-37.

28. SIDRAUSKI, MIGUEL. "Rational Choice and Patterns of Growth in a Monetary Economy," *American Economic Review*, May 1967, *57*(2), pp. 534-44.

29. TOBIN, JAMES. "Money and Economic Growth," *Econometrica*, Oct. 1965, *33*(4), pp. 671-84.

30. ____. "A General Equilibrium Approach to Monetary Theory," *Journal of Money, Credit, and Banking*, Feb. 1969, *1*(1), pp. 15-29.

31. ____. "Inflation and Unemployment," *American Economic Review*, March 1972, *62*(1), pp. 1-19.

32. ____, and BUITER, WILLEM. "Long-Run Effects of Fiscal and Monetary Policy on Aggregate Demand," in *Monetarism*. Edited by JEROME STEIN. Amsterdam: North-Holland, 1976.

Reprinted from THE JOURNAL OF FINANCE, Vol. XX, No. 4, December, 1965

THE BURDEN OF THE PUBLIC DEBT: A REVIEW ARTICLE

JAMES TOBIN*

DOES DEBT-FINANCING of public expenditure place a "burden" on future generations? The answer has long been "yes" in conservative financial and political circles, but "no" among academic economists. A lively controversy on the question has raged in economic journals in recent years, provoked mainly by the iconoclastic writings of James Buchanan, who contends that his fellow economists are much farther from the truth than the laymen whom they accuse of primitive error.

Mr. Ferguson has collected twenty-three of the most important and representative contributions to the debate.[1] Three of these, including one previously unpublished paper, are by Buchanan. The anthology is quite different from most of the readings volumes which are pouring from the presses these days to cash in on the growing student market. Although it will be useful to students, Ferguson's volume also serves a definite scholarly and professional purpose. The volume is carefully organized to achieve the unity which a well-defined topic makes possible. The editor has provided the "names and numbers of all the players" in an introduction, a final comment, and a bibliography. His contributions are a useful guide for the reader venturing on to this murky battleground for the first time.

Two ground rules are almost universally respected by the combatants. One is to assume full employment. The other is to assume a fixed program of government expenditure; the "gross" burden in question results from financing a fixed program by issuing debt instead of levying taxes. The debate does not concern the merits of debt-financed government expenditure, which would have to be judged by the "net" burden allowing for benefits. In logic at least, these ground rules deny the political champions of fiscal orthodoxy much of the comfort which the arguments of Buchanan and other discoverers of debt burden might seem to provide. President Eisenhower's strictures, which are much quoted in the book, made no fine distinctions between full employment and unemployment. They were, moreover, directed against increases in public expenditure, without nice calculation whether the benefits to future generations might outweigh the burdens.

No one disputes the fact that in a closed economy with full employment the resources used for government expenditure are drawn from other *current* uses of resources. Given the government program, the reduction in resources available for *current* nongovernment use is independent of the method of financing the government. This reasoning has traditionally led economists to deny that the burden of public expenditure can be shifted forward in time by issuing

* Yale University.

1. *Public Debt & Future Generations.* Edited by JAMES M. FERGUSON. University of North Carolina Press, 1964. Pp. 234. $6.75.

Reprinted by permission from *Journal of Finance* 20(4) (December 1965):679–682.

internal debt rather than taxing. The debt can be no burden, because future payments of interest or principal from taxpayers to bondholders will be transfers involving no aggregate draft on resources. They may involve a redistribution of income. They may even impose a "deadweight loss" because taxes distort incentives. But these recognized qualifications of the traditional view are not what the new heretics have in mind.

They are not all of the same mind. Three views may be distinguished. One is Buchanan's. Stripped of all embellishment, it reduces to the assertion that payment of taxes is *per se* a burden—whether or not the taxes affect incentives and resource allocation. Since debt finance postpones the levy of taxes, it obviously shifts Buchanan's burden to future generations. The justification for this definition is that taxes are compulsory and involuntary. In contrast, market transactions, including the purchase of public debt, are voluntary agreements. Buchanan's view implies that democratic societies "burden" themselves whenever they agree to a social compact binding on all their members. On the other hand, agreements which do not involve governmental coercion evidently burden none of the participants.

The political theory is questionable, and so is the economics. Does Buchanan really mean that government imposes no burden when it acts through the market? It is true that purchasers of government bonds are willing lenders. But is there no burden on would-be private borrowers whom government borrowing displaces from the bond market by raising interest rates? Do excise taxes involve no burden because they are paid only as an incident of voluntary market transactions? Buchanan's simplistic view of burden throws away the whole "incidence and effects" literature of public finance.

The second concept of burden, most forcefully advocated by Modigliani in this volume, is closer to the traditional analysis, of which it is more a refinement than a rejection. The method of financing government expenditure does not alter the size of the draft on current resources. But it may alter the nature of the private uses of resources which are displaced. Modigliani argues that debt finance will displace mainly investment, and tax finance mainly consumption. The burden of debt finance on future generations is that they inherit a smaller capital stock than if tax finance had been used. This is indeed an implication of the widely held view that, while full employment can be maintained by tight money and deficit spending, such a policy mix is unfavorable to capital accumulation and growth. (Modigliani goes further. On the basis of his life-cycle consumption-saving model he contends that each generation will do only so much saving; the more of this which is absorbed by government debt the less will be available for capital formation. Thus even anti-recession deficit finance impairs the inheritance of the next generation.)

Two main comments on the Modigliani view are suggested in or by the debate. First, the crucial matter is the national rate of capital formation, not debts or deficits *per se*. On Modigliani's logic, we impose a burden on future generations whenever we fail to run a surplus, or a bigger surplus, not just when we engage in debt finance. Taxes are not intrinsically virtuous. Some forms of current taxation shift the burden to the future by discouraging current investment; and debt finance keeps the burden in the present to the extent that it discourages consumer borrowing.

More broadly, there are many sins of omission and commission by which the present generation can contrive to bequeath to the future a smaller capital stock than it might. Why single out debt finance to bear the whole burden of guilt? Is it not more to the point, as Mishan argues in his contribution, to ask what is intergenerational equity anyway? If some "burden" of current public expenditure is shifted to the future, so what? Perhaps it should be. The answer cannot be found in any simple budgetary rule. It will depend on the nature of the public expenditure, and it will involve a judgment of the adequacy or over-adequacy of the provisions for the future the current generation is already making through private and public investment.

The second comment questions the consumption-saving behavior assumed in the Modigliani notion of the burden. Is it not based on some asymmetrical illusion? Society fools itself into consuming more, thinking that possession of government paper provides for its future. Why don't those who will have to pay taxes to service the debt—or even those who will be squeezed out of consumer goods markets when the holders of government paper spend it—consider themselves poorer and save more accordingly?

This observation threatens not only Modigliani's concept of debt burden but equally the belief that the government can influence investment and growth by varying the fiscal-monetary mix. Indeed it comes dangerously close to denying that any internal financial and monetary arrangements are of any real consequence. One does not have to assume inconsistent expectations or irrational money illusion to believe that financial intermediation—whether through government or through banks and insurance companies—can by pooling and reallocating risks diminish some of the needs which generate saving. Ultimately this is an empirical question, and the weight of evidence is that, illusion or not, the private income and wealth corresponding to government deficit and debt stimulate consumption.

Bowen, Davis, and Kopf—whose original essay is reprinted here along with several critiques and rejoinders—seem to provide still a third account of how the burden is shifted to future generations. The burden they have in mind seems to be the same as Modigliani's, but in Bowen *et al.* the shift is delayed. They assume that the initial public expenditure, although debt-financed, draws resources from consumption, not from investment. Thus "Generation I" appears to have shouldered the burden squarely, but the authors are at pains to point out how they may later try to unload it on to their heirs. By going on a consumption binge in retirement, financed by selling their government securities, Generation I forces Generation II either to accept a smaller inheritance of real capital or to finance their parents' binge by extra saving. In either case Generation II can play the same game with Generation III. And so on. (Perhaps President Eisenhower would have been less distressed had he known that any burdens we transmit to our grandchildren they can simply pass on to their grandchildren, *ad infinitum.*)

While the authors have provided an interesting account of the possibilities in wars between overlapping generations, it is not clear why government debt should be the central battlefield. Even if Generation I had taxed itself to pay for the government expenditure, they might still have both the desire and the means for compensatory high living in retirement.

Finally, nothing in this volume—unless one accepts Buchanan's identification of burden with tax payments—disturbs economists' customary insistence on the essential difference between internal and foreign debt. This is a distinction which lay critics of debt finance do not respect. For this reason alone, burden finders like Bowen, Davis, and Kopf should never have begun by saying they proposed to prove their fellow economists wrong and President Eisenhower right.

MARTIN NEIL BAILY
Yale University

JAMES TOBIN
Yale University

Macroeconomic Effects of Selective Public Employment and Wage Subsidies

DIRECT JOB CREATION and selective wage subsidies are policies designed to alter the mix of employment in favor of workers who, in the normal course of economic events, experience high rates of unemployment. As instruments of macroeconomic policy, these measures are intended to mitigate the conflict between society's goals for unemployment and inflation. The hope is to "cheat the Phillips curve." For the short run, as in the current cyclical recovery, this means to diminish the inflationary consequences of higher rates of employment. For the long run, it means to diminish the natural rate of unemployment—or, to use a more neutral term, the minimal nonaccelerating-inflation rate of unemployment

Note: This paper presents the analytical framework for the principal arguments, and some related empirical evidence, underlying a paper, "Direct Job Creation, Inflation, and Unemployment," delivered by the authors at the Conference on Direct Job Creation sponsored by the Brookings Institution and the Institute for Research on Poverty, held in Washington in April 1977. The conference paper, as revised, will be published in a Brookings volume devoted to the papers presented at the conference.

We would like to thank participants in the conference for helpful comments, and to acknowledge with gratitude the excellent research assistance of Richard Kolsky, Hiroshi Yoshikawa, and David Coppock. We are grateful also for the financial support provided by the institutions sponsoring the conference and by the National Science Foundation.

(NAIRU). In general, the purpose is to allow standard fiscal and monetary policy to achieve more satisfactory joint paths of output, employment, and prices.

The basic strategy is simple: Shift labor demand to types of workers who are—because of high unemployment, weak bargaining power, rigid wages, or other characteristics—on relatively flat Phillips curves. Let the government hire, or induce other employers to hire, workers whose unemployment does little or nothing to restrain the advance of wage costs in the aggregate. The idea is appealing, and our purpose is to examine it systematically. Most of our discussion concerns the long run—the possibility of reducing the NAIRU—because it is in that context that the strategy is most likely to encounter complications and pitfalls.

For the strategy to have a chance, selective eligibility is essential. Public employment opportunities or wage subsidies must be confined to workers whose supply and demand have relatively little to do with economy-wide inflation. From a macroeconomic viewpoint, this is the reason for eligibility criteria whose rationales may vary greatly: low income, low wage, welfare dependency, previous unemployment, residence in a labor surplus area, youth. Open-ended "employer of last resort" programs and general employment subsidies would not carry out the macroeconomic strategy to which our paper is directed.

We will present two analyses of the way selective employment policies may work. The first is an aggregative model of frictional unemployment and its possible reduction. The second is an explicitly disaggregated model of labor markets, in which the power of selective employment policies comes from exploiting differences among markets in wage responses.

Reducing Frictional Unemployment

Excess demand in any labor market is measured conceptually by the algebraic excess of jobs over the labor force, or of job vacancies over the unemployed. For given excess demand, both vacancies and unemployment may be high, or they may be low. Unemployment matched by simultaneous vacancies is frictional unemployment. It is a reasonable assumption that inflationary pressure on wages is proportional to excess demand, or depends separately on its components, vacancies and unemployment. If so, both the inflation-unemployment tradeoff and the NAIRU can be improved by reductions of frictional unemployment. Some labor-market policies—retraining, relocating, and more efficient exchanges of information—are specifically designed to place unemployed workers in existing vacancies, or to facilitate job searches and shifts without intervening spells of unemployment.

These aims are not central features of direct job creation. Nevertheless, such programs may indirectly diminish frictional unemployment. Job vacancies connected with direct job creation should be minimal, while the program itself could be a channel for routing unemployed workers to vacancies in the private sector as long as the wages and duration of the jobs did not reduce incentives to look for alternatives. Their availability may brake market wage increases nearly as much as if they were actually unemployed.

Wage subsidies per se do not promise the same reductions in frictional unemployment. If the subsidy for employing an eligible worker is permanent and the wage is uncontrolled, search behavior will not be modified. The mechanism by which wage subsidies could be effective is described by the second model below.

The first model is as follows:[1]

(1) $$UL(J, x) - L(J, x) + N(J, x) = 0, \quad 0 < L_J < N_J < 1.$$

Here U is the unemployment rate; L is the labor force, a function of the number of jobs (or slots), J, and of a policy parameter, x; and N is employment, a function of the same two variables.

(2) $$VJ - J + N(J, x) = 0.$$

The vacancy rate, V, is measured relative to the number of jobs:

(3) $$\dot{W} = f(U, V, x) + \dot{W}^e, \quad f_U < 0, f_V > 0.$$

Here, $\dot{W}$ is the proportional rate of wage inflation $(1/W \cdot dW/dt)$, and depends on built-in or expected inflation, $\dot{W}^e$, and on the vacancy and unemployment rates. The NAIRU condition is

(4) $$f(U, V, x) = 0.$$

---

1. This is an elaboration of a model one of us presented previously to serve as an organizing framework for examining ways in which labor-market policies, direct job creation and others, could alter the inflation-unemployment tradeoff and the NAIRU. See the comment by James Tobin (on Michael Wiseman, "Public Employment as Fiscal Policy") in *BPEA, 1:1976*, pp. 107–10.

For long-run equilibrium the three equations 1, 2, and 4 determine U, V, and J as a function of the policy variable, x. The number of jobs, J, is directly related to aggregate real demand, and thus to monetary and fiscal policies that affect it. Nevertheless, J is an endogenous variable in long-run analysis, in the sense that the monetary and fiscal policymakers seek the maximum J consistent with nonaccelerating inflation.

The solution of the system gives the NAIRU, $\bar{U}$, and

(5) $\qquad \Delta \dfrac{dU}{dx} = -N_x f_V[1 - V - L_J(1 - U)] + L_x(1 - U)f_V(1 - V - N_J)$
$$- f_x J[L_J(1 - U) - N_J],$$

where

$$\Delta = L f_V(1 - V - N_J) + J f_U[L_J(1 - U) - N_J].$$

Assume that, with unchanged policy x, increasing J raises the vacancy rate $(1 - V > N_J)$ and decreases the unemployment rate—$L_J(1 - U)$ $< N_J$. Equation 5 shows that a policy x will tend to reduce the NAIRU if:

(a) $N_x > 0$; that is, the policy diminishes the slippage between jobs and employment. This reduction in the vacancy content of jobs works only if $f_V > 0$—that is, if the vacancy rate, as well as the unemployment rate, affects the rate of wage inflation.

(b) $L_x < 0$; that is, the policy diminishes the endogenous response of the labor force to the number of jobs. This also works only if $f_V > 0$.

(c) $f_x < 0$; that is, the policy diminishes wage inflation for a given combination of vacancies and unemployment.

The short-run Phillips tradeoff is $(d\dot{W}/dJ)/(dU/dJ)$. Using equations 1, 2, and 3, and taking $\dot{W}^e$ as given,

(6) $\qquad \dfrac{d\dot{W}/dJ}{dU/dJ} = \dfrac{f_V(1 - V - N_J)L}{[L_J(1 - U) - N_J]J} + f_U.$

Policy will make the Phillips curve flatter if (a) it raises N_J, (b) it lowers L relative to J or reduces L_J, (c) it lowers f_V or the absolute size of f_U or both. These three points correspond to the three points for NAIRU. As in that case, points (a) and (b) apply only if $f_V > 0$.

This model is illustrated in figure 1, in which the number of jobs J is measured horizontally, the labor force L and employment N, vertically. The curve $L(J)$ indicates the dependence of the labor force on job availability; its positive slope represents the well-known fact that labor-force participation is responsive to job opportunities. The curve $N(J)$ represents the transformation of jobs into actual employment. Be-

Figure 1. Effects of Labor-Market Policy in Reducing Frictional Unemployment

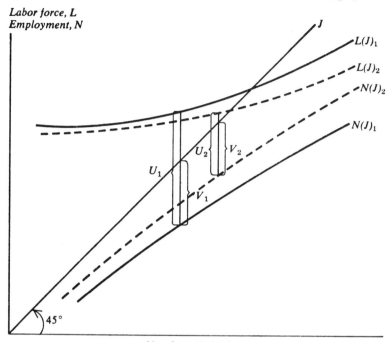

Number of jobs, J

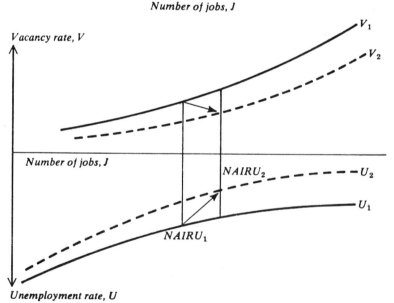

cause of "friction," the transformation is imperfect. The vertical shortfall of $N(J)$ from the 45° reference line J indicates the number of vacancies. Unemployment is the vertical distance $L - N$. In the lower panel, the vacancy rate, relative to jobs, and the unemployment rate, relative to the labor force, are shown. One pair of these rates is consistent with stable wage inflation, and this determines the NAIRU and corresponding jobs, vacancies, employment, and labor force.

The dashed lines represent some favorable shifts due to policy actions, perhaps direct job creation. As indicated, these permit increases in the long-run equilibrium levels of jobs and employment, and a reduction in the NAIRU. The gains arise from reducing the vacancy rate corresponding to any given unemployment rate. The necessary assumption is that vacancies have an independent inflationary effect on wages. On this assumption, a policy that will reduce the vacancy slippage in $N(J)$ or reduce the induced labor-supply response in $L(J)$ will diminish the NAIRU. Such a policy will also flatten the short-run Phillips curve and improve the trade off.

Direct job creation could have both effects. The key points are the limited eligibility of workers for the program and control of the wage rates. Vacancies, if they exist, would not have the normal effects on wages, and would not be a reason for job-seeking workers to decline other jobs at going wage rates. Similarly, the selective eligibility criteria could hold below normal the response of entrants or reentrants into the labor force to the creation of new jobs.

The third possible policy effect is reduction in the wage pressure associated with a given state of the labor market. Direct job creation could contribute to this result insofar as employees under the program continued to look for and be available for other jobs in nearly the same degree as if they were unemployed. Keeping wage rates for the program below the market, limiting tenure in the jobs, and providing placement service would encourage such behavior.

Segmented Labor Markets and the NAIRU

This section explores the conditions under which direct job creation could exploit differences among labor markets in order to reduce the NAIRU. In the next section the same apparatus is used to analyze a wage subsidy.

Unemployment is measured in persons. But persons differ widely in the effective labor input they provide per hour. A natural first approximation is that effective labor is proportional to the hourly wage. At the margin, substitution of two workers at $2.50 an hour for one worth $5.00 an hour leaves effective labor input unchanged, and presumably gross national product as well. However, it increases employment and reduces unemployment, measured in persons (though the unemployment reduction may be partially offset by induced labor-force entry).

Suppose that the true aggregate Phillips curve relates inflation of the wage *per effective worker* to the rate of unemployment *per effective worker*. A low-wage worker has a relatively low weight in the wage index, and his unemployment exerts correspondingly little restraint on increases in the index. The NAIRU would be determined as a certain amount of wage-weighted unemployment. The equilibrium unemployment count could vary, but not effective labor input or GNP.[2]

Substitutions of low-wage for high-wage workers, diminishing the number of persons unemployed, might be regarded as socially desirable even though total output is not increased. The social disutility of unemployment may depend in part on the number of persons affected, not just on the sum of labor resources wasted. The substitution of low-wage for high-wage employment may result in a fairer allocation of the unemployment required for restraining inflation. The formation of human capital via work experience, an output not included in GNP, may be greater the more persons are employed. Some of these considerations apply also to other proposals for sharing work and unemployment—for example, forced reductions in hours of work.

As a numerical illustration, consider a two-way split of the labor force into adults and teenagers. The ratio of an individual adult to an individual teenager in Perry's wage-weighted unemployment measure is 3.05.[3] Assuming that substitution in production can be made at this ratio over a relevant range, employment of one hundred teenagers would displace

2. George L. Perry estimated such an equation in "Changing Labor Markets and Inflation," *BPEA, 3:1970*, pp. 411–41. The unemployed were classified by demographic groups defined by age and sex. Smaller wage weights per person were given to unemployed teenagers and females than to adult males. Thus a redistribution of unemployment at the expense of high-wage workers would lower the NAIRU in persons, but not lower the NAIRU in weighted persons or raise GNP.

3. This was computed from Perry's "Changing Labor Markets" (p. 440). Since Perry has finer disaggregation, his weights were reaggregated for the two-way classification.

thirty-three adults. The weighted unemployment rate and GNP would be unchanged, but the unemployment count would be down by sixty-seven.[4] This calculation will be a convenient reference point for further illustrative estimates, using the same two-way break of the labor force.

The aggregate model, however, raises troubling questions. If the labor inputs of different workers are perfectly substitutable at prevailing wages, what determines the distribution of employment? Why are there such great differences in unemployment rates among the demographic groups? If the various types of workers are not good substitutes, what determines their relative wages and their differential impacts on average wage inflation?

The most appropriate model to deal with these questions seems to us to be one that (a) permits some flexibility in relative wages and determines equilibrium relative wages for the long run; (b) allows for some substitution in production among workers of different types; and (c) explains the determination of wages in different markets. Continuing illustratively to use two demographic groups, adults (group 1) and teenagers (group 2), let L_1 and L_2 be the sizes of the labor force of the two groups, and α_1 and α_2 the shares $[\alpha_i = L_i/(L_1 + L_2)]$.[5] The Ls are assumed constant for the present, an important assumption discussed below. Two wage rates call for two wage equations. Our specification is

(7) $\dot{W}_1 = f^1(\alpha_1 U_1, \alpha_2 U_2, -\ln R) + h_1^1 \dot{W}^e + h_2^1 \dot{W}_2^e,$

$\qquad f_1^1 < f_2^1 < 0, f_3^1 > 0; h_1^1, h_2^1 \geqq 0, h_1^1 + h_1^2 = 1;$

$\dot{W}_2 = f^2(\alpha_1 U_1, \alpha_2 U_2, \ln R) + h_1^2 \dot{W}_1^e + h_2^2 \dot{W}_2^e,$

$\qquad f_2^2 < f_1^2 < 0, f_3^2 > 0; h_1^2, h_2^2 \geqq 0, h_1^2 + h_2^2 = 1.$

Both unemployment rates appear in each equation. The two types of workers are in some degree substitutes, and unemployment of each type restrains both wage rates. However, the "own" effects should be stronger

4. This example does not take account of changes in labor-force participation. A reduction in the rate of unemployment of teenagers might encourage more of them to enter the labor force. To some extent this would be offset—in its impact on the unemployment rate—by a reduction in adult participation.

5. Other divisions of the labor force, with n groups rather than two, could be handled by the same type of analysis. A more realistic formulation would be to distinguish m labor markets—say, industries—in which distinct wages are determined. The n types of labor would participate in varying degrees in each of the markets. In the illustrative two-group model, however, labor markets and wage rates are identified with the two demographic groups.

—that is, each wage rate is more sensitive to unemployment of the type of labor in that market. The unemployment rates are weighted by shares in the labor force; the arguments $\alpha_1 U_1$ and $\alpha_2 U_2$ are proportional to the number of persons of each type unemployed. The ratio of the levels of the two wage rates, W_1/W_2, is expressed as R. The assumption is that each sectoral wage rises faster, other things equal, when it is low relative to the other wage. The h functions are the feedback or expectational terms. The specification says that an equal increase in the two expected rates of wage inflation will raise both actual rates of wage increase $\dot{W}_i$ one for one. However, the two expected rates may, if they differ, have different effects in the two markets.

Inclusion of R in the sectoral Phillips curves requires further explanation. Sectoral Phillips curves are "reduced form" equations that reflect forces from both sides of the labor market—firms and workers. Behavior on both sides suggests that the relative wage $R = W_1/W_2$ should be an argument in f^1 and f^2. First, employers pay attention to relative wage levels when establishing their wage offers to the two types of labor.[6] Second, and perhaps more compelling, the job-search and turnover behavior of teenagers or other secondary workers will be affected by their relative wage. At the point $f^2 = 0$, the excess supply (unemployment) of group 2 workers balances the inflation pressure from excess demand (vacancies). Much of the problem of teenage unemployment, it is often observed, comes from dissatisfaction with the available jobs, a gap between expectations or aspirations and the realities of miserable wages and working conditions. One consequence is the high turnover among teenagers. The $f^2 = 0$ equilibrium, therefore, occurs with very high U_2, because an individual unemployed teenager does not exert much excess-supply pressure on the market. If the relative position of teenagers were improved—in practice, by improving working conditions as well as by raising wages—each unemployed teenager would exert more effective pressure, and the equilibrium would involve less dissatisfaction and lower turnover. In short, for a given W_2 the required U_2 is smaller when R is lower—that is, when the relative position of teenagers is better. Third, when adult workers are bargaining for wage increases they, as well as their employers, consider

6. The relative wage is, of course, relevant for employers' demand for labor of the two types. This effect is in the labor-demand functions implicit in equation 17 below. The behavior of employers embedded in the f functions has to do with hiring and turnover strategy.

the potential for substituting secondary workers. When the relative wage is high, group 1 workers may moderate their own wage demands or even bargain for higher group 2 wages in order to protect their own jobs.[7] Long-run equilibrium requires that the relative wage R be constant and that expectations are realized: $\dot{W}_1 = \dot{W}_2 = \dot{W}_1^e = \dot{W}_2^e$. Thus the NAIRU condition is that $f^1 = f^2 = 0$.[8] The aggregate NAIRU in persons is $\alpha_1 U_1 + \alpha_2 U_2$. The aggregate NAIRU in wage-weighted persons is $\bar{R}\alpha_1 U_1 + \alpha_2 U_2$, where $\bar{R}$ is a reference relative wage.

If the relative wage, R, is omitted from equations 7, they determine unique values of both unemployment rates in the NAIRU equilibrium. Specifically, they determine a pair of unemployment rates $(\alpha_1 U_1, \alpha_2 U_2)$ at which $\dot{W}_1 = \dot{W}_2 = \dot{W}_1^e = \dot{W}_2^e$.[9] If this were the correct specification, direct job creation would be unavailing in the long run. Hiring teenagers in public jobs would lower their unemployment rate in the short run, drive up their relative wage, and lead to the substitution of adults for teenagers in private employment. This process, plus the necessary policy adjustment of output to avoid wage acceleration, would not stop until a number of teenagers equal to the number employed in public jobs had been displaced from private employment.

With R included, the two equations $f^1 = 0$, $f^2 = 0$ determine $\alpha_1 U_1$ and $\alpha_2 U_2$, each as a function of R:

$$(8) \qquad \alpha_1 U_1 = s^1(R),\ s_R^1 < 0,$$
$$\alpha_2 U_2 = s^2(R),\ s_R^2 > 0.$$

Type 1 unemployment falls with R; a high W_1 relative to W_2 dampens the pressure for wage increases and thus allows a lower unemployment rate. For like reasons, type 2 unemployment rises with R. In figure 2 the locus of combinations $(\alpha_1 L U_1, \alpha_2 L U_2)$ that meet the NAIRU condition is shown graphically as the curve marked $f^1 = f^2 = 0$ in the upper right.

7. Some analysis of behavior of this kind appears in Martin Neil Baily, "Contract Theory and the Moderation of Inflation by Recession and by Controls," *BPEA*, 3:1976, pp. 585–622.

8. An expected-*price* feedback formulation would imply that the *f*s are equal to the normal growth of labor productivity. We abstract from changes in raw-material prices, taxes, and other external price determinants, so the difference between the two formulations is not significant.

9. If the cross-effects are ignored, the monotonicity of the two *f*s ensures that there are uniquely determined values of $\alpha_1 U_1$ and $\alpha_2 U_2$. Allowing for the cross-effects does open the technical possibility of multiple equilibria, but this possibility does not look very interesting as an avenue by which to lower the NAIRU.

274

Figure 2. Impact of a Program of Direct Jobs Creation for Teenagers (Group 2)

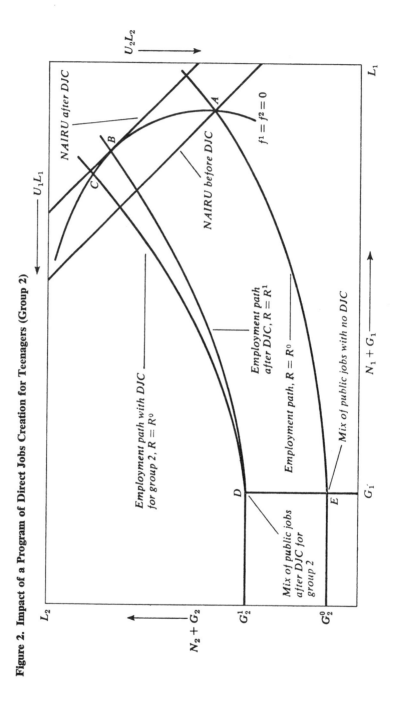

The slope of this NAIRU locus $[\partial(\alpha_2 U_2)]/[\partial(\alpha_1 U_1)]$ is s_R^2/s_R^1 and is negative. Movement down the locus, as oriented in figure 2, is associated with increases in R.[10]

The steeper the locus is at the point the economy reaches in the absence of policy—for example, A in figure 2—the greater is the potential reduction in aggregate unemployment from policies varying U_1 and U_2 along the locus. The total unemployment count is $L_1 U_1 + L_2 U_2$, and points of equal count, therefore, lie along straight lines of slope -1 in figure 2. At point A, the locus is steeper than such a line, indicating the potential for reducing the number of persons unemployed by moving up the locus.[11]

Aggregate unemployment in "teenage equivalent" units, with persons weighted in proportion to their wage rates at point A, is $\bar{R} L_1 U_1 + L_2 U_2$. Points of equal wage-weighted unemployment lie along lines of slope $-\bar{R}$, steeper than $45°$. Only if the slope of the locus is steeper than the relative wage is it possible to reduce wage-weighted unemployment and to increase GNP (assuming that relative wages match relative marginal products).

We will now show that, under plausible assumptions, the slope of the

10.
$$s_R^1 = \frac{1}{R\Delta} (f_3^1 f_2^2 + f_3^2 f_2^1);$$

$$s_R^2 = \frac{1}{R\Delta} (-f_3^2 f_1^1 - f_3^1 f_1^2);$$

$$\Delta = f_1^1 f_2^2 - f_2^1 f_1^2.$$

Δ is positive by assumption of dominance of "own" effects. The signs of s_R^1 and s_R^2 asserted in the text follow from the other assumptions in equations 7.

11. The locus is shown as concave from below. The concavity is not necessary for the results derived here; it is only necessary that the locus be steeper than the $45°$ line at point A. Concavity is extremely plausible, however. It suggests decreasing returns to successive application of direct job creation in reducing the NAIRU. The diagram suggests that there is, in fact, a limit to the process—shown as the minimum NAIRU. According to note 10, the locus slope is

$$-\frac{f_3^2 f_1^1 + f_3^1 f_1^2}{f_3^1 f_2^2 + f_3^2 f_2^1}.$$

As U_1 increases, U_2 decreases, and R falls, what happens to the value of this slope? To justify the convex locus shown in figure 2, it must fall. From the curvature of Phillips curves, $|f_1^1|$ falls and $|f_2^2|$ rises; these "own" effects tend to flatten the locus. The decline in R would be expected, if anything, to raise f_3^1 and lower f_3^2, reinforcing the "own" effects. The cross terms in the numerator and denominator work the other way, but seem likely to be weaker.

locus is likely to be steeper than the relative wage. To simplify the exposition, we shall ignore the cross-effects in 7 of one group's unemployment rate on the other's rate of wage increase, and take the functions to be linear in R and in the reciprocal of unemployment. Thus:

$$(9) \qquad \dot{W_1} = a_1 + \frac{b_1}{U_1} - c_1 R + \text{feedback terms};$$

$$\dot{W_2} = a_2 + \frac{b_2}{U_2} + c_2 R + \text{feedback terms}.$$

Each of these equations defines a family of conventional, sectoral Phillips curves. The higher the value of R, the lower the position of the particular group 1 curve that is relevant and the higher the position of the relevant group 2 curve.

Moreover, each equation implies a tradeoff between R and the "own" unemployment rate consistent with equilibrium:

$$(10) \qquad \left(\frac{-b_1}{U_1^2}\right) dU_1 - c_1 dR = 0;$$

$$\left(\frac{-b_2}{U_2^2}\right) dU_2 + c_2 dR = 0.$$

Directly from 10,

$$(11) \qquad \frac{dU_1}{dR} = \frac{-c_1 U_1^2}{b_1}; \qquad \frac{dU_2}{dR} = \frac{c_2 U_2^2}{b_2}.$$

Now the slope of the locus of equilibria in figure 2 can be written as

$$(12) \qquad \frac{L_2 dU_2}{L_1 dU_1} = \frac{-L_2 c_2 U_2^2 b_1}{L_1 c_1 U_1^2 b_2}.$$

Next, for the present assume that changes in R do not alter aggregate inflation; that is, the dollar value of the reduced wage increase in group 1 from a higher R is exactly offset by increased wages in group 2. Then, $c_1 N_1 W_1 = c_2 N_2 W_2$, or

$$(13) \qquad \frac{c_2}{c_1} = \frac{N_1 W_1}{N_2 W_2} = \left(\frac{N_1}{N_2}\right) R.$$

Using equation 13 in 12 and simplifying leads to another expression for the locus slope:

$$(14) \qquad \frac{L_2 dU_2}{L_1 dU_1} = -R \left(\frac{b_1(1 - U_1)U_2^2}{b_2(1 - U_2)U_1^2}\right).$$

If the fraction that multiplies R on the right side of 14 is unity, then any movement along the locus simply changes the number of unemployed teenagers by R times the change (in the opposite direction) in the number of unemployed adults. In that event, no improvements in wage-weighted unemployment or in GNP are possible through policies that alter the mix of unemployment, although a reduction of the head-count NAIRU is possible.

There are analytical reasons for thinking this outcome is too pessimistic. To accept it is tantamount to asserting that the labor market is operating efficiently—one can redistribute unemployment at the margin, but one cannot gain anything overall. Not only the minimum wage, but institutional factors such as union hiring rules, employer discrimination, inadequate information, geographic separation of jobs and inner-city youths—and perhaps more diffuse sociological factors such as the legacy of alienation and disillusionment of younger workers—all surely contribute to a labor market that is not efficient. Intervention in this labor market, whether by direct job creation or by a wage subsidy, in favor of disadvantaged workers, whether teenagers or some other group, should do better than the reference outcome.

There is, moreover, crude empirical support for the same conclusion, stemming from equation 14. In 1974, the unemployment rates for adults and teenagers were 4.5 and 16 percent, respectively. For the expression that multiplies R to be unity with those sharply contrasting values of U_1 and U_2, the ratio of b_2 to b_1 would have to be 14.4. At the same unemployment rate for both groups, the sectoral Phillips curve for teenagers would have to be more than fourteen times as steep as that for adults! Any ratio of slopes below that would mean that a lowering of U_2, with its inflationary effect just neutralized by a rise of U_1, would lead to more GNP as well as a cut in the overall head count of unemployment. To be sure, there are reasons to believe that b_2 exceeds b_1 by some margin. It would be extreme to suppose that the Phillips curve for teenagers is simply a vertical displacement of the adult curve. Entry, reentry, and search are much more important for teenagers than for adults. But a ratio of 14 to 1 seems implausible. We feel justified in suggesting that the slope of the locus may well be above the reference value of R.

Adding the impact of cross-effects should steepen the locus slope further. The impact of teenage unemployment on prime-wage inflation

(f_2^1) is negligible compared with the effect of adult unemployment on secondary-wage inflation (f_2^2).

So far our model explains (1) how, via a decline in R, the adult wage relative to the teenage wage, it may be possible to reduce teenage unemployment while increasing adult unemployment; (2) how such a change in the mix may reduce aggregate unemployment counted in persons; and (3) how it may even diminish wage-weighted unemployment. The argument refers to a "long-run" equilibrium, to rates of unemployment that meet the conditions for the NAIRU, and to shifts of that equilibrium when the composition of labor demand is shifted in favor of teenagers.

However, we have not so far taken account of endogenous effects on labor demand resulting from the adjustment of relative wages. The decline in R is crucial to the mechanism described here, but it should induce substitution of adult workers for teenage workers in private employment, diminishing the effectiveness of direct job creation. The offset is depicted qualitatively in figure 2. In the absence of direct job creation the expansion path of private employment is EA. This describes the mix of employment of the two types of labor that employers will offer at a given relative wage R^0, specifically the relative wage that corresponds to point A on the NAIRU locus CBA. Path DC is the same, displaced vertically by the number of public jobs provided for type 2 workers. However, on the NAIRU locus, C requires a lower R than R^0. Unless the proportions in which workers are used is insensitive to the relative wage, the expansion path will shift against teenagers, rotating clockwise around point D. A new equilibrium—for example, B—will be associated with a lower R than the initial equilibrium A, and with lower private employment of both teenagers and adults. Private employment will be lower for both groups—this would also be true in the absence of substitution, as at point C—and especially for teenagers.

An extreme case, the polar opposite of zero substitution in private employment, is that the two types of workers are perfect substitutes, and that the relative wage R indicates the constant rate of substitution. If R^0, corresponding to point A, is that rate, then point A is the only possible equilibrium, whether public jobs are at E or at D. In this case, direct job creation will be fruitless; an equal number of teenagers will lose private jobs.

To analyze substitution formally, suppose that private output Q is produced by the two types of workers, along with capital and other factors, assumed constant. The production function $Q(N_1, N_2)$ has diminishing returns to scale; N_1 and N_2 represent employment of the two types of workers:

$$(15) \qquad N_1 = L_1 - G_1 - U_1 L_1 = L_1 - G_1 - s^1(R)L,$$

$$N_2 = L_2 - G_2 - U_2 L_2 = L_2 - G_2 - s^2(R)L.$$

Here G_1 and G_2 are the numbers of workers of the two types in government jobs. From equation 9, $(L_i/L)U_i = s^i(R)$ in the NAIRU equilibrium. The following system of equilibrium equations determines Q; w_2, the real wage of group 2 workers; and Rw_2, the real wage of group 1 workers, all as functions of the policy variables G_1 and G_2. Private output Q is a variable in the sense that, whether by demand-management policy or by price and wage flexibility, Q adjusts to the NAIRU level in the long run.[12]

$$(16) \quad Q = Q[L_1 - G_1 - s^1(R)L, L_2 - G_2 - s^2(R)L], Q_1, Q_2 > 0;$$

$$Rw_2 = Q_1[L_1 - G_1 - s^1(R)L, L_2 - G_2 - s^2(R)L], Q_{11} \leqq 0;$$

$$w_2 = Q_2[L_1 - G_1 - s^1(R)L, L_2 - G_2 - s^2(R)L], Q_{22} \leqq 0.$$

The second and third equations set each wage equal to the marginal product of labor.

Consider variation of G_2 by direct job creation:

$$(17) \quad \begin{pmatrix} 1 & Q_1 s_R^1 L + Q_2 s_R^2 L & 0 \\ 0 & Q_{11} s_R^1 L + Q_{12} s_R^2 L + w_2 & R \\ 0 & Q_{21} s_R^1 L + Q_{22} s_R^2 L & 1 \end{pmatrix} \begin{pmatrix} \partial Q/\partial G_2 \\ \partial R/\partial G_2 \\ \partial w_2/\partial G_2 \end{pmatrix} = \begin{pmatrix} -Q_2 \\ -Q_{12} \\ -Q_{22} \end{pmatrix}.$$

Recall that $s_R^1 < 0$, $s_R^2 > 0$. If the two kinds of labor were perfect substitutes at the relative wage R, then an addition of R units of type 2 labor would have the same effects as that of one unit of type 1. Adding to N_1 reduces Q_1 at the rate Q_{11}; hence adding to N_2 would reduce Q_1 at the rate Q_{11}/R. If the substitution is less than perfect, Q_{12} will exceed, algebraically, Q_{11}/R. The assumption of imperfect substitution—$RQ_{12} - Q_{11}$

12. There is no explicit modeling of the determination of the general price level. It is simply assumed that in any steady state the price level increases at the same rate as the two wage rates (we have abstracted from productivity change). The comparative-statics analysis says that the price level will in the long run adjust so that the two real wages rates w_2 and Rw_2 satisfy equation 16.

> 0 and $RQ_{22} - Q_{12} < 0$—guarantees that the determinant Δ of the Jacobian in equation 12 is positive. Also

(18)
$$\frac{\partial Q}{\partial G_2} = -w_2 + \frac{w_2}{\Delta} L(Rs_R^1 + s_R^2)(Q_{12} - RQ_{22});$$

$$\frac{\partial R}{\partial G_2} = \frac{1}{\Delta}(RQ_{22} - Q_{12}) < 0;$$

$$\frac{\partial w_2}{\partial G_2} = \frac{1}{\Delta}[-Q_{22}w_2 - Ls_R^1(Q_{11}Q_{22} - Q_{12}^2)] > 0.^{13}$$

The first term of $\partial Q/\partial G$ is simply the loss of the marginal product of a type 2 worker transferred from private employment to public employment. But if he is worth his wage in the public job, there is no loss to society. The GNP outcome therefore depends on the second term, which has the sign of $(s_R^2/-s_R^1) - R$. As we have argued above, GNP will increase—and weighted unemployment will decrease—if the slope of the NAIRU locus is in absolute value bigger than the relative wage R.

In order to provide a concrete example and, subsequently, to give some rough estimates for our findings, we have used the Cobb-Douglas and constant-elasticity-of-substitution production functions as specific forms for the production function. Define σ as the elasticity of substitution between the two types of workers: $\sigma = 1$ is the Cobb-Douglas case. It will be convenient to define a term D, equal to the determinant Δ divided by $s_R^1 L(RQ_{22} - Q_{12})$. This term is positive and, with the CES production function, it is given by

(19)
$$D = \frac{N_2\sigma}{LR(-s_R^1)} + \frac{N_2}{N_1} + \frac{s_R^2}{-s_R^1}.$$

The impact of direct job creation (a change in G_2) on GNP is then (from equation 18) given by

(20)
$$\frac{dGNP}{dG_2} = \frac{w_2}{D}\left(\frac{s_R^2}{-s_R^1} - R\right).$$

Inclusion of the production side of the model allows us not only to find the impact of a change in G_2 on GNP, but also to give specific expressions for the impact of G_2 on adult and teenage unemployment. In other words,

13. The inequalities above imply that $Q_{11}Q_{22} > Q_{12}^2$.

we can evaluate (at least for small changes) the movements around the equilibrium locus achieved for a given magnitude of government employment.[14] These are given by

$$(21) \qquad \frac{dL_2 U_2}{dG_2} = \frac{s_R^2 / s_R^1}{D} < 0, \frac{dL_1 U_1}{dG_2} = \frac{1}{D} > 0,$$

so that

$$\frac{dLU}{dG_2} = [(s_R^2 / s_R^1) + 1]/D.$$

Consider the interpretation of the conditions 21. The expression of D, equation 19, has three terms, all of them positive. If the first two terms were zero, then hiring one teenager into public employment ($dG_2 = 1$) would reduce the number of teenagers unemployed by one ($dL_2 U_2 / dG_2$ goes to unity in this case). The increase in the number of adult unemployed would be $s_R^1 / -s_R^2$—that is, the reciprocal of the slope of the NAIRU locus. This is just enough to keep the economy in equilibrium. Since the first two terms of 19 are not in fact zero, the overall impact of an increase in G_2 is scaled down. There are two reasons in the model why hiring one teenager into a directly created job reduces teenage unemployment by less than one. First, as was discussed earlier, the rise in the teenage relative wage causes employers to substitute adults for teenagers at the margin. The measure of this is the term $N_2 \sigma / LR(-s_R^1)$.

Second, to achieve the increase in adult unemployment that is required in order that the economy remain on the NAIRU locus after the increase in G_2, private output Q must be reduced.[15] The reduction of Q has the side effect of reducing N_2 as well as N_1. In the example of the CES production function, the adjustment of N_2 and N_1 at the margin, following the change in Q, occurs in the same proportions as the proportions on average $—N_2 / N_1$.

In order to provide some orders of magnitude for the impact of direct job creation, estimates of the parameters can be inserted into equations 20 and 21. Values for $N_1, N_2,$ and $L_1,$ and L_2 are taken from data for

14. Since $L_i U_i = L s^i(R)$, it follows that $dL_i U_i / dG_2$ is $L s_R^i dR / dG_2$, which can be found easily from equation 17.

15. This reduction of Q occurs either by demand-management policies or by price-level adjustment. The change in Q must be large enough first to overcome the tendency to increase N_1 generated by the substitution effect described above, and then further to reduce N_1. Adult unemployment must end up higher.

1974.[16] Two values of the locus slope $s_R^2 / - s_R^1$ have been tried—3.05 and 6.1—and results for both of these values are given. The value 3.05 is Perry's estimate of R; it is selected to illustrate the case in which GNP is unaffected. The value 6.1 is simply twice 3.05. Two values of σ are used, $\sigma = 0.5$ and $\sigma = 1.0$; higher substitution elasticity seems unlikely. In addition to the ratio of the ss, we need an estimate for s_R^1, which appears in D. We know of no hard evidence on this parameter.[17] One way of expressing s_R^1 is to ask: if the adult relative wage fell by 10 percent, how much would the adult unemployment rate have to rise to maintain equilibrium? We experiment with two answers. The first is 10 percent also— for example, from 4.5 percent to 4.95 percent. The second is 5 percent— for example, from 4.5 percent to 4.73 percent.

Table 1 shows, for different parameter values, answers to the following questions: if 100 teenagers are hired into directly created jobs, how much does (1) teenage unemployment (in persons) fall? (2) total unemployment fall? (3) GNP rise? The range of outcomes is wide. The table indicates how changes in values of strategic parameters affect the outcome, but where the actual parameter values lie cannot be known without difficult empirical research.

Variations in the two labor forces, L_1 and L_2, were ignored in the analysis. Changes in these variables will not affect the locus of sustainable combinations of U_1 and U_2. However, an increase in L_2 induced by the lower U_2 and higher relative wage of this group will make the reduction in its measured unemployment smaller than that derived above. At the same time, the production outcome Q will be more favorable on this account: some of the induced entrants will be employed. Some new entrants will be drawn from the ranks of the discouraged workers or the actually or potentially delinquent. Even if they were not previously counted as unemployed, it is desirable to enable them to work.

Induced reductions in L_1 are likely to be small, and hence to reduce Q only slightly.

16. From *Employment and Training Report of the President, 1976* (Government Printing Office, 1976).
17. Robert E. Hall, "The Process of Inflation in the Labor Market," *BPEA*, *2:1974*, pp. 343–93, discusses the process by which equilibrium levels of scale wages are restored through changes in rates of wage increase. Michael L. Wachter in his paper in this issue, gives data showing how relative wage incomes of certain cohorts have changed. If these data are compared with unemployment-rate data that suggest persistent changes in relative unemployment rates for these same groups, the overall picture is consistent with our story—although we make no claim that it proves it.

Table 1. Effect on Unemployment and Gross National Product of Hiring 100 Teenagers into Public Jobs

Unemployment in persons; GNP in thousands of dollars

Change in unemployment and GNP	Relative-wage responsiveness[a]	
	High value (10%–10%)	Low value (10%–5%)
$\sigma = 0.5$; NAIRU locus slope = 3.05		
Fall in unemployment		
Teenage	73.4	59.1
Total	49.4	39.7
Rise in GNP[b]	0	0
$\sigma = 1.0$; NAIRU locus slope = 3.05		
Fall in unemployment		
Teenage	59.1	42.5
Total	39.7	28.5
Rise in GNP[b]	0	0
$\sigma = 0.5$; NAIRU locus slope = 6.1		
Fall in unemployment		
Teenage	84.7	74.3
Total	70.8	62.1
Rise in GNP[b]	158.8	139.3
$\sigma = 1.0$; NAIRU locus slope = 6.1		
Fall in unemployment		
Teenage	74.3	59.6
Total	62.1	49.9
Rise in GNP[b]	139.3	111.8

Source: Based on text equations 20 and 21. See accompanying text discussion, where the symbols are defined.

a. Assumes that the adult relative wage falls by 10 percent. For the high value, the adult unemployment rate rises 10 percent; for the low value, 5 percent.

b. GNP calculations assume that the teenage wage is $2.50 an hour and that teenagers work 1,500 hours per year. If the same is true in directly created jobs, then, ignoring overhead, the budgetary cost of 100 such jobs is $375,000.

Wage Subsidies and the NAIRU

The idea of paying a wage subsidy to increase employment has been around for a long time. Recently, renewed interest has centered on two main forms. First, temporary but general wage subsidies have been proposed as a remedy for high unemployment, possibly confined to incremental hiring. The second, the one considered here, is a selective wage subsidy limited to particular categories of workers. For example, Feldstein has suggested giving to all teenagers vouchers that could be used either for schooling or to subsidize employers who hire them.[18] The Orcutts have recently proposed a wage subsidy payable to all persons who, during the preceding twelve months, have been unemployed for more than some stated amount of time.[19]

Feldstein's proposal fits our analysis, since it is intended to improve the position of a particular demographic group. The Orcutts' proposal is not covered under any of the classifications listed earlier. It would presumably give the most assistance to those with the highest unemployment rates, whatever their demographic group. In Phillips-curve terms, the argument must be that the disadvantaged—defined by high incidence of unemployment in the preceding period—exert less restraint on wages. This is probably true, although a counterargument is that persons who have been unemployed a long time are more anxious to find new jobs and more willing to accept a low wage.[20]

Whatever the details of particular proposals, we should like to consider a wage-subsidy scheme that benefits the same "group 2" workers as direct job creation was assumed to do, applying the apparatus used earlier to analyze the impact of a wage subsidy on the NAIRU. The basic assumption is that expressed in equation 16. A subsidy is used to change the relative wage paid by employers for the two types of labor. Let β be the policy variable such that βw_2 is the real wage *paid* by employers for group 2 workers, where the subsidy implies $\beta < 1$. The model used in the previous section remains valid with βw_2 substituted for w_2 in the third part of equation 16.[21] The demand-for-labor equations are combined, as before, with the Phillips curves for equation 7. Presumably, it is the relative wage received R that appears in equation 7 rather than the relative

18. Martin S. Feldstein, *Lowering the Permanent Rate of Unemployment*, A Study for the Joint Economic Committee, 93:1 (GPO, 1973).

19. Guy Orcutt and Geil Orcutt, "A Proposal to Increase Employment" (Yale University, February 1977; processed).

20. There is even some evidence to support this—at least the acceptance-wage part; see Hirschel Kasper, "The Asking Price of Labor and the Duration of Unemployment," *Review of Economics and Statistics*, vol. 49 (May 1967), pp. 165–72. Another potential difficulty with the Orcutt proposal is the "moral hazard": it is difficult and costly to determine whether someone is really looking for work or is out of the labor force. In addition, firms would have an incentive to concentrate temporary layoffs on a small group of workers (even more than they already do) rather than spreading the burden more evenly (by short-term plant closings, for example). By this means, some workers will build up eligibility for the subsidy.

21. We will continue to define R as W_1/W_2—that is, the relative wage *received*. Thus w_1, the real wage for group 1, is still equal to Rw_2.

wage paid R/β.[22] Lowering β has an impact on the NAIRU that can be analyzed in a manner similar to the analysis of direct job creation. In the case of a CES production function, the outcome of the wage subsidy is quite closely related to the outcome of direct job creation:

$$(22) \qquad -\frac{dGNP}{d\beta} = \frac{w_2 N_2 \sigma}{D}\left(\frac{s_R^2}{-s_R^1} - R\right);\, \frac{dL_1 U_1}{d\beta} = \frac{-N_2\sigma}{D};$$

$$\frac{dL_2 U_2}{d\beta} = \frac{N_2\sigma}{D}\frac{s_R^2}{(-s_R^1)};\, \frac{dLU}{d\beta} = \frac{N_2\sigma}{D}\left(\frac{s_R^2}{-s_R^1} - 1\right),$$

where the derivatives are evaluated starting from $\beta = 1$. They are simply $N_2\sigma$ times the corresponding derivatives from direct job creation. The counterpart of dG_2 is $N_2\sigma(-d\beta)$, the number of additional teenagers hired *on the first round* as a result of a wage subsidy of $-d\beta$. Subsequent adjustments to maintain NAIRU equilibrium are the same in both cases.

The working of the wage subsidy is illustrated in figure 3, which is analogous to figure 2. As before, the locus CBA gives the combinations of adult and teenage unemployment that equilibrate both labor markets. Each point on the locus is associated with a relative wage, with higher values of R occurring at points further to the southeast. Point E represents the demographic mix of government employment; EA gives the path of total private and public employment for various levels of real private output at a given relative wage paid by employers. The slope of the path depends upon this relative wage paid; the path EA is drawn for the wage R^0 that corresponds to point A on the NAIRU locus. If a wage subsidy β is introduced and the relative wage *received* remains R^0, then the relative wage *paid* by firms is R^0/β and the path EA shifts to EC. But R^0 is no longer consistent with stability when the unemployment combination is C instead of A. The relative wage received decreases (W_2 rises relative to W_1) and the employment path rotates clockwise to EB. In the new equilibrium (that is, in C as compared to the original A), (1) the relative wage paid by employers is higher; (2) the relative wage received is lower (teenagers get relatively more and firms pay relatively less, the gap being the subsidy); (3) teenage unemployment is lower, adult unemployment is higher, and the unemployment count is lower.

22. Workers presumably respond to R in their search and turnover behavior and firms know this when they set wage offers. Note, however, that we do *not* assume R remains constant. A wage subsidy for teenagers would increase the demand for teenagers and change the equilibrium R—that is part of the process described below.

Figure 3. Impact of a Wage Subsidy for Teenagers (Group 2)

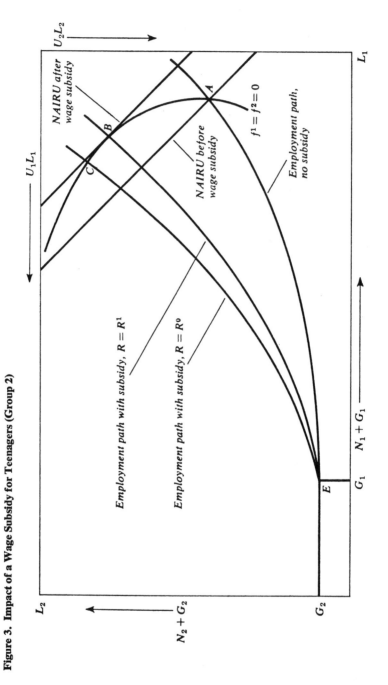

The figures given in table 1 also illustrate the impact of a wage subsidy of the same total budget cost as direct job creation. If a CES function with elasticity σ is assumed, a wage subsidy is σ times as effective *per dollar* as direct job creation. Thus, if $\sigma = 0.5$, the figures given for direct job creation in table 1 should be reduced by one-half to give the effect of the same expenditure on a wage subsidy. The two policies are equivalent in this sense if $\sigma = 1$ (Cobb-Douglas).

Effectiveness per budget dollar is only one consideration in comparison of direct job creation and wage subsidy. More important is an evaluation of output resulting from direct job creation relative to that from increased private employment. Another dimension is the possible political resistance of unions to a wage subsidy paid to private employers.

THE SHORT-RUN TRADEOFF

Currently, direct job creation is proposed as an instrument of short-run fiscal policy, as part of a package to stimulate economic recovery. How does the short-run impact of direct job creation differ from the long-run results obtained above?

If $\dot{W}_1$ and $\dot{W}_2$ are given by equation 7, then the overall rate of wage inflation $\dot{W}$ is given by

(23) $$\dot{W} = \theta_1 f^1 + \theta_2 f^2 + \text{feedback terms},$$

where θ_1 and θ_2 are the payroll shares. If one concentrates employment gains (unemployment reductions) on group 2 workers, under what conditions can one (a) lower overall unemployment, $U = \alpha_1 U_1 + \alpha_2 U_2$, in the short run and keep $\dot{W}$ constant (in other words, improve the short-run Phillips curve); and (b) raise GNP (which implies lowering wage-weighted unemployment, $R\alpha_1 U_1 + \alpha_2 U_2$) in the short run and keep $\dot{W}$ constant?

For our purposes "short run" involves holding the relative wage R constant and the feedback terms constant. Cross-unemployment effects will also be ignored. If $\dot{W}$ is held constant this gives

(24) $$d\dot{W} = \theta_1 f_1^1 d(\alpha_1 U_1) + \theta_2 f_2^2 d(\alpha_2 U_2).$$

The change in overall unemployment is simply

(25) $$dU = d(\alpha_1 U_1) + d(\alpha_2 U_2).$$

The short-run Phillips curve is then improved by programs for group 2 workers provided that

$$(26) \qquad -\theta_1 f_1^1 > -\theta_2 f_2^2.$$

This is a weaker condition than those for long-run improvement, since it does not involve relative-wage effects.

The change in wage-weighted unemployment is

$$(27) \qquad dU_w = Rd(\alpha_1 U_1) + d(\alpha_2 U_2).$$

Since it is approximately true that $R\theta_2/\theta_1 = \alpha_2/\alpha_1$, it follows that a non-inflationary short-run gain in GNP can be made provided that

$$(28) \qquad -\alpha_1 f_1^1 > -\alpha_2 f_2^2.$$

Recall that f^1 and f^2 are defined as functions of $\alpha_1 U_1$ and $\alpha_2 U_2$. Thus 28 is simply the condition that the Phillips curve for adults (defined with respect to U_1) be steeper than the Phillips curve for teenagers (defined with respect to U_2).[23]

Empirical Evidence

The possibilities of "cheating the Phillips curve" by direct job creation, selective wage subsidies, or other labor-market policies, depend, according to the theories presented in previous sections, on three hypotheses: (1) Vacancies are, independently of unemployment rates, important for wage inflation. (2) Primary unemployment—of adult males or of all adults—is relatively more important for wage behavior than unemployment of other workers. (3) Relative-wage levels affect adjustments of wages in specific markets or industries.

We have attempted some econometric calculations bearing on these propositions, and we present some of them in this section. Our confidence in these results is limited.

23. Lags in the wage equations will affect short-run outcomes. In econometric Phillips curves the unemployment variable is often a distributed lag. For long-run analysis the lags do not matter. But the relevant lag distribution on U_1 may differ from that on U_2, perhaps because wage contracts are more important in labor markets for adults. Even if the Phillips curve for teenagers is fundamentally flatter than that for adults, this may not translate into improvement in the short-run tradeoff if the wage effects of unemployment of teenagers occur with shorter lags.

Table 2. Coefficients Explaining the Rate of Change of Hourly Wages, Private Nonfarm Economy[a]

| Equation | Constant | Cyclical variable | | | | | Feedback term | | | | Regression statistic | |
| | | Reciprocal of unemployment rate[b] | | | | Help-wanted index | Wages | Consumer price index | Private nonfarm GNP deflator | Minimum wage | ρ | Standard error |
		Adults over 25	Youths 20-24	Teen-agers	Males over 25							
2-1	0.0195 (1.67)	0.000863 (3.59)	...	...	...	...	-0.292 (-0.76)	0.655 (2.74)	...	0.0263 (1.57)	0.753	0.0057
2-2	0.0457 (3.37)	0.00134 (3.57)	-0.000216 (-1.43)	-0.000145 (-0.83)	...	...	-0.264 (-0.70)	0.431 (1.99)	...	0.0267 (1.72)	0.609	0.0054
2-3	0.0399 (3.69)	0.00115 (4.88)	-0.000168 (-1.38)	-0.000185 (-1.22)	...	...	...	0.291 (3.48)	...	0.0296 (1.99)	0.581	0.0054
2-4	-0.00977 (-1.19)	0.000362 (1.90)	...	...	...	...	1.02 (3.47)	...	-0.177 (-0.89)	0.0474 (2.92)	0.583	0.0060
2-5	0.0291 (2.15)	0.000675 (1.45)	-0.0000515 (-0.29)	-0.000313 (-1.79)	...	...	0.711 (1.64)	...	-0.150 (-0.64)	0.0407 (2.71)	0.525	0.0056
2-6	0.000333 (0.03)	-0.000323 (-0.84)	...	...	...	0.000442 (3.22)	-0.0993 (-0.31)	0.448 (2.25)	...	0.0276 (1.77)	0.620	0.0055
2-7	-0.0188 (-2.79)	-0.000639 (-2.09)	...	...	...	0.000427 (3.67)	0.816 (3.25)	...	-0.149 (-0.91)	0.0471 (3.27)	0.472	0.0057
2-8	0.00103 (0.12)	...	...	...	...	0.000332 (5.35)	-0.070 (-0.23)	0.461 (2.61)	...	0.0282 (1.84)	0.623	0.0055
2-9	-0.0138 (-1.94)	...	...	...	...	0.000222 (3.50)	0.743 (2.70)	...	-0.0475 (-0.27)	0.0447 (2.95)	0.528	0.0058
2-10	-0.000642 (-0.05)	...	...	...	-0.0000994 (-0.57)	0.000413 (2.93)	-0.131 (-0.041)	0.486 (2.49)	...	0.0275 (1.75)	0.631	0.0055

Sources: The help-wanted index was provided by the Conference Board. Other data are from the official series of the U.S. Bureau of Labor Statistics and the U.S. Bureau of the Census. The numbers in parentheses are t statistics.

a. The period of estimation is 1958:1 to 1976:4, using quarterly observations. See the text for specific details on each variable.

b. Seasonally adjusted, except for males over 25.

In table 2 we report several alternative regressions "explaining" economy-wide inflation. The observations are quarterly, spanning 1958 through 1976. The dependent variable is the four-quarter proportional rate of change of private nonfarm hourly wage rates. The explanatory variables are of three types: The first are reciprocals of unemployment rates for demographic groups, adjusted for the relative size of the groups in the overall labor force. The variable is entered as a four-quarter average, lagged one quarter behind the dependent variable. The groups used were adults over twenty-five, youths twenty to twenty-four, and teenagers. An additional regression uses the unadjusted rate for males over twenty-five, a popular variable in other studies. The second set of explanatory variables was the help-wanted index published by the Conference Board, deflated by total employment. A linear four-quarter average lagged one quarter is used. The third set were wage and price feedback variables. In all cases the variables used were averages of the four-quarter proportional rates of change. The averages were for eight quarters, lagged one quarter. The wage itself, the consumer price index, and the deflator for private nonfarm GNP were used.

Partly on theoretical grounds and partly based on Gramlich's findings, the four-quarter proportional rate of change of the legal minimum wage is included as a feedback variable.[24] It is not averaged but is lagged one quarter. It enters with a very small coefficient and is intermittently significant.

The macroeconomic wage regressions of table 2 support the proposition that vacancies, via their proxy, the help-wanted index, are important. Indeed, as a measure of labor-market tightness, this demand-side variable appears to be stronger than unemployment rates. Equation 2-10 of table 2 attributes a stronger effect to the index than to the reciprocal of the unadjusted unemployment rate for males over twenty-five.[25]

So far as the adjusted unemployment rates are concerned, the regressions confirm the differential importance of primary unemployment. Indeed, the secondary rates are insignificant and their coefficients have the wrong sign. Doubtless, collinearity is part of the reason why it is

24. Edward M. Gramlich, "Impact of Minimum Wages on Other Wages, Employment, and Family Incomes," *BPEA, 2:1976*, pp. 409–51.
25. We make no claim that the help-wanted index explains the shifting Phillips curve. "Other factors" may have caused trends in the index that are correlated with the inflationary spurt of the 1970s. Our purpose is just to show that vacancies matter.

difficult to estimate the relative importance of several unemployment rates in wage behavior.

Partly to see how well the findings of the aggregate wage equations held up at a slightly lower level of aggregation, and partly to test the importance of relative-wage levels, various Phillips curves were estimated for wages in seven major sectors. The results are shown in table 3.[26]

The same adjusted unemployment rates and deflated help-wanted index were used as in the aggregate wage equations. Of the feedback variables, only the two price indexes and the minimum wage were used. Experiments with wage feedbacks, both sector own wage and aggregate wage, were not encouraging. Collinearity was a severe problem. We concluded that wage-feedback terms were not so appropriate in sectoral equations including relative-wage levels. In practice, the wage-feedback variables generally reduced the significance of the relative wage.[27]

The relative-wage variable is important in specification of the sectoral equations. The hypothesis used in the theoretical analysis was that a rise in the wage of a sector relative to other wages would reduce the rate of increase of the sector's wage. A variable defined as the ratio of the sector's wage to the index of private nonfarm wages was included as a moving average from $t - 1$ to $t - 8$. The results are reported in column 9 of table 3. The hypothesis receives rather strong empirical support. For the six sectors excluding construction, there are sixteen equations with the expected sign and two with perverse signs—neither significantly positive. Many of the negative signs are significant. Even including construction, the sign count is sixteen to five. Such a consistent pattern would be unlikely if the true coefficient were zero or positive. Construction wages behaved in a notoriously unpredictable way over the period. The finding that construction workers, having achieved a high relative wage, were induced to bargain for even larger wage increases is not inconsistent with anecdotal evidence about the industry.

The hypothesis that unemployment among older adults (column 2) is more important as a determinant of wage inflation than the unemployment

---

26. The sectors are manufacturing; wholesale and retail trade; services; mining; transportation; construction; finance, insurance, and real estate. The wage data are from *Employment and Earnings,* various issues. More complete results, matching those of table 2, are available from the authors.

27. An exception is the construction industry, in which wage feedbacks turned perverse signs on relative wages into expected negative coefficients, some significant.

among youths and teenages (columns 3 and 4) is generally confirmed by the sectoral equations.

The superiority of the deflated help-wanted index as a measure of labor-market tightness is supported by the manufacturing, transportation, and mining equations, but not by the other sectoral equations.

The coefficient of the minimum-wage variable, though generally small, continued to be both significant and robust across specifications. The service sector was the only one with consistently perverse negative signs. It is not unreasonable that an increase in the minimum wage would throw workers into the service sector, causing a downward pressure on wages there. The coefficients and statistical significance of the minimum-wage variable in finance, insurance, and real estate seem too good to be true. There are other odd features of this sector—the relative-wage variable has an incorrect sign, for example.

Our general conclusion from the regressions is that the hypotheses necessary for success of direct job creation, wage subsidies, and kindred policies are empirically supported, at least qualitatively. But our previous analysis makes us skeptical of the more extravagant hopes and claims for these policies, especially in the long run. Gains in GNP are harder to come by than reduction in unemployment counts. In the long run, displacements of workers from private employment, both in and outside the target population, will offset some of the direct employment gains. A large share of the case for direct job creation or selective subsidies depends on important effects not captured in aggregate measures of employment and production: improved distribution of income and opportunity.

Table 3. Coefficients Explaining the Rate of Change of Wages, by Sector[a]

| | Cyclical variable | | | | | Feedback term | | | | Regression statistic | |
| | Reciprocal of unemployment rate | | | | | | | | | | |
Equation	Constant (1)	Adults over 25 (2)	Youths 20–24 (3)	Teen-agers (4)	Help-wanted index (5)	Consumer price index (6)	Private nonfarm GNP deflator (7)	Minimum wage (8)	Relative wage (9)	ρ (10)	Standard error (11)
					Manufacturing (1958:1 to 1976:4)						
3-1	0.193 (1.32)	0.000505 (0.81)	−0.000203 (−1.22)	0.000385 (1.32)	...	0.379 (2.74)	...	0.0651 (3.66)	−0.990 (−1.24)	0.596	0.0062
3-2	0.233 (2.90)	0.000273 (1.01)	...	...	...	...	0.276 (1.81)	0.0620 (3.31)	−1.08 (−2.90)	0.737	0.0065
3-3	0.160 (1.68)	−0.000316 (−0.55)	...	...	0.000262 (1.13)	...	0.327 (2.26)	0.0618 (3.33)	−0.774 (−1.83)	0.702	0.0065
					Wholesale and retail trade (1967:1 to 1976:4)						
3-4	0.310 (2.20)	0.00158 (2.18)	0.0000738 (0.38)	−0.000794 (−0.78)	...	0.101 (0.98)	...	0.0615 (3.66)	−1.80 (−1.63)	0.393	0.0054
3-5	0.450 (5.44)	0.000912 (3.89)	...	...	...	...	−0.0089 (−0.08)	0.0615 (3.92)	−2.87 (−5.03)	0.451	0.0054
3-6	0.644 (3.76)	0.00176 (2.51)	...	...	−0.000328 (−1.27)	...	−0.0935 (−0.78)	0.0599 (3.88)	−4.05 (−3.78)	0.386	0.0053
					Services (1967:1 to 1976:4)						
3-7	−0.639 (−0.94)	0.00240 (4.73)	−0.0000546 (−0.27)	−0.00118 (−1.43)	...	0.466 (2.79)	...	−0.0424 (−2.47)	4.41 (1.06)	0.365	0.0051
3-8	1.03 (0.95)	0.000319 (0.55)	...	...	...	...	0.048 (0.16)	−0.0309 (−1.44)	−6.31 (−0.92)	0.874	0.0059
3-9	1.19 (1.03)	0.000931 (0.98)	...	...	−0.000255 (−0.77)	...	−0.054 (−0.17)	−0.0312 (−1.46)	−7.16 (−0.99)	0.933	0.0059

293

					Mining (1958:1 to 1976:4)					
3-10	0.0941 (0.44)	0.00107 (0.88)	-0.000186 (-0.70)	-0.000247 (-0.36)	...	0.751 (4.03)	...	0.0102 (0.29)	-0.291 (-0.27)	0.373	0.0145
3-11	0.263 (2.94)	0.000160 (0.41)	...	...	...	...	0.815 (5.03)	0.0105 (0.28)	-1.08 (-3.19)	0.491	0.0149
3-12	0.132 (1.49)	-0.00153 (-2.17)	...	0.000769 (2.66)	...	...	0.719 (5.20)	0.0187 (0.56)	-0.666 (-2.09)	0.357	0.0145
					Transportation (1967:1 to 1976:4)					
3-13	0.472 (2.62)	0.0000888 (0.11)	-0.000441 (-1.21)	-0.000364 (-0.25)	...	-0.155 (-1.29)	...	0.0150 (0.69)	-1.44 (-2.22)	0.307	0.0071
3-14	0.662 (3.29)	-0.00133 (-2.64)	...	...	...	...	0.118 (0.49)	0.00165 (0.06)	-2.44 (-2.78)	0.771	0.0075
3-15	0.770 (4.18)	-0.00251 (-3.08)	...	0.000490 (1.45)	...	...	0.0787 (0.41)	0.0118 (0.45)	-3.03 (-3.48)	0.648	0.0076
					Construction (1958:1 to 1976:4)					
3-16	-0.349 (-1.43)	0.000451 (0.88)	0.000376 (1.42)	-0.000134 (-0.49)	...	0.671 (3.48)	...	0.0215 (0.93)	1.18 (1.42)	0.697	0.0080
3-17	-0.170 (-0.94)	0.00116 (4.77)	...	...	...	...	0.472 (4.06)	0.0233 (1.03)	0.596 (0.94)	0.686	0.0080
3-18	-0.232 (-1.41)	0.00194 (3.28)	...	-0.000294 (-1.39)	...	...	0.552 (4.47)	0.0223 (1.00)	0.841 (1.44)	0.634	0.0079
					Finance, insurance, real estate (1967:1 to 1976:4)					
3-19	-0.242 (-1.94)	0.00112 (1.35)	-0.000573 (-2.48)	0.000430 (0.30)	...	0.441 (2.89)	...	0.109 (5.29)	1.48 (1.76)	0.457	0.0063
3-20	0.0666 (0.61)	0.000540 (1.36)	...	...	...	...	0.287 (1.43)	0.0884 (3.77)	-0.303 (-0.47)	0.605	0.0071
3-21	0.621 (4.86)	0.00362 (5.38)	...	-0.00123 (-4.83)	...	...	-0.206 (-1.36)	0.0757 (4.44)	-3.08 (-4.60)	0.341	0.0060

Sources: Sector data, *Employment and Earnings*, various issues; other data, same as table 2.

a. The periods of estimation are indicated after each sector designation; all observations were quarterly. See the text for specific details on each variable. The numbers in parentheses are t statistics.

Reflections Inspired by Proposed Constitutional Restrictions on Fiscal Policy

James Tobin

Public sector budgets have become big political issues. Popular opinion is that federal, state, and local governments are too big, that they spend too much, tax too much, and borrow too much. Fiscal sins are commonly blamed for inflation, dollar depreciation, lagging capital investment, productivity slowdown, low stock prices, and other economic disappointments of the 1970s. Politicians do not debate these premises; they embrace them in greater or lesser degree and argue about who should wield the axe and how, where, and when.

The wave of sentiment for fiscal reform has taken various shapes including: President Carter's promises to balance the federal budget and reduce its economic size to 21 percent of the gross national product (GNP); proposed congressional resolutions to limit and reduce future federal budgets relative to GNP; the Kemp-Roth bills for drastic reductions of federal taxes; Proposition 13 in California and other constitutional limits on state and local spending and taxation, adopted in several states and proposed in many others; and proposals

From *Economic Regulation: Essays in Honor of James R. Nelson*, eds. Kenneth D. Boyer and William G. Shepherd, East Lansing, MI: Bureau of Research, Michigan State University, 1981, 341–347. Reprinted by permission of the publisher, Division of Research, Graduate School of Business Administration, Michigan State University.

to amend the United States Constitution to limit federal spending or to require annual budget balance.

Crusades with one or another of these objectives have received considerable support from professional economists. The so-called Laffer curve is the intellectual foundation for the Kemp-Roth proposal.[1] The argument is that lowering tax rates will so increase incentives to work, produce, bear risk, save, invest, and obey the tax code that revenues will actually increase. Simultaneously, the burst of supply will cool inflation and create jobs for the unemployed. Several economists, including Peter Gutmann[2] and Edward Feige,[3] strike receptive chords when they argue that high taxes are responsible for the growth of a vast underground economy, unrecorded and untaxed. Martin Feldstein — Harvard professor, American Economic Association Clark medalist, president of the National Bureau of Economic Research — tells Congress, readers of two-page advertisements in news magazines, and fellow scholars how federal taxes stifle capital formation and productivity.

Attacks on Keynesian economics in general and Keynesian fiscal policies in particular crowd the popular media, business press, after-dinner circuits, publishers' lists, and even learned journals. A proposed constitutional amendment to limit federal spending is the brainchild of Milton Friedman, aided by other economists and legal scholars. The budget balance amendment, supported by petitions from some thirty state legislatures, has many fathers, among them James Buchanan and Richard Wagner in their anti-Keynesian tract, *Democracy in Deficit.*[4]

The subject in question is an important one and deserves the serious attention of economists. Elsewhere I have examined the macroeconomic theory and history involved in the Buchanan-Wagner polemic.[5] My purpose here is twofold: to review the major facts about government budgets and finance in the United States in order to provide some perspective for contemporary alarms, and to consider some implications of the fiscal rules proposed as amendments to the federal Constitution.

The Size and Growth of Government in the United States

In presenting relevant statistics, I am not under the illusion that the prevailing antigovernment mood is closely linked to facts, correctly or incorrectly perceived. Vietnam and Watergate, reinforced by diffuse economic discontents, are doubtless important sources.

Businessmen complain of federal interference and overregulation by government; anecdotes of mindless interferences by OSHA are a staple of business lunches, whether or not fueled by deductible martinis. Distaste for regulation is spread widely throughout the economy and across the political spectrum. To the satisfaction of most economists, deregulation is an idea whose time has come. Although the budget impact is trivial, reaction against regulation heightens receptivity to the generic charge that government is a monster out of control.

Measures of Government Size. How big is government relative to the economy? What has been the trend in its size? The answers, as I shall explain, are not as simple as the questions. In Table 1, I have assembled some of the simple measures of government size often cited. These are presented for five representative years, all years of prosperity: 1956, midway in the Eisenhower era; 1965, just before the military and fiscal escalation of the Vietnam war and at the beginning of President Johnson's Great Society programs; 1969, when both these initiatives were affecting the budget and the economy; 1973, midway in the Nixon-Ford administration, before OPEC and acute stagflation; and 1978, after three years of recovery from recession and a year or so of President Carter. All figures, except those in columns 1.1.2, 1.1.3, and 1.1.4 regarding employment, are ratios of dollar amounts to the dollar gross national product of the year. Both numerators and denominators of these ratios have grown since 1956, with population, production, and inflation.

Governments engage in several kinds of economic activities and transactions, as follows:

1. Governments themselves *produce* goods and services, in this country mostly services: for example, schooling, military and police protection, streets, sometimes water and electricity.
2. Governments purchase goods and services and use them for public purposes. Most goods and services produced by government are also, in effect, purchased by government; they are not sold to the private sector. In addition, most goods, and some services, used by governments are purchased from private contractors or suppliers. Purchases, in this inclusive sense, are often called *exhaustive expenditures*. The point of the word *exhaustive* is that productive resources that could have been used to meet private demands are used to meet public demands.

TABLE 1. Measures of Government Size, United States, Selected Years.

1.1 Government as producer and employer.

	Share of constant (1972) dollar GNP originating in gov't., federal, state, & local (1.1.1)	Fraction of civilian workforce employed by government			Number of civilian employees: all governments. (millions) (1.1.5)
		Federal (1.1.2)	State & local (1.1.3)	All (1.1.4)	
1956	.145	.034	.080	.114	7.3
1965	.138	.034	.108	.142	10.1
1969	.141	.036	.121	.157	12.2
1973	.127	.032	.135	.167	14.1
1977	.124				
1978		.029	.134	.163	14.4

1.2 Government as purchaser of goods and services.

Purchases in current dollars as fraction of GNP in current dollars.

	All governments (1.2.1)	Federal (1.2.2)	State & local (1.2.3)	Defense (1.2.4)	Civilian (1.2.5)
1956	.189	.109	.080	.096	.093
1965	.201	.097	.104	.072	.129
1969	.222	.104	.118	.081	.141
1973	.206	.078	.128	.056	.150
1978	.206	.073	.113	.047	.159

Purchases in 1972 dollars relative to private purchases in 1972.

	All governments	
	Total (1.2.6)	Civilian (1.2.7)
1956	.288	.142
1965	.289	.186
1969	.317	.201
1973	.259	.189
1978	.254	.196

1.3 Government as transferor.

	Transfers to persons, as fraction of GNP			Federal transfers to State & local governments	
	All governments (1.3.1)	Federal (1.3.2)	State & local (1.3.3)	($ billion) (1.3.4)	(fraction of GNP) (1.3.5)
1956	.041	.032	.009	3.3	.008
1965	.055	.044	.011	11.1	.012
1969	.067	.054	.013	20.3	.022
1973	.087	.071	.016	40.6	.031
1978	.102	.086	.016	76.6	.036

1.4 Government as tax collector.

	All outlays as fraction of GNP All governments (1.4.0)	Tax revenues as fraction of GNP			Personal taxes as fraction of:	
		All governments (1.4.1)	Federal (1.4.2)	State & local (1.4.3)	Personal income (1.4.4)	Personal income, excluding transfers (1.4.5)
1956	.248	.260	.185	.075	.14	.15
1965	.273	.274	.181	.093	.15	.16
1969	.305	.317	.211	.106	.19	.21
1973	.309	.315	.198	.117	.18	.21
1978	.325	.324	.205	.119	.19	.22

SOURCE: National income accounts, Department of Commerce. Employment statistics, Bureau of Labor Statistics.

3. Governments make *transfers* to private individuals. Transfers, as distinct from purchases, are payments for which the government receives currently no goods or services in return. Examples are Social Security benefits, welfare checks, and veterans' pensions. Expenditures by the transferees are private purchases, not government uses of resources. By transfers, the government redistributes purchasing power among private individuals, but it does not "exhaust" resources available to meet private demands.

4. Governments collect revenues, mostly by *taxation*, but also by various user charges and fees.

5. Governments *borrow* and *lend*. Their debt issues are not counted as revenues, and for consistency their loans should not be counted as expenditure. This is the treatment of financial transactions in the national income accounts that estimate GNP and related magnitudes. (Interest subsidies, however, are expenditures.) Therefore, I use the national income accounting estimates of government receipts and outlays, which are somewhat different from the comprehensive cash figures usually cited.

Figures bearing on (1) through (4) are shown in Table 1; I will comment on them in turn. Deficits and debt will be discussed later in the paper.

Production. Anyone worried that the United States is going socialist in the classic sense that the government is owning, operating, and organizing an increasing share of productive activity will be relieved by Table 1, columns 1.1.1 through 1.1.4. This has not been happening, but neither is it the burden of recent complaints.

Purchases. The fraction of GNP purchased for governmental use is more germane (columns 1.2). A common conservative complaint is that people as private citizens have too little control over how the country's productive resources are to be used. Household and business spending in commercial markets gives people what they really want. Government spending diverts resources to purposes chosen by bureaucrats and politicians, without any market test of their value.

There is little trend in the total government share. Federal defense purchases have declined as a share of GNP, while state and local civilian activities have increased. The increase in purchases by state and local governments was facilitated by federal transfers to those governments, shown in columns 1.3.4 and 1.3.5. A Vietnam war and Great Society bulge is apparent in 1969, but the current government total is about the same as in 1965. The 1970s display no increasing government appetite that could account for the emergence of the current charge that the government is devouring too much of the economy's substance.

The steady growth of purchases by state and local governments responded to strongly felt needs for the services they provide: education, roads and streets, fire and police protection, sanitation, public housing and urban redevelopment, hospitals and public health, parks and other recreational facilities. In the two decades after 1950, the nation's population grew by one-third, 51 million persons. All of the net growth occurred in urban areas.

It is instructive to examine the growth of expenditures for education, which amount to about 45 percent of state and local purchases. Between 1960 and 1976, dollar expenditures multiplied five times. In real terms, after correcting for increases in prices of teachers, school buildings, and other inputs, they doubled. The number of enrolled students grew by nearly 50 percent. In the end, real expenditure per pupil increased by 40 percent from $940 to $1340 in 1972 dollars. Virtually all of that increase occurred before 1972. Contributing factors included the rapid growth of state-supported higher education and the deliberate effort to equalize educational inputs between wealthier and poorer localities and between pupils of different economic and racial backgrounds.

How has the growth in the *real volume* of government purchases compared with that of private purchases? Such comparisons are tricky. Our national income accounts use 1972 as a reference year for calculating changes in real magnitudes. They correct for price changes by estimating for each year how GNP and its components would have been valued at 1972 prices. Prices do not move in step. In particular, the prices of the goods and services governments buy rise, over the years, faster than the prices of things private households and businesses buy. There are several reasons. Government activities are generally quite labor intensive, and, throughout the economy, wages and the prices of labor-intensive commodities and services rise faster than other prices. These activities do not generally share the gains in productivity achieved in other sectors by a combination of capital investment and technological innovation. In any case, national income statisticians do not know how to measure changes in the productivity of government inputs. Government "output" is not priced in any market, and for the most part the accountants simply value it at input cost. The services of teachers, soldiers, policemen, and judges are instructive examples. The upshot is that to purchase a 1972 dollar's worth of government activity, which by assumption costs a 1972 dollar's worth of privately used commodities in 1972, cost more than that in 1978 and less in 1956. The rising relative price of government is indicated by the following numbers for our five selected years in chronological order: .81, .87, .90, 1.00, 1.02.

What is the effect of the increasing relative cost of government on the social choice between government and private purchases? Simply to keep the *real* quantities of the two in step would require a growing proportion of government purchases in current dollars (the sort of ratio displayed in columns 1.2 of Table 1). For example, to maintain the 1965 relation of real quantities in 1978 would have required an increase in the government share of dollar GNP from 20.1 percent in 1965 to 23.1 percent in 1978. In actuality, the figure rose only to 20.6 percent, and thus the real volume of government purchases declined relative to private purchases. The history of this ratio is in column 1.2.6. Some substitution against commodities that become relatively dear is to be expected and, in fact, occurred.

In Figure 1, the two axes measure government purchases and private purchases, both in billions of constant 1972 dollars. The points labeled with the five dates show the actual combinations. The ray from the origin reflects the proportions of the 1965 combination, which happened to be the same as for 1956. The 1969 point is more government oriented, the 1973 and 1978 points considerably more private oriented. The downward sloping line through the 1978 point depicts the terms on which society could have traded private for government purchases in 1978, at a price of 1.02 government for one private. Within limits, the United States could have chosen any point on that line, including the several lettered alternatives. In fact, the point chosen was almost precisely that which repeated the 1965 dollar proportions (an outcome economists would describe by saying the elasticity of substitution with respect to the price change was unity).

The substitution, it is true, was almost wholly against defense purchases. Since 1965, public civilian purchases have grown in real terms somewhat faster than private purchases, even though gov-

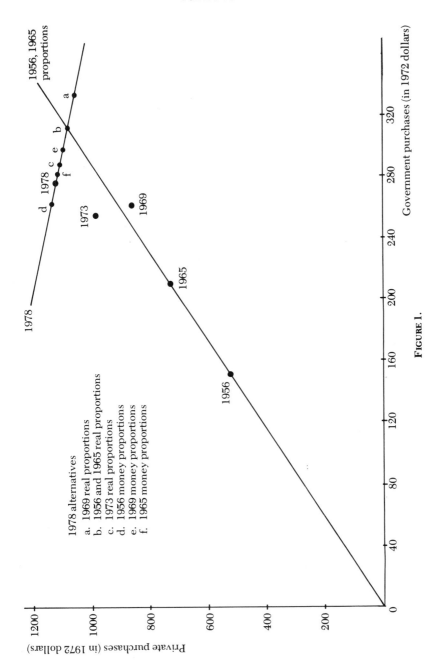

FIGURE 1.

ernment goods and services became more expensive (column 1.2.7). In recent years, the political process apparently has treated defense and civilian purchases as substitutes, in the sense that civilian government programs either crowd some defense funds out of the budget or are priority claims for resources released by exogenous reductions in defense needs.

Transfers

As columns 1.3 of Table 1 indicate, transfers have grown much faster than GNP. The ratio of transfers to GNP has little conceptual justification as a measure, or even as a part of a measure, of the economy-wide burden of government. Here, unlike the ratios for government as producer and as purchaser, the numerator is not a part or a share of a total represented by the denominator. Transfers are not an exhaustive component of GNP. Resources are still used to meet private demands, individually determined and signaled by market spending.

No doubt a fractional social loss results from taxing *A* one dollar and paying it to *B*. I refer not to the possible inequity, a matter of judgment, but to the inefficiency. *A* may work somewhat less because of the tax, for example, and *B* may work less because of the terms of the transfer. There are leaks in the buckets that move wealth from rich to poor, or from young to old, or from well to sick; but it is the leaks that are the social burden, not the contents of the bucket. No one knows the size of the social costs of transfers. We do know they are a fraction of the amounts transferred.

Of course, antigovernment sentiment may reflect dislike of redistribution and of the supposed beneficiaries of transfers, as well as opposition to government consumption of resources. To taxpayers, the fact that the transferees are private consumers who spend the benefits in private markets is immaterial.

A surge of transfer payments began with Lyndon Johnson's Great Society and continued under Republican presidencies. A breakdown of the sources of this expansion is given in Table 2, which compares 1977 and 1965. The bulk of the expansion was in Social Security; Medicare and Medicaid, begun in 1966, were major factors. Social Security became virtually universal, and generous provisions for disabled of all ages were added. Benefits were increased much faster than the cost of living. Cash welfare, including food stamps, increased in coverage and real benefits.

TABLE 2. Government Transfer Payments to Persons (Including Payments to Vendors of Medical Care).

	Federal	State & local	Total
	(Billion dollars of 1977 consumption purchasing power)		
1977	169.5	47.3	216.8
1965	57.7	16.6	74.3
Difference	111.8	30.7	142.5

Increases in Real Transfers, 1965 and 1977

	Billions of 1977 dollars	Percent of total increase	Percentage growth Aggregate real outlays	Number of beneficiaries
Old age, survivors, disability insurance	48.8	34.2	141	63
Medicare (begun 1966)	21.7	15.2		
Medicaid (begun 1966)	15.0	10.5		
Other retirement insurance (civil service, railroad, workmen's comp., and so forth)	22.2	15.6	153	81
Veterans' pensions and benefits	4.6	3.2	56	11
Cash public assistance (incl. food stamps)	22.1	15.5	156	110
Unemployment compensation	8.1	5.7	184	92
	142.5	99.9		
For reference: National consumption:			54	
U.S. population				12

SOURCE: Statistical Abstract of the United States 1978.

Welfare, however, is a small fraction of the total, compared to the programs that benefit middle America.

Indications are that Social Security benefits will continue to rise relative to GNP, and the burden on contributing workers will also rise. Reasons are the aging of the population and the increasing costs of medical care relative to other wages and prices. Most economists agree that a solution other than repeated raising of payroll taxes needs to be found.

A considerable factor in the growth of government outlays for health care has been the rapid relative increase in costs of hospitals, physicians, and drugs. Private households and insurers have faced the same problems. No doubt the government programs themselves, along with the expansion of private plans with third-party payment, contributed to the escalation of costs. The Carter administration has been trying to get hospital costs under control; somehow discipline by direct controls, if not market competition, must be introduced in the industry. There are already signs of strong substitution against medical care; average real expenditure per beneficiary has recently been declining.

Taxation. Columns 2.4 of Table 1 show tax takes relative to GNP and personal taxes to personal income. Since some taxes are transferred back to the private sector, the same strictures as in the previous section apply. Taxes to make transfers are only fractionally a burden on the private sector as a whole. They are, or course, a burden on taxpayers, especially on those who have no sympathy for the redistribution. A rough measure of this burden is in column 2.4.5, the ratio of personal taxes to personal income other than transfers. The Great Society surge of transfers is reflected in the three or four point jump in these measures of tax take after 1965. Very little has happened since; tax burdens, on average, have not increased in the 1970s. Although many tears have been shed about the supposed hidden tax of inflation — it pushes people into brackets with higher rates although their real incomes have not risen — Congress has taken pleasure in making periodic corrections.

The United States in International Perspective. The burden of government expenditure and taxation is frequently blamed for the slowing of real economic growth in the 1970s. Considerable caution is prudent in diagnosing recent disappointments in our economic performance. Serious students of productivity, notably Edward Denison,[6] find the recent slowdown a mystery yet to be explained. After all, the quarter century from 1946 to 1970 was a period of per capita economic progress unparalleled in U.S. statistical history, and also a period when taxes and government expenditures were larger factors in the economy than ever before in peacetime.

Comparisons with other advanced national economies, many of which have outshone the United States in economic growth, do not suggest that the size and growth of the public sector are decisive determinants. By almost any measure of government size, the United States is well below the advanced countries of Western Europe, including Germany and France. (Employment is an exception, because of our armed forces.) Moreover, from the mid-1960s to the mid-1970s our public sector showed less net growth than that of any of those European countries except France. The two major OECD countries that have smaller governments are Japan and Australia; Japan is catching up fast. Why Germany and Japan, the two economies with which the United States is so often unfavorably compared, have both grown so rapidly is a challenging question, one that certainly is not easy to answer by reference to government expenditures and taxes. In these respects, those two nations could hardly be more different from each other. Selected figures comparing eight countries in these dimensions are given in Tables 3 and 4.

The Proposed Constitutional Limit on Growth of Federal Outlays. The proposal of the National Tax Limitation Committee reflects the ideas of Milton Friedman. Its central provision is: "Total outlays in any fiscal year shall increase by a percentage no greater than the percentage increase in nominal gross national product in the last calendar year ending prior to the beginning of said fiscal year. If inflation for that calendar year is more than three percent, the permissible percentage of increase in total outlays shall be reduced by one-fourth of the excess of inflation over three percent." An escape is provided in presidentially declared emergencies, with consent of two-thirds of both houses. Some attention is paid to the technicalities of measuring inflation and defining outlays, and provision is made for judicial enforcement. State and local governments are protected against reductions of federal grants and against federal mandates for additional costly activities.

The budget involves many technicalities of accounting, statistics, and definition. So many differences of interpretation are possible that compliance with the amendment could be the subject of endless dispute and litigation. Conceivably, the amendment could become meaningless as formal cosmetic compliance disguises violations of intent. Consider some examples: Budget outlays can be reduced, at least for the time being, by renting rather than building office space. Subsidies and grants are outlays, but tax credits to the same beneficiaries for the same purposes are reductions in revenues, even if paid in cash. All expenses of the postal service were outlays when it was a federal department; now it is a public corporation and only the subsidy is an outlay. The GNP is calculated in the Department of

TABLE 3. Public Sectors in Selected Countries — Percentage of Gross Domestic Product in Current Prices: Three-year Averages.

Year	Sweden	Nether-lands	United Kingdom	Germany	France	United States	Australia	Japan	OECD average (unweighted)
Total expenditures									
1955–1957		31.1	32.3	30.2	33.5	25.9	21.7		28.5
1967–1969	41.3	42.6	38.5	33.1	39.4	31.7	26.4	19.2	34.5
1974–1976	51.7	53.9	44.5	44.0	41.8	35.1	32.8	25.1	41.4
Purchases of goods and services									
1955–1957		18.6 (5.7)	20.1 (7.4)	15.2 (2.9)	16.4 (5.9)	18.8 (9.5)	13.2 (3.2)		17.0 (4.0)
1967–1969	26.3 (4.3)	21.0 (4.3)	23.8 (6.1)	17.9 (3.0)	17.6 (4.7)	22.0 (8.4)	16.7 (2.6)	13.4 (1.0)	19.0 (3.4)
1974–1976	29.3 (3.4)	22.0 (3.0)	26.3 (5.0)	24.2 (3.1)	18.1 (3.8)	20.9 (5.8)	20.4 (2.4)	16.7 (0.9)	22.5 (2.7)
Transfers									
1955–1957	8.2	9.3	7.9	12.5	15.0	4.5	5.6	4.0	8.8
1967–1969	12.3	18.1	11.3	13.2	19.2	7.1	6.4	5.2	12.2
1974–1976	19.3	27.3	14.7	16.9	21.9	11.2	9.3	8.4	16.1
Tax revenues									
1955–1957	26.2	29.0	28.6	31.4	30.9	24.8	22.0	18.0	24.6
1967–1969	38.8	38.4	34.1	33.6	36.2	29.1	23.9	18.8	30.1
1974–1976	47.0	46.2	36.0	38.3	37.2	27.5	29.1	22.1	33.9

SOURCE: *Public Expenditure Trends*, OECD Studies in Resource Allocation, No. 5, Paris: Organization for Economic Cooperation and Development, 1978.

TABLE 4. Public Sector Employment (Including Armed Services) as Share (Percentage) of Total Employment.

	1965	1974	Percentage growth of share
Sweden	15.3	24.8	62.1
Netherlands	11.5	13.2	14.8
United Kingdom	15.7	19.8	26.1
Germany	9.8	13.1	33.7
France	12.4	13.7	10.5
United States	18.0	19.1	6.1
Australia	20.5	21.9	6.8
Japan	3.1	3.7	19.3

SOURCE: *Public Expenditure Trends,* OECD Studies in Resource Allocation, No. 5, Paris: Organization for Economic Cooperation and Development, 1978.

Commerce by a group of professional economic statisticians who have made some arbitrary conceptual decisions and a host of *ad hoc* numerical approximations. What if for any reason, professional or political, they change definitions and procedures? One could go on and on. However, it is prudent to assume that the amendment, seriously intended, would be seriously construed.

The Friedman amendment is not as devastating to economic stabilization as the balanced budget proposal, to be discussed below. The proposal does not require the federal government to take measures that intensify cyclical fluctuations affecting its revenues, nor does it outlaw discretionary tax policies to combat recessions or restrain booms. Nonetheless, it would have some bizarre and awkward consequences. As GNP growth fell below par or actually became negative in cyclical recessions, the permissible growth of outlays would fall correspondingly; yet, at the same time, a number of uncontrollable outlays, those with open-ended entitlements such as unemployment insurance, would grow faster than normal. The squeeze on the rest of the budget would be very tight and very disruptive to the continuity of programs, not excluding national defense. Moreover, the enforced procyclical variation of outlays would put much greater burdens of stabilization on tax variation and on monetary policy.

The appendix at the end of this paper contains some formal multiplier algebra analyzing the effects of various fiscal rules on the multipliers for fiscal policy variables and for exogenous shocks to private spending. In section A.4, it is shown that the multiplier for private spending, whether exogenous or induced by tax cuts or transfer payments, would be raised by the proposed rule. In the numerical illustration used in the appendix, the multiplier rises from two to three.

An important feature of the Friedman proposal is the floating base. The allowed growth of the budget is always measured in terms of the preceding year's budget. If that budget had for any reason grown less than the permitted amount, or if it had been penalized for excessive inflation, future budgets would be constitutionally smaller as a result. The consequence — desired by the proponents but probably not eternally by the nation — would be a gradual decline in budget relative to GNP. Or, alternatively, Congress could pad the budget inefficiently in order to preserve the base for future years. In any event, those who share my concern that Congress and the president need some flexibility in national defense outlays without chronic or periodic declarations of emergency should be particularly alarmed by the Friedman straitjacket.

I have simulated the budgetary consequences of the Friedman amendment by supposing it had been introduced in time to affect the budget for fiscal year 1975 and subsequent budgets through fiscal year 1979. I have assumed, somewhat implausibly, that the mandated budget reductions would have had no effect on the track of the economy, GNP, and prices. To achieve this result, taxes would have to have been reduced and/or credit conditions eased relative to actual history. These were cyclical years, in which the 1974–1975 recession and the subsequent recovery would have influenced the workings of the proposed rule. They are also years in which the penalty for exceeding three percent inflation would be consequential. The outlay budget for fiscal year 1979, estimated to be $493 billion, would have been $412 billion under the proposed regime, 18.1 percent of GNP instead of 21.9 percent.

Government Deficits and the Balanced Budget Rule

Since World War II, the federal debt has steadily declined relative to the scale of the economy. Its ratio to GNP was 1.03 in 1946, .47 in 1960, .30 in 1970, and .28 in 1978. Over the ten fiscal years from 1970 to 1979, federal deficits (on national income account) cumulated to $281 billion. However, at the end of the period the real value of the outstanding debt, in terms of the GNP deflator, was $290 billion in 1970 dollars. Debt service increased from $14 billion a year in 1970 to $43 billion a year in 1979. However, $11 billion could be considered repayment of real value principal in 1970, and $48 billion as such repayment in 1979.

These figures suggest that the popular picture of the growth of federal debt is exaggerated, even for the last decade. This should be some comfort to those worried about the burden of debt service on taxpayers. But inflation is a considerable part of this story, particularly for the 1970s. People who regard federal deficits in current dollars as the chief inflationary villain will not be consoled by the news that inflation itself reduced the debt burden.

Inflation. Are the huge federal deficits of the 1970s responsible for our inflation? The answer, contrary to pious conventional wisdom, is generally no. The budget was virtually in balance in 1973. Agricultural shortages and OPEC made double-digit inflation in 1974, and the Federal Reserve responded with a tight credit crunch that sent the economy reeling into recession. That produced the big deficits, which were inflationary only in the sense that maybe inflation would have abated further if the recession had been longer and deeper and the recovery slower. The disappointing acceleration of inflation in 1978–1979, which occurred while the deficit was declining, was due in part to the pace and extent of recovery, which, in turn, might have been slower with a more restrictive budget.

Contrary to the premise of much rhetoric of media and politics, there is no direct link between budget and inflation. There is indirect linkage: budget to economic conditions to inflation. Thus, budgets are inflationary when, as in Lyndon Johnson's Vietnam war escalation of 1966–1969, they overheat the economy, contributing to excess demand and to shortages of goods and labor. They are disinflationary when they slow the economy down and contribute to unemployment and excess capacity. But anyone who expects that balancing the budget would all of a sudden eliminate inflation is living in a dream world. Our current domestic inflation, due in part to Johnson's fiscal mistakes a decade ago, has acquired a stubborn life of its own, a recurrent and self-perpetuating pattern of wage and price increases. It succumbs very slowly to restrictions of aggregate demand, whether due to fiscal restraint or to other causes. Added to the wage-price cycle are the specific supply and price shocks, external to the country or at any rate to its industrial sector. In 1979–1980, as in 1973–1974, these inflationary impulses are beyond the reach of conventional macroeconomic policy.

The New Federalism. In describing or prescribing fiscal policy, it is a mistake to concentrate on the federal government rather than to consider the public sector as a whole. Thanks to federal grants-in-aid and to revenue-sharing — the new federalism common to presidents Johnson and Nixon — the finances of federal, state, and local governments are intertwined. In 1978, federal transfers to those other governments amounted to $77 billion. As a consequence, state and local governments have been running surpluses while the federal government has been in deficit. As Tables 5 and 1 (columns 1.4.0 and 1.4.1) reveal, the consolidated fiscal record shows much less red ink than the federal accounts alone.

Deficits, Passive and Active. The timeworn fallacy of advocates of the budget balance rule is that Congress can control the federal budget outcome. In fact, that outcome is sensitive to the state of the economy. Business conditions for the fiscal year beginning 1 October are quite uncertain the previous January when the president submits the budget, and they continue to be so throughout the session of Congress. Profits, personal incomes, sales, and other tax bases fall in recessions and rise in recoveries. Entitlements to unemployment insurance, food stamps, and other welfare benefits also vary with economic conditions, as do revenues and outlays. Every $100 billion shortfall of GNP increases the federal deficit by $40 billion and the

TABLE 5. Government Surpluses (+) or Deficits (−), National Income Accounts.

		1973	1975	1978
Federal government				
(1) Actual	($ billion)	− 6.7	− 70.6	− 29.4
	(percent of GNP)	− 0.5	− 4.6	− 1.4
(2) High employ-	($ billion)	− 8.4	− 29.6	− 12.9
ment	(percent of GNP)	− 0.6	− 1.8	− 0.6
(3) Cyclical	($ billion)	+ 1.7	− 41.0	− 16.5
(1) − (2)	(percent of GNP)	+ 0.1	− 2.8	− 0.8
All governments				
(4) Actual ($ billion)		+ 6	− 64	− 1
(5) High employment ($ billion)		+ 4	− 14	+ 18
(6) Cyclical ($ billion)		+ 2	− 50	− 19
(4) − (5)				
Memo: GNP shortfall ($ billion)		− 8	+ 100	+ 38

SOURCE: *Economic Report of the President,* 1978 and 1979. Estimates of high employment budget and of GNP shortfall are those of the Council of Economic Advisers.

all-governments deficit by $50 billion. For example, in 1975 the federal deficit was $71 billion, compared to $7 billion in 1973. Of the difference, $41 billion was due to the 1974–1975 recession; only $23 billion was due to congressional initiatives — outlays and tax cuts — designed to stimulate the economy or alleviate economic distress. The high employment rows of Table 5 eliminate cyclical influences on government receipts and outlays in order to isolate the effects of variation in government expenditure programs and tax laws.

Stabilization. Should a Congress, observing that its budget has fallen into deficit because of unexpected recession, cut expenditures and/or raise taxes to restore budget balance? To do so is to intensify the recession. Herbert Hoover pursued this course in 1930–1932, without notable success for either budget or economy. The willingness of the federal government to accept cyclical swings in budget outcome is one of the reasons the economy has been much more stable since World War II. Another important reason has been the use of deliberate countercyclical fiscal policy, varying government spending and taxation to compensate for swings in private spending.

The destabilizing effects of the balanced budget rule are shown algebraically in the appendix. The rule is compared with a standard multiplier model with constant expenditure and income-related tax revenues, and with a Keynesian rule for countercyclical compensatory spending. It is shown that the budget balance rule enlarges the range of parameter values incompatible with a positive static multiplier, a necessary condition for stability. Nonetheless, the multiplier for private expenditure will be positive under the balanced budget rule so long as the parameters are such that an increase in spending or reduction in taxes would in the standard model *increase* the deficit. But the multiplier will be considerably larger than the standard multiplier. For example, the same plausible parameter values that give an illustrative standard multiplier of two will yield a multiplier of eight under the rule. Exogenous shocks in private or external spending will make bigger cyclical waves, and greatly increase the burden of stabilization on the monetary authority.

The Proposed Amendment. Some thirty state legislatures have petitioned Congress to call a convention to propose a balanced budget amendment to the Constitution or to propose one itself. The texts of the desired amendment vary, but the most frequent language requires "that the total of all federal appropriations made by the

Congress for any fiscal year may not exceed the total of all estimated federal revenues for that fiscal year." In some state resolutions, exceptions are allowed by two-thirds vote of both houses during national emergencies proclaimed by the president. No enforcement procedure is specified, and no rules for estimating revenues are prescribed. Presumably, these would be added with more careful drafting. An amendment of this type proposed by two economists, Buchanan and Wagner, provides that in the event a deficit occurs the president must propose, and Congress must adopt, expenditure cuts of 20 percent each year until the deficit is eliminated.

From the standpoint of economic stabilization, the amendment would turn the clock back a half-century. With the federal budget so much larger than in Hoover's time, trying to keep it balanced could be even more perverse and futile than it was then. However, since deficit spending *can* overheat the economy and speed up inflation and has done so on occasions, some voters may find the amendment worthwhile in spite of its costs. I believe this would be a mistake. The occasions have almost always been wars. The amendment would not have helped — the national emergency escape hatch would have been used. Any Congress that would vote the Tonkin Gulf Resolution would go along with the president's fiscal policy as an emergency measure.

Concluding Remarks

Perhaps the present revolt against government expenditures and taxes is Barry Goldwater's revenge. Goldwater ran against the Great Society in 1964 and was defeated by a landslide. Now, many years later, the taxpaying public seems to find the costs of the surviving Great Society programs excessive. Johnson tried to have both "guns and butter." To preserve the butter from a potentially skeptical Congress, he declined in 1966 to ask for taxes to pay for the guns. The legacy of the resulting inflation is one source of the discontents that now threaten the butter, the health and welfare initiatives of the 1960s.

There is nothing in the record I have reviewed to justify a hysterical rush to arrest government's supposed insatiable appetite by constitutional amendment or other drastic departures from regular political process. The Johnson administration's transfer and health programs have been absorbed into budgets and taxes. They have contributed to a sizable reduction in poverty in this country, and to a generally more humane society. Demographic changes are creating difficult financial problems for the Social Security system, but the same trends are bringing to an end a long period of growth in public outlays for education. Politicians, from the president down, understand the current frugal national mood. Right or wrong, it is already influencing budget outcomes via the normal workings of representative democracy. Let us not tie the hands of future voters and their elected servants, or clutter the Constitution with fiscal rules.

Notes

1. For history and exposition of this idea, see Jude Wanniski, *The Way the World Works* (New York: Simon and Schuster, 1978).
2. Peter Gutmann, "The Subterranean Economy," *Financial Analysts Journal* (November/December 1977).
3. Edward Feige, "The Irregular Economy: Its Size and Macroeconomic Implications," unpublished paper, Social Systems Research Institute Workshop Series, May 1979.
4. James M. Buchanan and Richard E. Wagner, *Democracy in Deficit: The Political Legacy of Lord Keynes* (New York: Academic Press, 1977).
5. James Tobin, "Comment from an Academic Scribbler," *Journal of Monetary Economics* 4 (October 1978):617–25.
6. Edward Denison, *Accounting for Slower Economic Growth* (The United States in the 1970s) (Washington, D.C.: Brookings Institution, 1979).

Appendix

Stability of Multiplier Models under Alternative Fiscal Policies

The purpose of this appendix is to examine the consequences of compensatory, balanced-budget and outlay-limiting rules for the size of the multiplier and for the stability of the economy. If aggregate demand changes exogenously and unpredictably, for example, because consumers or businessmen spend less, what happens to GNP? I begin with the standard analysis of fiscal policy, and then show how it is altered by the two rules in turn.

A.1. A Standard Multiplier Model

Aggregate demand in any period, t, is the sum of private expenditure on goods and services, E_t, and government purchases, G_t. Demand must be equal to production, Y_t:

$$Y_t = E_t + G_t. \qquad (1)$$

I assume that private expenditure depends on current and lagged earnings from production, Y, and on current and lagged taxes, T. Transfers are regarded as negative taxes. Other factors are embodied in an additive constant, A. Thus,

$$E_t = a_1 Y_t + a_2 Y_{t-1} - b_1 T_t - b_2 T_{t-1} + G_t + A \qquad (a_1, a_2, b_1, b_2 \geqq 0). \qquad (2)$$

Taxes are a linear function of contemporaneous income:

$$T_t = T_0 + \tau Y_t.$$ (3)

Here T_0 may well be negative, reflecting transfers and a progressive schedule of taxes.

Combining equations (1), (2), and (3) gives:

$$Y_t (1 - a_1 + b_1\tau) = Y_{t-1}(a_2 - b_2\tau) + G_t + A - T_0 (b_1 + b_2).$$ (4)

For unchanging G, the equilibrium Y^* is found by setting Y_t and Y_{t-1} equal:

$$Y^*(1 - a + b\tau) = G + A - bT_0,$$ (5)

where $a = a_1 + a_2, b = b_1 + b_2$.

Thus, the multiplier for G and for A is

$$\mu = 1/(1 - a + b\tau) = \frac{\partial Y^*}{\partial G} = \frac{\partial Y^*}{\partial A}.$$ (6)

The multiplier is positive for $1 > a - b\tau$, that is, if the increase in private spending induced by a dollar increase of income and output is smaller than one. This "marginal propensity to spend" is the net of the positive response to higher income, a, and the negative response to the higher taxes levied on the income, $-b\tau$. Note that an increase in the tax rate, τ, makes the multiplier smaller, and thus dampens the change in Y^* due to any sustained change in the autonomous part of private spending, A.

The government deficit is

$$D_t = G_t - T_0 - \tau Y_t.$$ (7)

The equilibrium deficit is

$$D^* = G - T_0 - \tau Y^*.$$ (8)

With equation (6), the response of the equilibrium deficit to G and A can be seen:

$$\frac{\partial D^*}{\partial G} = 1 - \mu\tau, \quad \frac{\partial D^*}{\partial A} = \mu\tau.$$ (9)

An old question of interest is whether D^* increases with G. Can more spending so stimulate the economy that the government collects enough additional taxes to pay for the increase in spending? From equation (9), we see that a positive answer requires that $\mu\tau$ equal or exceed 1.

$$\frac{\partial D^*}{\partial G} \gtrless 0 \text{ as } 1 \gtrless \mu\tau,$$

that is, as $1 - a + b\tau \gtrless \tau$ or $1 - a \gtrless \tau(1-b)$.   (10)

This assumes that μ is positive. Thus, the condition for automatic balancing or overbalancing is that τ exceeds $(1-a)/(1-b)$. For $\tau < 1$, this can happen only if a is larger than b, that is, the marginal spending response to earned income is larger than that to tax cuts or transfers. A possible scenario is that business investment depends on total income, Y, while consumption depends only on disposable income, $Y(1-\tau)$. Then the excess of a over b represents a marginal propensity to invest.

The stability of the process can be examined by looking at the deviations of Y_t from equilibrium Y^*. Let $y_t = Y_t - Y^*$ and subtract equation (5) from equation (4) for constant G:

$$y_t(1 - a_1 + b_1\tau) = y_{t-1}(a_2 - b_2\tau). \tag{11}$$

The process is stable if and only if

$$\left| \frac{a_2 - b_2\tau}{1 - a_1 + b_1\tau} \right| < 1. \tag{12}$$

For the normal case with $a_1 - b_1\tau$, $a_2 - b_2\tau$ both positive but less than one, the necessary and sufficient condition is that $(1 - a + b\tau) > 0$, that is, the static multiplier, equation (6), is positive. This condition is in any case necessary to have positive solutions Y^* in equation (5) for positive values of the multiplicand on the right-hand side. Instability could happen, with a positive static multiplier, if and only if $a_2 - b_2\tau$ is negative and exceeds $1 - a_1 + b_1\tau$ in absolute value. This would lead to sawtooth oscillations of increasing amplitude.

A.2. Compensatory Fiscal Policy

A Keynesian compensatory fiscal policy can be described as one that sets G_t endogenously in an attempt to stabilize Y at a target value $\overline{Y}$. Suppose that this is done by moving G in the opposite direction from the last observed deviation of Y from $\overline{Y}$:

$$G_t = G_{t-1} + c(\overline{Y} - Y_{t-1}), c > 0. \tag{13}$$

Substituting equation (13) in equation (4) gives a new difference equation for Y:

$$Y_t(1 - a_1 + b_1\tau) = Y_{t-1}(a_2 - b_2\tau) + G + c\overline{Y} + A - bT_0. \tag{14}$$

The equilibrium of the system (13) and (14) is:

$$Y^* = \overline{Y}$$

$$G^* = \overline{Y}(1 - a + b) - A + bT_0. \tag{15}$$

That is, for given A and T_0, G will in equilibrium be the amount needed to make aggregate demand sum to $\overline{Y}$. Letting y and g denote deviations from equilibrium,

$$\begin{cases} g_t - g_{t-1} & + cy_{t-1} & = 0 \\ -g_t + y_t(1 - a_1 + b_1\tau) - y_{t-1}(a_2 - b_2\tau) & = 0 \end{cases} \tag{16}$$

Eliminating g, the difference equation for y is:

$$y_t + y_{t-1} \left\{ \frac{-1 + (a_1 - a_2) - (b_1 - b_2)\tau + c}{1 - a_1 + b_1\tau} \right\} + y_{t-2} \left\{ \frac{a_2 - b_2\tau}{1 - a_1 + b_1\tau} \right\} = 0. \tag{17}$$

There are three necessary and sufficient conditions for stability. Assuming that $(a_1 + b_1\tau) < 1$, these amount to the following:

(i) $(1 - a + b\tau) > 0$
(ii) $c > 0$
(iii) $c/2 - (a_2 - b_2\tau) < (1 - a_1 + b_1\tau)$. $\hspace{2cm}$ (18)

Condition (i) is simply that the standard multiplier be positive, as before.

Condition (ii) is simply the assumption that the change in G is compensatory. Condition (iii) says that c must not be too large. *Too large* means that the current public and private spending induced from last period's Y must not exceed in absolute value the "leakage" induced by the increase in current Y that it generates. Otherwise, there will be oscillations of increasing amplitude. This is like the unstable case of the previous model, except that the introduction of c allows it to happen even if $a_2 - b_2\tau$ is positive. The common sense is that exaggerated fiscal response could overshoot.

A.3. A Balanced Budget Rule

I turn now to a fiscal rule that simulates the proposed constitutional amendment requiring a balanced budget. In practice, this too would be a feedback rule, for example:

$$G_t = G_{t-1} + s(T_0 + \tau Y_{t-1} - G_{t-1}). \tag{19}$$

Following the same procedure as for the Keynesian fiscal rule gives:

$$Y_t(1 - a_1 + b_1\tau) = Y_{t-1}(a_2 - b_2\tau + s\tau) \\ + (1-s)G_{t-1} + A - (b-s)T_0. \tag{20}$$

In equilibrium, the budget is balanced:

$$G^* = T_0 + \tau Y^*$$
$$Y^*(1 - \tau - a + b\tau) = T_0(1-b) + A. \tag{21}$$

Thus, the static multiplier for autonomous expenditure A is:

$$\frac{\partial Y^*}{\partial A} = 1/(1 - \tau - a + b\tau). \tag{22}$$

This is larger than the standard multiplier because of the term $-\tau$ in the denominator. Note also that the denominator is related to the condition (10), as follows: The new multiplier is positive when in the standard model $\partial D^*/\partial G$ is positive, that is, the deficit rises when spending is increased. The new multiplier is negative — a clue that the equilibrium is unstable — when in the standard model $\partial D^*/\partial G$ is negative.

We can also derive a multiplier for an increase in T_0, the constant in the tax function:

$$\frac{\partial Y^*}{\partial T_0} = \frac{1-b}{1 - \tau - a + b\tau} = (1-b)\frac{\partial Y^*}{\partial A}. \tag{23}$$

This is greater than zero if the denominator in these multipliers is positive. The reason, of course, is that an increase in taxation will in equilibrium be accompanied by an increase in spending, and the celebrated balanced budget multiplier theorem tells us that the higher budget must increase Y. Note also that if $a = b$, the multiplier in equation (23) becomes $1/(1-\tau)$.

Once again, there are two simultaneous difference equations in the deviations from equilibrium y and g:

$$g_t - (1-s)g_{t-1} \qquad\qquad - s\tau y_{t-1} \qquad\qquad = 0$$
$$- (1-s)g_{t-1} + y_t(1 - a_1 + b_1\tau) - y_{t-1}(a_2 - b_2\tau + s\tau) = 0 \tag{24}$$

The second-order difference equation in y is:

$$y_{t+1} + y_t \left[\frac{(s-1)(1-a_1+b_1\tau)}{1-a_1+b_1\tau} \right]$$

$$+ y_{t-1} \left[\frac{(1-s)(a_2-b_2\tau)}{1-a_1+b_1\tau} \right] = 0. \tag{25}$$

The three stability conditions are (assuming $1 - a_1 + b_1\tau > 0$):

(i) $-s(a_2 - b_2\tau) < 1 - a + b\tau$
(ii) $1 - \tau - a + b\tau > 0$
(iii) $(2-s)(1-a_1+b_1\tau) + s\tau > 0.$ (26)

The second condition is the one foreshadowed, that the static multiplier (22) is positive. The first is automatically met if $(a_2 - b_2\tau)$ is positive. So is the third, unless s is larger than 2; it may be met anyway.

Thus, the balanced budget feedback rule is compatible with stability under plausible conditions, the most important of which is that an increase in spending increases the deficit. Compared with the other two models, however, it does enlarge the range of parameter values incompatible with stability, that is, incompatible with a positive static multiplier for autonomous expenditure. In any event, it makes that multiplier large, and increases the amplitude of fluctuations for given fluctuations of autonomous spending. For example, suppose that $a = b = .8$ and $\tau = .4$. The standard multiplier is then $1/(1 - .48) \approx 2$. The multiplier under the budget balance feedback rule is $1/(.6 - .48) \approx 8$.

A diagrammatic exposition of the several models may be useful. In Figure A.1, the diagrams show G vertically and Y horizontally. In each case, two lines are shown, one the locus along which ΔG is zero, the other the locus along which ΔY is zero. The intersection of the two is the equilibrium. The arrows show the direction of movement of G and Y in the various regions defined by the two lines.

In Figure A.1-a, for the standard multiplier model with G exogenous, the zero ΔG locus is horizontal, and all movements occur on the line. The zero ΔY locus is the multiplier relationship (5). Stability is assured for the positive multiplier depicted. Only if the zero ΔY locus were negatively sloped would the equilibrium be unstable.

Figure A.1-b applies to the compensatory fiscal rule. Here the zero ΔG locus, corresponding to (13), is vertical at the target $\bar{Y}$. The zero ΔY locus, derived most easily from the second equation of (16), has the same slope as in Figure A.1-a, $1/(1 - a + b\tau)$. [Stability condition (i) of equation (18).] Here both G and Y can be changing, in the directions indicated by the arrows. The system is oscillatory. In principle, it could be either damped or antidamped. In the formal model above, this depends on condition (iii) of equation (18).

Figures A.1-c and A.1-d both refer to the balanced budget rule. The zero ΔG locus is simply the tax function. The zero ΔY line is the standard multiplier relation, with slope $1/(1 - a + b\tau)$. [See equation (22) and stability condition (ii) of equation (26).] As the phase diagrams indicate, stability depends on the relative slopes of the two relations.

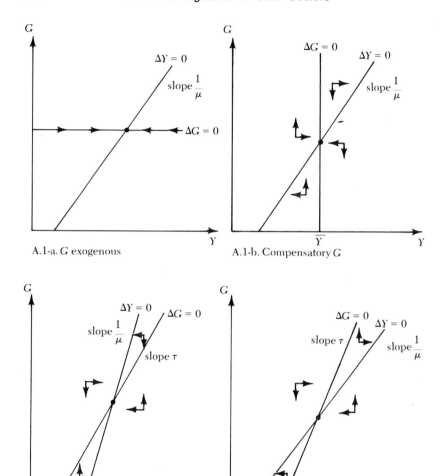

A.1-a. G exogenous   A.1-b. Compensatory G

A.1-c. Balanced budget rule, stable   A.1-d. Balanced budget rule, unstable

FIGURE A.1.

The active parameter of fiscal policy in all three models has been taken to be government purchases G. It could have been taxation, either T_0 or τ or both, without altering the qualitative results.

A.4. Limiting Expenditure Growth

As an alternative to the balanced budget amendment, a constitutional limit on the growth of federal outlays has been proposed. The rule would restrict the growth of outlays to the previous year's growth of GNP. To simulate this type of restriction, assume:

$$G_t \leqq \alpha Y_{t-1} \tag{27}$$

where α is the historical ratio that the amendment seeks to freeze. Like the balanced budget proposal, the rule is an inequality; assuming the government is always against the constraint, it can be taken as an equality. All this does is convert equation (4) into the following:

$$Y_t(1 - a_1 + b_1\tau) = Y_{t-1}(a_2 - b_2\tau + \alpha) + A - T_0b. \tag{28}$$

The multiplier for A becomes $1/(1 - \alpha - a + b\tau)$. Compared with the standard case, our first model, the denominator is reduced by α. The scope for instability via a negative static multiplier is increased; and if it is still positive, it is larger. With the illustrative parameter values used above, and assuming $\alpha = .2$, the multiplier would become $1/(.8 - .48) \approx 3$.

This exercise does not capture the full spirit of the proposal. For one thing, the proposal contains a penalty for inflation, not considered here. For another, the outlays limited by the amendment include transfers as well as purchases. This second is not a significant matter for our purpose, especially if the affected transfers carry a b close to one.

Technological Development and Employment

James Tobin

Yale University

For developing economies, the process of economic growth can be described as one of shifting resources from one known technology to another. Modern technologies used in advanced countries are more productive than traditional technologies. But their adoption generally requires saving to accumulate new forms of capital. The capital used in old technology cannot be transformed into modern capital, except possibly by the slow process of depreciation and replacement.

Typically, the newer technologies also require human capital not needed in the older processes: not only different manual and physical skills but also literacy and managerial capacity. But though they require more skilled labour, the modern technologies require much less unskilled labour, and less labour *in toto*, per unit of output. It is precisely this labour saving that makes their adoption the eventual avenue to higher standards of living.

The other side of the coin, of course, is the structural unemployment that typically accompanies economic development. Concentration of available saving on the accumulation of modern capital often appears to accentuate the problem of surplus labour. Sometimes it appears that the allocation of investment to older and more labour-intensive techniques would be more rational. Employment would be greater, and national output would benefit accordingly, even though the capital stock would be less productive than if investment had been otherwise directed. An important issue of development strategy is how to allocate available saving among alternative forms of capital accumulation.

The issue of investment strategy is the main subject of this paper. I come to it in Section 5. In the earlier sections I set up a simple model within which the problem can be discussed. There are two technologies, old and modern. Their difference is embodied in capital: that is, capital useable in one technology is not useable in the other. Both technologies involve fixed input-output coefficients. This makes unemployment due to capital shortage a logical possibility. At the same time, the modern technology requires skilled labour, trained either on the job or by educational investment. Unlike modern capital, skilled labour is not completely specific. Lacking skilled jobs, these workers are suitable for employment as unskilled labour

Reprinted by permission from *Eastern Africa Economic Review* 6(1) (June 1974):1–26.

on either technology. Typically skilled labour can command a premium wage, even when general labour is surplus.

The economy's propensity to save is assumed to be adequate to accumulate the physical and human capital required under the modern technology as rapidly as the total labour force is growing. Otherwise full development, a full shift of resources to modern technology, would not be a feasible long-run objective. Of course in many actual economies insufficiency of the propensity to save may be a fundamental obstacle to development. But here my interest is in a different question. Assuming the propensity to save is adequate for full development, is it possible 'to get there from here', and if so, how?

The economy starts with a considerable portion of its capital and employment in the old technology, and possibly with unemployment. Generally it is feasible to achieve both full employment and a full shift of resources, although the optimal path may involve a detour during which investment is concentrated in the older sector until unemployment is eliminated. In some circumstances, however, there can be an impasse, with no feasible path to the ultimate goal—even though the position of full development and full employment would be sustainable once reached. The answer turns on the relative capital requirements of the two sectors. If the modern technology is the more capital using, as well as the more labour saving, there is always a feasible path. The impasse arises if the modern technology saves capital as well as labour.

I have assumed throughout this paper that the economy under discussion is closed, although I am aware that in reality development is always intertwined with foreign trade and capital transactions. More precisely, the economy here need not be literally closed; the essential assumption is that it is dependent on its own saving. Although the capital goods needed for modern technology may be imported, they must be purchased with exports from either sector of the developing economy, at constant terms of trade. Foreign aid and foreign loans are not available. Realistically, they could provide an escape from the detours or impasses that, according to the analysis of the paper, might complicate the process of self-contained development.

1. THE TECHNOLOGIES AVAILABLE

There are two technologies, using different kinds of capital, but producing commensurable outputs. Both are characterized by fixed proportions. The amounts of inputs required for a unit of gross output are given in Table 1.

Technology 1 is the modern technology. It is the more capital intensive in the sense that more physical capital is required per unit of gross output ($\alpha_1 > \alpha_2$), and it requires less total labour per unit of output ($\beta_1 < \beta_2$). However, technology 1 requires some input (β_{11}) of skilled labour, and only a part of the labour force is skilled ($\ell_1 < \ell$). Skilled labour can also

TABLE 1

Technology	1	2	
			Total supplies
(i) Capital type 1	a_1	0	k_1
(ii) Capital type 2	0	a_2	k_2
(iii) Skilled labour	β_{11}	0	ℓ_1
[Unskilled labour	β_{21}	β_{22}]	
(iv) All labour	$\beta_1 (= \beta_{11} + \beta_{21})$	$\beta_2 (= \beta_{22})$	ℓ
Total output	y_1	y_2	y

perform in unskilled jobs, just as well as unskilled labour. Thus the supply of unskilled labour *per se* is not a resource constraint. The resource constraints are for skilled labour, line (iii) of the table, and for all labour, line (iv) of the table. Here is a summary of the four resource constraints at any moment of time, given the supplies of the four resources:

(1.1)   (i) $a_1 y_1 \qquad \leq k_1$

       (ii) $a_2 y_2 \qquad \leq k_2$

       (iii) $\beta_{11} y_1 \qquad \leq \ell_1$

       (iv) $\beta_1 y_1 + \beta_2 y_2 \quad \leq \ell.$

Unless the four supplies stand in particular ratios to each other, not all of these four relations will hold with equality. Whatever the supplies of resources, an efficient use of them implies full employment of at least two of the resources. The most interesting regimes are:

I. General Capital Shortage

Constraints (i) and (ii) are binding, i.e. hold with equality. Resources (iii) and (iv), both kinds of labour, are in surplus; the corresponding relations are inequalities. The efficiency prices or shadow prices of the four resources are respectively $1/a_1$, $1/a_2$, 0, 0. (These are found by solving the two break-even equations for the technologies. Let r_1 and r_2 be the rents per time period for the use of the two types of capital. Let w be the wage rate of labour in unskilled jobs, and w_1 be the premium paid for skilled labour in jobs requiring skill—the total wage rate of such a worker is $w+w_1$. The two breakeven equations are:

(1.2) $1 = a_1 r_1 \qquad + \beta_{11} w_1 + \beta_1 w$

         $1 = \qquad a_2 r_2 + \beta_2 w.$

Whenever a resource is slack, its marginal productivity—and hence its efficiency price—is zero. In the present case, then, $w_1 = w = 0$, and therefore $r_1 = 1/a_1$, $r_2 = 1/a_2$.)

II. Shortage of Skilled Labour and Labour-Intensive Capital

Constraints (ii) and (iii) are binding; the others are slack. The efficiency prices, calculated by the same procedure as above, are 0, $1/\alpha_2$, $1/\beta_{11}$, 0. There is general unemployment of unskilled labour, because of a shortage of suitable capital for technology 2. Modern capital is not fully used, for lack of skilled labour to man it. Skilled labour commands a wage, even though general manpower is surplus.

III.   *Shortage of Labour-Intensive Capital*

Constraints (i), (ii), and (iii) are binding, but general labour is surplus. This requires that the supplies of modern capital and skilled labour are in balance: $k_1/\alpha_1 = \ell_1/\beta_{11}$. In this case the breakeven equations for prices are:

$$1 = \alpha_1 r_1 + \beta_{11} w_1; \quad 1 = \alpha_2 r_2.$$

Here we know that the general wage $w = 0$, and that $r_2 = 1/\alpha_2$. However r_1 and w_1 are indeterminate. Since neither can be less than zero, we have $0 \leq r_1 \leq 1/\alpha_1$ and $0 \leq w_1 \leq 1/\beta_{11}$.

IV.   *Full Employment of Labour, Surplus of Labour-Intensive Capital*

Constraints (i), (iii), (iv) are binding. As in III, k_1 and ℓ_1 must be in balance and their prices are indeterminate. Old-technology capital is in excess supply, and its rent is zero. The wage of general labour is $1/\beta_2$.

V.   *Full Employment of Labour, Only Modern Technology in Use*

Constraints (i), (iii), (iv) are binding, and $\beta_1 y_1 = \ell$. There is no labour left over for technology 2, even though some capital for that technology is available. Since $\beta_1 < \beta_2$ it would clearly be inefficient to reduce y_1 in order to release labour for the older technology. In this case there is only one break-even equation:

$$1 = \alpha_1 r_1 + \beta_{11} w_1 + \beta_1 w.$$

The other one is an inequality, showing that operation of technology 2 is unprofitable:

$$1 < \alpha_2 r_2 + \beta_2 w.$$

We know that $r_2 = 0$, given the excess supply of k_2. Therefore, $w > 1/\beta_2$. At the same time $w \leq 1/\beta_1$. The upper limit on r_1 is found by setting w_1 and w at their lower limits, 0 and $1/\beta_2$ respectively:

$$1 = \alpha_1 \bar{r}_1 + \beta_1/\beta_2, \quad \bar{r}_1 = \frac{1 - \beta_1/\beta_2}{\alpha_1}.$$ Similarly the upper limit on w_1 is

$$\bar{w}_1 = \frac{1 - \beta_1/\beta_2}{\beta_{11}}.$$

VI.   *All Resources Fully Employed*

All the four constraints of (1.1) apply. Thus,

$$(1.3) \qquad \frac{k_1}{\ell_1} = \frac{\alpha_1}{\beta_{11}}$$

$$\text{and} \quad \frac{\beta_1 k_1}{\alpha_1} + \frac{\beta_2 k_2}{\alpha_2} = \ell.$$

Prices are indeterminate, within the constraints (1.2).

2. Depreciation, Accumulation, and Net Output

To complete the description of the technologies, I must specify the mechanisms of depreciation and accumulation of the stocks of physical capital k_1 and k_2, and of the stock of human capital ℓ_1.

Physical capital

I assume that each capital stock k_i depreciates at the constant exponential rate d_i. Let $I_i(t)$ be the rate of gross investment in physical capital of type i at time t, and let the stock of such capital at time t be $k_i(t)$, its time rate of change $k_i'(t)$. (I will suppress the notation (t) whenever it is clear that the variable is a function of time.) The familiar expression for net accumulation is:

(2.1) $\qquad k_i' = I_i - d_i k_i \qquad (i = 1, 2)$.

Since $I_i \geq 0$ (capital in existence cannot be converted into another type of capital or into consumable goods),

(2.2) $\qquad k_i' \geq d_i k_i \qquad (i = 1, 2)$.

Skilled labour

Without new recruits, the supply of skilled labour would decline by attrition due to retirement, disability, and death. This attrition is analogous to the depreciation of physical capital. It is assumed to occur at an exponential rate of m_1 per year.

New recruits to the cadre of skilled labour occur in two ways. One is educational training. Let the rate of recruitment from this source be $n_1(t)$ per year, and the cost per recruit be e units of output. The implicit assumption is that education is performed by technology 1, with the same capital, skilled labour, and general labour requirements of that modern technology. Thus training costs $e n_1(t)$ are a claim on y_1, the output of technology 1. A more elaborate model would, of course, specify a distinct educational technology, and in addition allow for the lengthy gestation of skilled manpower over successive grades of education.

The other source of skilled manpower is learning by doing, or more accurately in this case learning by observation and contact. Upgrading of unskilled personnel associated with modern technology is a normal method of enlarging the availability of skilled labour, perhaps more important than formal education off the job. Here it is assumed that a fraction μ of the unskilled labour employed in technology 1 (ℓ_{21}) becomes skilled each year.

This on-the-job training is a special advantage of producing by modern technology. Unskilled labour employed in technology 2 does not become skilled.

Taking account of attrition and of both sources of recruitment, we have the growth of the supply of skilled labour:

(2.3) $\ell_i'(t) = -m_1\ell_1(t) + n\ell_{21}(t)$.

We know that $\ell_{21} = \beta_{21}y_1(t)$. Likewise, provided skilled manpower is fully employed, $\ell_1'(t) = \beta_{11}y_1(t)$. In this case we can write (2.3) as:

(2.4) $\ell_i'(t) = n_1(t) + y_1(t)(\mu\beta_{21} - m_1\beta_{11})$.

Conceivably the term in brackets, which represents the net of attrition and upgrading is positive, i.e. the use of technology 1 generates human capital faster than it depreciates.

The total capital requirement, human plus physical, in technology 1, is $\alpha_1 + e\beta_{11}$ per unit of gross output. In later sections I shall find it convenient to aggregate the two capital requirements of technology 1, on the assumption that within the sector balance between the two kinds of capital is maintained. I shall use $\hat{a}_1$ to refer to the aggregate capital requirement:

(2.5) $\hat{a}_2 = \alpha_1 + e\beta_{11}$.

The parameter, e, educational cost, converts the skilled labour requirement into units of output, commensurate with the physical capital requirement.

The *net* output of sector 1, $\bar{y}_1$ must allow for the depreciation of the two kinds of capital:

(2.6) $\bar{y}_1 = y_1 + d_1k_1 - em_1\ell_1 + e\mu\ell_{21}$.

Assuming both kinds of capital are fully used, this can be written as:

(2.7) $\bar{y}_1 = y_1(1 - d_1\alpha_1 - em_1\beta_{11} + e\mu\beta_{21})$.

In these circumstances, it is convenient to have a summary depreciation rate $\bar{d}_1$ for sector 1, defined so that

(2.8) $\bar{y} = y_1(1 - \bar{d}_1\alpha_1)$.

It follows that

(2.9) $\bar{d}_1 = \dfrac{d_1\alpha_1 + em_1\beta_{11} - e\mu\beta_{21}}{\alpha_1 + e\beta_{11}}$.

These definitions would not be appropriate in regimes where either physical or human capital were in surplus. In that case no deduction for depreciation of the surplus stock should be made in going from gross to net output.

Sector 2 is less complicated. Net output is simply:

(2.10) $\bar{y}_2 = y_2(1 - d_2\hat{a}_2)$.

Once again the deduction for depreciation is appropriate only when k_2 is fully employed.

To find the input coefficient for net output, it is only necessary to divide the coefficients in Table 1 by the appropriate ratio of net to gross output. When no capital resources are redundant, these ratios are respectively $1 - \bar{d}_1\hat{a}_1$ and $1 - d_2\alpha_2$.

I have already assumed that the physical capital requirement per unit of gross output is larger in sector 1 ($\alpha_1 > \alpha_2$) and in the same spirit I would assume also that the physical capital requirement per unit of *net* output is larger in sector 1 $\left(\dfrac{\alpha_1}{1-\alpha_1 d_1} > \dfrac{\alpha_2}{1-\alpha_2 d_2} \right)$. Otherwise I would be allowing greater durability of capital in technology 1 to offset its greater capital coefficient.

But the distinctive learning-by-doing capacity of technology 1 suggests keeping open the interesting possibility that technology 1 is not the more capital using when human as well as physical capital is taken into account. I shall analyse both cases:

sector 1 the more capital using

$\left(\dfrac{\hat{a}_1}{1-\hat{a}_1 \bar{d}_1} > \dfrac{\alpha_2}{1-\alpha_2 d_2} \right)$ and sector 1 the less capital using (the inequality reversed).

3. Total Labour Supply

The growth of total labour supply is taken to be exogenous, at a constant exponential rate μ. It is possible to interpret this 'natural rate' to include labour-augmenting technological progress as well as population growth proper, provided that such progress is costless and 'disembodied', and applies impartially to all labour, wherever employed and whether skilled or unskilled. Under this interpretation labour supplies and employments ℓ, ℓ_1, ℓ_{21}, ℓ_2 are numbers of effective man-hours; the effective man-hours associated with a natural man-hour grows at the rate of technological progress. The education or training cost e, which is assumed to be constant, is then the cost of turning an effective unit of unskilled labour into an effective unit of skilled labour. Since educating one man converts more effective units this year than last, constancy of e implies that the education cost *per man* grows at the rate of general labour-augmenting progress. This is probably a reasonable assumption, more so than the more optimistic opposite assumption that education costs *per natural man* remain constant. Education is notoriously immune to the forces of progress that pervade other sectors. Moreover, it makes highly intensive use of labour (and skilled labour at that), at wages that rise along with economy-wide productivity.

In what follows we shall not make the distinction between natural and effective labour, counting on the reader to remember the alternative interpretations of the model.

4. Golden Ages

In a 'golden age' the economy grows at its natural rate n. All outputs, capital stocks, labour supplies grow at this common rate, and all resources are fully utilized. There are two possible polar golden ages, one with exclusive use of technology 1 ($y_2=0$), one with exclusive use of technology 2 ($y_1=0$). Mixtures of these polar cases are also conceivable, as the proportion of y_2, in total output y varies from 0 to 1, and that of y_1 correspondingly from 1 to 0.

Consider first the golden age in which $y_1=0$ and technology 2 is used exclusively. Capital of type 2 must be sufficient to employ the whole labour force: $k_2 = a_2y_2 \cdot \dfrac{a_2\ell}{\beta_2}$. The net saving required to make k_2 grow at the same rate as the labour force is

$$k_2'(t) = nk_2(t) = na_2y_2(t) = na_2y(t).$$

Therefore the fraction of net income which must be saved, s, is given by $s(y_2(t)-d_2k_2(t)) = s(1-d_2a_2)y_2(t) = na_2y(t)$, and

(4.1) $$s = \frac{na_2}{1-d_2a_2}.$$

Consumption per worker in the golden age of old technology is:

(4.2) $$\frac{c}{\ell} = \frac{1-a_2(n+d_2)}{\beta_2}.$$

In the other polar case, the golden age of the modern technology, the required saving propensity is $s = \dfrac{n\hat{a}_1}{1-\hat{a}\bar{d}_1}$, and consumption per worker is:

(4.3) $$\frac{c}{\ell} = \frac{1-\hat{a}_1(n+\bar{d}_1)}{\beta_1}.$$

I assume, of course, that consumption per worker is larger in (4.3) than in (4.2). Otherwise there is no reason for the economy to modernize. In other words,

(4.4) $$\beta_2(1-\hat{a}_1\bar{d}_1)-\beta_1(1-a_2d_2)>n(\beta_2\hat{a}_1-\beta_1a_2)>0.$$

Golden ages are also possible with both technologies in use. To examine them, let the ratio of employment in the modern sector, ℓ_1, to the total labour force ℓ be x. On the assumption that full employment obtains in these golden ages, the fraction of the labour force employed with technology 2 is $\ell_2/\ell = 1 - x$. For given x ($0 \leq x \leq 1$):

$$c_1 = \frac{x\ell(1-\hat{a}_1(n+\bar{d}_1)}{\beta_1}$$

(4.5) $$c_2 = \frac{(1-a)\ell(1-a_2(n+d_2))}{\beta_2}$$

$$\frac{c}{\ell} = \frac{c_1+c_2}{\ell} = x\frac{(1-\hat{a}_1(n+\bar{d}_1))}{\beta_1} + (1-x)\frac{(1-a_2(n+d_2))}{\beta_2}.$$

Evidently c/ℓ is a linear function of x, with a slope which I have already, in comparing (4.3) and (4.2), assumed to be positive.

A larger allocation of labour to sector 1—a higher value of—also means a larger capital stock per worker, as follows:

$$(4.6) \qquad \frac{k}{\ell} = x \frac{\hat{a}_1}{\beta_1} + (1-x) \frac{\alpha_2}{\beta_2}.$$

The gross marginal product of capital is equal to the increment of gross output associated with an increase in x, divided by the increment in capital stock associated with an increase in x:

$$(4.7) \qquad \frac{\partial\left(\frac{y_1+y_2}{\ell}\right)}{\partial(k/\ell)} = \frac{\beta_2 - \beta_1}{\beta_2\hat{a}_1 - \beta_1\alpha_2} \qquad (0 \leq x \leq 1).$$

The net marginal product must allow for the increase in depreciation and training requirements associated with an increment in the capital stock

$$(4.8) \qquad \frac{\partial\left(\frac{\bar{y}_1+\bar{y}_2}{\ell}\right)}{\partial(k/\ell)} = \frac{\beta_2(1-\hat{a}_1\bar{d}_1) - \beta_1(1-\alpha_2 d_2)}{\beta_2\hat{a}_1 - \beta_1\alpha_2}.$$

Normally we expect a net marginal product to be less than the gross marginal product. Here, however, it is conceivable that the reverse is true; $\beta_2\hat{a}_1\bar{d}_1$ may be smaller than $\beta_1\alpha_2 d_2$.

Neo-classical growth theory tells us that a shift to a more capital-intensive golden age will increase consumption per worker if and only if the net marginal product exceeds the rate of growth n. As is evident from (4.4) and (4.8), this is another way of expressing the assumption that an increase in x augments consumption per worker.

Alternative golden ages are summarized graphically in Figures 1a and 1b. These give the standard diagrams of growth theory for the two cases. In Figure 1a, the normal case, technology 1 is the more capital-using technology in all the senses discussed above. In Figure 1b technology 1 requires less total capital per unit of net output. This leads to a number of anomalies: the net marginal product of capital is higher than the gross marginal product, and also higher than the net average product. In the upper panel of each diagram a dashed broken line represents the net saving generated by a saving propensity ŝ adequate to support the maximum-consumption golden age, the golden age which corresponds to the allocation of all productive resources to the new technology. In the normal case, Figure 1a, this propensity to save is more than adequate for any less capital-intensive golden age. In the other case, Figure 1b, it is not; the maximum-consumption golden age is the only one it will support. I will return to this theme in section 5.

5. DEVELOPMENT STRATEGY: SAVING AND ITS ALLOCATION

I assume now that the economy is not initially in a golden age, and that its ultimate objective is to reach the maximum-consumption golden age, with all labour and capital allocated to modern technology. This objective is feasible only if the economy's propensity to save is sufficient to maintain that golden age, and accordingly I assume such a propensity to save. This is defined as a suitable constant ratio $\hat{s}$ of net saving to net income. Gross saving also includes allowance for depreciation of capital not in surplus.

To simplify the analysis, I assume that sector 1 is kept in balance as between physical capital and skilled labour by appropriate allocation of gross investment between capital investment and training expenditure. This enables me to treat sector 1 symmetrically with sector 2, each dependent on two factors, capital and labour. The 'capital' of sector 1 is an amalgam of physical and human capital, with the input and depreciation parameters α_1 and $\bar{d}_1$ defined in (2.5) and (2.9). The assumption that the propensity to save is adequate to support a golden age with all resources in sector 1 means simply:

$$(5.1) \qquad \hat{s}\bar{y} \;=\; \frac{n\hat{a}_1}{1-\bar{d}_1\hat{a}_1} \; \bar{y}.$$

I recall the other assumptions made about the technological and behavioural parameters of the system:

$$(5.2) \qquad \begin{cases} \hat{a}_1 > \alpha_2, \; \beta_1 < \beta_2, \; \hat{a}_1\beta_2 - \alpha_2\beta_1 > 0 \\ \beta_2(1-\bar{d}_1\hat{a}_1) - \beta_1(1-d_2\alpha_2) > n(\hat{a}_1\beta_2 - \alpha_2\beta_1) > 0. \end{cases}$$

The last inequality, repeated from (4.4), can be written

$$(5.3) \qquad \beta_2 - \gamma\beta_1 > 0 \text{ where } \gamma \;=\; \frac{1-d_2\alpha_2}{1-\bar{d}_1\hat{a}_1}.$$

Normally, γ would be expected to be greater than 1. But for reasons already stated, I do not exclude the possibility that it is less than 1, and indeed less than $\alpha_2/\hat{a}_1$.

The problem of development strategy is how to allocate the available saving between investments in the two sectors. The proper strategy for reaching the maximum-consumption golden age depends on the technological parameters just discussed and also on the initial position of the economy. I will consider three cases: (A) Initially there is full employment, and the stock of capital in sector 2, k_2, is just adequate to provide jobs for everyone who cannot be employed in sector 1. This corresponds to Regime VI in section 1 above. (B) Initially there is full employment, and the stock of type 2 capital is actually redundant (Regime IV). (C) Initially there is surplus labour. The stock of type 2 capital k_2 is insufficient (Regime III). In all three cases, I assume that sector 1 is initially balanced and remains so. The third case is the one of greatest interest, but it is instructive to discuss the other cases first.

(a)   *Full Employment of all Resources*

Consider the constraints on the increments of gross output in the two sectors, $y_1'(t)$ and $y_2(t)$. There are two constraints. The first is the labour

FIGURE 1a

ALTERNATIVE GOLDEN AGES
Technology 1: the More Capital-Using

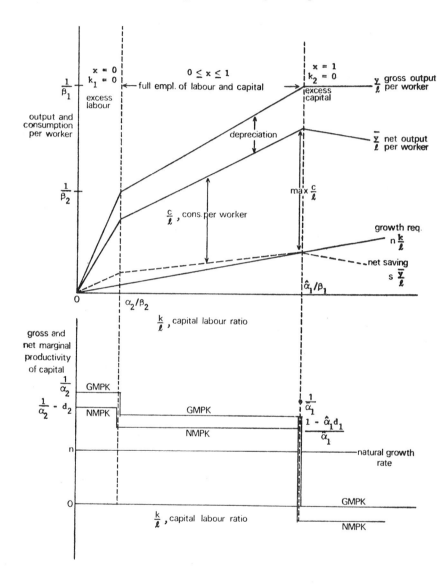

FIGURE 1b

ALTERNATIVE GOLDEN AGES
Technology 1: The Less Capital-Using

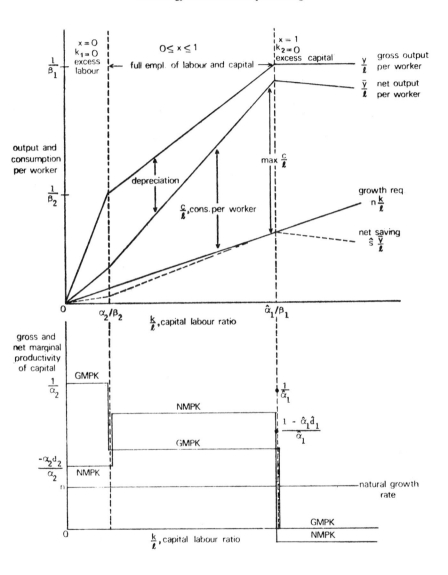

force. Outputs cannot increase faster than the growth of the labour force permits. The second is capital. Output cannot grow faster than the overall propensity to save allows the two capital stocks to grow. The two constraints are as follows:

(5.4)   Labour $\beta_1 y_1' + \beta_2 y_2' \leq n\beta_1 y_1 + n\beta_2 y_2$

Saving $\hat{a}_1 y_1' + \alpha_2 y_2' = \hat{s}(1 - \bar{d}_1 \hat{a}_1)y_1 + \hat{s}(1 - d_2\alpha_2)y_2$, or

(5.5) $\hat{a}_1 y_1' + \alpha_2 y_2' \leq n\hat{a}_1 y_1 + n\hat{a}_1\gamma y_2$.

If both constraints are satisfied with equality, I can solve the two simultaneous equations in y_1' and y_2' in terms of y_1 and y_2, as follows:

(5.6) $y_1' = ny_1 + ny_2 \dfrac{\beta_2(\hat{a}_1\gamma - \alpha_2)}{\beta_2\hat{a}_1 - \beta_1\alpha_2}$

(5.7) $y_2' = ny_2 \dfrac{\hat{a}_1(\beta_2 - \gamma\beta_1)}{\beta_2\hat{a}_1 - \beta_1\alpha_2}$.

The constraints are pictured diagrammatically in Figure 2. Here y_2 is plotted vertically and y_1' horizontally. If y_1' is less than the indicated point $-\bar{d}_1 y_1$, capital in sector 1 becomes redundant, because this represents the maximum speed at which type 1 capital can be consumed. The point $-d_2 y_2$ on the vertical axis has an analogous interpretation. The line LL, with slope of $-\dfrac{\beta_1}{\beta_2}$, less than 1 in absolute value, is the labour constraint (5.4). The line SS, with slope of $-\dfrac{\hat{a}_1}{\alpha_2}$ greater than 1 in absolute value, is the saving constraint (5.5). Point E represents the solution (5.6) and (5.7). The ray through the origin ZZ is the line $y_2 = \dfrac{y_2}{y_1} \cdot y^1$. A point on the line means that the relative rates of growth of the two outputs are the same, so that y_2/y_1 remains unchanged. A point below the line, like E in Figure 2, means that y_2/y_1 is declining, while a point above the line means that y_2 is growing faster than y_1. The point (ny_1, ny_2), represented by N in Figure 2, is common to the lines LL and ZZ. In the normal variant, depicted in Figure 2a, γ exceeds 1 and *a fortiori* exceeds $\alpha_2/\hat{a}_1$. Then (5.6) and (5.7) say that the solution value of y_1' exceeds ny_1 while that of y_2' is positive but less than ny_2.

Consider also the growth of aggregate *net* output $\bar{y}$, defined as $\bar{y}_1 + \bar{y}_2 = y_1(1 - \hat{a}_1\bar{d}_1) + y_2(1 - \alpha_2 d_2)$. The combinations (y_1', y_2') that yield any given increment in total net output are given by:

(5.8) $y_1'(1 - \hat{a}_1\bar{d}_1) + y_2'(1 - \alpha_2 d_2) = \bar{y}'$.

One such line, the one through E, is shown in Figure 2a as YY. Its slope is $-\dfrac{1}{\gamma}$, always greater in absolute value than β_1/β_2, by (5.2) but normally less than one in absolute value. A faster growth of net income would be indicated by a line parallel to, but above YY'.

FIGURE 2

2a. NORMAL VARIANT

Technology 1: More Capital-Using

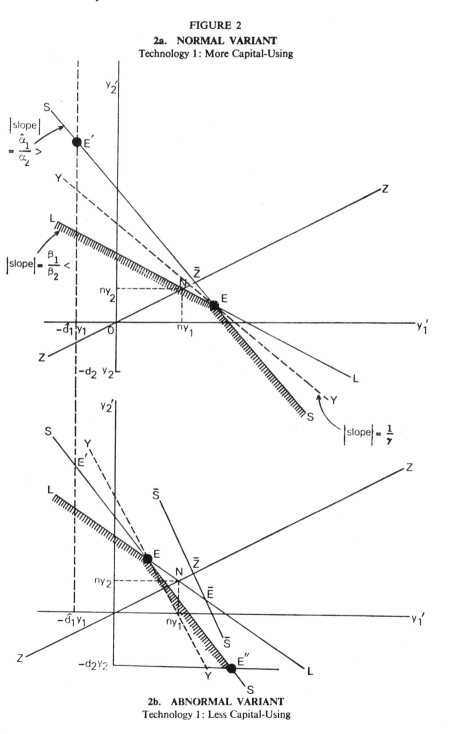

2b. ABNORMAL VARIANT

Technology 1: Less Capital-Using

Figure 2a makes two things clear. First, departure from point E by increasing y_2 could not increase $\bar{y}'$ without violating the labour constraint. To the left of E, LL lies below YY. Likewise, second, departure from point E to the right, increasing y'_1, could not increase $\bar{y}'$ without violating the capital constraint. In other words, the answer to the question, 'Would it be possible to grow faster by shoving all saving into the modern sector even though it produces unemployment?', is no. Point E, which maintains full employment, is also the best that can be done with respect to increasing net income.

Note that everything said about aggregate net income applies also to the more fundamental variable consumption, which is a constant proportion $1-\hat{s}$ of net income.

The abnormal variant, where γ is smaller than $a_2/\hat{a}_1$, and $1/\gamma$ is larger than $\hat{a}_1/a_2$, is shown in Figure 2b. Now the solution point E is northwest of point N. But it is also clear that, so far as short-run growth of net income and consumption is concerned, a better strategy can be found. Consider point E'', where all possible gross saving, including depreciation allowances generated in sector 2, is invested in sector 1. Compared to point E, point E'' will increase the growth of income. But it will also create unemployment, as indicated by the fact that E'' is well inside the labour constraint. Here there is a conflict, at least in the short run, between employment and income growth. Note also that if E'', or any other point to the right of E, is chosen, the economy shifts from full employment, case (A), to unemployment, case (C). Further analysis is deferred to the discussion of that case.

(b) Full Employment of Labour, Capital Surplus

If type 2 capital is in surplus, there is no reason to invest any gross saving in sector 2. The two constraints become:

(5.9)   Labour $\beta_1 y'_1 + \beta_2 y'_2 \leq n\beta_1 y_1 + n\beta_2 y_2$

(5.10)   Saving $\hat{a}_1 y'_1 \quad \leq n\hat{a}_1 y_1 + \dfrac{n\hat{a}_1 y_2}{1-\hat{a}_1 \bar{d}_1}$

The saving constraint differs from (5.5) in allowing for zero gross investment in type 2 capital. This alters the definition of net income. At the same time, since type 2 capital is redudant, no allowance is made for its depreciation, so this source of gross saving is lost.

When the constraints are both met with equality, the solutions are:

(5.11) $$y'_1 = ny_1 + ny_2 \frac{1}{1-\hat{a}_1 \bar{d}_1}$$

(5.12) $$y'_2 = ny_2 \left(1 - \frac{\beta_1}{\beta_2(1-\hat{a}_1 \bar{d}_1)} \right).$$

The normal variant is depicted in Figure 3a, constructed in the same fashion as Figure 2a. The saving constraint SS is now a vertical line, since capital growth places no limit on the growth of output in sector 2. Point E represents the solution given above. It will be southeast of point N, so that y_2/y_1 will be declining. In Figure 3a the solution for y_2' is shown as positive, i.e.

$\dfrac{\beta_2}{\beta_1} > \dfrac{1}{1-\hat{a}_1\bar{d}_1}$. This would be our normal expectation, but (5.3) does not

permit us to exclude the contrary. If y_2' is positive, or indeed even if it is negative but declining less rapidly than the depreciation of the capital used in its production, the redundancy of capital in sector 2 will be only temporary. With the passage of time case (B) will evolve into case (A).

In case (B) the condition for constant increment to net income is

(5.13) $y_1'(1-\hat{a}_1\bar{d}_1) + y_2' = \bar{y}'.$

This differs from (5.8) by omitting any deduction for the depreciation of k_2. The slope of such a line, YY, is $-(1-\hat{a}_1\bar{d}_1)$. In the normal variant illustrated in Figure 3a the slope of YY exceeds β_1/β_2, the slope of LL, in absolute value. There is no way to make net income grow faster than at point E.

Should point E lie below the horizontal axis, it will also be true that YY is flatter than LL, as illustrated in Figure 3b. Here net income could grow faster by staying inside the saving constraint SS and later shifting as much to sector 2 as the capital stock in that sector permits. But then it would no longer be proper to ignore the depreciation of sector 2 capital, and the situation would be immediately transformed into the normal variant of case (A), depicted in Figure 2a.

To avoid confusion, I should point out that the distinction between normal and abnormal variants of case (B) is not the same distinction as in the other cases. In case (B) it does not turn on the question of which technology is the more capital using. That question is irrelevant when capital is in surplus.

(c)   Unemployment of Labour and Capital Shortage: Normal Variant

Given initial unemployment, capital and its accumulation are the binding constraints on production and its growth. Constraint (5.5) applies, but (5.4) does not. In Figure 2, LL can be ignored. Points above it are not unattainable. They simply indicate that unemployment is declining.

In the normal variant of Figure 2a, it is clear that the short run growth of net income and consumption, as well as the growth of employment, will be maximized by placing all gross saving in sector 2 and letting sector 1 decline at its rate of depreciation (Point E'). As y_2 grows relative to y_1, the line ZZ will rotate counter-clockwise. With the passage of time, this strategy will run out of surplus labour, and the conditions for case (A), Figure 2a, will be established. With the achievement of full employment, the allocation of investment will shift (to a point like E in Figure 2a), and sector 1 will from that time on grow faster than sector 2.

FIGURE 3

3a. NORMAL VARIANT

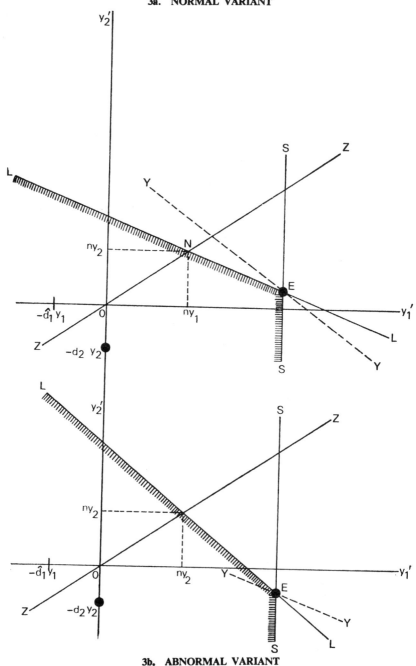

3b. ABNORMAL VARIANT

Some re-interpretation of Figure 2a is required for a strategy like E' which puts zero gross investment into sector 1. This strains my simplifying assumption that the two kinds of capital, physical and human, can always be kept balanced by shuffling of funds within sector 1. The spirit of the model is that depreciation is more rapid for physical capital: that

$d_1 > \bar{d}_1 > m_1 - \mu \dfrac{\beta_{21}}{\beta_{11}}$. When sector 1 is getting no investment funds, it is

unreasonable to expect that human capital can be converted into physical capital. Consequently sector output will dwindle at the rate of depreciation of physical capital, d_1, rather than $\bar{d}_1$. Skilled labour will be surplus. The saving constraint (5.5) becomes

$$(5.5)' \qquad a_1 y_1' + a_2 y_2' \leqq \frac{n\hat{a}_1}{1 - \bar{d}_1 \hat{a}_1} (1 - d_1 a_1) y_1 + n\hat{a}_1 \gamma y_2.$$

In Figure 2a, SS moves in and has a gentier slope. Likewise the lower limit to y_1' becomes $-d_1 y_1$, lower than the limit indicated in Figure 2a. These amendments do not change the essentials of the argument.

Once full employment is attained by strategy E', investment begins again in sector 1. At first all such investment will be in the physical capital of sector 1. Only when the stock of physical capital catches up will investment in human capital become necessary.

But is it really correct to let sector 1 dwindle and then build it up again? One answer, of course, is that only mistaken investment allocation permitted it to become so large in the first place, while the shortage of saving in sector 2 was creating unemployment. But we must let bygones be bygones and compare the strategy indicated by E' in Figure 2a with alternatives.

First, note that among the points on SS, it takes one to the left of E to reduce unemployment at all. And unless full employment is achieved, the maximum-consumption golden age can never be reached. Indeed full employment must be achieved before sector 2 is phased out. Otherwise a pseudo golden age of technology 1 will be reached with surplus labour, and with a propensity to save that creates enough capital to expand employment at the same rate as the labour force is growing but never enough to keep unemployment from growing at that same rate also.

Second, note that an intermediate strategy, between E and E', sacrifices net income and consumption in the short run, while reaching full employment later than strategy E' and with a lower ratio y_2/y_1. For example, the policy indicated by $\bar{Z}$ would maintain unchanged the initial ratio y_2/y_1 while slowly diminishing unemployment. I show now that Path I, the path of net income, and therefore of consumption, under initial strategy E' dominates the path corresponding to any intermediate strategy. That is, Path I is sometimes higher and never lower than the alternative, call it Path II. I have already argued that Path I is higher throughout the time corresponding to its unemployment phase. If Path II ever overtakes Path I their intersection occurs during the second or full employment phase of Path I.

At the time of any such overtaking, Path II must have no higher a ratio y_2/y_1 than Path I. If the alleged overtaking occurs when both paths are at full employment, they can show the same total net income only with an identical mixture of y_2 and y_1. If it occurs while Path II still displays unemployment, the ratio y_2/y_1 must be smaller for Path II. They can have the same total net income only if greater weight of the high productivity sector 1 in path II makes up for its unemployment. Now if path II has the same or lower ratio y_2/y_1 and the same total income, it must have at least as large a total capital stock as path I. Since the two paths started with the same capital stocks, this means an equal or larger aggregate accumulation along Path II. But this is impossible, because in the intervening period net income, to which net saving is proportional, has always been higher along Path I than Path II. Thus it is proved that Path I—the strategy indicated initially by point E — dominates all alternatives.

The key point is that none of the accumulation of type 2 capital during the phase of diminishing unemployment ever becomes redundant. This is clear from (5.7) and point E in Figure 2a, which indicate that sector 2 continues to expand in absolute size even during the full employment phase of development. Its continuing expansion, of course, in no way contradicts the fact that in the limit its relative share of the economy approaches zero.

Figure 4 shows schematically the fastest development path in the case under discussion, compared with a typical alternative.

(d)   Unemployment of Labour and Capital Shortage: Abnormal Variant

In the abnormal variant pictured in Figure 2b, there is a conflict between growth of income and consumption and growth of employment. With initial unemployment, the labour constraint LL in Figure 2b does not apply. Points on SS to the left of E are feasible, and they will reduce unemployment. Points to the right of E will increase income faster, but actually increase unemployment.

Indeed, 'you can't get there from here'. Getting there means two things— achieving full employment, and shifting all resources to the modern sector. In this case, these two developments are contradictory. As Figure 2b makes clear, if unemployment is to be reduced or even kept from rising, sector 2 has to grow relative to sector 1. On the other hand, if resources are to be shifted to the modern sector, saving is insufficient to keep up with the growth of the labour force, much less to reduce unemployment.

The essential problem was already clear in Figure 1b. The dashed broken line in that figure represents net saving generated by the propensity to save I have been assuming. The saving propensity is adequate to sustain a maximum-consumption golden age once established. (In Figure 2b ZZ would coincide with the horizontal axis, and points E, N, and E″ would all

FIGURE 4

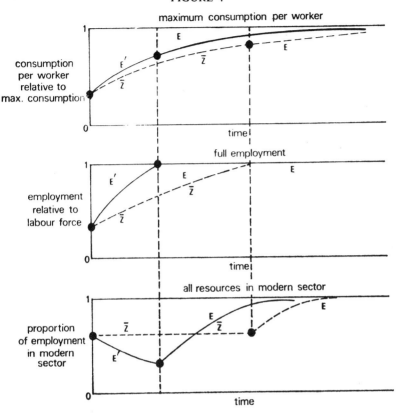

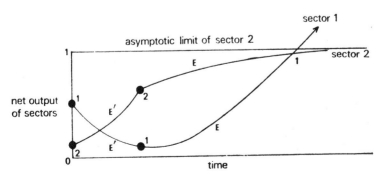

Optimal path (solid line), following strategy E' (Figure 2a) until full employment, then strategy E.

Alternative path (dashed line), following strategy Z (Figure 2a) until full employment, then strategy E.

converge at the point ny_1 on that axis.) From any initial position in which sector 2 is operating, the assumed saving propensity generates inadequate saving. This is because sector 2 is more capital-using than sector 1, in the sense already discussed. From such a starting point, the economy needs a temporary burst of saving to make up for the fact that its permanent propensity to save yields too little from sector 2.

In these circumstances, the concentration of investment in sector 2 is not even a permanent solution to unemployment. For as sector 1 vanishes, the saving generated by sector 2 alone is not enough to keep its capital stock growing at the pace of the labour force. This is true because the propensity to save is just adequate to give sector 1 a rate of growth of n, but not high enough to give sector 2 a growth rate of n. If the saving constraint (5.5) is solved for y_2' on the assumption that $y_1' = d_1 y_1$—all gross investment is diverted to sector 2—we have

(5.14)
$$y_2' = (n + d_1)\, \frac{\hat{a}_1}{a_2}\, y_1 + n\, \frac{\hat{a}_1}{a_2}\, \gamma y_2.$$

Since $\frac{\hat{a}_1 \gamma}{a_2}$ is less than 1 in the variant under discussion, $\frac{y_2'}{y_2}$ is less than n when $y_1 = 0$ and even when y_1 is small. (Graphically, as ZZ swings to the vertical axis in Figure 2b, point N becomes point ny_2 on that axis but SS is still below N.)

A higher propensity to save would escape the impasse. Suppose, for example, that the propensity to save $\hat{s}$ were sufficient to support steady golden-age growth of sector 2, the more capital-using sector in the case under discussion, namely $\hat{s} = \dfrac{na_2}{1 - d_2 a_2}$. Then the saving constraint (5.5) would be

(5.15)
$$\hat{a}_2 y_1' + a_2 y_2' = \frac{na_2}{\gamma}\, y_1 + na_2 y_2.$$

With $\gamma < a_{21}\hat{a}_1$ this is a less confining constraint than (5.5). Now the line SS in Figure 2b would cross ZZ above and to the right of N, like $\overline{SS}$. This can be seen by noting that if $y_2' = ny_2$, $y_1' = \dfrac{a_2}{\gamma \hat{a}_1} ny_1 > ny_1$. Consequently point E moves to the south-east of point N, like É, indicating that it is possible to shift resources to the modern sector while maintaining or even diminishing the unemployment rate.

Consider two possible strategies for exploiting the higher propensity to save. One is to abolish unemployment first, and then shift resources—follow the strategy indicated by point $\overline{Z}$ until the labour constraint becomes binding, and then shift to $\overline{E}$. The other is to shift resources first—point $\overline{E}$ from the very beginning. As resources shift, ZZ rotates clockwise and $\overline{E}$ ends up on the horizontal axis to the right of ny_1. So unemployment will continue to fall after sector 2 is phased out. Once full employment is restored, a lower saving rate, $\hat{s} = \dfrac{n\hat{a}_1}{1-\hat{a}_1\bar{d}_1}$, will suffice to maintain it. As between the two strategies the second makes aggregate net income and consumption grow faster; given the slope of YY, income growth is greater at $\bar{E}$ than at $\bar{Z}$. But the first one might be preferred nonetheless if reduction of unemployment is valued *per se*, independently of its contribution to consumable output.

6. Prices and Rates of Return Along Development Paths

I return now to the price calculations of section 1. These gave wage rates and capital rents in various regimes. The capital rents can be converted into net rates of return by subtracting depreciation per unit of capital. Net rates of return should be equal in the two sectors when non-zero gross investments are being made in both. Along paths where gross investment is being made only in one sector, the rate of return for that technology should exceed the other one.

Consider first case (A) of section 5 (which corresponds to regime VI in section 1), with full employment of all resources. With the skilled labour or sector 1 amalgamated into capital, the basic price equations (1.2) become

(6.1)
$$1 = \hat{a}_1\bar{r}_1 \quad\quad + \beta_1 w$$
$$1 = \alpha_2 r_2 \quad\quad + \beta_2 w.$$

Let the rate of return on type 1 capital be $\bar{p}_1 = \bar{r}_1 - \bar{d}_1$, and on type 2 capital $p_2 = r_2 - d_2$. The two equations of (6.1) become:

(6.2)
$$1 - \hat{a}_1\bar{d}_1 = \hat{a}_1\bar{p}_1 + \beta_1 w$$
$$1 - \alpha_2 d_2 = \alpha_2 p_2 + \beta_2 w.$$

If $\bar{p}_1 = p_2 = p$, the solutions for p and w are:

(6.3)
$$p = \frac{\beta_2(1 - \hat{a}_1\bar{d}_1) - \beta_1(1 - \alpha_2 d_2)}{\hat{a}_1\beta_2 - \beta_1\alpha_2}$$

$$w = \frac{\alpha_1(1 - \alpha_2 d_2) - \alpha_2(1 - \hat{a}_1\bar{d}_1)}{\hat{a}_1\beta_2 - \beta_1\alpha_2}.$$

The solution for p is the net marginal product of capital in Figure 1a and 1b, for the range of golden ages ($0 \le x \le 1$). It is always positive, and greater than n, by (4.4). In the normal case—sector 1, the more capital-using—the solution for w is also positive. A positive wage and equal rates of return are consistent with the discussion of the normal variant of case (A), where it turned out that the optimal path involved positive investment in both sectors and also maintained full employment of labour.

In the abnormal case—sector 1, the less capital-using—(6.3) gives a nonsense negative solution for w. If w is set at zero (6.2) tells us that $\bar{p}_1$ and p_2 must be different, each equal to the average net product of capital in its sector. Since that is greater in technology 1, all investment should be allocated to that sector. This is precisely the conclusion of the analysis of section 5. In the abnormal case, concentration of investment in modern capital maximizes income growth, while at the same time making labour increasingly redundant.

If the economy begins with unemployment—case (C) of section 5 above —the wage rate will be zero and (6.2) will give divergent values of $\bar{p}_1$ and p_2. In the normal case, p_2 will be the larger. As already concluded, growth is maximized by concentrating investment in that sector.

A word is in order regarding the interpretation of $\bar{p}_1$. If both kinds of capital in sector 1 are binding constraints and are receiving non-zero gross investment, they must have equal rates of return:

(6.4) $$\bar{p}_1 = r_1 - d_1 = \frac{w_1}{\ell} - m_1 + \mu \frac{\beta_{21}}{\beta_{11}}.$$

It follows then from the definitions of $\hat{a}_1$ and $\bar{d}_1$, (2.5) and (2.9) that:

(6.5) $$1 - \beta_1 w = \alpha_1 r_1 + \beta_{11} w_1 = \hat{a}_1(\bar{p}_1 + \bar{d}_1).$$

When skilled labour is in excess supply, w_1 is zero. The rate of return on physical capital in sector 1 can then be found by substituting α_1, d_1 and p_1 for $\hat{a}_1$, $\bar{d}_1$ and $\bar{p}_1$ in the first equation of (6.2).

CONCLUSIONS

In the normal case, when the modern technology is the more capital using, the proper strategy is to eliminate unemployment first and only then to attend to the shift of resources to the modern sector. The elimination of unemployment requires channelling of all gross saving to the old technology, temporarily reducing the size of the modern sector. There is nevertheless no conflict of objectives. The strategy that eliminates unemployment most rapidly also maximizes the growth of net income and consumption. Once full employment is achieved, it can be maintained while the relative allocation of resources shifts in favour of the modern sector. But none of the interim investment in old-technology capital is lost; the older sector grows absolutely even while it declines relatively.

In the abnormal case, when the modern sector is the less capital using, an impasse arises. The propensity to save is geared to the eventual low capital requirements of that sector and is inadequate to expand the capital stock as fast as the labour force is growing when the older technology is still operating. The impasse can be escaped only by a temporary burst of saving. If this is available, there is a conflict between rapid reduction of unemployment and rapid growth of income and consumption. Channelling saving predominantly to the modern sector is the way to maximize income growth, but it postpones the day when unemployment is eliminated.

The essential conclusions of the paper can be obtained without finding explicit expressions for the various development paths discussed. But these expressions can be obtained, and the method is described in the Appendix for interested readers.

Appendix

Along the development paths discussed in the paper, the exponential rate of growth of each sectoral output is a linear function of the ratio of the two outputs:

$$(A.1) \quad \begin{cases} \dfrac{y_1'}{y_1} = b_1 + c_1 \dfrac{y_2}{y_1} \\[2mm] \dfrac{y_2'}{y_2} = b_2 + c_2 \dfrac{y_2}{y_1} \end{cases} \quad (y_1 \neq 0).$$

The parameters b_i and c_i vary with the path under discussion. In at least one case the two rates of growth are linear functions of y_1/y_2 ($y_2 \neq 0$) instead of y_2/y_1. But the same method of solution applies symmetrically.

Let $y_2/y_1 = z$, $b_2 - b_1 = b$, and $c_2 - c_1 = c$. Then:

$$(A.2) \quad \begin{cases} y_1 = y_1(0)e^{b_1 t}\, e^{c_1 \int_0^t z(\tau)d\tau} \\[4mm] y_2 = y_2(0)e^{b_2 t}\, e^{c_2 \int_0^t z(\tau)d\tau} \\[4mm] z = z(0)e^{bt}\, e^{c \int_0^t z(\tau)d\tau} \end{cases}$$

The last equation may be written:

$$(A.3) \quad \ell n\, z = \ell n\, z(0) + bt + c \int_0^t z(\tau)d\tau.$$

Differentiating (A.3) with respect to time t gives:

$$(A.4) \quad z' = bz + cz^2.$$

The solution to the differential equation (A.4) is:

$$(A.5) \quad z = \frac{z(0)e^{bt}}{1 + \dfrac{c}{b}z(0) - \dfrac{c}{b}z(0)e^{bt}} = \frac{1}{\left(\dfrac{1}{z(0)} + \dfrac{c}{b}\right)e^{-bt} - \dfrac{c}{b}}.$$

Moreover,

(A.6) $\quad \int_0^t z(\tau)d\tau = -\frac{tb}{c} - \frac{1}{c}\, \ell n\left(\left(\frac{1}{z(0)} + \frac{c}{b}\right)e^{-bt} - \frac{c}{b}\right) + \frac{1}{c}\, \ell n\, \frac{1}{z(0)}$

(A.7) $\quad e^{\displaystyle c_i \int_0^t z(\tau)d\tau} = \left(\frac{c}{b}\, z(0)\,(1 - e^{bt}) + 1\right)^{-\frac{c_i}{c}}.$

These results can be used to obtain explicit descriptions of paths discussed in section 5 of the text. Consider, for example, case (A), full employment of all resources, with the solutions for y_1' and y_2' given by (5.6) and (5.7). These may be put in the form of (A.1) with:

(A.8) $\quad \begin{cases} b_1 = n \quad c_1 = n\, \dfrac{\beta_2(\hat{a}_1\gamma - \alpha_2)}{\beta_2\hat{a}_1 - \beta_1\alpha_2} \\[2em] b_2 = 0 \quad c_2 = n\, \dfrac{\hat{a}_1(\beta_2 - \gamma\beta_1)}{\beta_2\hat{a}_1 - \beta_1\alpha_2} \\[2em] b = -n \quad c = n\, \dfrac{\hat{a}_1(\beta_2 - \gamma\beta_1) - \beta_2(\hat{a}_1\gamma - \alpha_2)}{\beta_2\hat{a}_1 - \beta_1\alpha_2}. \end{cases}$

From (A.2) and (A.7) may be obtained solutions for y_1, y_2, and z in terms of basic parameters and initial conditions. From these, of course, the paths for $\bar{y}_1$, $\bar{y}_2$, $\bar{y}_1 + \bar{y}_2$, and for employment variables, sectoral and aggregate, may be derived.

For another example, take the case where the labour force constraint does not apply and the strategy is to place all investment in sector 1.

(A.9) $\quad \begin{cases} b_1 = n \qquad\qquad c_1 = n\gamma + \dfrac{\alpha_2}{\hat{a}_1}\, d_2 \\[2em] b_2 = -d_2 \qquad\quad c_2 = 0 \\[2em] b = -(n + d_2) \quad c = -\left(n\gamma + \dfrac{\alpha_2}{\hat{a}_1}\, d_2\right). \end{cases}$

If the saving constraint is (5.15) instead of (5.5), the parameters are different:

(A.10) $\quad \begin{cases} b_1 = \dfrac{n\alpha_2}{\gamma} \qquad\qquad c_1 = \dfrac{\alpha_2}{\hat{a}_1}\,(n + d_2) \\[2em] b_2 = -d_2 \qquad\qquad c_2 = 0 \\[2em] b = -\left(\dfrac{n\alpha_2}{\gamma} + d_2\right) \quad c = \dfrac{\alpha_2}{\hat{a}_1}\,(n + d_2). \end{cases}$

Finally, for the path along which all saving is allocated to sector 2—discussed under (C) in section 5—the rates of growth are linear functions of $1/z$ instead of z. Essentially the same set up as (A.10) applies, but with the roles of the y_1 and y_2 interchanged.

Journal of Development Economics 1 (1974) 7–18. © North-Holland Publishing Company

NOTES ON THE ECONOMIC THEORY OF EXPULSION
AND EXPROPRIATION*

James TOBIN

Yale University, New Haven, Conn., U.S.A.

Received May 1973, revised version received November 1973

1. Introduction

When aliens are expelled from a nation, what is the effect on the economic welfare of the remaining residents? The question is suggested in General Amin's expulsion of Asians and Europeans from Uganda.[1] A quieter, slower, and more humane policy of Africanization continues in Kenya, as non-citizens are gradually denied renewal of trade licenses and work permits. These policies are explicitly premised, at least in part, on the expectation that the economic welfare of African citizens will be improved, certainly in the long run if not immediately. Against this official premise stand the dire predictions of some observers and commentators, mostly foreigners, that these countries will suffer great economic loss by forcing productive members of their economies to depart.

What can economic theory say about this conflict of analysis and prediction? It is too much to expect to answer empirical questions without empirical research, which will not be able to provide conclusive answers for some time to come if ever. But theory should at least be able to offer some guidance for such research, delineating the facts on which the answers depend.

To avoid misunderstanding at the outset I stress two points. First, I am not concerned here with the ethics of policies of Africanization, either their objectives or the means by which they are pursued. The paper concerns only the efficacy

*The paper was written at the Institute of Development Studies, University of Nairobi, Kenya, where the author was a Visiting Professor 1972–73. I am grateful to the Rockefeller Foundation, the University, and the Institute for making the visit possible. To say the needless, they are in no way responsible for anything in the paper. The paper was originally written, and presented at an I.D.S. seminar, to provoke some *economic* discussion of the most striking and widely discussed current events in East Africa.

[1] I am aware that Amin expelled Ugandan citizens of non-African descent as well as aliens proper. Throughout the paper I use the terms 'aliens' and 'citizens', but I do not mean them in a literal juridical sense. In East Africa some citizens have more citizenship than others, and it is to describe the true sons and daughters of the land that the term *wananchi* has become current.

of the policies with respect to their stated objectives. Second, I am concerned only with the economic objectives and motivations of the policies. I recognize that the policies could have, doubtless do have, important political and social goals as well. Conceivably the majority of East Africans and their leaders would find the gains of 'controlling our own economy' worth some loss of per capita income and consumption, should that price have to be paid. Conceivably improvements in the positions of certain native elites might have decisive weight in political evaluation of the merits of expulsion, for national as well as self-interested reasons. I confine myself to the narrower question, the effect on the average per capita income of citizens.

The loss of human capital by expulsion is in many ways analogous to its loss via voluntary emigration, the 'brain drain' which has already been extensively analyzed by economists.[2] In both cases the basic theoretical presumption is the same. If just one worker who has been receiving his marginal product goes, voluntarily or involuntarily, the output available for those left behind is unchanged. This is true for any withdrawal which can be regarded as infinitesimal. But if a finite withdrawal occurs, the country loses some of the 'surplus' formerly obtained from productive inputs complementary to those of the remaining residents. The dominance of the complementary effects follows from the customary assumption that production sets are convex.

There are, however, some differences between 'brain drain' and expulsion. Expulsion without expropriation leaves the economy with a foreign debt burden. Expelled aliens have typically accumulated considerable property. Some of it they will manage to export in one form or another, and for immovable properties left behind they may be entitled to compensation. Young professional emigrants are likely to be less well endowed with non-human capital and will probably remit to the home country some of their earnings abroad. On this score, expulsion (without expropriation) is more damaging to the economy than brain drain.

A second difference that works the other way may be important. It is sometimes argued that brains are paid less than their marginal social product in poor developing countries. If there are real external benefits to the presence of natives of high education and professional skill, the standard argument understates the loss from their emigration. Such externalities seem less likely in the case of aliens, even those who are highly trained professionals. Just because they form a tightly knit community apart from the general culture, they have little spill-over as models or teachers for the native population. To the extent they have succeeded in erecting barriers to entry to certain occupations – a possibility analyzed below – their private product exceeds their social product.

---

[2]I am indebted to Jagdish Bhagwati (1973) for illuminating the similarities and difficulties. On 'brain drain', see his article with Hamada in this issue, and the literature there cited.

2. The standard argument

I will begin by rehearsing the standard argument. The first approximation it provides is a useful point of reference for further considerations. The proposition is that expulsion without expropriation cannot increase but may well decrease the average income of the remaining residents. This answer depends on certain assumptions which it is well to put on the table right away; some consequences of possible failure of these assumptions will be discussed in later sections. The assumptions are:

(a) As already stated, there is no expropriation of the non-human properties of the expelled aliens. They are paid full value for properties they leave behind, though they are not compensated for the loss of their incomes from personal labor and skill, 'human capital'.

(b) Before and after expulsion the economy is in competitive equilibrium, in which factors of production are paid their marginal private and social products.

(c) Production is subject to constant returns to scale in the economy, and production sets are convex. [That is, if x_1 and x_2 are any two feasible vectors of inputs and outputs, then any linear combination of them $bx_1 + (1-b)x_2$ ($0 \leq b \leq 1$) is also feasible.]

(d) The output of the economy can be regarded as a single homogeneous commodity produced by a large number of inputs. This is a convenient, and I think innocuous, simplification. It enables me to define income unambiguously and to avoid welfare calculations in terms of utilities.

There is no need to prove the theorem here. Instead, I shall sketch the result, using a linear activity model of production. This will be convenient later for discussing some qualifications to the argument, but of course the basic proposition does not depend on this specialization of the production model.

The homogeneous output is produced by n inputs. The quantity of the ith input initially owned by citizens is c_i; the quantity initially owned by aliens is a_i; of this a_i' remains in the country after expulsion, while the remainder departs with the aliens ($0 \leq a_i' \leq a_i$). The price of the ith factor, measured in terms of output, is p_i before expulsion and p_i' after expulsion. In each case the price of the factor is its marginal product. Initially, before expulsion, total output Y is $\Sigma p_i(c_i + a_i)$; this equality is assured by the assumption of constant returns to scale, which implies that payment of marginal products to all inputs just exhausts output. Of this total Y citizens receive $\Sigma p_i c_i$, which I will denote as y. After expulsion, total output Y' is $\Sigma p_i'(c_i + a_i)$. The income of citizens is $\Sigma p_i'(c_i + a_i') - \Sigma p_i a_i'$, y' for short. The second term in y' is the compensation annually paid to aliens, in the case of no expropriation, for the productive properties they left in the country. Note that this compensation is paid at the initial prices p_i, the earnings of these factors of production prior to expulsion. The 'first approximation' proposition is that y' is at most equal to y.

A further word about compensation is in order. We do not have to imagine a literal annual payment to the former alien owners. More likely they will have sold the properties outright and obtained in exchange foreign assets previously owned by the citizens or government of the country they left. Or that economy will have borrowed abroad the sums needed to pay the aliens full capital value. Either way there is an increase in the net annual interest burden on the economy payable abroad, equal to $\Sigma p_i a_i'$.

In summary:

$$y = Y - \Sigma p_i a_i = Y - \Sigma p_i a_i' - \Sigma p_i (a_i - a_i'), \tag{1}$$

$$y' = Y' - \Sigma p_i a_i', \tag{2}$$

$$y = y' = [Y - \Sigma p_i (a_i - a_i')] - Y'. \tag{3}$$

The question at issue is the value of $y - y'$ as given in eq. (3).

Production is a set of linear activities or processes. Each process is subject to constant returns to scale and is characterized by fixed requirements of various inputs per unit of output. Production of the homogeneous output can be carried out by any number of the m available processes, each one using some or all of the n factors of production. A competitive equilibrium is the solution of a linear programming problem, maximizing output subject to the constraints imposed by the n factor supplies. In the equilibrium some s processes are operated, where s cannot exceed either m or n. Correspondingly, s of the factor supply constraints – obviously never more than n or m – will be binding, while the remaining $n - s$ factors will be in excess supply. In linear programming jargon the selection of s operating processes and s fully employed factors is a *basis*, and the programming problem is to find that basis which maximizes total output, given the factor supply constraints.

Factor prices are marginal productivities. The prices of all the surplus factors are zero. The prices of the other s factors are found by imputing the value of the production of each operating process to the s non-surplus inputs used in its operation. They may be found by solving s simultaneous break-even equations, one for each process in the basis, for the prices of the s factors in the basis. At these factor prices, any process not in the solution basis, i.e., any process that is inefficient to use, would cost more to operate than it could produce.

How does the competitive equilibrium, the solution of the linear programming problem, change when factor supplies are altered by expulsion? There are two possibilities. One is that the solution basis is unchanged. This will certainly be the case if expulsion simply scales down all inputs proportionately. Constant returns to scale are built into the model. In this case, expulsion simply reduces the scale of the economy. Prices are unchanged, and so are the incomes of residents. If 5% of factor inputs are lost, production declines by 5%, but there are 5% fewer mouths to feed.

It is also possible that the basis is unchanged even if the relative supplies of inputs are changed. Geometrically, the production function consists of plane facets. Each facet corresponds to a different basis, as do the boundary lines and points between facets. The tangent or 'supporting' plane, instead of touching the production surface only along one line, the ray from the origin, may coincide with a whole facet. The change in factor supplies may not be so great as to move out of this facet. In this case, since the basis is unchanged, factor prices are

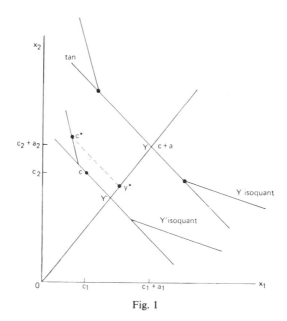

Fig. 1

unaffected and $y = y'$. A two-factor example is diagrammed in fig. 1. Here x_1 and x_2 are the two factors, owned in amounts c_1, c_2 by citizens and a_1, a_2 by aliens. For simplicity I take the a_i', alien-owned properties left behind, to be zero. Broken-line isoquants for outputs Y, obtainable with inputs $c_i + a_i$ and Y', obtainable with inputs c_i, are shown. Input prices before expulsion are represented by the slope of the isoquant through point $c + a$; citizen income before expulsion is indicated by a parallel line through point c. The output equivalent of citizen income before expulsion can be gauged by observing where this line intersects the ray from the origin to point $c + a$. In the case shown the value of citizen income is Y', which is also the value of output and citizen income after expulsion. This equality will be true so long as c is located anywhere on the middle segment of the y' isoquant. Suppose, however, it had been located on one of the other segments, say at c^*. Then initial citizen income would exceed y', and citizens would lose by expulsion. In the diagram this would be indicated by the fact that a line through c^* parallel to the original price line ('tan') would intersect the ray OY above Y'.

This illustrates the second and more interesting possibility, namely that the equilibrium basis is altered. Some processes formerly in operation may drop out, while others previously unused become efficient. Some factors initially surplus may become binding constraints, while others become unemployed for lack of cooperating factors. The dimension of the basis s may rise or fall. In any event the following is true: Let the prices p_i correspond to the initial basis B for factor supplies $c_i + a_i$, and the prices p_i' correspond to the post-expulsion basis B' for factor supplies $c_i + a_i'$. Then if B' is different from B, $\Sigma p_i(c_i + a_i')$ exceeds $\Sigma p_i'(c_i + a_i')$. Therefore $\Sigma p_i c_i$ exceeds $\Sigma p_i'(c_i + a_i') - \Sigma p_i a_i'$. That is, y exceeds y'.

The general proposition is the duality theorem of linear programming. The minimum valuation of given factor supplies occurs with the prices of that basis which maximizes the objective function (here total output) with those factor supplies. The prices of some other basis, one which would be the maximizing solution for a different set of factor supplies but not for this set, will give a larger valuation of the actually given factor supplies. [3]

There is another interesting and intuitively reasonable implication. The inputs withdrawn by the aliens are in aggregate more valuable, anyway not less, at the factor prices that prevail *after* their expulsion. It is not surprising; the factors most heavily reduced in supply would be expected to become relatively scarce and high-priced. To see this, use in reverse the theorem discussed and employed above: $\Sigma p_i'(c_i + a_i) \geqq \Sigma p_i(c_i + a_i)$, that is:

$$\Sigma p_i'(c_i + a_i') + \Sigma p_i'(a_i - a_i') \geqq \Sigma p_i(c_i + a_i') + \Sigma p_i(a_i - a_i').$$

But

$$\Sigma p_i'(c_i + a_i) \leqq \Sigma p_i(c_i + a_i').$$

Therefore

$$\Sigma p_i'(a_i - a_i') \geqq \Sigma p_i(a_i - a_i').$$

Before discussing below the limitations of the first approximation, I should emphasize what it does *not* mean. Let us assume, realistically I think, that the loss of inputs due to expulsion is uneven rather than proportionate, that aliens were not providing the same mixture of inputs as citizens. Let us assume indeed that the changes of relative factor supplies are drastic enough to alter the basis. So the first approximation conclusion is the stronger one that aggregate citizen

---

[3]Ties are of course possible. Two or more bases may be solutions for a given set of factor supplies. Prices will be indeterminate between them, but total output and factor income will be the same whichever basis and price system is used. I assume that if the basis and prices that prevailed before expulsion continue to be one of the possible solutions, even though not the only one, after expulsion they will continue to prevail.

income is lower after expulsion. This does not imply that *every* marginal product, every factor price, declines. Some citizens, those who can supply factors formerly provided substantially by aliens, will enjoy increases in their incomes. Others, those who supply factors complementary to aliens' productive inputs, will suffer losses. Convexity implies that in aggregate the complementary effects dominate, so the gains are smaller than the losses. But substantial shifts of income distribution can certainly occur.

If the East African stereotype of aliens as shopkeepers, traders, independent professionals or semi-professionals, and small business managers is accurate, citizens with these capacities will be in scarce supply after expulsion. Their marginal products and earnings will rise. On the other hand, citizens whose jobs and productivity depend on having shopkeepers, traders, professionals, and managers to assist will suffer.

I have distinguished between those alien inputs which are physically withdrawn from the country and those which remain after compensation of former alien owners. What difference does it make how alien inputs are divided between these two categories? At one extreme, if all alien inputs remained in the country – as would happen if all aliens were simply rentiers and absentee landlords – the argument implies that expulsion does not alter citizen income: $y = y'$. Indeed it does not even alter the distribution of citizen income. It doesn't matter whether the aliens are resident capitalists or non-resident capitalists.

We have no way to compare intermediate cases with each other or with the other extreme, where all alien factors are physically withdrawn. But realistically it is quite conceivable that citizen losses are especially acute when alien inputs are partly immobile and partly mobile. The immobile inputs may well be especially complementary to the mobile ones, so that the prices of the immobile inputs are especially depressed by expulsion. Yet the citizen economy is saddled with a debt for these immobile properties, calculated at the pre-expulsion prices. High complementarity of this kind seems likely between shops, workshops, and professional equipment and the self-employed proprietors and professionals who formerly owned and operated them. In other words, if the citizen economy had the option of destroying the immobile properties without compensating their alien owners rather than preserving and operating them while paying full compensation, the former alternative might well be chosen.

3. Alternative compensation and expropriation

It is time to recognize the third alternative, to keep the properties without full compensation at pre-expulsion values. Clearly citizens can gain by full or partial expropriation of aliens, or of non-residents for that matter. In the algebra, $\Sigma p_i'(c_i + a_i')$, with little or no deduction for debt to former owners of the a_i', may easily exceed $\Sigma p_i c_i$, even if the p_i are on balance better prices for citizen inputs than the p_i'. No one ever doubted that expropriation pays, at least in the short run before repercussions on foreign investment are felt. The basic first approximation proposition is that expropriation is the only aspect of expulsion that promises gains.

I have used 'expropriation' to refer to compensation less than the initial market values of the properties, the pre-expulsion prices p_i. But an alternative principle of compensation is to use the new prices p'_i, and perhaps this does not merit the pejorative term 'expropriation'. In effect, the expelled aliens retain equity in the

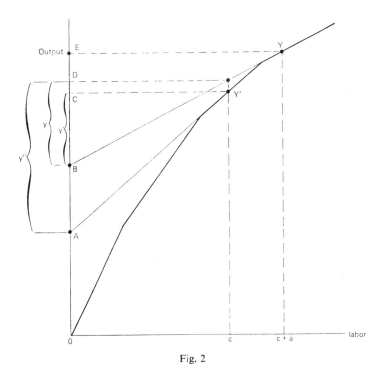

Fig. 2

properties they leave behind, and their earnings depend on the marginal productivities of these properties in the post-expulsion economy.

With this form of compensation, it is conceivable that citizens gain in aggregate. They will gain if their inputs are highly substitutable for the withdrawn alien inputs but complementary to the retained alien inputs. Imagine, for example, a two-factor economy, in which the ratio of alien-owned capital to alien labor is much higher than the ratio of citizen-owned capital to citizen labor. Expulsion of alien labor raises the overall capital–labor ratio and raises wages. The marginal product of capital declines, and with respect to alien-owned capital the decline is absorbed by alien owners rather than by citizens. The country is not burdened with the obligation to pay the aliens the pre-expulsion earnings of their properties.[4]

This case is illustrated in fig. 2, where the broken line $OY'Y$ represents the relationship of output to labor input, on a given capital stock, assumed for convenience to belong wholly to aliens. Before expulsion total labor input is $c+a$, of which c is provided by citizens. Expulsion reduces output from Y to Y'. Initially the wage rate is the slope of the line BY. Total labor income is BE, but only y of it (BD) is earned by citizens. Capital income is OB. On the first principle of compensation, capital will continue to earn OB, and citizen income after paying the compensation will be only y' (BC). The competitive wage rate after expulsion is the slope of AY', and the competitive earnings of capital are reduced to OA. On the second principle of compensation, citizens as workers earn and retain y'' (AC).

Two questions arise, one ethical and one empirical. The ethical question is difficult. On the one hand, aliens could argue that the decline in the value of their property is not a normal risk of ownership, but a consequence of their own expulsion, injury added to injury. In response, citizens could complain that aliens never had the right to believe their capital would be immune to the residential and citizenship policies of the nation.

The empirical question is whether citizens would in fact gain by expulsion even with the second method of remuneration. The example just described is only a possibility, and it depends on a high and perhaps unrealistic degree of substitutability between citizen and alien labor.

4. Occupational barriers

The argument so far was based on the assumption that factor incomes are competitively determined, equal to the marginal products of available factor supplies. But, it will be asked, what if the aliens had some monopolistic market power?

The first answer is merely an extension of previous arguments. If the monopolies were attached to particular immobile properties and sites owned by aliens, and if the compensation paid them fully capitalized the monopoly incomes, transfer of these properties and sites to citizen ownership and operation cannot increase aggregate citizen income. Of course the new owners and managers may not shoulder any or all of the debt burden, so that they personally benefit. But other citizens, taxpayers or consumers, will suffer correspondingly. Once again the gain, if any, can only come from expropriation.

If expulsion were the occasion for eliminating the monopolies associated with these properties, the citizen economy could gain whatever deadweight loss had been due to the previous distortion and misallocation. But this could presumably

[4] I am indebted to Richard C. Porter for insistently calling my attention to this possibility.

have been accomplished without expulsion. Indeed one may suspect that monopolistic power will be reinforced by the loss of potential competitors.

Other monopolies may have been attached to the mobile human capital or
labor skills of the expelled aliens. Suppose that there had been artificial restrictions on entry into occupations where aliens were heavily represented but
qualified citizens were excluded. Excluded citizens were forced into lower-
paying occupations below their capacities, occupations where their marginal
products were further depressed by the artificially swollen supplies. When the
aliens leave, citizens take their slots. Here there is a potential gain in citizen
income. The loss of alien inputs is at least partially compensated by an upgrading
of marketable citizen factor supplies.

An extreme example will make the point. Suppose that all aliens benefited,
so far as their mobile inputs are concerned, from restrictions on entry to their
occupations. Suppose that exclusion of qualified citizens from these high-paid
occupations resulted, via a chain of bumpings down the ladder, in an actual
surplus of general unskilled citizen labor. (The linear production model allows
for the possibility of surpluses of some factors.) The marginal product and price
of this labor is then zero. Suppose that this unemployment was no larger than
the number of privileged skilled aliens expelled. After expulsion the citizen labor
force shuffles up the skill ladder. At every rung qualified recruits replace departing aliens or replace other citizens who move up to fill higher-level vacancies.
There is a new set of citizen factor supplies c_i', identical to the old factor supplies
$c_i + a_i - a_i'$, which were distorted by monopolistic restrictions before expulsion.
Therefore the total output of the economy will be unchanged, but now all of it,
except the compensation for aliens' immobile inputs $\Sigma p_i a_i'$, belongs to citizens.
Citizen income gains by $\Sigma p_i(a_i - a_i')$.

The analysis is the same in principle but more complex in detail if the
restrictions took the form of excluding potentially qualified citizens from education and training. For example, maybe citizen children capable of acquiring
the same human capital as aliens were prevented from doing so by allocation of
school slots to alien children. Presumably then the returns on investment in
citizen human capital, especially in view of the low opportunity cost of diverting
young citizens from labor force to schooling, exceeded the social interest rate.
In the long run the human capital of the departing aliens is replaced, and the
returns on it all accrue to the citizen economy. And these returns, thanks to the
sub-optimal level of education and training in the first place, exceed the interest
costs of the investment.

Others can judge better than I the realism of these scenarios, or of less extreme
scenarios with the same qualitative results. They cannot be either excluded or
accepted a priori. Were aliens in East Africa in fact able to restrict citizen entry
and competition in their professions and lines of business? Were they in fact able
to keep citizens out of scarce school slots or to prevent the expansion of educational opportunities for citizens? If so, an economist is bound to observe that

anti-monopoly pro-competitive measures were an alternative to expulsion. Indeed the argument above suggests that these measures would add more to citizen income than expulsion could. Better to retain the aliens and their skills, but to pay them only their true competitive marginal products, the prices they would command in competition with all qualified citizens.

5. Other possible qualifications

The assumption of constant returns to scale may not be justified. How would the first approximation conclusions have to be modified? On the one hand, it might be argued that there are diminishing returns to scale in the inputs of labor and reproducible capital because of limited supplies of natural resources, for example unimproved land. On these grounds diminution in population, even accompanied by a proportionate curtailment of capital inputs, could be welcomed because it would raise output per unit of input. I doubt the applicability, or at least the importance, of this consideration in East Africa, where population density is not high and much land and space are unused.

On the other hand, the national markets may be so small that many economies of scale have yet to be fully exploited. Even though the countries engage in international trade, the size of their domestic markets is relevant, given the natural obstacles and costs of distance as well as tariffs and other governmental barriers to free trade. On this score, reduction in the size of the domestic market by expulsion is, other things equal, bad for per capita income. Expelled aliens in England and India are not a substitute, so far as the size of the market is concerned, for aliens in Nairobi and Mombasa and Kampala – a fact reinforced by the likelihood that their marginal productivities are lower in their new and strange locales.

Another assumption that might be challenged is the aggregation of output into a single homogeneous good in the models analyzed above. Departure of aliens probably changes the mix of output, since their tastes are not the same as those of citizens. Some may wonder whether aliens' high incomes were due to the fact that their inputs were especially well adapted to the pre-expulsion final bill of goods and would not be so valuable in producing the goods and services favored in a citizen economy. The question almost refutes itself. In the extreme, the aliens might have been a separate economy, producing for themselves to satisfy their own tastes. If so, their departure – regardless of how rich they were – could neither help nor harm the separate citizen economy. To the extent that their incomes were due to their own tastes, their influence on the rest of the economy was neutral. If they earned incomes by selling to citizens, it is because their inputs were in some degree adapted to citizen tastes, and their withdrawal has the kind of effects already described.

One could indeed apply a two-country international trade model to the alien and citizen communities and obtain the standard conclusion that normally each side gains from trade, or at worst does not lose. The extreme possibility that aliens manipulate the terms of trade so as to capture all the gains for themselves means that citizens would not lose by the termination of the trade when the aliens depart. It does not mean that they would gain. Anyway this suspicion is just the question of alien monopolies in another guise, a subject already discussed in the previous section.

6. Concluding remarks

Sometimes official economic rationales of policies of Africanization, implicit and explicit, seem to be based on an image of the economic process quite different from the models discussed above. The image is an economy whose aggregate wealth and income are naturally and exogenously determined, independently of the effort, skill and saving of the inhabitants. Jobs and shops and businesses are just tickets that allow the holders to claim shares of these exogenously fixed, though it is hoped growing, amounts of wealth and output. The tickets can be reassigned without danger to the total, so obviously the lot of citizens can be improved by giving them tickets formerly held by aliens. Maybe such an economy is approximated by an oil-rich sheikdom or by a country whose land effortlessly yields crops for export or home consumption or displays scenic beauties greatly prized by foreigners. But it is a dangerous model for almost all real countries, and a possibly serious consequence of expulsion policies may be that these rationales will be believed by the governments that espouse them and the people the policies are supposed to benefit.

Economics and economic theory cannot evaluate that danger, and they are equally helpless to appraise an intangible effect of great potential importance in the opposite direction. This is the response of the populace to national challenge, evoked by the political appeal of economic independence and self-sufficiency and even accentuated by the initial hardships and disruptions incident to expulsion. (Let us show the world and ourselves that we can do it on our own, just as the Egyptians confounded skeptical prophecies and operated the Suez canal.) The example of communist China shows that nationalistic and patriotic motivations, tinged until fairly recently with xenophobia, can support indigenous economic progress. Whether the example can be copied in Africa or elsewhere, with or without communism, only the future can tell. But the Chinese case suggests one more lesson, namely that economic progress occurs after 'wars' of economic independence stop and are supplanted by hard work and careful administration, sustained by appropriate shift in the party line. In some ways the Great Cultural Revolution of the 1960's in China was the moral and political equivalent of the policies of expulsion and Africanization in East Africa. It did considerable economic damage, but the Chinese leadership knew when to declare peace and to shift the emphasis of policy and propaganda from blaming economic ills on enemies to extolling hard work and self-reliance.

Is Growth Obsolete?

William Nordhaus and James Tobin

Yale University

A long decade ago economic growth was the reigning fashion of political economy. It was simultaneously the hottest subject of economic theory and research, a slogan eagerly claimed by politicians of all stripes, and a serious objective of the policies of governments. The climate of opinion has changed dramatically. Disillusioned critics indict both economic science and economic policy for blind obeisance to aggregate material "progress," and for neglect of its costly side effects. Growth, it is charged, distorts national priorities, worsens the distribution of income, and irreparably damages the environment. Paul Erlich speaks for a multitude when he says, "We must acquire a life style which has as its goal maximum freedom and happiness for the individual, not a maximum Gross National Product."

Growth was in an important sense a discovery of economics after the Second World War. Of course economic development has always been the grand theme of historically minded scholars of large mind and bold concept, notably Marx, Schumpeter, Kuznets. But the mainstream of economic analysis was not comfortable with phenomena of change and progress. The stationary state was the long-run equilibrium of classical and neoclassical theory, and comparison of alternative static equilibriums was the most powerful theoretical tool. Technological change and population increase were most readily accommodated as one-time exogenous shocks; comparative static analysis could be used to tell how they altered the equilibrium of the system. The obvious fact that these "shocks" were occurring continuously, never allowing the

Note: We would like to express our appreciation to Walter Dolde, James Pugash, Geoffrey Woglom, Hugh Tobin, and especially Laura Harrison, for assistance in the preparation of this paper. We are grateful to Robin Matthews for pointing out some problems in our treatment of leisure in the first draft.

Reprinted by permission from *Economic Growth: Fiftieth Anniversary Colloquium V*, New York: National Bureau of Economic Research, distributed by Columbia University Press, New York and London, 1972, pp. 1–80; and from *The Measurement of Economic and Social Performance*, ed. Milton Moss, New York: National Bureau of Economic Research, distributed by Columbia University Press, New York and London, 1973, pp. 554–564.

system to reach its equilibrium, was a considerable embarrassment. Keynesian theory fell in the same tradition, attempting rather awkwardly, though nonetheless fruitfully, to apply static equilibrium theory to the essentially dynamic problem of saving and capital accumulation.

Sir Roy Harrod in 1940 began the process, brought to fruition by many theorists in the 1950s, of putting the stationary state into motion. The long-run equilibrium of the system became a path of steady growth, and the tools of comparative statics could then be applied to alternative growth paths rather than to alternative stationary states. Neo-Keynesian macroeconomics began to fall into place as a description of departures from equilibrium growth, although this task of reinterpretation and integration is still far from a satisfactory completion.

By now modern neoclassical growth theory is well enough formulated to have made its way into textbooks. It is a theory of the growth of potential output, or output at a uniform standard rate of utilization of capacity. The theory relates potential output to three determinants: the labor force, the state of technology, and the stock of human and tangible capital. The first two are usually assumed to grow smoothly at rates determined exogenously by noneconomic factors. The accumulation of capital is governed by the thrift of the population, and in equilibrium the growth of the capital stock matches the growth of labor-*cum*-technology and the growth of output. Simple as it is, the model fits the observed trends of economic growth reasonably well.

The steady equilibrium growth of modern neoclassical theory is, it must be acknowledged, a routine process of replication. It is a dull story compared to the convulsive structural, technological, and social changes described by the historically oriented scholars of development mentioned above. The theory conceals, either in aggregation or in the abstract generality of multisector models, all the drama of the events — the rise and fall of products, technologies, and industries, and the accompanying transformations of the spatial and occupational distribution of the population. Many economists agree with the broad outlines of Schumpeter's vision of capitalist development, which is a far cry from growth models made nowadays in either Cambridge, Massachusetts, or Cambridge, England. But visions of that kind have yet to be transformed into a theory that can be applied in everyday analytic and empirical work.

In any case, growth of some kind is now the recognized economic norm. A symptom of the change in outlook can be found in business cycle semantics. A National Bureau *recession* was essentially a period in which aggregate productive activity was declining. Since 1960 it has become increasingly customary to describe the state of the economy by the gap between its actual output and its growing potential. Although the word recession is still a source of confusion and controversy, almost everyone recognizes that the economy is losing ground — which will have to be recaptured eventually — whenever its actual rate of expansion is below the rate of growth of potential output.

In the early 1960s growth became a proclaimed objective of government policy, in this country as elsewhere. Who could be against it? But like most value-laden words, growth has meant different things to different people and at different times. Often growth policy was simply identified with measures to expand aggregate demand in order to bring or keep actual output in line with potential output. In this sense it is simply stabilization policy, only more gap-conscious and growth-conscious than the cycle-smoothing policies of the past.

To economists schooled in postwar neoclassical growth theory, growth policy proper meant something more than this, and more debatable. It meant deliberate effort to speed up the growth of potential output itself, specifically to accelerate the productivity of labor. Growth policy in this meaning was not widely understood or accepted. The neoclassical model outlined above suggested two kinds of policies to foster growth, possibly interrelated: measures that advanced technological knowledge and measures that increased the share of potential output devoted to accumulation of physical or human capital.[1] Another implication of the standard model was that, unless someone could find a way to accelerate technological progress permanently, policy could not raise the rate of growth permanently. One-shot measures would speed up growth temporarily, for years or decades. But once the economy had absorbed these measures, its future growth rate would be limited once again by constraints of labor and technology. The level of its path, however, would be permanently higher than if the policies had not been undertaken.

Growth measures nearly always involve diversions of current resources from other uses, sacrifices of current consumption for the benefit of succeeding generations of consumers. Enthusiasts for faster

---

[1] The variety of possible measures, and the difficulty of raising the growth rate by more than one or two percentage points, have been explored by Edward Denison in his influential study, *The Sources of Economic Growth in the United States and the Alternatives Before Us*, New York, Committee for Economic Development, January 1962, Supplementary Paper No. 13.

growth are advocates of the future against the present. Their case rests on the view that in a market economy left to itself, the future would be shortchanged because too small a fraction of current output would be saved. We mention this point now because we shall return later to the ironical fact that the antigrowth men of the 1970s believe that it is they who represent the claims of a fragile future against a voracious present.

Like the enthusiasts to whom they are a reaction, current critics of growth are disenchanted with both theory and policy, with both the descriptive and the normative implications of the doctrines of the previous decade. The sources of disenchantment are worth considering today, because they indicate agenda for future theoretical and empirical research.

We have chosen to direct our attention to three important problems raised by those who question the desirability and possibility of future growth: (a) How good are measures of output currently used for evaluating the growth of economic welfare? (b) Does the growth process inevitably waste our natural resources? (c) How does the rate of population growth affect economic welfare? In particular, what would be the effect of zero population growth?

MEASURES OF ECONOMIC WELFARE

A major question raised by critics of economic growth is whether we have been growing at all in any meaningful sense. Gross national product statistics cannot give the answers, for GNP is not a measure of economic welfare. Erlich is right in claiming that maximization of GNP is not a proper objective of policy. Economists all know that, and yet their everyday use of GNP as the standard measure of economic performance apparently conveys the impression that they are evangelistic workshipers of GNP.

An obvious shortcoming of GNP is that it is an index of production, not consumption. The goal of economic activity, after all, is consumption. Although this is the central premise of economics, the profession has been slow to develop, either conceptually or statistically, a measure of economic performance oriented to consumption, broadly defined and carefully calculated. We have constructed a primitive and experimental "measure of economic welfare" (MEW), in which we attempt to allow for the more obvious discrepancies between GNP and economic welfare. A complete account is given in Appendix A. The main results will be discussed here and summarized in Tables 1 and 2.

In proposing a welfare measure, we in no way deny the importance of the conventional national income accounts or of the output measures based upon them. Our MEW is largely a rearrangement of items of the national accounts. Gross and net national product statistics are the economists' chief tools for short-run analysis, forecasting, and policy and are also indispensable for many other purposes.

Our adjustments to GNP fall into three general categories: reclassification of GNP expenditures as consumption, investment, and intermediate; imputation for the services of consumer capital, for leisure, and for the product of household work; correction for some of the disamenities of urbanization.

1. Reclassification of GNP Final Expenditures

Our purposes are first, to subtract some items that are better regarded as instrumental and intermediate than as final output, and second, to allocate all remaining items between consumption and net investment. Since the national accounts do not differentiate among government purchases of goods and services, one of our major tasks will be to split them among the three categories: intermediate, consumption, and net investment. We will also reclassify some private expenditures.

Intermediate products are goods and services whose contributions to present or future consumer welfare are completely counted in the values of other goods and services. To avoid double counting they should not be included in reckoning the net yield of economic activity. Thus all national income accounts reckon as final consumption the bread but not the flour and as capital formation the finished house but not the lumber. The more difficult and controversial issues in assigning items to intermediate or final categories are the following:

Capital Consumption. The depreciation of capital stocks is a cost of production, and output required to offset the depreciation is intermediate as surely as materials consumed in the productive process. For most purposes, including welfare indexes, NNP is preferable to GNP. Only the difficulties and lags in estimating capital consumption have made GNP the popular statistic.

However, NNP itself fails to treat many durable goods as capital, and counts as final their entire output whether for replacement or accumulation. These elementary points are worth repeating because some of our colleagues are telling the public that economists glorify wasteful "through-put" for its own sake. Focusing on NNP, and accounting for all durables as capital goods, would avoid such foolish paradoxes as the implication that deliberate efforts to make goods more perishable raise national output. We estimate, however, that proper treatment of consumer durables has little quantitative effect (see Table 1, lines 3 and 5).

The other capital consumption adjustments we have made arise from allowing for government capital and for the educational and medical capital embodied in human beings. In effect, we have reclassified education and health expenditures, both public and private, as capital investments.

Growth Requirements.   In principle net national product tells how much consumption the economy could indefinitely sustain. GNP does not tell that; consuming the whole GNP in any year would impair future consumption prospects. But *per capita* rather than aggregate consumption is the welfare objective; neither economists nor other observers would as a rule regard sheer increase in the numbers of people enjoying the same average standard of living as a gain in welfare. Even NNP exaggerates sustainable *per capita* consumption, except in a society with stationary population — another example of the pervasiveness of the "stationary" assumption in the past. Per capita consumption cannot be sustained with zero net investment; the capital stock must be growing at the same rate as population and the labor force. This capital-widening requirement is as truly a cost of staying in the same position as outright capital consumption.[2]

This principle is clear enough when growth is simply increase in population and the labor force. Its application to an economy with technological progress is by no means clear. Indeed, the very concept of national income becomes fuzzy. Should the capital-widening requirement then be interpreted to mean that capital should keep pace with output and technology, not just with the labor force? If so, the implied sustainable consumption per capita grows with the rate of technological progress. This is the point of view which we have taken in what follows. On the other hand, a given level of consumption per capita could be

---

[2] Consider the neoclassical model without technological change. When labor force is growing at rate g, the capital-labor ratio is k, gross product per worker is $f(k)$, net product per worker is $f(k) - \delta k$, then the net investment requirement is gk, and sustainable consumption per worker is $f(k) - \delta k - gk$. Denoting the capital-output ratio as $\mu = [k/f(k)]$, sustainable consumption per worker can also be written as $f(k)[1 - \mu(\delta + g)]$. Although NNP embodies in principle the depreciation deduction δk, it does not take account of the capital-widening requirement gk.

sustained with a steady decline in the capital-output ratio, thanks to technological progress.[3]

The growth requirement is shown on line 7 of Table 2. This is clearly a significant correction, measuring about 16 per cent of GNP in 1965.

Our calculations distinguish between actual and sustainable per capita consumption. *Actual MEW* may exceed or fall short of *sustainable MEW*, the amount that could be consumed while meeting both capital consumption and growth requirements. If these requirements are met, per capita consumption can grow at the trend rate of increase in labor productivity. When actual MEW is less than sustainable MEW, the economy is making even better provision for future consumers; when actual MEW exceeds sustainable MEW, current consumption in effect includes some of the fruits of future progress.

Instrumental Expenditures. Since GNP and NNP are measures of production rather than of welfare, they count many activities that are evidently not directly sources of utility themselves but are regrettably necessary inputs to activities that may yield utility. Some consumer outlays are only instrumental, for example, the costs of commuting to work. Some government "purchases" are also of this nature—for example, police services, sanitation services, road maintenance, national defense. Expenditures on these items are among the necessary overhead costs of a complex industrial nation-state, although there is plenty of room for disagreement as to the necessary amounts. We are making no judgments on such issues in classifying these outlays as intermediate rather than final uses of resources. Nevertheless, these decisions are difficult and controversial. The issues are clearly illustrated in the important case of national defense.

We exclude defense expenditures for two reasons. First, we see no direct effect of defense expenditures on household economic welfare. No reasonable country (or household) buys "national defense" for its own sake. If there were no war or risk of war, there would be no need

---

[3] As is well known, the whole concept of equilibrium growth collapses unless progress is purely labor-augmenting, "Harrod-neutral." In that case the rate g above is $n + \gamma$, where n is the natural rate of increase and γ is the rate of technological progress, and "labor force" means effective or augmented labor force. In equilibrium, output and consumption per natural worker grow at the rate γ, and "sustainable" consumption per capita means consumption growing steadily at this rate. Clearly, level consumption per capita can be sustained with smaller net investment than $g\mu f(k)$; so μ and k steadily decline. See section A.2.3, below.

for defense expenditures and no one would be the worse without them. Conceptually, then, defense expenditures are gross but not net output.

The second reason is that defense expenditures are input rather than output data. Measurable output is especially elusive in the case of defense. Conceptually, the output of the defense effort is national security. Has the value of the nation's security risen from $0.5 billion to $50 billion over the period from 1929 to 1965? Obviously not. It is patently more reasonable to assume that the rise in expenditure was due to deterioration in international relations and to changes in military technology. The cost of providing a given level of security has risen enormously. If there has been no corresponding gain in security since 1929, the defense cost series is a very misleading indicator of improvements in welfare.

The economy's ability to meet increased defense costs speaks well for its productive performance. But the diversion of productive capacity to this purpose cannot be regarded simply as a shift of national preferences and the product mix. Just as we count technological progress, managerial innovation, and environmental change when they work in our favor (consider new business machines or mineral discoveries) so we must count a deterioration in the environment when it works against us (consider bad weather and war). From the point of view of economic welfare, an arms control or disarmament agreement which would free resources and raise consumption by 10 per cent would be just as significant as new industrial processes yielding the same gains.

In classifying defense costs — or police protection or public health expenditures — as regrettable and instrumental, we certainly do not deny the possibility that given the unfavorable circumstances that prompt these expenditures consumers will ultimately be better off with them than without them. This may or may not be the case. The only judgment we make is that these expenditures yield no direct satisfactions. Even if the "regrettable" outlays are rational responses to unfavorable shifts in the environment of economic activity, we believe that a welfare measure, perhaps unlike a production measure, should record such environmental change.

We must admit, however, that the line between final and instrumental outlays is very hard to draw. For example, the philosophical problems raised by the malleability of consumer wants are too deep to be resolved in economic accounting. Consumers are susceptible to influence by the examples and tastes of other consumers and by the sales efforts of producers. Maybe all our wants are just regrettable necessities; maybe productive activity does no better than to satisfy the wants which it generates; maybe our net welfare product is tautologically zero. More seriously, we cannot measure welfare exclusively by the quantitative flows of goods and services. We need other gauges of the health of individuals and societies. These, too, will be relative to the value systems which determine whether given symptoms indicate health or disease. But the "social indicators" movement of recent years still lacks a coherent, integrative conceptual and statistical framework.

We estimate that overhead and regrettable expenses, so far as we have been able to define and measure them, rose from 8 per cent to 16 per cent of GNP over the period 1929–65 (Table 2, line 4).

2. Imputations for Capital Services, Leisure, and Nonmarket Work

In the national income accounts, rent is imputed on owner-occupied homes and counted as consumption and income. We must make similar imputations in other cases to which we have applied capital accounting. Like owner-occupied homes, other consumer durables and public investments yield consumption directly, without market transactions. In the case of educational and health capital, we have assumed the yields to be intermediate services rather than direct consumption; that is, we expect to see the fruits of investments in education and health realized in labor productivity and earnings, and we do not count them twice. Our measure understates economic welfare and its growth to the extent that education and medical care are direct rather than indirect sources of consumer satisfaction.

The omission of leisure and of nonmarket productive activity from measures of production conveys the impression that economists are blindly materialistic. Economic theory teaches that welfare could rise, even while NNP falls, as the result of voluntary choices to work for pay fewer hours per week, weeks per year, years per lifetime.

These imputations unfortunately raise serious conceptual questions, discussed at some length in section A.3, below. Suppose that in calculating aggregate dollar consumption the hours devoted to leisure and nonmarket productive activity are valued at their presumed opportunity cost, the money wage rate. In converting current dollar consumption to constant dollars, what assumption should be made about the unobservable price indexes for the goods and services consumed during those hours? The wage rate? The price index for marketed con-

TABLE 1

Measures of Economic Welfare, Actual and
Sustainable, Various Years, 1929–65
(*billions of dollars, 1958 prices, except lines 14–19, as noted*)

	1929	1935	1945	1947	1954	1958	1965
1 Personal consumption, national income and product accounts	139.6	125.5	183.0	206.3	255.7	290.1	397.7
2 Private instrumental expenditures	−10.3	−9.2	−9.2	−10.9	−16.4	−19.9	−30.9
3 Durable goods purchases	−16.7	−11.5	−12.3	−26.2	−35.5	−37.9	−60.9
4 Other household investment	−6.5	−6.3	−9.1	−10.4	−15.3	−19.6	−30.1
5 Services of consumer capital imputation	24.9	17.8	22.1	26.7	37.2	40.8	62.3
6 Imputation for leisure							
B	339.5	401.3	450.7	466.9	523.2	554.9	626.9
A	339.5	401.3	450.7	466.9	523.2	554.9	626.9
C	162.9	231.3	331.8	345.6	477.2	554.9	712.8
7 Imputation for nonmarket activities							
B	85.7	109.2	152.4	159.6	211.5	239.7	295.4
A	178.6	189.5	207.1	215.5	231.9	239.7	259.8
C	85.7	109.2	152.4	159.6	211.5	239.7	295.4
8 Disamenity correction	−12.5	−14.1	−18.1	−19.1	−24.3	−27.6	−34.6
9 Government consumption	0.3	0.3	0.4	0.5	0.5	0.8	1.2
10 Services of government capital imputation	4.8	6.4	8.9	10.0	11.7	14.0	16.6
11 Total consumption = actual MEW							
B	548.8	619.4	768.8	803.4	948.3	1,035.3	1,243.6
A	641.7	699.7	823.5	859.3	968.7	1,035.3	1,208.0
C	372.2	449.4	649.9	682.1	902.3	1,035.3	1,329.5
12 MEW net investment	−5.3	−46.0	−52.5	55.3	13.0	12.5	−2.5
13 Sustainable MEW							
B	543.5	573.4	716.3	858.7	961.3	1,047.8	1,241.1
A	636.4	653.7	771.0	914.6	981.7	1,047.8	1,205.5
C	366.9	403.4	597.4	737.4	915.3	1,047.8	1,327.0
14 Population (no. of mill.)	121.8	127.3	140.5	144.7	163.0	174.9	194.6

(*continued*)

Table 1 (concluded)

	1929	1935	1945	1947	1954	1958	1965
Actual MEW per capita							
15 Dollars							
B	4,506	4,866	5,472	5,552	5,818	5,919	6,391
A	5,268	5,496	5,861	5,938	5,943	5,919	6,208
C	3,056	3,530	4,626	4,714	5,536	5,919	6,832
16 Index (1929 = 100)							
B	100.0	108.0	121.4	123.2	129.1	131.4	141.8
A	100.0	104.3	111.3	112.7	112.8	112.4	117.8
C	100.0	115.5	151.4	154.3	181.2	193.7	223.6
Sustainable MEW per capita							
17 Dollars							
B	4,462	4,504	5,098	5,934	5,898	5,991	6,378
A	5,225	5,135	5,488	6,321	6,023	5,991	6,195
C	3,012	3,169	4,252	5,096	5,615	5,991	6,819
18 Index (1929 = 100)							
B	100.0	100.9	114.3	133.0	132.2	134.3	142.9
A	100.0	98.3	105.0	121.0	115.3	114.7	118.6
C	100.0	105.2	141.2	169.2	186.4	198.9	226.4
19 Per capita NNP							
Dollars	1,545	1,205	2,401	2,038	2,305	2,335	2,897
1929 = 100	100.0	78.0	155.4	131.9	149.2	151.1	187.5

Note: Variants A, B, C in the table correspond to different assumptions about the bearing of technological progress on leisure and nonmarket activities. See section A.3.2, below, for explanation.
Source: Appendix Table A.16.

sumption goods? Over a period of forty years the two diverge substantially; the choice between them makes a big difference in estimates of the growth of MEW. As explained in Appendix A, the market consumption "deflator" should be used if technological progress has augmented nonmarketed uses of time to the same degree as marketed labor. The wage rate should be the deflator if no such progress has occurred in the effectiveness of unpaid time.

In Tables 1 and 2 we provide calculations for three conceptual alternatives. Our own choice is variant B of MEW, in which the value of leisure is deflated by the wage rate; and the value of nonmarket activity, by the consumption deflator.

TABLE 2
Gross National Product and MEW, Various Years, 1929–65
(*billions of dollars, 1958 prices*)

	1929	1935	1945	1947	1954	1958	1965
1. Gross national product	203.6	169.5	355.2	309.9	407.0	447.3	617.8
2. Capital consumption, NIPA	−20.0	−20.0	−21.9	−18.3	−32.5	−38.9	−54.7
3. Net national product, NIPA	183.6	149.5	333.3	291.6	374.5	408.4	563.1
4. NIPA final output reclassified as regrettables and intermediates							
a. Government	−6.7	−7.4	−146.3	−20.8	−57.8	−56.4	−63.2
b. Private	−10.3	−9.2	−9.2	−10.9	−16.4	−19.9	−30.9
5. Imputations for items not included in NIPA							
a. Leisure	339.5	401.3	450.7	466.9	523.2	554.9	626.9
b. Nonmarket activity	85.7	109.2	152.4	159.6	211.5	239.7	295.4
c. Disamenities	−12.5	−14.1	−18.1	−19.1	−24.3	−27.6	−34.6
d. Services of public and private capital	29.7	24.2	31.0	36.7	48.9	54.8	78.9
6. Additional capital consumption	−19.3	−33.4	−11.7	−50.8	−35.2	−27.3	−92.7
7. Growth requirement	−46.1	−46.7	−65.8	+5.4	−63.1	−78.9	−101.8
8. Sustainable MEW	543.6	573.4	716.3	858.6	961.3	1,047.7	1,241.1

NIPA = national income and product accounts.

Note: Variants A, B, C in the table correspond to different assumptions about the bearing of technological progress on leisure and nonmarket activities. Variant A assumes that neither has benefited from technological progress at the rate of increase of real wages; variant C assumes that neither has so benefited; variant B assumes that leisure has not been augmented by technological progress but other nonmarket activities have benefited. See section A.3.2, below, for explanation.

Source: Appendix Table A.17.

3. Disamenities of Urbanization

The national income accounts largely ignore the many sources of utility or disutility that are not associated with market transactions or measured by the market value of goods and services. If one of my neighbors cultivates a garden of ever-increasing beauty, and another makes more and more noise, neither my increasing appreciation of the one nor my growing annoyance with the other comes to the attention of the Department of Commerce.

Likewise there are some socially productive assets (for example, the environment) that do not appear in any balance sheets. Their services to producers and consumers are not valued in calculating national income. By the same token no allowance is made for depletion of their capacity to yield services in the future.

Many of the negative "externalities" of economic growth are connected with urbanization and congestion. The secular advances recorded in NNP figures have accompanied a vast migration from rural agriculture to urban industry. Without this occupational and residential revolution we could not have enjoyed the fruits of technological progress. But some portion of the higher earnings of urban residents may simply be compensation for the disamenities of urban life and work. If so we should not count as a gain of welfare the full increments of NNP that result from moving a man from farm or small town to city. The persistent association of higher wages with higher population densities offers one method of estimating the costs of urban life as they are valued by people making residential and occupational decisions.

As explained in section A.4, below, we have tried to estimate by cross-sectional regressions the income differentials necessary to hold people in localities with greater population densities. The resulting estimates of the disamenity costs of urbanization are shown in Table 1, line 8. As can be seen, the estimated disamenity premium is quite substantial, running about 5 per cent of GNP. Nevertheless, the urbanization of the population has not been so rapid that charging it with this cost significantly reduces the estimated rate of growth of the economy.

The adjustments leading from national accounts "personal consumption" to MEW consumption are shown in Table 1, and the relations of GNP, NNP, and MEW are summarized in Table 2. For reasons previously indicated, we believe that a welfare measure should have the dimension *per capita*. We would stress the per capita MEW figures shown in Tables 1 and 2.

Although the numbers presented here are very tentative, they do suggest the following observations. First, MEW is quite different from conventional output measures. Some consumption items omitted from GNP are of substantial quantitative importance. Second, our preferred variant of per capita MEW has been growing more slowly than per capita NNP (1.1 per cent for MEW as against 1.7 per cent for NNP, at annual rates over the period 1929–65). Yet MEW has been growing. The progress indicated by conventional national accounts is not just a myth that evaporates when a welfare-oriented measure is substituted.

GROWTH AND NATURAL RESOURCES

Calculations like the foregoing are unlikely to satisfy critics who believe that economic growth per se piles up immense social costs ignored in even the most careful national income calculations. Faced with the finiteness of our earth and the exponential growth of economy and population, the environmentalist sees inevitable starvation. The specter of Malthus is haunting even the affluent society.

There is a familiar ring to these criticisms. Ever since the industrial revolution pessimistic scientists and economists have warned that the possibilities of economic expansion are ultimately limited by the availability of natural resources and that society only makes the eventual future reckoning more painful by ignoring resource limitations now.

In important part, this is a warning about population growth, which we consider below. Taking population developments as given, will natural resources become an increasingly severe drag on economic growth? We have not found evidence to support this fear. Indeed, the opposite appears to be more likely: Growth of output per capita will accelerate ever so slightly even as stocks of natural resources decline.

The prevailing standard model of growth assumes that there are no limits on the feasibility of expanding the supplies of nonhuman agents of production. It is basically a two-factor model in which production depends only on labor and reproducible capital. Land and resources, the third member of the classical triad, have generally been dropped. The simplifications of theory carry over into empirical work. The thousands of aggregate production functions estimated by econometricians in the last decade are labor-capital functions. Presumably the tacit justification has been that reproducible capital is a near-perfect substitute for land and other exhaustible resources, at least in the perspective of heroic aggregation customary in macroeconomics. If substitution for natural resources is not possible in any given technology, or if a particular resource is exhausted, we tacitly assume that "land-augmenting" innovations will overcome the scarcity.

These optimistic assumptions about technology stand in contrast to the tacit assumption of environmentalists that no substitutes are available for natural resources. Under this condition, it is easily seen that output will indeed stop growing or will decline. It thus appears that the substitutability (or technically, the elasticity of substitution) between the neoclassical factors, capital and labor, and natural resources is of crucial importance to future growth. This is an area needing extensive further research, but we have made two forays to see what the evidence is. Details are given in Appendix B, below.

First we ran several simulations of the process of economic growth in order to see which assumptions about substitution and technology fit the "stylized" facts. The important facts are: growing income per capita and growing capital per capita; relatively declining inputs and income shares of natural resources; and a slowly declining capital-output ratio. Among the various forms of production function considered, the following assumptions come closest to reproducing these stylized facts: (a) Either the elasticity of substitution between natural resources and other factors is high — significantly greater than unity — or resource-augmenting technological change has proceeded faster than overall productivity; (b) the elasticity of substitution between labor and capital is close to unity.

After these simulations were run, it appeared possible to estimate directly the parameters of the preferred form of production function. Econometric estimates confirm proposition (a) and seem to support the alternative of high elasticity of substitution between resources and the neoclassical factors.

Of course it is always possible that the future will be discontinuously different from the past. But if our estimates are accepted, then continuation of substitution during the next fifty years, during which many environmentalists foresee the end to growth, will result in a small increase — perhaps about 0.1 per cent per annum — in the growth of per capita income.

Is our economy, with its mixture of market processes and governmental controls, biased in favor of wasteful and shortsighted exploitation of natural resources? In considering this charge, two archetypical cases must be distinguished, although many actual cases fall between them. First, there are appropriable resources for which buyers pay market values and users market rentals. Second, there are inappropriable resources, "public goods," whose use appears free to individual producers and consumers but is c)stly in aggregate to society.

If the past is any guide for the future, there seems to be little reason to worry about the exhaustion of resources which the market already treats as economic goods. We have already commented on the irony that both growth men and antigrowth men invoke the interests of future generations. The issue between them is not whether and how much provision must be made for future generations, but in what form it should be made. The growth man emphasizes reproducible capital and education. The conservationist emphasizes exhaustible resources —minerals in the ground, open space, virgin land. The economist's initial presumption is that the market will decide in what forms to transmit wealth by the requirement that all kinds of wealth bear a comparable rate of return. Now stocks of natural resources—for example, mineral deposits—are essentially sterile. Their return to their owners is the increase in their prices relative to prices of other goods. In a properly functioning market economy, resources will be exploited at such a pace that their rate of relative price appreciation is competitive with rates of return on other kinds of capital. Many conservationists have noted such price appreciation with horror, but if the prices of these resources accurately reflect the scarcities of the future, they must rise in order to prevent too rapid exploitation. Natural resources *should* grow in relative scarcity—otherwise they are an inefficient way for society to hold and transmit wealth compared to productive physical and human capital. Price appreciation protects resources from premature exploitation.

How would an excessive rate of exploitation show up? We would see rates of relative price increase that are above the general real rate of return on wealth. This would indicate that society had in the past used precious resources too profligately, relative to the tastes and technologies later revealed. The scattered evidence we have indicates little excessive price rise. For some resources, indeed, prices seem to have risen more slowly than efficient use would indicate ex post.

If this reasoning is correct, the nightmare of a day of reckoning and economic collapse when, for example, all fossil fuels are forever gone seems to be based on failure to recognize the existing and future possibilities of substitute materials and processes. As the day of reckoning approaches, fuel prices will provide—as they do not now—strong incentives for such substitutions, as well as for the conservation of remaining supplies. On the other hand, the warnings of the conservationists and scientists do underscore the importance of continuous monitoring of the national and world outlook for energy and other resources. Substitutability might disappear. Conceivably both the market and public agencies might be too complacent about the prospects for new and safe substitutes for fossil fuels. The opportunity and need for fruitful collaboration between economists and physical scientists has never been greater.

Possible abuse of public natural resources is a much more serious problem. It is useful to distinguish between *local* and *global* ecological disturbances. The former include transient air pollution, water pollution, noise pollution, visual disamenities. It is certainly true that we have not charged automobile users and electricity consumers for their pollution of the skies, or farmers and housewives for the pollution of lakes by the runoff of fertilizers and detergents. In that degree our national product series have overestimated the advance of welfare. Our urban disamenity estimates given above indicate a current overestimate of about 5 per cent of total consumption.

There are other serious consequences of treating as free things which are not really free. This practice gives the wrong signals for the directions of economic growth. The producers of automobiles and of electricity should be given incentives to develop and to utilize "cleaner" technologies. The consumers of automobiles and electricity should pay in higher prices for the pollution they cause, or for the higher costs of low-pollution processes. If recognition of these costs causes consumers to shift their purchases to other goods and services, that is only efficient. At present overproduction of these goods is uneconomically subsidized as truly as if the producers received cash subsidies from the Treasury.

The mistake of the antigrowth men is to blame economic growth per se for the misdirection of economic growth. The misdirection is due to a defect of the pricing system—a serious but by no means irreparable defect and one which would in any case be present in a stationary economy. Pollutants have multiplied much faster than the population or the economy during the last thirty years. Although general economic growth has intensified the problem, it seems to originate in particular technologies. The proper remedy is to correct the price system so as to discourage these technologies. Zero economic growth is a blunt instrument for cleaner air, prodigiously expensive and probably ineffectual.

As for the danger of global ecological catastrophes, there is probably very little that economics alone can say. Maybe we are pouring pollutants into the atmosphere at such a rate that we will melt the polar icecaps and flood all the world's seaports. Unfortunately, there seems to be great uncertainty about the causes and the likelihood of such occurrences. These catastrophic global disturbances warrant a higher priority for research than the local disturbances to which so much attention has been given.

POPULATION GROWTH

Like the role of natural resources, the role of population in the standard neoclassical model is ripe for re-examination. The assumption is that population and labor force grow exogenously, like compound interest. Objections arise on both descriptive and normative grounds. We know that population growth cannot continue forever. Some day there will be stable or declining population, either with high birth and death rates and short life expectancies, or with low birth and death rates and long life expectancies. As Richard Easterlin argues in his National Bureau book,[4] there surely is some adaptation of human fertility and mortality to economic circumstances. Alas, neither economists nor other social scientists have been notably successful in developing a theory of fertility that corresponds even roughly to the facts. The subject deserves much more attention from economists and econometricians than it has received.

On the normative side, the complaint is that economists should not fatalistically acquiesce in whatever population growth happens. They should instead help to frame a population policy. Since the costs to society of additional children may exceed the costs to the parents, childbearing decisions are a signal example of market failure. How to internalize the full social costs of reproduction is an even more challenging problem than internalizing the social costs of pollution.

During the past ten years, the fertility of the United States population has declined dramatically. If continued, this trend would soon diminish fertility to a level ultimately consistent with zero population growth. But such trends have been reversed in the past, and in the absence of any real understanding of the determinants of fertility, predictions are extremely hazardous.

The decline may be illustrated by comparing the 1960 and 1967 net reproduction rates and intrinsic (economists would say "equilibrium") rates of growth of the United States population. The calculations of Table 3 refer to the asymptotic steady-state implications of indefinite continuation of the age-specific fertility and mortality rates of the year 1960 or 1967. Should the trend of the 1960s continue, the intrinsic growth rate would become zero, and the net reproduction rate 1.000, in the 1970s. Supposing that the decline in fertility then stopped. The actual population would grow slowly for another forty or fifty

---

[4] *Population, Labor Force, and Long Swings in Economic Growth: The American Experience,* New York, NBER, 1968.

TABLE 3
U.S. Population Characteristics in Equilibrium

	Intrinsic Growth Rate (per cent per year)	Net Reproduction Rate	Median Age
1960 fertility-mortality	2.1362	1.750	21–22
1967 fertility-mortality	0.7370	1.221	28
Hypothetical ZPG	0.0000	1.000	32

years while the inherited bulge in the age distribution at the more fertile years gradually disappeared. The asymptotic size of the population would be between 250 million and 300 million.

One consequence of slowing down the rate of population growth by diminished fertility is, of course, a substantial increase in the age of the equilibrium population, as indicated in the third column of Table 3. It is hard to judge to what degree qualitative change and innovation have in the past been dependent on quantitative growth. When our institutions are expanding in size and in number, deadwood can be gracefully bypassed and the young can guide the new. In a stationary population, institutional change will either be slower or more painful.

The current trend in fertility in the United States suggests that, contrary to the pessimistic warnings of some of the more extreme antigrowth men, it seems quite possible that ZPG can be reached while childbearing remains a voluntary private decision. Government policy can concentrate on making it completely voluntary by extending the availability of birth control knowledge and technique and of legal abortion. Since some 20 per cent of current births are estimated to be unintended, it may well be that intended births at present are insufficient to sustain the population.

Once the rate of population growth is regarded as a variable, perhaps one subject to conscious social control, the neoclassical growth model can tell some of the consequences of its variation. As explained above, sustainable per capita consumption (growing at the rate of technological progress) requires enough net investment to increase the capital stock at the natural rate of growth of the economy (the sum of the rate of increase of population and productivity). Given the capital-output ratio, sustainable consumption per capita will be larger the lower the rate of population increase; at the same time, the capital-widening requirement is diminished.

This is, however, not the only effect of a reduction of the rate of population growth. The equilibrium capital-output ratio itself is altered. The average wealth of a population is a weighted average of the wealth positions of people of different ages. Over its life cycle the typical family, starting from low or negative net worth, accumulates wealth to spend in old age, and perhaps in middle years when children are most costly. Now a stationary or slow-growing population has a characteristic age distribution much different from that of a rapidly growing population. The stationary population will have relatively fewer people in the early low-wealth years, but relatively more in the late low-wealth

TABLE 4
Illustrative Relationship of Sustainable Per Capita Consumption to Marginal Productivity of Capital and to Capital-Output Ratio

Marginal Productivity of Capital					Index of Consumption Per Capita (c)		
Gross (R)	Net of Depreciation ($R - \delta$)	Ratio of Capital to GNP (μ')	Ratio of Capital to NNP (μ)	Index of NNP per Capita (y)	1960 Pop. Growth	1967 Pop. Growth	ZPG
(1)	(2)	(3)	(4)	(5)	(6)	(7)	(8)
.09	.05	3.703	4.346	1.639	1.265	1.372	1.426
.105	.065	3.175	3.637	1.556	1.265	1.344	1.386
.12	.08	2.778	3.125	1.482	1.245	1.309	1.343
.15	.11	2.222	2.439	1.356	1.187	1.233	1.257

Note: A Cobb-Douglas production function is assumed for GNP, with constant returns to scale, with an elasticity of output with respect to capital (α) of $\frac{1}{3}$, and with the rate (γ) of labor-augmenting technological progress 3 per cent per year. The depreciation rate (δ) is assumed to be 4 per cent per year. GNP per capita (Y) is $ae^{\gamma t}k^{\alpha}$ and NNP per capita (y) is $Y - \delta k$, where k is the capital-labor ratio.
Column 3: Since $Rk = \alpha Y$, $\mu' = k/Y = \alpha/R$.
Column 4: $\mu = \mu'/(1 - \delta\mu')$.
Column 5: $y = (1 - \delta\mu')Y$. For the index, $ae^{\gamma t}$ is set equal to 1.
Columns 6, 7, and 8: $c = [1 - (n + \gamma)\mu]y$. Given $\gamma = 0.03$, $n + \gamma$ is 0.0513 for 1960, 0.0374 for 1967, 0.0300 for ZPG.

TABLE 5
Desired Wealth-Income Ratios Estimated for Different Rates of Population Growth (and for Different Equivalent Adult Scales and Subjective Discount Rates [a])

Net Interest Rate $(R - \delta)$	Desired Wealth-Income Ratio (μ)		
	1960 Pop. Growth (.021)	1967 Pop. Growth (.007)	ZPG
Teenagers, 1.0; Children, 1.0; Discount, 0.02			
.05	−1.70	−1.46	−1.24
.065	0.59	0.91	1.16
.08	2.31	2.70	2.90
.11	4.31	4.71	4.95
Teenagers, 0.8; Children, 0.6; Discount, 0.01			
.05	0.41	0.74	0.97
.065	2.36	2.75	3.00
.08	3.74	4.16	4.41
.11	5.17	5.55	5.75
Teenagers, 0.8; Children, 0.6; Discount, 0.02			
.05	−1.17	−0.95	−0.75
.065	1.08	1.38	1.60
.08	2.74	3.11	3.34
.11	4.61	4.98	5.18
Teenagers, 0.0; Children, 0.0; Discount, 0.02			
.05	−0.40	−0.15	0.02
.065	1.93	2.20	2.36
.08	3.56	3.85	4.01
.11	5.20	5.47	5.61

Note: The desired wealth-income ratio is calculated for a given steady state of population increase and the corresponding equilibrium age distribution. It is an aggregation of the wealth and income positions of households of different ages. As explained in Appendix C it also depends on the interest rate, the typical age-income profile and the expected growth of incomes ($\gamma = 0.03$), the rate of subjective discount of future utility of consumption, and the weights given to teenagers (boys 14–20 and girls 14–18) and other children in household allocations of lifetime incomes to consumption in different years. See Appendix C for further explanation.
   [a] Shown in boldface.

TABLE 6
Estimated Equilibrium Capital-Output Ratios
and Per Capita Consumption Rates [a]

Population Growth Rate	Interest Rate $(R - \delta)$	Capital-Output Ratio (μ)	Consumption Index (c)	Per Cent Increase in c over 1960
Teenagers, 1.0; Children, 1.0; Discount, 0.02				
1960	.089	2.88	1.23	
1967	.085	2.99	1.30	5.62
ZPG	.082	3.07	1.34	9.04
Teenagers, 0.8; Children, 0.6; Discount, 0.01				
1960	.074	3.28	1.25	
1967	.071	3.38	1.33	6.23
ZPG	.069	3.47	1.37	9.74
Teenagers, 0.8; Children, 0.6; Discount, 0.02				
1960	.084	3.00	1.24	
1967	.080	3.11	1.31	5.82
ZPG	.078	3.16	1.35	8.97
Teenagers, 0.0; Children, 0.0; Discount, 0.02				
1960	.077	3.22	1.25	
1967	.074	3.28	1.32	6.42
ZPG	.073	3.33	1.36	9.99

Note: Estimated by interpolation from Tables 4 and 5. See Figure 1.
[a] Equivalent adult scales and subjective discount rate are shown in boldface.

years. So it is not obvious in which direction the shift of weights moves the average.

We have, however, estimated the shift by a series of calculations described in Appendix C. Illustrative results are shown in Tables 4–6 and Figure 1. Evidently, reduction in the rate of growth increases the society's desired wealth-income ratio. This means an increase in the capital-output ratio which increases the society's sustainable consumption per capita.[5]

On both counts, therefore, a reduction in population increase

[5] Provided only that the change is made from an initial situation in which the net marginal productivity of capital exceeds the economy's natural rate of growth. Otherwise the increased capital-widening requirements exceed the gains in output.

FIGURE 1
Determination of Equilibrium Capital-Output Ratio and Interest Rate
(equivalent adult scale for teenagers and children = 1.0; subjective discount rate = 0.02)

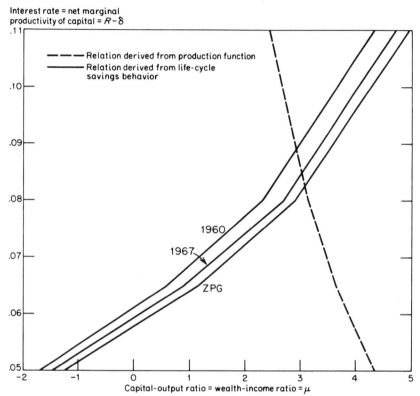

Source: Tables 4 and 5.

should raise sustainable consumption. We have essayed an estimate of the magnitude of this gain. In a ZPG equilibrium sustainable consumption per capita would be 9–10 per cent higher than in a steady state of 2.1 per cent growth corresponding to 1960 fertility and mortality, and somewhat more than 3 per cent higher than in a steady state of 0.7 per cent growth corresponding to 1967 fertility and mortality.

These neoclassical calculations do not take account of the lower pressure of population growth on natural resources. As between the 1960 equilibrium and ZPG, the diminished drag of resource limitations is worth about one-tenth of 1 per cent per annum in growth of per capita consumption. Moreover, if our optimistic estimates of the ease of substitution of other factors of production for natural resources are wrong, a slowdown of population growth will have much more important effects in postponing the day of reckoning.

Is growth obsolete? We think not. Although GNP and other national income aggregates are imperfect measures of welfare, the broad picture of secular progress which they convey remains after correction of their most obvious deficiencies. At present there is no reason to arrest general economic growth to conserve natural resources, although there is good reason to provide proper economic incentives to conserve resources which currently cost their users less than true social cost. Population growth cannot continue indefinitely, and evidently it is already slowing down in the United States. This slowdown will significantly increase sustainable per capita consumption. But even with ZPG there is no reason to shut off technological progress. The classical stationary state need not become our utopian norm.

APPENDIX A: A MEASURE OF ECONOMIC WELFARE

The purpose of this appendix is to explain the "measure of economic welfare" (MEW) introduced in the text. Conceptually it is a comprehensive measure of the annual real consumption of households. Consumption is intended to include all goods and services, marketed or not, valued at market prices or at their equivalent in opportunity costs to consumers. Collective public consumption is to be included, whether provided by government or otherwise; and allowance is to be made for negative externalities, such as those due to environmental damage and to the disamenities and congestion of urbanization and industrialization. Real consumption is estimated by valuing the flows of goods and services at constant prices.

We distinguish sustainable welfare (MEW-S) from actual welfare (MEW-A). Sustainable MEW is the amount of consumption in any year that is consistent with sustained steady growth in per capita consumption at the trend rate of technological progress. MEW, whether sustainable or actual, can be expressed either in aggregate or in per capita terms. For obvious reasons set forth in the text, we regard the per capita measure as the more relevant one, a judgment that enters into the very definition of MEW-S.

Actual MEW excludes all final output actually devoted to capital replacement and accumulation. Sustainable MEW excludes the capital expenditures needed to sustain the capital-output ratio. It allows for capital depreciation, for equipping new members of the labor force, and for increasing capital per worker at the trend rate of productivity change. MEW-S will be greater than MEW-A in years when the economy is investing more than these requirements, and smaller when it is investing less. In a neoclassical growth model, an excess of MEW-S over MEW-A means that the capital-output ratio is rising, the economy is moving to a higher equilibrium growth path, and MEW-S is increasing faster than the trend rate of technological progress. An excess of MEW-A over MEW-S means the opposite.

We have not attempted to estimate a concept of "potential MEW" — analogous to potential GNP — which would correct for fluctuations in utilization of the labor force and the capital stock. Consequently comparisons of MEW, actual or sustainable, are best confined to periods of comparable utilization. The end points of our trial calculations, 1929 and 1965, are roughly comparable in this respect.

We are aiming for a consumption measure, but we cannot of course estimate how well individual and collective happiness are correlated with consumption. We cannot say whether a modern society with cars, airplanes, and television sets is really happier than the nation of our great-grandparents who lived without use or knowledge of these inventions. We cannot estimate the externalities of social interdependence, of which Veblen, Galbraith, and other social critics have complained. That is, we cannot tell to what degree increases in consumption are offset by displeasure that others are also increasing their consumption. Nor can we tell how much consumption is simply the relief of artificially induced cravings nurtured by advertising and sales effort.

In suggesting a consumption-oriented measure, we do not in any way derogate the importance of the conventional national income accounts. They are, of course, the chief and indispensable source of our calculations, which are for the most part simply a rearrangement of the data the Department of Commerce faithfully and skillfully provides. Gross national product and net national product are measures of output performance. As such, they are the relevant measures both for short-run stabilization policy and for assessing the economy's long-run progress as a productive machine.

Our purpose is different and suggests a different measure. Consider, for example, the treatment of defense expenditure, which rose from less than 1 per cent of GNP in 1929 to 10 per cent in 1965. The capacity of the economy to meet this rise in defense demands, along with others, certainly deserves to be counted in assessing its gains in productive performance between the two dates. But we exclude defense expenditures because they add to neither actual nor sustainable household consumption. This exclusion does not charge the rise in defense expenditures as an inevitable by-product of the growth of the economy, nor does it imply any judgment as to their necessity or desirability. It simply acknowledges that this component of GNP growth, whatever its causes and consequences, does not enter via normal economic processes into the consumption satisfactions of households.

We recognize that our proposal is controversial on conceptual and theoretical grounds and that many of the numerical expedients in its execution are dubious. Nevertheless, the challenge to economists to produce relevant welfare-oriented measures seems compelling enough to justify some risk-taking. We hope that others will be challenged, or provoked, to tackle the problem with different assumptions, more refined procedures, and better data. We hope also that further investigations will be concerned with the distribution, as well as the mean value, of a measure of economic welfare, an aspect we have not been able to consider.

In the remaining sections of this appendix we explain the details of the calculations presented in text Table 1. Section A.1 concerns reclassification of expenditures reported in national income accounts to obtain a more comprehensive concept of consumption. This reclassification implies some adjustments in the capital accounts presented in section A.2. In section A.3 we describe our imputations for consumption yielded by nonmarket activities; and in section A.4, our adjustments for the disamenities of urban growth. Section A.5 describes the final estimates, and section A.6 contains some discussion of their reliability.

A.1 Reclassification of Final Expenditures

A.1.1 Government Purchases. In the United States income and product accounts, government purchases of goods and services are counted as final output and are not classified as consumption and investment. For our purposes, we need to classify government uses of resources as (a) consumption, (b) replacement and accumulation of capital contributing to future consumption possibilities, (c) "regrettable" outlays that use resources for national purposes other than consumption or capital formation supportive of future consumption, and

TABLE A.1
Reclassification of Government Purchases of Goods and Services, Various Years, 1929–65
(billions of dollars, 1958 prices)

	1929	1935	1945	1947	1954	1958	1965
1 Public consumption	0.3	0.3	0.4	0.5	0.5	0.8	1.2
2 Public investment, gross	15.0	19.3	9.7	18.6	30.6	37.0	50.3
3 Regrettables	1.7	2.0	139.7	14.4	49.4	46.4	47.6
4 Intermediate goods and services	5.0	5.4	6.6	6.4	8.4	10.0	15.6
5 Total government consumption and investment	15.3	19.6	10.1	19.1	31.1	37.8	51.5
6 Total government purchases	22.0	27.0	156.4	39.9	88.9	94.2	114.7

Note: For 1954–65, based on current-dollar figures for federal and state and local purchases of goods and services, NIP Table 3.10 (see note 6, above), deflated by government purchases deflator, NIP Table 8.1. Line 6 is also line 20 of NIP Table 1.2.

Consumption: postal service (line 52) and recreation (line 61).

Investment: one-half atomic energy development (line 4), education (line 16), health and hospitals (line 21), commerce, transportation, and housing (line 39), conservation and development of resources (line 60), and agriculture (line 54).

Regrettables: national defense (line 2) less one-half atomic energy development (line 4), space research and technology (line 6), international affairs and finance (line 13), and veterans benefits and services (line 33).

Intermediate: everything else, including general government (line 7), sanitation (line 22), and civilian safety (line 28).

For 1929–47, NIP Table 3.10 is not available, and the breakdowns were based on estimates by broad expenditure category.

(d) provision of intermediate goods and services instrumental to final production. The results of our classifications are shown in Table A.1.

Very little government expenditure on goods and services can be considered consumption. From the functional breakdown in the national accounts, we take as consumption only the subsidy of the post office and recreation outlays (NIP Table 3.10).[6]

We have counted as gross investment only items that raise productivity (education, medicine, public health) or yield services directly consumed by households (housing, transportation). Investment so defined represents 65 per cent of government purchases in 1929 and 43

[6] References to NIP tables are to the standard tables of the Department of Commerce, *National Income and Product Accounts of the United States, 1929–1965* and to the annual extensions or revisions of these data in July issues of the *Survey of Current Business.*

per cent in 1965. It is, of course, necessary to account for the yield of government capital investments. In some cases the yield consists of increased factor incomes and is automatically registered. In other cases imputations for the consumption of the services of government capital are necessary. This is discussed in section A.2, below.

"Regrettables" represent final expenditures — made for reasons of national security, prestige, or diplomacy — which in our judgment do not directly increase the economic welfare of households. We will discuss further the most important case, national defense; the reasoning is similar for other regrettables.

Defense expenditures have no direct value in household consumption. No reasonable nation purchases defense because its services are desired per se. The product of defense outlays is national security, but it is clearly not true that our security has increased as the outlays rose a hundredfold from 1929 to 1965. Changes in international relations and in military technology have vastly multiplied the costs of providing a given level of security. Just as we count the fruits of scientific progress, managerial improvement, and mineral discovery when they make it easier for the nation to wrest its living from the environment, so we must count the results of deterioration in the nation's economic or political environment. This procedure does not blame the economy for unfavorable international political events any more than recording a reduction in food crops due to bad weather or a plague of locusts means that the agricultural economy has become any less efficient.

The final category, "intermediate goods and services," is clearest when the government is providing direct services or materials to business enterprises. It also includes more diffuse instrumental outlays: the costs of maintaining a sanitary and safe natural and social environment. There is no sharp dividing line between intermediate overhead expenditures and regrettables. Police protection, for example, might fall under either category.

A.1.2 Private Purchases.   We have also made some reclassifications of private expenditures: (a) Personal business expenses and one-fifth of personal transportation expenses (an estimate of the fraction devoted to commutation) are subtracted from consumption and regarded as intermediate or instrumental (Table A.16, line 2). (b) Educational and medical outlays are regarded as gross investments (Table A.16, line 4). (c) All outlays for consumer durables, not just purchases of residences, are treated as investments (Table A.16, line 3). (d) Imputations are made for those services of consumer capital that are directly consumed (Table A.16, line 5); these are described in section A.2.

A.2 Adjustments for Capital

Conventional national income accounting limits investment to domestic business investment and residential construction. Economists have come to include a much wider group of expenditures in this category. Table A.2 gives a list of the conventional items and those added for our present purposes, for the year 1958.

The three important accounting problems introduced by this treatment of capital are (a) calculation of the net stock of wealth; (b) calculation of imputed services from capital to be added to consumption; (c) decomposition of gross investment into capital consumption and net investment to calculate sustainable MEW.

A.2.1 Net Stock of Wealth. Most of the figures for components of wealth have been gathered from other sources. They are shown in Table A.3. The figures for educational capital and health capital have

TABLE A.2
Items of Gross Investment, 1958
(*dollars in billions*)

	Investment	Per Cent of Total
Conventional items		
1. Business investment	$ 40.1	25.4%
2. Residential construction	20.8	13.2
New items		
3. Government investment	37.0	23.5
4. Consumer durables	37.9	24.0
5. Other consumer investments	19.6	12.4
6. Net foreign investment	2.2	1.4
Total	$157.6	100.0%

Source (for NIP, see note 6, above):
Line
1 NIP Table 1.2, lines 8–14
2 NIP Table 1.2, line 11
3 Table A.1, line 2
4 NIP Table 1.2, line 3
5 NIP Table 2.5, lines 42 plus 93 less 44
6 NIP Table 1.2, line 6

TABLE A.3

Net Stock of Public and Private Wealth, Various Years, 1929–65

(billions of dollars, 1958 prices)

	1929	1935	1945	1947	1954	1958	1965
1 Net reproducible capital	765.6	742.3	832.5	895.3	1,186.6	1,367.6	1,676.2
2 Nonreproducible capital *a*	299.0	276.1	245.9	262.2	299.9	335.4	392.4
3 Educational capital	91.2	120.2	253.2	269.0	447.2	581.6	879.4
4 Health	7.2	28.7	44.5	49.5	74.8	89.5	121.2
5 Total	1,163.0	1,167.3	1,376.1	1,476.0	2,008.5	2,374.1	3,069.2

Source: Lines 1 and 2: 1929–58 from Raymond W. Goldsmith, *The National Wealth of the United States in the Postwar Period*, Princeton for NBER, 1962, Tables A-1, A-2, and A-16; 1965, from John Kendrick's estimates presented in *Statistical Abstract of the United States*, 1967, Tables 492 and 494. Figures for 1935 and 1965 are linear interpolations.

Line 3: See text.

Line 4: Deflated health expenditures, public and private, cumulated on the assumption of an exponential depreciation rate of 20 per cent per annum. Public health expenditures are given in NIP Table 3.10, line 21; private expenditures, NIP Table 2.5, line 42 (see note 6, above).

a Nonreproducible capital covers five categories, which are listed below with their relative importance in 1958:

	Share of Total Value of Nonreproducible Assets, 1958 (per cent)
Agricultural land	30.2
Residential land	18.1
Nonresidential land	32.2
Public land	12.2
Net foreign assets	7.3
Total	100.0

been constructed in part by us. The estimates of tangible capital, reproducible and nonreproducible, are from Goldsmith and Kendrick.[7] The data on nonreproducible wealth are dubious. In principle, the increased value in constant prices of nonreproducible assets comes primarily through upgrading land from agricultural to nonagricultural

[7] Raymond W. Goldsmith, *The National Wealth of the United States in the Postwar Period*, Princeton for NBER, 1962; and John W. Kendrick, *Productivity Trends in the United States*, Princeton for NBER, 1961.

uses.[8] In practice, given the nature of the estimates, some of the recorded increase may be due to improper deflation.

The value of educational capital is based on Schultz's estimates of the cost per pupil of attained education, valued at 1956 costs of each level of education. This assumes no technological change in education. We preferred to treat education in a similar way to other forms of wealth and to value it at replacement cost at constant prices rather than at constant 1956 costs. We therefore used Machlup's series of average cost per pupil to get an index of cost per pupil in constant prices. We then recalculated Schultz's figures to obtain the value of educational capital per member of the labor force.[9]

The value of health capital was constructed by cumulating deflated public and private medical health and hospital expenditures. These were cumulated assuming exponential depreciation at 20 per cent per annum.

A.2.2 Services from Wealth. Having shifted some public and private expenditures from consumption to investment, we must impute consumption of services of those types of capital whose yield does not take the form of explicit factor earnings. Such imputations are made in the national accounts only for owner-occupied housing.

For both consumer durable expenditures and government structures (excluding military), Juster has prepared estimates of capital services.[10] We have used his estimates for services, and these are presented in Table A.4. It should be noted that this imputation is not entirely appropriate, since some of the imputed output is intermediate (that is, used by business). On the other hand, his assumed rates of return seem quite low, and this low estimate may offset the erroneous inclusion of some intermediate product.

We do not impute any consumption services to health or educational capital. To the extent that health and education expenditures lead to higher productivity, there is no need for further imputation. We make the admittedly extreme assumption that no direct gains in satisfaction are produced by these categories of wealth. Since they have

[8] See Goldsmith, *National Wealth*, p. 48, n. 2.

[9] Data are from Theodore Schultz, "Education and Economic Growth," in N. B. Henry, ed., *Social Forces Influencing American Education*, Chicago, University of Chicago Press, 1961; Fritz Machlup, *The Production and Distribution of Knowledge in the United States*, Princeton, Princeton University Press, 1962.

[10] F. Thomas Juster, *Household Capital Formation and Its Financing, 1897–1962*, New York, NBER, 1966, App. B.

TABLE A.4
Imputed Services from Consumer Durables and Civilian Government
Structures, Various Years, 1929–65
(*billions of dollars*)

	1929	1935	1945	1947	1954	1958	1965
Current Prices							
Imputed net rental							
Consumer	3.6	1.9	3.5	5.6	10.6	13.9	23.2
Government	0.4	0.5	1.8	2.8	3.8	5.0	6.3
Capital consumption							
Consumer	6.2	4.2	7.9	12.2	21.7	26.9	44.9
Government	1.5	1.7	2.8	3.9	6.4	9.0	11.8
Total services	11.7	8.3	16.0	24.5	42.5	54.8	86.2
1958 Prices							
Consumer services	24.9	17.8	22.1	26.7	37.2	40.8	62.3
Government services	4.8	6.4	8.9	10.0	11.7	14.0	16.6
Total services	29.7	24.2	31.1	36.7	49.0	54.8	78.9

Source: Figures in current prices are from F. Thomas Juster, *Household Capital Formation and Its Financing, 1897–1962*, New York, NBER, 1966, Tables B-2 and B-4. The constant-price series is obtained by dividing by the deflator for fixed investment.
The figures for 1965 were extrapolated from 1962 using data on purchases and depreciation of consumer durables.

been growing faster than the other stocks, our assumption may lead to understatement of the growth of welfare.

A.2.3   Capital Consumption and Net Investment.   In Table A.5 we show first, in lines 1, 6, and 7, the national accounts figures for gross investment, capital consumption, and net investment. For our MEW we have, as explained above, broadened the concepts of capital and investment. Lines 5, 8, and 9 give estimates for the MEW concepts of gross investment, capital consumption, and change in capital stock. Capital consumption, line 8, is estimated from the wealth data of Table A.3 above.

In addition, we have estimated a new concept of net investment, called net MEW investment. This is the amount of investment to be added to actual MEW to obtain sustainable MEW. Zero net MEW investment corresponds to that gross investment which would keep per capita consumption growing at the rate of technological progress. In

TABLE A.5
Gross and Net Investment in National Accounts (NIPA) and in Measure of Economic Welfare (MEW), Various Years, 1929–65

	1929	1935	1945	1947	1954	1958	1965
1. Gross investment, NIPA	40.4	18.0	19.6	51.5	59.4	60.9	99.2
2. Government purchases re-classified as investment for MEW	15.0	19.3	9.7	18.6	30.6	37.0	50.3
3. Consumer purchases reclassified as investment for MEW							
a. Consumer durables	16.7	11.5	12.3	26.2	35.5	37.9	60.9
b. Education and health	6.5	6.3	9.1	10.4	15.3	19.6	30.1
4. Net foreign investment, NIPA and MEW	1.5	−1.0	−3.8	12.3	3.0	2.2	6.2
5. Gross investment, MEW	80.1	54.1	46.9	119.0	143.8	157.6	246.7
6. Capital consumption, NIPA	20.0	20.0	21.9	18.3	32.5	38.9	54.7
7. Net investment, NIPA	20.4	−2.0	−2.3	33.2	26.9	22.0	44.5
8. Capital consumption, MEW	39.3	53.4	33.6	69.1	67.7	66.2	147.4
9. Change in capital stock, MEW	40.8	0.7	13.3	49.9	76.1	91.4	99.3
10. Growth requirement, MEW	46.1	46.7	65.8	−5.4	63.1	78.9	101.8
11. Net investment, MEW	−5.3	−46.0	−52.5	55.3	13.0	12.5	−2.5

Source (for NIP, see note 6, above):

Line
1   NIP Table 1.2, line 6
2   Table A.1, line 2
3a NIP Table 1.1, line 3, deflated by the consumption deflator
3b NIP Table 2.5, lines 42 plus 93 less 44, all deflated by consumption deflator, NIP Table 8.1, line 2
4   NIP Table 1.2, line 17
5   Sum of lines 1–4
6   NIP Table 1.9, line 2, deflated by fixed investment deflator, NIP Table 8.1, line 7
7   Line 1 minus line 6
8   Line 5 minus line 9
9   Estimated on per annum basis from Table A.3
10 Annual increase in capital stock necessary to keep up with trend growth of labor forces and productivity. See text.
11 Line 8 minus line 10, or line 5 minus sum of lines 9 and 10

the standard neoclassical growth model, with labor-augmenting technical progress and a constant rate of labor force participation, this is also the gross investment necessary to maintain a constant ratio of capital to the effective or augmented labor force and a constant ratio of capital to output. The conventional net investment needed for this purpose we call the growth requirement (Table A.5, line 10). Net MEW investment (line 11) is change in capital stock less the growth requirement.

If NNP is a desirable measure of social income in a stationary economy, sustainable MEW is a natural analogue for a growing economy.[11] Indeed, in the special case of zero population growth and no technological change, sustainable MEW and NNP are identical. NNP, it will be recalled, is the amount of consumption that leaves the capital stock "intact." The reason for keeping *capital* intact in a stationary economy is that the same amount of consumption, in aggregate and per capita, will be available in future years. The reason for keeping the *capital-output ratio* intact in a growing economy is that per capita consumption will grow at the rate of technological progress.

An alternative concept of social income would be sustainable per capita consumption, which will be larger than sustainable MEW when there is technological progress. Per capita consumption can be sustained by technological advance even while the capital-output and capital-labor ratios steadily decline. With a production function that allows factor substitution, today's consumption standard could eventually be produced with a capital-labor ratio asymptotically approaching zero. During this process the marginal productivity of capital would steadily rise. Our proposed measure of social income is more austere and, we believe, more consonant with revealed social preference. We do not observe current generations consuming capital on the grounds that their successors will reap the benefits of technological progress.

A guiding principle for a definition of social income is the following: The social income is that amount of consumption that is consistent with the social valuation of investment at its current opportunity cost in terms of consumption. The social value of giving up an extra dollar of current consumption in favor of capital accumulation is the sum of the resulting increments to future consumption, each discounted by the appropriate social discount rate. When this value exceeds a dollar, investment is less than optimal and consumption should be reduced until

[11] See P. A. Samuelson, "The Evaluation of 'Social Income,'" in F. A. Lutz and D. C. Hague, eds., *The Theory of Capital,* London, Macmillan, 1961.

lowered capital yield and increased social discount rates combine to lower the value of investment to par. Similarly, when the stream of returns from a marginal dollar of investment sums to less than a dollar, current investment is too large and consumption too small. The amount of current consumption at which the marginal social value of investing a dollar at the expense of consumption is precisely a dollar may be regarded as the social income. It follows that the optimal amount of MEW net investment – defined as social income less actual consumption – is zero.

How do sustainable MEW and NNP relate to this principle? Under what conditions will these be the definitions of social income that follow from the valuation principle given above? Sufficient conditions can be presented formally. Let $c(t)$ be consumption per worker at time t and $L(t)$ the size of the work force. We assume that the labor force is a fixed proportion of the population; therefore, $c(t)$ can also be regarded as an index of per capita consumption. The labor force L is growing exponentially at rate n. Labor-augmenting technical progress is occurring at rate γ; so $L(t)e^{\gamma t}$ is the effective labor force, which is growing at rate $g = n + \gamma$. Gross output per worker is $e^{\gamma t}f(k)$, where k is the ratio of capital stock to effective labor force $K/Le^{\gamma t}$ and k' is the rate of change of k. Capital depreciates at the exponential rate δ.

The equation relating consumption, output, capital, and investment at every moment of time is:

$$c(t) = e^{\gamma(t)}\{f[k(t)] - (g + \delta)k(t) - k'(t)\}. \tag{A.1}$$

Consider a feasible and efficient consumption plan: a sequence $c(t)$ for $t \geqq 0$, feasible in the sense that it is consistent with (A.1), given the initial capital stock, $k(0)$, efficient in the sense that it would not be possible to increase any $c(t)$ without diminishing some other $c(t)$. We can then ask: What is the increase in per capita consumption at time θ that can be obtained by a unit reduction of per capita consumption at time 0 – the present – keeping the rest of the plan unchanged?

Let $r(t) = f'[k(t)] - \delta$, the net marginal productivity of capital at time t. Since the population is growing exponentially at rate n, the rates that transform per capita saving and investment today into per capita consumption in the future are $r(t) - n$; that is, a unit reduction of the rate of per capita consumption at time 0 will yield an increase of per capita consumption at time θ of

$$\exp\left\{\int_0^\theta [r(t) - n]dt\right\}$$

if consumption rates at all other times before and after θ are unchanged.[12]

If the consumption plan corresponds to a neoclassical growth equilibrium, k and r are constants and per capita consumption is growing at rate γ. The marginal trade-off of later for earlier consumption is $e^{(r-n)\theta}$ and depends only on the intervening time θ.

We turn now to the other half of the story, the social valuation of increments of future consumption yielded by current saving. Suppose that society's intertemporal preferences, at any current date designated by 0, can be described by a social welfare function,

$$U = \int_0^\infty u[c(t)]e^{-\rho t}dt,$$

where u is the one-period utility of consumption, and ρ is the constant pure rate of time preference at which utility is discounted. Let the one-period utility function be of the form $A + Bc^{1-\alpha}$ so that marginal utility $u'(c) = (1 - \alpha)Bc^{-\alpha}$, where α and $(1 - \alpha)B$ are positive. Furthermore, the elasticity of marginal utility with respect to consumption is $u''c/u' = -\alpha$. Holding U constant, the marginal rate of substitution between per capita consumption rates at θ and 0 is

$$\frac{u'[c(0)]}{u'[c(\theta)]} = \left[\frac{c(0)}{c(\theta)}\right]^{-\alpha} e^{\rho\theta}.$$

Thus the slope of any indifference curve between $c(\theta)$ and $c(0)$ is $-e^{-\rho\theta}$ along the 45° ray and $-e^{(\rho+\alpha\gamma)\theta}$ along the ray $c(\theta) = c(0)e^{\gamma\theta}$ (see Figure A.1).

---

[12] The rate at which incremental saving at time t can increase k, the ratio of capital to effective labor, is $r(t) - g$. Over the interval $(0, \theta)$ continuous reinvestment of the proceeds of incremental saving at time 0 will compound the increase in k to

$$\exp\left\{\int_0^\theta [r(t) - g]dt\right\}.$$

The increase of the aggregate capital stock will then be

$$L(0)e^{g\theta} \cdot \exp\left\{\int_0^\theta [r(t) - g]dt\right\} = L(0) \exp\left[\int_0^\theta r(t)dt\right].$$

This increment can be consumed during a small interval following time θ while leaving subsequent values of $k(t)$ at their original values, so that the initial consumption plan can be executed thereafter. Divided among the population $L(0)e^{n\theta}$ this gives an increment of per capita consumption of

$$\exp\left\{\int_0^\theta [r(t) - n]dt\right\}.$$

FIGURE A.1
Illustration of Balanced Growth as Optimal Consumption Plan
(*ρ = pure rate of social time preference; α = −elasticity of marginal
utility; γ = rate of technological progress*)

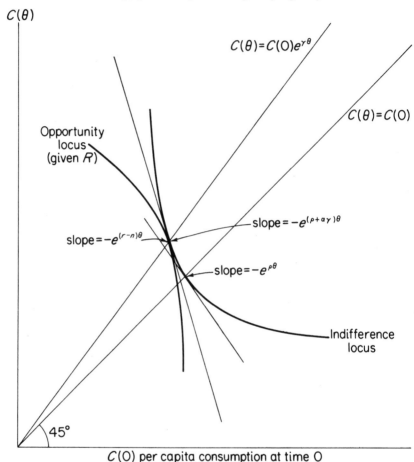

$C(0)$ per capita consumption at time O

Under these assumptions the basic condition that must be met in order that the social valuation of investment equal its cost in current consumption is equality of the two intertemporal substitution rates, the one reflecting production possibilities and the other social preferences. They must be equal for every time interval θ:

$$\left[\frac{c(0)}{c(\theta)}\right]^{-\alpha} e^{\rho\theta} = \exp\left\{\int_0^\theta [r(t) - n]dt\right\}.$$

For a consumption path in equilibrium growth at rate γ, the condition reduces to $e^{(\rho+\alpha\gamma)\theta} = e^{(r-n)\theta}$. This will be true for all θ provided that $\rho + \alpha\gamma = r - n$.

If this condition is met, as illustrated in Figure A.1, the path of sustainable MEW – per capita consumption growing at rate γ – fulfills the basic principle for definition of social income.[13]

In the absence of technological progress and population growth, the condition is simply $\rho = r$. The path of NNP – constant per capita and aggregate consumption – meets the condition that the net marginal productivity of capital equal the pure social rate of time preference.

To summarize, social income is the amount society can consume without shortchanging the future. Thus social income refers to a consumption path along which saving and investment are, according to social valuations of their future yields, just worth their cost in current consumption. Under special conditions this path may be one with per capita consumption growing steadily at the rate of technological progress, and sustainable MEW is then the appropriate measure of social income. In our economy revealed social preference seems to support our inference that the consumption plan is one of ever-growing consumption per capita and our use of social valuations that are consistent with steady growth.

A.3   Imputation for Nonmarket Activities: Time Components of Consumption

Only a fraction of a lifetime is spent in gainful employment, but it is that fraction alone that shows up in output and consumption as ordinarily measured. Leisure and nonmarket work grow steadily in importance, and their omission can bias downward estimates of trends

---

[13] The result can also be derived by explicitly maximizing U with respect to $k'(t)$, given $k(0)$, using (A.1). The first-order conditions are:

$$\int_t^\infty u'[c(v)]e^{\gamma v}\{f'[k(v)] - (g + \delta)\}e^{-\rho(v-t)}dv = e^{\gamma t}u'[c(t)] \text{ for all } t \geq 0.$$

Differentiating this with respect to t gives

$$-u'[c(t)]e^{\gamma t}[r(t) - g]e^{-\rho t} = (\gamma - \rho)e^{(\gamma-\rho)t}u'[c(t)] + e^{(\gamma-\rho)t}u''[c(t)]c'(t).$$

Using $-\alpha = u''c/u'$ we have the general requirement that

$$r(t) - g = \rho - \gamma + \alpha \frac{c'(t)}{c(t)}.$$

An equilibrium growth path will meet this condition if and only if the constant value of k that characterizes it produces a value of r such that $r - n = \rho + \alpha\gamma$.

of per capita consumption. Imputation of the consumption value of leisure and nonmarket work presents severe conceptual and statistical problems. Since the magnitudes are large, differences in resolution of these problems make big differences in overall MEW estimates.

A.3.1 Conceptual Issues. Consider an individual dividing a fixed endowment of time R among gainful employment W, leisure L, and nonmarket productive activity H. From the earnings of his employment he purchases consumption C. Let v_t be the real wage; $v_t p_t^C$, the money wage; and p_t^C, the price of market consumption goods, all for year t. These prices can be observed. Let p_t^L be the price of an hour of the consumption good leisure, and p_t^H the price of an hour's worth of the consumption good produced by home activity. These prices cannot be observed, and this is the source of the problem. Take all base-period prices, v_0, p_0, p_0^c, p_0^L, p_0^H, to be 1.

On the principle that the individual can on the margin exchange leisure or nonmarket activity for market consumption at the money wage $v_t p_t^C$, we can estimate the total money value of his consumption as $v_t p_t^C W_t + v_t p_t^C H_t + v_t p_t^C L_t$. But what did he get for his "money"? The three components of consumption must be "deflated" by the relevant prices p_t^C, p_t^H, p_t^L. This gives an expression for real consumption

$$v_t W_t + \frac{v_t p_t^C}{p_t^H} H_t + \frac{v_t p_t^C}{p_t^L} L_t.$$

Since real consumption at time zero is by definition R, the consumption index is:

$$v_t \frac{W_t}{R} + \frac{v_t p_t^C}{p_t^H} \frac{H_t}{R} + \frac{v_t p_t^C}{p_t^L} \frac{L_t}{R}. \tag{A.2}$$

The basic issue is whether the consumption prices of nonmarket uses of time have (a) risen with wage rates, or (b) risen with the prices of market consumption goods. On the first assumption, an hour not sold on the market is still an hour, the same in 1965 as in 1929. The only gains in consumption that can be credited on this account are the reductions in hours of work. On the second assumption, an hour not sold in the market has increased in consumption value the same as an hour worked, namely, by the increase in the real wage.

In our numerical estimates below we have calculated three variants:

Variant A: $p_t^H = p_t^L = v_t p_t^C$. The index (A.2) is then $1 + (v_t - 1)(W_t/R)$.
Variant B: $p_t^H = p_t^C$; $p_t^L = v_t p_t^C$. The index is $1 + (v_t - 1)[(W_t + H_t)/R]$.
Variant C: $p_t^H = p_t^L = p_t^C$. The index is $1 + (v_t - 1) = v_t$.

Variant A is the most conservative alternative. (C) is the most optimistic alternative.

The essential question is whether nonmarket activities have shared in the technical progress that has raised real wages. If this progress has been time-augmenting, not simply work-augmenting, then the optimistic alternative is correct. But if technology has increased solely the effectiveness of on-the-job work, the pessimistic alternative is correct.

The alternatives can be shown diagrammatically if we confine ourselves to two instead of three uses of time. In Figure A.2, the horizon-

FIGURE A.2

Alternative Interpretations of Welfare Gains Accompanying Wage Increases

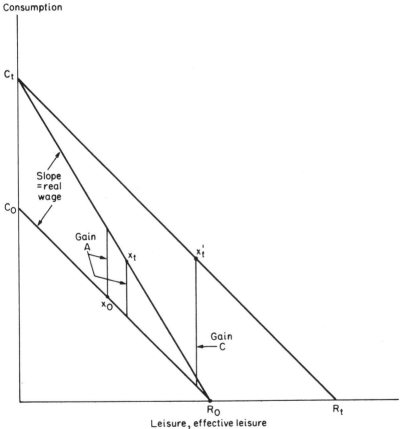

tal axis measures leisure; and the vertical axis, market consumption. The line R_0C_0 represents the opportunity locus in the base period; its slope is -1, on the convention that the base-period real wage is scaled at unity. The point x_0 represents the individual's choice. In period t the real wage has increased to v_t, the slope of the new opportunity locus is R_0C_t, and the selected point is x_t. According to the pessimistic interpretation, the gain in welfare, measured in market consumption, is approximated by the vertical difference between the two lines R_0C_0 and R_0C_t, measured either up from x_0 or down from x_t. The individual's time has not increased, and he gains from the higher real wage only in the degree that he works.

The optimistic interpretation is that technological progress has augmented his time, so that in terms of *effective* leisure and consumption the opportunity locus has shifted outward to R_tC_t. The real wage per effective hour is unchanged, although it has increased in terms of natural hours. The point x_t is, in terms of effective leisure, really x_t'. The increment in welfare is approximated by the vertical difference between the parallel lines R_0C_0 and R_tC_t, and is independent of the amount of time the individual works in either period.

Formally, let the individual maximize $U(v_tW_t, h_tH_t, l_tL_t)$,[14] subject to $W_t + H_t + L_t = R$, where h_t and l_t are augmentation indexes for household production and leisure, with $h_0 = l_0 = 1$. The first-order conditions are $v_tU_1 = h_tU_2 = l_tU_3 = \lambda_t$.

If (W_0, H_0, L_0) is the maximizing decision at time zero and (W_t, H_t, L_t) at time t, what is the measure of the change in welfare? The change in utility can be linearly approximated as

$$U_1(v_tW_t - W_0) + U_2(h_tH_t - H_0) + U_3(l_tL_t - L_0)$$
$$= [U_1(W_t - W_0) + U_2(H_t - H_0) + U_3(L_t - L_0)]$$
$$+ [U_1(v_t - 1)W_t + U_2(h_t - 1)H_t + U_3(l_t - 1)L_t].$$

The first of the two terms is the substitution effect, which is approximately zero because with $v_0 = h_0 = l_0 = 1$, $U_1 = U_2 = U_3 = \lambda_0$ and $W_t + H_t + L_t = W_0 + H_0 + L_0 = R$. The second term is the income effect, the gain in utility we seek. Dividing by U_1, we convert the utility gain into its equivalent in market consumption:

$$(v_t - 1)W_t + (h_t - 1)H_t + (l_t - 1)L_t.$$

[14] We have assumed that work does not enter directly into the utility function. We do not consider complications that may arise if work is a direct source of satisfaction or pain, nor do we see any way to measure the marginal utility of work.

TABLE A.6
Rise in Three Price Indexes, 1929–65

	Ratio: 1965 to 1929	Average Annual Growth Rate
Consumption deflator	1.97	1.9%
Service deflator	2.06	2.0
Wage index	4.65	4.3

Source: NIP Table 8.1 (see note 6, above) and Table A.11 below.

Expressed as a ratio of base-period consumption R, this gives the results cited above: (A) if $h_t = l_t = 1$, (B) if $h_t = v_t$, $l_t = 1$, (C) if $h_t = l_t = v_t$.

Nonmarket activity. Housework is not directly productive of satisfaction, but rather yields a range of end products (meals, healthy children, gardens, etc.). Given the increase in household equipment and consumer durables, it would be surprising if nonmarket activities did not share in at least part of the advances in technologies that have raised productivity in the market economy.

The proper deflation of housework would be a base-weighted price of the bundle of home-produced services. In the absence of such an index, the closest measure is the deflator for the service component of consumption expenditures in the national accounts. This is compared with the total consumption deflator and the wage index in Table A.6.

It is clear that the price deflators for services and for consumption as a whole moved together over this period, while the wage index rose more than twice as fast. Table A.7 gives the growth of price indexes for important categories of consumption related to housework.

Leisure poses a deeper problem. To the extent that time itself is the final good – daydreaming, lounging, resting – then the conservative interpretation is indicated. But if leisure time is one among several inputs into a consumption process, then it may well have been augmented by technological progress embodied in the complementary inputs – television, boats, cars, sports equipment, etc.

A.3.2 Measurement.   We are not aware of any reasonably comprehensive estimates of the use of time over the period 1929–65. Data on the average workweek are available and are used below. Ta-

TABLE A.7
Rise in Prices of Various Household Services, 1929–65

	Ratio: 1965 to 1929	Average Annual Growth Rate
Transportation	2.12	2.1%
Cleaning	2.06	2.0
Domestic service	3.39	3.4
Barbershops	3.03	3.1
Medical care	2.71	2.8
Purchased meals and beverages	2.35	2.4

Source: NIP Table 8.6 (see note 6, above). Note that the index of domestic service is an index of costs rather than a proper price index of output.

ble A.8 gives the results of a large sample survey conducted in 1954. We are doubtful about its reliability, but at present we have no choice but to base our estimates on this survey.

According to this survey leisure time of those surveyed amounted to about 47.6 hours per week for the men and 49.7 hours per week for the women. We will regard personal care and cost of work as instrumental maintenance items and exclude them from consumption. The

TABLE A.8
Use of Time, 1954
(average hours per day, between
6 A.M. to 11 P.M.)

	Men	Women
Gainful work	6.0	1.5
Cost of work	1.4	0.7
Personal care	0.6	0.9
Housework	2.2	6.7
Leisure	6.8	7.1

Note: Leisure includes time at restaurant, tavern; at friend's or relative's home; in games, sports, church; recreation at home; reading; and sleep during this seventeen-hour period.
Source: A Nationwide Study in Living Habits, cited in Sebastian de Grazia, *Of Time, Work, and Leisure,* New York, Twentieth Century Fund, 1962.

TABLE A.9
Principal Occupation of Population, 14 and Over,
Various Years, 1929–65
(*millions of persons*)

	Total Population	Em- ployed	Unem- ployed	Keeping House	School	Other
1929	88.0	47.9	1.5	28.1	6.0	4.5
1935	95.5	42.5	10.6	30.3	6.6	5.5
1945	106.7	64.3	1.0	27.8	4.8	8.8
1947	108.8	59.6	2.4	32.4	6.4	8.0
1954	117.7	64.3	3.6	33.9	6.3	9.6
1958	123.1	66.5	4.7	34.2	7.5	10.2
1965	137.6	74.6	3.5	35.6	11.1	12.8

Source: Economic Report of the President, 1967, Table B-20, for employed and unemployed. Other series from U.S. Department of Commerce, *Statistical Abstract of the United States*, various years; U.S. Department of Commerce, *Historical Statistics of the United States*, various editions. Since series are not always compatible, some adjustments have been made to link them. For 1929 and 1935, the last three columns are estimated from data on female population and employment, school enrollment, and population over 65 years, with the total constrained to equal total population.

important item other than leisure is housework, which takes 46.9 hours a week for women and 15.4 hours per week for men.

Table A.9 makes a breakdown of the population age 14 and over [15] by five time occupations for different years.

Table A.10 estimates the average hours of leisure and nonmarket activity for the five groups of the population described in Table A.9. Table A.11 shows the wage rates applicable to each group.

The general problem of valuation of housework and leisure time was discussed above. In addition, there are some special problems:

Unemployment: In general, time is to be valued at its opportunity cost, the wage rate. Should the unemployed be treated as having zero wage? Clearly this is not the proper treatment for the frictionally or voluntarily unemployed, whose opportunity cost should be close to the market wage rate. On the other hand, during the Great Depression, most unemployed persons could not have obtained work at anywhere near the prevailing wage. Our compromise is to treat unemployment

[15] Why do we exclude children under 14? Because the market value of their time is very low, not because we undervalue the joys of childhood.

TABLE A.10
Hours of Leisure and Nonmarket Work, Persons Over 14,
Various Years, 1929–65
(hours per week)

	Employed and Unemployed			Keeping House			School			Other		
	L	NM	Tot	L	NM	Tot	L	NM	Tot	L	NM	Tot
1929	39.4	15.4	54.8	49.7	46.9	96.6	50	13	63	50	10	60
1935	45.5	15.4	60.9	49.7	46.9	96.6	50	13	63	50	10	60
1945	43.1	15.4	58.5	49.7	46.9	96.6	50	13	63	50	10	60
1947	45.7	15.4	61.1	49.7	46.9	96.6	50	13	63	50	10	60
1954	47.6	15.4	63.0	49.7	46.9	96.6	50	13	63	50	10	60
1958	48.6	15.4	64.0	49.7	46.9	96.6	50	13	63	50	10	60
1965	48.1	15.4	63.5	49.7	46.9	96.6	50	13	63	50	10	60

L = leisure hours.
NM = nonmarket hours.
Tot = total hours.
Source: Hours of leisure are obtained by using the benchmark estimates for 1954 and then making estimates using data on average hours worked for other years. Thus the number of leisure hours for any year is obtained by subtracting from 47.6 (the number of hours of leisure for 1954) the difference in hours between the reference year and 1954. Hours data from John W. Kendrick, *Productivity Trends in the United States,* Princeton for NBER, 1961, Table A-X and A-VI. It is assumed that unemployed workers had the same number of hours of leisure and nonmarket work as employed workers. Further, it is assumed that nonmarket activity has stayed the same since 1929. Those keeping house were assumed to have no change from the total number of hours available in 1954 (96.6 per week). Arbitrary numbers were chosen for students and other persons.

as involuntary and thus assign a zero price to the normal working hours of the unemployed. On the other hand, we continue to value their leisure time at the going wage.[16]

Keeping house: The majority of those keeping house are women, and we thus choose the average hourly earnings for women as the proper valuation.

School: Since those in school are primarily under age 20, we use the wage for that age group as the proper valuation of school time.

[16] An alternate imputation is to value *all* time of unemployed workers at zero. For the depression year 1935, this lowers our final estimate of MEW (B variant) by 10 per cent. It makes very little difference for movements over the entire period.

TABLE A.11
Manufacturing Wage Rate and Wage Rate for Different Groups
in Population, Various Years, 1929–65
(current dollars per hour)

Year	Em- ployed	Unem- ployed	Females	Under 20 Years Old	Over 65 Years Old	Wage Index (1958 = 1.00)
1929	0.56	0.56	0.34	0.19	0.49	0.2654
1935	0.54	0.54	0.32	0.18	0.47	0.2559
1945	1.016	1.016	0.61	0.35	0.89	0.4815
1947	1.217	1.217	0.73	0.42	1.06	0.5768
1954	1.78	1.78	1.07	0.61	1.55	0.8436
1958	2.11	2.11	1.27	0.72	1.84	1.000
1965	2.61	2.61	1.57	0.89	2.28	1.237

Source: Basic wage data from *Economic Report of the President* and *Historical Statistics of the United States.* The basic figure is average hourly earnings in manufacturing, which is the only series available back to 1929. (This differs slightly but not appreciably from the ratio of total labor income to Kendrick's man-hour estimate.) Wage rates for females, and for those in the labor force who are under 20 or over 65 years old are calculated as a fraction of the manufacturing wage rate (these numbers being 0.58, 0.34, and 0.81). The data used to calculate the fractions are median incomes of persons who are year-round, full-time workers. Thus the ratio of median incomes of females to males is 4,560/7,814 = 0.58. (Data given in U.S. Department of Commerce, *Current Population Reports, Consumer Income,* Series P-60, No. 66, December 23, 1969, p. 90.)

The wage index is constructed from the data for employed workers with 1958 as the base.

"Other": The final category is "other persons," primarily retired. For this group, we choose the wage rate for persons over 65.

Finally in Table A.12 we calculate the total value of leisure, non-market activity, and the sum which we call the "time component" of MEW. Column 1 of Table A.12 gives the current dollar value of the three series. For the reasons given above, two alternative constant-dollar values are calculated for both leisure and nonmarket activity, one using the wage rate as deflator, the other using the consumption price index. Column 2 of Table A.12 shows the result if price deflation is used, while column 3 shows the result of using the wage deflator.

We feel that price deflation is probably superior for nonmarket activity, but that for leisure there is no general presumption. We have, therefore, proceeded with the three variants shown in Table A.12.

TABLE A.12
Value of Leisure and Nonmarket Activity,
Various Years, 1929–65
(billions of dollars)

	Current Prices (1)	Deflated by Consumption Deflator (2)	Deflated by Wage Rates (3)
A. Leisure			
1929	90.1	162.9	339.5
1935	102.7	231.3	401.3
1945	217.0	331.8	450.7
1947	269.3	345.6	466.9
1954	441.4	477.2	523.2
1958	554.9	554.9	554.9
1965	775.5	712.8	626.9
B. Nonmarket Activity			
1929	47.4	85.7	178.6
1935	48.5	109.2	189.5
1945	99.7	152.4	207.1
1947	124.3	159.6	215.5
1954	195.6	211.5	231.9
1958	239.7	239.7	239.7
1965	321.4	295.4	259.8
C. Total, Time Component			
1929	137.5	248.6	518.1
1935	151.2	340.5	590.8
1945	316.7	484.2	657.8
1947	393.6	505.2	682.4
1954	637.0	688.7	755.1
1958	794.6	794.6	794.6
1965	1,096.9	1,008.2	886.7

Note: Column 1: For each group, total hours per week times total persons times hourly wage rate times 52, and sumed across all groups. Data are from Tables A.9, A.10, and A.11.

Column 2: Column 1 deflated by consumption deflator.

Column 3: Column 1 deflated by index of wage rate (last column of Table A.11).

TABLE
Preferred County Regression of the Logarithm
(*figures in parentheses*

Area	Con-stant (α_0)	Log of Popu-lation (α_1)	Log of Density (α_2)	Migra-tion Rate (α_3)	Log of % Urban Popu-lation (α_4)	Popu-lation Negro (α_5)
Mass., R.I.,	7.9 ‡	0.039 †	−0.020 *	0.00045	0.0595 *	−0.0089
Conn.	(17.1)	(1.89)	(0.92)	(0.24)	(0.93)	(−1.0)
New Mexico	2.85 †	0.093 *	−0.087 *	−0.00079	−0.073 †	−0.031 *
	(1.8)	(0.94)	(1.2)	(−0.58)	(1.5)	(1.0)
New York	7.7 ‡	0.010	0.035 ‡	0.0012 ‡	0.035 †	−0.011 ‡
	(15.3)	(0.65)	(2.98)	(0.25)	(1.3)	(2.9)
Wisconsin	7.74 ‡	−0.036 †	0.091 ‡	0.0029 ‡	0.035 ‡	−0.010
	(15.7)	(1.3)	(3.1)	(2.6)	(3.1)	(0.6)
Indiana	7.15 ‡	−0.0014	0.065 ‡	0.0017 ‡	0.0173 †	−0.0072 †
	(22.7)	(0.06)	(2.7)	(2.4)	(1.7)	(1.5)

NA = not available.
* Significant at 75 per cent confidence level.
† Significant at 90 per cent confidence level.
‡ Significant at 99 per cent confidence level.

Variant A: It is assumed that there has been no technological change in the time component, and deflation is therefore by wage rates.

Variant B: This is a hybrid, in which it is assumed that technological change has been occurring at the average rate for non-market activity, but that no technological change has taken place in leisure. For this variant, leisure is deflated by the wage index, while nonmarket activity is deflated by the consumption deflator.

Variant C: It is assumed that technological change has been occurring at the average rate for leisure and nonmarket activity, and both are therefore deflated by the consumption deflator.

For most of our discussion below and in the text, our preferred variant is B.

A.13
of Median Income on Selected Variables
are t ratios)

Population over 65 (α_6)	Log of Median Years of Schooling (α_7)	Log of Property Tax per Capita (α_8)	Log of Local Expenditures per Capita (α_9)	Observations	R^2	F Test	Mean of Dependent Variable	Standard Error of Estimate	Mean of Median Income per Household
−0.017 (0.021)	0.182 * (0.73)	0.627 ‡ (4.13)	−0.603 ‡ (3.09)	25	.76	5.45	8.72	.061	$6,180
−0.031 * (0.93)	1.86 ‡ (4.21)	0.264 ‡ (1.70)	0.014 (0.035)	22	.91	14.4	8.38	.127	4,614
−0.011 † (1.9)	0.44 ‡ (3.0)	0.17 ‡ (3.6)	−0.22 ‡ (2.9)	62	.85	35.0	8.64	.540	5,761
−0.020 ‡ (2.7)	0.383 ‡ (2.5)	−0.004 (0.061)	0.012 (0.13)	70	.88	49.4	8.46	.074	NA
−0.020 ‡ (4.6)	0.413 ‡ (4.4)	0.114 ‡ (2.2)	−0.038 (0.61)	89	.87	60.6	8.52	.036	NA

A.4 Disamenities and Externalities

In principle those social costs of economic activity that are not internalized as private costs should be subtracted in calculating our measures of economic welfare. The problems of measurement are formidable, and we have been able to do very little toward their solution.

One type of social cost not recorded in the national income accounts is the depletion of per capita stocks of environmental capital. Nonappropriated resources such as water and air are used and valued as if they were free, although reduction in the per capita stocks of these resources diminishes future sustainable consumption. If we had estimates of the value of environmental capital, we could add them to the national wealth estimates of Table A.3 and modify our calculations of MEW net investment accordingly. We have not been able to make this adjustment, but given the size of the other components of wealth, we do not believe it would be significant.

Some unrecorded social costs diminish economic welfare directly rather than through the depletion of environmental capital. The disamenities of urban life come to mind: pollution, litter, congestion, noise, insecurity, buildings and advertisements offensive to taste, etc. Failure to allow for these negative consumption items overstates not only the level but very possibly the growth of consumption. The fraction of the population exposed to these disamenities has increased, and the disamenities themselves may have become worse.

We have attempted to measure indirectly the costs of urbanization. Our measure relies on the assumption that people can still choose residential locations, urban or nonurban, high density or low density. Individuals and families on the margin of locational decisions will, we would expect, require higher incomes to live in densely populated cities than in small towns and rural areas. Urban areas do have higher wage rates and incomes. We interpret this differential as the "disamenity premium" compensating for living in less pleasant surroundings. From the estimated per capita income premium and the locational distribu-

TABLE A.14
Disamenity Estimates

Area	Total Population Effect $(\alpha_1 + \alpha_2)$	Urbanization Effect (α_4)
Massachusetts, Rhode Island, Connecticut	.019	.059
New Mexico	.006	−.073
New York	.045	.035
Wisconsin	.055	.035
Indiana	.064	.017
Disamenity per Unit Change of Income, 1958 Prices		
	1.75 [a]	3.75 [b]

[a] The coefficient is $1.75 of average household income (1958 prices) per 1 million of population: 1.75 = 0.06 (5,421/180.7) (1.0/1.029), where 5,421 = median family income in the sample states, 180.7 is the population of the United States in millions, 1.0 and 1.029 are consumer deflators for 1958 and 1960, respectively, and 0.06 is the elasticity between income and population change.

[b] The coefficient for urbanization is $3.75 of average household income per percentage point rise in average urbanization: 3.75 = 0.04 (5,421/56.2) (1.0/1.029), where 56.2 is average urbanization, 0.04 is the elasticity between income and the urbanization effect, and all the other figures are as described in note a, above.

TABLE A.15
Corrections for Disamenities of Population and Urbanization,
Various Years, 1929–65

	1929	1935	1945	1947	1954	1958	1965
1. Households (no. of mill.)	29.5	32.5	38.9	40.3	46.9	51.0	59.0
2. Disposable personal income per household (1958 prices)	5,105	4,055	5,904	5,409	5,934	6,251	7,389
3. Per cent urbanization	56.2	56.3	58.0	58.6	61.4	62.2	65.1
4. Total population (no. of mill.)	121.8	127.3	140.0	144.1	163.0	174.9	194.6
5. Population density (persons per square mile)	40.3	42.1	46.5	47.9	53.9	57.8	64.4
6. Total correction per household (1958 prices)	425.1	435.1	464.7	474.4	517.2	541.1	586.6
7. Total correction (billions of dollars, 1958 prices)	12.5	14.1	18.1	19.1	24.3	27.6	34.6

Source (for NIP, see note 6, above):

Line

1 *Historical Statistics* and *Statistical Abstract*, various years. Linear interpolation is used to estimate households in noncensus years.
2 Personal disposable income in 1958 prices (NIP Table 2.1) divided by line 1.
3 Same as line 1.
4 *Economic Report of the President, 1968*, Table B-21.
5 Line 4 divided by 3,022,387 square miles.
6 Equals $1.75 times line 4 plus $3.75 times line 3.
7 Equals line 6 times line 1.

tion of the population we can compute an aggregate correction and observe its changes over time.

Urban income differentials also reflect, of course, technological productivity advantages. The uncorrected national accounts claim all the gains in productivity associated with urbanization; our correction removes some of them on the ground that they merely offset disamenities. We would not be justified in cancelling out income differentials which are still inducing migration. We have therefore allowed for observed migration and estimated an equilibrium zero-migration differential. We have also attempted to standardize for other factors affecting locational decision besides density and for other sources of income differences.

Our estimates are based on a single cross section, the 1960 census. Consequently we do not know whether the disamenity premium has

TABLE A.16
Measures of Economic Welfare, Actual and
Sustainable, Various Years, 1929–65
(*billions of dollars, 1958 prices, except lines 14–19, as noted*)

	1929	1935	1945	1947	1954	1958	1965
1 Personal consumption, national income and product accounts	139.6	125.5	183.0	206.3	255.7	290.1	397.7
2 Private instrumental expenditures	−10.3	−9.2	−9.2	−10.9	−16.4	−19.9	−30.9
3 Durable goods purchases	−16.7	−11.5	−12.3	−26.2	−35.5	−37.9	−60.9
4 Other household investment	−6.5	−6.3	−9.1	−10.4	−15.3	−19.6	−30.1
5 Services of consumer capital imputation	24.9	17.8	22.1	26.7	37.2	40.8	62.3
6 Imputation for leisure							
B	339.5	401.3	450.7	466.9	523.2	554.9	626.9
A	339.5	401.3	450.7	466.9	523.2	554.9	626.9
C	162.9	231.3	331.8	345.6	477.2	554.9	712.8
7 Imputation for nonmarket activities							
B	85.7	109.2	152.4	159.6	211.5	239.7	295.4
A	178.6	189.5	207.1	215.5	231.9	239.7	259.8
C	85.7	109.2	152.4	159.6	211.5	239.7	295.4
8 Disamenity correction	−12.5	−14.1	−18.1	−19.1	−24.3	−27.6	−34.6
9 Government consumption	0.3	0.3	0.4	0.5	0.5	0.8	1.2
10 Services of government capital imputation	4.8	6.4	8.9	10.0	11.7	14.0	16.6
11 Total consumption = actual MEW							
B	548.8	619.4	768.8	803.4	948.3	1,035.3	1,243.6
A	641.7	699.7	823.5	859.3	968.7	1,035.3	1,208.0
C	372.2	449.4	649.9	682.1	902.3	1,035.3	1,329.5
12 MEW net investment	−5.3	−46.0	−52.5	55.3	13.0	12.5	−2.5
13 Sustainable MEW							
B	543.5	573.4	716.3	858.7	961.3	1,047.8	1,241.1
A	636.4	653.7	771.0	914.6	981.7	1,047.8	1,205.5
C	366.9	403.4	597.4	737.4	915.3	1,047.8	1,327.0
14 Population (no. of mill.)	121.8	127.3	140.5	144.7	163.0	174.9	194.6

(*continued*)

Table A.16 (concluded)

	1929	1935	1945	1947	1954	1958	1965
Actual MEW per capita							
15 Dollars							
B	4,506	4,866	5,472	5,552	5,818	5,919	6,391
A	5,268	5,496	5,861	5,938	5,943	5,919	6,208
C	3,056	3,530	4,626	4,714	5,536	5,919	6,832
16 Index (1929 = 100)							
B	100.0	108.0	121.4	123.2	129.1	131.4	141.8
A	100.0	104.3	111.3	112.7	112.8	112.4	117.8
C	100.0	115.5	151.4	154.3	181.2	193.7	223.6
Sustainable MEW per capita							
17 Dollars							
B	4,462	4,504	5,098	5,934	5,898	5,991	6,378
A	5,225	5,135	5,488	6,321	6,023	5,991	6,195
C	3,012	3,169	4,252	5,096	5,615	5,991	6,819
18 Index (1929 = 100)							
B	100.0	100.9	114.3	133.0	132.2	134.3	142.9
A	100.0	98.3	105.0	121.0	115.3	114.7	118.6
C	100.0	105.2	141.2	169.2	186.4	198.9	226.4
19 Per capita NNP							
Dollars	1,945	1,205	2,401	2,038	2,305	2,335	2,897
1929 = 100	100.0	78.0	155.4	131.9	149.2	151.1	187.5

Source (for NIP, see note 6, above):

Line
1 NIP Table 1.2, line 2.
2 NIP Table 2.5, line 52 (personal business), plus one-fifth of line 60 (transportation), deflated by consumption deflator, NIP Table 8.1, line 2.
3 NIP Table 1.1, line 3, deflated by consumption deflator, NIP Table 8.1, line 2.
4 NIP Table 2.5, lines 42 plus 93 less 44, all deflated by consumption deflator, NIP Table 8.1, line 2.
5 Table A.4.
6 Table A.12, part A. Variants B and C from column 3; C, from column 2.
7 Table A.12, part B. Variants B and C from column 2; A, from column 2.
8 Table A.15.
9 Table A.1, line 1.
10 Table A.4.
11 Sum of lines 1–10.
12 Table A.5, line 11.
13 Line 10 plus line 11.
14 *Economic Report of the President, 1971*, Table C-21, p. 221.
15 Line 11 divided by line 14.
17 Line 13 divided by line 14.
19 NNP (NIP Table 1.9) divided by GNP deflator (NIP Table 8.1) times population (Table A.15, line 4).

increased over time. We have simply applied the 1960 premium to population distributions 1929–65.

The unit of observation is the county. It was desired to include sparsely populated areas, and this would not be possible with cities or standard metropolitan statistical areas. The basic data are from the U.S. Department of Commerce *City and County Data Book,* 1960. Regressions were run separately across the counties in each of four states, and in three New England states as a unit. This procedure was followed because we thought that pooling across states and regions would introduce additional sources of variation in locational decision and income choice and obscure the density effects we were seeking to estimate.

The regressions are reported in Table A.13. The dependent variable is the log of median family income for the county. The relevant coefficients are α_1, α_2, and α_4, referring to county population, density, and per cent of county population in urban areas. The other regression variables are included to allow for other sources of income differences. Table A.14 summarizes the regression results for the population variables and shows the values used in the MEW calculations carried out in Table A.15.

The disamenity adjustment is not insubstantial: In 1965 it was about 8 per cent of average family disposable income. If the population were completely urbanized, the adjustment would be about one-third of income. But the correction as a fraction of income has not risen since 1929. Although the population has become more urban and more dense, incomes have grown relative to the disamenity differential.

A.5   Estimates of MEW

We now assemble the components of MEW in Table A.16, which is the same as text Table 1. We also show, in Table A.17, a reconciliation of MEW and GNP. In Table A.18, we show growth rates of NNP and of the three variants of MEW-S. These four series are plotted in Figure A.3.

MEW looks quite different from NNP. It is roughly twice as large. Our preferred variant of MEW-S — variant B, which deflates nonmarket activity by the consumption price index and leisure by the wage rate — has grown somewhat more slowly than NNP: 2.3 per cent per annum compared with 3.0 per cent. The more optimistic variant C has risen faster than NNP. Even the most conservative estimate of MEW-S,

TABLE A.17
Gross National Product and MEW, Various Years, 1929–65
(billions of dollars, 1958 prices)

	1929	1935	1945	1947	1954	1958	1965
1. Gross national product	203.6	169.5	355.2	309.9	407.0	447.3	617.8
2. Capital consumption, NIPA	−20.0	−20.0	−21.9	−18.3	−32.5	−38.9	−54.7
3. Net national product, NIPA	183.6	149.5	333.3	291.6	374.5	408.4	563.1
4. NIPA final output reclassified as regrettables and intermediates							
a. Government	−6.7	−7.4	−146.3	−20.8	−57.8	−56.4	−63.2
b. Private	−10.3	−9.2	−9.2	−10.9	−16.4	−19.9	−30.9
5. Imputations for items not included in NIPA							
a. Leisure	339.5	401.3	450.7	466.9	523.2	554.9	626.9
b. Nonmarket activity	85.7	109.2	152.4	159.6	211.5	239.7	295.4
c. Disamenities	−12.5	−14.1	−18.1	−19.1	−24.3	−27.6	−34.6
d. Services of public and private capital	29.7	24.2	31.0	36.7	48.9	54.8	78.9
6. Additional capital consumption	−19.3	−33.4	−11.7	−50.8	−35.2	−27.3	−92.7
7. Growth requirement	−46.1	−46.7	−65.8	+5.4	−63.1	−78.9	−101.8
8. Sustainable MEW	543.6	573.4	716.3	858.6	961.3	1,047.7	1,241.1

Source (for NIP, see note 6, above):

Line
1 NIP Table 1.2, line 1.
2 Table A.5, line 6.
3 Line 1 minus line 2.
4a Table A.1, line 3 plus line 4.
4b Table A.16, line 2.
5a Table A.16, line 6.
5b Table A.16, line 7.
5c Table A.16, line 8.
5d Table A.4.
6 Table A.5, line 9 minus line 6.
7 Table A.5, line 10.
8 Sum of lines 3–7; equals Table A.16, line 13.

414

TABLE A.18
Rates of Growth of NNP and of Sustainable MEW,
Various Periods, 1929–65
(*average compound growth rate, per cent per year*)

	1929–47	1947–65	1929–65
Total			
NNP	2.6	3.6	3.1
MEW variant			
A	2.1	1.5	1.8
B	2.6	2.0	2.3
C	4.0	3.3	3.6
Per capita			
NNP	1.4	2.0	1.7
MEW variant			
A	1.1	−0.1	0.5
B	1.6	0.4	1.0
C	2.3	1.6	2.3
Population	0.96	1.65	1.3

Source: Tables A.16 and A.17.

variant A, shows progress, though only at a rate of 0.5 per cent per year.

The modifications of the national accounts which make the most difference are the omissions of regrettables and the imputations for leisure and nonmarket work.

The net MEW investment rate was negative before the Second World War and mainly positive since. Since 1945 sustainable MEW has, in the main, exceeded actual MEW (Figure A.4). We have been investing enough to move the economy to a higher consumption path.

A.6 Reliability of the Estimates

In national accounting, reliability cannot be calculated like statistical sampling error but only judged, for the most part subjectively, by those familiar with the data and the adjustments made in them. We have attempted to estimate very roughly the reliability of our measure of MEW and of its components. These judgments are presented in Table A.19.

FIGURE A.3
Per Capita Net National Product (NNP) and Per Capita Sustainable
MEW, 1929–65
(*1958 prices*)

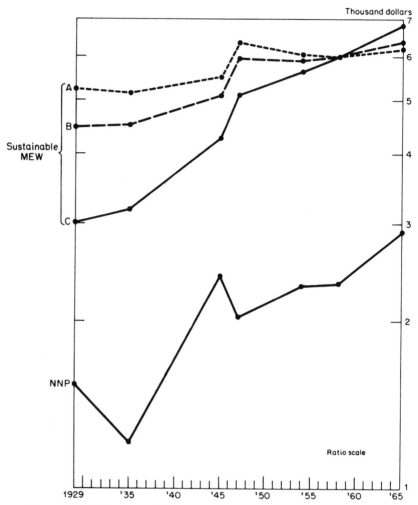

Source: See Table A.16 and lines 17 and 19.

FIGURE A.4
Per Capita Net National Product (NNP) and Per Capita Actual MEW,
1929–65
(*1958 prices*)

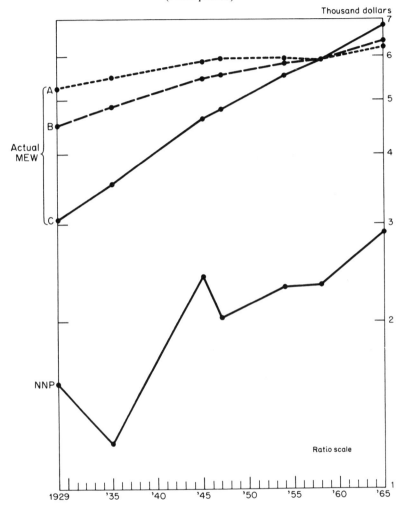

Source: See Table A.16, lines 15 and 19.

TABLE A.19
Reliability of the Estimates of MEW

Item	Reliability
Consumption expenditures in national accounts	low error
Corrections for	
Instrumental expenditures	medium error
Capital consumption	high error
Growth requirement	high error
MEW net investment	very high error
Imputations for	
Capital services	high error
Leisure	very high error
Nonmarket activity	very high error
Disamenity	very high error
Totals	
GNP	low error
MEW	
Excluding time component	medium error
With time component	high error

Source: Authors' judgment.

We have used as a benchmark the reliability of the gross national product estimates, which we call (for reference) "low error." [17] An item with "medium error" is one with a percentage error we feel to be about twice the percentage error of the GNP. "High error" is about five times the percentage error of GNP. "Very high error" is about ten times the percentage error of GNP.

The sources of unreliability lie both in the data (especially in the case of the time components of MEW) and in the concepts used (such as the proper deflator for leisure or the proper regression for calculating the disamenity premium). There are no independent estimates of comparable totals, as is sometimes the case in the income and product accounts. Totals therefore have all the unreliabilities that their components in combination contribute.

[17] Although no official estimate of the unreliability of GNP exists in the United States, the official estimate in the United Kingdom is that three percentage points either way includes a 90 per cent confidence interval. (See Rita Maurice, ed., *National Accounts Statistics, Sources and Methods,* London, Central Statistical Office, 1969, pp. 42 and 52.)

We must in all candor recognize that in moving away from the conventional accounting framework, we must accept sizable losses in the precision of the estimates.

APPENDIX B: NATURAL RESOURCES

B.1 The Role of Natural Resources in Economic Growth

In this appendix we consider the importance of natural resources in measured economic growth. In comparison with the usual neoclassical growth model, the laws of production are more complex. There are not simply constant returns to scale in capital and labor. The easiest way to view the problem is to assume a constant-returns-to-scale aggregate production function of the form

$$Y = F(A_K K, A_L L, A_R R) \qquad (B.1)$$

where Y is output, and K, L, and R are the services from capital, labor, and natural resources, respectively. All technological change is assumed to be factor-augmenting, and A_i is the augmentation level of factor i.

In general, resources might be renewable and augmentable, like capital, or exhaustible, like stocks of minerals. But we shall confine ourselves to the case typified by "land," where the stock is constant — neither augmentable nor destructible — and the services are proportional to the stock.

We can take the logarithmic derivative of (B.1) to obtain:

$$\hat{Y} = \xi_K(\hat{A}_K + \hat{K}) + \xi_L(\hat{A}_L + \hat{L}) + \xi_R(\hat{A}_R + \hat{R}) \qquad (B.2)$$

where hats over variables represent proportional rates of growth, and ξ_i is the elasticity of output with respect to factor i.

Since our main interest is the movement of per capita quantities, we define y as per capita income Y/L, k as capital per head K/L, and r as land per head R/L. From (B.2) we derive

$$\hat{y} = \hat{Y} - \hat{L} = \hat{A} + \xi_K(\hat{K} - \hat{L}) + \xi_R(\hat{R} - \hat{L}) + (\xi_K + \xi_R + \xi_L - 1)\hat{L}$$

where $\hat{A} = \hat{A}_K \xi_K + \hat{A}_L \xi_L + \hat{A}_R \xi_R$.

On the assumption of constant returns to scale, the sum of the elasticities of the three factors is unity. If $\hat{L}$ is the constant n, then $\hat{r} = \hat{R} - \hat{L} = -n$, and we have

$$\hat{y} = \hat{A} + \xi_K \hat{k} - \xi_R n, \qquad (B.3)$$

and

$$\hat{k} = (sy/k) - n. \tag{B.4}$$

The production function (B.1) can be converted to the intensive form

$$y = A_L f(a_k k, a_r r) = A_L F(A_K K/A_L L, 1, A_R R/A_L L).$$

Balanced growth could occur with constant elasticities ξ_i, constant rates of technical progress, and a constant capital-output ratio k/y. The balanced growth rate is obtained by letting $\hat{k} = \hat{y}$ in (B.3). It is $(\hat{A} - \xi_R n)/(1 - \xi_K)$. The drag due to resource limitation is indicated by the second term in the numerator, as well as by the possibility that ξ_K is smaller than it would be in a two-factor economy.

The share of natural resource owners in national income appears to have fallen over time. This trend is not compatible with balanced growth, and there are several possible interpretations of it. One is the following combination of circumstances: The elasticity of substitution resources for the other two factors taken jointly is greater than 1, and the *effective* quantity of resources per effective worker, $a_r r$, is declining. This implies that the elasticity of output with respect to resources, ξ_R, is falling, and therefore that the drag on growth is progressively diminishing.

A second interpretation is quite the opposite: The elasticity of substitution is less than 1, but effective resources per effective worker are growing, thanks to the speed of resource-augmenting progress.

A third possible mechanism is a shift in demand away from resource-intensive goods, as a result either of income or of price effects. This mechanism cannot be easily described in a one-sector aggregative model. But price-induced shifts of demand are similar in effect to price-induced shifts of factor proportions. A high elasticity of substitution will lower the income shares of resource owners. Inelasticity of demand for resource-intensive products with respect to income growth has the same qualitative effects as rapid land-augmenting progress.

To the central question—How important are natural resources in measured growth?—we seem to get an unambiguous answer: less important than they were. Table B.1, from Denison, indicates that the share of land declined from about 9 per cent to 3 per cent from 1900 to 1950.[18] Denison concludes that while land slowed down the growth rate 0.11 per cent per annum for the period 1909–29, this drag was only

[18] *Sources*, p. 30.

TABLE B.1
Shares of Factors in National Income, Various Periods, 1909–58

Period	National Income	Labor	Land	Total	Reproducible Capital Goods				
					Nonfarm Residential Structures	Other Structures and Equipment	Inventories	U.S. Holdings of Private Assets Abroad	Less: Foreign Holdings of U.S. Private Assets
1909–13	100.0	69.5	8.9	21.6	3.3	13.9	4.6	0.4	.6
1914–18	100.0	67.0	8.8	24.2	3.5	15.3	5.3	0.4	.3
1919–23	100.0	69.5	7.0	23.5	3.4	14.8	4.7	0.8	.2
1924–28	100.0	69.7	6.4	23.9	4.3	14.6	4.3	0.9	.2
1929–33 [a]	100.0	69.2	6.2	24.6	4.5	15.3	4.2	1.0	.4
1934–38 [a]	100.0	70.4	5.6	24.0	3.6	15.6	4.3	0.8	.3
1939–43 [a]	100.0	72.1	4.9	23.0	2.8	15.5	4.3	0.6	.2
1944–48 [a]	100.0	74.9	4.0	21.1	2.2	14.6	3.9	0.5	.1
1949–53	100.0	74.5	3.4	22.1	2.5	15.4	3.8	0.5	.1
1954–58	100.0	77.3	3.0	19.7	3.0	13.1	3.0	0.7	.1
1909–58 [a]	100.0	71.4	5.8	22.8	3.3	14.9	4.2	0.6	.2
1909–29	100.0	68.9	7.7	23.4	3.7	14.6	4.8	0.6	.3
1929–58 [a]	100.0	73.0	4.5	22.5	3.1	15.0	3.9	0.7	.2

Source: Reproduced from Denison, *Sources,* p. 30.

[a] For 1930 through 1940 and 1942 through 1946 these represent interpolated distributions, not the actual distribution for those dates. See text.

0.05 per cent for 1929–57 and would fall slightly more for the next twenty years.[19] In subsequent work, Denison has also examined the extent to which differences in supplies of land and natural resources can account for differences in productivity and growth between the United States and Western European countries. He finds the differences negligible.[20]

A closer look at specific products which are resource-intensive confirms the general suspicion that resources have not been a drag. In a careful study of the relative costs and prices of major categories of

[19] *Ibid.,* p. 270.
[20] See Edward F. Denison, *Why Growth Rates Differ,* Washington, D.C., Brookings, 1967, Chap. 14. The difference ranges between 0.5 and 0.6 per cent of per capita national income.

421

resource-intensive goods, Barnett and Morse conclude that, with the exception of forestry products, none appears to have become relatively more scarce than goods in general.[21] They examine reasons for this paradox and show that the most important reason is pervasive technological change. Moreover, in those resource-using industries where technology has not come to the rescue of scarcity, substitution of other goods has been significant (substitution away from lead and zinc, from forestry products, from animal power in agriculture).[22]

B.2 Simulations of Three-Factor Production Functions

Our brief review of historical tendencies in resource industries has led us to conclude tentatively that natural resources have not become an increasing drag on economic growth. One possible explanation for this result is that technology allows ample means for substituting away from increasingly scarce natural resources.

In an attempt to make this speculation more concrete, we have studied several three-factor aggregate production functions. Although two-factor (labor-capital) production functions have been widely studied, there does not appear to be comparable work on three-factor (labor-capital-land) functions. Moreover, the only analytical results available are for production functions with constant partial elasticities of substitution between different factors. Consequently, our first step was to examine different functional forms and parameter combinations to see which seemed to exhibit plausible behavior. The final choice between the simulations was on the basis of a comparison of the simulated results with the "revised stylized facts" of growth reviewed above.

B.2.1 Parameters.   Four functional forms were tested:

$$Y = [\alpha_1(A_K K)^{-\rho} + \alpha_2(A_L L)^{-\rho} + \alpha_3(A_R R)^{-\rho}]^{-1/\rho} \qquad \text{(PF1)}$$

$$Y = \{\alpha_1[(A_K K)^{1/4}(A_L L)^{3/4}]^{-\rho} + \alpha_2(A_R R)^{-\rho}\}^{-1/\rho} \qquad \text{(PF2)}$$

$$Y = (\alpha_1\{[\beta_1(A_K K)^{1/2} + \beta_2(A_L L)^{1/2}]^{1/2}\}^{-\rho} + \alpha_2(A_R R)^{-\rho})^{-1/\rho} \qquad \text{(PF3)}$$

$$Y = (\alpha_1\{[\beta_1(A_K K)^{-1} + \beta_2(A_L L)^{-1}]^{-1}\}^{-\rho} + \alpha_2(A_R R)^{-\rho})^{-1/\rho} \qquad \text{(PF4)}$$

[21] See Harold J. Barnett and Chandler Morse, *Scarcity and Growth*, Baltimore, Johns Hopkins University Press, 1963, Part III. The other broad sectors were agriculture, extractive industries, and minerals.

[22] "A rough calculation based on Btu's of mineral fuel indicates that if the United States today has to rely upon work animals for its 'horsepower,' the feed would require 15 to 30 times as many acres of cropland as are in use in the country" (*ibid.*, p. 185).

The first one is a general three-factor production function with constant elasticity of substitution (CES). The others are two-stage CES functions, in which production depends on two factors, resources and a capital-labor composite. In PF2 the capital-labor composite is a Cobb-Douglas function of capital and labor, with assumed elasticities of $\frac{1}{4}$ for labor and $\frac{3}{4}$ for capital. In PF3 and PF4 the composite is itself a CES function of the two "neoclassical" factors, with different elasticities of substitution between them. Unlike PF1, the two-stage functions imply a different partial elasticity of substitution between capital and labor from that between resources and the other two inputs.

In summary, the assumed elasticity between (K, L) and R is the same for all four production functions, namely, $1/(1 + \rho)$. The assumed elasticity between K and L is as follows:

PF1	$1/(1 + \rho)$	PF3	2
PF2	1	PF4	1/2

The parameter values tested in simulations were as follows: For ρ, $-9/10$, $-1/2$, $-1/3$, 1. For the rate of labor-augmenting progress, $(g_A)_L$; the rate of capital-augmenting progress, $(g_A)_K$; and the rate of resource-augmenting progress, $(g_A)_R$, the values are 0.0, 0.015, and 0.03.

The numerical specifications were completed with the following parameters: $\alpha_1 = 0.9$; $\alpha_2 = 0.1$; $\beta_1 = 0.25$; $\beta_2 = 0.75$; s = net savings rate $(\Delta K/Y) = 0.1$; g_L = natural growth rate of labor = 0.01; g_R = growth rate of resource input = 0.0. All values were indexed at 100 at time $t = 0$.

Altogether there were 405 specifications, differing in the form of the function (PF1–PF4) and in the numerical values of their parameters. Each case was simulated for 300 "years." The results were compared with the following stylized facts:

Factor shares are labor 0.73; capital, 0.22; resources, 0.05 (Denison, *Sources*).
Capital growth exceeds output growth by 1 per cent per year.
Output growth is 3.5 per cent per year.
The marginal product of capital (MPK) is constant at 0.15.

Simulations were scored by their conformity to these "facts." Two scoring procedures were used.

The first was based on an arbitrarily weighted sum of squared deviations of simulated results from the facts:

$(L$ share $- 0.73)^2 + (K$ share $- 0.22)^2$

$$+ 2(R \text{ share} - 0.05)^2 + 3[(g_K - g_Y) - (-0.01)]^2$$
$$+ 10(g_Y - 0.035)^2 + 0.2(MPK - 0.15)^2. \quad \text{(B.5)}$$

For each simulation, this sum was computed for each period, and its minimum value found. The minimum value was Score I for the simulation. The lower the score, the more acceptable the simulation.

Score II was simply the number of individual criteria met in the year 100 of the simulation, to a maximum of 10 criteria. The criteria were:

> (i) $(g_K - g_Y)$ in $[-0.02, 0.005]$ (B.6)
> (ii) $(g_{MPL} - g_Y)$ in $[-0.01, 0.01]$
> (iii) g_{MPK} in $[0.02, 0.02]$
> (iv) g (share of labor) $\geqq 0$
> (v) share of labor in $[0.6, 0.8]$
> (vi) g (share of K) in $[-0.005, 0.005]$
> (vii) share of K in $[0.15, 0.30]$
> (viii) (share of R) $\leqq 0$
> (ix) share of R in $[0.02, 0.10]$
> (x) g_Y in $[0.03, 0.04]$

Conditions (v), (vii), (ix), (i), and (x) in (B.6) are analogous to the first five terms in (B.5) in that order.

B.2.2 Results.   The two scoring functions are quite consistent. Score I ranged from 0.001183 to more than 3.0. The 51 lowest scores, ranging from 0.001183 to 0.003998, are analyzed below. None of the 405 cases scored 10 on the second test; ten scored 9. All ten of these cases are among the 51 cited above and listed in Table B.2, below. Other summary compilations appear in Table B.3, below.

Two fairly definite conclusions emerge from these simulations. The elasticity of substitution between resources and the capital-labor composite is greater than 1 in all 51 cases. Secondly, the partial elasticity of substitution between K and L is greater than 1 in the top seven cases, and equal to 1 (Cobb-Douglas) in 35 of the next following cases. Only one out of the 102 substitution elasticities in these 51 cases is less than unity.

The findings relating to the rates of labor- and capital-augmenting technical change are somewhat clouded since in the Cobb-Douglas case factor-augmenting change is indistinguishable from Hicks-neutral

TABLE B.2
Fifty-One Best-scoring Simulations

PF	$\sigma_{(K,L),R}$ $= \dfrac{1}{1+\rho}$	$\sigma_{K,L}$	$(g_A)_R$	$(g_A)_K$	$(g_A)_L$	Score I
1	1.5	1.5	0	0	.03	.001183
(1,3)	2	2	0	0	.03	.001250
1	1.5	1.5	.03	0	.03	.001283
3	1.5	2	0	0	.03	.001303
(1,3)	2	2	.015	0	.03	.001325
3	10	2	.015	0	.03	.001344
(1,3)	2	2	.03	0	.03	.001456
2	2	1	.03	0	.03	.001516
1	10	10	0	0	.03	.001531
3	10	2	0	0	.03	.001535
2	1.5	1	.03	0	.03	.001559
2	2	1	0	0	.03	.001634
2	10	1	.03	.03	.015	.001642
2	1.5	1	.015	.03	.015	.001646
2	10	1	.015	.03	.015	.001688
2	10	1	.015	0	.03	.001704
2	1.5	1	0	0	.03	.001719
2	2	1	.015	.03	.015	.001723
2	2	1	.03	.03	.015	.001732
1	10	10	.015	0	.03	.001753
2	2	1	0	.03	.015	.001799
3	1.5	2	.03	0	.03	.001828
2	2	1	.015	0	.03	.001872
2	10	1	0	.03	.015	.001887
2	1.5	1	.03	.015	.03	.001975
2	10	1	0	0	.03	.001994
3	10	2	.03	0	.03	.002125
3	1.5	2	.015	0	.03	.002147
2	10	1	.03	0	.03	.002171
1	1.5	1.5	.015	0	.03	.002208
2	2	1	.03	.015	.03	.002272
2	1.5	1	.015	0	.03	.002285
2	1.5	1	0	.015	.03	.002302
2	1.5	1	0	.03	.015	.002346
2	1.5	1	.015	.015	.015	.002382
1	10	10	.03	0	.03	.002407
2	2	1	.015	.015	.03	.002441
2	1.5	1	.03	.03	.015	.002480

(continued)

425

Table B.2 (concluded)

PF	$\sigma_{(K,L),R}$ $= \dfrac{1}{1+\rho}$	$\sigma_{K,L}$	$(g_A)_R$	$(g_A)_K$	$(g_A)_L$	Score I
2	2	1	.015	.015	.015	.002759
2	2	1	0	.015	.03	.002779
2	10	1	.03	.015	.03	.002795
2	1.5	1	.015	.015	.03	.003123
2	1.5	1	.03	.03	.03	.003155
2	10	1	.015	.015	.03	.003288
2	10	1	.015	.015	.015	.003360
2	1.5	1	0	.015	.015	.003462
2	2	1	0	.015	.015	.003588
4	1.5	0.5	.015	0	.015	.003630
2	1.5	1	.015	0	.015	.003634
2	10	1	0	.015	.015	.003883
2	1.5	1	0	.03	.03	.003907

(separable) technical change. There is, however, some reason to favor an estimate of $(g_A)_L$ of 0.03 and of $(g_A)_K$ of 0.0. Of the sixteen cases in Table B.1 which are not Cobb-Douglas, fifteen have $[(g_A)_K, (g_A)_L] =$ (0, 0.03). In 26 of the 35 Cobb-Douglas cases, $(1/4)(g_A)_K + (3/4)(g_A)_L$ was in the range $[2 - (1/8), 2 - (5/8)]$.

No conclusions are possible regarding the growth rate of resource-augmenting change. In all cases effective resources grow less rapidly than effective capital plus effective labor; therefore, with $\sigma_{(K,L),N}$ greater than unity the share of resources declines. If higher rates of g_R had been chosen, this conclusion might have been reversed.

One final note of interest is that the simulations *did* produce a declining capital-output ratio. Since the "apparent" decline of the capital-output ratio has been a puzzle to analysts, it is of some interest to see how this arises in the present model. As is well known, the capital-output ratio in balanced growth is the ratio of the saving rate to the rate of growth of the exogenous factor (usually labor). In a three-factor model, the composite exogenous factor is the combination of labor and resources, weighted by their relative shares. But inputs of resources are growing more slowly than labor inputs, and the share of resources is declining relative to labor's. Therefore, the growth rate of the composite exogenous factor is speeding up over time and the equilibrium capital-output ratio is falling.

B.2.3   The Next Fifty Years?   Under the assumption that the models which best correspond to the stylized facts will apply to the future, we can draw inferences about the next few decades. All of the best simulations indicate the same trends; the exact numbers given below are from the best Cobb-Douglas case (PF2), which had $\sigma_{(K,L),R} = 2$, and $[(g_A)_R, (g_A)_K, (g_A)_L] = [0.03, 0, 0.03]$, beginning at year 150.

Briefly, very little changes. The K/Y ratio declines slightly (2.53 to 2.52), while shares of capital and labor increase slightly at the expense of resources (0.237 to 0.240, 0.711 to 0.719, 0.052 to 0.041, respectively). The marginal product of capital rises (0.0936 to 0.0952). The growth rate of output rises slightly (0.0397 to 0.0398), while the rate of change of wages (marginal product per natural worker) approaches 0.03 (up from 0.0296 to 0.0297).

B.3   Production Models Including Natural Resources: Econometric Estimates

The simulations described in the last section are quite optimistic about the effects of natural resources on future growth. They imply that growth will accelerate rather than slow down even as natural resources become more scarce in the future. Since the models used there are only suggestive, it is perhaps useful to check the results with a more formal approach.

One of the best simulations was of the following form, PF2: [23]

$$Y = \{\alpha_1[(A_KK)^\epsilon(A_LL)^{1-\epsilon}]^{-\rho} + \alpha_2(A_RR)^{-\rho}\}^{-1/\rho} \qquad \text{(B.7)}$$

where ϵ was assumed to be $1/4$. In this specification, capital and labor are combined with an elasticity of substitution of 1, while the composite capital-labor factor and natural resources are combined with an elasticity of substitution of $1/(1 + \rho)$. Let us designate the composite factor as:

$$N = K^\epsilon L^{1-\epsilon} e^{ht} \qquad \text{(B.8)}$$

where $h = (g_A)_K\epsilon + (g_A)_L(1 - \epsilon)$.

One way to calculate ρ is as follows. The ratio between the shares of the composite factor and natural resources is:

$$z = \frac{\text{share of } N}{\text{share of } R} = \frac{\alpha_1}{\alpha_2}\left(\frac{R}{N}\right)^\rho e^{\lambda\rho t} \qquad \text{(B.9)}$$

where $\lambda = (g_A)_R - h$.

[23] This form won 15 of the top 24 places on Score I.

TABLE B.3
Distribution of Fifty-one Lowest Scores

By Elasticity of Substitution Between Capital and Labor		By Rates of Factor-Augmenting Technical Change			
$\sigma_{(K,L),R}$	No.	Rate	$(g_A)_R$	$(g_A)_K$	$(g_A)_L$
0.5	0	0	17	26	0
1.5	21	.015	19	14	17
2.0	14	.03	15	11	34
10.0	17				

By Production Function			By Combinations of Rates of Technical Change	
Function	$\sigma_{K,L}$	No.	$(g_A)_R, (g_A)_K, (g_A)_L$	No.
PF1	^{a}	9 ^{b}	(0, 0, .03)	8
PF2	1.0	35	(.015, 0, .03)	8
PF3	2.0	9 ^{b}	(.03, 0, .03)	8
PF4	0.5	1	All others ^{c}	27
				51

^{a} Same as $\sigma_{(K,L),R}$.
^{b} In three cases, PF1 and PF3 are identical.
^{c} Fewer than 4 each.

We use data from Denison for both shares and inputs.[24] These are given in Table B.4. The basic estimation is obtained by taking the logarithms of (B.9).

$$\ln z = A + \rho \left[\ln \left(\frac{N}{R} \right) + \lambda t \right] \qquad (B.10)$$

where A is a constant. N is calculated from (B.8), taking ϵ equal to 0.242 from Table B.1 above.

$$\ln z = 1.797 - .5046 \ln (N/R) - .0319t \qquad R^2 = .9816 \quad (B.11)$$
$$(0.026) \quad (.3486) \qquad\qquad (.0169) \qquad SE = .026$$

This regression implies an elasticity of substitution between neo-classical factors and resources of about 2 and a value of λ of 0.06. It

[24] One should give the usual caveats about the data. The labor and capital figures are probably good, but Denison assumes that inputs of natural resources are constant due to the domination of land in natural resource inputs. Since the nonland component in resources has certainly been rising, we understate the growth of R, and consequently we probably overstate ρ.

TABLE B.4
Factor Inputs
(*1929 = 100;*
in each period, resources equal
100.0 on the 1929 base)

	Capital	Labor
1909–13	57.28	67.58
1914–18	65.48	76.10
1919–23	77.00	79.32
1924–28	90.94	92.12
1929–33	101.60	88.74
1934–38	99.44	95.76
1939–43	106.36	132.06
1944–48	114.28	154.14
1949–53	136.92	160.68
1954–58	162.30	174.40

Source: Denison, *Sources*, pp. 85 and 100.

is consistent with the general impression given by the simulation tests — either the elasticity of substitution is high or technological change is relatively resource-saving or both.

APPENDIX C: POPULATION GROWTH AND SUSTAINABLE CONSUMPTION

Equilibrium or Intrinsic Population Growth

A population is in equilibrium when the number of persons of any given age and sex increases at the same percentage rate year after year. This constant rate is the same for all age-sex classes, and therefore for the aggregate size of the population and for the numbers of births and deaths. In equilibrium the relative age-sex composition of the population remains constant.

Such an equilibrium will generally be reached asymptotically if the fertility and mortality structure of the population remains constant. Mortality structure means the vector of death rates by age and sex. Fertility structure means the vector of male and female births as a proportion of the female population of various ages. The equilibrium rate of growth of a population and its equilibrium age distribution will be different for different fertility and mortality structures.

The net reproduction rate, for a given fertility and mortality structure, is the average number of females who will be born to a female baby during her lifetime. For zero population growth (ZPG) this rate must be 1.000. When it is higher, the equilibrium rate of population growth per year will depend also on how early or late in life the average female gives birth.

In the text three equilibrium populations are compared, one corresponding to the 1960 fertility and mortality structure, one to the 1967 structure, and one to an assumed ZPG structure. The 1960 and 1967 structures were obtained from the U.S. Census. The ZPG estimates use the 1967 mortality structure, and a fertility vector obtained by proportionately scaling down the 1967 vector enough to obtain a net reproduction rate of 1.000. Figure C.1 shows the three vectors of birth rates by age of woman: 1960, 1967, ZPG.

The differences in equilibrium age distribution associated with differences in fertility structure are illustrated in Figures C.2, C.3, and C.4. These figures also show actual age distributions for 1960 and 1967. The differences between actual and equilibrium age distributions are, of course, responsible for the considerable discrepancies between actual and equilibrium rates of population growth.

Finally, Figures C.5, C.6, and C.7, show for each of the three structures (a) the hypothetical "projection" which the population would follow if the fertility-mortality structure remained constant, given the initial disequilibrium, and (b) the "constant rate" equilibrium path to which the projected path would converge.

These calculations make no allowance for net immigration, which amounts to 300,000 to 400,000 persons per year under current legislation.

Life Cycle Saving and Aggregate Wealth

As explained in the text, the effect of a change in the equilibrium rate of population growth on sustainable consumption depends in part on the change in the stock of wealth the society desires to hold relative to its income. We have taken the "life cycle" approach to this problem, as described in Tobin's paper "Life Cycle Saving and Balanced Growth."[25]

[25] In *Ten Economic Studies in the Tradition of Irving Fisher,* ed. William Fellner, New York, Wiley, 1967, pp. 231–56.

FIGURE C.1
Actual U.S. Birth Rates, 1960 and 1967, and Rates Assuming Zero
Population Growth (ZPG)

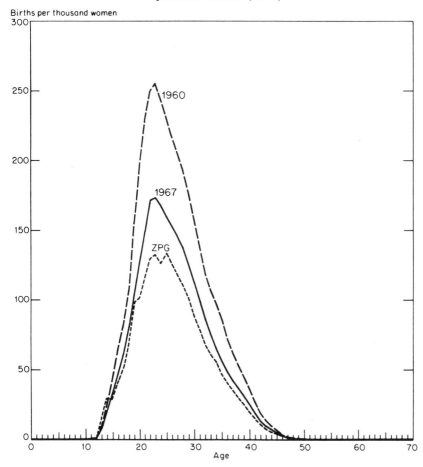

The population is assumed to be in equilibrium, and the calculations have been made for the three fertility-mortality structures already
described: 1960, 1967, ZPG. It is necessary further to group the populations in households. This is done arbitrarily by associating with each
female 18 or older: (a) her pro rata share of the living males two years
older, and (b) all the surviving children ever born to an average female
of her age. Males are children until 20, females until 18; at those ages

FIGURE C.2
Actual 1960 Age Distribution and Equilibrium Distribution of the
U.S. Female Population

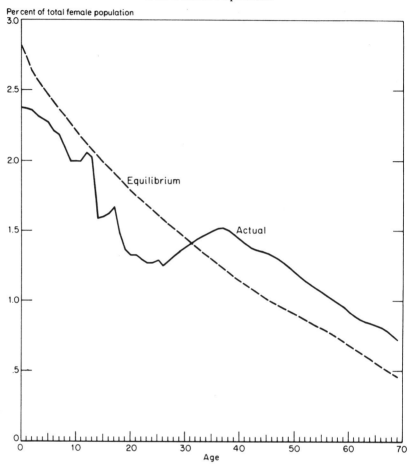

they create new households. Over the life of a household its average size varies as births and deaths occur.

The household's income each year is the sum of the incomes of its various members. These vary with age and sex, according to profiles published by the Census Bureau and based on the Current Population Survey. The 1960 profile was used with the 1960 demographic structure, the 1967 profile with the 1967 and ZPG structures. The whole

FIGURE C.3
Actual 1967 Age Distribution and Equilibrium Distribution of the
U.S. Female Population

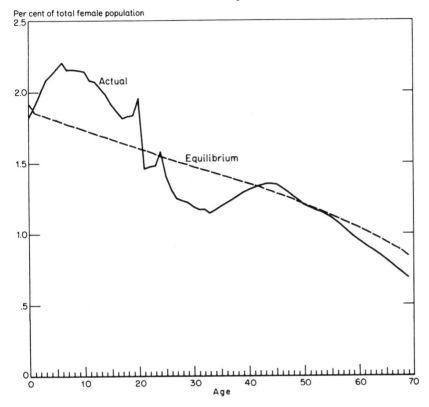

profile is assumed to shift upward at 3 per cent per year, the assumed
rate of increase of productivity due to labor-augmenting technological
progress. Labor inputs of different ages and sexes are assumed to be
perfect substitutes, at rates indicated by the profiles.

Each household is assumed to know its future size, n, its labor income, y and the interest rate, r. Over its lifetime the average household
consumes all of its income, including interest on any savings accumulated along the way. The household spreads its consumption more
evenly than its income, saving in high-income years in order to dissave
in low-income years. The utility, u, of consumption at any time is taken
to be a function of the consumption, c, per surviving equivalent adult

FIGURE C.4
Actual 1967 Age Distribution and ZPG Equilibrium Distribution of
U.S. Female Population

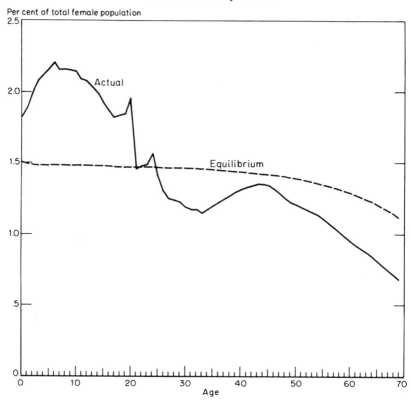

Per cent of total female population

member of the household at that time. The household maximizes over its lifetime the sum of the utilities of this consumption at each age, a, weighted by the expected number of equivalent adult members in the household at that age, $n(a)$, discounted by a subjective rate of time preference, ρ: $\int e^{-\rho a} u[c(a)] n(a) da$, where the limits of integration are from $a = 0$ to $a = A$. This is maximized subject to the budget constraint that expected lifetime income equals expected lifetime consumption:

$$Y = \int e^{-ra} y(a) da = \int e^{-ra} c(a) n(a) da$$

where the integration limits are the same as before and where $y(a)$ is the expected labor income of a household at age a. The calculations

FIGURE C.5
Projected and Equilibrium U.S. Population, 1960 Fertility-Mortality
Structure

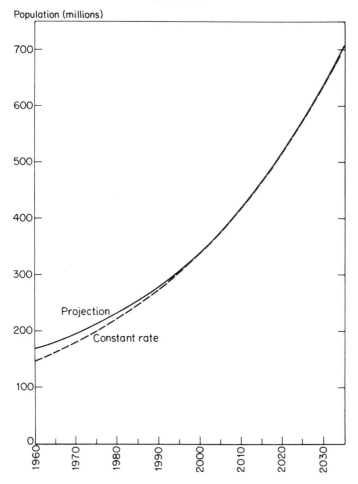

have been made for the specific utility function $u(c) = \ln c$. This leads
to the following rule:

$$c(a) = \frac{e^{(r-\rho)a}Y}{\int e^{-\rho a}n(a)da}$$

where the limits of integration are the same as before; Y is the present
value, at household age 0, of its expected lifetime labor income; and

FIGURE C.6
Projected and Equilibrium U.S. Population, 1967 Fertility-Mortality
Structure

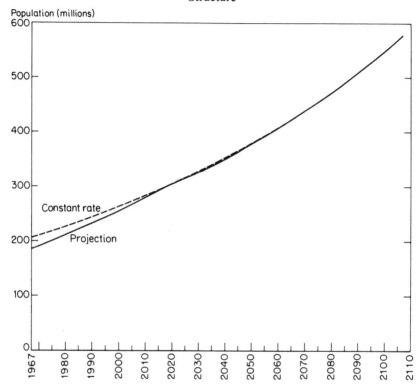

the denominator is the discounted sum of expected equivalent adult years of household life and consumption. If the market and subjective discount rates were equal, the rule says that lifetime income should be spread evenly in consumption, so that consumption per equivalent adult would be constant. To the extent that r exceeds ρ the household is induced to postpone consumption until later in life.

As this exposition makes clear, the household's consumption pattern depends on (a) the way in which its members are counted—the equivalent adult scale, and (b) the subjective discount rate. Calculations have been made for various equivalent adult scales, ranging from counting teenagers and other children as full members to counting them not at all. In one case the parents are diminishing their old-age consumption in order to increase household consumption during the

FIGURE C.7
Projected and Equilibrium U.S. Population for ZPG Fertility-Mortality
Structure

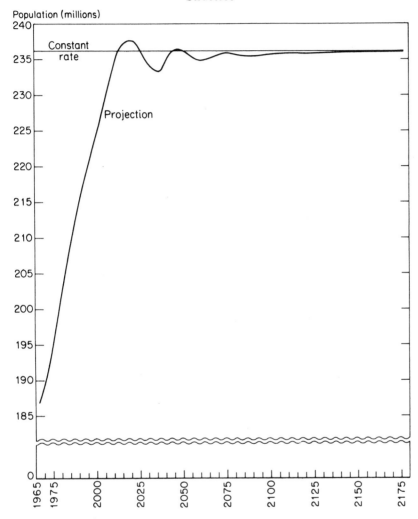

Population (millions)

years children are at home; in the other case they are not. Likewise a
number of values of subjective discount rate have been assumed. Some
of the combinations are shown in text Tables 2–4. For the present purpose, which is to exhibit the effects of changes in the fertility-mortality
structure, the assumed equivalent adult scales and subjective discount

rate matter very little. They would matter if they were thought to vary systematically with the rate of population growth, but there is no reason to expect that.

On the other hand, the response of consumption patterns to market interest rates does matter. It is this response that makes the aggregate wealth-income ratio respond to market interest rates, as illustrated in the upward sloping curves of text Figure 1.

Household consumption planning is assumed to be actuarial. A given cohort of households breaks even over its lifetime. Some households last longer than average, and some dwindle away sooner. Life insurance and annuities enable the excess consumption of some members of a cohort to be met by the excess saving of other members.

Similarly, households are assumed to be able to borrow, as well as lend, at will at the prevailing interest rate, so long as they have expected future labor income to borrow against. This assumption of a perfect capital market has less effect than might have been supposed, because in most cases households have few or no years of negative net worth.

Given the consumption plan of an average household, it is possible to compute at any time the number, the net worth positions, and the income of households of every age. From this the aggregate wealth-income ratio can be computed. Along a path of equilibrium population and economic growth this ratio will be a constant, dependent on the characteristics of the path but unchanging over time. The reasons that it is a constant of this kind are essentially that (a) the lifetime propensity to consume equals unity regardless of the absolute size of income, and (b) all the demographic and economic variables that determine the pattern of consumption of a household over its lifetime, and the age distribution of households and their members, are constant along an equilibrium path.

As indicated in text Tables 4–6, the key economic variable, the interest rate, is identified with the net marginal productivity of capital and depends on the capital-output ratio. Here we have also made the capital-output ratio and the wealth-income ratio identical. This would not be the case if we allowed for accumulation of wealth in forms other than capital.[26] Then the two ratios would differ, but our conclusions about the effects of population growth would not be affected so long as

[26] See James Tobin, "Money and Economic Growth," *Econometrica,* October 1965, pp. 671–84; and Tobin, "Notes on Optimal Monetary Growth," *Journal of Political Economy,* August 1968, pp. 833–59.

the monetary-fiscal policies that determine the difference remained the same.

How does the fertility-mortality structure affect the aggregate wealth-income ratio? The most obvious way is that it determines the equilibrium age distribution. For example, ZPG puts relatively more households in the retirement years, when wealth declines to zero. On the other hand, it also puts more households in the high-wealth years just before retirement, and fewer in the early, low-wealth years. A less obvious effect is the life cycle of household size. With ZPG, there are fewer children to claim consumption as against the retirement consumption of the adults. When children are counted in the consumption plan, therefore, ZPG raises the peak wealth accumulations of middle-aged households. The upshot is, as reported in text Tables 4–6 and Figure 1, that reduction in fertility raises aggregate wealth-income ratios at all interest rates.

REPLY BY NORDHAUS AND TOBIN

DENISON AND USHER

Both Denison and Usher direct their comments to the valuation of leisure. Their emphasis is natural, because difficult conceptual issues are involved and substantial quantitative differences are at stake.

We regard all our quantitative estimates as extremely tentative, and especially the leisure components. To begin with, the data on allocation of time are inadequate. We derived them from a single benchmark survey. What is needed is a periodic sample survey of household uses of time. What is happening to hours spent in preparing meals, laundering, and cleaning; in do-it-yourself repair and construction; in child care; in commuting? Is it really true, as we assumed, that the number of hours in nonmarket productive activity, as distinguished from recreational leisure, has remained constant? Or has the increase in the household capital-labor ratio released time for leisure activities? A careful survey might enable us to distinguish better among leisure, home production, and uses of time that do not contribute to household utility either directly or indirectly.

Even with improved data, difficult conceptual issues will remain. In discussing them here, we will ignore the distinction of our paper between household work and leisure proper and refer to both as "leisure." Incidentally, Denison is incorrect in attributing to us a preference for variant C, our most optimistic procedure. Our expressed preference was for variant B, which assumes that the productivity of work at home has increased with the real wage while the yield of leisure proper has remained constant.

One conceptual issue is how to count leisure in estimating the *absolute* increments of total consumption between two dates. The contribution of leisure is obviously greater if technical progress is assumed to have augmented leisure time (variant C) than if an hour of leisure time is assumed always to be the same hour, no more, no less (variant A). Denison seems to believe it is more likely less than more. Unfortunately no one can marshal arguments much above the level of anecdote and casual empiricism on either side of this debate. Perhaps careful detailed surveys of time allocation, repeated periodically, could enable us to do better.

An even more difficult conceptual issue arises in estimating the *relative* growth of total consumption between two dates. Once we agree on how to estimate the absolute increment in total consumption, we have the numerator. But what is the right denominator? What is the proper estimate of total consumption in the base period? Both Usher and Denison think that the procedures of our paper overstate base-period consumption and therefore understate the rate of growth.

Usher objects to the fact that if, as in variant A, the value of an hour of leisure is assumed not to have increased, inclusion of leisure in a consumption index is almost bound to diminish the estimated rate of increase. This will happen whenever the percentage increase in leisure is smaller than the percentage increase in consumption. The greater the amount of nonwork time assigned to leisure, rather than to maintenance items such as sleep, the more likely is this result. Usher correctly points out that this assignment is arbitrary. His solution is extreme—do not count leisure in base-period income. On the other hand, our estimates of percentage growth in leisure, and in consumption inclusive of leisure, would have been even smaller if we had used 24 hours instead of 18 hours as the day to allocate among welfare-generating activities. We chose 18 hours as the available time simply because this was the way the sample study was designed.

Usher's preferred procedure is to add to the increment in market consumption the value—imputed at the wage rate—of any increase in leisure at the expense of work. We have no quarrel with this estimate of the *absolute increase* in total consumption. But Usher uses only the base-year value of market consumption as the denominator in calculating the *percentage increase* in total consumption. His exclusion of leisure from base-period income is not a procedure that could logically be repeated in successive calculations. Once the year 1950 has been credited with leisure equal to reduction in hours of work since 1929, it is hardly possible to pretend that there was no leisure in 1950 in calculating the relative gain of 1965 over 1950.

Denison also regards our base-period consumption as too large, but for a different reason. He raises the interesting and difficult question of the disutility of work itself, a question we explicitly finessed. The real wage measures the sum of the marginal disutility of work and the marginal utility of leisure, both relative to the marginal utility of market consumption. There is no observed variable that enables us to decompose the real wage into these two components. We explicitly assumed the marginal disutility of work was zero. If it is really positive, then at least part of the market consumption purchased from wages simply offsets the unpleasantness of work, and the net contribution to welfare from working is smaller than wage income. The procedure of our paper, therefore, by exaggerating the value of base-period consumption, understates the percentage growth of welfare.

Denison comes close to asserting that the wage rate represents exclusively the marginal disutility of work, or at least did so in some base year, like 1958. We do not see the empirical basis for this assertion, or for Denison's evident belief that traditional economic theory regards the wage wholly as compensation for the unpleasantness of work rather than for leisure foregone.[1]

We now realize that the estimation of percentage gains and rates of growth is even more arbitrary than we originally understood. We have two unobservable strategic quantities—the rate of augmentation of leisure time, and the marginal disutility of work. Here is the algebra of the problem:

Let R_t, L_t, and W_t be total hours, leisure hours, and work hours, all during period t. Let v_t be the wage rate, and λ_t the leisure-augmentation factor. Take $\lambda_0 = 1$. Note that $R_t = R_0 = R$. In each period the consumer is to maximize, with respect to W_t, his utility $V(v_t W_t, L_t, W_t) = U(v_t W_t, R - W_t, W_t)$. The condition for the maximum at time 0 is:

$$v_0 U_1 - U_2 + U_3 = 0, \text{ or } v_0 = \frac{U_2}{U_1} - \frac{U_3}{U_1}, \tag{1}$$

where U_2/U_1 is the marginal utility of leisure in terms of goods and $-U_3/U_1$ the marginal disutility of work in terms of goods. Here is the linear approximation of the gain in utility, time t compared to base-period 0:

$$\Delta U = U[v_t W_t, (R - W_t)\lambda_t, W_t] - U[v_0 W_0, (R - W_0), W_0]$$
$$= U_1(v_t W_t - v_0 W_0) + U_2[(R - W_t)\lambda_t - (R - W_0)]$$
$$+ U_3(W_t - W_0).$$

[1] Denison goes even further—or one might say further backward in the history of economic thought toward "real cost" doctrine—in suggesting a symmetrical proposition for capital incomes, that they represent compensation for the pain of abstinence, rather than the opportunity cost of current consumption. In this way Denison reaches the conclusion that the net utility value of all production and exchange is zero. Wages just pay for the pain of work, property incomes for the pain of waiting. At least this was so in 1958. Denison intimates that productivity gains may have made positive contributions since then, though he does not discuss the implication that net welfare was negative before 1958.

Some manipulation shows that:

$$\Delta U = U_1 W_t (v_t - v_0) + U_2 (R - W_t)(\lambda_t - 1)$$
$$+ v_0 U_1 (W_t - W_0) - U_2 (W_t - W_0) + U_3 (W_t - W_0).$$

By (1) the last three terms sum to zero. Hence the gain in utility is

$$\Delta U = U_1 W_t (v_t - v_0) + U_2 (R - W_t)(\lambda_t - 1). \tag{2}$$

To convert this into an equivalent amount of market consumption we divide by the marginal utility of such consumption, U_1, and we obtain

$$\frac{\Delta U}{U_1} = W_t(v_t - v_0) + \frac{U_2}{U_1}(R - W_t)(\lambda_t - 1) \tag{3}$$

$$= W_t(v_t - v_0) + \left(v_0 + \frac{U_3}{U_1}\right)(R - W_t)(\lambda_t - 1).$$

Now we have several cases:

a. No Augmentation of Leisure; No Marginal Disutility of Work. Then (3) becomes:

$$\frac{\Delta U}{U_1} = W_t(v_t - v_0). \tag{3a}$$

The denominator, base-period consumption, inclusive of leisure, is unambiguously the equivalent of Rv_0 of market consumption. Therefore the proportionate gain is, as in our variant A:

$$\frac{W_t}{R} \cdot \frac{v_t - v_0}{v_0}. \tag{4a}$$

b. Augmentation of Leisure; No Marginal Disutility of Work.

$$\frac{\Delta U}{U_1} = W_t(v_t - v_0) + v_0(R - W_t)(\lambda_t - 1), \tag{3b}$$

and the proportionate gain is:

$$\frac{W_t}{R} \cdot \frac{(v_t - v_0)}{v_0} + \frac{(R - W_t)}{R}(\lambda_t - 1). \tag{4b}$$

If $\lambda_t - 1 = (v_t - v_0)/v_0$, we have the result of variant C of our paper. The proportionate increase in welfare is equal to the increase in the real wage rate.

c. No Augmentation of Leisure; Positive Marginal Disutility of Work. The absolute gain, measured in market consumption, is the same as (3a):

$$\frac{\Delta U}{U_1} = W_t(v_t - v_0). \tag{3c}$$

But now it is not obvious what the denominator should be. One candidate, as before, is Rv_0. But another candidate is the "net" consumption:

$$W_0 v_0 + (R - W_0)\frac{U_2}{U_1} + W_0 \frac{U_3}{U_1}$$

$$= W_0 v_0 + (R - W_0)\left(v_0 + \frac{U_3}{U_1}\right) + W_0 \frac{U_3}{U_1} = R\left(v_0 + \frac{U_3}{U_1}\right).$$

The first candidate values all the time available at the market wage of the base period. The second candidate values the time at the *net* wage, i.e., the market wage minus the marginal disutility of work. The first procedure gives the result (4a). The second procedure gives a larger relative gain:

$$\frac{W_t(v_t - v_0)}{R\left(v_0 + \dfrac{U_3}{U_1}\right)}. \tag{4c}$$

d. Augmentation of Leisure, Positive Marginal Disutility of Work.

$$\frac{\Delta U}{U_1} = W_t(v_t - v_0) + \left(v_0 + \frac{U_3}{U_1}\right)(R - W_t)(\lambda_t - 1). \tag{3d}$$

This is smaller than (3b). Thus the assumption of our paper that marginal disutility of work is zero may exaggerate the absolute increment of welfare. Technological progress has the effect of giving the representative consumer additional leisure. He gets it even if he does not reduce his hours of work. How should this extra leisure be valued? The wage rate, used in (3b), overvalues the gift to the extent that the wage is compensation for disutility of work. Indeed, if that is *all* the wage represents, the augmentation of leisure has no value at all.

Moreover, we have the same ambiguity about the denominator as in the previous case. If Rv_0 is used, relative gain is greater than (4a), smaller than (4b). If $R[v_0 + (U_3/U_1)]$ is used, relative gain is

$$\frac{W_t}{R}\left(\frac{v_t - v_0}{v_0 + \dfrac{U_3}{U_1}}\right) + \frac{(R - W_t)}{R}(\lambda_t - 1). \tag{4d}$$

This is the largest of the several estimates. Although the marginal disutility of work scales down the value of the incremental leisure, it scales down the value of base-period time even more.

A summary comparison of alternatives is shown in Table 1. The table shows the value of the growth of welfare for the different assumptions

TABLE 1

Summary of Alternative Measures of Growth
of Consumption Including Leisure

Assumption [a]	Rate of Growth of Welfare	Rank
(4a) (4c-I) } (variant A)	$\dfrac{(v_t - v_0)}{v_0}\dfrac{W_t}{R}$	5
(4b) [b] (variant C)	$\dfrac{v_t - v_0}{v_0}$	2 or 3
(4c) II	$\dfrac{v_t - v_0}{v_0}\left\{\dfrac{W_t v_0}{R[v_0 + (U_3/U_1)]}\right\}$	2 or 3
(4d) [b] I	$\dfrac{v_t - v_0}{v_0}\left[\dfrac{W_t}{R} + \dfrac{v_0 + (U_3/U_1)}{v_0}\cdot\dfrac{R - W_t}{R}\right]$	4
(4d) II	$\dfrac{v_t - v_0}{v_0}\left\{\dfrac{R - W}{R} + \dfrac{W}{R}\left[\dfrac{v_0}{v_0 + (U_3/U_1)}\right]\right\}$	1

[a] Assumption I used the gross wage, thus setting initial consumption at v_0R. Assumption II uses the net wage, with consumption being $R[v_0 + (U_3/U_1)]$.
[b] Assumes rate of augmentation, λ, is equal to rate of growth of real wage rate, v.

discussed above and shows how the magnitudes are ranked (1 showing the most rapid growth, and so forth). Our preferred variant was variant A for leisure, which is indeed the most pessimistic, and variant C for home production. It should be noted that all other variants require knowledge of the marginal disutility of work.

It will be helpful to visualize the two candidates for denominator. Imagine indifference surfaces in three-dimensional space with axes representing work, leisure, and market consumption. Given the constraint on time, the consumer is confined to the plane Work + Leisure = Total hours available. Within this plane he is further constrained by the relationship: Work × Wage = Market consumption. We would like to obtain the market consumption equivalent of the indifference surface he reaches. One procedure is to stay within both constraining planes, and follow the tangent line to the maximum market consumption, obtained by setting leisure equal to zero and work equal to R. This gives the conventional measure, Rv_0. The other procedure is as follows: There is a plane tangent to the attained indifference surface at the chosen point. The plane does not represent choices effectively open to the consumer, since it departs from the clock constraint on leisure and work. Nevertheless we can follow this tangent plane to the market consumption axis, where both work and leisure are hypothetically zero, and read off the height of the intersection. This gives to the denominator the value $R[v_0 + (U_3/U_1)]$. Measuring along an axis which the consumer cannot reach may seem farfetched. But we see no compelling logic in favor of one approximation over the other.

In Figures 1 to 4 we illustrate graphically the four measures just discussed. In Figure 1, E_0 and E_t are the chosen work, leisure, and consumption points in the two periods. N_a is the estimate of the increment of consumption, or the numerator. D_a is the estimate of the equivalent market value of the base-period consumption, the denominator.

In Figure 2, the augmentation of leisure is represented by shifting

FIGURE 1

No Disutility of Work; No Time Augmentation

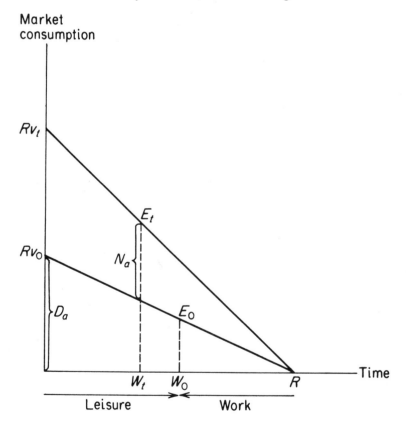

FIGURE 2

No Disutility of Work; Positive Time Augmentation

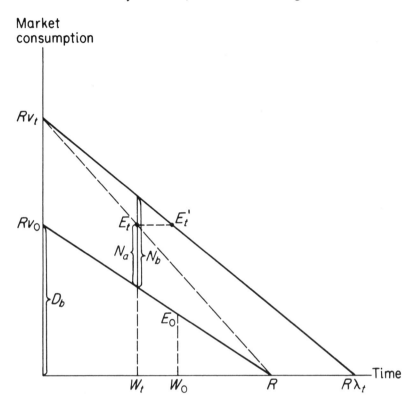

point R out to $R\lambda_t$. The observed point E_t is the equivalent of E'_t in base-period hours. The market consumption value of this augmentation is added to N_a. Therefore, the numerator, N_b, is larger than in Figure 1, while the denominator is the same.

In Figure 3 the dashed curve RA represents the marginal disutility of work (in market consumption units) times the hours of work, $-W(U_3/U_1)$. The slope of a line from R to the dashed curve at $W = W_0$ is the marginal disutility of work in the base period. Subtracting an allowance for this disutility reduces the denominator to D_c.

In Figure 4, the calculation of the denominator follows Figure 3. The augmentation of leisure from point E_t to E'_t is the same as in Figure 2, but in the valuation of this leisure the wage rate used in Figure 2 is diminished by the marginal disutility of labor.

FIGURE 3

Positive Disutility of Work; No Time Augmentation

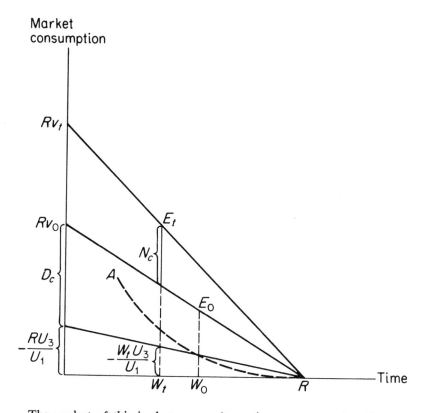

The upshot of this is that many alternative measures of welfare are plausible, and that there is no unambiguous answer to the question, how fast has welfare grown? Nevertheless, until some reasonable method for measuring utility or the disutility of work has been devised, we see no plausible alternative to the variants we presented in the original paper.

FIGURE 4

Positive Disutility of Work; Positive Time Augmentation

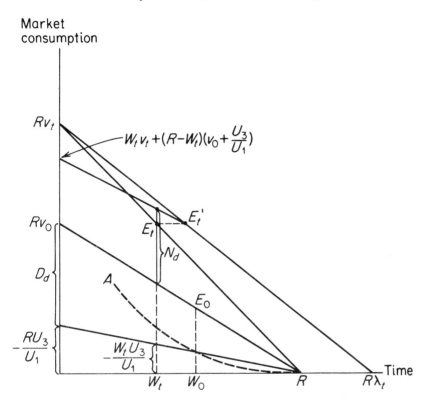

MEYER

John Meyer's comments refer mainly to other aspects of our paper, and call for a separate response. We certainly concur with the main thrust of his remarks, that much remains to be done.

Meyer does make one point on the valuation of leisure, namely, that overvaluation of leisure is responsible for our finding that MEW (variant B) was 8 per cent higher in 1935 than in 1929, a finding which Meyer regards as counter-intuitive. The 22 per cent decline in NNP per capita corresponds better to his impression. We did not, of course, count unemployment as leisure. But we did attribute positive value to time outside normal working hours, for the unemployed as well as the employed. It might be argued that the opportunity cost of time is effectively zero for people who cannot find jobs. We thought it more reasonable to assume that the unemployed would have chosen the normal amounts of work and leisure if they could have found jobs at the prevailing wages. But we stressed in the original paper, and we stress again now, that MEW is designed for secular rather than cyclical comparisons.

Meyer also suggests that allowance should be made for depreciation of human capital during the Depression, nonuser cost, so to speak. We accept in general the point that experience as well as education should be reckoned in human capital. But this cannot affect the NNP-MEW comparison, because neither concept makes such an allowance.

As Meyer points out, the disamenity calculations need to be refined in a number of directions: (1) Cross-sectional regressions should be run for various census dates; the disamenity premium of urban living may have changed. (2) At least some of the variables in the regressions should refer to finer geographical areas than our counties. (3) Nonlinear relationships and threshold effects should be examined. Meyer also suggests that higher incomes in cities may reflect the higher intelligence of urban residents rather than any compensation for disamenities. It would indeed be desirable to add intelligence to the variables we used to control for nongeographical sources of income differentials. The calculations Meyer reports do not tell us whether controlling for intelligence would increase or decrease our disamenity estimates.

Part III
INTERNATIONAL MONETARY ECONOMICS

Adjustment Responsibilities of Surplus and Deficit Countries

JAMES TOBIN

• 1 •

THESE observations concern the conditions for maintaining
fixed exchange parities among the currencies of a group of
countries. I take fixed exchange rates as an assumption,
though it is apparent that some imbalances may be so
extreme and so persistent that the only way out is a change
in parities. Exchange-rate readjustment is, of course, envis-
aged in the Bretton Woods Agreement. But the recent
practices and pronouncements of the major developed
countries, though they do not altogether rule out parity
changes, seem to have established *de facto* a greater fixity of
rates than was originally contemplated. When the deficit
countries are reserve-currency countries, there are special
difficulties in devaluation. And upward revaluation, never
a popular remedy for surplus countries, is apparently even
less popular in the wake of the difficulties associated with
the 1961 revaluations of the Deutsche Mark and the guilder.
The Group-of-Ten (plus) countries seems to be determined
to fashion an international monetary system in which
exchange-rate adjustments would be quite exceptional. It is
useful, therefore, to consider whether, and how, such a system can work, and perhaps to define the exceptional circumstances in which its failure to work makes exchange-rate
adjustment necessary.

• 2 •

I shall also exclude from consideration another adjustment mechanism, very popular in practice if not in doctrine.
This is the use of direct controls, compulsory or voluntary,
on international transactions. After all, the *raison d'être* of
fixed rates is precisely to extend to private transactions

Reprinted by permission from *Maintaining and Restoring Balance in International Payments* by William Fellner, Fritz Machlup, Robert Triffin, et al., Princeton: Princeton
University Press, 1966, pp. 201–211. Copyright © 1966 by Princeton University Press.

across international boundaries the freedom which the countries concerned generally accord to internal transactions. By eliminating major exchange risks, the fixed-rate system is intended to foster, through trade and capital movements, efficient use of the world's productive resources. Protracted or frequent use of direct controls to maintain fixed rates is surely a subversion of ends to means. We must try to construct a system in which this does not happen.

· 3 ·

A group of countries can keep the exchange rates among their currencies unchanged only if they are reasonably compatible—compatible in the objectives of their economic policies, in the battery of instruments they command to achieve their goals, and in the economic circumstances and institutions governing their wages, prices, and interest rates. The absence of such compatibility is the essential reason that fixed parities are generally regarded as impracticable for the world as a whole, including developing as well as developed countries. But it is by no means clear that the objectives, instruments, and institutions of the developed countries themselves—Western Europe, North America, and Japan—are sufficiently compatible.

· 4 ·

The most important question about compatibility is this: Will the pursuit by these countries of their individual objectives for employment and economic growth lead to such widely divergent trends in money wages and prices that exchange rates can be maintained, if at all, only by resort to permanent and progressively restrictive direct controls? I am not sure that the Group of Ten has confronted this question realistically. Collective failure to face up to the question is understandable, because none of the countries individually admits candidly and realistically the problems of reconciling its several economic goals. Full employment and price stability are universally avowed objectives. But the fact is that it is virtually impossible to achieve them both simultane-

202

ously. It is commonly and piously said that the international monetary system and adjustment mechanism should preserve stability in world prices, on average across countries and in the long run. This seems to me a dangerously unrealistic premise, because an adjustment mechanism strong enough to achieve this goal would inflict on each of the participating countries, whenever it was in deficit, severe and protracted unemployment. I do not think the participating countries are in fact prepared to take the consequences, in unemployment, lost production, and interrupted growth, of such an international monetary system. Nor do I think they should.

· 5 ·

It is a fact of life in the developed countries that downward stickiness of prices makes it almost impossible to expect actual price deflation in any country for very long without intolerably high rates of unemployment and excess capacity. It is very difficult, except with severe unemployment, to keep money wages from advancing at a rate at least equal to the long-run trend in labor productivity. In the long run, increases in money wages at a rate faster than productivity rises must normally increase prices.[1]

I do not think we are entitled to expect that "incomes policy" offers an escape from this dilemma. This is discussed in Chapter 13 by Professor Niehans. Experience indicates, I believe, that in free industrial economies incomes policies can at best moderate, but not overcome, the conflict between price stability and full employment.

The implication of this fact of life for the adjustment process should be clear: One major adjustment mechanism involves divergence between deficit and surplus countries in price movements, or in movements of money costs rela-

---

[1] The price level I am referring to relates to value added by economic activity within the country. At times the price of final output may fall because of declining prices of imported raw materials. But the developed countries neither can nor should, as a matter of policy, count on improving their terms of trade with raw-material-producing countries.

203

tive to uniform world market prices for homogeneous commodities. This cannot be expected to take a symmetrical
form—cost and/or price increases in surplus countries balanced by decreases in deficit countries. Rather, it will generally take the form of higher rates of inflation in surplus
countries against lower—and at the lowest, zero—rates of
inflation in deficit countries. This means inevitably that
there will be an upward trend in the average price index
for the group as a whole. Realistically, therefore, the adjustment obligations of surplus and deficit countries, so far as
they relate to prices, will probably have to be expressed in
terms of deviations from a positive trend rather than deviations from zero. It would be desirable for the group of
developed countries to recognize this fact and to consider
frankly the order of magnitude of an acceptable positive
trend.

• 6 •

In this consideration, two relevant factors are worth men-
tioning here. The first, obviously, is the weight which the
group of countries—not just their central banks and finance
ministries—really wish to give to employment and output
relative to the containment of inflation. Obviously, the more
willing the group is, individually and collectively, to sacrifice employment and output, the more moderate will be the
price trend. But, as I argued above, it does no good to set
a less inflationary target than is actually feasible. If this is
done, deficit countries will simply choose exchange controls
in preference to the deflationary consequences to which the
adjustment process would otherwise subject them.

The second concerns the time and finance allowed for
adjustment to imbalances of a structural nature. If little
time and finance are allowed, and if exchange controls are
excluded, then most of the burden of adjustment will take
the form either of severe income deflation and unemployment in the deficit country or of general price and cost
increases in the surplus country. If more generous finance
is available to permit more gradual adjustment, time-con-

204

suming structural processes—shifts in allocation of resources in the countries involved and in the composition of trade among them—can assume some of the burdens that would otherwise fall on inflation and deflation in surplus and deficit countries. Therefore, in the long run, a group of countries will suffer either a higher price trend or a higher average rate of unemployment if rapid adjustments are forced than if slow adjustments are permitted. Indeed, given the floor to price-trend adjustment by deficit countries, speedy adjustments can be accomplished, if at all, only by more inflation in the surplus countries and, on average over the long run, for the group as a whole than if structural adjustment processes and policies are given time to work themselves out.

· 7 ·

The group of countries needs to reach a realistic consensus on the above points, that is, rough targets for employment, growth, and the rate of price increase for the group as a whole. If such a consensus could be reached, it might be possible to define the adjustment obligations of deficit and surplus countries by relation to the rates of utilization and of price change in those countries. The adjustment obligations of surplus and deficit countries should be defined by their circumstances relative to the economic objectives of the group of countries. Responsibilities should be related to measurable circumstances rather than to sources of imbalance. It is rarely possible to assign "blame" for imbalances, and it is a fruitless quest. But in those cases where blame is easily assigned—for example, when a country suffers a payments deficit as a result of policies that produced rapid inflation—obligations implied by circumstances will coincide with those that would be assigned on the basis of "blame."

· 8 ·

An assignment of adjustment obligations carries with it a set of financial rights and duties. If a deficit country has

205

TABLE 1
DEFICIT COUNTRIES

Rate of increase of money costs and/or prices	Rate of unemployment		
	Low	Moderate	High
High	**I** Must take restrictive monetary-fiscal measures regardless of reserve position. Must use own reserves. Low claim to finance.	**II** Must take restrictive measures as a condition of finance.	**III** Normal claim to finance. Should devalue situation persists?
Moderate	**IV** Must take restrictive measures as condition of finance.	**V** Should take fiscal-monetary measures to maintain situation. Normal claim to finance.	**VI** May take expansionary measures. Normal claim to finance.
Low	**VII** Should take fiscal-monetary measures to maintain situation. Normal claim to finance.	**VIII** High claim to finance.	**IX** May take expansionary measures. Entitled to generous finance while promoting structural adjustments.

responsibility for speedy adjustment, it has relatively little claim for assistance in financing its deficits. The country must rely mainly on its own reserves, augmented only by its drawing rights in the IMF. But in other circumstances, the rules may impose on the deficit country no obligation for speedy correction—for example, when slow structural change rather than income deflation is the appropriate

206

TABLE 2

SURPLUS COUNTRIES

Rate of increase money costs and/or prices	Rate of unemployment		
	Low	Moderate	High
High	**I** May take restrictive monetary-fiscal measures. No special obligation to lend surpluses.	**II** May take restrictive measures without special obligation to lend surpluses.	**III** Normal obligation to give finance, the more so if restrictive measures are taken.
Moderate	**IV** Should take fiscal-monetary measures to maintain situation. Normal obligation to give finance.	**V** Should take fiscal-monetary measures to maintain situation. Normal obligation to give finance.	**VI** Must take expansionary measures, or else give abnormally large finance.
Low	**VII** High obligation to give finance. Should revalue if situation persists?	**VIII** Must take expansionary measures, or else give abnormally large finance.	**IX** Must take expansionary measures regardless of reserve position and lend surpluses.

adjustment. Then, by the same token, the country is entitled to receive financing from surplus countries. Similarly, a surplus country whose circumstances oblige it to make speedy adjustment is required meanwhile to lend its surpluses, directly or indirectly, to deficit countries. But a surplus country with no such adjustment obligation would be allowed more latitude to accumulate owned reserves.

· 9 ·

For illustrative purposes, a code is suggested in Tables 1 and 2. Table 1 sets forth schematically the adjustment

207

obligations, and corresponding financial rights and responsibilities, for deficit countries in various circumstances. Table 2 does the same for surplus countries. "Circumstances" are defined by two variables, rates of unemployment and rates of price increase. Each variable is classified in three intervals, although obviously finer distinctions could and perhaps should be made. It would be necessary to specify the period of time (six months? one year?) to which the measures must refer in defining the category into which a country falls, as well as to determine the specific measure to be used. The targets of the group, for unemployment and inflation, would lie in the middle intervals. The rules are intended to achieve these targets in the long run, as individual countries shift between Tables 1 and 2 and between cells.

I do not speculate here on the numerical values of the boundaries between cells, for either unemployment or inflation. As already suggested, this is a matter for high-policy decision. Perhaps these numbers would have to be different for different countries, to take account of differences in geography, tradition, institutions, and statistics. Some countries may wish to operate at higher pressure (lower unemployment, more inflation) than others and at the same time be able to do so without either biasing their balance of payments toward deficit or forcing other countries to miss their own targets. But even if the numbers used to define categories are different for different members of the group, their selection must be a collective decision. Everyone must have the same agreed understanding as to where country X falls at any particular time. If such a collective understanding cannot be reached, it may be doubted that the group constitutes a solid enough community to operate what amounts to a common currency, that is, a system of fixed exchange rates.

· 10 ·

The adjustment obligations suggested in the tables refer to the management of aggregate demand by fiscal and mone-

208

tary policies. Restrictive policies are those that reduce aggregate demand relative to the productive capacity of the economy. Such policies increase unemployment while relieving upward pressure on prices and money costs. Expansionary policies, of course, do the opposite. Restrictive policies are assumed to improve the balance of payments on current account, and expansionary policies to reduce the current-account surplus or increase the current-account deficit. Naturally the links between policy instruments and demand, between demand and unemployment and prices, and between these variables and the balance of payments differ widely among countries. But it must be assumed that each member of the group commands monetary and fiscal instruments adequate to manage total demand and fulfill its adjustment obligations. If, for political, constitutional, or traditional reasons, this assumption is not met by various members of the group, the system cannot work. Members cannot be expected to accept more than their share of adjustment responsibilities simply because they have and can use the requisite tools of policy while their neighbors cannot or do not. This is why, at the beginning of these observations, I included international similarity in command of policy instruments among the prerequisites for operating a fixed-rate system.

· 11 ·

Given the proper direction and dosage of aggregate-demand policy in each country, there remains the question of the proper mixture of monetary and fiscal policies. I will not take up this question here. It is admirably treated in Professor Johnson's paper (Chapter 8). He suggests, among other things, that countries that would fall in cells IX of Tables 1 and 2 in this paper should rely mainly on fiscal policy for achieving the desired effects on internal demand. The question of appropriate monetary-fiscal mixture requires, like the assignment of adjustment obligations, an international consensus. In a world of convertible currencies and mobile capital, national interest rates must be kept in rough alignment. National deviations from the general

209

461

international structure of rates may assist in balance-of-payments adjustment. But private responses to rate differentials may be so large that, if rates are not in line, capital movements are overwhelming. Therefore an important policy question is, what is the appropriate general international level of rates? The growth of the economies of the group of countries may depend on whether their monetary rates of interest are set high, with correspondingly loose fiscal policies, or low, with tight fiscal policies. This decision should not be left, by default, to the decision of those surplus countries with the tightest monetary policies. It should be a coordinated decision by the group as a whole, like the unemployment and price targets discussed above.

· 12 ·

Would a set of rules like those in the tables work? Would the obligations and rights of the several countries mesh with each other, so that imbalances are cured within the time and finance allowed? When a deficit country is entitled to finance, will there be a surplus country that is obligated to provide it? When a surplus country has no obligation to take expansionary measures, is there a deficit country which does have obligations to adjust? Clearly there is no guarantee that these questions can be answered affirmatively. The system must be able to stand temporary incompatibilities. This is indeed the purpose of owned reserves and of central facilities for creating additional owned reserves. Note also that a country would move from one category to another as its circumstances changed, whether as a result of policy measures or because of other events. Thus, for example, a deficit country with high unemployment and a low rate of inflation would cease to qualify for generous international financing with freedom to follow expansionary policies at home once these policies really worked. Still, it is possible that countries may get stuck for extended periods in particular cells where neither surplus nor deficit countries can contribute to the balance-of-payments adjustment without acting counter to the primary economic goals of the

210

country and the group. If surplus countries consistently fall in category VII and deficit countries in category III, exchange-rate readjustments may be the only way out.

211

THE SHORT-RUN MACROECONOMICS OF FLOATING EXCHANGE RATES: AN EXPOSITION

JAMES TOBIN and JORGE BRAGA DE MACEDO

1. Introduction

Egon Sohmen was ahead of his time. During the heyday of Bretton Woods, when floating exchange rates were a thing of the past and international capital movements were still restricted, he began to examine the macroeconomics of open economies with floating rates and capital mobility. His 1958 M.I.T. dissertation, expanded into his *Flexible Exchange Rates* published in 1961 while he was a colleague of one of us at Yale, undertook among other things to compare fixed and floating-rate regimes with respect to an economy's vulnerability to external shocks and with respect to the workings of fiscal and monetary policies. Sohmen anticipated qualitative results that later became standard. His strong support of floating rates was, so far as it depended on macroeconomic grounds, based on his views that floating rates provided greater insulation from external shocks and that monetary policy would be relatively more effective than under fixed parities.[1]

Formal macroeconomic analysis of open economies with capital mobility began with the work of Fleming (1962) and Mundell (1961, 1963, 1964). They extended standard *IS/LM* analysis to open economies and examined the effects of domestic demand-management policies and other shocks, comparing fixed and floating-exchange-rate regimes. For the floating-rate-regime, their analysis implied three strong propositions: (1) A market-determined floating rate would enable a "small" open economy to use domestic monetary policy to control its own macroeconomic outcomes, national output or price or some domestically feasible combination of them. (2) With money stock given, the exchange rate

[1] Sohmen (1961, pp. 83–90 and 123–124). The revised edition, Sohmen (1969), draws on the formal analysis in Sohmen (1967) and Sohmen and Schneeweiss (1969).

Flexible Exchange Rates and the Balance of Payments, edited by John S. Chipman and Charles P. Kindleberger
©North-Holland Publishing Company, 1980

would wholly absorb changes in foreign demand for exports or other shocks to the current external account. In this sense the domestic macro-economy would be "insulated" from external disturbances. (3) Fiscal policy would be impotent as a tool of macroeconomic policy. Indeed any shifts in aggregate domestic demand for goods and services—*IS* shifts—would be, via exchange rate adjustment, completely offset by changes in the external balance on current accounts.

Twenty years of theoretical and empirical research, and six years of experience with floating rates, have raised doubts about these propositions. But they are still widely held.[2] Our purpose in this paper is to review the application of macroeconomic theory to the questions addressed by Fleming and Mundell, and many successors. Our perspective is the same as theirs, the extension of simple short-run macroeconomic models to open economies. We do not consider long-run equilibria or the dynamics of adjustment to them, nor do we treat the formation of expectations of exchange rates and other variables. We do try to provide a more careful, more appropriate, and more general specification of the *IS/LM* model for open economies, and we show that this model does not support the three strong propositions.

The crux of the matter is the modeling of asset markets. There are several related issues:

(1) Omission of the exchange rate from the asset-demand functions is necessary for the three strong propositions. It means that all the mutual adjustments of aggregate demand and the exchange rate must occur within the *IS* equation. That is, exchange-rate movements do not feed through financial markets and interest rates into domestic investment and consumption demand. This assumption, not as sometimes thought perfect substitutability between foreign and domestic assets, is the crucial one. If the exchange rate does not belong in the asset-demand equations, then the strong propositions apply in a Fleming-Mundell-type model even if the interest differential between domestic and foreign assets varies endogenously.

(2) Following traditional practice, Fleming and Mundell took interest rates and asset prices to be determined in markets that equate stock demands to existing stocks. Yet the solution of the model generally implies that stocks are changing, and conclusions about effects of policies and other shocks may be misleading if the changes in stocks are not tracked. This caution applies to domestic assets, capital and government debt, and thus applies to closed-economy models. It could be even more important for the net external position of an open economy, where the flow, the current-account surplus or deficit, may be large relative to the stock.

---

[2] Recent surveys of theoretical developments are in Mussa (1979) and in Myhrman (1976). Other useful references are Branson (1977), Dornbusch (1976), Kouri (1975). Earlier contributions are surveyed in Whitman (1970).

(3) Twenty years ago, the current account was regarded both by practical men and by economists as the locus of exchange-rate determination. Or, if the rate was pegged, the current account was expected to absorb the shocks that would otherwise move the exchange rate. In a world of controls restricting inter-currency capital movements, this was not surprising. Though emphasizing capital mobility, Fleming and Mundell were still in this tradition, thanks to the features of their model just discussed. More recently, analysts of the international monetary scene have discovered that the exchange rate is an asset price, determined by portfolio preferences in markets for asset stocks. This useful insight is overdone if it leads to neglect of the relation between the exchange rate and the current account, as occurs for example in models where domestic and foreign goods are perfect substitutes.[3]

These points are elaborated in Sections 2 and 3 of this paper. We show how exchange rates enter asset-market equations, and what difference their inclusion makes. In the course of the analysis, we also emphasize the macroeconomic importance of export and import elasticities, and of the net creditor or debtor position of the country vis-à-vis the rest of the world. To handle the stock-flow issues mentioned in points (2) and (3) above, we introduce and analyze a discrete-time model with four asset markets. Finally, in Section 4, we depart from the small-country assumption and show how to extend our modeling procedure to a two-country world. Unfortunately, the results of such analysis depend on more restrictions of the behavior equations than are required in the single-country analysis.

2. A standard *IS/LM* model of a small open economy

Suppose there are just three distinct assets available to savers and wealth-owners in a small open economy. Their values in domestic currency and their descriptions are as follows:

H Government-issued base (high-powered) money with zero nominal interest.

$q_V V$ Domestic interest-bearing assets with a market-determined nominal yield r_V. Their aggregate value, in domestic currency, is $q_V(r_V)V$, where the asset valuation q_V is an inverse function of the yield. V includes both the par value of government bonds, all of which we take for convenience to be consols paying the same annual coupon, and equities in the domestic capital stock valued at current commodity prices. Following the usual assumption of the Hicksian

---

[3] An analogous insight is that the commodity price level is an asset price, in the sense that its reciprocal is the real value of money. It is likewise overdone when the next step is to ignore the flow markets for commodities themselves, in which the price level is determined.

IS / LM framework, these are perfect substitutes and must yield the same real rates of return (or one rate of return must be an invariant function of the other).

eF Foreign assets, denominated in foreign currency, and bearing a foreign-currency yield of r_F^* exogenous to our small country. The domestic-currency price of foreign currency is *e*. The domestic-currency yield r_F is r_F^* plus the expected change in the exchange rate, $(\dot{e}/e)_{\text{exp}}$.

Domestic private economic agents must have, individually and in aggregate, non-negative holdings of *H* and *V*. They may have either positive or negative holdings of *F*. The government does not hold any foreign assets or have a foreign debt; it does not intervene in the exchange market. Foreigners do not hold any part of *H* or *V*. We will not consider here changes in expected inflation rates. Thus the nominal rates of interest specified above also stand for real rates.

At any point in time, the net wealth of domestic residents is given by their past savings and past capital gains or losses. Subject to this constraint, they are in portfolio equilibrium, holding the stock of each asset that they desire at prevailing interest rates, prices, and incomes. Likewise, government's total debt in money and consols is determined by the past history of its budget, though the market value of its consols depends endogenously on the current interest rate. By open-market operations the government can change instantaneously the form of its liabilities, buying or selling a $1 consol for q_V high-powered money. The real capital stock is predetermined, but its nominal market value is endogenous and need not be the same as its replacement value. The quantity of foreign assets, positive or negative, is predetermined by the history of current-account surpluses and deficits. The domestic value of this stock depends on the exchange rate, which is endogenous. These predeterminations of stocks do not mean that they are not changing. A government deficit may be increasing *H* or *V* or both, capital investment may be occurring, and the country may be earning or losing foreign assets in trade. But at a point in continuous time, these rates of flow do not affect stocks.

The analysis can be carried out either for the extreme Keynesian case, with price level fixed at least for the moment and with output endogenous, or for the classical case, with price level flexible and output supply-determined. Indeed it can be carried out with any intermediate rule relating price level and national product. Like Fleming and Mundell, we present the analysis for the polar Keynesian case and assume the price level predetermined arbitrarily at 1.[4]

Let domestic private purchases of goods and services, including both con-sumption and investment, be $E(\overset{-}{r_V}, \overset{-}{r_F}, \overset{+}{Y})$ where *Y* is real (and nominal) national product. The signs over the arguments, here and elsewhere in the paper, refer to

---

[4] The formulation of models of this type with *P* rather than *Y* endogenous is described in Tobin and Buiter (1980).

the respective partial derivatives. Let G be government purchases, the quantity to be varied exogenously by fiscal policy. Taxes are, for the purposes of this model, behind the scenes, the $E(\cdot)$ function allows for their influence on private demands. Let $X(\overset{-}{e}, \overline{Y}) + x$ be the export surplus, positive or negative. The shift parameter x is a favorable shock to the export surplus, e.g. an improvement of export demand. If the Bickerdike-Robinson-Metzler condition for successful devaluation is satisfied, $X_e > 0$. The current-account surplus also includes $er_F^* F$, the earnings from foreign investment.

Our rendition for a Fleming-Mundell model is:

(1) $E(\overset{-}{r_V}, \overset{-}{r_F}, \overset{+}{Y}) + G + X(\overset{+}{e}, \overline{Y}) + x = Y$ (*IS* equation)

(2) $A^H(\overset{-}{r_V}, \overset{-}{r_F}, \overset{+}{Y}) = H$ (High-powered money)

(3) $A^V(\overset{+}{r_V}, \overset{-}{r_F}, \overset{?}{Y}) = q_V(r_V)V$ (Domestic interest-bearing assets)

(4) $A^F(\overset{-}{r_V}, \overset{+}{r_F}, \overset{?}{Y}) = eF.$ (Foreign assets)

(5) $H + q_V(r_V)V + eF = H_0 + q_V(r_V)V_0 + eF_0$ (Wealth constraint)

(6) $X(e, Y) + x + er_F^* F = e\dot{F}.$ (Balance of payments)

The A^S ($S = H, V, F$) are demand functions for asset stocks as valued in domestic currency. They are functions of income and interest rates; the indicated signs correspond to the assumption of gross substitutability. These stocks, as equation (5) says, must add up to the current value of home residents' wealth. This depends on the composition, as well as the amount, of their previous accumulations (H_0, V_0, F_0). Discrete instantaneous transactions are allowed between the public and the government in domestic assets at the initiative of the government. Otherwise the public cannot change its holdings without the passage of time. Thus $F = F_0$; by assumption foreigners are not interested in acquiring H or V.

By Walras's law, the sum of the three A^S functions is equal to the sum of the right-hand sides of equations (2), (3) and (4) for any arguments in the functions. One of these equations may be derived from the other two and (5). The system will determine five endogenous variables. For the flexible-exchange-rate regime here analyzed, these can be (r_V, Y, e, V, F) given the exogenous variables (H, $H_0, V_0, F_0 = F, G, x, r_F^*$). Here r_F is tied to r_F^* if exchange-rate expectations are not endogenous.

If V and F were, for domestic wealth-owners, perfect substitutes, then equations (3) and (4) added together become a single equation and r_V and r_F collapse into a single exogenous interest rate. This leaves two asset equations, of which one is redundant. Dropping the combined equation (3) & (4), we see that (2) will determine Y. Given Y so determined, equation (1) determines e. The three strong propositions cited at the beginning follow immediately. Clearly H determines Y, and neither G nor x can affect Y. All demand shocks can do is change the exchange rate. Under our assumptions about the X function, an increase in G or x will lower e, i.e., appreciate the exchange rate. These are the Fleming-Mundell conclusions for perfect substitutability of foreign and domestic assets.

But perfect substitutability is not necessary to obtain these conclusions from system (1)–(6). They still follow if the domestic interest rate r_V can diverge from r_F. Equations (2) and (3)—letting (4) be the redundant asset equation—together determine Y and r_V. Then equation (1) again determines only e, and the conclusions of the preceding paragraph still apply. With $E_Y < 1$, $X + x$ will be larger the higher is Y, and so e will be higher (the currency depreciated) with higher Y.

Monetary policy, all-powerful under floating rates, may be analyzed from the subsystems of equations (2) and (3). An open-market operation that increases H by a dollar diminishes $q_V V$ by a dollar. Thus differentiation of (2) and (3) with respect to H gives:

$$\begin{bmatrix} \overset{-}{A_{r_V}^H} & \overset{+}{A_Y^H} \\ A_{r_V}^V - q'_V\left(\overset{+}{r_V}\right)V & \overset{?}{A_Y^V} \end{bmatrix} \begin{bmatrix} \dfrac{\partial r_V}{\partial H} \\ \dfrac{\partial Y}{\partial H} \end{bmatrix} = \begin{bmatrix} 1 \\ -1 \end{bmatrix}. \qquad (7)$$

We know from Walras's law that $A_{r_V}^H + A_{r_V}^V + A_{r_V}^F = 0$, and the gross-substitutability assumption says that the cross-effects $A_{r_V}^H$ and $A_{r_V}^F$ are both non-positive. Likewise $A_Y^H + A_Y^V + A_Y^F = 0$. Customarily we take A_Y^H to be positive, to reflect transactions demands for money. Suppose also $A_Y^V \geqslant -A_Y^H$, implying $A_Y^F \leqslant 0$. In words, the public does not shift into foreign assets at the same time that increased transactions demands compel them to add to their holdings of domestic money. These assumptions suffice to make negative the determinant of the Jacobian of (7), $[-A_{r_V}^V A_Y^H + A_{r_V}^H A_Y^V] + A_Y^H q'_V = \Delta$ and:

$$\frac{\partial Y}{\partial H} = \frac{A_{r_V}^F + q_V V}{\Delta} > 0, \qquad \frac{\partial r_V}{\partial H} = \frac{-A_Y^F}{\Delta} \leqslant 0. \qquad (8)$$

The effect of monetary policy on the exchange rate is not the same, possibly not even the same in sign, as if perfect capital mobility tied the domestic interest rate to the exogenous foreign rate. It hinges on whether the rise in Y engineered by monetary expansion creates more room in the economy for the export surplus X or less room. If it creates more room, the exchange rate must depreciate (e rise) to induce the export demand to fill it, the more so because the direct effect of Y is to diminish X via the marginal propensity to import. If it creates less room, while the k effect in contracting net export demand is weak, then the exchange rate will have to appreciate (e fall). We cannot be sure whether it creates more room or less. By itself expansion of Y creates more, by our assumption that $E_Y < 1$. But in addition there is the increase in E, most likely investment, induced by the concurrent interest-rate reduction. The ambiguity is due to this effect, which is absent when the domestic interest rate is tied to the foreign rate by perfect substitutability.

The situation is pictured in Figure 1. In traditional (Y, r) space the asset equations (2) and (3) jointly determine a locus HV as open-market operations change the quantities of the two assets. Monetary expansion moves the economy down and to the right. The slope of the locus, from (8), is $-A_Y^F/(A_{r_V}^F + q_V'V)$. Great (negative) sensitivity of foreign asset demand to income makes it steep; high substitutability of foreign for domestic assets makes it flat. The economy must be on this locus. The IS curves comes from equation (1), and each is drawn for a given value of exchange rate e. In Figure 1a, the IS curves are steeper than HV. If monetary policy shifts the economy from point 1 to point 2, the IS curve must be shifted out to go through point 2, and this requires exchange depreciation, $e_2 > e_1$. In Figure 1b, the IS curves are flatter than HV, and exchange appreciation ($e_2 < e_1$) brings the requisite leftward shift. In case domestic and foreign assets are prefect substitutes, HV is horizontal. This is just an extreme case of Figure 1a.

A related graphical version is Figure 2, in (Y, e) space. The LM locus (from equation (2) is vertical, shifted right by monetary expansion. For a given domestic interest rate the IS curve is upward sloping: to keep equation (1) satisfied, an (export-increasing) increase in e must be offset by an (import-increasing) increase in Y. Figure 2 also shows, of course, how IS shifts resulting from increases in G and x, with no LM shift, will be completely absorbed in exchange appreciation. But a decline in the interest rate moves the IS locus to the right. Thus an expansionary monetary policy shifts both curves, and the result may be either Figure 2a or Figure 2b.

Formally, using (1) and (8) gives:

$$\frac{\partial e}{\partial H} = \frac{\left(1 - \overset{+}{E_Y} - X_Y\right)\overset{+}{\frac{\partial Y}{\partial H}} - E_{r_V}\overset{-}{\frac{\partial r_V}{\partial H}}}{\overset{+}{X_e}}$$

$$= \frac{\left(A_{r_V}^F + \overset{-}{q_V'}V\right)(1 - \overset{-}{E_Y} - X_Y) + \overset{-}{A_Y^F}\overset{-}{E_{r_V}}}{\underset{-}{\Delta}\overset{+}{X_e}}. \tag{9}$$

The second term in the numerator is what introduces the ambiguity regarding the sign. The numerator has the sign of the difference between the slope of the

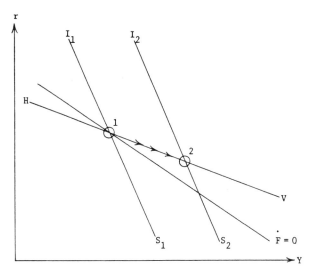

Fig. 1a.

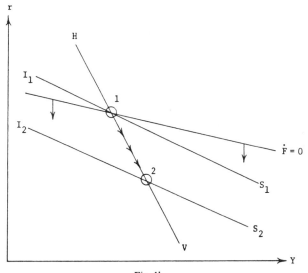

Fig. 1b.

IS locus and the slope of the *HV* locus. If, in absolute value, $(dr/dY)|_{IS} >$ $(dr/dY)|_{HV}$ as in Figure 1a, then $(\partial e/\partial H) > 0$ as in Figure 2a.

Equation (6) reminds us that foreign asset holdings will generally be changing as a byproduct of the solution. In Figures 1 and 2 we also show a locus for $\dot{F} = 0$, but nothing compels the solution to lie on this locus. In (Y, r) space this is

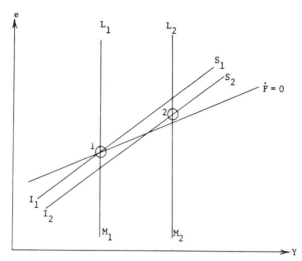

Fig. 2a.

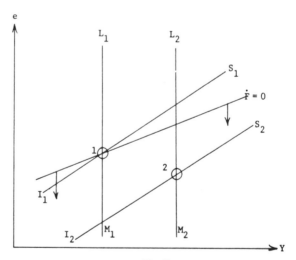

Fig. 2b.

essentially the *IS* curve with *X* deleted, and it is flatter than the true *IS* curve because the import leakage is omitted. For similar reasons, it is flatter than the true *IS* in (Y, e) space, Figure 2. In each case points to the right have $\dot{F} < 0$, to the left $\dot{F} > 0$. These current-account balance curves will move right in Figure 1 by increases in *G*, and move down in Figure 2 by increases in *x*. As for monetary expansion, in the normal case, Figures 1a and 2a, it is not possible to say whether $\dot{F}$ will be increased or lowered. But in the abnormal case, Figures 1b and 2b, when Y increases and the currency appreciates, clearly $\dot{F}$ will decline.

Unless monetary or fiscal policy forces a solution with $\dot{F} = 0$, the solution will not be stationary but will change as F_0 changes with the passage of time. This impermanence has rightly worried theorists. But it would nonetheless be a mistake to impose the condition $\dot{F} = 0$ on this model. Its solution is transient anyway, because other stocks—domestic financial assets, capital, total wealth—are not stationary either. Point-of-time models should be used with caution, especially for policy implications.[5]

An obvious objection to the above analysis is the omission of the wealth constraint from the portfolio equations. If wealth-owners have a non-zero position in foreign assets, their domestic value depends on the exchange ratio e. So, of course, does the total value of their wealth, W_0, given in (6) as $H_0 + q_V V_0 + eF_0$. Omitting this total or its separate constituents from the asset-demand functions A^S amounts to assuming that, for example, increases in value of wealth due to exchange depreciation are held entirely in the foreign assets whose domestic value has risen. If there were spillovers into domestic money and other domestic assets, then an increase in e would shift upward the LM curve in (Y, r) space (not drawn in Figure 1) and make the LM curve in (Y, e) space (Figure 2) downward sloping instead of vertical. An IS shift due to fiscal policy or a favorable foreign demand shock lowers e. Therefore it increases Y, as it would in a closed economy or with fixed exchange rates. The strong propositions of the Fleming-Mundell model no longer hold. They do not hold even if, because of perfect substitutability, the domestic interest rate is controlled by the foreign rate.

What if the country is a net debtor on foreign account? Then depreciation, an increase in e, augments the domestic-currency value of the debt, lowers wealth, and induces some depletion of domestic financial assets. Hence the LM curve in (Y, e) space is upward sloping. A positive IS shift which raises Y also raises e, depreciating the currency. But LM might be steeper than IS in (Y, e) space. Then the IS/LM comparative statics gives perverse results: increases in G or x lower both e and Y.

Qualitatively similar modifications arise from endogenous expectations of changes of exchange rates.[6] The rate of return on foreign assets, expressed in domestic currency, is $r_F^* + (\dot{e}/e)_{\text{exp}}$. If the exchange-expectation term is lower

---

[5] On the transition from temporary to steady-state equilibrium in the standard macroeconomic model, see Tobin and Buiter (1980).

[6] The importance of modeling exchange rate expectations was noted by Sohmen (1966, p. 34, n. 29), where he criticizes Mundell's analysis for assuming that "spot and forward exchange rates as well as expected future spot rates are identical, even though exchange rates may be perfectly free to find their monetary equilibrium levels at all times." The formal introduction of exchange-rate expectations in the Fleming-Mundell apparatus is due to Argy and Porter (1972).

the higher is current *e*, then a high current *e* means bigger demands for money and other domestic assets. Substitution effects with respect to the foreign interest rate so adjusted work in the same direction as wealth effects on positive foreign holdings. They apply even if those holdings are initially zero, and even if r_V must be equal to the foreign interest rate corrected for exchange expectation.

Since these amendments to the Fleming-Mundell model and their implications are familiar, we will not show them formally. Instead in the next section we will incorporate them in a somewhat different model.

3. A discrete-time model with four assets

The model we propose uses discrete rather than continuous time. The motivation is to include some of the effects of finite stock accumulations, which as we observed above are not captured at all when asset markets are modeled as stock equilibrium at a point in time. The same technique has been applied in closed-economy analyses of government fiscal policies and of capital accumulation.

Here we split *V* into its constituents, capital *K* and government bonds *B*, no longer assuming them to be perfect substitutes. The market valuation of an equity claim to a unit of physical capital is q_K, inversely related to yield r_K from equity ownership for a period and positively related to the net rate of return *R* earned by the capital in use. The marginal efficiency *R* may depend on income *Y* of the period, as well as on future *Y*'s. Bonds are consols paying $1 a period, valued at $q_B(\bar{r}_B)$, where r_B is the yield from bond ownership for a period. Clearly in both cases, the interest rate depends on the *q* expected to prevail next period. In this regard all we need for present purposes is to assume that the expected *q* moves if at all less than proportionately to current period *q*. In other respects, we follow the first model and its notation.

$$(10) \quad A^K(\cdot) - q_K(r_K)K_{-1} = I(\overset{-}{r_K}, \overset{+}{R}) \tag{Capital}$$

$$(11) \quad A^B(\cdot) - q_B(r_B)B_{-1} = \gamma_B(G + B_{-1} - T(\overset{+}{Y})) + Z_B \tag{Government bonds}$$

$$(12) \quad A^F(\cdot) - eF_{-1} = X(\overset{+}{e}, \bar{Y}) + x + er_F^* F_{-1} \tag{Foreign assets}$$

$$(13) \quad A^H(\cdot) - H_{-1} = \gamma_H(G + B_{-1} - T(\overset{+}{Y})) + Z_H \tag{High-powered money}$$

$$(14) \quad S_P = G + B_{-1} - T + I + X + x + er_F^* F_{-1}. \tag{Private saving}$$

Here the A^S ($S = K, B, F, H$) are the domestic-currency values of asset stocks desired at the end of the period. The arguments of the functions (·) include variables endogenous within the period ($r_K, r_B, r_F(e), e, Y$), predetermined variables ($H_{-1}, B_{-1}, K_{-1}, F_{-1}$), and in the background parameters such as those of the tax function $T(Y)$, which we will not vary in the present analysis. All interest rates are one-period yields. The foreign interest rate in domestic currency r_F allows for exchange-rate expectations; as argued before, these may be a function of the current exchange rate; $r_F(e)$, with r_{F_e} negative. Of course, r_F also depends on the exogenous foreign interest rate r_F^*. The exchange rate enters additionally as a carrier of wealth effects when F_{-1} is non-zero. Capital appreciation will be distributed among the several assets. We assume therefore that each partial derivative A_e^S has the same sign as F_{-1} but is smaller than F_{-1} in absolute value.

The parameters γ_H and γ_B, which are non-negative and sum to one, are the shares of this period's government deficit financed by base money and bonds respectively. Open-market purchases of bonds with money occur in amount Z_H, equal to $-Z_B$.[7] $I(\cdot)$ is the amount of capital investment during the period valued at q_K, thus $I = q_K dK$.

The strategy of the model is simple. Each asset equation has the period's incremental demand on the left, and the new supply on the right. The incremental demand is the difference between the stock desired at end of period and the value of the pre-existing stocks at this period's asset prices, $q_K K_{-1}, q_B B_{-1}, e F_{-1}$, H_{-1}. On the right, new investment adds to the capital stock, government deficits and open-market operations supply money and bonds, and the current-account balance changes the stock of foreign assets. The sum of the first four equations gives the *IS* equation (14), private saving S_P on the left equal to government dissaving plus domestic investment plus foreign investment on the right. One of the five equations is redundant. In what follows we find it convenient to drop the *IS* relation.

Walras's law and gross substitutability among assets, used in the analysis of the first model, take somewhat different form in this one. The partial derivatives of the A^S with respect to any yield or to income do not sum to zero. Their sum is the partial derivative of total desired end-of-period wealth with respect to the same variable. We assume this sum to be non-negative for every interest rate and positive for Y. That is, an increase in any interest rate increases saving, or at least does not reduce it. We assume, however, that such increase occurs wholly in the asset whose rate is increased, and that to this is added any pure portfolio substitutions against other assets. Thus, cross-partials of the A^S with respect to interest rates are non-positive. A standard assumption will also be that all A_Y^S are positive.

---

[7] Here in this clean-floating regime the government is assumed to stay out of the foreign asset markets; otherwise a γ_F and Z_F would be added for foreign assets. This is further elaborated in Kouri and de Macedo (1978).

Differentiating totally the system (10)–(13) gives (15). Note that for symmetry the differential of the exchange rate de is entered with a minus sign.

$$
\begin{bmatrix}
A_{r_K}^K - I_{r_K} - q_K' K_{-1} & A_{r_B}^K & -A_{r_F}^K r_{F_e} - A_e^K & A_Y^K - I_R R_Y \\
A_{r_K}^B & A_{r_B}^B - q_B' B_{-1} & -A_{r_F}^B r_{F_e} - A_e^B & A_Y^B + \gamma_B T_Y \\
A_{r_K}^F & A_{r_B}^F & -A_{r_F}^F r_{F_e} - A_e^F & A_Y^F - X_y \\
& & + F_{-1}(1 + r_F^*) + X_e & \\
A_{r_K}^H & A_{r_B}^H & -A_{r_F}^H r_{F_e} - A_e^H & A_Y^H + \gamma_{I'} T_Y
\end{bmatrix}
\begin{bmatrix}
dr_K \\
dr_B \\
-de \\
dY
\end{bmatrix}
$$

$$
= \begin{bmatrix}
0 & 0 & 0 \\
\gamma_B & 0 & -1 \\
0 & 1 & 0 \\
\gamma_H & 0 & 1
\end{bmatrix}
\begin{bmatrix}
dG \\
dx \\
dZ_H
\end{bmatrix}.
\tag{15}
$$

Beyond the assumptions already described, two more suffice to establish the sign pattern of the Jacobian of (15). One refers to the entry in the last column, first row. It is that $A_Y^K > I_R R_Y$. This means that an increase in Y generates investment. It is analogous to the assumption in standard IS/LM analysis that the marginal propensity to save exceeds the marginal propensity to invest, the assumption that keeps the IS curve from sloping upward. The other is that $F_{-1} \geqslant 0$. (We have already alluded to the reversals that occur via the wealth effect of changes in exchange rates when the country is a debtor on external accounts, and we shall return to this question.) With these assumptions—ignoring for the moment the possibility of zeros, and recording at the bottom the signs of column sums—the sign pattern of the Jacobian is

$$
\begin{bmatrix}
+ & - & - & + \\
- & + & - & + \\
- & - & + & + \\
- & - & - & + \\
\hline
+ & + & + & +
\end{bmatrix}.
$$

The determinant Δ of such a matrix is positive. The pattern of $\Delta(\partial Y / \partial G)$ is

$$
\begin{bmatrix}
+ & - & - & 0 \\
- & + & - & \gamma_B \\
- & - & + & 0 \\
- & - & - & \gamma_H \\
\hline
+ & + & + & 1
\end{bmatrix},
$$

also positive. That of $\Delta(\partial Y/\partial x)$ is

$$\begin{bmatrix} + & - & - & 0 \\ - & + & - & 0 \\ - & - & + & 1 \\ - & - & - & 0 \end{bmatrix}$$
$$\quad + \quad + \quad + \quad 1$$

likewise positive. That of $\Delta(\partial Y/\partial Z_H)$ is

$$\begin{bmatrix} + & - & - & 0 \\ - & + & - & -1 \\ - & - & + & 0 \\ - & - & - & 1 \end{bmatrix}$$
$$\quad + \quad + \quad + \quad 0$$

positive too, as can be seen by adding the fourth row to the second, changing it to $[- \; + \; - \; 0]$ without altering the value of the determinant.

These results contradict the strong propositions cited at the beginning. More important, those propositions do not all stand even under the following assumptions: (i) $F_{-1} = 0$, erasing the wealth effect of exchange-rate variation, (ii) $\gamma_H = 0$, eliminating any monetary accumulation of fiscal policy and unbalanced budgets, (iii) $r_{F_e} = 0$, eliminating any change in expectation of exchange-rate movement accompanying variation in the current level of e. With these restrictions, the pattern of the Jacobian is

$$\begin{bmatrix} + & - & 0 & + \\ - & + & 0 & + \\ - & - & + & + \\ - & - & 0 & + \end{bmatrix}$$
$$\quad + \quad + \quad + \quad +$$

and Δ is still positive. $\Delta(\partial Y/\partial G)$ is

$$\begin{bmatrix} + & - & 0 & 0 \\ - & + & 0 & 1 \\ - & - & + & 0 \\ - & - & 0 & 0 \end{bmatrix},$$
$$\quad + \quad + \quad + \quad 1$$

also positive. The essential reason for this may be seen by going back to the first model and observing that a hypothetical increase in $q_V V$ in (3)—*not* offset by a reduction of H—would raise Y. (If $[0, 1]$ replaces the second column of the Jacobian in (7), the determinant remains negative.) In the second model, with discrete time, this is precisely what happens when there is an increase in G wholly financed by issuing bonds.

However, the insulation proposition, $\partial Y/\partial x = 0$, holds in the special case under consideration:

$$\Delta \frac{\partial Y}{\partial x} \text{ is } \begin{bmatrix} + & - & 0 & 0 \\ - & + & 0 & 0 \\ - & - & + & 1 \\ - & - & 0 & 0 \\ + & + & + & 1 \end{bmatrix} = 0.$$

An increase in export demand, at a given Y, lowers e. But now this appreciation alters neither the amounts the public wants to save in domestic assets at that Y nor the incremental supplies of those assets. So if the exchange rate appreciates enough to keep the trade surplus unchanged, the same old Y will still be a solution.

The conclusions just reached could have been obtained by dynamic analysis of a continuous-time model tracking the moving equilibrium of stock demands and supplies. The discrete-time model here analyzed reaches the conclusions in a simpler way. The showing that fiscal policy works even when e is not in asset demand functions arises naturally from the balance-of-payments equation (12), where e is a price equilibrating capital and current-account transactions.

If the country is a debtor to foreigners ($F_{-1} < 0$), wealth effects are reversed. This does not necessarily change the qualitative comparative-static results, because portfolio substitution and trade substitution effects may still dominate. An interesting special case occurs if the signs of the $-de$ column are all reversed, as could happen with negative F_{-1} and wealth effects—or *a fortiori* if r_{F_e} is zero or positive and the trade elasticities are perverse, $X_e < 0$. The analysis then stands with the exception that the exchange rate moves in the opposite direction. For example, monetary expansion makes it appreciate, and a jump in export demand makes it depreciate. Wonders about the dynamic mechanics and the stability of this case are beyond the scope of this paper. More complex troubles arise from other combinations of the entries of the third column of the Jacobian. The results so far are collected in Table 1.

We can improve the model by allowing the large rest of the world to hold the small home country's assets. Unfortunately notation becomes complex. An asset stock S_{-1} ($S = K, B, H$) is held partly by domestics, $^A S_{-1}$ and partly by foreigners $^J S_{-1}$. At this point we continue to represent foreign investments available to domestic savers simply by a single asset F with a fixed interest rate in foreign currency r_F^*. The demand for a stock by foreigners will be denoted by $J^S(\cdot)$. Those demands are for stocks at market value in the foreigners' currency, let us call it marks. They must be converted into domestic currency, dollars, in the asset equations. The endogenous variables on which they depend are the home-country yields $r_S - (de/e)_{\exp}$, interpreting r_H to be zero. In keeping with the designation of rest-of-world as "large," we ignore at this stage any wealth

Table 1.   Effects of exogenous variables on output and exchange rate

	Fiscal Policy Effects of G on						Foreign Demand		Monetary Policy	
	Y			*e*			Effects of *x* on:		Effects of Z_H on:	
	(1) Gen.	(2) $\gamma_B = 1$	(3) $\gamma_H = 1$	(1) Gen.	(2) $\gamma_B = 1$	(2) $\gamma_H = 1$	*Y*	*e*	*Y*	*e*
Standard case	+	+	+	?	?	+	+ −	+	+	
No wealth or asset substitution effects of exchange rates	+	+	+	?	?	+	0	−	+	+
Negative foreign assets, zero or positive substitution effects of exchange rates, perverse relation of trade balance to exchange rate	+	+	+	?	?	−	+	+	+	−

(1) General case
(2) All bond finance of government deficits
(3) All money finance of government deficits

effects of *e* on foreign portfolios. The current level of *e* may, however, affect foreign demands via expected changes in *e*. For domestic savers, the endogenous variables in $A^S(\cdot)$ are as before the two local r_S, the foreign interest rate $r_F^* + (de/e)_{\text{exp}}$, domestic income *Y*, and *e* as a carrier of wealth effects. The model now looks like this:

$$\text{Domestic Demands} \qquad \text{Foreign Demands} \qquad \text{Supply}$$

$$A^K(\cdot) - q_K{}^A K_{-1} + eJ^K(\cdot) - q_K{}^J K_{-1} = I(r_K, R) \tag{16}$$

$$A^B(\cdot) - q_B{}^A B_{-1} + eJ^B(\cdot) - q_B{}^J B_{-1} = \gamma_B (G + B_{-1} - T) + Z_B \tag{17}$$

$$A^F(\cdot) - e^A F_{-1} - \sum_S \left(eJ^S(\cdot) - q_S{}^J S_{-1} \right) = X(e, Y) + x + er_F^* F_{-1} - R^J K_{-1} - {}^J B_{-l} \tag{18}$$

$$A^H(\cdot) - {}^A H_{-1} + eJ^H(\cdot) - {}^J H_{-1} = \gamma_H (G + B_{-1} - T) + Z_H. \tag{19}$$

   In the balance-of-payments equation (18), *S* takes on (K, B, H) and q_H is identically 1. On the right-hand side interest and dividend payments to foreigners must now appear. The arguments of the A^S and J^S functions have been described above.

With some plausible additional assumptions, the amendment of the model leaves the conclusions unaltered. Consider, as an example that applies to all the asset equations, the differentiation of the capital equation (16) with respect to $(r_K, r_B, -e, Y)$:

$$
\begin{array}{cccc}
r_k & r_B & -e & Y \\[4pt]
A^{K}r_K - q'_K K_{-1} & A^{K}_{r_B} + eJ^{K}_{r_B} & -A^{K}_{r_F}r_{F_e} - A^{K}_{e} & A^{K}_{Y} - I_R R_Y \\[8pt]
- I_{r_K} + eJ^{K}_{r_K} & & -J^{K} + er_{F_e}\sum_{S} J^{K}_{r_S} &
\end{array}
\tag{20}
$$

This row, we assert, has the same sign pattern as in (15), namely $[+\ -\ -\ +]$. Consider the four entries in turn:

To the first, for dr_K, is added foreigners' positive response to an increase in equity yield.

To the second, for dr_B, is added foreigners' negative response to an increase in bond yield.

The third entry, for $-de$, now includes two effects of a decline in the exchange rate, an appreciation of the dollar, on foreigners' demand for equity in dollars. The first term $(-J^{K})$ says the same demand in marks amounts to less in dollars. The second term says that a decline in the exchange rate brings expectation of a subsequent rise, which makes dollar investments, whether in equity or bonds or money, less attractive. Our new assumption, which seems innocuous, is that $\sum_S J^{K}_{r_S}$ is positive. That is, if the yields of all three assets decrease by the same amount—the yield differences among them remain unchanged but their differential over foreign assets declines—then foreigners' demand for equity will be smaller. Thus the third entry remains unambiguously negative.

The fourth entry is unamended, since Y is not in foreigners' asset demand functions.

The same argument maintains the sign patterns for the bond and money rows, from equations (17) and (19).

The balance-of-payments equation (18) now gives the following partial derivatives:

$$
\begin{array}{cccc}
r_K & r_B & -e & Y \\[4pt]
A^{F}_{r_K} - e\sum_{S} J^{S}_{r_K} & A^{R}_{r_B} - \sum J^{S}_{r_B} & -A^{F}_{r_F} - A^{F}_{e} + F_{-1}(1 + r^{*}_{F}) + X_e & A^{F}_{Y} - X_R \\[8pt]
+ q'_K{}^{J} K_{-1} & - q'_B{}^{J} B_{-1} & + \sum J^{S} - er_{F_e}\sum \left(J^{S}_{r_K} + J^{S}_{r_B} + J^{S}_{r_H} \right) & + R_Y{}^{J} K_{-1}
\end{array}
\tag{21}
$$

In (15) this row had the signs $[- - + +]$ for $F_{-1} \geqslant 0$, $r_{F_e} < 0$, $X_e > 0$. Recall that a positive sign means that an increase in the variable tends to worsen the home country's balance of payments. We must look at the additions to the entries.

To the first two entries, for r_K and r_B, the additions reinforce the negative sign. We assume $\sum J^S_{r_K}$ and $\sum J^S_{r_B}$ are both positive, meaning that an increase in any one domestic yield attracts capital from abroad, not just substitutions by foreigners among domestic assets. Naturally, foreigners' holdings ${}^J S_{-1}$ are all nonnegative.

The third entry, for e, looks the most complicated, but the new entries reinforce its positive sign. We already justified, using the capital equation as an example, the assumption that $J^S_{r_K} + J^S_{r_B} + J^S_{r_H}$ is positive.

The only addition to the fourth entry, for Y, is positive, reflecting a possible income-associated increase in the earnings of foreign owners of domestic equity.

Thus the amendments to (15) leave intact its sign pattern. They also leave intact the dominant-diagonal quality of the matrix, indicated above by the positive signs for column sums. The sum of the four equations (16)–(19) is still the home country's *IS* equation, (14).

Consequently all the qualitative conclusions of the simpler model stand. Note, however, that even stronger conditions are now necessary for insulation. It is not enough that r_{F_e} and F_{-1} be zero, or even that the net foreign assets of the country be zero. It is necessary that F^{-1} and each J^S be zero. Otherwise there will be non-zero off-diagonal entries in the third $(-de)$ column of the matrix. The reason the J^S are involved is that they are stock demands in marks. The exchange rate is involved in converting them into dollars, even though it appears nowhere inside the J^S functions directly or indirectly.

4. A two-country world

In this section, we will discuss briefly the problems of modeling a two-country world, with each country large enough to affect the asset markets of the other. Think of North America vis-à-vis the Common Market, dollars vis-à-vis marks. Each country will be described in the way the home country was modeled in Section 3. However, for simplicity of exposition, we will return to one of the assumptions of Section 2, that the capital and bonds of a country are perfect substitutes for each other, though not for the capital and bonds of its partner. No issue of principle is involved in this condensation. In this world there are four distinct assets, two for each country, money and capital-cum-bonds. The corresponding four equations, plus the balance-of-payments equation, determine five endogeous variables: two interest rates, two incomes, one exchange rate.

To write down the model, we need one bit of additional notation beyond that of Sections 2 and 3. The variables for the second region will be distinguished by asterisks. Here then is the model:

	American Demands	European Demands	Supply
(22) (American capital & bonds)	$A^V(\cdot) - q_V{}^A V_{-1} + eJ^V(\cdot) - q_V{}^J V_{-1}$		$= I(r_V, R)$ $+ \gamma_B(G - B_{-1} - T)$ $+ Z_B$
(23) (European capital & bonds)	$A^{V^*}(\cdot) - eq_{V^*}{}^A V^*_{-1} + eJ^{V^*}(\cdot) - eq_V{}^J V^*_{-1}$		$= eI^*(r_{V^*}, R^*)$ $+ e\gamma_{B^*}\!\cdot\!(G^* - B^*_{-1} - T^*)$ $+ Z_{B^*}$
(24) (American money)	$A^H(\cdot) - {}^A H_{-1} + eJ^H(\cdot) - {}^J H_{-1}$		$= \gamma_H(G - B_{-1} - T) + Z_H$
(25) (European money)	$A^{H^*}(\cdot) - e^A H^*_{-1} + eJ^{H^*}(\cdot) - e^J H^*_{-1}$		$= e\gamma_{H^*}\!\cdot\!(G^* - B^*_{-1} - T^*)$ $+ Z_{H^*}$
(26) (Balance of payments)	$\sum_{S^*}\left(A^{S^*}(\cdot) - eq_{S^*}{}^A S^*_{-1}\right) - \sum_S\left(eJ^S(\cdot) - q_S{}^J S_{-1}\right)$		$= X(\overset{+}{e}, \overset{-}{Y}, \overset{+}{Y^*}) + x$ $+ eR^{*A}K^*_{-1} + e^A B^*_{-1}$ $- R^J K_{-1} - {}^J B_{-1}$

Note that the sum of the four equations ((22) through (25)) is the world IS equation, the sum of the two American asset equations and the balance-of-payments equation ((22) + (24) + (26)) is the American IS equation, the sum of the two European asset equations less the balance-of-payments equation ((22) + (24) − (26)) is the European IS equation in dollars.

The endogenous arguments of the A functions are (r_V, r_V^*, Y, e). Those of the J functions are (r_V, r_V^*, Y^*, e). American incomes does not affect European residents' asset demands, or vice versa. The trade-balance function X now includes both Y and Y^*, with partial derivatives of opposite signs. The assumptions and reasoning of the last part of Section 3, now applied to both countries, gives a set of simultaneous equations in differentials as follows:

$$
\begin{bmatrix}
+ & - & + & + & - \\
- & + & + & + & + \\
- & - & ++ & + & - \\
- & - & + & ++ & + \\
- & + & + & - & + \\
+ & + & + & + & ?
\end{bmatrix}
\begin{bmatrix}
dr_V \\
dr_{V^*} \\
dY \\
dY^* \\
-de
\end{bmatrix}
=
\begin{bmatrix}
\gamma_B & 0 & -1 & 0 & 0 \\
0 & \gamma_{B^*} & 0 & -1 & 0 \\
\gamma_H & 0 & 1 & 0 & 0 \\
0 & \gamma_{H^*} & 0 & 1 & 0 \\
0 & 0 & 0 & 0 & 1
\end{bmatrix}
\begin{bmatrix}
dG \\
dG^* \\
dZ_H \\
dZ_{H^*} \\
dx
\end{bmatrix}. \quad (27)
$$

The sign pattern for $-de$ in the final column requires explanation. In connection with equation (20), we concluded that the effect of an increase in the mark price of dollars on European demand for an American asset would be negative. To hold the same value in marks, European investors would sell some of their holdings. Against this is the wealth effect, which we did not previously allow. Having gained wealth, European investors might wish to increase the mark value of any one of their dollar holdings. But the wealth elasticity would have to exceed one—indeed equal the reciprocal of the asset's share in the portfolio— to induce them not to sell any of the dollar asset. For example, if the holding was $1/4$ of the portfolio, then a 1 percent increase in the exchange rate would increase wealth by $1/4$ of 1 percent, and it would take a wealth elasticity of 4 to make the exchange rate elasticity unity. Formally in equation (20), third entry, we add a term $-eJ_e^K > 0$. But it can be expected to be smaller in absolute value than $-J^K$.

For the same reasons that depreciation of the mark decreases dollar demand for American assets, it increases dollar demand for European assets. That is why the signs in the $-de$ column alternate. The last entry says that depreciation of the mark deteriorates the American balance of payments, which does not require any new assumptions.

The two income columns are shown in (27) as non-negative, as before. But the $++$ for the diagonals denote a new condition, namely that the maximum non-diagonal entry in the column is smaller that the average of the first four entries. This ensures that the first four rows and columns are a dominant diagonal matrix. The economic meaning is the same that motivated our assumption in the continuous-time model of Section 2, that transactions demands for cash are met by substitutions against all other assets. In that model, money was the only asset with a positive income elasticity. Here, however, wealth is not predetermined and saving offsets the portfolio substitutions. Transactions demand gives money that dominant positive income effect.

The significance of the dominant-diagonal structure of the 4×4 matrix can be seen if we abstract from all effects of exchange rate on asset demands, via wealth or expected exchange-rate appreciation or depreciation, making all the entries except the bottom one zero in the last column. We then find the following: (i) A trade shock x affects only the exchange rate; the insulation property of the floating exchange rate holds as before. (ii) Expansionary monetary action—open market purchases or increases in government spending financed wholly or predominantly by monetary issue—in one country raises income in that country and *lowers* it in the other. (iii) Expansionary fiscal action—increases in government spending financed wholly or predominantly by bond issue—raises income in both countries. These conclusions arise from manipulations of determinants familiar by now to a studious reader, and they are omitted here to spare space and tedium.

The second and third results may seen surprising, especially the second, but the explanations are straightforward. Expansionary monetary policy is essentially a method of exchange depreciation. The resulting trade surplus—always assuming well-behaved elasticities—raises the country's income and lowers its partner's income.[8] Bond-financed fiscal stimuli raises interest rates and induces capital inflows that appreciate the exchange rate. The resulting trade deficit moderates, but does not cancel, the fiscal stimulus in the home country and raises income in the other country.

With respect to (ii), remember that if the period of our discrete-time model were very short, the portfolio substitution effects of Y and Y^* would dominate the accumulation effects. The two income columns would then have non-positive entries everywhere but the diagonals. Then expansionary monetary policy in either country would raise incomes in both countries. In a short period, the contagion of lower interest rates is stimulative in the second country as well as the first. It is the build-up of desired saving, strong enough to make the income columns non-negative, that reverses the effect on the second country over longer time periods. The reason is that the second country's trade deficit reduces the net wealth available to its savers, and a fall in income is the only way to reconcile them to that fact. This effect is ignored or deferred in a continuous-time snapshot in which exchange-rate determination is detached from the asset markets. Imagine the second country to be the small open economy of the model of Section 2, faced with a decline in the outside interest rate r_F^* combined with a negative shock x to its trade balance. The decline in r_F^* will be stimulative, but the model says that in the assumed circumstances the economy is insulated from the trade shock by movement of the exchange rate. Only later would accumulation of foreign debt or decumulation of foreign assets have repercussions on domestic saving and portfolio choices that cause income to decline.

The general case (27), with wealth and expectation effects of exchange rate movements, is very messy. We will not attempt a taxonomy here.

We can, nevertheless, point out the relevance of the simplification used so far by partitioning the Jacobian in (27) as

$$
J = \begin{bmatrix}
J_1 & B \\
(4 \times 4) & (4 \times 1) \\
\hline
\Theta & \theta_e \\
(1 \times 4) & (1 \times 1)
\end{bmatrix}.
$$

[8] The practical value of domestic monetary policy in a floating-rate system is diminished by the fact that it is a "beggar-my-neighbor" policy. In 1972, during the transition from fixed to floating rates, one of us wrote, "Since monetary policy is the more responsive instrument of domestic stabilization, perhaps we should welcome an exchange rate regime that increases its potency relative to that of fiscal policy. However, when the export-import balance becomes the strategic component of aggregate demand, one country's expansionary stimulus is another country's deflationary shock. We can hardly imagine that the Common Market will passively allow the U.S. to manipulate the dollar exchange rate in the interests of U.S. domestic stabilization. Nor can we imagine the reverse. International coordination of interest-rate policies will be essential in a regime of floating exchange rates, no less than in a fixed-parity regime." (Tobin, 1974, pp. 91–92).

Since J_1 is a dominant-diagonal matrix, $\det(J_1) > 0$. Also $\theta_e > 0$. Furthermore,

$$\det(J) = \theta_e \det(J_1 - B\Theta/\theta_e).$$

Denoting the total effects of the exchange rate on the first four rows by V, V^*, H and H^* and the first four columns of the last row by Θ, the structure and sign pattern of the $-B\Theta$ matrix is:

$$
-\begin{bmatrix} V_e \\ V_e^* \\ H_e \\ H_e^* \end{bmatrix} \begin{bmatrix} \theta_{r_V} & \theta_{r_{V^*}} & \theta_Y & \theta_{Y^*} \end{bmatrix} = \begin{bmatrix} - & + & + & - \\ + & - & - & + \\ - & + & + & - \\ + & - & - & + \end{bmatrix}
$$

The sign of the determinant of the difference $J_1 - B\Theta/\theta_e$ is thus ambiguous. The stronger the effect of the exchange rate on the balance of payments θ_e the smaller are the elements of the matrix $B\Theta/\theta_e$ and therefore the less likely it is that the sign of the determinant of the Jacobian J will be different from the sign of the determinant of the J_1 matrix. For large θ_e in this sense, the effect of an increase in the demand for American exports will appreciate the dollar as before, even though B is not a zero vector.

5. Concluding remarks

The analysis in the preceding sections has referred to a Keynesian economy, in which real output is flexible but price is fixed for the point or period of of time to which the models refer. This follows the Fleming-Mundell analysis with which we began, and it is of intrinsic interest. But the applicability of the method is by no means restricted to this Keynesian case. Indeed, with few qualifications, the analysis applies to the polar opposite classical case, with price level endogenous and output exogenously supply-determined. Anyone is free to re-read the article, substituting P for Y throughout.

We have tried to provide a framework for analysis of the short-run effects of macroeconomic policies and other events on economies linked by trade, capital markets, and floating exchange rates. Some conclusions of previous analysis, it turns out, do not survive in our models. The points we emphasize are: (i) Assets, ranging from capital to base money, are imperfect substitutes both within and across countries. (ii) Changes in stocks, including particularly those resulting from imbalances in external current accounts, have important effects not captured in conventional point-in-time specification of asset stock equilibrium. (iii) Floating rates do not insulate economies from shocks in their external trade accounts when exchange-rate movements induce portfolio shifts either by influencing expectations of appreciation or depreciation or by altering the wealth of portfolio owners. (iv) Although we are able to obtain some definite qualitative results in standard cases, they depend on a series of conditions that might not be met. It is easy to imagine plausible configuration in which the comparative statics would yield results counter to conventional intuition and wisdom, e.g., when a country is in debt to the rest of the world, when the trade-balance elasticities are perversely low, when exchange-rate expectations are extrapolative instead of regressive, when the income effects on asset demands are irregular. (v) Our framework can be applied not only to a small economy in a large world but to two, and by extension more, large economies or currency areas connected by commodity and financial markets.

References

Argy, Victor and Porter, Michael G., 1972, "The Forward Exchange Market and the Effects of Domestic and External Disturbances Under Alternative Exchange Rate Systems," *International Monetary Fund Staff Papers* 19, November, 503–532.

Branson, William H., 1977, "Asset Markets and Relative Prices in Exchange Rate Determination," *Sozialwissenschaftliches Annalen*, Physica-Verlag, Vienna, 1, Heft 3, 69–80.

Dornbusch, Rudiger, 1976, "Flexible Exchange Rates, Capital Mobility and Macroeconomic Equilibrium." In Emil-Maria Claassen and Pascal Salin, eds., *Recent Issues in International Monetary Economics* (Amsterdam: North-Holland), pp. 261–278.

Fleming, J. Marcus, 1962, "Domestic Financial Policies Under Fixed and Under Floating Exchange Rates," *International Monetary Fund Staff Papers* 9, November, 369–379.

Kouri, Pentti J. K. , 1975, *Essays in the Theory of Flexible Exchange Rates*. Ph.D. Dissertation, Massachusetts Institute of Technology.

Kouri, Pentti, J. K. and de Macedo, Jorge Braga, 1978, "Exchange Rates and the International Adjustment Process," *Brookings Papers on Economic Activity*, No. 1, 111–150.

Mundell, Robert A., 1961, "Flexible Exchange Rates and Employment Policy," *Canadian Journal of Economics and Political Science* 27, November, 509–517.

Mundell, Robert A., 1963, "Capital Mobility and Stabilization Policy Under Fixed and Flexible Exchange Rates," *Canadian Journal of Economics and Political Science* 29, November, 475–485.

Mundell, Robert A., 1964, "Capital Mobility and Size: A Reply," *Canadian Journal of Economics and Political Science* 30, May, 421–431.

Mussa, Michael, 1979, "Macroeconomic Interdependence and the Exchange Rate Regime." In Rudiger Dornbusch and Jacob Frenkel, eds., *International Economic Policy* (Baltimore and London: The Johns Hopkins Press), pp. 160–203.

Myhrman, Johan, 1976, "Balance of Payments Adjustment and Portfolio Theory: A Survey." In Emil-Maria Claassen and Pascal Salin, eds., *Recent Issues in International Monetary Economics* (Amsterdam: North-Holland), pp. 203–237.

Sohmen, Egon, 1961, *Flexible Exchange Rates: Theory and Controversy* (Chicago: University of Chicago Press).

Sohmen, Egon, 1866, *The Theory of Forward Exchange*. Princeton Studies in International Finance No. 17 (Princeton, N.J.; Princeton University, International Finance Section).

Sohmen, Egon, 1967, "Fiscal and Monetary Policies Under Alternative Exchange-Rate Systems," *Quarterly Journal of Economics* 81, August 515–523.

Sohmen, Egon, 1969, *Flexible Exchange Rates*, Revised Edition (Chicago: University of Chicago Press).

Sohmen, Egon and Schneeweiss, Hans, 1969, "Fiscal and Monetary Policies Under Alternative Exchange-Rate Systems: A Correction," *Quarterly Journal of Economics* 83, May 336–340.

Tobin, James, 1974, *The New Economics One Decade Older* (Princeton, N.J.: Princeton University Press).

Tobin, James and Buiter, Willem H., 1980, "Fiscal and Monetary Policies, Capital Formation, and Economic Activity." In George von Furstenberg, ed., *The Government and Capital Formation* (Cambridge, Mass.: Ballinger Publishing Co.), pp. 73–151.

Whitman, Marina v. N., 1970, *Policies for Internal and External Balance*. Special Papers in International Economics No. 9 (Princeton. N.J.: Princeton University, International Finance Section).

A Proposal for International Monetary Reform*

JAMES TOBIN
Yale University

Over the last twenty years economists' prescriptions for reform of the international monetary system have taken various shapes. Their common premise was dissatisfaction with the Bretton Woods regime as it evolved in the 1950s. Robert Triffin awakened the world to the contradictions and instabilities of a system of pegged parities that relied on the debts in reserve currencies, mostly dollars, to meet growing needs for official reserves. Triffin and his followers saw the remedy as the internationalization of reserves and reserve assets; their ultimate solution was a world central bank. Others diagnosed the problem less in terms of liquidity than in the inadequacies of balance of payments adjustment mechanisms in the modern world. The inadequacies were especially evident under the fixed-parity gold-exchange standard when, as in the 1960s, the reserve currency center was structurally in chronic deficit. These analysts sought better and more symmetrical "rules of the game" for adjustments by surplus and deficit countries, usually including more flexibility in the setting of exchange parities, crawling pegs, and the like. Many economists, of whom Milton Friedman was an eloquent and persuasive spokesman, had all along advocated floating exchange rates, determined in private markets without official interventions.

By the early 1970s the third view was the dominant one in the economics profession, though not among central bankers and private financiers. And all of a sudden, thanks to Nixon and Connally, we got our wish. Or at least we got as much of it as anyone could reasonably have hoped, since it could never have been expected that governments would eschew all intervention in exchange markets.

Now after five to seven years—depending how one counts—of unclean floating there are many second thoughts. Some economists share the nostalgia of men of affairs for the gold standard or its equivalent, for a fixed anchor for the world's money, for stability of official parities. Some economists, those who emphasize the rationality of expectations and the flexibility of prices in all markets, doubt that it makes much difference whether exchange rates are fixed or flexible, provided only that government policies are predictable. Clearly, flexible rates have not been the panacea which their more extravagant advocates had hoped; international monetary problems have not disappeared from headlines or from the agenda of anxieties of central banks and governments.

I believe that the basic problem today is not the exchange rate regime, whether fixed or floating. Debate on the regime evades and obscures the essential problem. That is the excessive international—or better, inter-currency—mobility of private financial capital. The biggest thing that happened in the world monetary system since the 1950s was

*This paper is Prof. Tobin's presidential address at the 1978 conference of the Eastern Economic Association, Wash. D.C.

Reprinted by permission from *The Eastern Economic Journal* 4(3–4) (July/October 1978):153–159. (A presidential address at Washington meeting, April 1978.)

the establishment of *de facto* complete convertibility among major currencies, and the development of intermediaries and markets, notably Eurocurrency institutions, to facilitate conversions. Under either exchange rate regime the currency exchanges transmit disturbances originating in international financial markets. National economies and national governments are not capable of adjusting to massive movements of funds across the foreign exchanges, without real hardship and without significant sacrifice of the objectives of national economic policy with respect to employment, output, and inflation. Specifically, the mobility of financial capital limits viable differences among national interest rates and thus severely restricts the ability of central banks and governments to pursue monetary and fiscal policies appropriate to their internal economies. Likewise speculation on exchange rates, whether its consequences are vast shifts of official assets and debts or large movements of exchange rates themselves, have serious and frequently painful real internal economic consequences. Domestic policies are relatively powerless to escape them or offset them.

The basic problems are these. Goods and labor move, in response to international price signals, much more sluggishly than fluid funds. Prices in goods and labor markets move much more sluggishly, in response to excess supply or demand, than the prices of financial assets, including exchange rates. These facts of life are essentially the same whether exchange rates are floating or fixed. The difficulties they create for national economies and policy-makers cannot be avoided by opting for one exchange rate regime or the other, or by providing more or different international liquidity, or by adopting new rules of the game of balance of payments adjustment. I do not say that those issues are unimportant or that reforms of those aspects of the international monetary system may not be useful.

For example, I still think that floating rates are an improvement on the Bretton Woods system. I do not contend that the major problems we are now experiencing will continue unless something else is done too.

There are two ways to go. One is toward a common currency, common monetary and fiscal policy, and economic integration. The other is toward greater financial segmentation between nations or currency areas, permitting their central banks and governments greater autonomy in policies tailored to their specific economic institutions and objectives. The first direction, however appealing, is clearly not a viable option in the foreseeable future, i.e., the twentieth century. I therefore regretfully recommend the second, and my proposal is to throw some sand in the wheels of our excessively efficient international money markets.

But first let us pay our respects to the "one world" ideal. Within the United States, of course, capital is extremely mobile between regions, and has been for a long time. Its mobility has served, continues to serve, important economic functions: mobilizing funds from high-saving areas to finance investments that develop areas with high marginal productivities of capital; financing trade deficits which arise from regional shifts in population and comparative advantage or from transient economic or natural shocks. With nationwide product and labor markets, goods and labor also flow readily to areas of high demand, and this mobility is the essential solution to the problems of regional depression and obsolescence that inevitably occur. There is neither need for, nor possibility of, regional macroeconomic policies. It would not be possible to improve employment in West Virginia or reduce inflation in California, even temporarily, by changing the parity of a local dollar with dollars of other Federal Reserve Districts. With a common currency, national financial and capital markets, and a single national monetary policy, movements of funds to exploit interest arbitrage or to speculate on exchange rate fluctuations cannot be sources of disturbances and painful interregional adjustments.

To recite this familiar account is to remind us how difficult it would be to replicate its prerequisites on a worldwide basis. Even for the Common Market countries, the goal is still far, far distant. We do not have to resolve the chicken-egg argument. Perhaps it is true that establishing a common currency and a central macro-economic policy will automatically generate the institutions, markets, and mobilities which make the system viable and its regional economic consequences everywhere tolerable. The risk is one that few are prepared to take. Moreover, EEC experience to date suggests that it is very hard to contrive a scenario of gradual evolution towards such a radically different regime, even though it could well be the global optimum.

At present the world enjoys many benefits of the increased worldwide economic integration of the last thirty years. But the integration is partial and unbalanced; in particular private financial markets have become internationalized much more rapidly and completely than other economic and political institutions. That is why we are in trouble. So I turn to the second, and second best, way out, forcing some segmentation of inter-currency financial markets.

My specific proposal is actually not new. I offered it in 1972 in my Janeway Lectures at Princeton, published in 1974 as *The New Economics One Decade Older*, pp. 88–92. The idea fell like a stone in a deep well. If I cast it in the water again, it is because events since the first try have strengthened my belief that something of the sort needs to be done.

The proposal is an internationally uniform tax on all spot conversions of one currency into another, proportional to the size of the transaction. The tax would particularly deter short-term financial round-trip excursions into another currency. A 1% tax, for example, could be overcome only by an 8 point differential in the annual yields of Treasury bills or Eurocurrency deposits denominated in dollars and Deutschmarks. The corresponding differential for one-year maturities would be 2 points. A permanent investment in another country or currency area, with regular repatriation of yield when earned, would need a 2% advantage in marginal efficiency over domestic investment. The impact of the tax would be less for permanent currency shifts, or for longer maturities. Because of exchange risks, capital value risks, and market imperfections, interest arbitrage and exchange speculation are less troublesome in long maturities. Moreover, it is desirable to obstruct as little as possible international movements of capital responsive to long-run portfolio preferences and profit opportunities.

Why do floating exchange rates not solve the problems? There are several reasons, all exemplified in recent experience.

First, as economists have long known, in a world of international capital mobility flexibility of exchange rates does not assure autonomy of national macroeconomic policy. The Mundell-Fleming models of the early 1960s showed how capital mobility inhibits domestic monetary policy under fixed parities and domestic fiscal policy under flexible rates. Moreover, the availability of the remaining instrument of macroeconomic policy in either regime is small consolation. Nations frequently face compelling domestic institutional, political, and economic constraints on one or the other instrument, or on the policy mix.

Second, it may seem that we should welcome an exchange rate regime that increases the potency of monetary policy relative to fiscal policy; after all, monetary policy is the more flexible and responsive instrument of domestic stabilization. But the liberation of domestic monetary policy under flexible rates is in large degree illusory. One reason is the attachment of central bankers to monetarist targets irrespective of exchange rate regimes and the openness of financial markets. More fundamentally, monetary policy becomes, under floating rates, exchange rate policy. The stimulus of expansionary monetary policy to domestic demand is limited by the competition of foreign interest rates for mobile funds. Thus much—in the limit, all—of the stimulus depends on exchange depreciation and its effects on the trade balance, namely on shifting foreign and domestic demand to home goods and services. The depreciation may occur all right, but its effects on the trade balance can be perverse for a disconcertingly long short run, during which further depreciation, perhaps reinforced by speculation, occurs. Meanwhile the effects of depreciation on domestic currency prices of internationally traded goods are inflationary, even for an economy with idle resources and no domestic sources of inflationary pressure.

Furthermore, there are international difficulties in reliance on monetary policy in a floating rate regime. I quote from my 1972 lecture: ". . . When the export-import balance becomes the strategic component of aggregate demand, one country's expansionary stimulus is another country's deflationary shock. We can hardly imagine that the Common Market will passively allow the U.S. to manipulate the dollar exchange rate in the interests of U.S. domestic stabilization. Nor can we imagine the reverse. International coordination of interest rate policies will be essential in a regime of floating exchange rates, no less than in a fixed parity regime." The bickering between Washington and Bonn about these issues in the last year is just what I had in mind.

Third, governments are not and cannot be indifferent to changes in the values of their currencies in exchange markets, any more

than they did or could ignore changes in their international reserves under the fixed-parity regime. The reasons for their concern are not all macroeconomic; they include all the impacts on domestic industries, export and import-competing sectors, that arise from exchange rate fluctuations originating in financial and capital transactions. The uncoordinated interventions that make floating dirty are the governments' natural mechanisms of defense against shocks transmitted to their economies by foreign exchange markets.

Fourth, another optimistic hope belied by events was the belief that floating rates would insulate economies from shocks to export and import demand. The same Mundell-Fleming type model that told us the relative impotence of fiscal policies and non-monetary demand shocks under floating rates also implied that trade balance shocks would be absorbed completely in exchange rates without adjustment of domestic output or prices. This will, of course, not be the case if the trade balance moves the wrong way (anti-Marshall-Lerner), or if, for any of the other understandable reasons enumerated above, governments intervene to prevent full exchange rate adjustment. It will not be the case anyway if exchange rate movements have consequences for asset demands and supplies, as they will, either via the capital gains or losses they produce for agents with long or short positions in foreign currency or via the expectations of future exchange rate movements which they generate.

The recent decline of the dollar against the Deutschmark, yen, and Swiss franc illustrates many of the above points. The U.S., on the one hand, and Germany and Japan on the other, clearly have divergent domestic histories, prospects, and objectives in terms of output growth and inflation. The changes in currency exchange rates have not served, as some proponents of flexible rates might have hoped, to permit these countries to pursue their differing policies without mutual interference. The Germans and Japanese have been reluctant to accept the effects of currency appreciation on their export industries, and so they have intervened to limit the appreciation. The Americans, concerned about the effects of depreciation on price indexes, have tightened monetary policy and raised interest rates in an attempt to stem the anti-dollar tide in the foreign exchange markets.

This history also supports the assertion I made above, that goods "arbitrage" is very slow relative to inter-currency financial speculation and portfolio shift. The net result of exchange rate movements and domestic price movements over the past few years has been to improve dramatically the competitive position of the U.S. vis-à-vis Germany and Japan. This is true when wholesale prices indices, converted to a single currency at prevailing exchange rates, are compared. Our trade-weighted real exchange rate is about 5% below 1977 and March 1973, and more than 7% below 1976. Germany's is 7% above 1973, though still below 1976 and 1977. Japan's is 3% above 1973, 7% above 1976, and 2% above 1977. The change is even more spectacular when labor costs are similarly compared. In 1970 U.S. hourly labor costs, including fringe benefits, were the highest in the world, 67% above Germany, 300% above Japan. In 1977 five countries had higher costs at exchange rates prevailing in December. Our costs were 16% below Germany, and now only 55% above Japan.* The U.S. is now a low-wage country! Yet we are suffering from the worst trade deficits in history.

I do not wish to be misunderstood. I think the hysteria over the recent decline of the dollar is greatly overdone, and that the

*For these calculations, made at the Institut der Deutschen Wirtschaft, Köln, I am indebted to Professor Herbert Giersch.

panicky pressure on our government to defend the dollar—pressure from European governments, from financial circles here and abroad, from the media—has been most unjustified. Moreover, anyone who thinks that the pre-1971 system of pegged rates would have handled better the recent flight from the dollar into marks, yen, and Swiss francs has a very short memory. Things would have been lots worse, with greater impacts on U.S. domestic policies and greater disruptions to international markets. My message is not, I emphasize again, that floating is the inferior regime. It is that floating does not satisfactorily solve all the problems.

One big reason why it does not is that foreign exchange markets are necessarily adrift without anchors. What we have is an incredibly efficient set of financial markets in which various obligations, mostly short-term, expressed in various currencies are traded. I mean the word "efficient" only in a mechanical sense: transactions costs are low, communications are speedy, prices are instantaneously kept in line all over the world, credit enables participants to take large long or short positions at will or whim. Whether the market is "efficient" in the deeper economic-informational sense is very dubious. In these markets, as in other markets for financial instruments, speculation on future prices is the dominating preoccupation of the participants. In the ideal world of rational expectations, the anthropomorphic personified "market" would base its expectations on informed estimates of equilibrium exchange rates. Speculation would be the engine that moves actual rates to the equilibrium set. In fact no one has any good basis for estimating the equilibrium dollar-mark parity for 1980 or 1985, to which current rates might be related. That parity depends on a host of incalculables—not just the future paths of the two economies and of the rest of the world, but the future portfolio preferences of the world's wealth-owners, including Arabs and Iranians as well as Americans and Germans. Reasonable economists and traders, not to mention unreasonable members of both species, can and do have diverse views. In the absence of any consensus on fundamentals, the markets are dominated—like those for gold, rare paintings, and—yes, often equities—by traders in the game of guessing what other traders are going to think.

As a technical matter, we know that a rational expectations equilibrium in markets of this kind is a saddle point. That is, there is only a singular path that leads from disequilibrium to equilibrium. If the markets are not on that path, or if they don't jump to it from wherever they are, they can follow any of a number of paths that lead away from equilibrium—paths along which, nonetheless, expectations are on average fulfilled. Such deviant paths are innocuous in markets—as for rare coins, precious metals, baseball cards, Swiss francs—which are sideshows to the real economic circus. But they are far from innocuous in foreign exchange markets whose prices are of major economic consequence.

This suggests that governments might contribute to exchange market efficiency by themselves calculating and publicizing estimates of equilibrium exchange rates, rates expected some years in future. The floating of the Canadian dollar in the 1950s was probably an empirical episode of considerable intellectual importance in solidifying economists' acceptance of the theoretical case for flexible rates. Floating rates had acquired a bad reputation, rightly or wrongly, in the interwar period. The Canadian experiment seemed to show that market speculation was stabilizing; certainly there were no gyrations greatly disturbing to Canadian-U.S. economic relations or to the two economies. One reason, among others, appears to have been a general belief in a long-run equilibrium not far from dollar-dollar parity, an equilibrium that

accorded both with the interconnected structures of the two economies and with the policy intentions of the Canadian government. Those who extrapolated from the model to the world-wide floating of the 1970s have been disappointed. It is scarcely conceivable that the various OECD countries could individually project, much less agree on, much less convince skeptical markets of, a system of equilibrium or target exchange rates for 1980 or 1985. So I must remain skeptical that the price signals these unanchored markets give are signals that will guide economies to their true comparative advantage, capital to its efficient international allocation, and governments to correct macroeconomic policies.

That is why I think we need to throw some sand in the well-greased wheels. Perhaps one might have hoped that the volatility of floating rates would do that automatically; given the limitations of futures markets, uncovered risks might permit wedges between national interest rates and currency diversification might limit intercurrency movements of funds. In my 1972 excursion into this subject I was skeptical on this point, and events since have vindicated my skepticism. I said, "Increasing exchange risk will help, but I do not think we should expect too much from it. Many participants in short term money markets can afford to take a relaxed view of exchange risk. They can aim for the best interest rate available, taking account of their mean estimate of gain or loss from currency exchange. Multinational corporations, for example, can diversify over time. They will be in exchange markets again and again: there are no currencies they cannot use."

Let me return to my proposed tax, and provide just a few more details. It would be an internationally agreed uniform tax, administered by each government over its own jurisdiction. Britain, for example, would be responsible for taxing all inter-currency transactions in Eurocurrency banks and brokers located in London, even when sterling was not involved. The tax proceeds could appropriately be paid into the IME or World Bank. The tax would apply to all purchases of financial instruments denominated in another currency—from currency and coin to equity securities. It would have to apply, I think, to all payments in one currency for goods, services, and real assets sold by a resident of another currency area. I don't intend to add even a small barrier to trade. But I see offhand no other way to prevent financial transactions disguised as trade.

Countries could, possibly subject to IMF consent, form currency areas within which the tax would not apply. Presumably the smaller EEC members and those ldc's which wished to tie their currency to a key currency would wish to do this. The purpose is to moderate swings in major exchange rates, not to break links between closely related economies.

Doubtless there would be difficulties of administration and enforcement. Doubtless there would be ingenious patterns of evasion. But since these will not be costless either, the main purpose of the plan will not be lost. At least the bank facilities which are so responsible for the current troublesome perfection of these markets would be taxed, as would the multinational corporations.

I am aware of the distortions and allocational costs that can be attributed to tariffs, including tariffs on imports of foreign-currency assets. I don't deny their existence. I say only that they are small compared to the world macroeconomic costs of the present system. To those costs, I believe, will be added the burdens of much more damaging protectionist and autarkic measures designed to protect economies, at least their politically favored sectors, from the consequences of international financial shocks.

I do not want to claim too much for my modest proposal. It will, I think, restore to national economies and governments some fraction of the short-run autonomy they enjoyed before currency convertibility became so easy. It will not, should not, permit governments to make domestic policies without reference to external consequences. Consequently, it will not release major governments from the imperative necessity to coordinate policies more effectively. Together the major governments and central banks are making fiscal and monetary policy for the world, whether or not they explicitly recognize the fact. Recently, it is quite clear from the differences and misunderstandings among the so-called three locomotives, they have not been concerting their policies very successfully. I would hope that, relieved of the need to stay in lockstep in order to avoid large exchange rate fluctuations, these governments might approach the task of policy coordination with a longer-range and more global view of their responsibilities.

Part IV
WELFARE AND INEQUALITY

JAMES TOBIN

On Improving the Economic Status of the Negro

I START from the presumption that the integration of Negroes into the American society and economy can be accomplished within existing political and economic institutions. I understand the impatience of those who think otherwise, but I see nothing incompatible between our peculiar mixture of private enterprise and government, on the one hand, and the liberation and integration of the Negro, on the other. Indeed the present position of the Negro is an aberration from the principles of our society, rather than a requirement of its functioning. Therefore, my suggestions are directed to the aim of mobilizing existing powers of government to bring Negroes into full participation in the main stream of American economic life.

The economic plight of individuals, Negroes and whites alike, can always be attributed to specific handicaps and circumstances: discrimination, immobility, lack of education and experience, ill health, weak motivation, poor neighborhood, large family size, burdensome family responsibilities. Such diagnoses suggest a host of specific remedies, some in the domain of civil rights, others in the war on poverty. Important as these remedies are, there is a danger that the diagnoses are myopic. They explain why certain individuals rather than others suffer from the economic maladies of the time. They do not explain why the over-all incidence of the maladies varies dramatically from time to time—for example, why personal attributes which seemed to doom a man to unemployment in 1932 or even in 1954 or 1961 did not so handicap him in 1944 or 1951 or 1956.

Public health measures to improve the environment are often more productive in conquering disease than a succession of individual treatments. Malaria was conquered by oiling and draining swamps, not by quinine. The analogy holds for economic maladies.

Reprinted by permission from *Daedalus* 94(4) (fall 1965):878–898. (Also in *The Negro American*, eds. T. Parsons and K. Clark, New York: Houghton Mifflin, 1966, pp. 451–471.)

Unless the global incidence of these misfortunes can be diminished, every individual problem successfully solved will be replaced by a similar problem somewhere else. That is why an economist is led to emphasize the importance of the over-all economic climate.

Over the decades, general economic progress has been the major factor in the gradual conquest of poverty. Recently some observers, J. K. Galbraith and Michael Harrington most eloquently, have contended that this process no longer operates. The economy may prosper and labor may become steadily more productive as in the past, but "the other America" will be stranded. Prosperity and progress have already eliminated almost all the easy cases of poverty, leaving a hard core beyond the reach of national economic trends. There may be something to the "backwash" thesis as far as whites are concerned.[1] But it definitely does not apply to Negroes. Too many of them are poor. It cannot be true that half of a race of twenty million human beings are victims of specific disabilities which insulate them from the national economic climate. It cannot be true, and it is not. Locke Anderson has shown that the pace of Negro economic progress is peculiarly sensitive to general economic growth. He estimates that if nationwide per capita personal income is stationary, nonwhite median family income falls by .5 per cent per year, while if national per capita income grows 5 per cent, nonwhite income grows nearly 7.5 per cent.[2]

National prosperity and economic growth are still powerful engines for improving the economic status of Negroes. They are not doing enough and they are not doing it fast enough. There is ample room for a focused attack on the specific sources of Negro poverty. But a favorable over-all economic climate is a necessary condition for the global success—as distinguished from success in individual cases—of specific efforts to remedy the handicaps associated with Negro poverty.

The Importance of a Tight Labor Market

But isn't the present over-all economic climate favorable? Isn't the economy enjoying an upswing of unprecedented length, setting new records almost every month in production, employment, profits, and income? Yes, but expansion and new records should be routine in an economy with growing population, capital equipment, and productivity. The fact is that the economy has not operated with reasonably full utilization of its manpower and plant capacity since

879

1957. Even now, after four and one-half years of uninterrupted expansion, the economy has not regained the ground lost in the recessions of 1958 and 1960. The current expansion has whittled away at unemployment, reducing it from 6.5 to 7 per cent to 4.5 to 5 per cent. It has diminished idle plant capacity correspondingly. The rest of the gains since 1960 in employment, production, and income have just offset the normal growth of population, capacity, and productivity.

The magnitude of America's poverty problem already reflects the failure of the economy in the second postwar decade to match its performance in the first.[3] Had the 1947-56 rate of growth of median family income been maintained since 1957, and had unemployment been steadily limited to 4 per cent, it is estimated that the fraction of the population with poverty incomes in 1963 would have been 16.6 per cent instead of 18.5 per cent.[4] The educational qualifications of the labor force have continued to improve. The principle of racial equality, in employment as in other activities, has gained ground both in law and in the national conscience. If, despite all this, dropouts, inequalities in educational attainment, and discrimination in employment seem more serious today rather than less, the reason is that the over-all economic climate has not been favorable after all.

The most important dimension of the overall economic climate is the tightness of the labor market. In a tight labor market unemployment is low and short in duration, and job vacancies are plentiful. People who stand at the end of the hiring line and the top of the layoff list have the most to gain from a tight labor market. It is not proves in a tight labor market and declines in a slack market. Unsurprising that the position of Negroes relative to that of whites imemployment itself is only one way in which a slack labor market hurts Negroes and other disadvantaged groups, and the gains from reduction in unemployment are by no means confined to the employment of persons counted as unemployed.[5] A tight labor market means not just jobs, but better jobs, longer hours, higher wages. Because of the heavy demands for labor during the second world war and its economic aftermath, Negroes made dramatic relative gains between 1940 and 1950. Unfortunately this momentum has not been maintained, and the blame falls largely on the weakness of labor markets since 1957.[6]

The shortage of jobs has hit Negro men particularly hard and thus has contributed mightily to the ordeal of the Negro family,

880

which is in turn the cumulative source of so many other social disorders.[7] The unemployment rate of Negro men is more sensitive than that of Negro women to the national rate. Since 1949 Negro women have gained in median income relative to white women, but Negro men have lost ground to white males.[8] In a society which stresses breadwinning as the expected role of the mature male and occupational achievement as his proper goal, failure to find and to keep work is devastating to the man's self-respect and family status. Matriarchy is in any case a strong tradition in Negro society, and the man's role is further downgraded when the family must and can depend on the woman for its livelihood. It is very important to increase the proportion of Negro children who grow up in stable families with two parents. Without a strong labor market it will be extremely difficult to do so.

Unemployment. It is well known that Negro unemployment rates are multiples of the general unemployment rate. This fact reflects both the lesser skills, seniority, and experience of Negroes and employers' discrimination against Negroes. These conditions are a deplorable reflection on American society, but as long as they exist Negroes suffer much more than others from a general increase in unemployment and gain much more from a general reduction. A rule of thumb is that changes in the nonwhite unemployment rate are twice those in the white rate. The rule works both ways. Nonwhite unemployment went from 4.1 per cent in 1953, a tight labor market year, to 12.5 per cent in 1961, while the white rate rose from 2.3 per cent to 6 per cent. Since then, the Negro rate has declined by 2.4 per cent, the white rate by 1.2.

Even the Negro teenage unemployment rate shows some sensitivity to general economic conditions. Recession increased it from 15 per cent in 1955-56 to 25 per cent in 1958. It decreased to 22 per cent in 1960 but rose to 28 per cent in 1963; since then it has declined somewhat. Teenage unemployment is abnormally high now, relative to that of other age groups, because the wave of postwar babies is coming into the labor market. Most of them, especially the Negroes, are crowding the end of the hiring line. But their prospects for getting jobs are no less dependent on general labor market conditions.

Part-time work. Persons who are involuntarily forced to work part time instead of full time are not counted as unemployed, but their number goes up and down with the unemployment rate. Just as Negroes bear a disproportionate share of unemployment, they

881

bear more than their share of involuntary part-time unemployment.[9] A tight labor market will not only employ more Negroes; it will also give more of those who are employed full-time jobs. In both respects, it will reduce disparities between whites and Negroes.

Labor-force participation. In a tight market, of which a low unemployment rate is a barometer, the labor force itself is larger. Job opportunities draw into the labor force individuals who, simply because the prospects were dim, did not previously regard themselves as seeking work and were therefore not enumerated as unemployed. For the economy as a whole, it appears that an expansion of job opportunities enough to reduce unemployment by one worker will bring another worker into the labor force.

This phenomenon is important for many Negro families. Statistically, their poverty now appears to be due more often to the lack of a breadwinner in the labor force than to unemployment.[10] But in a tight labor market many members of these families, including families now on public assistance, would be drawn into employment. Labor-force participation rates are roughly 2 per cent lower for nonwhite men than for white men, and the disparity increases in years of slack labor markets.[11] The story is different for women. Negro women have always been in the labor force to a much greater extent than white women. A real improvement in the economic status of Negro men and in the stability of Negro families would probably lead to a reduction in labor-force participation by Negro women. But for teenagers, participation rates for Negroes are not so high as for whites; and for women twenty to twenty-four they are about the same. These relatively low rates are undoubtedly due less to voluntary choice than to the same lack of job opportunities that produces phenomenally high unemployment rates for young Negro women.

Duration of unemployment. In a tight labor market, such unemployment as does exist is likely to be of short duration. Short-term unemployment is less damaging to the economic welfare of the unemployed. More will have earned and fewer will have exhausted private and public unemployment benefits. In 1953 when the over-all unemployment rate was 2.9 per cent, only 4 per cent of the unemployed were out of work for longer than twenty-six weeks and only 11 per cent for longer than fifteen weeks. In contrast, the unemployment rate in 1961 was 6.7 per cent; and of the unemployed in that year, 17 per cent were out of work for longer

882

501

than twenty-six weeks and 32 per cent for longer than fifteen weeks. Between the first quarter of 1964 and the first quarter of 1965, overall unemployment fell 11 per cent, while unemployment extending beyond half a year was lowered by 22 per cent.

As Rashi Fein points out elsewhere in this volume, one more dimension of society's inequity to the Negro is that an unemployed Negro is more likely to stay unemployed than an unemployed white. But his figures also show that Negroes share in the reduction of long-term unemployment accompanying economic expansion.

Migration from agriculture. A tight labor market draws the surplus rural population to higher paying non-agricultural jobs. Southern Negroes are a large part of this surplus rural population. Migration is the only hope for improving their lot, or their children's. In spite of the vast migration of past decades, there are still about 775,000 Negroes, 11 per cent of the Negro labor force of the country, who depend on the land for their living and that of their families.[12] Almost a half million live in the South, and almost all of them are poor.

Migration from agriculture and from the South is the Negroes' historic path toward economic improvement and equality. It is a smooth path for Negroes and for the urban communities to which they move only if there is a strong demand for labor in towns and cities North and South. In the 1940's the number of Negro farmers and farm laborers in the nation fell by 450,000 and one and a half million Negroes (net) left the South. This was the great decade of Negro economic advance. In the 1950's the same occupational and geographical migration continued undiminished. The movement to higher-income occupations and locations should have raised the relative economic status of Negroes. But in the 1950's Negroes were moving into increasingly weak job markets. Too often disguised unemployment in the countryside was simply transformed into enumerated unemployment, and rural poverty into urban poverty.[13]

Quality of jobs. In a slack labor market, employers can pick and choose, both in recruiting and in promoting. They exaggerate the skill, education, and experience requirements of their jobs. They use diplomas, or color, or personal histories as convenient screening devices. In a tight market, they are forced to be realistic, to tailor job specifications to the available supply, and to give on-the-job training. They recruit and train applicants whom they would otherwise screen out, and they upgrade employees whom they would in

883

slack times consign to low-wage, low-skill, and part-time jobs. Wartime and other experience shows that job requirements are adjustable and that men and women are trainable. It is only in slack times that people worry about a mismatch between supposedly rigid occupational requirements and supposedly unchangeable qualifications of the labor force. As already noted, the relative status of Negroes improves in a tight labor market not only in respect to unemployment, but also in respect to wages and occupations.

Cyclical fluctuation. Sustaining a high demand for labor is important. The in-and-out status of the Negro in the business cycle damages his long-term position because periodic unemployment robs him of experience and seniority.

Restrictive practices. A slack labor market probably accentuates the discriminatory and protectionist proclivities of certain crafts and unions. When jobs are scarce, opening the door to Negroes is a real threat. Of course prosperity will not automatically dissolve the barriers, but it will make it more difficult to oppose efforts to do so.

I conclude that the single most important step the nation could take to improve the economic position of the Negro is to operate the economy steadily at a low rate of unemployment. We cannot expect to restore the labor market conditions of the second world war, and we do not need to. In the years 1951-1953, unemployment was roughly 3 per cent, teenage unemployment around 7 per cent, Negro unemployment about 4.5 per cent, long-term unemployment negligible. In the years 1955-57, general unemployment was roughly 4 per cent, and the other measures correspondingly higher. Four per cent is the official target of the Kennedy-Johnson administration. It has not been achieved since 1957. Reaching and maintaining 4 per cent would be a tremendous improvement over the performance of the last eight years. But we should not stop there; the society and the Negro can benefit immensely from tightening the labor market still further, to 3.5 or 3 per cent unemployment. The administration itself has never defined 4 per cent as anything other than an "interim" target.

Why Don't We Have a Tight Labor Market?

We know how to operate the economy so that there is a tight labor market. By fiscal and monetary measures the federal government can control aggregate spending in the economy. The govern-

884

ment could choose to control it so that unemployment *averaged* 3.5 or 3 per cent instead of remaining over 4.5 per cent except at occasional business cycle peaks. Moreover, recent experience here and abroad shows that we can probably narrow the amplitude of fluctuations around whatever average we select as a target.

Some observers have cynically concluded that a society like ours can achieve full employment only in wartime. But aside from conscription into the armed services, government action creates jobs in wartime by exactly the same mechanism as in peacetime—the government spends more money and stimulates private firms and citizens to spend more too. It is the *amount* of spending, not its purpose, that does the trick. Public or private spending to go to the moon, build schools, or conquer poverty can be just as effective in reducing unemployment as spending to build airplanes and submarines —if there is enough of it. There may be more political constraints and ideological inhibitions in peacetime, but the same techniques of economic policy are available if we want badly enough to use them. The two main reasons we do not take this relatively simple way out are two obsessive fears, inflation and balance of payments deficits.

Running the economy with a tight labor market would mean a somewhat faster upward creep in the price level. The disadvantages of this are, in my view, exaggerated and are scarcely commensurable with the real economic and social gains of higher output and employment. Moreover, there are ways of protecting "widows and orphans" against erosion in the purchasing power of their savings. But fear of inflation is strong both in the U.S. financial establishment and in the public at large. The vast comfortable white middle class who are never touched by unemployment prefer to safeguard the purchasing power of their life insurance and pension rights than to expand opportunities for the disadvantaged and unemployed.

The fear of inflation would operate anyway, but it is accentuated by U.S. difficulties with its international balance of payments. These difficulties have seriously constrained and hampered U.S. fiscal and monetary policy in recent years. Any rise in prices might enlarge the deficit. An agressively expansionary monetary policy, lowering interest rates, might push money out of the country.

In the final analysis what we fear is that we might not be able to defend the parity of the dollar with gold, that is, to sell gold at thirty-five dollars an ounce to any government that wants to buy. So great is the gold mystique that this objective has come to occupy a niche in the hierarchy of U.S. goals second only to the military de-

885

fense of the country, and not always to that. It is not fanciful to link the plight of Negro teenagers in Harlem to the monetary whims of General de Gaulle. But it is only our own attachment to "the dollar" as an abstraction which makes us cringe before the European appetite for gold.

This topic is too charged with technical complexities, real and imagined, and with confused emotions to be discussed adequately here. I will confine myself to three points. First, the United States is the last country in the world which needs to hold back its own economy to balance its international accounts. To let the tail wag the dog is not in the interests of the rest of the world, so much of which depends on us for trade and capital, any more than in our own.

Second, forces are at work to restore balance to American international accounts—the increased competitiveness of our exports and the income from the large investments our firms and citizens have made overseas since the war. Meanwhile we can finance deficits by gold reserves and lines of credit at the International Monetary Fund and at foreign central banks. Ultimately we have one foolproof line of defense—letting the dollar depreciate relative to foreign currencies. The world would not end. The sun would rise the next day. American products would be more competitive in world markets. Neither God nor the Constitution fixed the gold value of the dollar. The U.S. would not be the first country to let its currency depreciate. Nor would it be the first time for the U.S.—not until we stopped "saving" the dollar and the gold standard in 1933 did our recovery from the Great Depression begin.

Third, those who oppose taking such risks argue that the dollar today occupies a unique position as international money, that the world as a whole has an interest, which we cannot ignore, in the stability of the gold value of the dollar. If so, we can reasonably ask the rest of the world, especially our European friends, to share the burdens which guaranteeing this stability imposes upon us.

This has been an excursion into general economic policy. But the connection between gold and the plight of the Negro is no less real for being subtle. We are paying much too high a social price for avoiding creeping inflation and for protecting our gold stock and "the dollar." But it will not be easy to alter these national priorities. The interests of the unemployed, the poor, and the Negroes are under-represented in the comfortable consensus which supports and confines current policy.

886

Another approach, which can be pursued simultaneously, is to diminish the conflicts among these competing objectives, in particular to reduce the degree of inflation associated with low levels of unemployment. This can be done in two ways. One way is to improve the mobility of labor and other resources to occupations, locations, and industries where bottlenecks would otherwise lead to wage and price increases. This is where many specific programs, such as the training and retraining of manpower and policies to improve the technical functioning of labor markets, come into their own.

A second task is to break down the barriers to competition which now restrict the entry of labor and enterprise into certain occupations and industries. These lead to wage- and price-increasing bottlenecks even when resources are not really short. Many barriers are created by public policy itself, in response to the vested interests concerned. Many reflect concentration of economic power in unions and in industry. These barriers represent another way in which the advantaged and the employed purchase their standards of living and their security at the expense of unprivileged minorities.

In the best of circumstances, structural reforms of these kinds will be slow and gradual. They will encounter determined economic and political resistance from special interests which are powerful in Congress and state legislatures. Moreover, Congressmen and legislators represent places rather than people and are likely to oppose, not facilitate, the increased geographical mobility which is required. It is no accident that our manpower programs do not include relocation allowances.

Increasing the Earning Capacity of Negroes

Given the proper over-all economic climate, in particular a steadily tight labor market, the Negro's economic condition can be expected to improve, indeed to improve dramatically. But not fast enough. Not as fast as his aspirations or as the aspirations he has taught the rest of us to have for him. What else can be done? This question is being answered in detail by experts elsewhere in this volume. I shall confine myself to a few comments and suggestions that occur to a general economist.

Even in a tight labor market, the Negro's relative status will suffer both from current discrimination and from his lower earning capacity, the result of inferior acquired skill. In a real sense both factors reflect discrimination, since the Negro's handicaps in

887

506

earning capacity are the residue of decades of discrimination in education and employment. Nevertheless for both analysis and policy it is useful to distinguish the two.

Discrimination means that the Negro is denied access to certain markets where he might sell his labor, and to certain markets where he might purchase goods and services. Elementary application of "supply and demand" makes it clear that these restrictions are bound to result in his selling his labor for less and buying his livelihood for more than if these barriers did not exist. If Negro women can be clerks only in certain stores, those storekeepers will not need to pay them so much as they pay whites. If Negroes can live only in certain houses, the prices and rents they have to pay will be high for the quality of accommodation provided.

Successful elimination of discrimination is not only important in itself but will also have substantial economic benefits. Since residential segregation is the key to so much else and so difficult to eliminate by legal fiat alone, the power of the purse should be unstintingly used. I see no reason that the expenditure of funds for this purpose should be confined to new construction. Why not establish private or semi-public revolving funds to purchase, for resale or rental on a desegregated basis, strategically located existing structures as they become available?

The effects of past discrimination will take much longer to eradicate. The sins against the fathers are visited on the children. They are deprived of the intellectual and social capital which in our society is supposed to be transmitted in the family and the home. We have only begun to realize how difficult it is to make up for this deprivation by formal schooling, even when we try. And we have only begun to try, after accepting all too long the notion that schools should acquiesce in, even re-enforce, inequalities in home backgrounds rather than overcome them.

Upgrading the earning capacity of Negroes will be difficult, but the economic effects are easy to analyze. Economists have long held that the way to reduce disparities in earned incomes is to eliminate disparities in earning capacities. If college-trained people earn more money than those who left school after eight years, the remedy is to send a larger proportion of young people to college. If machine operators earn more than ditchdiggers, the remedy is to give more people the capacity and opportunity to be machine operators. These changes in relative supplies reduce the disparity both by competing down the pay in the favored line of work and by

888

raising the pay in the less remunerative line. When there are only a few people left in the population whose capacities are confined to garbage-collecting, it will be a high-paid calling. The same is true of domestic service and all kinds of menial work.

This classical economic strategy will be hampered if discrimination, union barriers, and the like stand in the way. It will not help to increase the supply of Negro plumbers if the local unions and contractors will not let them join. But experience also shows that barriers give way more easily when the pressures of unsatisfied demand and supply pile up.

It should therefore be the task of educational and manpower policy to engineer over the next two decades a massive change in the relative supplies of people of different educational and professional attainments and degrees of skill and training. It must be a more rapid change than has occurred in the past two decades, because that has not been fast enough to alter income differentials. We should try particularly to increase supplies in those fields where salaries and wages are already high and rising. In this process we should be very skeptical of self-serving arguments and calculations —that an increase in supply in this or that profession would be bound to reduce quality, or that there are some mechanical relations of "need" to population or to Gross National Product that cannot be exceeded.

Such a policy would be appropriate to the "war on poverty" even if there were no racial problem. Indeed, our objective is to raise the earning capacities of low-income whites as well as of Negroes. But Negroes have the most to gain, and even those who because of age or irreversible environmental handicaps must inevitably be left behind will benefit by reduction in the number of whites and other Negroes who are competing with them.

Assuring Living Standards in the Absence of Earning Capacity

The reduction of inequality in earning capacity is the fundamental solution, and in a sense anything else is stopgap. Some stopgaps are useless and even counter-productive. People who lack the capacity to earn a decent living need to be helped, but they will not be helped by minimum wage laws, trade union wage pressures, or other devices which seek to compel employers to pay them more than their work is worth. The more likely outcome of such regula-

889

tions is that the intended beneficiaries are not employed at all.

A far better approach is to supplement earnings from the public fisc. But assistance can and should be given in a way that does not force the recipients out of the labor force or give them incentive to withdraw. Our present system of welfare payments does just that, causing needless waste and demoralization. This application of the means test is bad economics as well as bad sociology. It is almost as if our present programs of public assistance had been consciously contrived to perpetuate the conditions they are supposed to alleviate.

These programs apply a strict means test. The amount of assistance is an estimate of minimal needs, less the resources of the family from earnings. The purpose of the means test seems innocuous enough. It is to avoid wasting taxpayers' money on people who do not really need help. But another way to describe the means test is to note that it taxes earnings at a rate of 100 per cent. A person on public assistance cannot add to his family's standard of living by working. Of course, the means test provides a certain incentive to work in order to get off public assistance altogether. But in many cases, especially where there is only one adult to provide for and take care of several children, the adult simply does not have enough time and earning opportunities to get by without financial help. He, or more likely she, is essentially forced to be both idle and on a dole. The means test also involves limitations on property holdings which deprive anyone who is or expects to be on public assistance of incentive to save.

In a society which prizes incentives for work and thrift, these are surprising regulations. They deny the country useful productive services, but that economic loss is minor in the present context. They deprive individuals and families both of work experience which could teach them skills, habits, and self-discipline of future value and of the self-respect and satisfaction which comes from improving their own lot by their own efforts.

Public assistance encourages the disintegration of the family, the key to so many of the economic and social problems of the American Negro. The main assistance program, Aid for Dependent Children, is not available if there is an able-bodied employed male in the house. In most states it is not available if there is an able-bodied man in the house, even if he is not working. All too often it is necessary for the father to leave his children so that they can eat. It is bad enough to provide incentives for idleness but even worse to legislate incentives for desertion.[14]

890

The bureaucratic surveillance and guidance to which recipients of public assistance are subject undermine both their self-respect and their capacity to manage their own affairs. In the administration of assistance there is much concern to detect "cheating" against the means tests and to ensure approved prudent use of the public's money. Case loads are frequently too great and administrative regulations too confining to permit the talents of social workers to treat the roots rather than the symptoms of the social maladies of their clients. The time of the clients is considered a free good, and much of it must be spent in seeking or awaiting the attention of the officials on whom their livelihood depends.

The defects of present categorical assistance programs could be, in my opinion, greatly reduced by adopting a system of basic income allowances, integrated with and administered in conjunction with the federal income tax. In a sense the proposal is to make the income tax symmetrical. At present the federal government takes a share of family income in excess of a certain amount (for example, a married couple with three children pays no tax unless their income exceeds $3700). The proposal is that the Treasury pay any family who falls below a certain income a fraction of the shortfall. The idea has sometimes been called a negative income tax.

The payment would be a matter of right, like an income tax refund. Individuals expecting to be entitled to payments from the government during the year could receive them in periodic installments by making a declaration of expected income and expected tax withholdings. But there would be a final settlement between the individual and the government based on a "tax" return after the year was over, just as there is now for taxpayers on April 15.

A family with no other income at all would receive a basic allowance scaled to the number of persons in the family. For a concrete example, take the basic allowance to be $400 per year per person. It might be desirable and equitable, however, to reduce the additional basic allowance for children after, say, the fourth. Once sufficient effort is being made to disseminate birth control knowledge and technique, the scale of allowances by family size certainly should provide some disincentive to the creation of large families.

A family's allowance would be reduced by a certain fraction of every dollar of other income it received. For a concrete example, take this fraction to be one third. This means that the family has considerable incentive to earn income, because its total income including allowances will be increased by two-thirds of whatever it

891

earns. In contrast, the means test connected with present public assistance is a 100 per cent "tax" on earnings. With a one-third "tax" a family will be on the receiving end of the allowance and income tax system until its regular income equals three times its basic allowance.[15]

Families above this "break-even" point would be taxpayers. But the less well-off among them would pay less taxes than they do now. The first dollars of income in excess of this break-even point would be taxed at the same rate as below, one-third in the example. At some income level, the tax liability so computed would be the same as the tax under the present income tax law. From that point up, the present law would take over; taxpayers with incomes above this point would not be affected by the plan.

The best way to summarize the proposal is to give a concrete graphical illustration. On the horizontal axis of Figure 1 is measured family income from wages and salaries, interest, dividends, rents, and so forth—"adjusted gross income" for the Internal Revenue Service. On the vertical axis is measured the corresponding "disposable income," that is, income after federal taxes and allowances. If the family neither paid taxes nor received allowance, disposable income would be equal to family income; in the diagram this equality would be shown by the 45° line from the origin. Disposable income above this 45° line means the family receives allowances; disposable income below this line means the family pays taxes. The broken line OAB describes the present income tax law for a married couple with three children, allowing the standard deductions. The line CD is the revision which the proposed allowance system would make for incomes below $7963. For incomes above $7963, the old tax schedule applies.

Beneficiaries under Federal Old Age Survivors and Disability Insurance would not be eligible for the new allowances. Congress should make sure that minimum benefits under OASDI are at least as high as the allowances. Some government payments, especially those for categorical public assistance, would eventually be replaced by basic allowances. Others, like unemployment insurance and veterans' pensions, are intended to be rights earned by past services regardless of current need. It would therefore be wrong to withhold allowances from the beneficiaries of these payments, but it would be reasonable to count them as income in determining the size of allowances, even though they are not subject to tax.

Although the numbers used above are illustrative, they are in-

892

Figure 1

Illustration of Proposed Income Allowance Plan
(Married couple with three children)

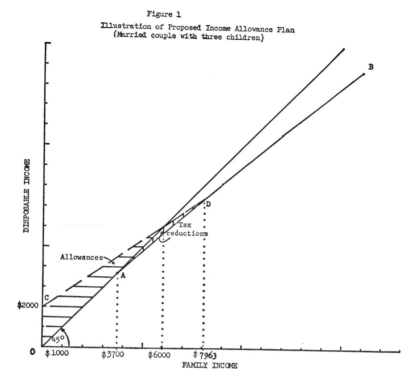

dicative of what is needed for an effective program. It would be expensive for the federal budget, involving an expenditure of perhaps fifteen billion dollars a year. Partially offsetting this budgetary cost are the savings in public assistance, on which governments now spend five and six-tenths billion dollars a year, of which three and two-tenths billion are federal funds. In addition, savings are possible in a host of other income maintenance programs, notably in agriculture.

The program is expensive, but it need not be introduced all at once. The size of allowances can be gradually increased as room in the budget becomes available. This is likely to happen fairly rapidly. First of all, there is room right now. The budget, and the budget deficit, can and should be larger in order to create a tight labor market. Second, the normal growth of the economy increases federal revenues from existing tax rates by some six to seven billion dollars a year. This is a drag on the economy, threatening stagnation and rising unemployment unless it is matched by a similar rise

893

in federal spending or avoided by cutting taxes. With defense spending stable or declining, there is room both for increases in civilian spending, as in the war on poverty, and for further tax cuts. Indeed, periodic tax reduction is official administration policy, and President Johnson agrees that the next turn belongs to low-income families. Gradually building an allowance system into the federal income tax would be the best way to lower the net yield of the tax—fairer and more far-reaching than further cuts in tax rates.

I referred to programs which make up for lack of earning capacity as stopgaps, but that is not entirely fair. Poverty itself saps earning capacity. The welfare way of life, on the edge of subsistence, does not provide motivation or useful work experience either to parents or to children. A better system, one which enables people to retain their self-respect and initiative, would in itself help to break the vicious circle.

The proposed allowance system is of course not the only thing which needs to be done. Without attempting to be exhaustive, I shall mention three other measures for the assistance of families without adequate earning capacity.

It hardly needs emphasizing that the large size of Negro families or non-families is one of the principal causes of Negro poverty. There are too many mouths to feed per breadwinner, and frequently the care of children keeps the mother, the only possible breadwinner, at home. A program of day care and pre-school education for children five and under could meet several objectives at once—enriching the experience of the children and freeing the mother for training or for work.

The quality of the medical care of Negroes is a disgrace in itself and contributes to their other economic handicaps.[16] Even so the financing of the care of "the medically indigent" is inadequate and chaotic. Sooner or later we will extend the principle of Medicare to citizens under sixty-five. Why not sooner?

As mentioned above, much Negro poverty in the South reflects the inability of Negroes to make a livelihood in agriculture. As far as the traditional cash crop, cotton, is concerned, mechanization and the competition of larger-scale units in the Southwest are undermining the plantation and share-cropping system of the Southeast. The Negro subsistence farmer has too little land, equipment, and know-how to make a decent income. Current government agricultural programs, expensive as they are to the taxpayer, do very little to help the sharecropper or subsistence farmer. Our whole

894

agricultural policy needs to be recast, to give income support to people rather than price support to crops and to take people off the land rather than to take land out of cultivation. The effects on the social system of the South may be revolutionary, but they can only be salutary. Obviously there will be a tremendous burden on educational and training facilities to fit people for urban and industrial life. And I must emphasize again that substantial migration from agriculture is only possible, without disaster in the cities, in a booming economy with a tight labor market.

Conclusion

By far the most powerful factor determining the economic status of Negroes is the over-all state of the U.S. economy. A vigorously expanding economy with a steadily tight labor market will rapidly raise the position of the Negro, both absolutely and relatively. Favored by such a climate, the host of specific measures to eliminate discrimination, improve education and training, provide housing, and strengthen the family can yield substantial additional results. In a less beneficent economic climate, where jobs are short rather than men, the wars against racial inequality and poverty will be uphill battles, and some highly touted weapons may turn out to be dangerously futile.

The forces of the market place, the incentives of private self-interest, the pressures of supply and demand—these can be powerful allies or stubborn opponents. Properly harnessed, they quietly and impersonally accomplish objectives which may elude detailed legislation and administration. To harness them to the cause of the American Negro is entirely possible. It requires simply that the federal government dedicate its fiscal and monetary policies more wholeheartedly and singlemindedly to achieving and maintaining genuinely full employment. The obstacles are not technical or economic. One obstacle is a general lack of understanding that unemployment and related evils are remediable by national fiscal and monetary measures. The other is the high priority now given to competing financial objectives.

In this area, as in others, the administration has disarmed its conservative opposition by meeting it halfway, and no influential political voices challenge the tacit compromise from the "Left." Negro rights movements have so far taken no interest in national fiscal and monetary policy. No doubt gold, the federal budget, and

895

the actions of the Federal Reserve System seem remote from the day-to-day firing line of the movements. Direct local actions to redress specific grievances and to battle visible enemies are absorbing and dramatic. They have concrete observable results. But the use of national political influence on behalf of the goals of the Employment Act of 1946 is equally important. It would fill a political vacuum, and its potential long-run pay-off is very high.

The goal of racial equality suggests that the federal government should provide more stimulus to the economy. Fortunately, it also suggests constructive ways to give the stimulus. We can kill two birds with one stone. The economy needs additional spending in general; the wars on poverty and racial inequality need additional spending of particular kinds. The needed spending falls into two categories: government programs to diminish economic inequalities by building up the earning capacities of the poor and their children, and humane public assistance to citizens who temporarily or permanently lack the capacity to earn a decent living for themselves and their families. In both categories the nation, its conscience aroused by the plight of the Negro, has the chance to make reforms which will benefit the whole society.

REFERENCES

1. As Locke Anderson shows, one would expect advances in median income to run into diminishing returns in reducing the number of people below some fixed poverty-level income. W. H. Locke Anderson, "Trickling Down: The Relationship between Economic Growth and the Extent of Poverty Among American Families," *Quarterly Journal of Economics,* Vol. 78 (November 1964), pp. 511-524. However, for the economy as a whole, estimates by Lowell Galloway suggest that advances in median income still result in a substantial reduction in the fraction of the population below poverty-level incomes. "The Foundation of the War on Poverty," *American Economic Review,* Vol. 55 (March 1965), pp. 122-131.

2. Anderson, *op. cit.,* Table IV, p. 522.

3. This point, and others made in this section, have been eloquently argued by Harry G. Johnson, "Unemployment and Poverty," unpublished paper presented at West Virginia University Conference on Poverty Amidst Affluence, May 5, 1965.

4. Galloway, *op. cit.* Galloway used the definitions of poverty originally suggested by the Council of Economic Advisers in its 1964 Economic Report, that is: incomes below $3000 a year for families and below $1500 a year

896

for single individuals. The Social Security Administration has refined these measures to take better account of family size and of income in kind available to farmers. Mollie Orshansky, "Counting the Poor: Another Look at the Poverty Profile, *Social Security Bulletin*, Vol. 28 (January 1965), pp. 3-29. These refinements change the composition of the "poor" but affect very little their total number; it is doubtful they would alter Galloway's results.

5. Galloway, *op. cit.*, shows that postwar experience suggests that, other things equal, every point by which unemployment is diminished lowers the national incidence of poverty by .5 per cent of itself. And this does not include the effects of the accompanying increase in median family income, which would be of the order of 3 per cent and reduce the poverty fraction another 1.8 per cent.

6. For lack of comparable nationwide income data, the only way to gauge the progress of Negroes relative to whites over long periods of time is to compare their distributions among occupations. A measure of the occupational position of a group can be constructed from decennial Census data by weighting the proportions of the group in each occupation by the average income of the occupation. The ratio of this measure for Negroes to the same measure for whites is an index of the relative occupational position of Negroes. Such calculations were originally made by Gary Becker, *The Economics of Discrimination* (Chicago, 1957). They have recently been refined and brought up to date by Dale Hiestand, *Economic Growth and Employment Opportunities for Minorities,* (New York, 1964), p. 53. Hiestand's results are as follows:

Occupational position of Negroes relative to whites:

	1910	1920	1930	1940	1950	1960
Male	78.0	78.1	78.2	77.5	81.4	82.1
Female	78.0	71.3	74.8	76.8	81.6	84.3

The figures show that Negro men lost ground in the Great Depression, that they gained sharply in the nineteen forties, and that their progress almost ceased in the nineteen fifties. Negro women show a rising secular trend since the nineteen twenties, but their gains too were greater in the tight labor markets of the nineteen forties than in the nineteen thirties or nineteen fifties.

Several cautions should be borne in mind in interpreting these figures: (1) Much of the relative occupational progress of Negroes is due to massive migration from agriculture to occupations of much higher average income. When the over-all relative index nevertheless does not move, as in the nineteen fifties, the position of Negroes in non-agricultural occupations has declined. (2) Since the figures include unemployed as well as employed persons and Negroes are more sensitive to unemployment, the occupational index understates their progress when unemployment declined (1940-50) and overstates it when unemployment rose (1930-40 and 1950-60). (3)

897

516

Within any Census occupational category, Negroes earn less than whites. So the absolute level of the index overstates the Negro's relative position. Moreover, this overstatement is probably greater in Census years of relatively slack labor markets, like 1940 and 1960, than in other years.

The finding that labor market conditions arrested the progress of Negro men is confirmed by income and unemployment data analyzed by Alan B. Batchelder, "Decline in the Relative Income of Negro Men," *Quarterly Journal of Economics*, Vol. 78 (November 1964), pp. 525-548.

7. This is emphasized by Daniel Patrick Moynihan in his contribution to this volume.

8. Differences between Negro men and women with respect to unemployment and income progress are reported and analyzed by Alan Batchelder, *op. cit.*

9. Figures are given in other papers in this volume: see, for example, the articles by Rashi Fein and Daniel Patrick Moynihan.

10. In 34 per cent of poor Negro families, the head is not in the labor force; in 6 per cent, the head is unemployed. These figures relate to the Social Security Administration's "economy-level" poverty index. Mollie Orshansky, *op. cit.*

11. See *Manpower Report of the President*, March 1964, Table A-3, p. 197.

12. Hiestand, *op. cit.*, Table I, pp. 7-9.

13. Batchelder, *op. cit.*, shows that the incomes of Negro men declined relative to those of white men in every region of the country. For the country as a whole, nevertheless, the median income of Negro men stayed close to half that of white men. The reason is that migration from the South, where the Negro-white income ratio is particularly low, just offset the declines in the regional ratios.

14. The official Advisory Council on Public Assistance recommended in 1960 that children be aided even if there are two parents or relatives *in loco parentis* in their household, but Congress has ignored this proposal. *Public Assistance: A Report of the Findings and Recommendations of the Advisory Council on Public Assistance*, Department of Health, Education, and Welfare, January 1960. The Advisory Council also wrestled somewhat inconclusively with the problem of the means test and suggested that states be allowed to experiment with dropping or modifying it for five years. This suggestion too has been ignored.

15. Adjusting the size of a government benefit to the amount of other income is not without precedent. Recipients of Old Age Survivors and Disability Insurance benefits under the age of seventy-two lose one dollar of benefits and only one dollar for every two dollars of earned income above $1200 but below $1700 a year.

16. See the statistics summarized by Rashi Fein elsewhere in this volume.

898

Is a Negative Income Tax Practical?

James Tobin,† Joseph A. Pechman†
and Peter M. Mieszkowski†

The war on poverty has brought emphatically to public attention the inadequacies of the nation's welfare system. The assistance given to the impoverished is pitifully inadequate in most states, and the rules under which it is given severely impair both the incentives and the potential of the recipients to help themselves. Most poor people are ineligible for public assistance, so restrictive are the eligibility requirements for the various categories of federal, state and local welfare programs. Many eligible poor people do not accept assistance from local welfare agencies because recipients are subject to numerous indignities by the procedures employed to enforce the means test and other conditions which determine who is entitled to help and to how much. The means test is in effect a 100 per cent tax on the welfare recipient's own earnings; for every dollar he earns, his assistance is reduced by a dollar. Administration of public assistance is now largely a matter of policing the behavior of the poor to prevent them from "cheating" the taxpayers, rather than a program for helping them improve their economic status through their own efforts. As a result poverty and dependence on welfare are perpetuated from one generation to the next, and the wall dividing the poor from the rest of society grows higher even as the nation becomes more affluent.

† James Tobin: Sterling Professor of Economics, Yale University; A.B. 1939, Ph.D. 1947, Harvard University.
Joseph A. Pechman: Director of Economic Studies, Brookings Institution; Irving Fisher Research Professor of Economics, Yale University, 1966-67; B.S. 1937, Coll. City N.Y.; Ph.D. 1942, University of Wisconsin.
Peter M Mieszkowski: Associate Professor of Economics, Yale University; B.S.C. 1957, McGill University; Ph.D. 1963, Johns Hopkins University.

1

Reprinted from YALE LAW JOURNAL, Vol. 77, No. 1, November, 1967

From *Yale Law Journal* 77(1) (November 1967):1–27. Reprinted by permission of the Yale Law Journal Company and Fred B. Rothman & Company.

Four ideas for reform of our present system of public assistance, none of them novel, have lately received serious attention from economists, social welfare experts, and public officials. One is that assistance should be available to everyone in need. Present welfare laws require not only a showing of need but also an acceptable reason for the need. Old age, physical disability, having children to feed but no husband to feed them—these are acceptable reasons. The inability or failure of the father of a normal, intact family to find a job that pays enough to support the family is not an acceptable reason. Such families cannot now receive welfare assistance in most localities. The second proposed reform is that need and entitlement to public assistance should be objectively and uniformly measured throughout the nation in terms of the size and composition of the family unit, its income, and its other economic resources. There would not be different calculations of need and entitlement from one state to another, one welfare administration to another, one case-worker to another. The third is that the public assistance to which people are entitled should be paid in cash for free disposition by the recipients, not earmarked for particular uses or distributed in kind as food, housing, or medical care. The fourth reform would modify the means test to reduce the "tax" on earnings below 100 per cent, in order to give the recipients of assistance some incentive to improve their living standards by their own efforts.

Some or all of these objectives are embodied in specific proposals that have entered public discussion under a confusing variety of names: "guaranteed income," "family allowance," "children's allowance," "negative income tax." These proposals can be described and compared in terms of two identifying features: the *basic allowance* which an eligible individual or family may claim from the government, and the *offsetting tax* which every recipient of the basic allowance must pay on his other income. The *net benefit* to the recipient is the basic allowance less the offsetting tax. The net benefit can be considered a "negative" income tax because it makes the income tax symmetrical. The regular or positive income tax allows the government to share in a family's earnings when those earnings exceed a minimum that depends on the number of exemptions and the size of allowable deductions. Under a negative income tax plan, the government would by providing benefits also share in any shortfalls of family income below a minimum similarly but not necessarily identically calculated.

The basic allowance can be regarded as the income guarantee. It is

2

the net benefit received by a person whose other income for a year is zero and who has no offsetting tax to pay. It is therefore the minimum total disposable income—income from all sources including basic allowance less offsetting tax and other income taxes—the recipient can receive.

The basic allowance depends on the size and composition of the recipient unit. Plans differ in the schedule of basic allowances they propose, both in the adequacy of the amounts and in the variations for family size and composition. Some plans contemplate a fixed per capita allowance. Some would allow more for adults than for children. Some would add diminishing amounts to the basic allowance of a unit for successive children and perhaps impose a ceiling on the amount a family unit can receive regardless of size. Some would give no allowance for adults and would perhaps count young children more heavily than older children.

With respect to the offsetting tax, the main issue is the rate at which other income should be taxed. As already noted, current public assistance procedures generally impose, in effect, a 100 per cent tax. Some proposals for a universal "income guarantee" retain this same tax, disguised as a federal commitment to make up any gap between a family's income and an established living standard. Other "family allowance" plans contemplate no special offsetting tax at all; other income would simply be subject to the regular federal income tax. Some variants of this proposal would count the basic allowance as taxable income. In either case everyone in the country eligible for a basic allowance would be a net beneficiary.

So-called "negative income tax" proposals typically subject allowance recipients to a special offsetting tax with a rate less than 100 per cent but greater than the low-bracket rates of the regular income tax. At sufficiently high incomes the offsetting tax produces a negative net benefit to the family unit as large as or larger than its liability under the regular income tax. Taxpayers in this position would exercise the option to decline the basic allowance and thereby avoid the offsetting tax.

The authors strongly support some sort of negative income tax (NIT) plan, and indeed we have, as will appear below, some specific proposals regarding basic allowance schedules and offsetting tax rates. But the purpose of this article is not to expound the merits of the negative income tax approach in general or of our proposal in particular. The primary purpose is the more limited one of examining some of the sticky technical problems that must be solved if any such

3

plan is to be implemented. The larger issues of social policy are doubt-less more important for the ultimate national decision, but the technical problems are neither trivial nor peripheral—nor can they be wholly divorced from the policy issues. The technical problems are in our opinion solvable. An analysis of at least one plan, with specific feasible solutions suggested for most of the problems, should advance understanding of the approach and meet some lines of criticism. A secondary purpose is to provide rough estimates of the cost of several alternative NIT plans; these are presented at the end of the article.

There are three major sets of problems in designing a workable plan: (1) How to define the family unit and relate basic allowances to its size and composition; (2) How to define the base for the offsetting tax and to relate NIT to the regular income tax and to existing governmental income assistance and maintenance programs; (3) How to determine eligible claimants, make timely payments to them, and collect offsetting taxes from them.

These questions are best discussed in the context of a specific proposal such as that described in section I. The three sets of problems are then considered in sections II, III and IV. The advantages and costs of the several variants of our proposal are described and evaluated in section V.

I. The Proposals

Under our NIT plan every family unit would be entitled to receive a basic allowance scaled to the number of persons in the family, provided it paid an offsetting tax on its other income. Two specific schedules of basic allowances are presented here; a High (H) Schedule which would guarantee allowances that approach the officially-defined "poverty lines" but would be relatively costly to the federal budget; and a Low (L) Schedule which would be relatively inexpensive but would guarantee only a fraction of poverty-line incomes. The schedules were chosen with some care. However, different numbers could be substituted for budgetary or other reasons.

The H Schedule would provide basic allowances ranging from $800 a year for a one-person family to $3,800 for an eight-person family. Under the L Schedule the allowances would range from $400 to $2,700. Two rates of offsetting tax are considered: 50 per cent and 33⅓ per cent. Table 1 describes two plans: H-50 and L-33⅓. Two other possible plans are the H Schedule with a tax rate of 33⅓ per cent and the L Schedule with a 50 per cent tax rate.

4

Negative Income Tax

To illustrate how the plan would operate, a four-person family under the H-50 Schedule would receive a basic allowance of $2,600, and its other income would be taxed at a 50 per cent rate. However, no family would be left with a smaller net disposable income than it would enjoy under the current federal income tax without a basic allowance. For every family size there is an income at which the net tax, *i.e.*, offsetting tax less basic allowance, under this new rule is the same as the tax under present rates. On higher incomes, the regular tax schedule would apply.

The proposal thus would not increase anyone's tax liability under

TABLE 1

BASIC ALLOWANCES, BREAK-EVEN POINTS, AND LEVEL AT WHICH PRESENT INCOME TAX
SCHEDULE APPLIES UNDER THE PROPOSED NEGATIVE INCOME TAXa

Family size (number of persons)b	Basic allowance (received by units with no income)	Break-even point (point at which no allowance is received and no taxes paid)	Level at which present tax rates begin to applyb	Present marginal tax rate at income in (4)
(1)	(2)	(3)	(4)	(5)
H Schedule (with a tax rate of 50%)				
1 adult	$ 800	$1,600	$1,876	15%
2 adults	1,600	3,200	3,868	16
3 including at least 2 adultsc	2,100	4,200	4,996	17
4	2,600	5,200	6,144	17
5	3,000	6,000	7,003	17
6	3,400	6,800	7,857	17
7	3,600	7,200	8,100	17
8	3,800	7,600	8,359	16
L Schedule (with a tax rate of 33⅓%)				
1 person	$ 400	$1,200	$1,420	15%
2 persons	800	2,400	3,007	15
3	1,200	3,600	4,633	16
4	1,600	4,800	6,279	17
5	2,000	6,000	7,963	19
6 including at least 2 adultsd	2,400	7,200	9,728	19
7	2,550	7,650	9,951	19
8	2,700	8,100	10,196	19

a The tax rates are 50 per cent for the H Schedule and 33⅓ per cent for the L Schedule.

b Assumes one-person family is a single unattached individual with no dependents and that families of two or more persons are husband and wife families and file joint returns. Assumes also that the families are entitled to the number of exemptions shown in column 1 (and no additional exemptions for blindness or old age) and use the standard deduction. Rates are those applicable to 1965 and 1966 incomes under the Revenue Act of 1964.

c A family of three or more receives basic allowances $300 less if only one of the members is adult.

d A family of six or more receives basic allowance $150 less if only one of the members is adult.

5

the regular federal income tax (unless, of course, taxes were increased generally to finance the plan). Under the NIT proposal the government would pay net benefits to many families who now pay no taxes. Some families who now pay taxes would be relieved of these and would qualify for net benefits. Some families who now pay taxes would pay less taxes. Other families, with relatively high incomes, would be unaffected.

Table 1 summarizes the proposal for families varying in size from one to eight members. Column 2 gives the basic allowance, the amount to which the family unit is entitled if it has no other income. Column 3, which is simply Column 2 multiplied by two for the H-50 Schedule and by three for the L-33⅓ Schedule, shows the "break-even income"; below it the family receives a net benefit equal to ½ or ⅓ of the short-fall from break-even income; above it the net benefit is negative, *i.e.*, the family pays a net tax. The net tax is ½ or ⅓ of the excess of the family's income over the break-even point so long as the tax so computed does not exceed the present federal tax liability. The income at which the two calculations are equal for typical taxpayers is given in Column 4, and the marginal tax rate applicable at that income under the regular tax schedule is shown in Column 5.

The best way to understand the proposal is to consider the disposable income (DY) after tax and allowance which corresponds to every income (Y) before tax or allowance. Aside from modifications which will be mentioned below, Y is the total income of the family before exemptions and deductions. In Figure 1 the solid line OAB shows the relationship between DY and Y under the present tax law for a married couple with two children filing joint returns. After starting from the origin with a slope of 1, since four-person families with incomes below $3,000 pay no tax, OAB then takes on successively lower slopes as income increases and progressively high tax rates apply. The total tax is the vertical distance between OAB and the 45° line.

The proposal under the H-50 Schedule is to substitute the relationship CDB for OAB. Below $6,144 (Column 4, Table 1) families will have larger disposable incomes than they do now; the dashed line CD is higher than the corresponding segment of OAB. Those with no income will get an allowance of $2,600. Those with incomes below the break-even level of $5,200 will get some net benefits—and this group includes some families, those between $3,000 and $5,200, who now pay tax. Families with incomes between $5,200 and $6,144 will pay a smaller tax than they do now; and those above $6,144 will not be affected.

6

The plan must include units with incomes somewhat higher than the break-even level of $5,200 in order to avoid confiscatory marginal tax rates at that point. The H Schedule would wipe out all tax payments on incomes below $5,200. If the regular tax schedules were applied to all income above $5,200 a four-person family with an income of $5,201 would pay a tax of $322, leaving it with a disposable income of $4,879. In other words, the additional dollar of earned income would cost the family $322. The plan avoids this problem by giving the family the option to remain under the negative income tax system until its disposable income is exactly the same under the positive and negative income tax. For a family of four persons, this point is reached under the H Schedule at a "tax-break-even" income of $6,144.

Figure 1 Illustration of Proposed Income Allowance Plan for 4-person family under the H-50 Schedule

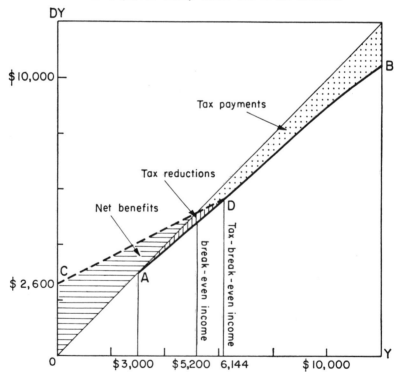

7

II. The Family Unit and the Allowance Schedule

A workable and equitable definition of the family unit is crucial to the success of a negative income tax plan. The two major problems are the relative amounts to be provided as basic allowances for families of different size, and the rules governing the assignment of individuals to units.

A. *Basic Allowances in Relation to Family Size and Composition*

One consideration in setting the schedule of basic allowances is the relative cost of supporting units of different sizes at the same standard of living. By this criterion a family of five should be given just enough more than a family of four so that neither is "better off" than the other. In principle a schedule of basic allowances so computed would be neutral as among families of different sizes. The basic allowance should rise with family size but not proportionately, since there are economies of scale in family consumption. Beyond this qualitative indication, the criterion is not an easy tool to apply; it tends to break apart in the hands of the user. Consumption patterns vary with income, and the economies of scale will be different for different consumption mixes. Whose consumption level should be maintained as family size increases? Parents presumably get some utility, or disutility, from having children; at any rate parents' consumption patterns are not the same as if they were childless.

Another major consideration is the possible impact of the basic allowance schedule on the stability and cohesion of the family as a unit. If there are large per capita differentials between small and large families—more than are justified by economies of scale—there will be an incentive to split up large units. For example, if a family unit of two gets a basic allowance of $2,000 and a family unit of four a basic allowance of $3,000, a group of four people could gain $1,000 by splitting into two two-person units.

In the vast majority of cases the factors governing family-unit formation or splits are largely non-pecuniary in nature. Nevertheless, it would be unwise to ignore the possibility that a financial incentive might cause families to break up, or to pretend to break up. Accordingly, the objective of scaling assistance to poor families of different sizes in proportion to their needs must be balanced against the possible incentive such a standard might provide for family disintegration. The basic allowance schedules shown in Table 1 were designed to strike such a balance. In both schedules the per capita allowance for the first

8

two members of the family unit is the same—$800 in the H Schedule and $400 in the L Schedule. Thus there is no incentive for a couple to define themselves as two single individuals. In the H Schedule the two $800 allowances are available only to adults; otherwise there would be an opportunity for financial gain by setting up one-adult units in which a child is listed as the second $800 member.

The allowance for children declines as the number of children increases. In the H Schedule, the allowances are $500 for each of the first two children, $400 for the third and fourth, and $200 for the fifth and sixth. In the L Schedule the allowances are $400 for each of the first four children, and $150 for the fifth and sixth. No additional allowance is provided for children after the sixth in order to give some incentive to limit family size. A corollary, in all justice, is that the government should make birth control information and supplies easily accessible.

Although the schedules provide larger per capita allowances for small than for large families, the incentive to split will normally not be great. For example, under the H Schedule a family of two adults and six children would receive $4,600 if it split into four-person families, as compared with $3,800 if the group remained together as one unit—a difference of only $800. Amounts of this size do not seem to be large. in comparison with the other considerations that are ordinarily significant in the decision to maintain or split a family unit. For the rare cases of families with very large numbers of children, a significant financial advantage for splitting is unavoidable. For example, the H Schedule would give a family of 12 $6,200 if it split in two but only $3,800 if it remained together.

B. *Membership Rules*

Definition of family units for NIT purposes may be the single most difficult legal and administrative problem. The intention is clear. A single adult is a unit. A married couple and their children are a unit. A widowed or divorced mother and her chidren are a unit. But rules must also cover other situations—children who live with grandmothers or aunts rather than their own parents, fathers who support children but do not reside with them, married teenagers, college students, self-supporting 19-year-olds, etc. The rules should provide for genuinely split families—some children living with father, others living elsewhere with mother—without giving too much financial incentive for apparent or real splitting of intact families. The following rules have been devised with some of these complexities in mind.

9

A family unit consists of an adult nucleus, plus any other persons claimed as members by the adult nucleus. Government checks are payable to the individual, or jointly to the individuals, who form the adult nucleus; and this nucleus is also responsible for payment of the offsetting tax. The following can be the adult nucleus of a family unit for the purpose of qualifying for NIT allowances:

(1) Any person 21 years of age or older.
(2) Any person 19 or 20 years of age who maintains a domicile separate from his parents or guardian and does not receive more than half his support from his parent or guardian, and is not studying full time for his first college degree. We would conclusively presume that any unmarried non-student below 19 years of age was not in fact maintaining a separate domicile.
(3) Any married couple, whatever their ages.

Individuals who are not eligible to be the adult nucleus of a unit are "children." The adult nucleus of a unit may claim children as other members of the unit as follows:

(1) Any child of whom he is (they are) the legal parent(s) or guardian(s) provided the child is living with him (them) in the same dwelling unit, or, if not, is receiving more than half support from him (them) or is studying full time for his first college degree.
(2) Any other children residing with him (them) in the same dwelling unit and receiving more than half support from him (them). An adult claiming someone else's child without the written consent of the child's parent or guardian would have to substantiate the claim.

However, no adult can claim a child without also including in the same unit any parent or guardian of the child residing in the same dwelling unit as the child. And, no adult nucleus can claim another adult without his consent.

No person can be a member of more than one unit. No person who is taken as an exemption on any regular income tax return can be claimed as a member of a family unit claiming NIT allowances. Likewise, if either husband or wife is a member of such a unit, they may not file a joint return under the regular income tax. The income of all members of a unit must be aggregated for the purposes of the offsetting tax.

In recognition of the additional expenses of college education, the

10

adult basic allowance might be allowed for a person engaged in full time study for his first college degree, and added to the basic allowance to which the unit would be entitled if the college student were not counted as a member. Suppose, for example, that one of the three children of a married couple goes to college. Under the H Schedule the basic allowance of the family unit would rise from $3,000 to $3,400 ($800 for the student plus the schedule allowance for a unit of four, $2,600).

These rules leave open at least two possibilities that might be regarded as loopholes, but there are good reasons for retaining both. The first is that any adult could qualify as a separate unit and receive an allowance while remaining residentially, economically, and socially a part of a unit with adequate income. If this is deemed a loophole, it would be possible to plug it. But it seems consistent with good social policy and certainly with horizontal equity to assist adults who are incapacitated for independent living and employment by physical or psychological difficulties, even if they are attached to families of high income. The other possible "loophole" is that married minors would be permitted to claim allowances even though they are living with a parent. Again, this is a possibility which could be eliminated. But the advantages of giving married couples of whatever age some financial independence, even if their parents are well off, seem worth the small cost involved.

III. Definition of Income

Since the basic purpose of the negative income tax is to alleviate economic need, the definition of income should not coincide with the definition used for positive income tax purposes. The latter excludes many items of income that contribute as much to the ability of the family unit to support itself at an adequate consumption level as do taxable items. To avoid paying benefits to those who are not needy, the definition of income should be comprehensive.

A. *Receipts To Be Included in Income*

Income for NIT purposes should include many items that are specifically excluded in whole or in part from the positive income tax base. Thus, tax-exempt interest, realized capital gains, and scholarships and fellowships in excess of tuition would be included in full; income from oil and other minerals would be computed after allowance for cost depletion only; and exclusions for dividends and sick pay would not be

11

allowed. In addition to these obvious changes from the positive income tax base, a number of other modifications seem to be necessary:

(1) The simplest procedure is not to allow any exemptions for dependents or deductions (standard or itemized) in computing income subject to the offsetting tax. The basic allowance schedule already reflects the size of unit and the standard costs of living for units of different sizes. Therefore, further refinement of the income concept seems unnecessary. The only exception might be to allow deductions for certain unusual but unavoidable expenditures, *e.g.*, medical expenses greater than some function of the unit's basic allowance.

(2) Exclusion of the value of the services of owner-occupied homes from the offsetting tax would create the same inequities as it does under the positive income tax. Mr. A does not own his home but pays rent with the $1,000 of taxable income he receives from $25,000 worth of securities; Mr. B, having sold his securities and bought a home with the proceeds, has no taxable income to report. To put these individuals on a par, the net value of the services provided by B's home should be imputed as taxable income to him. For this reason we would favor inclusion of the value of the services of owner-occupied homes under the positive as well as the negative income tax. But general reform of income taxation is not our present purpose, and it is not necessary to make the definition of taxable income the same for both the positive and negative income taxes. The reason for taxing this type of income under the negative income tax is to gear net benefits more accurately and equitably to the true economic need of the family.

The problem of calculating the imputed net rental value of owner-occupied homes is admittedly difficult. However, most persons should be able to estimate the market value of their homes by correcting their property tax assessments for the generally known rate of underassessment in their locality. The rate of return on this market value must be imputed on an arbitrary basis. At recent interest and dividend levels, a 5 per cent rate would seem fair. As under the ordinary income tax, actual interest paid on a home mortgage would be deductible from income. Alternatively, at the taxpayer's option, the canonical 5 per cent rate of return could be applied to his equity in the home—that is, its market value less the outstanding principal of the mortgage.

(3) The value of food grown and consumed on the farm should also be imputed as income. The federal income tax law and most state tax laws omit this imputation, but it would be undesirable to extend this omission to a negative income tax. It should be possible to settle on a flat per capita amount for each state (if not for each region) to be added

12

to the money income of farmers for this purpose. Farm families could declare a smaller amount, but the burden of proof would be on them. In addition, the value of meals and lodging provided by employers should be included in employees' incomes, at least up to the amount that the individual would normally spend for the same purposes.

(4) Whether government transfer payments should be regarded as income subject to offsetting tax will depend in large measure on how the plan is integrated with other public welfare and social insurance programs. This problem is discussed in Section III *infra*. In general we recommend that if a transfer is intended not as a payment based on need but as deferred compensation for previous work it should be counted as income. Unemployment compensation and veterans' pensions, for example, would thus be included in the NIT base. If on the other hand a payment is based on need and is designed to supplement the benefits of the NIT program, it should not be counted as income. Public assistance, the benefits of the food stamp program, and rent subsidies would accordingly be excluded from income if these programs are continued unchanged after the negative income tax took effect.

Pensions and annuities from pension plans other than social security should be included in income to the same extent that they are included in the positive income tax base. Social security benefits are not included in the positive income tax base. But if social security beneficiaries are eligible for NIT, their benefits under Federal Old Age Survivors and Disability Insurance—but not their Medicare benefits—should be subject to the offsetting tax, at least in part. They might well be included in full, since the proportion of benefits paid for by the recipients is currently relatively low, particularly among those with very small benefits. Alternatively, a standard fraction of these social security benefits might be excluded as a return of contributions previously made from taxed income.

(5) Transfer payments from relatives, friends, and private charities are as helpful in maintaining consumption as are government transfers. These gifts should not be discouraged, but neither should the government assist individuals with easy access to private sources of aid as generously as it assists others. If gifts from relatives were to be wholly excluded from the negative income tax base, adult children of very wealthy families might be eligible for negative income tax allowances. Also, inequities might arise if some individuals were more fortunate than others in the amounts of assistance they receive from private charities. We propose as a compromise that transfer income from individuals and private charities be excluded from the tax base up to an

13

amount equal to half the basic allowance shown in Column 2, Table 1. Amounts in excess of half the basic allowance would be included in the tax base.

B. *Integration with Public Assistance Programs*

Current disparities among states in public assistance standards greatly exceed differences in cost-of-living; they reflect other political and economic differences among the states. They are inequitable and lead to uneconomic migrations. Although migration from agriculture and low income rural areas should be encouraged, it might well be desirable on both economic and social grounds to reverse the present tide of migration into a limited number of large northern urban areas. One of the purposes of establishing a national NIT program is to guarantee a decent minimum standard of life to Americans wherever they reside.

Nevertheless, it is probably desirable to encourage states to maintain public assistance programs as supplements to the national NIT system. This is particularly true if basic allowances are on the scale of the L Schedule, since these amounts would be inadequate substitutes for existing public assistance in most states (though of course much more comprehensive in coverage). Even the H Schedule falls short of welfare payments now made in some jurisdictions. State and even local supplementation is an attractive economical way to adjust for cost-of-living differentials. States with a greater than average sense of obligation to their less fortunate residents should not be discouraged from implementing it.

However, if the states continue to administer public assistance with a 100 per cent tax on other income, the value of the NIT as a device to maintain work incentives will be diluted. Suppose, for example, that the H Schedule is in effect nationally and a state wishes to add $400 to the $2,600 basic allowance for a family of four. If the state reduces its aid dollar-for-dollar for other income earned up to $400, the incentive effect of the 50 per cent NIT rate would be negated unless the family could earn more than $400. To be sure, the family certainly has more incentive than under present welfare laws; with a $3,000 basic allowance and 100 per cent tax the family must find a way of jumping from zero earnings to more than $3,000 before there is any financial reward for self-help. But it is undesirable for even small amounts of income to be subject to 100 per cent marginal tax rates.

States should therefore be encouraged to modify their rules to avoid

14

inconsistencies with the national plan. One possibility is to condition a federal subsidy for supplementary state allowances on adoption by the states of the federal negative income tax rules. That is, to be entitled to a federal grant-in-aid equal to, say, 50 per cent of the cost of a supplementary program, the states would be required to use the same rate of offsetting tax as used in the federal negative income tax.

At present the federal government pays an average of 59 per cent of the cost of federally aided categorical public assistance. The basic nationwide NIT program would be entirely federal; thus sizable state funds would be freed for the supplements or other purposes. The attraction of the optional state supplement plan is that it allows adequate guarantees to be offered in high cost-of-living states without entailing the expense of providing the same scale of allowances throughout the country. Also, individual states may find it desirable to allow for variations in the supplement plan within the state if there are substantial cost-of-living differences between rural and urban areas.

Ideally, the federal NIT program should be so generous that state supplements would be unnecessary. Although political and budgetary considerations probably make this impossible in the beginning, we believe that once an NIT program was adopted the federal minima would eventually become adequate. The welfare-minded states would have strong financial incentives to make the federal government solely responsible for income maintenance.

Since we view the negative income tax as a superior alternative to such welfare programs as Old Age Assistance and Aid to Dependent Children, we expect these and other categorical income-maintenance programs to be scaled down or eliminated if the negative income tax is adopted.

Whether assistance in kind should be abolished once cash assistance is increased in amount and in coverage is more doubtful. In general, we suggest that if public housing, the food stamp program and medical programs for the poor are to be continued, they should be justified, and modified, by considerations other than income maintenance. For example, under an adequate negative income tax the means test presently used in the determination of eligibility for public housing could be eliminated, and rent subsidies eventually could be eliminated. Eligibility for housing built under government programs would not depend on income levels. Public funds might still be made available by the government at rates below the market rate of interest, but these loans would be related to urban renewal programs and to the elimination of discrimination in the housing market—and not to con-

15

siderations of income maintenance. On the other hand, society will not allow anyone to be without essential medical care, even if his inability to pay for it reflects improvidence rather than poverty. Therefore, it is unlikely that direct assistance in kind in the health field can be eliminated until a comprehensive, compulsory health insurance plan is adopted.

C. *Integration with Social Security*

The negative income tax might be integrated with social security in two ways. One approach would be to cover people by both social security and NIT allowances. In this case, as explained above, social security benefits would be counted partially or fully as income subject to offsetting tax.

Alternatively, if minimum social security benefits were set at levels adequate for all groups, it would be unnecessary to include the aged and the disabled covered by OASDI in the negative income tax plan. Those who are not now eligible under the social security system could be blanketed in, and the cost of their benefits reimbursed to the social security trust fund from the general treasury. This cost would be relatively small since the vast majority of retired people are already covered by social security.

Nevertheless, to raise the benefits of social security to levels high enough to make the negative income tax unnecessary for retired people would probably be too expensive to be feasible. The present minimum social security benefits of $792 a year for a retired worker and his wife would have to be raised substantially, and it is unlikely that this could be done without increasing OASDI benefits across the board. This would be an expensive and inefficient way to meet the objectives of income assistance, because large amounts of additional social security benefits would be paid to people whose incomes are adequate.

In general, it seems advisable to separate income assistance from the other objectives of the social security system and to meet the minimal needs of retired people by NIT allowances rather than by blanketing them under social security. The two systems are based on quite different principles; they can and should be operated independently.

D. *Application of the Offsetting Tax to Wealth*

There are a number of arguments for and against taking wealth into account in computing the offsetting tax. The major argument

16

Negative Income Tax

against "taxing" wealth is that *income* is the basic measure of ability to pay in the positive tax system. Reducing NIT benefits on the basis of wealth as well as income seems to impose a discriminatory capital levy on those with very low incomes. Moreover, the use of a comprehensive income tax base would prevent most "tax avoidance" on the part of recipients of NIT allowances.

On the other hand, it may be argued that the analogy between positive and negative income taxation is not appropriate. Isn't a government providing financial assistance to a family on a need basis entitled to ask the family to use at least part of its wealth in its own support? Some would argue that the family should be required to exhaust its capital before becoming eligible for NIT allowances. This is an unappealing view, and not only because it is inhumane. A 100 per cent capital levy is surely a disincentive to rainy-day saving, an invitation to improvidence for anyone who thinks it likely he will be needing government help.

In practice, the use of any except the harshest capital test would have little effect on the vast majority of poor persons. It has been estimated that only 39 per cent of all family units with incomes below $3,000 have a net worth of more than $5,000. The average net worth of all families in these income classes was $7,609, of which owner-occupied homes acounted for $3,204.[1]

Nevertheless, it seems desirable to take some account of wealth, if only to avoid the charge that the program would subsidize wealthy persons who prefer to hold their capital in forms that yield little or no current income. Currently, an individual owning $100,000 worth of IBM stock receives cash dividends of less than $1,000 per year. While it is highly unlikely that such an individual would not have enough other income to disqualify him for NIT benefits, the mere possibility that the public might be obliged to such a capitalist could discredit the program.

One possibility is to deny eligibility to any individual or family unit with a net worth of more than, say, $25,000. This solution has the merit of simplicity. However, a fixed limit would deny benefits to families with wealth just above the limit, while others just below it would be eligible. Such a "notch" would be inequitable and would create incentives to conceal or even give away wealth in order to preserve eligibility for negative income tax.

1. D. PROJECTOR & G. WEISS, SURVEY OF FINANCIAL CHARACTERISTICS OF CONSUMERS, table A-1, at 96, table A-8, at 110 (1966).

17

A much more equitable approach would be to impose an offsetting tax on capital as well as on income, though not at the same rate. The offsetting tax on capital would in effect require the family to use a portion of its wealth to maintain its consumption. The capital tax would be a flat percentage, say 10 per cent, of the family's net worth above an exemption, most simply stated as some multiple of the basic allowance. Thus, for example, if the minimum allowance for a family of four is $3,000, an exemption of eight times the allowance would be $24,000. A family with a net worth of $50,000 would have to pay 10 per cent of $26,000 or $2,600 as offset against the NIT allowance to which it would otherwise be entitled.

There is room for difference of opinion on how large the exemption should be. The arguments are qualitatively the same as those for and against imposing any capital tax at all. Our own balance of these considerations leads us to suggest an exemption between four and eight times the basic allowance.

Net worth should be comprehensively calculated, with the family's debts deducted from its total assets. Valuations should be made on a current market basis; where market valuations are not available, they should be approximated by expert appraisers. As observed above, the value of owner-occupied homes may be estimated in most parts of the country by reference to the average ratio of market values to assessed values in the community.

Including the value of the equity in owner-occupied homes in net worth may be regarded as too strict. This rule might force some poor people to sell or mortgage their homes. But it would be highly inequitable to require a capital offset on the part of families with other types of assets and to exclude homes altogether. Since in any case the proposal would exempt a substantial amount of wealth for each family unit, any hardship that might be imposed on poor homeowners would be minimal. If further protection against the danger of forced sales is desired, the value of the home might be reckoned, not as market value, but as the maximum first mortgage for which it would stand as collateral.

An alternative method of dealing with wealth is to disregard property income in defining taxable income and to impose an appropriately larger offsetting tax on capital. For example, a total of 15 per cent might be imputed to the family's net worth and taxed as income. The 15 per cent equals the sum of a 5 per cent rate of return plus the 10 per cent capital offset discussed above. This procedure has the advantage of correcting for differential yields on assets; it would even

18

impute a rate of return to cash holdings. To provide for the exemption proposed earlier, the imputation might be set at the rate of 5 per cent on net worth up to eight times the minimum allowance and 15 per cent above this point. This method has the additional virtue that the form filed by the family would require only two items of information—total family earnings and net worth—whereas the other method would require the family to report property income as well. On balance, there is little to choose between the two.

E. *Fluctuating Incomes*

It is well known that a progressive income tax based on a one-year accounting period imposes a heavier tax burden on persons with fluctuating annual incomes than on those with stable incomes. For example, under present law, the federal income taxes on a single person with an income of $25,000 in each of two successive years total $17,060; if the individual receives $50,000 in one year and has no income in the second year, his two-year tax would be $22,500, or almost a third higher. To reduce this inequity, sections 1301-04 of the *Internal Revenue Code of 1954* allow a measure of "income averaging" in federal taxation. Under these provisions, taxpayers are generally permitted to average their income for individual income tax purposes if "averageable income" (current year income minus 133⅓ per cent of the average of the four prior years' income) exceeds $3,000.[2]

Similar inequities could arise under negative income taxation. But here the rate structure benefits rather than penalizes recipients of fluctuating incomes. Fluctuations in and out of the NIT income range are advantageous. Consider an individual at the tax-break-even income level, with a regular marginal tax rate of 20 per cent and an NIT rate of 50 per cent. If his income exceeds that level by $1,000 he is taxed $200. If his income falls short by $1,000, he gains $500. Over a two-year cycle he is $300 better off than if he had received the same total in equal installments.

Under plan H-50 a family of four which earns a *total* of $10,000 spread evenly over a three year period will receive $2,800 in NIT benefits. The same family, if it earned $10,000 in one year and nothing in the two following years, would pay $1,114 in positive tax and

---

2. INT. REV. CODE OF 1954, § 1301, provides:
. . . the tax imposed by Section 1 for the computation year which is attributable to averagable income shall be 5 times the increase in tax under such section which would result from adding 20 per cent of such income to . . . 133⅓% of [the average income of the previous four years].

19

receive $5,200 in net NIT benefits during the two years of zero income: its net receipts from government over the three-year period would thus be $4,086.

Moreover, there will doubtless be some instances in which the use of an annual accounting period for negative income tax purposes will provide benefits to persons who are not "poor" by most standards. Consider, for example, an individual who spends all his income when he earns it, with violently fluctuating annual income. Most people would not regard it as proper to provide negative income tax payments in one year to an individual who earned $25,000 in the year before.

In spite of these inequities and anomalies, it does not seem desirable to try to enforce income-averaging by NIT allowance recipients. Most eligible people, the real poor, gear their outlays closely to their incomes. They would suffer real hardships if their current NIT benefits were cut back because of their past income, or if in their more prosperous years they had to repay NIT benefits received in the past. The rich man who by design or misfortune turns up with no income in one particular year will usually be disqualified by the offsetting capital levy already discussed. If not, the best protection is simply to deny him the privilege of averaging for regular income tax purposes if he has received negative income tax benefits in any of the four preceding years. A rule of this sort would require any individual with wide income fluctuations to weigh the advantage of receiving negative income tax against the disadvantage of losing the benefits of income averaging. It has the obvious attraction that it is entirely self-administering and does not complicate the negative or positive income taxes.[3]

IV. Methods of Payment

Although the calendar year should be the basic accounting period, there is every reason to adopt a short payment period. Benefits should be paid weekly or twice monthly to prevent real distress among those who have little capital or credit. Such an arrangement would be analogous to the positive income tax, which is withheld weekly or twice monthly for most wage earners and is then subject to a final reconciliation for the entire year when the final tax return is filed.

Government welfare and other agencies have substantial experience

---

3. A statement of the rule might be included with the averaging form. It is doubtful that this refinement needs to be mentioned on the form filed by the negative income tax recipient.

20

in the payment of transfers to individuals and families, so that the mere preparation and mailing of NIT allowance checks poses no great administrative difficulties. The problem is to devise a method of payment prompt enough to prevent distress among those eligible and in great need for assistance while avoiding the paternalistic rules now imposed by the nation's welfare programs. Among the methods we have considered, two meet the requirements: (1) automatic payments of full basic allowances to all families,[4] except those who waive payment in order to avoid withholding of the offsetting tax on other earnings; (2) payment of *net* benefits upon execution of a declaration of estimated income, patterned along the lines now used for quarterly payments of federal income tax by persons not subject to withholding.

A. *Automatic Payments of the Full Basic Allowance*

Under this system, the full basic allowance would be mailed out at the beginning of each period—week, or half-month—to all families. The checks would be received by families who may ultimately have incomes in excess of the break-even point, as well as those who will be eligible for net benefits. Likewise, all families would be subject to withholding at the rate of the offsetting tax on the first X dollars of their earnings, and would be required to pay the offsetting tax on other income by quarterly declaration. Final adjustment would be made by the tax return for the year filed the next April 15th.

This method may be illustrated for a family of two which, on the basis of the H-50 Schedule, has a basic allowance of $1,600, a break-even point of $3,200 and an offsetting tax rate of 50 per cent, and a tax-break-even point of $3,868. The basic allowance would be mailed to all families in 24 installments of $66.67. However, withholding tables would be adjusted so that 50 per cent of earnings up to $322.33 per month ($3,868 a year) would be withheld. Taxpayers not subject to withholding would be expected to pay the offsetting tax quarterly.

---

4. This is the procedure used for "demogrants" or family allowances in other countries. The essential characteristic of demogrants is that the payment is made to all families in the potential eligible group, regardless of income. In some cases, the allowances are subject to positive income tax, but this is not a necessary condition. Family allowances are used in many countries, including Canada, Belgium, France, West Germany, Italy, Luxemburg, Netherlands, Sweden and the United Kingdom. For data on the European countries, see Joint Economic Committee, European Economic Systems, Economic Policies and Practices, Paper No. 7, 89th Cong., 1st Sess. (1965). It should be noted that universal payment of basic allowances under an NIT program does not mean everyone is benefited by the program. Most people would pay an offsetting tax large enough to repay the allowance checks. Therefore the NIT program differs in essential respects from programs under which everyone benefits, no matter how wealthy. There is only an apparent procedural similarity.

21

There is no reason, of course, to burden the government and the population with unnecessary exchanges of payments. Any family which does not expect to be eligible for significant net NIT benefits can always elect to withdraw. The family will not then receive the periodic basic allowance payment from the government, and its working members will not be subject to withholding (or quarterly payments) of the offsetting tax. This election could be made in writing either to the Internal Revenue Service or to the employer. In the former case, the IRS would inform the employer not to withhold the offsetting tax. In the latter, the employer would inform the government through the IRS to stop the payments.

B. *Declarations by Benefit Claimants*

The declaration method would operate as follows: At any time families who believe they are or will be eligible for net NIT benefits could prepare a declaration of expected income for the current year. The declaration might be a simple post-card form requiring information only on family composition, expected income for the year, income in the prior quarter, and (if the proposed offsetting tax on wealth were adopted) net worth. The federal government—whether the IRS or some other agency—would compute the estimated *net* benefit, basic allowance less offsetting tax, for the year. Taking account of payments already made to the family during the year and taxes already collected from the family, the agency could estimate the remaining net benefit due and pay it in weekly or twice-monthly installments. Families whose incomes increased above expectation would be required to file a new declaration to stop or reduce the benefit payments. Families whose income fell short of expectation could make a new declaration at any time. Even if circumstances do not change, a renewed declaration would be required at the beginning of each year.

The withholding system would not need to be changed to collect the offsetting tax, because it would be deducted in determining net benefits to be paid.

The declaration method would not, of course, avoid the necessity of a final accounting and settlement between the family and the government for the year as a whole. This would be accomplished, as now, by the final income tax return on April 15, which would cover obligations under both the NIT and the regular income tax. At this time the family would either claim any net benefits not previously received or pay any net amount due the government.

The major drawback of the declaration method is that it would

22

Negative Income Tax

invite many families to underestimate their income in order to obtain current payments. Claims for benefit payments would have to be compared with income information already available from prior years, from prior declarations, and employers' withholding. The computer makes prompt cross-checking of this kind feasible. Nevertheless, some families will use the NIT facility as an easy source of credit. This is not wholly undesirable, because many poor people lack credit facilities. But it would be reasonable to charge an interest penalty for underpayment of taxes or over-claiming of benefits. There will also be cases of outright fraud and these will have to be handled as severely as is fraud in the positive income tax. However, it should be remembered that the amounts potentially involved in "negative" fraud are small fractions of the sums often at stake in "positive" fraud.

It is difficult to choose between the two methods of payment. Both are workable. The declaration method would limit payments to families who expect to be eligible for net benefits and would not require any changes in the present withholding system. The automatic payment method, on the other hand, would be less likely to be abused by persons who are willing to take the chance of defrauding the government. The declaration method imposes the burden of initiative on those who need payments; the automatic payment method places the burden on those who do not want them. It may be argued that the latter are more likely to have the needed financial literacy and paperwork sophistication.

V. Budgetary Cost of the Plans

We have made a tentative and preliminary attempt to estimate the cost of the plans to the federal government. These estimates should be regarded as merely indicative and very rough. The costs are defined as the net reduction in income tax revenues which would result from superimposing the plans on the 1965 income tax code; this sum is the equivalent of the total increase in family incomes after taxes and allowances resulting from the plan. Although the tax law and rates applicable in 1965 are the reference point, the cost estimates are based on the 1962 population and the 1962 distribution of families by size and income. The reason is that 1962 was the last year for which *Statistics of Income: Individual Income Tax Returns* was published when work on these estimates commenced.

We made four sets of cost estimates covering each of the two allowance schedules in turn at the rates of 50 per cent and 33⅓ per cent.

23

The costs are broken down into three parts: (A) the net benefits to family units which did not pay taxes in 1962; (B) net NIT benefits, plus reduction in income tax payments, for units which paid taxes in 1962 and which would receive net benefits under the negative income tax plan (*i.e.*, families whose incomes are below the break-even points); (C) the reduction in taxes for units which paid income taxes in 1962 whose net benefits would be negative under NIT but smaller than their regular income tax liability. The cost estimates for each of the four plans are given in Table 2.

TABLE 2

Estimates of Alternative Negative Income Tax Plans
(billions of dollars)[5]

	H Schedule		L Schedule	
The status under present law	33⅓% tax rate	50% tax rate	33⅓% tax rate	50% tax rate
A. Nontaxable	22.3	18.2	10.0	6.7
B. Taxable, income below break-even point	23.2	6.7	3.3	.2
C. Taxable, income above break-even point	3.8	1.1	1.0	.1
Total cost	49.3	26.0	14.3	7.0

The estimates are based on data found in Table 18 of the *Statistics of Income*;[6] this is the basis for an estimate of the distribution of tax-paying families by size and income. In deriving these distributions we assumed that families who claim children as exemptions do not have other dependents and families who have other dependents do not have children. Secondly, it was necessary to account for the 14.1 million people who do not appear on tax returns. It was assumed that they have the same family size and income characteristics as the non-tax-paying units who filed returns in 1962. This last assumption probably leads to a downward bias in the cost estimates, as families who do not file tax returns can be expected to have very low income.

On the other hand, the costs are over-estimated to the extent that the "adjusted gross income" concept on which they are based is nar-

---

5. These estimates are based upon a distribution of taxpaying families by size and income estimated from U.S. Treasury Dep't, Internal Revenue Service, Statistics of Income—1962: Individual Tax Returns table 18 (1965).

6. *Id.*

24

rower than the income concept proposed for NIT. Also, against the cost of the NIT program must be set the saving on other governmental income assistance programs which it will, at least in time, substantially replace. The federal government spends $3.2 billion for categorical public assistance, and the states and localities dispense another $2.4 billion.

On the assumption that people receiving social security also qualify for negative income tax, the single largest downward adjustment in the cost estimate would result from the inclusion of social security and veterans' pensions in the tax base. On the basis of information from the Social Security Administration,[7] it is estimated that about $4 billion of OASDI benefits and veterans' pensions are paid to married couples whose total income (including social security) is less than $3,000 and to single men and women whose income is less than $1,500. Since this type of income accounts for between 50 and 60 per cent of the total income of these groups, its inclusion in the tax base under plan H-50 would increase the base by at least $4 billion and decrease the cost of the plan by at least $2 billion.

In 1962 the gross rental value of owner-occupied dwellings was estimated to be $37 billion. From the 1960 Census of Housing[8] we estimated that about 12.8 per cent of the total value of owner-occupied homes was owned by people whose income was less than $3,000. We estimate that imputing a 5 per cent return on owner-occupied residences would increase the negative income tax base by about $2 billion and decrease the cost of plan H-50 by about $1 billion. Other items, part of which would be included in the broader negative income tax base include: $500 million of capital gains accruing to tax-paying units whose adjusted gross income was less than $3,000, $1 billion of unemployment compensation and $2.2 billion of food consumed on farms.

Although our analysis is very imprecise, we estimate that the broadened tax base would save between $3 and $5 billion for plan H-50. It is not obvious whether the saving for plan H-33 would be higher or lower. For this plan the break-even levels of income are higher; therefore larger amounts of income that is not now taxed

7. See Merriam, Social Welfare Expenditures, 1963-64, in Social Security Administration Bulletin, table 3, at 3, 9 (October, 1964); Palmove, Differences in Sources and Size of Income: Findings of the 1963 Survey of the Aged, in Social Security Administration Bulletin, table 1, at 3 (May, 1965).
8. 2 U.S. Dep't of Commerce, Bureau of the Census, Census of Housing pt. 1, table A-3, at 1-5 (1963).

25

would be included in the negative income tax base. On the other hand, the tax rate is lower.

Taking into account the fact that a substantial proportion of the $5.6 billion of categorical assistance would be replaced by NIT, the net cost of H-50 would be about $20 billion, while plan H-33 would cost at least twice that amount. The net cost of plan L-33 would be around $10 billion, while the cost for L-50 would be less than $5 billion.

Clearly these rough estimates do not even begin to take account of:

(1) The growth of population and income since 1962: There are more people, but the incidence of poverty has declined. How the costs of various NIT programs have been affected is hard to say.

(2) Induced responses to the program itself: Some people may work and earn more when their marginal tax rate is reduced from 100 per cent to 50 per cent or 33 per cent, while others work and earn less when the government makes them better off and raises their marginal tax rate from zero or 14-20 per cent to 33 or 50 per cent. These responses will change the tax base, but in the absence of experience or experiment it is not possible to estimate in which direction or how much.

(3) Savings in government expenditures other than income assistance: To an unknown degree NIT benefits may reduce the need for assistance in kind such as medical care, housing and food. We believe that a generous NIT program would also in time diminish expenditures now devoted to controlling and suppressing the symptoms of poverty—crime, social disorder, unsanitary environments—rather than to eliminating poverty. But budgetary savings are the smallest consideration in this anticipated consequence of the program, and they neither can be nor need to be estimated.

Although the authors believe that it is well within the fiscal capacity of this country to adopt a generous negative tax plan, there may be in the first instance a conflict between cost, the adequacy of the basic allowances, and the objective of keeping the offsetting tax rate as low as possible. The allowance levels for plan L are inadequate for many parts of the country and this plan would have to be supplemented in some way. On the other hand, if plan H were adopted for the country as a whole, the offsetting tax rate would probably have to be considerably higher than 33 per cent because of cost considerations. High tax rates unfortunately weaken one of the basic objectives of NIT, namely to improve upon the disincentive aspects of existing welfare programs.

The course of action which we think best balances these considera-

26

tions is federal enactment of plan L with a tax rate of 40 per cent. The basic allowances of this plan would then, we hope, be supplemented by individual high cost-of-living states along the lines outlined above. As the federal budgetary situation eases, the national basic allowance schedule could be gradually improved to approach plan H.

27

JAMES TOBIN

RAISING THE INCOMES OF THE POOR

The revolt against poverty and economic inequality in the United States began some time in the middle 1960s. Like many revolutionary movements, it arose and grew in intensity not when conditions were getting worse but when they were getting better, not when the ruling authorities were insensitive and oppressive but when they proclaimed commitment to the revolutionary cause. No doubt the natural progress of the American economy and the normal course of American politics would suffice, as they have in the past, gradually to raise the standards of life of the poorest fifth of the population. But neither the poor themselves nor their many sympathizers among the affluent majority are content with business and politics as usual. That is why the revolt against poverty is today the main item on the nation's domestic economic agenda.

It was not so eight years ago, when full employment and growth were the main economic issues. In terms of the aspirations of 1960–61, both private enterprise and public economic policy have performed very successfully. Unemployment, which was 7 percent of the labor force on the eve of the Kennedy administration, has been reduced well below the administration's interim full employment target of 4 percent. The growth rate of gross national product (GNP), adjusted for price changes, rose from 2.4 percent per year over the period 1953–60, to 6.5 percent per year over the period 1961–67.

As predicted, the restoration of full employment and the growth of national output significantly diminished the prevalence of poverty. By the income criteria of the federal government, 38.9 million persons, 22.1 percent of the population, were poor in 1959. By 1967 these numbers had been reduced to 25.9 million persons, 13.3 percent of the population.[1] What was

1. Bureau of the Census, *Current Population Reports*, Series P-60, No. 55, Aug. 5, 1968.

Reprinted by permission from *Agenda for the Nation*, ed. K. Gordon, Washington, DC: Brookings Institution, 1968, pp. 77–116.

not predicted was that after this performance poverty and economic inequality would be more acute and divisive social problems than they had been for a generation, more compelling than at any time in this century save the depths of the Great Depression.

The Revolt against Poverty and the Negro Revolution

Aspirations have outrun performance. The major factor in widening the gap was the Negro civil rights revolution. Its essential message, to blacks and whites alike, was that Negroes count fully and equally as people and as U.S. citizens.

The determination that Negroes shall no longer be second-class citizens soon extended to the economic sphere. This is what gives the revolt against poverty its cutting edge—the disproportionately heavy burden of poverty and economic disadvantage on black people. And this is why the major battlefront of the war on poverty is the large northern city—that is where they live, the black people who aspire to a better life. It is statistically true that there are more whites than blacks among the poor, and that most poor people do not live in urban ghettos. Nevertheless it seems very doubtful that there would be either a revolt or a war against poverty in this decade if poverty were as rare and as unconcentrated among blacks as it is among white people.

TABLE 1. *Selected Statistics on the Prevalence and Distribution of Poverty*

	Persons in poor households				Percentage of poor persons living in central cities (1964)
	As percentage of all persons		Number (millions)		
Race	1966	1967	1966	1967	
White	11.5	10.2	19.5	17.6	23.8
Nonwhite	40.0	35.3	9.3	8.3	41.7

Sources: Persons in poor households—Bureau of the Census, *Current Population Reports,* Series P-60, No. 55, Aug. 5, 1968; percentage of poor in central cities—*Report of the National Advisory Commission on Civil Disorders,* Mar. 1, 1968, p. 127.

Prior to the civil rights revolution, almost all people of both races took for granted the second-class economic status of the Negro. Negroes were just not expected to enjoy the same standards of life, health, and education as whites; it was normal for them to put up with conditions that would be regarded as pathological for whites. Even optimists and well-wishers were content to reflect that time and education would slowly ameliorate the economic condition of the Negro. This racial double standard made the nation conveniently unconscious of the extent of poverty in its midst, and gave the national conscience a ready excuse for doing very little about it. (The nationwide attitude toward Negro poverty was similar to that of the ingenuously puzzled and indignant white residents of a northern Wisconsin county on learning that the federal government considered it to be one of severe poverty; it did not occur to them that the dismally low incomes of the many Chippewa Indian residents would count in this assessment.) When the Negro became a first-class citizen, the psychological and political dimensions of the poverty problem were suddenly magnified.

Poverty per se is by no means the only focus of discontent. The poor want more of the good things of American life, to be sure. They also want, especially for their children, the opportunities other Americans have for social, occupational, and economic advancement. Here again, the Negro revolution has revealed the vast failure of the society to live up to its professed ideals of equality of opportunity, a discrepancy that enrages middle-class Negroes no less than the poor. Essential as it is to raise the living standards of the poor, simply lifting the bottom of the income distribution will not set the situation right so long as Negroes feel that the institutions of the society conspire to confine them to the bottom.

The Revival of Inequality as a Social and Political Issue

The revolt against poverty has made the distribution of income, wealth, and economic power a live social and political issue in the United States once again. Periodically throughout American history the poorer classes have expressed severe discontent with their shares of the pie, regarding them as both inadequate and unfair. But for most of the postwar era—certainly after the war in Korea distracted President Truman from domestic reform—the issue of inequality was quiescent. Even John F. Kennedy and Lyndon B. Johnson tried not to revive it explicitly, although they presided over large increases in the scope and size of federal domestic civilian spending. They hoped to build a wide consensus in support of their war on poverty and related welfare measures. An essential part of this strategy was to rely on growth in the pie rather than on new ways of slicing it up. Corporate and personal income taxpayers would not be antagonized by demands to dip deeper in their pockets to pay the bills. As their profits and incomes rose under benign fiscal and monetary policies that sustained prosperity and encouraged steady growth, the yield of existing tax rates would grow too. In addition there would be savings in defense outlays as the cold war gradually thawed. These fiscal resources would permit a steady expansion of federal programs to aid the poor, even with occasional tax cuts for everyone else.

This strategy foundered for two reasons. One was the war in Vietnam and the associated jump in defense spending. The other was the impatience of the poor and their allies; they now want measures that will require actual sacrifices by the affluent majority; perhaps they want the sacrifices for their own sake. As Charles Schultze's calculations in this volume show, there is little prospect, even with optimistic assumptions about peace and the domestic economy, that federal fiscal resources for a major initiative in the war on poverty will develop painlessly.

The consensus which seemed so broad and so firm after the election of 1964 has broken down, and with it the faith that economic growth is the solvent for all potentially divisive domestic issues. In the coming years the issue of distribution may be squarely joined: Will the affluent majority explicitly tax itself to improve the lot of the poorest fifth of the population? Is the majority wise enough or frightened enough to do so? How can the poor, with so little national electoral force, bring effective political pressure for redistributive measures? If their disaffection cannot find political outlet, will it pour forth into the streets?

The Agricultural Revolution, Migration, and Contemporary Poverty

Poverty in the United States in the second half of the twentieth century is in substantial degree a final and painful phase of the liquidation of the nineteenth century agricultural system of the South. Ever since the Industrial Revolution, transfer of manpower from farm to factory, from country to city, has been a major feature of economic progress throughout the Western world.

So spectacular has been man's progress in extracting the basic necessities of life from the land that most of the U.S. labor force has been released for the satisfaction, and indeed the creation, of other wants. The percentage of the labor force in agriculture declined from 53 in 1870 to 27 in 1920 and to 5 in 1967. In urban occupations, which also benefit from the endless advance of science, the wages of labor steadily rise. But the gains in the standard of life of the industrial worker have not been available in the countryside. To enjoy them, the vast majority of farmers, farmworkers, and their children must leave the farm. In order to earn from agricultural work a standard of life comparable to that of the urban worker, a man must till an ever-increasing number of acres, using up-to-date knowledge and equipment.

Attracted by job opportunities and high wages in industry and in cities, discouraged by the prospects in agriculture, rural Americans have been migrating to towns and cities on a tremendous scale for many decades. Between 1959 and 1966 the number of farms fell by 20 percent and the number of poor farm households by two-thirds.[2]

But the process has by no means run its course. Net emigration from the farm is declining, but it is still nearly a million persons a year. There are still 1.7 million farms with annual sales under $5,000. And though a subsistence farm can probably produce at least as much as twenty or fifty years ago, the living it provides a family is poverty by modern standards. Moreover, the subsistence tenant farmer or sharecropper is often simply displaced from the land, as the landowner diverts it to more profitable uses under the competitive spur of modern technology or the incentives of federal subsidies. The same developments, of course, greatly curtail the demand for hired farm labor, a work force which is 27 percent nonwhite. The President's National Advisory Commission on Rural Poverty estimates that in 1965, 25 percent of rural residents, 13.8 million persons, were poor. They accounted for 41 percent of the poor population of the nation. Rural poverty extends beyond the farms to the villages and towns they once supported. Only a quarter of the rural poor live on farms.

Although the continuing obsolescence of rural labor is nationwide, it has been especially acute in the Southeast. The southern agricultural economy was built on highly labor-intensive techniques of cultivation, and the work force was organized in a feudal manner. It is of course Negroes, the descendants of men and women who were enslaved to the land, who are now too numerous for it to support. Therefore, the required migration is disproportionately a Negro migration, and in large part a migration from the South to the Northeast and the West.

Emigration from the South, and migration into metropolitan areas, by both whites and nonwhites, have declined in this decade. But 100,000 Negroes are still leaving the South every year, and the growing Negro popu-

2. *Economic Report of the President, January 1968*, pp. 132–38.

lation in the South will support continuing emigration. Negroes are becoming more urban and industrial in the South as well as the North and West. The nonwhite population of metropolitan areas is still increasing at 3.1 percent per year; two-thirds of the growth can be attributed to natural increase. Within metropolitan areas, nonwhites are increasingly concentrated in the central cities, while the white population declines in the central cities and grows rapidly in the suburbs.

It is not farfetched to describe the contemporary urban crisis and revolt against poverty as side effects and aftereffects of the industrial transformation of the American economy, perhaps the more frustrating, painful, and dangerous because the transformation is so nearly completed. The danger and pain are the legacy of peculiarly American institutions and developments: southern slavery, the Civil War, and the long survival in the South of a feudal organization of agriculture and of race relations. It is Negroes who must migrate to new jobs and urban locations. But their experience and education in the rural South have not prepared them for urban employment and residence. In a real sense, the population displaced from southern agriculture has become the social problem of the northern cities, and the centuries of southern neglect of Negro education and rights explode in violence on the streets of the North.

Several lessons can be drawn. First, the problems of the northern cities are national in origin, scope, and responsibility. No city can be expected to handle them with its own limited legal powers and fiscal resources.

Second, improvement of the social and economic environment for immigrants to northern cities and their families is going to be a prolonged and difficult and expensive task. These cities face, for some years to come, what amounts to a Malthusian problem, a large potential supply of new residents from immigration and natural increase. Efforts to improve the housing, employment, and welfare of ghetto residents can easily be swamped by waves of immigration, partly inevitable, partly induced by the improvements themselves. This does not mean that such efforts should not be made; it does mean that lots of running is required just to stay in the same place.

The objective is, after all, to improve the conditions of people, not of places. A welfare family in New York City or Milwaukee is certainly not living at standards other residents of those areas consider tolerable for themselves; yet the family is better off than in a tar-paper shack in rural West Virginia or Mississippi. A residential neighborhood may deteriorate as it passes from established workers moving to the suburbs to recent immigrants from the South. Yet both the new and the old residents are better off than before.

Third, urban poverty must be attacked not only in the cities but in rural areas, especially in the South. It is just as important to improve education in the rural South as in the ghettos of northern cities. Many of the pupils in southern schools will end up as school children and adults in the North. It is just as important to bring industrial jobs to the South—for example, through subsidies for the employment and training of men and women displaced from agriculture—as to urban ghettos in the North.

Finally, it is important to remove the artificial incentive to migration to the urban North provided by the immense differences among states in public assistance benefits and eligibility rules. This can be done only by nationalization of public assistance. The southern states do not have the fiscal resources, even on a matching basis, to pay adequate benefits, even if they had the political will to do so.

The Measurement of Poverty and the Objectives of Policy

The federal war on poverty, whatever else it has accomplished, has established an official measure of the prevalence of poverty in the United States. Adoption of a specific quantitative measure, however arbitrary and debatable, will have durable and far-reaching political consequences. Administrations will be judged by their success or failure in reducing the officially measured prevalence of poverty. So long as any family is found below the official poverty line, no politician will be able to claim victory in the war on poverty or to ignore the repeated solemn acknowledgements of society's obligation to its poorer members. A similarly binding commitment to a specific measure of full employment, the adoption of 4 percent unemployment as the "interim target" of the Kennedy administration in 1961, strengthened the political forces on the side of expansionary fiscal and monetary policy in the early 1960s.

The official count of the poor is based on annual income. A four-person nonfarm family, two adults and two children, is considered poor if its income is less than $3,335 at 1966 prices of consumer goods. Adjustments are made for family size, so that the 1966 poverty line varies from $1,635 for a single individual to $5,430 for a family of seven or more. Because farm families have less need for cash incomes, they are not considered poor if their incomes exceed 70 percent of the nonfarm standards. The standards themselves are based on estimates of the realistically minimal costs of nutritionally adequate food for adults and children. Generally speaking, a household[3] is taken to be poor if its income does not exceed three times the cost of this food budget.[4]

Since this measure of poverty has become so important in government policy, a number of comments on it are appropriate:

1. It is an absolute rather than a relative measure. The dollar amount of the cutoff line is, of course, recomputed for changes in the cost of living. But as time goes on, the official poverty line will fall further and further behind the average and median incomes of the population.[5] Thus it would be conceivable gradually to eliminate poverty, thus defined, without any equalization in the relative distribution of income.

On the other hand, there will certainly be strong political and social forces working to scale up the income definition of poverty as the majority of the population becomes more and more affluent. In terms of absolute real income rather than relative position in the national distribution of income, the Great Society counts as poor many people whom the New Deal did not, and some crusade on behalf of the "forgotten man" or the "other America" of tomorrow will further revise upward society's notion of a tolerable minimum standard of life.

2. Annual income is not a wholly satisfactory criterion of poverty, although a more sophisticated measure would probably not change appreciably the estimated prevalence of poverty. According to estimates made in 1964 by the Council of Economic Advisers, based on the Current Population Surveys of the Census Bureau, 69 percent of households with poverty incomes in 1963 also had poverty incomes in the previous year. This figure indicates considerable turnover, but the CEA also calculated that the estimated prevalence of poverty would not be changed by basing it on average income for the two years.[6]

The normal life cycle of income presents a somewhat different problem in the definition of poverty. The low incomes of some young people are not indicative of poverty: Consider impecunious students of law or medi-

3. The term "household" includes both families and unrelated individuals.
4. Mollie Orshansky, "Counting the Poor: Another Look at the Poverty Profile," *Social Security Bulletin,* January 1965, and Mollie Orshansky, "The Shape of Poverty in 1966," *Social Security Bulletin,* March 1968.
5. For four-person families, the national median income was twice the poverty-line income in 1959, two and a half times in 1966. Orshansky, "Counting the Poor," p. 6.
6. *Economic Report of the President, January 1964,* pp. 164–65.

cine with years of lucrative practice ahead of them. Neither are the low incomes of many old people who are living comfortably by gradually consuming assets they accumulated before retiring. Distributions of annual income exaggerate economic inequality by including differences due to age and position in the life cycle. Unfortunately we do not have good estimates of inequality of lifetime incomes.

When wealth is considered, along with one-year income, in the definition of poverty, the estimated prevalence of poverty among the aged is reduced by about a third. But the aggregate estimate of its prevalence is lowered only by two or three percentage points. Few people who have low annual incomes have much wealth.[7]

3. The strategists of the official war on poverty have focused attention on the poverty count: the number and proportion of households below the official poverty line and the number and proportion of persons in those households. But the importance of moving households from the wrong side of the arbitrary line to the right side should not be emphasized to the exclusion of other dimensions of progress in the campaign. Any increase in the income of poor families is desirable, even if it is insufficient to move them out of the "poor" classification. Indeed, it is probably more important to give $100 to a family with no income than to a family within $50 of the poverty line.

The aggregate poverty income "gap" is a useful and simple supplement to the poverty count in assessing the aggregate amount of poverty. The gap is the total of all the shortfalls of incomes of poor families below poverty-line standards. This was estimated at $13.7 billion, and 2.8 percent of GNP, in 1959, and at $11 billion, and 1.6 percent of GNP, in 1965.

Neither of these aggregate measures, the count or the gap, awards any points for increasing the incomes of the near-poor, those households falling, say, between one and one and a half times the poverty line. The line is, after all, arbitrary and minimal, and it would be a hollow victory over poverty just to move all the poor a few inches beyond it. Some income supplementation proposals spill benefits on the near-poor. Quite apart from the fact that this spillover may be necessary for reasons of incentive, equity, and continuity, the near-poor should not be considered undeserving beneficiaries.

7. B. A. Weisbrod and W. Lee Hansen, "An Income-Net Worth Approach to Measuring Economic Welfare," unpublished, Department of Economics, University of Wisconsin, 1967.

Full Employment, Inflation, and Poverty

Most poor households contain workers or potential workers. Fifty-four percent of the poor families in 1966 were headed by persons in the labor force; this includes 39 percent of families headed by females. Only 4 percent of poor family heads reported themselves as unemployed. Of male heads of households under 65 years of age, 82 percent had work experience in 1966. Unrelated individuals in poverty are mostly aged 65 or more, and mostly female; even so, 28 percent are in the labor force, including 2 percent unemployed.[8] Many more heads of poor households would have been in the labor force if job opportunities had been available, or if they had not been discouraged by disincentives connected with their public assistance or social insurance benefits. In the population at large, one of every ten persons not seeking work really wants a regular job.[9] About one-fifth of poor families had more than one earner. But unemployment rates were high for teenagers and other potential secondary workers.

Jobs, more and better jobs, are certainly the most appealing solutions for these poor families—let them earn their way out of poverty. This is undoubtedly the path that they would prefer. It is also, the public opinion polls tell us, the path that the general American public prefers. It accords with the work ethic of the society, strongly ingrained in both the poor minority and the affluent majority. Moreover, so long as there are socially useful tasks to be done, it is a national economic waste to leave willing and able hands unemployed or underemployed.

But this solution is easier said than done; otherwise the normal processes of the labor market would long since have absorbed most of the potential workers among the poor. Since the winter of 1965–66 labor markets have been tight in the United States, with the unemployment rate confined to the narrow range between 3.5 and 4.3 percent. Most of this unemployment may be regarded as transitional or "frictional." In an average month in 1967, only 15 percent of the unemployed had been out of work for as long as fifteen weeks, and only 6 percent for as long as twenty-seven weeks. In 1961, of the 3.7 million unemployed in an average month, two-thirds were

8. Orshansky, "Counting the Poor," pp. 10–12.
9. Robert L. Stein, "Reasons for Nonparticipation in the Labor Force," *Monthly Labor Review*, Vol. 90 (July 1967), pp. 22–27.

males 20 years of age or older. In 1967, of the 3 million unemployed, only 36 percent fell in this group, and 43 percent were teenagers. Job vacancy statistics are not yet available in the United States, but it is likely that over the last two or three years vacancies have exceeded the number unemployed. The index of help-wanted advertising shot up 20 percent in 1966.

The problem is that the vacancies and the unemployed do not match. They diverge in location, in specifications of skill and experience, in wages and other terms of employment, and in other dimensions—including race, sex, age—of the preferences of employers and the characteristics of potential employees.

Labor markets could be tightened still further, the number of vacancies increased, the rate of unemployment diminished. Tipping the balance of labor markets further in favor of workers, as against employers, is within the well understood capacity of federal fiscal and monetary policy. Since 1961 expansion of aggregate demand for goods and services has lowered the unemployment rate from 7 percent to 3.5 percent, the equivalent today of 2.7 million workers, while at the same time providing jobs for an increase of more than 10 million in the civilian labor force. The same techniques of fiscal and monetary policy that engineered or allowed this expansion could bring the unemployment rate down to 3 percent or lower.

Such a tightening of the labor market, like previous turns of the same screw, would be of particular benefit to the disadvantaged workers in poor families. As employers compete for increased work forces to meet the new demands for their products, they find workers tailored to their job specifications increasingly scarce and expensive. They reach further back in the queue of unemployed workers. They relax their requirements and broaden their preferences; they overlook deficiencies in education and skills and undertake themselves the expense and trouble of training. From 1961 to 1967, for example, while white unemployment fell from 6.0 to 3.4 percent, nonwhite unemployment fell from 12.4 to 7.4 percent. Workers at the rear of the queue gain not only in reduction of unemployment, but also in greater availability of full-time work and chances for advancement. In other words, private employers and free markets do much of the work of the war on poverty—without public expenditure and government bureaucracy.

Experience also shows, however, that tightening the labor market—increasing the excess of unfilled vacancies over unemployed workers—accelerates inflation. Skilled and qualified workers, whether organized or not, acquire greater bargaining power. Employers' adjustments to accommo-

date or train less desirable substitutes add to their costs. Reduction of unemployment below 4 percent has been accompanied by acceleration of the
increase in the consumer price index from less than 1½ percent per year,
1960–65, to more than 3 percent per year, 1965–68. Reducing the unemployment rate from 3.5 percent to 3 percent would further increase the
speed of inflation, perhaps to 4 or 5 percent per year. On the other hand,
it would at the same time raise real GNP about $4 billion or $5 billion.
More important in this context, it could be expected to lower the prevalence of poverty in the population by four-tenths of a percentage point,
or about 2 percent. This is the same order of magnitude as the normal year-
to-year reduction in poverty due to economic growth at a constant unemployment rate; a once-for-all half-point reduction in the unemployment
rate would speed the attrition of poverty by about one year.[10]

How the society balances the cost in inflation of a monetary-fiscal
policy aimed at tighter labor markets against the advantages in real income and poverty reduction is one of its most important and difficult
political decisions. Some believe that we have already erred too far on the
inflationary side; others, like me, favor pushing the unemployment rate
still lower. But everyone would draw the line somewhere, if not at 4 percent
unemployment, then at 3.5; if not at 3 percent, then at 2.5. At some point,
certainly far short of zero unemployment, the distortions and inequities of
inflation, and the risks that inflation will be constantly accelerating, will be
deemed too great. Recent experience suggests that the political balance of
forces in this country places this point somewhere between 3.5 and 4 percent unemployment. The inflationary pressures generated at such rates lead
to restrictive monetary policies, as in the summer of 1966 and the winter of
1968, and eventually to deflationary changes of fiscal policy, as in mid-
1968. Of course, the political balance is not immutable, and a greater understanding of the advantages of a tight labor market in the war on poverty
may lead to a more inflationary resolution of the dilemma.

But even if the balance of forces determining fiscal and monetary policy
changed in an expansionary and inflationary direction, total demand could
not generate enough jobs to solve the problem of underemployment of the
disadvantaged. Left to itself, the normal operation of labor markets cannot
place these people in jobs unless the balance of demand and supply in

10. Estimates from Lester Thurow, *Poverty and Discrimination*, Chap. 4, to be
published by the Brookings Institution. Experience with tight labor markets in recent
years suggests that these may be underestimates.

many of them is tilted heavily in favor of excess demand and unfilled vacancies. This is why specific labor market policies, designed to match vacancies with unemployed workers, are necessary. This is, indeed, why they were inaugurated in 1961 and have been pursued with increasing vigor, if not with spectacular success, ever since. Elsewhere in this book, James Sundquist describes and evaluates these measures, and discusses government policy to create or to subsidize jobs tailored to the qualifications of the unemployed.

If the poor are employed, must someone else become unemployed? At first glance, this seems to be the implication if the economy and the body politic cannot tolerate the inflationary by-products of holding unemployment below a certain level. A good case could be made for the equity of some redistribution of the burden of unemployment, between black and white, poor and rich, unskilled and skilled. To equalize black and white unemployment rates in 1967 without changing the national average, for example, the black rate would have had to come down by 3.6 percentage points while the white rate rose by only 0.4 percentage point.

But in fact an increase in employment engineered by tailoring some existing vacancies to the type of workers who are in excess supply would not upset the balance of the labor markets. It is not these workers whose employment removes an important competitive check on the speed of wage increases. Indeed, filling vacancies with them reduces competitive upward pull on wages. Hence, successful labor market policy should dampen inflationary pressure even while lowering the unemployment rate.

If new jobs were especially created to absorb the disadvantaged unemployed, there would be no reduction in the excess of vacancies over unemployed. But there would be no increase either; the presumption is that unemployment would decline without increasing inflationary pressure. Of course the spillovers of demand from the newly employed workers into markets where products or skills are in short supply must be offset. Otherwise aggregate demand and inflationary pressure will increase. The necessary offset comes from sale of the products of the newly employed workers or from taxes levied to finance or subsidize the specially created jobs. These sales or taxes will cut down on spending elsewhere in the economy by roughly as much as the new employees spend. The conclusion is that policies to place disadvantaged unemployed workers in jobs, whether existing vacancies or new jobs, can reduce total unemployment at no inflationary cost. Therefore, these policies do not take jobs from other workers.

Structural and Distributive Strategies in Anti-Poverty Policy

The basic problem of poverty is that the earning capacities of many individuals and households fall short of socially defined standards of living. Continued prosperity and economic growth would, without any special governmental efforts, gradually narrow and eliminate these gaps. In ten years general economic progress would, it is estimated, diminish the prevalence of poverty by at least five percentage points. The response of poverty to economic growth might then diminish significantly, because most of the remaining poor would have personal disabilities isolating them from the mainstream of the economy. In any case, the prospective pace of attrition is not fast enough to satisfy the aspirations of the poor or the conscience of the nation.

Public policy can take two basic approaches to the war on poverty. One is structural: to raise earning capacities, equipping the poor of this generation and the potential poor of the next with the means to earn above-poverty incomes through normal employment. The other is distributive: to make up income deficiencies by direct government grants in cash or in kind or by subsidized employment.

The structural approach has two facets, the market and the individual. Labor markets, as currently organized, prevent many individuals from exploiting fully the earning capacities they have. Racial discrimination in employment and housing, restrictions on entry into organized trades, minimum wage regulations, failures of communication between employers with vacancies and potential applicants—these and other labor market imperfections bar some workers from competing for jobs they could perform and shunt them into unemployment, underemployment, or low-paid work. Public policy could try to promote more effective competition in labor markets, though not without encountering strong opposition from workers and employers who are sheltered by the existing barriers.

With respect to the individual, structural policy seeks to build up what economists call his human capital—the health, education, skill, experience, and behavior on which the future market value of his labor depends. This general principle is so clearly in accord with American ideals of fair play and equality of opportunity that it receives wide assent. An improved distribution of human capital poses a competitive threat to those who benefit from scarcity, but it is a diffuse and remote one. The trouble is that we are not very expert in making social investments in human capital. Adult education, training, and retraining are difficult, slow, and costly processes, as the review of past experience by James Sundquist makes clear. Our main hope must be in the education of children, where, as Ralph Tyler demonstrates, we are finding our belated commitment to equality of educational opportunity vastly more difficult and expensive to implement than anyone anticipated.

The two approaches, structural and distributive, compete for the taxpayer's dollar. But they are in an important sense complementary, for the following reasons:

1. There are some deficiencies of earning power that structural policy and economic progress can never wholly remedy: large families, families without breadwinners, blindness and other physical disabilities, obsolete skills, old age, and so on. Programs to maintain and supplement incomes are necessary to handle these cases.

2. The structural approach, even under the most favorable circumstances and with the most generous financing, is bound to take a long time. Labor markets and educational systems cannot be changed quickly. Furthermore, many of the necessary changes in these institutions will not bear fruit for a generation. Meanwhile people are poor.

3. It is tempting to dismiss the distributive approach as a palliative that deals only with symptoms, and to favor the structural approach as an attack on basic causes. But the metaphor is false. Poverty today leads to poverty tomorrow. Inequality of condition means inequality of opportunity. Poverty and inequality perpetuate themselves in children whose capacities and motivations to learn are impaired—perhaps by physical handicaps due to malnutrition or inadequate medical care before or after birth, perhaps by intellectually and culturally deprived homes and neighborhoods. Improvement in the conditions under which children are born and raised will increase, not diminish, their earning capacities as adults.

Investment in Human Capital

The principal objective of the structural strategy must be to increase the society's investment in human capital and to make the distribution of human capital much less unequal. The three major processes available are public primary and secondary education, higher education and vocational training for youth and adults, and experience in regular employment.

These processes, and policies to improve them, are discussed elsewhere in this book. I will confine myself to one suggestion before turning to distributive policy.

After high school, every youth in the nation—whatever the economic means of his parents or his earlier education—should have the opportunity to develop his capacity to earn income and to contribute to the society. To this end the federal government could make available to every young man and woman, on graduation from high school and in any case at the age of 19, an "endowment" of, for example, $5,000. He could draw on this "National Youth Endowment" for authorized purposes until his twenty-eighth birthday; the period of eligibility would be extended to allow for military service. Authorized purposes would include higher education, vocational training, apprenticeship, and other forms of on-the-job training. To be eligible, educational and training programs would have to be approved by the federal agency administering the endowment. The endowment would pay tuition and other fees to the educational institutions or employers operating the programs; the individual could also draw on the fund for subsistence while enrolled in an approved program.

For every dollar used, the individual would incur liability for payment of extra federal income tax after he reaches the age of 28. The terms of this contingent repayment would be set so that the average individual would over his lifetime repay the fund in full, plus interest at the government's borrowing rate. However, the government might decide to set less stringent terms and to subsidize the endowment, recognizing that some of the advantages of the program accrue to the nation as a whole and are not reflected in higher taxable incomes of the specific individuals assisted.

This proposal is a mixture of the GI bill of rights and the "Educational Opportunity Bank" proposed in recent years. It has a number of important advantages. Individuals are assisted directly and equally, rather than indirectly and haphazardly, through government financing of particular programs. The advantages of background and talent that fit certain young people for university education are not compounded by financial favoritism. Within the broad limits of approved programs, individuals are free to choose how to use the money the government is willing to invest in their development. No individual misses out because there happen to be no training courses where he lives, or because his parents' income barely exceeds some permissible maximum.

Every year 3½ million people become 18 years old and, under the proposal, they would acquire drawing rights in aggregate of $17½ billion.

Eventually repayments will cover most of the outlays. But meanwhile the government will build up a substantial claim. Since this is a social investment project it would not be necessary to meet the initial cash deficits by taxation. It would be entirely appropriate for the responsible government agency to borrow the funds in the capital markets, even though the monetary authorities would have to neutralize the inflationary impact by tightening credit and raising interest rates, temporarily displacing other investments, public and private, of lower social priority.

Income Maintenance and Public Assistance: The Legacy of the New Deal

The United States already has a large, complex system of income maintenance and public assistance. In 1967, cash transfers to persons by all levels of government totaled $48.6 billion, 8 percent of total personal income. In addition, other government expenditures provided benefits in kind to individuals or subsidized their consumption of certain goods or services. Among these expenditures the most important were $8 billion for health and hospitals and $3 billion for public housing and other welfare services. These transfers make an important contribution to the relief of poverty. It is estimated that slightly more than half of them went to people who would have been poor in their absence.[11]

A special Census survey for 1965 indicates that 55 percent of households receiving public cash income payments had other incomes below the poverty lines and that the total count of poor households would have been 42 percent higher in the absence of these programs. However, 31 percent of the households receiving transfers were still poor, and 32 percent of the pre-transfer poor, or 54 percent of the post-transfer poor, received no governmental payments.[12]

Why is the system so incomplete an antidote to poverty? The answer lies in the philosophy of the social security legislation of the 1930s, which

11. Figures from "U.S. National Income and Product Accounts," *Survey of Current Business*, Vol. 48 (July 1968), pp. 31, 32, 35, and 36, and from unpublished calculations kindly made available by Robert Lampman. He estimates also that $36 billion was transferred through the public educational system, of which $18 billion went to the pre-transfer poor. But in view of the long-established commitment of the nation to universal public education, without test of need, this "transfer" is quite different in nature from the others.

12. Mollie Orshansky, "The Shape of Poverty in 1966," pp. 26-30.

still provides the basic framework for social insurance and public assistance in this country. Its purpose was to provide protection against the unavoidable hazards of life. Some of the hazards are natural, biological; others, like involuntary unemployment, are incidents of our complex, interdependent industrial society. Some are highly probable, like outliving one's capacity to earn a living; others, like congenital or accidental physical disability, are very unusual. But they are hazards to which every individual and family is subject.

The major programs are the federal system of Old Age, Survivors, Disability, and Health Insurance (OASDHI) and the state-federal system of unemployment insurance. Over the years OASDHI has grown in coverage of the population, in scale of benefits and contributions, and in scope of contingencies insured. In 1967 the system disbursed benefits of $25.7 billion to a monthly average of 23 million recipients. Three-quarters of all jobs in the United States are covered by unemployment insurance or other public programs of unemployment compensation; and $2.2 billion in benefits were paid in 1967 to 5 million people.

These social insurance systems continue to be directed more against insecurity than against poverty. On the one hand, they protect people against economic reverses whether they are poor or not. The unemployed worker collects his compensation as a right earned during his employment and in a loose sense paid for by contributions levied on him and his employer. His benefits are not conditional on a showing of need; indeed benefits go up rather than down with his previous earnings. Similarly, OASDHI benefits must be earned in "covered" employment; their amount is positively related to pre-retirement earnings; no test of need or means is imposed; no reduction of benefits is made for property income or other pensions.

The other side of the coin is that these social insurance programs do not protect or assist chronically poor people. There is no unemployment compensation for the man who has never had a job, no OASDHI payment for the man with an insufficient history of covered employment.

Social insurance in the United States does, it is true, accomplish some redistribution of income in favor of the poor. In particular, transfers through OASDHI are the most important government mechanism for moving people, especially old people, out of poverty. The OASDHI system is a pragmatic mixture of contributory insurance and redistribution. There is no case-by-case actuarial correspondence between the contributions an individual and his employer make by payroll taxes during his working years and the benefits to which he is entitled. For some participants, the expected value, on a probability basis, of the benefits exceeds the contributions paid on their behalf. Others, correspondingly, pay more in taxes than the expected value of their benefits. Much of this redistribution is unsystematic and arbitrary. Much of it, however, is welfare-oriented, in the sense that the minimum benefits provided exceed the minimum tax contributions required.

Unfortunately OASDHI is not a suitable mechanism for redistribution. On the one hand, the absence of an effective test of needs and resources means that the beneficiaries may be better off than the contributors. Although the system contains a benefit-reducing "tax" on earnings by beneficiaries under 72, it contains no similar penalty for property income and wealth. On the other hand, the excess contributions redistributed are levied not in accordance with ability to pay, but by proportional taxes on total wages, salaries, and earnings from self-employment, up to an annual ceiling. The exemption of high earnings and of property income means that the transfers effected by the system are not financed on an equitable ability-to-pay basis.

The system as now financed and administered should, therefore, not be used for further income redistribution. It is true that minimum old age benefits are below the official poverty line and that increasing them would bring almost all old people out of poverty. But benefits would rise for all participants regardless of need. The same effect can be more equitably and efficiently achieved by a general system of income supplementation. A second-best alternative would be to use general federal tax revenues rather than payroll taxes to finance a welfare-oriented increase in the low end of the OASDHI benefit scale.

The social security legislation of the 1930s attempted to fill some of the gaps left by social insurance by providing for public assistance unrelated to previous earnings or employment. State and local governments spent $9.3 billion for public assistance and relief in 1967, of which $4.9 billion was for cash transfers and $4.2 billion for medical care. They financed more than half of the total with federal grants-in-aid. But these programs too are dominated and limited by the spirit of protecting people against the inexorable hazards of life. Thus public assistance is not available to everyone who is poor, but only to those whose poverty society recognizes as in large degree beyond their own control. The chief categories of needs recognized as legitimate are old age, blindness, physical disability, and absence or disability of one or both of a child's parents.

Several features of these categories are noteworthy. First, they were expected to dwindle in importance as, thanks to general economic prosperity and progress and to the widening of coverage of social insurance programs, more and more people earned protection against insured hazards and fewer and fewer people required assistance conditioned by need.

Second, the categories were carefully selected to minimize what insurance experts call "moral hazard"—risk to the insurer that some people will be induced deliberately to make themselves eligible for benefits.

Unfortunately these expectations have not proven to be true of the category of broken or incomplete families. Aid for Dependent Children (AFDC) was designed to help women who have to raise children without the help of a male breadwinner—principally widows, divorcées, wives of disabled workers, and mothers deserted by the fathers of their children. This category too was expected to decline relative to the population as more of these cases were covered by survivors' and disability insurance. It was never expected that the definition of the category would encourage desertion and paternal irresponsibility. The tacit assumption was that the institution of the nuclear family, the taboo on illegitimacy, and the ethic of paternal responsibility were too strong to be affected by financial incentives.

The enormous mushrooming of AFDC in recent years suggests that this has turned out to be a serious miscalculation. The number of cases rose by 25 percent between January 1961 and December 1965, a period of economic boom; only half of the increase can be attributed to liberalization of eligibility requirements.[13] Although the majority of AFDC cases are white, the increase is predominantly nonwhite, especially in the central cities.[14] No doubt the growth in the number of Negro households with female heads is a complex phenomenon, related to the matriarchal tradition inherited from slavery and to the submergence of the nuclear family in the extended family in rural agricultural settings. These traditions have left many urban immigrants unprepared for life in cities, where the culture and

13. *Welfare in Review*, Vol. 5 (May 1967), p. 10.
14. See Daniel J. Moynihan, "The Crises in Welfare," *The Public Interest*, Winter 1968.

economy are adapted to the nuclear family. Yet it is in the city that the Negro male encounters formidable disadvantages and difficulties. The incentives the man faces are certainly perverse when the government will help his children and their mother if and only if he disappears. Reform of this insane piece of social engineering has become a first order of business on the national agenda.

Social insurance and categorical assistance programs exclude able-bodied adults of working age, whether single or members of intact families, and their dependents. In 1966, there were 6 million poor households of this type, 54 percent of the total; they contained 17½ million people, 59 percent of the total. They are poor but few of them are eligible for assistance. Some local governments assist them from their own funds, and some states help intact families under the federally aided AFDC program when the breadwinner has become unemployed. But generally speaking, these people are not considered deserving poor with legitimate need for help. Able-bodied men are supposed to be able to take care of themselves and their dependents, no matter how large their family responsibilities. To give them assistance is regarded as an invitation to idleness at government expense, with ultimately incalculable damage to the national character and fisc.

The biggest issue the nation faces in the war on poverty and in the reform of its system of income supplementation and maintenance is how to handle this category. Can they be assisted in a way that preserves their incentives to work and to save to improve their own lot? Can they be assisted in a way that encourages them to form and maintain stable families? Can employment and training opportunities be found or provided for them? Do they need, and should they receive, assistance other than pay for employment or training?

The Philosophical Conflict

These questions are the battleground of a conflict among several American principles. One may be called the Puritan ethic: He who does not work should not eat.

Americans seem very firmly to believe themselves an indolent people, preferring idleness and meager subsistence to work and high income. In a society in which achievement and career success are so clearly honored and valued for their own sake as well as for their material rewards, in which wives work and workers "moonlight" not to eke out subsistence but to buy boats, vacation homes, and college educations, this appears a dubious collective introspection. Nevertheless, it has led to strong opposition in public opinion polls to unconditional cash assistance to potential workers, and to very substantial support for providing income via employment.

The second contesting principle is the social responsibility, accepted as an obligation of government since New Deal days, to see that no one falls below a decent minimum standard of living. How can this responsibility be discharged without making it a de facto or de jure guarantee? And how can such a guarantee be given without impairing the work incentive by which the Puritan ethic sets such store?

The third contesting principle is the American ideal of equality of opportunity. We like to think of the competition for career achievement, recognition, and material reward as a fair race, in which the success of every runner depends on his own talent and effort. This image underlies the strong conviction that the distribution of income and wealth resulting from competition in the marketplace is fair. Departures from it may be called for in the name of charity, but not in the name of justice.

This comforting view of the world assumes that everyone starts the race on a par, and America has had better cause than most societies to take pride in its record of individual opportunity and social mobility. Millions of immigrants came to these shores to escape limits on their social and economic status prescribed at birth. In a country free of the residue of feudalism, they could aspire to a better life. Most important, they could see their children surpass them in education, occupational status, and prosperity.

But this proud history does not mean that America has equality of opportunity and a fair race today. First of all, the concept has never fitted the Negro, the victim of America's own brand of feudalism and prescribed inferiority. Second, the inequalities of achievement and reward in one generation are inequalities of opportunity for the next. The United States allows vast differences in inherited material wealth and, what is probably even more important, vast differences in the health, informal education, and formal schooling which children bring to adulthood. The black son of a welfare mother in an urban ghetto and the son of a backwoods Appalachian subsistence farmer simply do not get the same start in life as the son of a suburban doctor or university professor. It is fatuous to pretend otherwise.

Some inherited inequality of opportunity is doubtless unavoidable where providing advantages for children is as important a motivation and incentive for parents as it is in our society. But this implies that children differ widely in their endowments. Distributing wealth and income in accordance with IQs or other genetic endowments is not inherently just. But actual inequalities far exceed innate differentials.[15] Public intervention is necessary to keep the race from becoming cumulatively more and more unfair and opportunity more and more unequal.

One obvious and recognized inequity is related to differences in family size. Wages and salaries are paid for work performed, without adjustment for family responsibilities or other dimensions of need. To do otherwise would certainly distort the allocation of manpower; family size should not be a factor in the assignment of jobs to men. Therefore, as between two workers of equivalent skill and wage, the one with the larger family is at a disadvantage, and so are his children. It is true that family size itself can be regarded as a voluntary decision, the more so as birth control technique is improved and widely disseminated. But if a poor family is too large, can we justify the children's sufferings on the grounds that they provide a salutary example for others? Discrepancies between earning capacity and family responsibility are inevitable in a society that entrusts economic decisions to the free market and child-rearing to the nuclear family. These discrepancies are particularly acute in the United States today; the prevalence of poverty rises dramatically with family size, in 1967 from 8.4 percent for families with one child to 35.0 percent for families with six or more children.

An increase in the legal minimum wage seems to many observers the obvious remedy for the inadequate incomes of the working poor. It is not. Employers can be required to pay higher wage rates but not to hire workers on whom they take a loss. The likely result of an increase in the minimum wage is to increase unemployment and involuntary part-time work among the very groups the measure aims to help. The way to increase the wages of the poor is to increase competition for their services and to increase their earning capacities.

15. Thurow, *Poverty and Discrimination.* Chaps. 5 and 6 show how inequality in education, experience on the job, and property ownership, together with racial discrimination, make the distribution of income much more unequal than the distribution of ability.

Reform of Public Assistance

The serious failings of the present system of public assistance can be summarized as follows:

1. *Inadequate coverage.* The restrictive categories of eligibility exclude millions of poor people, especially among the working or employable poor. Even within the eligible categories, many people in need receive no assistance because of state residence requirements, over-strict local administration, or simple ignorance.

2. *Anti-family incentives.* Eligibility rules for AFDC penalize financially the formation and maintenance of intact families.

3. *Inadequacy of benefits.* In most states benefits are inadequate. Under AFDC the states determine their own standards of need and decide how fully to meet them. The needs of a mother and three children, as estimated by the states, varied in January 1965 from $124 per month in Arkansas to $376 per month in Alaska. In most states actual benefit payments fall short of their own calculations of need. As a result, actual maximum payments to a mother with three children varied from $50 per month in Mississippi to $246 in New York. No state was paying benefits to families at the official poverty level.[16]

4. *Incentives for uneconomic migration.* The wide differences in benefits, eligibility rules, and administrative practices encourage migration to the wealthier and more liberal states, compounding the problems of northern cities. AFDC cases have more than doubled in New York and California since 1961, and these two states alone account for more than half of the one million increase in the case load since 1964.

5. *Disincentives to work and thrift.* Reduction of benefits on account of the recipient family's own earnings and savings amounts to a heavy tax on work and thrift.

6. *Excessive surveillance.* Complex administrative determinations concerning the eligibility, need, and resources of every applicant and recipient must be continuously made. The overburdened caseworker is a combination detective, social worker, advocate, and judge. This surveillance is costly; administration takes about 10 percent of the costs of public assis-

16. In August 1968, however, the maximum in New York was $344 per month.

tance. At the same time, the system often increases and perpetuates the recipients' incapacity to manage their own affairs.

7. *Inequities.* The present system gives rise to serious inequities. Unlike income taxation, which is designed to narrow but not to reverse initial differences in income, the present system changes economic ranks in an arbitrary and haphazard manner. Eligible households are made better off than ineligible households with the same or higher initial income. Households in generous states are better off than similar households in low-benefit states. Some taxpaying families are worse off than some households receiving aid.

This list of problems suggests the agenda of issues in reform of public assistance: How should benefits be related to household size and composition, and to the earnings and other resources of the recipient? How should assistance be financed? How should it be administered? Should there be a nationally uniform system?

I shall discuss these issues on the assumption that the objectives of the public assistance system are to reduce, indeed overcome, poverty; to reinforce measures to remedy the deficiencies of earning capacity that create the need for assistance; to treat recipients, nonrecipients, and taxpayers equitably—specifically to narrow income differences but not to reverse or to create them; to avoid financial penalties for work, thrift, and family stability.

In recent years a number of steps have been taken to remedy defects in the present welfare system.

Since 1962 federal legislation has permitted states to extend AFDC to families in need because of the unemployment of a parent. By 1968, twenty-one states had adopted this program, and 75,000 families were being assisted. Congress has not yet been willing to make the program compulsory for the states. The 1967 amendments to the Social Security Act imposed strict tests of "recent and substantial attachment to the labor force."

Three recent judicial decisions also work in the direction of extending eligibility. One, if sustained on appeal, will overturn residence requirements. One limits administrative discretion by establishing the principle that a citizen has a legal right to welfare benefits for which he meets the criteria. A third strikes down the practice of some states of denying AFDC when there is a "substitute father" in the house.

Thanks both to private initiatives and to public announcements, particularly in connection with Medicaid, more eligible applicants are becoming aware of their welfare rights.

Recent legislation has recognized the disincentive to work and self-reliance involved in 100 percent taxation—in reducing benefits one dollar for every dollar of earnings. States have had the option to disregard earnings of AFDC children, up to $50 a month per child or $150 per month per family. Now the states will be compelled to disregard all earnings of school children and the first $30 per month of other family earnings plus a third of the remainder. A two-thirds marginal tax rate is still very high—the President had proposed 50 percent—but it is an improvement over 100 percent. The 1967 amendments also required certain aid recipients to report to Department of Labor offices for employment or training.

Some states and localities are experimenting with streamlined methods of administration: greater reliance on declarations of applicants and less on investigation; greater use of flat cash payments and less of special appropriations for particular needs.

These are forward steps, but they leave untouched two major defects: the exclusion of the working poor, the inadequacy and diversity of benefits. The 1966 Report of the Advisory Council on Public Welfare recommended "a nationwide comprehensive program based upon a single criterion: need";[17] but neither the administration nor the Congress has yet seriously considered scrapping the existing categorical restrictions.

President Johnson proposed in 1967 to require states to pay benefits that meet the full need of eligible individuals by their own standards, under all federally aided assistance programs. The administration proposal also contained provisions to prevent erosion of the states' definitions of need. Unfortunately Congress ignored this recommendation, probably because many states would find it difficult to meet their share of the additional costs.

It is doubtful that the inadequacy of benefits in many states can be remedied without revamping the fiscal basis of public assistance. The Advisory Council on Public Welfare recommended in 1966 that all states be required to meet, or exceed, a minimum national standard for public assistance payments. A state's contribution to the cost of the required stan-

17. *"Having the Power, We Have the Duty,"* Report of the Advisory Council on Public Welfare to the Secretary of Health, Education, and Welfare, June 1966.

dard would depend on its fiscal capacity, as measured by state personal income and other economic indicators. The federal government would pay the rest of the bill.

Although nationwide standards of benefits, eligibility, and administration could in principle be imposed on the states, there are good reasons to move instead to a system wholly financed and administered by the federal government. The problem is national, and the population is mobile. It is no accident that the most successful social security program, OASDHI, is a federal program. Interstate differences in policy and administration have plagued the federal-state programs of unemployment insurance and public assistance. In the case of public assistance, state and local administrations differ widely in efficiency, sympathy, and impartiality. These differences can hardly be erased by federal edict alone. In particular, federal administration could make rural southern Negroes financially independent of the local white power structures.[18]

Another reason for nationalizing public assistance is to facilitate its integration with income taxation. As benefits and eligibility rules are liberalized, the need to mesh the two systems will become acute. Definitions of income and of household units need to be consistent. Otherwise there will be many anomalies and inequities, especially as individuals' circumstances change and they shift in and out of taxpaying status and in and out of eligibility for assistance. Later sections, therefore, consider how public assistance and income taxation could be integrated.

"Costs" of Redistributions to the Poor

From the point of view of the nation as a whole, a pure internal income transfer is, as a first approximation, costless. That is, no productive resources are used; no labor or capital or land needs to be diverted from other purposes, public or private. In this sense, transfers are fundamentally different from other government expenditures, which divert productive resources into, say, fighting wars or building schools. Transfer programs may, of course, have secondary consequences for the size and composition of national output. Administrative costs are real enough, though fractional;

18. See the eloquent testimony of John F. Kain before the U.S. Commission on Civil Rights, Montgomery, Alabama, May 2, 1968.

taxes and benefits may affect the behavior of the individuals involved, by altering their incentives to work, for example; and the beneficiaries of transfers may use the funds differently from the taxpayers. But exhaustive government expenditures have these consequences too, in addition to their primary claim on productive resources.

The costs that concern taxpayers are not the social costs but the additional taxes they will have to pay—or tax cuts they will have to forgo—in order to increase the incomes of the poor. There are many different ways in which this burden might be distributed among the non-poor. In the discussion that follows it is assumed that the additional taxes are federal taxes on personal income. A measure of the cost of a public assistance program is then the additional income tax which must be collected from the non-poor, taken as a group. This may be measured either in dollars of total additional revenue as of any given year, or in the equivalent increase in the effective average rate of tax on the personal income of the non-poor.

But under many proposals, benefits would not be confined to the poor. Indeed, it would not be fair or sensible to aid households with initial incomes of $2,999 at the expense of households with initial incomes of $3,001. Therefore, the burden on the non-poor as a group is a net figure, concealing some redistribution within the group from higher to lower income taxpayers. "Horizontal" redistributions may be involved as well, for example, between taxpayers with different numbers of dependents or different kinds of income. Some proposals draw a simple sharp line between beneficiaries and payers of additional tax, and in those cases it is possible to calculate the transfer between these two groups as well as the net transfer between poor and non-poor. The redistribution from non-poor to poor may be called the *primary redistribution* of a program of public assistance, and the transfers within the non-poor group the *secondary redistribution*.

The poor received $16 billion in 1966 and needed $27 billion. The poverty "gap"—the aggregate deficit of the incomes of the poor below their poverty thresholds—was $11 billion in 1966, less than 2 percent of total personal income, 69 percent of the actual personal income of the poor. This was the gap remaining after the incomes of the poor had benefited from existing governmental transfers, including $4½ billion of cash public assistance. It is an illusion, of course, to think that poverty could be eliminated by $11 billion additional expenditures. For if the government guaranteed everyone a poverty-line income, in the sense of making up any shortfalls, the poor would have no reason—and many non-poor very little reason—to earn as much as they do now. The poor would not lose by working less, or gain by working more. This would be the 100 percent tax rate implicit in old-fashioned public assistance.

Suppose the government pays every household its poverty-line income and takes back not 100 percent but some fraction of the poor household's initial income. How much transfer to the poor would then have to be made? How much would this exceed current public assistance? Initial incomes of the poor, before public assistance, aggregated $11.7 billion in 1966. Assuming that this figure is unaffected by the tax rate, the calculation is the simple one given in Table 2. Making up the $11 billion gap requires $15 billion with a rate of two-thirds, $22.8 billion with no tax. The table makes clear a general point: the redistributive cost of guaranteeing any level of income is greater the lower the tax rate—at least before allowance is made for the unknown incentive effects of the rates themselves.

TABLE 2. *Transfer to Poor Required in 1966 To Eliminate $11 Billion Poverty Gap, at Selected Tax Rates*
(*In billions of dollars*)

Item in calculation	Tax rate			
	2/3	1/2	1/3	0
1. Total poverty-line income	27.1	27.1	27.1	27.1
2. Offsetting tax on initial income of poor (tax rate × $11.7 billion)	7.8	5.9	3.9	0
3. Required benefit payments (1—2)	19.3	21.2	23.2	27.1
4. Current public assistance	4.3	4.3	4.3	4.3
5. Additional transfer required to eliminate gap (3—4)	15.0	16.9	18.9	22.8

The Credit Income Tax

The credit income tax, proposed by Earl Rolph and others, is a scheme for integrating public assistance with a vastly simplified and reformed system of income taxation. Radical as it is, the proposal deserves a serious hearing. It serves, moreover, as a convenient point of reference for considering less far-reaching reforms.

Suppose that every man, woman, and child in the country was entitled to receive $750 a year from the federal government, and obligated to pay the government one-third of his income (not including the $750). The $750 is a credit against the tax. It is also a guaranteed income, the final income an individual would receive if he had none of his own. Anyone else would end up with more final income, even though he would receive a smaller net amount from the government, or actually pay tax to the government. The system is summarized in Table 3.

Individuals with incomes of $2,250 would receive no net benefit and pay no net tax; $2,250 (more generally, the credit divided by the tax rate) can be termed the *break-even income*. If an individual has an initial income above $2,250, the government takes one-third of the excess. Symmetrically, if an individual's initial income is below $2,250, the government makes up one-third of the shortfall. The net benefits can be regarded as "negative income taxes."

TABLE 3. *Effect of the Credit Income Tax at Selected Initial Income Levels*

Initial income before payment to or from government	Gross offsetting tax (1/3 of 1)	Net benefit (+) or tax paid (−) ($750 − 2)	Final income after payment to or from government (1 + 3)
$ 0	$ 0	$+ 750	$ 750
300	100	+ 650	950
600	200	+ 550	1,150
900	300	+ 450	1,350
2,100	700	+ 50	2,150
2,250ᵃ	750	0	2,250
3,000	1,000	− 250	2,750
9,000	3,000	−2,250	6,750
12,000	4,000	−3,250	8,750

a. Break-even income.

Under the proposal, a family could pool its guarantee credits provided it also pooled its members' incomes. In the example of Table 4, the addition of another dependent would be worth $750 in reduced net taxes or added net benefits. Credits play a role in this scheme similar to that of personal exemptions in the present federal income tax. But there is one important difference. The guarantee or credit is of the same value, $750 in the example, whatever the income of the taxpayer. A personal exemption for a dependent is worth more to a high-bracket than a low-bracket taxpayer. The prevailing $600 exemption is worth $420 to a taxpayer rich enough to be taxed at a marginal rate of 70 percent; $84 to a lowest-bracket taxpayer; and nothing to a family too poor to pay income tax. To help large rich families but not large poor families is anomalous social policy.

TABLE 4. *Effect of Credit Income Tax on Initial Income of $6,000, by Selected Size of Family*

Size of family	Net benefit (+) or tax (−)	Final income
1	$−1,250	$4,750
2	− 500	5,500
3	+ 250	6,250
4	+1,000	7,000

Part of the logic of a negative income tax is that poor families should in equity be able to cash in their unused exemptions.

A simple proposal like the one illustrated in Table 4 is neutral with respect to the grouping of individuals. A person is worth the same—$750 in the example—whether he is a dependent member of a large taxpaying unit or a separate one-person unit. His income is subject to the same tax—one-third in the example—in either case. No set of individuals can gain at the expense of the government either by splitting into several units or by combining into one.

The average per capita net benefit or tax depends in a simple manner on average per capita income:

$$net\ revenue\ per\ capita = (tax\ rate \times initial\ income\ per\ capita) - tax\ credit,$$

or:

$$\frac{net\ revenue\ per\ capita}{initial\ income\ per\ capita} = tax\ rate - \frac{tax\ credit}{initial\ income\ per\ capita}$$

At the 1966 level of $3,000 personal income per capita, the average gross tax under the illustrative proposal would be $1,000, the average net tax $250. Thus the tax would yield the government 8⅓ percent of personal income (33⅓ percent − 25 percent) after all benefits or negative taxes were paid. (The federal income tax now yields about 10 percent of personal income, but little more than 9 percent after current public assistance transfers are paid.) Raising the guarantee from 25 to 30 percent of average income, that is, to the poverty line of $900 per capita, would require an increase of five points in the tax rate.

Real income per capita increases 2½ percent per year. Assuming the guarantee is held constant in purchasing power, net revenue from a credit income tax will rise as a share of personal income 2½ percent per year. Alternatively, this is the amount by which the flat tax rate can be reduced if no increase in revenue, relative to personal income, is needed.

A hypothetical redistribution to the poor is calculated in Table 5.

The proposal also involves, of course, a large secondary redistribution

TABLE 5. Hypothetical Redistribution from Non-Poor to Poor in 1966, Comparing Existing Public Assistance with Credit of $750 per Capita and Tax Rate of One-Third

Characteristic	Poor	Non-poor	Total
1. Number of persons (millions)	29.7	163.7	193.4
2. Percent of total population	15.3	84.7	100.0
3. Average income per capita			
a. Before taxes and public assistance	$ 395	3,471	$3,000
b. After taxes and public assistance a	$ 539	3,150	$2,750
4. Credit income tax			
a. Gross (1/3 3a)	$ 132	$1,157	$1,000
b. Net ($750 − 4a)	+$ 618	−$ 407	−$ 250
c. Final income (3a + 4b)	$1,013	$3,064	$2,750
5. Additional redistribution			
a. Per capita (4c − 3b)	+$ 474	−$ 86	0
b. Aggregate (billions)	+$ 14.1	−$ 14.1	0

a. These entries assume actual public assistance totalling $4.3 billion and an income tax that raises from the non-poor this amount and additional revenue of 8⅓ percent of personal income.

among the non-poor. A family of four would pay no tax unless its income exceeded $9,000. Benefits to non-poor families below the break-even incomes might total $29 billion. The burden would fall mainly on higher-income taxpayers, and among them mainly on taxpayers with income not now taxable. At present taxable income is only 46 percent of personal income. With this degree of slippage it would take a nominal tax rate of 70 percent to produce an effective tax rate of one-third. That is why the advocates of the credit income tax propose wholesale elimination of exclusions, deductions, and exemptions.

The uniform tax rate has great technical advantages; it eliminates all incentive to shift income, either in fact or in appearance, from one year to another or from one taxpaying unit to another. The structure is still progressive because of the tax credit or guarantee, which diminishes relative to income as income rises. As for progression in the rate structure itself, it is argued, the high rates applicable to high incomes are more apparent than real; the law is riddled with ways to escape these rates, particularly when the high incomes are derived from property. But marginal rates could be increased at high incomes.

Children's Allowances and Adults' Allowances

The credit income tax proposal can be modified in a number of different ways. The most important are the schedule of credits for households of varying size and composition and the structure of tax rates in relation to income.

A uniform per capita guarantee makes no allowance for economies of scale in family living or for differences in consumption requirements between adults and children. It favors large families, especially those with young children, as against single adults and small families. A high cash value for an additional child may be an undesirable incentive. For these reasons, it might be better to provide higher credits for adults, single or married, than for children, and also to reduce and eventually eliminate credit for an additional child as the size of family rises. An example is given in column 2 of Table 6. A schedule of this kind, however, introduces legal

TABLE 6. *Illustrative Schedules Relating Credits to Family Size*

	Household's credit or guaranteed income				
	(1)	(2)	(3)	(4)	(5)
			Half of personal exemptions and minimum standard deductions	Children's allowances	
Size of family	Constant per capita	Guarantees near poverty lines		Modest	Anti-poverty
1	$ 750	$1,000	$ 450	$ 0	$ 0
2	1,500	2,000	800	0	0
3	2,250	2,600	1,150	200	1,800
4	3,000	3,200	1,500	400	2,400
5	3,750	3,600	1,850	600	3,000
6	4,500	4,000	2,200	800	3,600
7	5,250	4,200	2,550	1,000	4,200
8	6,000	4,400	2,900	1,200	4,800
9	6,750	4,400	3,250	1,400	5,400

Note: The table assumes that the first two members of a household are adults. If there is only one adult, entries in column 2 for households of two or more persons would be $400 less, and entries in columns 4 and 5 would be moved up one line.

and economic problems that the flat per capita allowance avoids. A youth's claim on the government may depend on whether he is an "adult" or a "child," and the value of a child may depend on what household claims him as a member. Nevertheless, it seems perfectly feasible to set up and enforce some reasonable legal definitions.[19]

An entirely different approach is to allow credits only for families with children. The United States is the only advanced country that does not

19. See James Tobin, Joseph Pechman, and Peter Mieszkowski, "Is a Negative Income Tax Practical?" *Yale Law Journal*, Vol. 77 (November 1967), pp. 1–27.

pay children's allowances. In other countries allowances are paid for all children, without regard to parents' income, although in some cases the allowances are taxable. But they are in almost all cases too small to be the major form of assistance to families in serious poverty. The purposes of the allowances are, rather, to improve "horizontal" equity between small and large families of the same incomes, whether poor or rich, and in some countries to *raise* the birth rate.

A children's allowance plan in this spirit is illustrated in column 4 of Table 6. Paid to the parents of all children under 19, of whom there were 75 million in 1966, these allowances would cost $15 billion gross, or about $12 billion net if they were subject to regular income tax. Of the net benefits, nearly 80 percent would go to families above the poverty line. If the program were financed by a uniform increase in income tax rates, the end result would be a modest but dubious redistribution from childless taxpayers to large families, and very little redistribution from rich to poor.

If children's allowances are intended to be of significant help to destitute families, they must be much more generous, as in column 5 of Table 6. Moreover, since no help is to be given to childless couples, the value of the first child would have to be very high indeed. To offer so large a financial incentive for women to start having children is risky social policy. With allowances on the scale of column 5, it is necessary to abandon the appealing idea of a universal payment subject to no test of need except the regular income tax. The net cost, of the order of $65 billion as of 1966, would exceed the yield of the federal income tax. Yet nothing would have been done for 18 million poor childless adults.[20]

Negative Income Tax Proposals

The credit income tax involves a large politically difficult secondary redistribution, which can be diminished in magnitude by abandoning the flat tax rate and by partially offsetting the credits or guarantees with a special high tax on low initial incomes. This is the technique of most negative income tax (NIT) proposals.

20. Recognizing these problems, Harvey Brazer has proposed a special tax that recoups part or all of the allowances, the fraction depending on the other income of the family. See his contribution to Eveline M. Burns (ed.), *Children's Allowances and the Economic Welfare of Children* (Citizens' Committee for Children of New York, Inc., 1968).

Consider, for example, the proposal made by Milton Friedman and others to pay each nontaxpayer half the difference between (1) the sum of his personal exemptions and standard deductions and (2) his initial income. The amounts that a household with no other income would receive are shown in Table 6, column 3. Benefits would decline by 50 percent of other income—that is, the income would be taxed at 50 percent. The break-even levels would be twice the entries in column 3. At those incomes households would begin to pay regular income tax, just as they do now. The tax rate would fall from 50 percent to the first-bracket rate under the tax code (14 percent in the absence of the temporary surcharge enacted in 1968).

If the Friedman plan were superimposed on existing public assistance, about half the poverty gap, $5.5 billion as of 1966, would be made up—a bit less because the break-even levels fall short of the poverty lines. To finance the plan, regular income tax rates would have to be raised two points. If the plan replaced current public assistance, as Friedman suggests, its net cost would be only $2½ billion or $3 billion as of 1966, but it would reduce the aggregate poverty gap only by the same amount.[21]

Column 2 of Table 6 shows a more generous schedule of guarantees. This too could be combined with a 50 percent offsetting tax on other income. Break-even incomes would range from $2,000 for a single adult to $8,800 for a family of eight. But the 50 percent tax rate would continue to apply at higher incomes until it produced the same tax liability as the regular income tax code. Above the "tax break-even" income the regular rates would apply. For illustration, the calculation of tax, negative or positive, for a couple with two children is given in Table 7. The tax break-even income is $7,920. For incomes above that point the normal tax calculation supersedes the special NIT calculation. The marginal tax rate falls abruptly from 50 percent to 17.1 percent, and then rises again with income.

The primary redistribution involved in this proposal is roughly the $17 billion required to close the poverty gap with a 50 percent tax, as calculated in Table 2. The secondary redistribution is difficult to estimate, but it is of the order of $5 billion. About half of four-person families, for example, had incomes below $7,920 in 1966 and would have benefited from the plan. Beneficiaries other than current recipients of public assistance would have been subject to higher marginal tax rates, 50 percent compared with 0 to

---

21. It is assumed that double exemptions for age and blindness would not be allowed for NIT purposes.

TABLE 7. *Comparison of Effects of Existing Income Tax and Proposed Negative Income Tax, for Married Couple with Two Children at Selected Income Levels*

Initial income	Net benefit (+) or tax (−)		Final income		Marginal tax rate	
	NIT[a]	1966 tax law	NIT	1966 tax law[b]	NIT	1966 tax law
$ 0	$+3,200	$ 0	$3,200	$ 0		
1,000	+2,700	0	3,700	1,000	50 %	0 %
2,000	+2,200	0	4,200	2,000	50	0
3,000	+1,700	0	4,700	3,000	50	0
4,000	+1,200	− 140	5,200	3,860	50	14
5,000	+ 700	− 290	5,700	4,710	50	15
6,000	+ 200	− 450	6,200	5,550	50	16
6,400[c]	0	− 511	6,400	5,889	50	15.3
7,000	− 300	− 603	6,700	6,397	50	15.3
7,920[d]	− 760	− 760	7,160	7,160	50	17.1
8,000	− 772	− 772	7,228	7,228	17.1	17.1
10,000	−1,114	−1,114	8,886	8,886	17.1	17.1

a. $3,200 less 50 percent of initial income, or the tax under the 1966 tax law, whichever is algebraically larger.

b. Figures shown assume standard deduction of $600 or 10 percent of initial income, whichever is larger. The 10 percent deduction when applicable makes the effective marginal tax rate 10 percent lower than the nominal rate for the bracket; that is why the marginal rate is 15.3 percent in the 17 percent bracket and 17.1 percent in the 19 percent bracket.

c. NIT break-even income.

d. Tax break-even income.

17 percent now. This change could have serious disincentive effects, just as the reduction in marginal rate of tax from 100 or 66⅔ percent would improve incentives for public assistance clients.

A proposal of this type is, in effect, a credit income tax grafted onto the present income tax structure. The dip in the marginal tax rate creates some problems. Whenever marginal tax rates vary there is an inducement to shift income, both in appearance and in reality, to tax returns with lower marginal rates. This may mean the return for this year, last year, or some other person. In the present instance, there would be some incentive for concentrating income in time, in order to have it taxed at low marginal rates rather than at 50 percent. A more serious difficulty is the incentive for family-splitting: A father or potential stepfather with a good income may do better for himself and for a mother and her children by filing separately and paying regular income tax; if he joins the group, his income will be taxed at the 50 percent rate, depriving the mother and children of benefits they could otherwise claim. Although cases of this kind would be by no means as frequent or as serious as under AFDC, they point up the advantages of a uniform tax rate.

The two NIT examples both assumed a 50 percent tax rate. There is nothing sacred about 50 percent, or even about a constant rate. Lowering the tax rate in the more generous plan, while keeping the same schedule of credits, would increase the costs of both the primary and secondary redistributions. The Friedman proposal could be modified to change the tax rate to 25 percent while holding the break-even incomes constant. Then the guarantee levels shown in column 3 of Table 6 would be cut in half. So would the aggregate transfer: The government would be making up only a quarter of the deficit of each poor family. As an interim measure, Robert Lampman has suggested guarantee levels at a quarter of the poverty line, zero tax on incomes up to half the poverty line, and 50 percent tax thereafter. His purpose is to concentrate aid on the working poor.

Taxable income as defined for the federal income tax is so poor a definition of need that to use it as the base for negative income tax payments would be a travesty of common sense and social justice. Society does not want to pay benefits to people with low taxable income but with ample resources—wealth, tax-exempt interest, capital gains, pensions, social security stipends, college fellowships, large itemized deductions, gift receipts, and so on. Consequently, negative income taxation requires a much more inclusive definition of income as the base for the offsetting tax.[22]

Such a definition is feasible but admittedly involves a philosophical inconsistency. If taxable income as now defined is so obviously deficient as a test of need, why is it a good test of ability to pay? The illogic here is what leads Rolph and other advocates of the credit income tax to insist on a thorough reform, resulting in a single inclusive definition of income.

Americans, as noted above, are mortally afraid that some potential workers will choose idleness even at the expense of income. The total disqualification of households containing potential workers, as attempted in the present system of public assistance in most states, has proved disastrous. But does sufficient incentive to work remain after a tax of one-third or one-half is levied on earnings? Does the carrot need to be supplemented by a stick?

One possibility would be not to count potential workers in reckoning the guarantees to which the household unit is entitled, to presume that they have incomes at least sufficient to wipe out their credits. Thus if the credit

22. Detailed suggestions for this definition are made in Tobin and others, "Is a Negative Income Tax Practical?"

for a potential worker were $1,000 and the offsetting tax rate were 50 percent, he would be presumed to be earning income at a rate of $2,000 a year even if his actual income were lower. This presumption would deprive his family of the $1,000 but not, as under AFDC, of the amounts to which it is entitled on account of its other members.

The presumption should be removed, and the potential worker's entitlement restored, in any month for which a federal manpower officer in his locality certified that, whether due to temporary personal disabilities or lack of suitable job or training opportunities, he could not earn income at the presumed rate. In this manner, a federal program of creating, financing, and coordinating job and training opportunities could be meshed with a program of income supplementation.

Concluding Remarks

Poverty in the United States, as officially measured, has declined dramatically in this decade, thanks to the sustained expansion of the economy and the restoration of full employment. But the poverty that remains has become a greater threat to the social order. This is the decade of the Negro's claim to full equality in all aspects of American life. Although the economic conditions of Negroes have markedly improved during the boom of the 1960s, they suffer much more than their share of poverty, unemployment, and urban squalor. The transformation of the American economy and population from rural to urban is still going on. Ultimately it will be the engine of great improvement in the lives of Negro immigrants to cities and their children, as it has been for previous immigrants. But the transition is long, difficult, and dangerous.

The acute problem is the inability of many employable males to earn enough to support their children. The result is usually a family in poverty unrelieved by public assistance. With increasing frequency, however, the mother and children are left on their own, and "go on welfare." The basic solution in the long run is to build up earning capacities by education and work experience. Meanwhile, people are poor, and their children are raised under handicaps that may destine them to be poor too.

The present system of public assistance has failed. Inadequate in coverage and in benefits, perverse in its incentives, it fosters the very conditions it is supposed to relieve.

We urgently need a reformed and nationalized system of income assistance that does not exclude employable men and their families. In my opinion, this should be meshed with the federal income tax. The credit income tax seems the fairest and simplest solution. But it will take a long time to develop political consensus for so drastic a reform, and meanwhile something must be done. The merit of the negative income tax approach is that a workable and equitable system of aiding the poor can be introduced within the framework of present federal income taxation.

Which NIT proposal should it be? On some of the questions involved in a choice—for example, how high a tax rate can be used without costly damage to incentives—we will gain light from the experiments in negative taxation now being conducted in New Jersey by MATHEMATICA and the Institute for Research on Poverty of the University of Wisconsin. Meanwhile, I would venture the opinion that the tax rate should not exceed 50 percent. I also find it hard to justify guarantee levels significantly below poverty lines except as a temporary and transitional feature of a new system.

Together these specifications imply a system like the one illustrated in Table 6, column 2, and in Table 7. This is a costly proposal, and if the budgetary resources could not be found at once, it could be gradually introduced as follows: Keep the suggested break-even incomes, which for most family sizes are roughly twice the poverty thresholds. Start by making up, say, only one-quarter of the amount by which a household's income falls short of this break-even level,[23] and step up the rate gradually until it reaches 50 percent. During the transition the existing public assistance system would be gradually phased out. But states and localities that wished to augment the benefits available to the poor under the federal NIT system would be able to do so, perhaps even with some federal financial help.

The main obstacles to reform are ideological and fiscal. The widespread, if largely groundless, fear of freeloading can be met by making part, not all, of the assistance to families conditional on the willingness of employable members to present themselves for work or training, and by providing assistance in a way that rewards self-reliance. The budgetary cost is formidable, especially if we impose on ourselves the rule that taxes can never be

23. The guarantees would be half those in column 2 of Table 6; the tax rate would be 25 percent up to break-even incomes and then 50 percent up to tax break-even incomes. The total cost would be $14 billion, with no allowance for reduction of public assistance.

increased. But the war on poverty is too crucial to be relegated to the status of a residual claimant for funds that peace in Asia and the normal growth of tax revenues may painlessly and gradually make available. When asked to make sacrifices for the defense of their nation, the American people have always responded. Perhaps some day a national administration will muster the courage to ask the American people to tax themselves for social justice and domestic tranquillity. The time is short.

TAX REFORM AND INCOME REDISTRIBUTION: ISSUES AND ALTERNATIVES

Redistribution through the Income Tax

1. The 1972 presidential campaigns evoked great popular interest in proposals for income redistribution through the federal income tax, though more confusion than understanding and more opposition than support. Of course, the income tax has always been an instrument of redistribution, in two senses: First, it embodies, though quite imperfectly, the principle that the burdens of federal expenditure should be borne in accordance with "ability to pay." Second, income tax revenues finance transfer payments and other programs with identifiable individual benefits; the resulting net redistributions are large and, on the whole, egalitarian.[1] The common novelty of various controversial schemes of recent years is the proposal that the income tax system itself should result not only in tax payments *from* most citizens but also in cash payments *to* others, that is, in negative taxes as well as positive taxes.

This proposal would make explicit the redistributional nature of income taxation. The same set of rules and criteria that determines whether citizens pay more or less taxes would also determine whether they pay taxes or receive transfers of smaller or larger amount. Some existing transfers, now administered separately from the income tax and by different criteria, would be replaced by negative taxes. Although the idea is not at the moment a very live option in American politics, thanks in no small part to the 1972 debacle, Britain is about to implement it.[2] Strangely enough, what is regarded here as a radical proposal is viewed there as conservative.

2. In this paper we consider some of the problems and issues in reforming the US federal income tax in the same direction. Our approach is quite pragmatic. We do not pretend that we are building from scratch a wholly new integrated system of taxes and transfers. We begin with the existing systems and we take some account, for reasons of both

The support of the National Science Foundation is gratefully acknowledged. We are also grateful for the assistance and advice of the Brookings Institution, Benjamin Okner, Joseph Pechman, and their staff, who made available to us the MERGE file on which our calculations are based. We have benefited from discussions with Boris Bittker, Robert Eisner, Edwin Kuh, Jon Peck, and Harold Watts. William Starnes assisted in the computations. We alone are responsible for the contents of the paper.

equity and political acceptability, of the interests of the current beneficiaries of tax concessions and special transfers.

We set forth below a number of specific plans and calculate their
redistributional impact as of 1970. The reference plan is the actual federal
personal income tax of 1970, together with the cash public assistance
program of 1970. Each proposal is required to produce the same aggregate
net revenue as the reference plan.

Families (including single individuals) are classified by several characteristics: size, income, age of head, home ownership. The redistributional impact of any proposal on an average family of any type is the
difference, positive or negative, between its tax liabilities under the proposal and under the reference plan. We shall present summary statistics
of the redistributions for several plans.

These gains and losses are the first-round effects of each proposal.
They are calculated on the assumption that the original distribution of
income, before taxes and transfers, is not changed by the reform. Revisions of the tax code will in general induce changes in behavior and
earnings that will modify the first-round redistribution. We make no
attempt to estimate these second-round effects. We are encouraged to
believe that the omission is not serious by the experimental findings in
New Jersey, where income guarantees and high marginal tax rates appear
to have had little effect on earnings.[3]

The Credit Income Tax and the Negative Income Tax

3. All reform proposals of the genus described in section 1 provide an
income guarantee, the amount of negative taxes a family receives when
it has zero income. The guarantee can be regarded as a universal cashable
tax credit—available to discharge gross income tax liabilities and receivable in cash to the extent the credit exceeds gross taxes.

Gross taxes must be large enough in aggregate to cover all the tax
credits of the population and to provide the net revenues needed for the
federal budget. A useful identity to bear in mind is the following:

$$\frac{\text{average gross tax}}{\text{average income}} = \frac{\text{average net tax}}{\text{average income}} + \frac{\text{average tax credit}}{\text{average income}}.$$

Thus, if the federal budget needs 10% of personal income and the tax
credit or income guarantee is set at 25% of average personal income,
gross taxes will have to be 35% of personal income.

There are many tax codes that could produce the required net revenues, differing from each other in guarantee schedules, tax rate sched-

ules, definition of taxable income, and other provisions. We make one basic distinction, between a unitary code and a dual code. A unitary code, also called a *credit income tax*, specifies a uniform method of calculating tax liabilities; another distinguishing feature is that the marginal tax rate is either constant or nondecreasing with income. A dual code, generally called a *negative income tax*, offers the citizen a choice between two codes, of which one will generally be advantageous for poorer families, the other for richer. The second code is just the current positive income tax, with rates scaled up as necessary to pay the negative taxes. The first code offers tax credits in place of deductions and exemptions and offsets them by taxing an inclusive definition of income at a high marginal tax rate, 50% for example. When a taxpayer reaches the income at which the regular income tax code is cheaper, he shifts abruptly to a lower marginal tax rate.

Dual plans, negative income tax plans, have been extensively discussed and calculated.[4] For that reason, our emphasis is on unitary plans. But we have included, for comparative purposes, one model negative income tax proposal.

Vertical Equity

4. Every concrete proposal for tax reform is a compromise among conflicting objectives. The important criteria that must be balanced are vertical equity, horizontal equity, historical equity, simplicity, and minimization of incentives for inefficient tax-avoiding behavior. We shall discuss these objectives in turn and point out the important ways in which they conflict. We shall also indicate the general nature of the compromises reflected in our specific proposals; the details are given below.

Vertical equity is of course a principal motivation for proposals of this type. Existing transfer programs miss many poor and near-poor families, particularly large families headed by men of working age.[5] Income guarantees, tax credits, are designed to shift income to the low-income brackets. As for the upper brackets, the loopholes, privileges, exclusions, and deductions that neutralize the theoretical progressivity of the income tax are well known.[6] It is natural, therefore, to seek at least part of the revenue for negative taxes by tightening the definition of taxable income.

The pure credit income tax, originally propounded by Earl Rolph,[7] involves tax credits c, a single gross tax rate t, and a tight comprehensive concept of taxable income y. The tax liability of a family is $ty - c$, and may of course be either positive or negative. The system is progressive in the sense that taxes are an increasing share of income, approaching t asymptotically.

But if the gross tax rate t is held to a level that is not a serious earnings disincentive for the bulk of the population, a single-rate schedule may not be sufficiently progressive. Some high-income taxpayers would gain substantially in comparison with the existing situation, and their gains would be at the expense of more adequate income guarantees for the poor. This dilemma becomes worse if the most inclusive income definition is eroded by deductions, for many of which there are good arguments grounded in horizontal or historical equity. For these reasons, we were led almost inevitably from the pure Rolph model to a progressive tax rate schedule.

Horizontal Equity: Personal Tax Credits and Family Size

5. *Horizontal equity* presents a host of tough problems. Perhaps the most important and difficult is the treatment of family size and composition. If tax credits are to be more than a gesture of income assistance for the poor, the average credit per family member must be much larger than the tax-reducing value of an exemption in the present tax code. Note the relation of official poverty lines to family size in table 3.

Tax credits must bear some relation to family "needs." This is particularly important for families with little or no income, who would be heavily dependent on their receipts of negative taxes. The marginal credit for an additional dependent will therefore generally exceed the amount implicit in the present tax system. A credit income tax almost inevitably redistributes income from small families to large, as well as from rich to poor, and this redistribution by family size occurs in all income brackets.

The marginal tax credit need not, of course, be identical to the average. No one would advocate demogrants of $1,000 for every man, woman, and child, even if he favored an *average* tax credit of that amount. Adults need more than dependent children, and large families need less per capita than small families.

There are several objections to gearing tax credits to the relative "needs" of families of different sizes and compositions, quite apart from the difficulty of estimating the need differentials themselves. First, whenever the tax credit of an individual varies with the family group of which he is declared a member, there is some incentive for him to be, or appear to be, in the grouping where he is most valuable. Two can live more cheaply than one, but if the tax credit for a couple is less than twice two single tax credits, there will be lots of single individuals, at least for tax purposes. Similarly, if the sixth child is worth a lot less than the third child, there is an incentive to create smaller families and to convert sixth children into third children. This is the argument for age-related rather than size-related tax credit schedules, even at some cost in horizontal equity.

Second is the fundamental objection that tax credits for children are an undesirable incentive for reproduction. Closely connected is the view that children are consumer goods and that parents who prefer them to other consumption packages merit no help from the state. We make no attempt to handle these issues. We do observe that fertility in the United States is already down to rates ultimately consistent with ZPG. We strongly suspect that inadequate birth control information rather than the prospect of financial gain is the main source of excessive fertility among welfare mothers. We do not see how a humane society can penalize children for being born, even if their deprivation were an effective disincentive for other potential parents.

However, the view that people who like children should spend their own money on them is more compelling for the rich. One might approve of differential credits to the advantage of large poor families but disapprove of them for others. In this spirit Harvey Brazer proposed many years ago a system of vanishing credits for children.[8] In effect, large families get not only large income guarantees, but also higher marginal tax rates to whittle down their differential advantage in tax credits. One of the variants we present below contains this feature. Fine-tuning for equity always complicates the system. It is also worth remembering that US tax and transfer programs value children much less, relative to mean incomes, than European programs commonly do.

Historical and Horizontal Equity: Deductions

6. Both *historical equity* and *horizontal equity* are at stake in questions raised by deductions allowed under present tax law. The standard and low-income deductions are superseded because they are awkward ways of accomplishing the same purposes as personal tax credits.

The pure credit income tax would wipe out item deductions ruthlessly and provide tax credits only on the personal bases discussed in section 5. This surgery is unrealistic and not really equitable.

The most important itemized deductions are connected with home ownership. The homeowner escapes tax on the imputed rental value of the home. Yet he can deduct his property taxes and mortgage interest. Neither the landlord nor the tenant in a rental transaction gets an equivalent break. As unfair as these provisions are in the abstract, the interests of existing homeowners deserve some respect. In the proposals presented below, we provide some tax credits for homeowners while also suggesting parallel credits for tenants.

Other deductions are generally of three types: (1) those that are essentially corrections to the calculation of income—expenses of earning income, alimony and support payments, interest payments; (2) those that are indicative of significant differences in need—medical expenses are the prime example; (3) those that reflect dispositions of income that Congress wishes to encourage as a matter of social policy—charitable contributions, state and local taxes. It would be very difficult to rationalize the particular set of deductions in our tax laws, as opposed to a larger or smaller set. But it is also hard to ignore the social and political consensus that supports the current list.

Our proposals are very pragmatic. We need to restrict the erosion of the income tax base in order to have reasonably large income guarantees without exorbitant tax rates. We wish to avoid complexity in tax returns for both the citizens and the government. Basically our proposals allow deductions of type (1), while limiting and converting into credits the other types. The main limitation is to take account of certain deductions only to the extent that they exceed a specified threshold, calculated to make itemization no more frequent than it is under the present law. A specific limitation is to allow no deduction or credit for state and local sales and excise taxes. Like less visible indirect taxes, these levies could be regarded as part of the price of commodities taxpayers choose individually to consume. In practice the deduction does not require an accounting of taxes paid. It is generally automatic, following a tabulated function of income and sales tax rate. The justification for so indirect and inefficient a method of aiding states and localities has been greatly diminished by the advent of revenue-sharing.

Historical and Horizontal Equity: Provisions for the Aged and for Welfare Beneficiaries

7. Complicated questions of equity arise also with respect to the aged, most of whom benefit from old age and survivors insurance and from special concessions in the income tax code. Our proposals leave social insurance untouched. They also allow some special credits for the aged, designed to improve the lot of old people at the bottom of the income spectrum without significantly damaging their more fortunate fellows.

Cash public assistance is the only welfare program that our tax proposals are assumed to replace. We recognize that in some jurisdictions, welfare benefits, under the Aid for Dependent Children program, exceed the income guarantees here contemplated. In those cases historical equity calls for supplements for current beneficiaries. This is a state and local responsibility, but the federal government might share the costs. Our calculations do not take account of supplementary payments. But neither do they allow for any possible savings from in-kind programs: food stamps, rent subsidies, medicaid, and others.

In combination, these in-kind programs generate many unintended inequities and inefficiencies, and their several income tests, piled on top of one another and on top of regular taxes, can build the marginal tax on earnings up to frightening levels, sometimes over 100%.[9]

The in-kind programs badly need to be rationalized and integrated with cash assistance and the tax laws. Food stamps could logically be discontinued once universal income guarantees were enacted. Rent subsidies and other public housing benefits are enjoyed by a small minority of those who meet the income test of eligibility. It would be reasonable to count such benefits, or a sizable fraction of them, as an alternative way of receiving tax credits. Medicaid, however, is probably best left as a separate system, to be replaced in a few years by national health insurance.

Avoiding Complexities and Disincentives

8. One appeal of the pure credit income tax is its *simplicity*. With a simple schedule of personal tax credits, a flat tax rate, and a standard inclusive definition of income, the tax liability of any breadwinner is very easy to compute. Under the projected new British system, the vast majority of the population will never file returns. Declare your dependents to your employer, and PAYE (withholding) does the rest. The savings in administrative costs are welcome, but as we have already seen, a simple scheme necessarily carries inequities.

Simplicity is complementary to another and more important goal, minimization of incentives for tax-reducing behavior. If tax credits are attached to the *person*, regardless of the family group to which he belongs, then family groupings will not be distorted by the credits. If income is taxed at the same rate regardless of the tax return where it is reported, then there is no incentive to shift income between years or between taxpayers in search of the lowest marginal tax rate. For this reason our principal unitary proposals keep a flat tax rate for 97% of the population, introducing surtaxes only above $35,000. (In the Brazer-type proposal with vanishing children's credits, a greater variety of marginal tax rates is essential.) The dual proposal, in which the marginal tax rate shifts from 50% to 14% at the crossover income, invites considerable effort to concentrate reported income at the lower rate.

A certain quantum of disincentives cannot be avoided. No plan escapes the arithmetic fact that decent income guarantees cannot be provided without a high average marginal tax rate, about 35%. The same gross revenue that can be raised by a flat 35% rate can also be raised by a variable marginal rate. In the case of the negative income tax, the low-income rate of 50% falls to 14% and gradually rises again. If we knew that work and enterprise were less sensitive to after-tax earnings at one income level than another, we could concentrate high marginal tax rates in the insensitive income brackets. But we are really quite ignorant of the empirical elasticities.

Description of Proposed Plans

9. Schedules of Cashable Tax Credits
Three alternative schedules of cashable tax credits are used, two related to age and one to family size. They are shown in table 1. Age-related

Table 1 **Alternative Schedules of Cashable Tax Credits**

Age-related schedules			TC-3 Size-related-schedule		
Age	TC-1 credit ($)	TC-2 credit ($)	Family size	Total credit ($)	Marginal credit ($)
0–17	300	540	1	1,320	1,320
18–64	900	900	2	1,980	660
≥65 (male), ≥62 (female), or blind or disabled	1,080	1,080	3 4 5	2,400 2,820 3,000	420 420 180
plus					
Dwelling Unit Credit	180	180	6 7	3,180 3,360	180 180
Memoranda:			8	3,540	180
Couple 18–64	1,980	1,980	>8	3,540	0
Parents 18–64, plus 2 children	2,580	3,060			
Parents 18–64, plus 4 children	3,180	4,140			

credits are supplemented by a cashable dwelling unit credit, $180 per dwelling unit whether owned or rented. This credit is designed to improve the status of single individuals and small families when they genuinely occupy separate dwellings. At the same time, it is a partial replacement for the home-ownership deductions allowed in current law. As table 1 shows, the amounts of the credits in schedules TC-1 and TC-3 are roughly comparable. Schedule TC-2 is used only in the Brazer-type plan; large children's credits are provided for poor families, but they are partially recaptured by special surtaxes.

Since the credits are hypothetical income guarantees for 1970, readers may wish to compare them with official poverty-line incomes for 1970, given in table 2.

10.   Tax Rate Schedules

Three tax rate schedules are used, as shown in table 3. The first one, TR-1, is used in the several variants of the credit income tax. The second one, TR-2, is used in the Brazer-type plan. The third one, TR-3, is for the dual plan, the negative income tax proper.

Tax rates in the table must be added to obtain marginal rates. For example, under TR-1 the marginal rate above $75,000 is the basic rate plus 15. Under TR-2 the marginal rate for a 2-2 family is the basic rate

Table 2   **Poverty-Line Incomes 1970**

Size of Family	Income ($)
All unrelated individuals	1,947
Under 65 years	2,005
65 years and over	1,852
All families	3,580
2 persons	2,507
Head under 65 years	2,569
Head 65 years and over	2,328
3 persons	3,080
4 persons	3,944
5 persons	4,654
6 persons	5,212
7 persons	6,407

Source: US Bureau of the Census, *Current Population Reports*, Series P-60, No. 81, "Characteristics of the Low-Income Population, 1970," US Government Printing Office, Wash., D.C., 1971, page 20, Table N.

Table 3 **Alternative Schedules of Tax Rates**

TR-1		TR-2		TR-3
Basic rate[a] on all income	32–37%	Basic rate[a] on all income	30–35%	50% tax rate until liability would exceed regular 1970 income tax, modified to increase all tax liabilities by 11.6%
Income in excess of ($)	*Surtax* (%)	*Income in excess of* ($)	*Surtax* (%)	
35,000	5	12,000	3	
50,000	5	35,000	4	
75,000	5	50,000	5	
		75,000	5	

Surtaxes for Children

	Children	*Surtax* (%)[b]	*Up to income* ($)
One adult	1	3	12,000
	2	6	12,000
	3	9	12,000
	4	9	16,000
	5	9	20,000
Two adults	1	0	—
	2	1	12,000
	3	4	12,000
	4	7	12,000
	5	9	17,333

a. Basic rate adjusted to yield same net revenue as reference plan.
b. The principle is to impose a surtax of one point for every $180 by which personal tax credits total more than $1,800, the personal tax credits for two adults, or a surtax of nine points, whichever is smaller. The surtax applies up to incomes at which two thirds of the excess personal tax credits have been recaptured. The rates shown in the table carry out this principle for tax credit schedule TC-2.

plus 6 up to income of $12,000, basic rate plus 3 from $12,000 to $35,000, and basic rate plus 7 from $35,000 to $50,000. The surtaxes for children are designed to reduce the marginal value of a child to $180 at high incomes.

11. Noncashable Housing Credits

In plans that allow a dwelling unit credit of $180, homeowners and renters are also entitled to noncashable credits up to $300. A noncashable credit cannot be used except to offset gross tax liabilities. Two systems are considered:

NHC-1

Homeowners All taxpayers are allowed to deduct interest payments from property income declared—receipts of interest, dividends, rents, and capital gains (see section 12). Any mortgage interest left over may be used in calculating the base for the noncashable housing credit; the base also includes the property taxes on the owner's principal residence. The credit is the amount by which 25% of the base exceeds $180, but the credit may not exceed $300.

Renters A tenant is allowed a noncashable credit equal to the amount by which 10% of the annual rent on his principal residence exceeds $180, but the credit may not exceed $300.

NHC-2

Homeowners are required to declare net imputed rent as income. Every taxpayer, whether homeowner or renter, is allowed a noncashable credit equal to the amount by which 10% of the annual (gross) rent on his principal residence exceeds $180, or to $300, whichever is smaller.

NHC-3

Same as NHC-1 without the $180 threshold and $300 ceiling.

These credits provide homeowners with benefits equivalent to the present tax law on owner-occupied homes up to about $40,000 in value. In addition, tenants receive benefits not provided by present law.

12. Deductions and Credits in Lieu of Deductions

1. Full deductions from income are allowed for

   interest payments up to the amounts of property income declared,

   other expenses of earning income now allowed—moving expenses, union dues, child care, etc.,

   alimony and support payments taxable to the recipient.

2. Miscellaneous itemized deductions would be converted into tax credits, by one of the following two systems:

IDC-1

Eligible deductions are pooled, and if the sum exceeds the larger of $1,000 or 10% of corrected income, a noncashable credit of 25% of the excess is allowed. Eligible deductions include those in the present law for medical expenses, charitable contributions, state and local income taxes, uninsured casualty losses. "Corrected income" is taxable income plus cashable tax credits claimed.

IDC-2

Deductions are treated separately, and credits of 25% of the following are allowed: medical expenses as under present law, charitable contributions, state and local income taxes, uninsured casualty losses.

The purpose of converting deductions into credits is to make their value the same to everyone, regardless of his marginal tax bracket. The purpose of the thresholds—for pooled deductions in IDC-1 and specific deductions in IDC-2—is to discourage itemization of outlays by families who now use the standard deduction. Eligible outlays up to the thresholds are regarded as standard items covered by the personal tax credits.

13. Provisions for the Aged

A-1

Persons not on social security would be entitled to the cashable tax credits shown in table 1. They would also be entitled to the Retirement Income Credit (RIC) of the current law: 15% of the first $1,524 of unearned income less certain exclusions for earned income.

Persons receiving OASDI would not be taxed on their social security benefits. Consequently they would not receive personal tax credits unless they chose to waive their OASDI benefits, an option that would almost never be advantageous. They would be allowed the dwelling unit credits, cashable and noncashable. They would be allowed RIC. As under present law, social security benefits must be deducted from the base for the RIC, which is therefore of value only if OASDI benefits fall short of $1,524.

Special tax credits of $840 for a single person and $1,260 for a couple would be provided for social security beneficiaries. These credits would be cashable to the extent that OASDI benefits fall short of $1,200 per person, $2,400 per couple. The remaining amounts of these special credits would be noncashable but available to offset gross tax liabilities on income other than social security benefits. (This provision guarantees social security beneficiaries minimum incomes somewhat higher than those of other retired persons.)

A-2

All aged persons receive the cashable tax credits of table 1, whether or not they *are on OASDI. Half of social insurance benefits are taxed—a treatment roughly analogous to that of private pensions under present law.*

A-3

All persons on OASDI remain subject to the present income tax code. This is done only for the dual plan.

14. Definition of Taxable Income

For the unitary plans, "taxable income" means the income to which the gross tax rates are applied. It is more inclusive than Adjusted Gross Income as defined for the current tax code, in subjecting the following to tax:

dividends now excluded;

state and local bond interest now tax-exempt;

interest on life insurance;

realized capital gains in full.

We recognize that interest on existing tax-exempt bonds cannot be made taxable. The full effect of this change would not be felt until outstanding issues matured and were replaced. Even then the federal government would probably have to compensate state and local governments by a subsidy equal to some fraction of the federal revenue loss due to the tax exemption. Consequently our treatment of this item exaggerates the improvement in the tax base from this source, especially in the short run.

As already stated, our taxable income allows deduction of all interest payments to the extent they are offset by property income, interest, dividends, rents, capital gains. It also allows deduction of other expenses of earning income.

Finally, in some of our variants imputed rent on owner-occupied homes is included in taxable income.

The following items are *not* included in taxable income: OASDI and railroad retirement benefits, the fractions of government and private pensions not now taxable, workmen's compensation, unemployment compensation.

However, the last two items are included in taxable income for the negative income tax side of the dual plan. The positive side utilizes, of course, the income definitions of the present tax code. In our calculations the additional revenue needed for the dual plan is assumed to be raised by a proportionate increase of all tax liabilities. An alternative possibility, of course, would be to enlarge the tax base by adding some or all of the items listed above.

Calculations of Redistributions

15. The data base for our calculations of redistributional impacts is the MERGE file of the Brookings Institution.[10] The basic file is for 1966, but

Okner and his associates have updated the file to 1970 by a series of item-by-item corrections designed to make the aggregates of the file approximately consistent with 1970 aggregate economic and demographic magnitudes. We used the 1970 file.

According to the 1970 file, total income tax liabilities for 1970 were $81.8 billion, slightly less than the $83.8 reported by the Internal Revenue Service. The file estimates welfare and public assistance receipts of $8.4 billion. These are assumed to be replaced by the negative taxes of our proposals. The net revenue requirement is therefore $73.4 billion, and the basic tax rates of our plans are adjusted to meet this requirement.

It is true that about 40% of the $8.4 billion of cash public assistance in 1970 was financed by state and local governments. We have pretended that all of the tax relief resulting from the replacement of these welfare programs occurs in the federal income tax. What is more likely is that net federal income taxes are somewhat higher than our calculations assume, and that state and local taxes are correspondingly lower. Since our taxable income base is $660 billion, our basic tax rates would have to be 0.65 points higher if the saving to the federal government were only half of the $8.4 billion. State and local taxpayers would save the other $4.2 billion.

We do not know how to estimate this secondary redistribution. Since our proposed federal tax is more progressive, and more favorable to large families than state and local taxes typically are, any secondary redistribution of this type would go further in the same general directions as the primary redistributions calculated.

Table 4 summarizes certain aggregate data, as estimated from the 1970 MERGE file, for the whole US population and four subpopulations. Our calculations, for both the whole population and each subpopulation, are based on tabulations of MERGE data by 207 cells: 23 income brackets × 9 family size categories. For any proposed new tax code, we calculate average and total tax liabilities, positive or negative, for each of the 828 possible cells, and compare them with actual income taxes paid less actual public assistance received in 1970. The difference is the estimated redistributional impact of the new code.

Since the proposed tax laws are nonlinear in important respects, these calculations require estimates of within-cell distributions of some relevant variables, not simply their average values. We shall not recount here the ad hoc procedures we have used, employing information from both the MERGE file itself and external data from census and *Statistics of Income*.

The definition of income by which families are classified for the purpose of the calculations is "census income" plus realized capital gains. Ag-

Table 4 Summary Statistics for Population and Subpopulations

	0 Entire population	1 Homeowners	2 Nonhome- owners	3 Aged	4 Nonaged
1. Number of families and single individuals (thousands)	67,133	38,846	28,287	16,181	50,952
2. Number of persons (thousands)	199,141	125,250	73,891	28,692	170,449
3. Average family size (persons)	2.97	3.22	2.61	1.77	335
4. Aggregate Income[a] ($ billion)	750.774	502.087	248.679	95.951	654.823
5. Average income per family ($ thousand)	11.183	12.925	8.790	5.930	12.263
6. Aggregate Taxable Income[b] ($ billion)	658.923	435.052	226.581	58.635	600.203
7. Aggregate Adjusted Gross Income 1970 ($ billion)	636.915	420.880	216.035	52.692	584.223
8. Aggregate Income Tax 1970 ($ billion)	81.825	48.883	32.942	5.065	76.760
9. Aggregate Welfare Receipts 1970 ($ billion)	8.442	3.099	5.343	3.433	5.009

a. Row 4: census income plus realized capital gains.
b. Row 6: defined in section 14.

gregate amounts of this income are shown in line 4 of table 4. Income, in this sense, is more inclusive than our taxable income as described in section 14, in the following respects:

Pensions are included in full.

There are no deductions for interest paid or for other expenses of earning income.

OASDI, railroad retirement benefits, workmen's compensation, and unemployment compensation are all included in full.

16. In table 5 we present summary results for twenty-one plans, twenty unitary plans, and one dual plan. The features of each plan—cashable tax credit schedules, tax rate schedules, noncashable housing credits, deductions and credits in lieu of deductions, and provisions for the aged—are identified by the symbols defined in sections 9–13. The table then shows the basic tax rate needed to meet the net revenue requirement and summarizes the redistributions for the whole population and each of the four subpopulations.

Conclusions

17. A credit income tax is feasible with a basic marginal tax rate of 30–35%. This is comparable to the flat rate of 30% to which almost all British taxpayers are subject. As of 1970 the income guarantees consistent with a tax rate of this order were only 60–75% of poverty lines. But if the fraction of the tax base required as net revenue for the federal budget remains constant, the same tax rate will permit credits to rise at $2\frac{1}{2}$–3% per year, the rate of growth of per capita income in the economy. By 1980, guarantees would be 75–100% of poverty lines.

The credit income tax involves a considerable redistribution, much more than the "dual" proposal, the negative income tax. Our unitary proposals transfer about $30 billion, roughly 4% of the tax base. Large minorities, 35–40% of families, are made worse off than they are under the present system. The losers are in the upper income brackets, especially single individuals and small families in those brackets. Of the $584 billion of taxable income left after the net taxes of $73.4 billion are taken for the budget, $149 billion—slightly more than 25%—is distributed on egalitarian principles by the tax credit. The remainder is distributed according to earning capacity, proportionately except for the surtaxes in high brackets.

There is a significant redistribution from homeowners to nonhomeown-

Table 5 **Summary of Redistributional Impacts of Alternative Tax Proposals, 1970**

Plan Number		I	II	III	IV	V	VI	VII	VIII	IX	X
Plan Characteristics											
Cashable Tax Credits	TC	1	1	1	1	2	2	2	2	1	1
Tax Rates	TR	1	1	1	1	2	2	2	2	1	1
Housing Credits	NHC	1	1	1	1	1	1	1	1	2	2
Itemized Deduction Credits	IDC	1	2	1	2	1	2	1	2	1	2
Provisions for Aged	A	1	1	2	2	1	1	2	2	1	1
Basic Tax Rate (%)		33.03	35.28	33.68	35.88	32.32	34.57	32.98	35.17	32.47	34.65
Whole Population											
1) Families better off (%)		63.3	65.7	59.9	60.0	61.8	64.2	59.3	59.3	63.3	64.6
2) Persons better off (%)		62.3	63.1	57.9	58.3	59.5	60.4	56.5	56.5	62.3	61.2
3) Total transfer ($ billion)		31.5	31.0	34.7	34.2	36.6	36.3	40.0	39.5	32.1	31.7
Redistribution thresholds ($ thousand)											
4) Family size 1		6.6	7.0	6.3	6.1	6.9	7.3	6.6	7.0	6.8	7.3
5) Family size 2		9.8	9.8	9.9	9.7	10.3	10.2	10.2	10.1	10.0	10.0
6) Family size 4		13.4	13.2	12.9	12.8	12.9	12.9	12.5	12.4	13.4	13.2
7) Family size 7		19.8	20.0	18.9	19.3	17.9	17.9	17.3	17.3	19.3	19.7
Average increase in taxes for four-person family ($ thousand)											
8) Income 0–$1000		−1.20	−1.31	−1.21	−1.32	−1.60	−1.71	−1.61	−1.72	−1.20	−1.30
9) Income $8,000–$10,000 (median)		−0.74	−0.73	−0.67	−0.65	−0.79	−0.77	−0.71	−0.69	−0.75	−0.74
10) Income $30,000–$40,000		3.24	3.09	3.46	3.29	3.82	3.67	4.05	3.87	3.37	3.21

Plan Number		XI	XII	XIII	XIV	XV	XVI	XVII	XVIII	XIX	XX	XXI
Plan Characteristics												
Cashable Tax Credits	TC	1	1	2	2	2	2	3	3	3	3	3
Tax Rates	TR	1	1	2	2	2	2	1	1	1	1	3
Housing Credits	NHC	2	2	2	2	2	2	3	3	3	3	3
Itemized Deduction Credits	IDC	1	2	1	2	1	2	1	2	1	2	—
Provisions for Aged	A	2	2	1	1	2	2	1	1	2	2	—
Basic Tax Rate (%)		33.07	35.2	31.70	33.88	32.31	34.44	32.05	34.30	32.73	34.92	11.6 surcharge
Whole Population												
1) Families better off (%)		59.9	59.9	64.2	64.2	59.3	61.7	65.9	65.9	64.4	63.2	33.0
2) Persons better off (%)		57.9	57.9	60.4	60.4	56.5	57.3	61.8	61.8	59.8	57.6	26.0
3) Total transfer ($ billion)		35.2	34.6	37.2	36.9	40.4	39.9	29.8	29.5	33.0	32.6	9.1
Redistribution thresholds ($ thousand)												
4) Family size 1		6.6	6.9	7.3	7.6	6.9	7.3	8.3	8.3	7.8	8.0	4.0
5) Family size 2		10.0	9.9	10.5	10.4	10.5	10.4	11.0	11.0	11.0	10.9	6.5
6) Family size 4		12.9	12.8	12.8	12.7	12.4	12.3	14.6	14.3	13.9	13.7	7.0
7) Family size 7		18.7	19.0	17.6	17.6	17.1	17.0	15.2	14.9	14.7	14.4	8.8
Average increase in taxes for four-person family ($ thousand)												
8) Income 0–$1000		−1.21	−1.32	−1.60	−1.70	−1.61	−1.71	−1.22	−1.33	−1.23	−1.34	−1.11
9) Income $8,000–$10,000 (median)		−0.68	−0.67	−0.79	−0.78	−0.72	−0.70	−0.84	−0.82	−0.76	−0.75	0.07
10) Income $30,000–$40,000		3.58	3.40	3.95	3.79	4.16	3.90	2.82	2.66	3.05	2.87	0.49

Table 5 (*continued*)

Homeowners and Nonhomeowners

	I	II	III	IV	V	VI	VII	VIII	IX	X
Homeowners										
11) Families better off (%)	51.3	49.8	52.6	52.6	49.3	49.3	51.5	51.5	49.8	49.8
12) Persons better off (%)	51.5	49.2	50.1	50.1	48.0	48.0	47.8	47.8	49.2	49.2
13) Net transfer ($ billion)	7.7	7.4	7.8	7.5	9.8	9.4	9.9	9.6	9.0	8.8
14) Average net transfer ($ thousand)	0.199	0.190	0.201	0.193	0.252	0.243	0.256	0.247	0.233	0.227
15) Average gain of families better off ($ thousand)	0.746	0.763	0.832	0.821	0.870	0.865	0.942	0.932	0.779	0.770
16) Average loss of families worse off ($ thousand)	1.193	1.134	1.347	1.319	1.343	1.321	1.529	1.500	1.235	1.216
Nonhomeowners										
17) Families better off (%)	74.1	77.8	73.0	73.0	76.1	76.1	72.0	73.7	77.9	77.9
18) Persons better off (%)	77.8	79.1	76.0	76.0	76.1	76.1	74.0	72.8	78.3	79.3
19) Net transfer ($ billion)	−7.6	−7.2	−7.9	−7.6	−9.7	−9.4	−10.0	−9.7	−8.9	−8.7
20) Average net transfer ($ thousand)	−0.268	−0.256	−0.279	−0.267	−0.343	−0.331	−0.354	−0.343	−0.314	−0.308
21) Average gain of families better off ($ thousand)	0.791	0.740	0.862	0.845	0.924	0.912	1.038	1.000	0.777	0.768
22) Average loss of families worse off ($ thousand)	1.229	1.441	1.300	1.296	1.506	1.518	1.407	1.496	1.315	1.309

	XI	XII	XIII	XIV	XV	XVI	XVII	XVIII	XIX	XX
Homeowners										
11) Families better off (%)	52.4	52.6	49.3	50.1	51.5	51.5	58.1	58.1	58.1	56.0
12) Persons better off (%)	49.6	50.1	48.0	47.3	47.8	47.8	53.5	53.5	53.5	50.7
13) Net transfer ($ billion)	9.3	9.1	11.3	11.1	11.6	11.4	5.8	5.4	5.9	5.5
14) Average net transfer ($ thousand)	0.240	0.235	0.290	0.285	0.299	0.294	0.148	0.139	0.151	0.142
15) Average gain of families better off ($ thousand)	0.834	0.816	0.876	0.853	0.937	0.923	0.664	0.660	0.757	0.777
16) Average loss of families worse off ($ thousand)	1.422	1.402	1.424	1.430	1.614	1.589	1.275	1.249	1.411	1.313
Nonhomeowners										
17) Families better off (%)	74.1	77.8	80.1	79.1	78.6	75.8	75.2	75.2	74.8	74.8
18) Persons better off (%)	77.7	78.9	80.5	79.0	78.0	75.4	73.5	73.5	72.7	72.7
19) Net transfer ($ billions)	-9.3	-9.2	-11.1	-11.0	-11.6	-11.4	-5.6	-5.2	-5.9	-5.5
20) Average net transfer ($ thousand)	-0.330	-0.324	-0.394	-0.388	-0.410	-0.404	-0.197	-0.185	-0.207	-0.196
21) Average gain of families better off ($ thousand)	0.878	0.824	0.905	0.906	0.979	1.005	0.690	0.679	0.754	0.741
22) Average loss of families worse off ($ thousand)	1.233	1.420	1.660	1.575	1.678	1.473	1.296	1.310	1.415	1.418

Table 5 (*continued*)

Aged and Nonaged Heads

	I	II	III	IV	V	VI	VII	VIII	IX	X
Aged Heads										
23) Families better off (%)	70.7	71.3	86.2	86.2	73.6	77.1	86.2	86.2	70.7	76.5
24) Persons better off (%)	76.5	77.5	86.6	86.6	79.8	82.4	86.6	86.6	76.5	81.4
25) Net transfer ($ billion)	-5.2	-5.6	-10.4	-10.6	-5.5	-5.8	-10.9	-11.0	-5.8	-6.7
26) Average net transfer ($ thousand)	-0.322	-0.344	-0.646	-0.654	-0.338	-0.361	-0.674	-0.683	-0.362	-0.381
27) Average gain of families better off ($ thousand)	0.717	0.732	0.941	0.946	0.711	0.700	0.976	0.982	0.763	0.724
28) Average loss of families worse off ($ thousand)	0.631	0.618	1.197	1.167	0.698	0.780	1.212	1.181	0.607	0.733
Nonaged Heads										
29) Families better off (%)	55.1	52.8	50.4	50.6	55.4	55.4	52.7	52.7	53.6	55.9
30) Persons better off (%)	57.3	54.0	52.9	53.3	54.8	54.8	53.1	53.1	55.2	55.8
31) Net transfer ($ billion)	6.4	6.7	10.5	10.7	6.8	7.1	11.1	11.2	6.9	7.2
32) Average net transfer ($ thousand)	0.125	0.132	0.206	0.210	0.133	0.140	0.218	0.220	0.136	0.141
33) Average gain of families better off ($ thousand)	0.822	0.834	0.861	0.836	0.986	0.966	1.000	0.979	0.850	0.796
34) Average loss of families worse off ($ thousand)	1.285	1.215	1.291	1.281	1.525	1.516	1.572	1.553	1.276	1.329

Note: Discrepancies between rows (25) and (31), which should sum to zero, are due to a programming error involving the distribution of OASDI payments between aged and nonaged, and especially the assignment of special credits (A-1) for OASDI recipients. This will be rectified in revision.

	XI	XII	XIII	XIV	XV	XVI	XVII	XVIII	XIX	XX
Aged Heads										
23) Families better off (%)	86.2	86.2	73.6	76.5	86.2	89.1	72.4	72.4	81.6	85.1
24) Persons better off (%)	86.6	86.6	79.8	81.4	86.6	88.2	75.4	75.3	79.6	82.3
25) Net transfer ($ billion)	−10.7	−10.8	−6.2	−6.5	−11.2	−11.3	−1.9	−2.3	−7.3	−7.4
26) Average net transfer ($ thousand)	−0.664	−0.670	−0.381	−0.401	−0.695	−0.701	−0.119	−0.142	−0.449	−0.458
27) Average gain of families better off ($ thousand)	0.959	0.961	0.761	0.752	0.997	0.968	0.436	0.460	0.772	0.745
28) Average loss of families worse off ($ thousand)	1.177	1.148	0.674	0.741	1.190	1.484	0.711	0.692	0.983	1.190
Nonaged Heads										
29) Families better off (%)	50.4	50.4	54.9	54.9	52.7	54.9	60.1	60.1	58.1	56.6
30) Persons better off (%)	52.9	52.9	53.8	53.8	53.1	52.8	58.7	58.7	56.3	53.9
31) Net transfer ($ billion)	10.9	10.9	7.4	7.7	11.5	11.5	3.0	3.4	7.3	7.4
32) Average net transfer ($ thousand)	0.213	0.214	0.145	0.150	0.225	0.217	0.059	0.066	0.143	0.145
33) Average gain of families better off ($ thousand)	0.869	0.847	1.001	0.982	1.007	0.947	0.785	0.765	0.771	0.774
34) Average loss of families worse off ($ thousand)	1.312	1.293	1.539	1.529	1.595	1.655	1.332	1.318	1.412	1.343

Table 5 (*continued*)
Notes

Plan Characteristics (see sections 9–13)

Cashable Tax Credits	TC	1 Age-related, plus dwelling unit credit	2. Age-related, plus dwelling unit credit, extra children's credit	3. Size-related, no cashable dwelling unit credit	
Tax Rate Schedule	TR	1. Four rates	2. Five rates, plus children's surtaxes	3. Dual system, 50% Negative Income Tax rate	
Noncashable Housing Credits	NHC	1. Parallel credits for owners and renters, with threshold and ceiling	2. Imputed rent taxed; credits based on rent, imputed or actual	3. Parallel credits for owners and renters, without threshold and ceiling	
Itemized Deduction Credits	IDC	1. Credit based on pooled deductions above threshold	2. Credits based on separate deductions		
Provisions for Aged and other Social Security Beneficiaries	A	1. No personal credits for OASDI recipients, but special credits usually not cashable. OASDI benefits not taxed	2. OASDI recipients get regular credits but are taxed on half of benefits	3. OASDI recipients remain under regular income tax code	

Rows 1, 11, 17, 23, 29	Percentage of families in population or subpopulation with less taxes (or more receipts from government) than in reference situation (1970 income tax and cash public assistance)
Rows 2, 12, 18, 24, 30	Percentage of persons in population or subpopulation in families with less taxes than in reference situation
Row 3	Total gains of families better off = total losses of families worse off.
Rows 4–7	Income (interpolated) below which families of indicated size are better off.
Rows 8–10	Average loss (−) indicates gain) for four-person family in indicated bracket
Rows 13, 19, 25, 31	Net transfer—+ means loss; − means gain—for subpopulation
Rows 14, 20, 26, 32	Average net transfer per family in subpopulation
Rows 15, 21, 27, 33	Average gain of those families in subpopulation who gain
Rows 16, 22, 28, 34	Average loss of those families in subpopulation who lose

ers. The main reason is that homeowners are more affluent. But, in addition, most of our proposals place a ceiling on credits available to owners and give renters roughly comparable tax concessions. In plans IX–XVI, imputed rent is taxed, and naturally the "losses" of homeowners are increased; this is especially true under the Brazer-type plans XIII–XVI, where high-income homeowners lose the high tax credits their large families give them in other plans.

Redistribution in favor of the aged is roughly comparable in aggregate magnitude to the redistribution from homeowners to nonhomeowners. Once again, the main source of the redistribution is simply that the aged are poorer. But there are strikingly few losers among the aged, thanks to the special credits introduced to protect them. The position of the aged is especially favorable when OASDI recipients are allowed personal tax credits in return for subjecting half of their OASDI benefits to tax (A-2). This is probably overgenerous treatment as the outcomes for the eight plans involving A-2 indicate.

The proposals contain, in various degrees, the natural tendency of the credit income tax to favor large families even at high incomes. The redistribution thresholds shown in table 5—the incomes that divide losers from gainers—are of course higher, the larger the family. But broadly speaking, the proposals benefit no higher a fraction of the population of persons than of the population of families. In this respect, the Brazer-type plans XIII–XVI and the plans with size-related tax credits XVII–XX are perhaps excessively protective of the interests of smaller units.

In conclusion, we reiterate that our main purpose was to exhibit some pragmatic versions of the credit income tax. It is not, in our opinion, just a far-out impractical idea or just a reference point for theoretical speculations about redistribution, as the $1,000-demogrant or the pure Rolph proposal might suggest. It can be adapted to depart less radically from the prevailing views of the society regarding the equities of large families and small, old and young. Once it is so adapted, the redistribution it accomplishes is mainly vertical; the beneficiaries are not just the poor who already benefit from public assistance, but also the working poor, the near-poor, and the not-so-poor half-way up the income distribution. Whether the country will ever be ready for that kind of move toward equality is, of course, another matter.

Notes

1. See R. J. Lampman, "How Much does the American System of Transfers Benefit the Poor?", in L. H. Goodman, ed., *Economic Progress and Social Welfare,* (New York:

Columbia University Press, 1966); and Benjamin A. Okner, "Transfer Payments: Their Distribution and Role in Reducing Poverty," in Kenneth E. Boulding and Martin Pfaff, eds., *Redistribution to the Rich and the Poor: The Grants Economics of Income Distribution* (Belmont, California: Wadsworth, 1972), pp. 62–77, also Brookings Reprint 254.

2. The proposal is described in the Green Paper on Proposals for a Tax-Credit System (Command Paper 5116), H.M.S.O., 1972, and in Report and Proceedings of Select Committee on Tax-Credit, Vol. I, H.M.S.O., 1973.

3. Harold W. Watts and Glen G. Cain, "Labor Supply Effects of the New Jersey-Pennsylvania Graduated Work Incentive Experiment," Mimeo, 1973, and *Final Report of the Graduated Work Incentives Experiment*, Institute for Research on Poverty, University of Wisconsin, 1973.

4. James Tobin, Joseph A. Pechman, and Peter Mieszkowski, "Is A Negative Income Tax Practical?", *Yale Law Journal*, Vol. 77, November 1967, pp. 1–27.

Poverty and Plenty: The American Paradox, Report of the President's Commission on Income Maintenance Programs, U.S.G.P.O., 1969.

Benjamin A. Okner, "Alternatives for Transferring Income to the Poor: The Family Assistance Plan and Universal Income Supplements," in Boulding and Pfaff, *op. cit.*, pp. 348–357, also Brookings Reprint 254.

5. This is documented by Harold W. Watts and Jon K. Peck, "On the Comparison of Income Redistribution Plans," Institute for Research on Poverty Discussion Paper 166–73.

6. Joseph A. Pechman and Benjamin A. Okner, "Individual Income Tax Erosion by Income Classes," in *The Economics of Federal Subsidy Programs*, A Compendium of Papers submitted to the Joint Economic Committee, Part 1, *General Study Papers*, 92 Congress, 2nd Session, 1972, pp. 13–40, also Brookings Reprint 230.

7. Earl R. Rolph, "The Case for a Negative Income Tax Device," *Industrial Relations*, Vol. 6, February 1967, pp. 155–165.
Watts and Peck, *op. cit.*, simulate and compare redistributions by a pure credit income tax.

8. Harvey E. Brazer, "Tax Policy and Children's Allowances," in Eveline Burns, ed., *Children's Allowances and the Economic Welfare of Children*, Citizens Committee for Children of New York, Inc., 1968, pp. 140–149.

9. On this disincentive and on the general problem of integrating in-kind and cash assistance, see Henry J. Aaron, *Why is Welfare So Hard to Reform?* (Washington: Brookings Institution, 1973).

10. For description see Benjamin A. Okner, "Constructing a New Data Base from Existing Micro Data Sets: The 1966 MERGE File," *Annals of Economic and Social Measurement*, Vol. 1, July 1972, pp. 325–342.

Reprinted for private circulation from The Journal of Law and Economics, Volume XIII (2), October, 1970, Copyright 1970, The University of Chicago.

ON LIMITING THE DOMAIN OF INEQUALITY*

JAMES TOBIN
Yale University

THE most difficult issues of political economy are those where goals of efficiency, freedom of choice, and equality conflict. It is hard enough to propose an intellectually defensible compromise among them, even harder to find a politically viable compromise. These are ancient issues. The agenda of economics and politics have always featured policies whose effects on economic inequality and on efficiency in resource allocation are hopelessly intertwined. But it is only in the last five years that they have regained the center of attention of American economists, with whom stabilization, full employment, and growth took the highest priority for the preceding three decades.

When a distinguished colleague in political science asked me about ten years ago why economists did not talk about the distribution of income any more, I followed my *pro forma* denial of his factual premise by replying that the potential gains to the poor from full employment and growth were much larger, and much less socially and politically divisive, than those from redistribution. One reason that distribution has returned to the forefront of professional and public attention is that great progress was made in the postwar period, and especially in the 1960's, toward solving the problems of full employment and growth.

It is natural that debate should now focus on intrinsically harder issues of the composition and distribution of the national product, and it is also natural, though disappointing, to find people with short memories questioning whether full employment and growth ever were problems worth worrying about. There are of course other reasons for the recent shift of emphasis, notably the belated commitment of the society to racial equality and the diffuse concern for social justice that is one feature of the cultural revolution of the young.

American attitudes toward economic inequality are complex. The egalitarian sentiments of contemporary college campuses are not necessarily shared by the not-so-silent majority. Our society, I believe, accepts and approves a large measure of inequality, even of inherited inequality. Americans commonly perceive differences of wealth and income as earned and

* The Fifth Henry Simons lecture, delivered at the Law School, University of Chicago, April 16, 1970.

regard the differential earnings of effort, skill, foresight, and enterprise as deserved. Even the prizes of sheer luck cause very little resentment. People are much more concerned with the legitimacy, legality, and fairness of large gains than with their sheer size.

But willingness to accept inequality in general is, I detect, tempered by a persistent and durable strain of what I shall call *specific egalitarianism*. This is the view that certain specific scarce commodities should be distributed less unequally than the ability to pay for them. Candidates for such sentiments include basic necessities of life, health, and citizenship. Our institutions and policies already modify market distributions in many cases, and the issues raised by specific egalitarianism are central to many proposals now before the country.

The trained instincts of most economists set them against these policies and proposals. To the extent that economists are egalitarians at all, they are general egalitarians. The reason is their belief that specific interventions, whether in the name of equality or not, introduce inefficiencies, and the more specific the intervention the more serious the inefficiency. Henry Simons eloquently articulated these instincts and proposed a clear-cut practical resolution of the conflict between efficiency and equality.[1]

Simons' design is a very attractive one, deceptively so. He splits economic policy into two departments, one for equity and one for efficiency. Problems of equity and social justice are resolved at the most general level, in legislation for taxation of income and wealth. As for efficiency, the objective of government policy is to make markets work competitively. The government does not intervene in particular labor or product markets on behalf of distributive justice. Reformers interested in reducing, or increasing, economic inequality are referred to the Ways and Means Committee. They cannot seek these ends by fixing milk prices or minimum wages or oil imports or apartment rents or wheat acreage or subway fares—or, for that matter, by rent subsidies or food stamps. Simons says, "It is urgently necessary for us to quit confusing measures for regulating relative prices and wages with devices for diminishing inequality. One difference between competent economists and charlatans is that, at this point, the former sometimes discipline their sentimentality with a little reflection on the mechanics of an exchange economy."[2]

While concerned laymen who observe people with shabby housing or too little to eat instinctively want to provide them with decent housing and adequate food, economists instinctively want to provide them with more cash income. Then they can buy the housing and food if they want to, and if they choose not to, the presumption is that they have a better use for the

[1] Henry Simons, Economic Policy for a Free Society (1948).
[2] *Id.* at 83.

money. To those who complain about the unequal distribution of shelter or of food, our first response—and Simons'—is that they should look at the distribution of wealth and income. If the social critics approve that distribution, then they should accept its implications, including the unequal distribution of specific commodities. If they don't like it, then they should attack the generalized inequality rather than the specific inequality. Economists, especially some trained at the University of Chicago, think they can prove that, given the distribution of generalized purchasing power, competitive production and distribution of specific commodities will be optimal.

This answer rarely satisfies the intelligent egalitarian layman. He knows, partly because he has learned it from economists, that there are pragmatic limits on the redistributive use of taxation and cash transfers. These instruments are not as neutral in their allocative effects as Simons appeared to believe; they may seriously distort choices between work and leisure, selections of occupations and jobs, allocations of savings among competing investments, etc. We have yet to conjure into reality the economist's dream tax— the lump sum tax that no one can avoid or diminish by altering his own behavior.

Simons knew, no doubt, that progressive taxation was not neutral in its allocative effect, but he was writing in the days of small government and was not contemplating very heavy taxes. Nor does he seem to have contemplated what we now call negative taxes, although such transfers would have been a logical extension of his program.

Serious redistribution by tax and transfer will involve high tax rates, as the following simple calculation illustrates. Suppose the government gives every citizen a certain amount $m (a guaranteed minimum income) and collects by income tax enough to pay these grants and to finance government activities which cost $c per capita. Tax rates must be high enough to collect the fraction $(m + c)/\bar{y}$ of total income, where $\bar{y}$ is average income per capita. If the guarantee level m is a quarter or a third of mean income, and especially if the government is purchasing for substantive use any significant fraction of national output, the necessary tax rates will be so high that incentive and allocational effects cannot be ignored.

The layman therefore wonders why we cannot arrange things so that certain crucial commodities are distributed less unequally than is general income —or, more precisely, less unequally than the market would distribute them given an unequal income distribution. The idea has great social appeal. The social conscience is more offended by severe inequality in nutrition and basic shelter, or in access to medical care or to legal assistance, than by inequality in automobiles, books, clothes, furniture, boats. Can we somehow remove the necessities of life and health from the prizes that serve as incentives for economic activity, and instead let people strive and compete for non-essential luxuries and amenities?

This is essentially what the United States and other countries did in the second World War when the supplies of normal consumption goods were drastically limited by the drafts of resources for the war effort. The public was not taxed enough to accomplish this transfer of resources in the market, in large part because of fear of the disincentive effects of the high tax rates that would have been necessary. Prices and wages were controlled to repress, and postpone, the latent inflation. At the controlled prices there was chronic excess demand for consumption goods, and market distribution of these goods was supplanted by a more egalitarian distribution via official and unofficial rationing. Incentives to work, beyond sheer patriotism, were maintained by the prospect that incomes, though inconvertible into consumption at the time, would become convertible later, after the end of the war.

Specific egalitarianism takes a number of different forms, with a number of different motivations and rationalizations. There are some commodities where strict equality of distribution is deemed a crucially important objective, so important that society cannot permit an individual even voluntarily to transfer his share to someone else. These "commodities" include civil rights and privileges—and their converse, civil obligations—where equality among citizens is basic to the political constitution. The vote is a prime example, the military draft possibly another. The category includes also biological or social necessities which are scarce in aggregate supply, so scarce that if they are unequally distributed, some citizens must be consuming below a tolerable minimum. Examples include essential foods in wartime, and probably medical care here and now. In these cases there is a strong paternalistic element in the state's insistence that the individual may not, even voluntarily, transfer his ration to someone else.

At the other end of the spectrum there are commodities of ample supply, or at least of potentially ample supply, where the egalitarian objective is, so to speak, one-sided, not a strictly equal distribution but an assured universal minimum. Ample aggregate supply means that if everyone received only the tolerable minimum, there would be a surplus. Food and possibly housing are examples in the United States today.

In every case a crucial issue is the elasticity of supply, in the short run and the long run, of the commodity in question. When the scarce commodity is in fixed supply, then arrangements for distributing it equally, or on any other non-market criterion, can be made without worrying about efficiency. This is also the case in which social concern about specific inequality makes the most sense.

In wartime Britain tea was in short and inelastic supply; there was no way by which selling it to the highest bidder could increase the imports; and it made sense to worry specifically about the fairness of the distribution of tea. In peacetime United States there is social concern about inequality of access to medical care: luxury medical care for the rich uses resources that could be saving the lives or life chances of the poor. Specific redistribution makes sense if medical care, like tea in wartime Britain, is in inelastic supply. It makes less sense if additional medical care can be obtained by drawing resources from other uses. To that degree the medical deprivations of the poor can be laid to rich consumers of automobiles, boats, and higher education as fairly as to rich over-consumers of the services of physicians and hospitals.

The state has at its disposal a number of instruments for modifying or supplanting the market distribution of a commodity. By market distribution, I mean the distribution among consumers that would result from the expenditure of their money incomes after taxes and cash transfer payments, in the absence of any interventions to set prices or allocations. The concept is clear for privately produced goods and services. But some "commodities" of interest are produced and dispensed by the state; indeed some are rights or privileges rather than goods and services in the usual sense. In the case of state-controlled commodities, I shall use the term market distribution to refer to the result of auctioning the supply to the highest bidders.

One instrument is to forbid the delivery of the commodity to consumers without the surrender of *ration tickets*, of which the government controls the allocation. Ration tickets may be either *personal* or *transferable*. A second instrument is the *commodity voucher* or *stamp*, of which the government likewise controls the allocation. The consumer can use the voucher or stamp only for a specific commodity or class of commodities. The government redeems in cash the vouchers presented by a supplier. Like ration tickets, vouchers can be either personal or transferable. Finally, although ration tickets are usually necessary but not sufficient to purchase a rationed good, it is possible for ration tickets to serve also as vouchers. I shall find it convenient to use these terms in a figurative sense, that is, to apply them to a number of situations which can be described as if there are ration coupons and vouchers even though such pieces of paper do not or need not literally exist.

I propose now to discuss a number of illustrative cases of specific egalitarianism, actual or proposed.

Wartime Rationing

The rationing of scarce necessities of life in time of war or its aftermath is, as noted above, a common example of specific egalitarianism. It is worth further brief discussion, because it illustrates some of the issues and problems that arise in contemporary manifestations of specific egalitarianism.

One common system was specific rationing. Ration tickets for a single commodity, sugar or orange juice or tea or meat or gasoline, were distributed equally or in relation to some criteria of need. They were not transferable, either for money or for other ration coupons. The rationale was a combination of egalitarianism and paternalism. Rich children should not have all the orange juice, and no family should bargain away its children's vitamins even if the parents want to do so. Of course, even though ration tickets themselves are not transferable, it is difficult to prevent informal or black market exchanges and sales of the commodities themselves, except when the commodities are highly perishable or personal.

Once delivery of a commodity is effectively forbidden except in exchange for ration tickets, the government has at least indirect control of the money price. Left to the market, the price will be set so that the available supply will be equal to ration-limited demand. This could be as low as zero if the ration coupons cover no more than the available supply. If the government sets a positive price, then it will induce some consumers to leave coupons unused; the real value of remaining coupons will correspondingly increase. Conversely, if coupon values are set too high then a positive money price will arise in order to squeeze out excess consumers.

If equality is really the aim, if consumption is to be strictly independent of unequal money income, then a positive money price must not be allowed to squeeze anyone out. Indeed, ration tickets must double as vouchers, with the government paying the suppliers by redeeming the ration-vouchers with money.

If the supply is inelastic, as was typically the case in wartime, the terms of redemption are purely a distributive matter, as between the general taxpayers and the suppliers of the scarce commodity. But if the supply is responsive, then the government's payment will be one of the determinants of the future supply.

Another model is the negotiable ration ticket. Ration coupons are equally distributed, and the scarce commodity cannot be purchased without one. But coupons can be transferred. The rich and eager can consume an above average share of the commodity, but only by transferring purchasing power over other goods to the poor and indifferent. Equality of specific consumption is not maintained, but those who wish more than their share must find and compensate someone willing to get along with less. The same effect could be achieved by giving everyone a lump sum dollar grant and levying a tax on the consumption of the commodity, just enough to pay for the grant. The advantage of the ration mechanism is that the market makes what would be à difficult calculation for the tax collector. The equity of the system is that high consumers of the scarce commodity, rather than general taxpayers, are made to subsidize the poor and other low consumers.

The transferable ration system does not give the right signals when supply is elastic. It does not make sense to levy an excise tax on an essential commodity in short supply. The way out is for the government, in effect, to buy the supply at its supply price and to distribute it by ration-vouchers at a lower money price or free.

VOTING

There are some rights and privileges, and some duties, which the society desires to distribute precisely equally among its members, or among a subgroup of its members. The distribution is supposed to be wholly independent of income and wealth. Furthermore the distribution is supposed to be independent of individual preferences; society would not approve an individual's voluntary assignment of his share to someone else even if the assignee were of equal or lower income.

Perhaps the clearest example is the vote in a democratic polity. The modern democratic ethic excludes property qualifications, obvious or disguised, for the suffrage. Votes are not transferable; buying or selling them is illegal, and the secret ballot makes such contracts unenforceable. In some countries, indeed, citizens are penalized simply for not voting. Any good second year graduate student in economics could write a short examination paper proving that voluntary transactions in votes would increase the welfare of the sellers as well as the buyers. But the legitimacy of the political process rests on the prohibition of such transactions. A vote market would concentrate political power in the rich, and especially in those who owe their wealth to government privilege.

The instrument used for equal distribution of the vote could be described, in the terms previously introduced, as a non-transferable combined ration ticket and voucher. Obviously an egalitarian distribution can be enforced without any loss of efficiency. The aggregate supply of votes is intrinsically inelastic. Allowing a free market in votes could not augment the power of the electorate as a whole; it would serve only to redistribute it differently.

THE DRAFT

Military service is a duty rather than a right, but the same issues arise with respect to its distribution. In some nations it is regarded as a non-negotiable obligation of citizenship, just as the vote is a non-negotiable right. This conception applies in some countries even in peacetime. But the notion that the obligation should not be distributed among citizens on the basis of income and wealth is of course strongest in wartime, when it becomes a matter of distributing risks of death and injury. The national conscience was scandalized, at the time and in retrospect, by the civil war spectacle of rich fathers' purchasing substitutes for their drafted sons. The power of the purse saved the life of one boy in exchange for the death of another. Subsequent draft laws in this country have excluded this kind of transaction.

Nevertheless many of the criteria of selective service are highly correlated with economic status. The correlation is difficult to avoid so long as selections must be made, so long as the number of persons needed in the armed services is smaller than the physically eligible population. That is one reason why the draft today is so much more difficult and socially divisive a problem than it was in the second World War. Although equality of exposure could be achieved in current circumstances by short enlistments, too rapid a turnover would make it impossible for the armed services to accomplish their missions.

In these circumstances a lottery, with no deferments, is the only egalitarian device available. Forbidding the exchange of a vulnerable draft number for a safe number is conceptually equivalent to prohibiting the sale of votes or of ration tickets—once again a paternalistic insistence on an egalitarian distribution takes precedence over the standard economist's presumption that a voluntary exchange increases the welfare of both parties.

A further condition of a strictly egalitarian solution is hardly ever squarely faced. The possibility that poor young men may risk their lives for money can be wholly avoided only by prohibiting volunteering or by setting soldiers' pay well below effective civilian alternatives.

A volunteer army is subject to the same objections on egalitarian grounds as a free market in negotiable military obligations. It is just a more civilized and less obvious way of doing the same thing, that is, allocating military service to those eligible young men who place the least monetary value on their safety and on alternative uses of their time. There is one important difference, however. With a volunteer army, the general taxpayer must provide the funds necessary to draw into military service the number of soldiers needed. With a free market in draft obligations, much of this burden is picked up by the draftees who are buying substitutes, or by their families. The general taxpayer bears only the costs of the official soldiers' pay, which in a draft system is of course below the market supply price. Young men who escape the obligation are, in effect, taxed to pay the young men who take it on. It is certainly not obvious that the volunteer army solution, whatever its other merits, is the more equitable of these two arrangements.

As for efficiency on the supply side, it is not clear whether the size of the armed forces should be regarded as a fixed demand for manpower independent of its cost. If so, then there is no problem of resource allocation, only a problem of equitable distribution, and nothing is lost by an egalitarian draft. It may be argued, on the other hand, that voters, the Congress, the President, and the Pentagon would and should attune their foreign policies and military technologies to the costs of military manpower, and that the draft biases their decisions toward using more military personnel than they would if defense budgets reflected the true marginal costs. The volunteer army solution would correct this distortion. In principle it could also be corrected within the framework of the opposite solution, a stochastic draft with volunteering prohibited, but with military pay set at the conjectural supply price of the size army the government wants.

RIGHTS TO BEAR CHILDREN

Contemporary worries about the prospects of overpopulation have led to spreading conviction that society will eventually have to control population growth by rationing births. The Zero Population Growth movement, popular on campuses, wants every mother to be limited to two children. We can imagine that medical technology will some day permit social control of periods of fertility.

I am not interested in discussing here whether worries about overpopulation are justified or whether, even if they are, society should in fact regulate births. What is relevant to my subject is how such regulation would be carried out. Should each and every mother be limited to two children or less? Or should each woman be issued two—or two and a fraction tickets, whatever is consistent with zero population growth—and be allowed to transfer whole or fractional tickets to other women? Or should the government fix an annual quota of births and auction the tickets to the highest bidders?

The first system is the most egalitarian, but excludes many voluntary transfers of "birth rights" that would in principle increase the utility of all parties concerned. The second system allows such transfers, but also opens up the possibility that rights to have children will be concentrated in the rich. At least the poor and others who give up their rights will be well compensated. This is not the case under the third system, the auction, where the rich can still buy up the rights but to the benefit of the general taxpayer rather than of would-be mothers who lose out in the auction.

EDUCATION

The American system of elementary and secondary education is one of non-transferable ration vouchers, along with a paternalistically motivated compulsory requirement for minimum consumption. Every child is entitled to free schooling. His "ticket" cannot be transferred to anyone else; there is no direct way in which one parent, by accepting less schooling for his child, can provide more for another. A child may use his "voucher" only in the public schools. If he does not use it, he must buy an approved substitute version of the same commodity. His voucher is no good for that purpose, but neither is he limited by his ration. His parent may purchase for him as much education, beyond the minimum requirement, as he chooses.

In recent years support has been growing for what I shall call an extended voucher system, under which the education voucher is usable in any approved school of the parent's choice, not just in public schools. I note in passing that the advocates of the extended voucher system find it possible to reconcile some paternalism with their libertarian principles. They do not propose to abandon compulsory education and to compensate non-consumers of public education in money.

One of the effects of the present arrangement is to require high income parents who wish their children to have more or better education than the public schools provide to pay not only the extra costs but also part of the expenses of educating the children of the less affluent. In this respect the present system is a measure of specific egalitarianism. The proposed reform would shift the burden now borne by those who opt out of the public system to the society at large in higher taxes, or to the lower-income consumers of public education in lower quality.

Reducing the cost of luxury education would no doubt increase the demand for it, and draw teachers and other resources into it, partly from the public schools, partly but more slowly from the rest of the economy. Whatever its other merits, principally in encouraging greater competition and innovation in the supply of education, the extended voucher proposal would increase the inequality of education. This effect could be largely avoided by restricting the use of the vouchers to those private schools that hold other charges on the parents to zero or within prescribed limits.

Another difficulty with the extended voucher proposal arises from the externalities of the educational process—that is, the contributions to the education of students made by other students. The relationships here are complex and uncertain, and excessive heterogeneity in schools and classrooms may be as unproductive as excessive homogeneity. But the evidence seems to be that some racial, social, and intellectual heterogeneity is productive. A major problem of American education today is that public schools, reflecting and in turn influencing residential patterns, are becoming increasingly homogenous. The proposed extension of the voucher system might well accentuate this trend, by making it cheaper for parents to group their children homogeneously in private schools.

This possibility raises the question of how much selectivity in admission and retention private schools eligible for parentally disposed funds would be allowed to practice. So long as schooling is compulsory, there must be some schools that cannot be selective. Are public schools to become the residual depository for all students that publicly financed private schools cannot or will not cope with? To some degree, this is already true, and private and parochial schools gain reputations for intellectual achievement, discipline, and good behavior, simply by pushing difficult and risky cases back to the public schools. Perhaps beneficiary schools should be required to admit all applicants—or in case of oversubscription to select among them in an unbiased way—and to dismiss or suspend students only by the same rules as apply to the public schools.

MEDICAL CARE

There are not many commodities in prosperous peacetime America that are scarce in the sense in which some necessities of life were scarce in wartime, but this could be said of medical care. The available supplies of physicians, hospitals, and other personnel and facilities are still low relative to the needs of the population. Even if the supplies were equally distributed, the medical needs unmet at the margin would evidently be far from trivial. This fact is, of course, the basic reason for social concern about the inequality of access to medical care. If people differed only in the attention they received with respect to cosmetic or orthodontic problems, or the number of psychoanalyses they enjoyed, or the hotel-like amenities provided to new mothers, inequality of medical care would not be a big issue. What is disturbing to many observers is the suspicion that chances of death and disability are unequally distributed, that some people consume for trivial purposes resources that could be crucial to the health of others.

In the case of medical care, equality would mean that the treatment of an individual depends only on his medical condition and symptoms, not on his ability or willingness to pay. Everyone would be compelled to have the same medical insurance policy, and no one could obtain medical care except on the terms prescribed in the common policy. This would be, in principle, a non-transferable ration-voucher system, as defined above in other illustrations. But ration-vouchers for medical care would be complicated contingent claims, and stating their value in services so as to balance demand and supply would be extremely difficult.

If medical care were delivered through a ration-voucher system, the government would in effect be purchasing *all* the services of physicians, hospitals, and other suppliers. The prices paid would have to be set so as to draw new resources into the medical industry. Past experience suggests, however, that the mechanism of supply response to price is slow and imperfect, and there may well be more effective ways to get new doctors, medical schools, hospitals, and clinics than simply to add to the rents of the present practitioners.

The system just sketched is compatible with a great deal of decentralization and free choice, but there is no getting around the fact that it is socialized medicine. It is hard to see how there can be equality of medical care otherwise. Although this prospect may shock many people today, including many at the University of Chicago, it would not have shocked Henry Simons. In 1934 he wrote, in connection with his proposal for a rigorously thorough and progressive income tax, as follows: "On the expenditure side, we may look forward confidently to continued augmenting of the 'free income' of the masses, in the form of commodities and services made available by government, either without charge or with considerable modification of prevailing price controls. There are remarkable opportunities for extending the range of socialized consumption (medical services, recreation, education, music, drama, etc.). . . ."[3]

The system toward which the country is moving is quite different. More and more medical vouchers are being provided, through Medicare, Medicaid, and perhaps in the not too distant future, universal health insurance. But no formal rationing is being imposed. Inequality is reduced as the medical care of the poor is brought up to a minimum standard, but the rich can buy medical care in higher quantity and quality. The addition of voucher demands to the unrestricted private market drives prices up. If the government fixes the money value of its vouchers too low, doctors shift their attention to other patients. If the government tries to regulate all fees, not just those charged voucher patients, the result is informal rationing and queuing, with considerable inefficiency, inequity, and annoyance. There will be no good solution short of the day when resources for medical care are so abundant that a hypochrondiac can consume them for low priority purposes, if that way of spending money suits his taste, without depriving someone else of vital care.

FOOD STAMPS

The society's propensity to give assistance to the poor in kind rather than in cash is most clearly evidenced by the political popularity of food stamps and housing subsidies. These are what I earlier called one-sided egalitarian measures. The intent is to increase the consumption of these necessities of life by the poorly nourished and poorly housed, not to reduce the luxury amounts going to heavy consumers. Indeed these commodities are not, in aggregate, scarce in the sense that medical care is in short supply. Food supplies can easily and quickly be expanded in response to new demand, and present supplies are ample, if equally distributed, for meeting socially accepted standards of nutrition. There is no reason that gourmets and gourmands in particular, rather than high-income people in general, should pay for raising the food consumption of the poor.

Paternalism is presumably the motive for assisting poor people with food

[3] *Id.* at 68.

vouchers rather than generalized purchasing power. But the actual and proposed systems do not live up to the rationale, which would imply compulsory nutrition in the manner of compulsory education. Given the fungibility of stamps and foods, the plans do not even insure adequate diets for their beneficiaries. And, although based on the premise that adequate income is no guarantee of adequate nutrition, income-conditioned food vouchers do nothing to insure adequate nutrition for those whose incomes make them ineligible. In short, food vouchers are just an inferior currency, and taxpayers' funds would be better spent in general income assistance. It is quite true that society has an obligation to protect children whose parents cannot be trusted to nourish them. But this obligation is independent of the size and source of the parents' income.

Subsidized Housing

Paternalism once again is a major reason for society's willingness to subsidize the housing rather than the incomes of the poor. No doubt the neighborhood effects of poor housing, including the fact that it is a particularly visible manifestation of poverty, help to explain the appeal of subsidized housing. A paternalistic policy of housing vouchers is far more likely to be successful than food vouchers, because housing services are much less transferable and fungible.

Engineering a less unequal distribution of housing services is, however, particularly difficult because the services are generated by a specific housing stock inherited from the past. No doubt the resources invested in the current stock are more than enough to meet minimal standards for the whole population. But the high degree of inequality of density and quality built into the present stock limits the possibilities of equalizing its use in the short run. Likewise, expansion of the supply of housing services can occur only as fast as the stock can be augmented. It would take a long time for the market by itself to adapt the supply of housing to a significantly less unequal distribution of general income and wealth.

Present policies are neither fair nor effective. The income tests for housing subsidies are not very severe compared to the tests imposed for current and proposed cash assistance programs. Housing subsidies would be very expensive if everyone who could meet the income tests actually received them. But the subsidies are available only for an accidentally or arbitrarily selected few. The result is that some low income taxpayers are subsidizing the rents of families with equal or higher incomes. One reason that the spread of subsidized low-rent housing is slow is that, with minor exceptions, subsidies are connected only with designated new construction. Perhaps the concentration on new construction reflects the ambivalence of motivation for the programs, which are designed to make cities look better as well as to help low-income families. If the latter purpose is to be sought with housing vouchers, it would make sense to use them to improve the allocation of existing as well as new structures. A disadvantage of the present approach is that it publicly tags the residents of subsidized projects as recipients of public assistance.

I personally see little convincing justification in the long run for specific egalitarianism in housing. There are numerous reasons for preferring a system in which everyone can and does buy decent housing to his taste in the same market. But it does not follow that the supply of housing can be left to the market as now organized and regulated. There are too many cases of racial discrimination, too many ways in which zoning ordinances, building codes, and land taxes favor low-density housing, too many restrictive practices in the home-building industry, too many government subsidies to affluent home-owners, etc. Poor people ought to be given dollars—or housing vouchers if that is preferred—that they can spend for housing anywhere. But at the same time governments do have an obligation to see that these dollars and vouchers have some value.

In conclusion, I believe that Simons and the mainstream of the economics tradition have been right to insist that general taxation, positive and negative, is the best way to moderate the inequalities of income and wealth generated by a competitive market economy. I have no doubt that a cash negative income tax would be, dollar for dollar, the most effective anti-poverty and pro-equality program that could be adopted at this time. At the other end of the economic spectrum, the urgency of reform of income and estate taxation was scarcely diminished by the tax legislation of 1969. The interests opposed to egalitarian reform of the tax-and-transfer system are formidable. The cause could use some enthusiastic and intelligent support, and it deserves more energy and attention than most youthful egalitarians in our midst have been giving it. Still more fundamental, and certainly more difficult, are policies to diminish the distribution of income before taxes and transfers. These include removal of those barriers to competition, whether private or governmental in origin, which protect some positions of high wealth and income. They include efforts to diminish inequalities of endowment of human capital and of opportunity to accumulate it.

These approaches to the problem of economic inequality deserve priority, but they do not entitle us to dismiss out of hand every proposal for specific egalitarianism or to acquiesce in a market distribution of every scarce commodity. It does make sense in some cases to adopt non-market egalitarian distributions of commodities essential to life and citizenship. It makes sense when the scarcity of the commodity cannot be overcome by drawing resources from the general economy. Difficult practical cases arise when, as in the cases of medical care and housing, supply is inelastic in the short run but responsive to increased demand in the long run. In some instances, notably education and medical care, a specific egalitarian distribution today may be essential for improving the distribution of human capital and earning capacity tomorrow.

**Part V
ECONOMISTS**

HANSEN AND PUBLIC POLICY *

James Tobin

Alvin Hansen was never close to Presidents or politicians, and he never held a major government office. Yet no American economist was more important for the historic redirection of United States macroeconomic policy from 1935 to 1965. As the principal intellectual leader of the Keynesian conquest, Hansen deserves major credit for the "fiscal revolution in America" [1] and for the commitments to employment policy embodied in the Employment Act of 1946. As Galbraith has said, "The debt to the courage and intelligence of Alvin Hansen is especially great. Next only to Keynes, his is the credit for saving what even conservatives call capitalism." [2]

The channels of Hansen's influence were indirect. By books, articles, speeches, research reports, and Congressional testimony, he changed the climate of opinion — in the economics profession, in Washington, and in the general informed public. Progress was slow, but Hansen was patient, persistent, and persuasive. During the second world war Hansen worked in Washington at the National Resources Planning Board (NRPB) and the Federal Reserve Board. His wartime campaign for full employment after the war had both an inside and an outside audience. Beginning in the academic year 1937–1938, Hansen's classes and seminars at Harvard graduated generations of economists into public service, where they applied and developed Hansen's ideas.

In Hansen's mind and work, scientific interests and policy applications went hand in hand. Galbraith described him as "a man for whom economic ideas had no standing apart from their use." [3] His writings are natural blends of the abstract and the concrete, of pure theory and case history, of exposition and advocacy. In these respects, though in scarcely any others, Hansen resembled the man whose doctrines he did so much to advance and adapt on this side of the Atlantic.

Hansen was a leading economist long before his move to Harvard and his conversion to Keynesianism in 1938. From his academic

* David Hsieh, Yale 1976, helped me with this paper and became an admirer of Alvin Hansen in the process.
    1. The title of Herbert Stein's indispensable history (Chicago: University of Chicago Press, 1969).
    2. J. K. Galbraith, "Came the Revolution," *New York Times Book Review*, May 16, 1965, reprinted in his *Economics, Peace, and Laughter* (Boston: Houghton Mifflin, 1971).
    3. *Ibid.*

base at the University of Minnesota he had taken an active part in public affairs; his commissioned studies, committee memberships, and consultantships ranged over state unemployment insurance, dominion-provincial relations in Canada, U. S. foreign economic policy, and social security.[4] But his debut as a major public figure came in 1939 when he testified before the Temporary National Economic Committee (TNEC).

Begun by Congress the previous year to investigate concentration of economic power, the TNEC hearings had turned into a "showcase for Keynesian economics,"[5] orchestrated by Lauchlin Currie from his new office in the White House. Currie had long been an advocate of expansionary fiscal and monetary policies. After he moved from Harvard to Washington in 1934, he was one of a small group of New Deal economists urging a bold policy of deficit spending. As he recalls, "we welcomed Alvin Hansen with open arms as our most important recruit. I recall very well arranging for him to be our star witness in the TNEC hearings. . . ."[6] Currie's appointment as a White House assistant in 1939 indicated that the Keynesians were making progress in what Herbert Stein calls "the struggle for the soul of FDR."[7] In the crusade launched at the TNEC, Currie was Mr. Inside, and Hansen, Mr. Outside.

For the Washington Keynesians Hansen was more than a recruit, public voice, and name. He articulated the intellectual foundations of their position and gave the Keynesians, according to one of them, Alan Sweezy, "new confidence in both the economic soundness and the social and moral rightness of their policy recommendations."[8] Characteristically, Hansen's TNEC testimony[9] went beyond exposition and advocacy to include a novel compilation and interpretation of the facts and figures of public and private investment, saving, and consumption.

4. See Hansen's *New Plan for Unemployment Reserves* (Minneapolis: University of Minnesota Press, 1933); and *Programs for Unemployment Insurance* (Minneapolis: University of Minnesota Press, 1934). Hansen was economic adviser to the prairie provinces before the Canadian Royal Commission on Dominion-Provincial Relations 1937–1938. He was chief economic consultant to the U. S. State Department 1934–1935, advising on reciprocal trade agreements. He was a "public" member of the Advisory Council on Social Security 1937–1938.

5. Stein, *op. cit.*, 167–68.

6. L. Currie, "The Keynesian Revolution and its Pioneers: Discussion," *American Economic Review*, LXII (May 1972), 141.

7. Stein, *op. cit.*, 128–30.

8. A. Sweezy, "The Keynesians and Government Policy, 1933–1939," *American Economic Review*, LXII (May 1972), 122.

9. Temporary National Economic Committee, *Verbatim Record of Proceedings*, Vol. 3 (Washington: Government Printing Office, 1939), 338–47, 356–66, 533–41.

The Keynesian circle in Washington was augmented by recruits from Hansen's Harvard seminars, and from 1940 to 1945 by Hansen himself. During those years Hansen dedicated himself completely to the cause of postwar prosperity in the United States and in the world. On this theme he published books and articles, wrote in whole or in part several NRPB pamphlets, contributed several pieces to periodicals of general circulation, and gave numerous speeches.[10]

More than any other single person, Hansen created in Washington and beyond the climate of opinion and understanding that led to the Employment Act of 1946. But his direct role in the history of the legislation was minimal. He was informally consulted at various stages of its tortuous progress.[11] He did not participate in drafting, and he did not testify publicly. The central goal of Hansen's crusade had been federal commitment to full employment. The Act expressed this commitment, though in the diluted compromise language necessary to muster bipartisan support. The Act also established machinery for policy advice and review in the Executive branch and in Congress. Hansen knew as well as anyone that actual policy would depend year after year on specific Presidential and Congressional actions.

After the war the teachings of Hansen, like those of Keynes, were absorbed into the general corpus of economics, from graduate courses to elementary texts. Modes of quantitative macroeconomic analysis that were novel when introduced by Hansen and Currie at the TNEC in 1939 or by Hansen and Samuelson at NRPB during the war became routine procedures for economists in Washington and elsewhere. Younger waves of Hansen students entered the arena of

10. The following citations are not exhaustive.
Economic Problems of the Postwar World (Washington: National Council for the Social Studies, National Association of Secondary-School Principals, Departments of the National Education Association, 1942); *The United States After the War* (Ithaca: Cornell University Press, 1945); "The Postwar Economy," *The Postwar Economic Problems*, Seymour Harris, ed. (New York: McGraw-Hill Book Co., Inc., 1943). National Resources Planning Board, *After Defense — What* (August 1941) is attributed to Hansen by D. Howard, *WPA and Federal Relief Policy* (New York: Russell Sage Foundation, 1943); National Resources Planning Board, *After the War — Full Employment* (January 1942) is also credited to Hansen. Together with G. Means, D. E. Montgomery, J. N. Clark, and M. Ezekiel, Hansen wrote NRPB study *The Structure of the American Economy, Part II, Toward Full Use of Resources* (June 1940). Articles by Hansen appeared in *Foreign Affairs* (April 1942); *Atlantic Monthly* (Oct. 1942 and Sept. 1943); *Harper's* (April 1942); *New Republic* (Feb. 1944); and *Nation* (Oct. 1944). Two addresses by Hansen appear in publications of the New York University Institute on Post-War Reconstruction. The *New York Times* reported six Hansen speeches in 1942–1944.
11. S. K. Bailey, *Congress Makes A Law* (New York: Columbia 1950), 24, 46.

public policy, accepted Washington assignments, or undertook careers in government service.

The Hansenian revolution has never lacked opponents, even enemies. Congress killed the NRPB in 1943 shortly after receiving its report on postwar goals. Fearing hostile reactions in Congress, Roosevelt tabled a 1944 "White Paper" on full employment proposed by a group of his economists led by Hansen and Gerhard Colm.[12] In 1945 Hansen was dropped as adviser to the Federal Reserve Board; according to the press account the reasons were complaints by bankers and disagreements between Hansen and Chairman Marriner Eccles on postwar fiscal policy.[13] Although the Committee for Economic Development endorsed compensatory fiscal policy, most business sentiment remained hostile at least until the sixties and seventies. The Eisenhower Administration purged Washington of Democratic Keynesians but found that many of the economists recruited in partial replacement were also contaminated. The opposition carried counterrevolution to Hansen's home base. A Harvard Alumni Visiting Committee chaired by Clarence Randall of Inland Steel solemnly complained to the President and Fellows of Harvard of the Keynesian bias of the Harvard economics department.[14]

Hansen must have found irony in the "new economics" label attached to the 1961–1965 revival of his central ideas, but he certainly rejoiced in the substance. Early in 1966 he joined some "new economists," many of them his own students, in informal celebration of both the achievement of the Kennedy goal of 4 percent unemployment and the twentieth anniversary of the Employment Act. At the time he and his admirers deplored President Johnson's failure to seek taxes to finance his Viet Nam adventure, but no one foresaw how costly that decision would be.

Hansen's central message on macroeconomic policy is familiar to everyone and need not be rehearsed here. But some features of his position are less well remembered and deserve brief reminders.

Hansen is well-known for advocating public expenditure to maintain full employment, not only to counter cyclical recession but also to escape long-run stagnation. What may be less appreciated is that Hansen favored certain government expenditures for their own sake, not just to absorb saving and provide jobs. This is why he said little about tax reduction as a route to full employment.

12. *Ibid.*, 27, 161.
13. *New York Times*, August 15, 1945, 27:4.
14. Galbraith, *op. cit.* For another account of the same incident, see J. B. Conant, *My Several Lives* (New York: Harper and Row, 1970), Ch. 32.

He had strong views about national priorities, and anticipating Galbraith, thought more resources should be allocated to the public sector. He described his postwar plan as a "compensatory and developmental fiscal program." [15] Government, he thought, should assure minimum standards of nutrition, medicine, housing, and education.[16]

> Government investment . . . is high on the priority list for the reason that many of the gravest deficiencies in our society cannot be met except by a very large increase in the volume of outlays on public improvement and developmental projects — schools, hospitals, urban redevelopment, slum clearance, public housing, flood control, reforestation, soil conservation, irrigation, hydroelectric power, regional resource development, harbor improvement, river transportation, air transport facilities, improved highways, streets, recreational facilities, including national, state, and local parks and playgrounds, and finally, facilities for public lectures, music, art, and cultural activities of all kinds.[17]

Clearly Hansen was very conscious of the capital deficiencies inherited from depression, war, and national neglect. The same sense led him to give priority to private investment over consumption in postwar economic planning. He opposed the consumption-oriented Keynesianism of John Pierson and others. He suggested in 1944 reductions in corporate tax rates and generous loss offsets and averaging privileges to encourage risk taking.[18] For the longer long run, however, Hansen, like Keynes, looked forward to the day when capital deficiencies would be made up and full employment would be maintained in an economy of high public and private consumption.[19]

Hansen's reputation as a deficit spender should not obscure the abundant evidence that he regarded compensatory fiscal policy as a two-way street, and his standing as the "fiscalist" *par excellence* should not obscure his recognition of the importance of monetary policy.

In 1940 and 1941 he and other Keynesians opposed premature imposition of anti-inflationary measures, correctly arguing — not only against conservative Americans but against Keynes himself when he visited Washington — that slack in the American economy

15. "Planning Full Employment," *Nation*, 159, October 21, 1944, 492.
16. *Economic Problems of the Postwar World*, 11.
17. *Economic Policy and Full Employment* (New York: Norton, 1947), 183.
18. "National Debt, Flexible Budget and Tax Cut," *National Tax Association Bulletin*, No. 8, May 1944, 245.
19. "Postwar Re-employment Problem," *International Postwar Problems*, Vol. 1, 38 (periodical published by N. Y. American Labor Conference on International Affairs).

was still enormous.[20] But when Pearl Harbor and full mobilization produced an inflationary gap, Hansen was a strong advocate of heavy taxation and not, one infers, enamored of Galbraith's "disequilibrium system."[21] As for the postwar economy Hansen was not one of those people who feared depression immediately upon demobilization. Pent-up demands and transitional shortages would lead to inflation, he thought, and he warned against precipitate repeal of wartime controls, price ceilings, and taxes.[22] His compensatory and developmental program would be needed after the transition, when unemployment would otherwise recur as the major threat. In 1949 he set forth a strong anti-inflationary program, involving both budget surpluses and restrictive monetary policies.[23] The same book contains an extensive and careful treatment of monetary theory and policy and makes clear that he would leave monetary policy out of the tool kit only in the extreme "liquidity trap" conditions of a great depression.[24]

In 1967 the American Economic Association awarded Alvin Hansen its Francis A. Walker Medal, and I had the honor to present it to him with the following citation:

> The American Economic Association awards its highest honor, the Francis A. Walker medal, to Alvin H. Hansen, a gentle revolutionary who has lived to see his cause triumphant and his heresies orthodox, an untiring scholar whose example and influence have fruitfully changed the directions of his science, a political economist who has reformed policies and institutions in his own country and elsewhere without any power save the force of his ideas. From his boyhood on the South Dakota prairie, Alvin Hansen has believed that knowledge can improve the condition of man. In the integrity of that faith he has had the courage never to close his mind and to seek and speak the truth wherever it might lead. But, Professor Hansen, we honor you with as much affection as respect. Generation after generation, students have left your seminar and your study not only enlightened but also inspired — inspired with some of your enthusiastic conviction that economics is a science for the service of mankind. By the printed page you have reached countless others throughout the world. Today, from the vantage of your eightieth year, you can see these men and women, in academic and public service everywhere, teaching, applying, adapting, and — you would be the first to hope — improving what you helped them to learn.

YALE UNIVERSITY

20. B. L. Jones, "The Role of Keynesians in Wartime Policy and Postwar Planning, 1940–46," *American Economic Review,* LXII (May 1972), 125–33.
21. "The Postwar Economy," *op. cit.,* 21.
22. *Economic Problems of the Postwar World,* 12; *New York Times,* July 7, 1956, VI, 5.
23. *Monetary Theory and Fiscal Policy* (New York: McGraw-Hill Book Co., 1949), 162.
24. *Ibid.,* pp. 185–98, 65–70.

KERMIT GORDON

(1916-1976)

The career of Kermit Gordon was an extraordinary combination of teaching, public service, and institutional leadership. It is exemplary proof that a scientific craft may be expertly and creatively practiced in oral communication and action as well as in conventional scholarly publication. Gordon's renown as an economist came principally from teaching undergraduates at Williams College and from

Reprinted from Year Book of The American Philosophical Society, 1978

84–91

Printed in U. S. A.

Reprinted by permission from *Year Book of the American Philosophical Society* (1978):84–91.

advisory and administrative roles in Washington. He published very little under his name and never bothered to acquire a Ph.D. His reputation for incisive analysis, wisdom, and judgment spread by word of mouth from students, colleagues, and all who observed him in action.

Kermit Gordon was on the Williams College faculty from 1946 to 1971, ultimately as David A. Wells Professor of Political Economy. From 1961 to 1965 he served Presidents Kennedy and Johnson: in 1961–1962 as a member of the Council of Economic Advisers, subsequently as director of the Bureau of the Budget. He became vice-president of the Brookings Institution in Washington in 1965 and was its president from 1967 until his untimely death on June 21, 1976.

In December, 1941, Gordon married Mary King Grinnell of Winnetka, Illinois. Kermit and Molly Gordon had two daughters and one son. He was survived in addition by his mother Ida Robinson Gordon of Philadelphia and his brother Lester of Cambridge, Massachusetts.

Born and reared in Philadelphia, Gordon was graduated from Swarthmore College in 1938 with highest honors in economics. The stimulation and inspiration Swarthmore students found in economics depended crucially then, and for many years, on Professor Clair Wilcox, with whom Gordon formed a lifelong friendship. Wilcox was an influential model. His talents, interests, and vocations were strikingly similar to those later displayed in his student's career. At Swarthmore Gordon's editorship of the student newspaper *Phoenix* became legendary; his journalistic experience also included police reporting for a Philadelphia daily. Gordon's devoted association with Swarthmore continued long after his graduation. He returned on several occasions as an external honors examiner. He was a member of the Board of Managers of the College from 1965 to 1972. Swarthmore conferred on him the honorary degree of Doctor of Laws in 1963.

A Rhodes Scholar, Gordon spent one academic year, 1938–1939, at University College, Oxford. Returning to the United States after the outbreak of war in Europe, he joined Wilcox to work on the Report of the Temporary National Economic Committee, then studied graduate economics at Harvard in 1940–1941. His studies once again interrupted by war, he was an economist at the Office of Price Administration in Washington from 1941 to 1943, gaining experience and wisdom for later assignments, notably his 1971–1972 service as a public member of President Nixon's Pay Board. As a soldier of the United States Army 1943–1945, Gordon was assigned to the Office of Strategic Services, the common training ground of many economists and public servants of subsequent distinction. A tour of duty at the Department of State, 1945–1946, added international economics to his experience and interest; he continued in consulting roles on foreign economic policies after he moved to Williamstown in 1946.

At Williams, a college dedicated to excellent teaching, he quickly became known as an exceptionally fine teacher. His style was informal, genial, and witty; but he relentlessly demanded rigor, precision, and clarity of thought and expression. As Clair Wilcox had done at Swarthmore, Gordon set a tone for economics at Williams that made a small liberal arts college department one of which a major university could be proud, and one from which able students derived not just intellectual nurture but the conviction that intelligent application of political economy could and should improve the human condition. The Gordons dearly loved Williams and Williamstown. They kept a residence there and expected to return in retirement. The college awarded him the LL.D. in 1974.

Gordon's reputation for wisdom, insight, and foresight in matters of policy, well established in 1946, grew during his years at Williams. The manifold extramural calls on his energy and talent included consultation for the State Department 1946–1953, for the White House in connection with the *Report on Foreign Economic Policies*, 1950, and for the Office of Price Stabilization, 1951; part-time administrative assistance to the Merrill Foundation for Advancement of Financial Knowledge, 1947–1956; full-time executive positions, 1956–1957 and 1960–1961, with the Ford Foundation, of which he was later a Trustee, 1967–1975; work for the Committee for Economic Development, of which he also became a trustee; and not least, active participation in Massachusetts political campaigns on behalf of Adlai Stevenson and local candidates for Congress and other offices.

In 1961 Gordon was a natural choice for President Kennedy's Council of Economic Advisers, complementing Walter Heller, Chairman, and James Tobin. He shared the primary responsibilities of the Council for advising the president on overall policies for economic stabilization and full employment. In addition, his professional experience and interest had prepared him to assume special surveillance of micro-economic issues, notably regulation of industry, federal subsidy programs, budget priorities, and policies affecting prices and wages.

Gordon was the initiator and principal author of President Kennedy's proposals for deregulation and promotion of competition in transportation, fifteen years before the approach became fashionable and politically acceptable. Gordon assembled in 1962 a long list of federal regulations and practices that compel or protect high and rising prices, twelve years before such lists of "sacred cows" made headlines at the 1974 White House anti-inflation summit. Again and again Gordon exposed the costly economic folly of federal programs beloved of special interests and their agents in Congress and the executive branch: merchant marine subsidies and cargo preferences, sugar import quotas, irrigation dams, non-competitive union wages imposed by legislation in government-financed construction—the list was endless. Gordon relished puncturing the pious phony arguments of supporters of such legislation, but he was too much a political realist to be downcast when economic reason did not prevail.

A unique feature of economic policy in the Kennedy administration was the attempt to obtain by presidential persuasion voluntary compliance by business and labor with "guideposts for non-inflationary price and wage behavior." This experiment was in large measure due to Kermit Gordon. Early in 1961 Gordon realized that the president's hopes for full recovery, reducing unemployment from seven per cent to four per cent, would fail if prices began to move up early in the recovery; the specter of inflation would doom expansionary fiscal and monetary policies. He realized also how crucial, if only psychologically, steel prices and wages would be. He instigated in 1961 presidential requests for company and union restraint; they were followed by Secretary of Labor Arthur Goldberg's success in steering the parties to a non-inflationary steel wage settlement in early 1962. When U.S. Steel nevertheless announced price increases as soon as the ink was dry on the wage contract, Gordon was heavily involved in the tactics and negotiations by which the president prevailed on the industry to rescind the increases.

The wage and price guideposts published in the Council's 1962 *Economic Report* generalized and rationalized the policy. The 1961–1965 expansion did reduce unemployment to four per cent without significant increase in the inflation rate. (Of course inflation accelerated in 1966–1969 under the pressures of deficit financing of the Vietnam war; the guideposts collapsed, as they were bound to do. No one ever expected them to restrain wages and prices in the face of general excess demand.) Whether the guideposts, unpopular as they were with both labor and management, contributed to the happy 1961–1965 outcome is a question on which scholars still differ widely. Evidence in the 1970's of the inflationary bias of the economy in the absence of any wage/price policy suggests that Gordon's guideposts deserve some credit. In various mutations the policy is under serious consideration once again.

The Bureau of the Budget (now the Office of Management and Budget) evaluates thousands of federal programs and, in preparing the president's annual budget proposals, determines funding priorities in the large and in the small. Faced with a task of such immense complexity, a director may work incredibly hard to achieve personal command of his budget; or he may rely on subordinates for detail and take refuge in "the big picture." Kermit Gordon is remembered as a director who learned the federal government inside out and knew precisely why his agency was recommending cuts for some programs and increases, perhaps even exceeding agency requests, for others. He could administer austerity; he could also persuade the president that foreign aid and the war on poverty should get more. Gordon is remembered too for his forthrightness and candor in dealings with executive departments and with Congress. His first appearance as director before the Senate Finance Committee is a memorable example. Senator Harry F. Byrd, Sr., a fiscal conservative, asked him what would be the effect of bringing the federal budget into balance immediately. After a few tense minutes of silent calculation, Gordon replied that it would "probably add about two and a half million people to the rolls of the unemployed, delay the recovery four years, and knock ten per cent off U.S. output." This was, of course, not the answer Byrd expected or wanted, and the senator immediately wired Kennedy to fire Gordon, only a month after his appointment. Fortunately the president did not comply.

Throughout his tenure in the executive office, Gordon never forgot he was serving the president of the United States. He was no sycophant and he was not afraid to express his views, even when they clearly ran counter to the president's predilections. Once decisions were made, he loyally played his part in carrying them out. On this basis he won the respect and trust of both John Kennedy and Lyndon Johnson. When Johnson took office after the assassination of Kennedy, the 1964 budget preparations were nearly complete. Gordon told the new President that he still had time to make the budget his own, and they worked together overtime to that end.

When Kermit Gordon undertook the leadership of the Brookings Institution both he and the Institution were half a century old. Brookings describes itself as "an independent organization devoted to nonpartisan research, education, and publication in economics, government, foreign policy, and the social sciences generally. Its principal purposes are to aid in the development of sound public policies and to promote public understanding of issues of national importance.'' Under the presidency of Robert Calkins, Gordon's predecessor, Brookings was already enjoying a renaissance. The Institution was an increasingly attractive milieu for high-caliber social scientists of all ages, and its staff embodied an impressive amount and variety of academic and government experience. Congress, government departments, scholars, foundations, journalists, and the general public were turning more and more to Brookings for independent authoritative research related to public policy. After two transitional years as vice president, Gordon assumed the presidency in 1967

He was a natural for this job, as for his previous assignments. He was universally respected in the economics profession, in governmental and political circles, and in the lay public among the businessmen, labor leaders, foundation officials, journalists and others who had come to know him over the years. He had a keen and sophisticated sense of relevance. He looked beyond the fashionable topics of policy debate today to the issues that would be significant tomorrow and years hence. He knew better than to waste resources in research either on transient and trivial topics or on important issues that research could help very little to resolve. He took deadly seriously his responsibility as president for decisions to publish manuscripts as Brookings monographs. They all benefited in content and prose style from his critical and inquiring scrutiny. He was a severe and demanding editor, intolerant of puffery, redundancy, and obscurity. He assembled a fine staff because he was an acute judge of people, quick to recognize and encourage talent, promise, and integrity, also quick to detect foolishness, hypocrisy, and corruption. Time and again his judgments of the survival values and payoffs of ideas, proposals, projects, and people turned out right.

During his tenure Brookings grew in the scope of its activities, the volume of its publications, the size and quality of its research staff, and the public impact of its findings. The Institution became internationally recognized as a research center unsurpassed in the effective application of economics and political science to problems of public policy. Perhaps most important, although the Institution continued to be responsive to outside requests and proposals, its agenda became increasingly self-generated. Among the initiatives that have turned out to be substantial contributions both to scholarship and to public policy are the annual reviews of federal budget issues entitled *Setting National Priorities;* the Brookings Panel on Economic Activity, which commissions, discusses and publishes papers related to macroeconomic stabilization; and the series of Foreign Policy Studies.

Gordon was determined to maintain the independent and non-partisan character of the Institution, and no informed fair-minded observer could doubt that he did so. He was greatly disturbed therefore by facile characterizations of Brookings as a citadel of liberalism or a Democratic government in exile. During the years of expansion under Calkins and Gordon, it is true, a number of eminent scholars became available to Brookings when, like Gordon himself, they left federal positions with Democratic administrations. But when he angrily erupted under provocation of a *New York Times* story referring to Brookings as "between-election stop for out-of-office Democrats," Gordon pointed out that of his forty-one senior fellows four had served in high positions in the Kennedy-Johnson administrations, five in high positions in the Nixon-Ford administrations, and four in both. (In addition, Gordon himself served under Nixon on advisory committees on social security and on arms control, as well as on the Pay Board.) Somewhat earlier Gordon had been more amused and gratified than scared and angered by Watergate disclosures of the awkward plans of the Nixon White House to set up a captive foundation to take business from Brookings and to bomb and burglarize the building.

Gordon was a member of the board of editors of the *American Economic Review*, 1958–1960. He was a member of Phi Beta Kappa, a Fellow of the American Academy of Arts and Sciences, and from 1971, a member of the American Philosophical Society. He loved dogs, softball, children, arguments, good stories, and the ironies of politics and life. He never took himself or anyone else too seriously, and he was a marvelous companion in work or play.

Gordon's political economy was pragmatic and eclectic. He distrusted ideology and saw through doctrinaire generalizations of all colors. He refused to take stands on sweeping but foolish questions. Is government spending too much or too little? He likened the question to asking an art museum curator whether he had the right square footage of canvas. It all depends on the quality of the paintings—or the government programs. Likewise Gordon found many government economic regulations counterproductive; but he had no illusion that free enterprise and unfettered markets would always perform for the best. His common sense came through, in all-too-rare written form, in a 1974 Williams convocation address called "Inflation: A Non-Apocalyptic View," a balanced, perceptive antidote to hysteria or complacency about the nation's economic problems. He saw many flaws in welfare state programs, but his consistent life-long objective was raising living standards of poor people in this country and throughout the world. He was a realist but not a cynic. He never expected miracles. He was an active optimistic practitioner of political economy because he thought it would make a difference. Kermit Gordon made a difference.

JAMES TOBIN

THE CAREERS OF PAUL DOUGLAS

In the Fullness of Time: Memoirs, *by* Paul H. Douglas, *Harcourt Brace Jovanovich.*

In the fullness of his time Paul Douglas, entering his ninth decade, can look back on no less than four careers of remarkable service to humanity and truth. Any one alone would fill with distinction the lifetime of a man of unusually prodigious talent and energy. Men of Paul Douglas's range, intensity, and dedication are not just unusual; they stride across the national scene only once or twice a generation. In the breadth of his intellectual interests and powers, the universality of his public concerns, the natural union of thought and action in his life, he brings to mind Franklin, Jefferson, and Wilson—and among his contemporaries Dean Acheson and Adlai Stevenson. But these scholarly statesmen were much more coolly intellectual and, save Franklin, more patrician than Douglas. In the moral fervor and passion with which he fueled his pursuits Douglas is in the tradition of the first Roosevelt, Robert LaFollette, and George Norris, men more likely to be in his personal galaxy of saints.

Douglas's overlapping careers were scholar and teacher of economics, crusader for social reform, soldier, politician, and Senator. He relates all of them in these memoirs, though three-fourths of the book is devoted to his eighteen years in the Senate. The emphasis is natural, but some readers may find the detail on specific Senatorial issues and struggles excessive. Besides personal memoirs and fascinating comments on political personalities, these chapters contain instructive accounts of the office of Senator, the organization of the Senate, and the substance of the many legislative problems that engaged the writer.

The book begins with a charming account of Douglas's boyhood and youth. He grew up in Maine handicapped by a broken family, a series of makeshift living arrangements, and precarious economic circumstances. His determination and ambition, the moral support of his stepmother and a perceptive high school teacher, and the financial help of his older brother took him to Bowdoin College and set him on the path through graduate school at Columbia and Harvard to the academic ladder. From 1920 to 1948 he was a professor at the University of Chicago.

In economics Douglas's pioneering and lasting achievement was his formulation and statistical estimation of "production functions" relating output to inputs of capital and labor. The Cobb-Douglas production function, first unveiled in 1927 by Douglas and his friend the mathematician Charles W. Cobb, is still the favorite formula of theorists, econometricians, and students everywhere. Its durable appeal stems from its simplicity (output is a logarithmic linear function of inputs) and from its consistent success in fitting diverse data at least as well as more complex alternatives. Even Douglas's original numerical estimates persist: 25-35 percent of output variation attributable to capital, 75-65 percent to labor. This research was no doubt the main factor in Douglas's election to the presidency of the American Economic Association in 1947. His masterful presidential address, "Are There Laws of Production"— "the best piece of economic work I had ever done"—was also his valedictory as a scholar. As he was about to deliver it in late December 1947, the Cook County Democratic leader Jake Arvey notified him that the State Committee would support him for the United States Senate in 1948. But evidently the address was not a final valedictory; it is a pleasure to read at the end of the book that Douglas is returning to this work in his retirement.

Douglas undertook to estimate production functions because he was interested in wages, and much of his research was published in his major work, *The Theory of Wages*. As he knew, orthodox theory is that the wage is equal to the marginal productivity of labor, and this is what he hoped to estimate statistically. His work turned out to be a major vindication of the orthodox theory, because his numerical estimates of the contributions of capital and labor to output correspond fairly closely to the shares of profits and wages in income. The implication is that not much can be done about the distribution of income between wages and profits by trade unions, minimum wage laws, or other social legislation. Douglas the scholar must have caused some discomfort to Douglas the reformer, but the memoirs give no hint.

The University of Chicago was a young and exciting campus in Douglas's day, and its economics department then as now was one of the very best. Yet much of the ferment in economics in the 1930's passed Douglas by. Keynes made little splash in Chicago, except to arouse scorn and opposition. Keynesian and post-Keynesian ideas do not seem to have significantly interested or influenced either Professor Douglas or Senator Douglas. In the Senate he was a tower of strength for the full employment objectives of the Employment Act of 1946, and his membership and chairmanship on the Joint Economic Committee elevated the national dialogue on economic policy. But he never expended much Senatorial energy on Keynesian fiscal policy as a route to full employment and economic stabilization. He was more likely to assign responsibility for these tasks to the monetary policies of the Federal Reserve.

From Chicago colleagues with whose policy predilections he was certainly not sympathetic Douglas seems to have absorbed the quantity theory of money, which he trotted out in simplistic form in his Senatorial crusade in 1951 to liberate the "Fed" from its wartime subservience to the Treasury. He was right on that issue, as on many subsequent occasions when he criticized Federal Reserve policy. But he paid too little attention to fiscal policy, which was after all a responsibility of Congress.

Basically Douglas was much more interested in micro-economic issues—the distribution of income, wealth, and economic power; economic justice and security; competition and monopoly—than in macro-economics. After he returned from the war he felt increasingly alienated from the economics profession. His Chicago department had come to be dominated by doctrinaire exponents of laissez-faire. The profession at large, he complains with the bitterness of a front-line soldier who feels no one backing him up, was indifferent and silent with respect to the wastes, injustices, and privileges he was fighting in the Senate.

Douglas's career as an activist social reformer began early. No man to be contained even within the spacious academic horizons of the Midway, he found many causes and projects in the city and beyond: labor arbitration, fact-finding in Haiti and Russia, crusading against Sam Insull; mobilizing the economics profession against the Smoot-Hawley tariff; trying to protect consumers within the National Recovery Act; designing and promoting unemployment insurance as well as other social security and labor legislation. Inevitably the path led to his third career, politics.

Somehow in 1939 he was elected to the Chicago City Council. Somehow he managed to be a crusading anti-machine reformer without completely alienating the professional politicians. He gained the respect of successive Chicago bosses Kelly, Arvey, and Daley as a man and a vote-getter. The Kelly-Nash machine successfully thwarted his first attempt, in 1942, to gain the nomination for United States Senator. But in 1948 things were different. The machine does like to win and correctly assessed Douglas's appeal in Republican territory downstate. He was one of the two logical Democratic choices for major office in 1948. Probably the state committee was right to ignore expressed preferences and to ticket Stevenson for Governor and Douglas for Senator.

In the interim Douglas had been a Marine. Characteristically, he enlisted as a private, pushed his fifty-year-old frame through the ordeal of boot camp, wheedled his way into combat, and finally on Okinawa felt "a deep wave of exaltation—that I had shed blood in defense of my country." He never recovered full use of his left hand and arm. Though the combat interlude surely did him no harm with voters, it would be a mistake to infer calculated political motivation. At critical junctures of his life Douglas always acted courageously, impetuously, and emotionally, testing himself against his own principles. For him, enlistment was a natural course just after he lost a primary campaign where he represented strong support of Roosevelt and the war against a lukewarm Democratic rival and an isolationist Republican incumbent. Moreover, Douglas had earlier been a converted Quaker, and taking up arms against the Axis confirmed his reluctant but firm conviction that defense of freedom took precedence over pacifism.

Like many interventionists of his generation, Douglas transferred his fears and hates from Hitler to Stalin after the war. Subsequently he stuck to a strong anti-Communist no-appeasement line long after it seemed to many others to be obsolete. Although these views provided political protection for a domestic liberal, Douglas's hawkish stance on the Vietnam war—considerably modified in the memoirs —blinded many youthful idealists to his substantial claims to their loyalty and affection.

Of all his careers Douglas obviously enjoyed his three terms as Senator the most. Obviously too, nothing hurt him as much as his defeat in 1966. He discusses that campaign at length: the tactics of his opponent Charles Percy, the impact of the tragic murder of Percy's daughter in the midst of the campaign. In the fullness of time he has no doubt come to see that the citizens of Illinois might vote to retire him in 1966 without in any way repudiating his record as their Senator.

He had served them well, never neglecting his duties as their ombudsman in Washington. He had shown that a Senator could serve his constituents without sacrificing high standards of personal morality and intellectual integrity. He had been a great national Senator —in the forefront of many battles, most of them lost at the time, many of them won later, many yet to be won. Civil rights, civil liberties, reapportionment, pork barrels, subsidies to private interests, monopolies and their regulation, social security, depressed areas, tax reform, housing, international trade and tariffs, truth in lending—on all these issues and more Douglas was on the side of the angels. Most of the time there were few if any fellow angels. But Douglas was indefatigable and persistent. More of a teacher than a legislative strategist, he doggedly educated his colleagues and the public to the facts and appealed to their sense of decency and justice.

Like his hero Norris, unlike his friend Hubert Humphrey, Douglas was never a member of the Senate's inner club. He was forever in conflict with the Senate Establishment, the Kerrs, Russells, and Johnsons. He was too personally involved in all his causes to make strategic compromises or to view dispassionately the maneuvers the Senate power structure used to get its way. His principled independence and his distaste for deals likewise impaired his relations with the Democratic Presidents of his era, and unhappily with his fellow-Illinoisan Adlai Stevenson. Among these leaders his affection and admiration were greatest for John Kennedy, with whom he had developed a warm friendship in the Senate.

Sometimes impetuosity and emotion got the better of judgment. Once Douglas left the Senate floor in audible pain when another Senator cast aspersions on his loyalty during debate on defense appropriations. In 1948 he made the mistake of supporting Eisenhower at the Democratic convention. In 1952 he put on a bizarre and distraught performance on the floor of the convention, where he was a Kefauver supporter and a possible dark-horse candidate himself. The conservative columnist Holmes Alexander wounded Douglas deeply with a psychological analysis accusing him of smugness and self-righteousness. Douglas is a big man, and all these incidents are candidly recounted in the book.

Back in Illinois he was an effective politician and campaigner, and the same voters who gave us Everett McKinley Dirksen gave us Douglas. For their perception we can be proud of the American political process and grateful that men of Douglas's gifts occasionally throw themselves into active politics.

JAMES TOBIN

HARRY GORDON JOHNSON

1923–1977

FOR the economics profession throughout the world the third quarter of this century was an Age of Johnson. Harry Gordon Johnson, who died in Geneva, 9 May 1977, at the age of 53, bestrode our discipline like a Colossus. Throughout his career he was an active leader in the professional and academic economics of three countries, Britain, the United States, and Canada. At the time of his death he held chairs at both the University of Chicago and the Graduate School of International Studies at Geneva. He had been a fellow and lecturer at Cambridge, a professor at Manchester and at the London School of Economics, a visiting professor at numerous universities including Northwestern, Queen's, Toronto, and Yale, an undergraduate at Toronto and Cambridge, and a graduate student at Toronto and Harvard.

Born in Toronto in 1923, Johnson liked to recall his boyhood on an Ontario dairy farm. But his home nurtured mind as well as body. The home was close to Toronto, where his parents worked and he and his brother attended school. His father was a prominent politician, secretary of the provincial Liberal party, one of the chief lieutenants of Ontario Premier Hepburn. His mother was a child psychologist at the University of Toronto. Harry was married to Elizabeth Scott Serson of Ottawa, a journalist and editor, in 1948. They had met as Toronto undergraduates in 1940; on the eve of Harry's emigration to take up a position at the University of Cambridge, they eloped to Cambridge, Massachusetts, where Harry was completing his resident study as a graduate student. For many years an editor of the Collected Papers of John Maynard Keynes, Elizabeth Johnson is now Economics Editor for the University of Chicago Press. The Johnsons had two children, both born in Cambridge, England, a son Ragnar, in 1949, and a daughter Karen, in 1951. Ragnar is now an anthropologist and Karen an actress, both residing in London. Harry Johnson is also survived by his brother, a pediatrician in Toronto.

The label 'economists' economist' is a cliché but never more appropriate than for Harry Johnson. It was his impact on his own profession, not on the public at large, that justifies calling

Reprinted by permission from *Proceedings of the British Academy* 64 (1978):443–458.

the era his Age. He wrote and published, it is safe to say, more than any contemporary economist; his bibliography will include nineteen books of his own, twenty-four books which he edited and contributed to, more than five hundred scientific articles, and numerous pamphlets and book reviews.[1] He ranks near the top of contemporary economists in citation counts.[2] He probably knew personally more economists of all ages and nationalities than any other leading scholar. Certainly no one had a more far-flung, numerous, and devoted band of students, friends, and admirers. Everyone referred to him simply as Harry. In our peripatetic profession Harry is generally conceded the all-time records for air travel for academic and scientific purposes and for hours spent in lectures, conferences, symposia, and colloquia. He was a great editor, to the benefit of five journals and numerous volumes of conference proceedings and contributions on particular topics. Under his editorship the Chicage-based *Journal of Political Economy* became in general opinion the liveliest and most influential scholarly periodical in economics.

Johnson did not serve governments and politicians, or advise them except in print and public speech. He did not write introductory textbooks; few undergraduate students ever read him or heard him. He did not write best-sellers or columns in the popular press. He did not crusade for an economic ideology. His recognition and reputation outside his profession do not compare with those of Samuelson, Friedman, and Galbraith or of Harrod, Kaldor, and Mrs Robinson.

[1] A definitive bibliography will be published in the *Journal of Political Economy* in 1979. Eric J. Belton, librarian of Lakehead University, Thunder Bay, Ontario, has compiled a Johnson bibliography through 1975. It is indicative of Johnson's productivity, even after the crippling stroke he suffered in 1973, that since Mr Belton's compilation more than one hundred additional items have been published or are in press. The Lakehead University library is collecting copies of all Johnson's publications. The University of Chicago library will be the depository for Johnson's papers. For this information and much else I am indebted to Elizabeth Johnson and to the memorial article by Grant L. Reuber and Anthony D. Scott (*Canadian Journal of Economics*, November 1977).

[2] According to the Institute for Scientific Information (*Current Comments*, 7 August 1978), data from the Social Sciences Citation Index for 1969–77 place ahead of Johnson only three authors, all Nobel laureates, Milton Friedman, Paul Samuelson, and Kenneth Arrow. An unpublished study by Herbert Grubel of Simon Fraser University concerns specialists in international economics 1970–6 and finds Johnson, the most prolific author, cited far more frequently than anyone but Samuelson.

Harry could have done any or all of those things extremely well. The prose that flooded from his pen is clear, cogent, and graceful. He could, if he wished, make economic theory easy to read, and fun. Many of his writings—for example, *Of Economics and Society* (1975), a collection of non-technical essays; *Economic Policies Towards Less Developed Countries* (1967); *World Economy at the Crossroads* (1965)—do just that. Although he believed that a scientist should maintain distance from governments and politics, he was by no means indifferent to economic and social policies and outcomes. Many of his writings are analytical critiques, often devastating, of actual and proposed policies and of their intellectual and political under-pinnings, in his three home countries and throughout the world. Yet for these essays, as for his more purely scientific contributions, appreciation and attention came mainly from his fellow economists.

One reason Harry had less public impact than he deserved is that he was uncompromisingly independent of intellectual and political fashion. He did not tell people what they wanted to hear. He took the long view. His strategy was first to set straight the economics profession, in the hope and belief that competent research, teaching, and analysis would ultimately improve policy advice and policy itself. Another limit on his direct public influence was his steadfast internationalism. Cosmopolitan in his personal life, he had no use for nationalism whether in his native Canada (see *The Canadian Quandary* (1963)), Britain, other advanced countries, or the third world. Most of his prodigious scholarly energy was devoted to international economics. His studies convinced him that autarkic policies were short-sighted, inefficient, and inequitable. This stance did not make his voice welcome in the economic politics of nation-states.

Let me elaborate the reasons for Johnson's extraordinary popularity and influence within economics. One reason was his unfailing accommodation of fellow scholars and students. No country was too remote, no university too obscure, no professional association too parochial for Harry to visit; invite him for lectures, seminars, or conferences and he would come. No journal was too local or special or new or mediocre for Harry to give it a boost; the struggling editor need only ask him to contribute a paper. No author was too young or too far from the mainstream to get from Harry constructive comment on his papers and indeed personal advice on his research and career.

As a journal editor he had to reject most submissions, but he told the authors why and offered suggestions. He tried hard to find the germ of a good idea in unpromising material and to help the author develop it.

A second reason was the power of Johnson's exposition of economic ideas. If his style did not quite carry the word to a large general audience, it was made to order for his professional constituency. His collected essays and lecture courses on international trade, money, growth, and distribution are the way thousands of graduate students and teachers learn economic theory.[1] Johnson was a master of creative synthesis. He could organize the confusing variety of ideas, findings, and approaches in a field into a coherent whole. The structure was his original design. An outstanding example is his survey article 'Monetary Theory and Policy' (*American Economic Review*, June, 1962).

The same qualities of discrimination and perspective made Harry a formidable critic. He would not suffer foolishness, especially pretentious foolishness from persons of high status and reputation. He unerringly winnowed the false from the true, the trivial from the significant, the ideological from the analytical, the special from the general, the imitative from the original, the irrelevant from the important. Mathematical and econometric jargon did not faze him; he saw through it to the essential message, if any. He could digest and evaluate a paper or a book with amazing accuracy and perception in less time than an ordinary mortal could turn the pages. His knowledge of the literature, old and new, seemed limitless. These qualities made him the great editor he was, a tough and informative book reviewer, a demanding and invaluable mentor of graduate and postdoctoral students.

Third, Harry's internationalism—which may have diluted his impact on lay publics—gave his writings and talks extraordinary relevance to economists everywhere. He knew, as theorists rarely do, about problems and policies of countries all over the world. He refused to let his economics be bounded by the interests or institutions of any country or region.

Finally, not least, Harry was a 'character', a legend. The stories are legion. They will be told with awe and delight for years to come, and lose nothing in the telling. The dismal science attracts few colourful personalities. In Harry we had a

[1] *International Trade and Economic Growth* (1958), *Essays in Monetary Economics* (1967), *Further Essays in Monetary Economics* (1973), *Macroeconomics and Monetary Theory* (Lectures, 1971), *Theory of Distribution* (Lectures, 1973).

hero whose style of life and work and talk were worthy of a genius of poetry or art. Physically he stood out of a crowd, a large man, incorrigibly overweight, loudly and informally dressed years before the unconventional became the fashion. Only his eyes betrayed the fire of his mind.

En route to a conference an ocean or continent away, Harry would write an article or two in flight. During the sessions he would whittle exotic fauna; he was an expert and imaginative wood sculptor, and his carvings are prized ornaments in hundreds of homes and offices. Or he would carve three-dimensional models of economic relationships. Or he would design puzzles. Meanwhile he would enter the discussion as necessary to keep it on track. Later, undeterred by jet lag or combat fatigue and fortified by the most sumptuous repast available, Harry would hold night-long court in the local pub, tossing off witty and often cutting verdicts on economics and economists to the delight of hosts of admirers. His appetite and capacity for whisky, as prodigious as everything else he did, will be part of the legend too. Intellectually he flourished with the lubrication; he flourished without it too, after his stroke in 1973. If the superhuman intensity of his habits and pursuits contributed to his disability and early demise, perhaps he had chosen consciously or unconsciously to cram several normal lifetimes into one short span.

Harry wanted economics to be a science cumulative in knowledge. All too often, he found, it was an unscientific arena of conflicting values, political preferences, and ideologies. All too often studies that passed as professional contributions added nothing to verified scientific knowledge—they were too trivial, too sloppy, too derivative. On these counts he became especially critical of economics in Britain and in particular at Cambridge. Early in his career he concluded that the way professional economists are trained is decisive for the future of the discipline. Over the years he spent a great deal of thought and energy in organizing the education of graduate students. One of his life's ambitions, three times frustrated, was to reform economic research and instruction in the United Kingdom.

Harry's love–hate affair with England began as love in 1945. He had been a soldier assigned to clerical duties at Canada House in London. The Canadian Army, short of shipping to take soldiers home, offered to send some to British universities. Harry had graduated from Toronto in political economy in

1943. Prior to his miltary service he had spent the year 1943-4 as the one-man economics faculty of St. Francis Xavier University in Antigonish, Nova Scotia. He jumped at the chance to go to Cambridge. In his soldier–student year there he picked up another bachelor's degree, indeed another First, the highest in the third-year economics Tripos. He returned triumphantly to Toronto to a junior teaching appointment, and he also earned an MA degree in 1947.

In the autumn of 1947 he enrolled in the Ph.D. programme in economics at Harvard. It was the time to be there. The place buzzed with excitement and confidence. Harvard's great pre-war faculty was still intact: Schumpeter, Hansen, Williams, Haberler, Leontief, Mason, Harris, Chamberlain. Several cohorts of graduate students and junior faculty, mostly war veterans, were bunched together, an unusual assemblage of talent. They were learning as much from each other as from their elders. Some were giving mathematical rigour and statistical content to Keynesian theory, encouraged by Alvin Hansen, its leading apostle in the United States. Others, stimulated by Schumpeter and Leontief and by the example of Samuelson, then at Massachusetts Institute of Technology a few miles down river, were doing the same for neoclassical microeconomics. Thanks to Haberler, Harris, and a number of younger economists, there was also lively activity in international economics. In his three semesters at Harvard, Johnson breezed through the course requirements and the oral qualifying exams for the Ph.D. He wrote a note on 'An Error in Ricardo's Exposition of His Theory of Rent' and with Joseph Schumpeter's encouragement published it in the *Quarterly Journal of Economics*. But he did not complete his doctorate until 1958, when he was already Professor of Economic Theory at Manchester and scarcely needed credentials. The collection of essays published as *International Trade and Economic Growth* served as his Harvard Ph.D. dissertation.

The reason Harry left the American Cambridge at the beginning of 1949, after only three terms, was to return to the English Cambridge. The Professor, Dennis H. Robertson, had noticed the Canadian during his student year, and when Johnson revisited Cambridge (crossing the Atlantic by cattle boat) in the summer of 1948, Robertson offered him a job as assistant lecturer. Harry accepted on the spot, and hurried through his Harvard requirements when he returned to America. And so the Canadian farm boy, the corporal, became a don, first an assistant lecturer and later a lecturer in the university faculty, first a research fellow at Jesus and then a fellow of King's, the very centre of economics.

Liberated from student status, Harry began to write in earnest. He burst into print with a series of pioneering and now classic papers in international trade, collected in *International Trade and Economic Growth* (1958). It is worth noticing what some of these papers are about, because they show the characteristic double purpose of Johnson's theorizing. They advance, generalize, and synthesize theory; simultaneously they shed light on real-world issues and policies.

In the early 1950s some British economists were attracted by the theoretical possibility that a nation could, by levying a tariff of the right amount, gain at the expense of its trading partners. The argument, they thought, could defend the protectionist measures of HM government against the objections of free-trade doctrine. Johnson undertook a thorough analysis of the theory of tariffs and optimal tariffs; one by-product was to cast doubt on the strategy, especially when other countries can retaliate.

Another subject Johnson illuminated was the dispute between Keynes and Bertil Ohlin about German reparations in the 1920s. Could, in principle, an exchange-rate adjustment accomplish such a transfer, or would the attempt necessarily be frustrated as in Germany by endless currency depreciation and inflation? Johnson found the conditions for the one result and for the other.

Balance of payments deficits were then, as now, very much in the news and in the minds of economists and policy-makers. Some analysts attributed them to comparative costs, some to excesses of domestic 'absorption' of goods over production, some to lagging economic growth, some to inflationary monetary policies. Johnson put the pieces together in a unified model, and foreshadowed his work in the 1970s on the 'monetary theory of balance of payments'.

Countries producing raw materials have long complained that the trend of terms of trade is against them, and some economists argued that technological progress was actually to their disadvantage. Along similar lines, some people feared that international differences in technological progress and capital accumulation could lead to chronic imbalances of payments. First applied to the dollar shortage, the idea reappears for the mark or yen shortage. Modelling the links between international

8704C78   G g

trade and economic growth, Johnson showed that these fears are unlikely to be justified.

In the course of this work, Harry got marvellous mileage from a simple diagram, the 'Edgeworth box' (named after its inventor, F. Y. Edgeworth, the Oxford mathematical economist, contemporary of Alfred Marshall), a device Johnson later exploited with similar powerful effect in other contexts. Gifted with geometrical intuition, he loved to use ingenious diagrams for expository purposes in articles and lectures. He used algebra too, but he was not a mathematical economist and did not need complex mathematics to convey with logical rigour the points he wanted to make. Some people regard him as the last great English-speaking economic theorist.

Harry's lectures on international economics at Cambridge in the 1950s were famous for their succinct and elegant coverage of the field. He attracted, befriended, encouraged graduate students and visiting scholars, and he tried valiantly to build a community of research economists in the fragmented Cambridge environment.[1]

In spite of his personal success and fulfilment, Harry's experience of Cambridge alienated him from English economics in general, from the dominant Keynesian establishment at Cambridge in particular, and from the smug parochialism and genteel amateurism of economics training in Oxford, Cambridge, and elsewhere. The structured system of graduate education at Harvard and the lively interaction among faculty and students there must have looked good in contrast. In his *Encounter* memoirs[2] Johnson embedded a scathing indictment of Cambridge economics and instruction in an entertaining narrative of his life at Cambridge and a fascinating excursion into the comparative sociology of academic communities. The indictment is summed up in two passages:

'... [The] modern post-Keynesian-Cambridge style ... has three major elements in it. All are directly traceable to salient characteristics of Cambridge as an academic environment. (1) The belief that fundamental questions of social and economic policy are ultimately determined by debate among a handful of academic economists, in Cambridge and at most two other British universities. (2) Policy failure is the result of bad—and bad means orthodox, or more generally

---

[1] See the personal reminiscence of Johnson by Jagdish Bhagwati (*Journal of International Economics*, 1977).

[2] 'Cambridge in the 1950s' (*Encounter*, January, 1974) and 'How Good was Keynes' Cambridge' (*Encounter*, August, 1976).

pedestrian, tedious, and unimaginative—economics. (3) The world is to be put right by instructing the undergraduate students at Cambridge and elsewhere in the complex fallacies committed by orthodox economics and the simple truth as derived by anti-orthodox economic theory.' (*Encounter*, August 1976, p. 90).

'... I began to appreciate the difference between scientific and ideological motivations for theoretical work. I began to realize that more and more Cambridge people in my judgment were perverting economics in order to defend intellectual and emotional positions taken in the 1930s. In particular, for them Keynesian economics was not a theoretical advance to be built on for scientific progress and improved social policy. It was only a tool for furthering left-wing politics at the level of intellectual debate. So I decided to leave Cambridge and go somewhere else where I might learn something useful—namely to Manchester [in 1956]. I eventually left Manchester to go to Chicago [in 1959] in spite of the fact that my days at Manchester were probably the happiest of my life, professionally speaking. Over the years I became fed up with the poverty of English economics, which provided increasingly inadequate compensation for the material poverty that English academic life in the provinces imposed.'

I can understand something of Harry's disenchantment. I first met Harry in 1948 at Harvard one Saturday afternoon in Alvin Hansen's fiscal policy seminar library. We spent the afternoon talking about everything and began a permanent friendship that survived geographical, doctrinal, and political separations. As it happened, I followed Harry to the other Cambridge in the autumn of 1949, to work for a year at Richard Stone's Department of Applied Economics. Liz and Harry Johnson welcomed Betty and me to England, showed us the ropes of practical living amidst austerity, guided and joined us in exploring Cambridge, shared with us the pleasures and trials of first-born babies. Harry and Jan Graaff took it upon themselves to insinuate me into economic circles beyond the Department of Applied Economics, which to my surprise was pretty much an island to itself, detached from college life and ignored by regular faculty.

Johnson and Graaff were apprentices to the Cambridge economics establishment. Graaff was an aristocratic South African, educated at Cambridge, now a graduate student. In contrast to Harry, Jan had impeccable establishment credentials, and he looked and acted the part. I went with them to the famous King's seminar founded by Keynes and continued by Richard Kahn. In their different ways they were both brash and outspoken. They got away with it because they were usually right and because they knew what was going on in economics outside Cambridge. That was unusual—an eminent Cambridge economist told me there was no need to read the literature because most good ideas originated in Cambridge and any others would be discovered there shortly. When Paul Samuelson threatened to visit Cambridge in 1948, Graaff had to brief his distinguished mentors on who Samuelson was and what he had contributed. When Samuelson came, Professor Pigou expressed interest in one of his papers and suggested he check the proofs with a mathematician. When Samuelson protested that he himself was a mathematician Pigou replied, 'Oh, I mean a British mathematician.' Perhaps the geocentrism of Cambridge— the home of Marshall, Keynes, Pigou, Robertson, Mrs. Robinson, Sraffa, Kahn, and other stars—was only natural. But it was infuriating, and it infuriated Harry. As for Jan Graaff, he showed his mastery of economic calculus in an elegant book based on his thesis, *Theoretical Welfare Economics*, and to our profession's misfortune turned to other pursuits in South Africa.

Arrogant, complacent parochialism was not all that alienated Harry. Cambridge economics was a bloody battleground. On one side were the veterans of the great Keynesian revolution of the 1930s. On the other were economists of the older tradition of Pigou and Robertson and Keynesians of less radical bent. The stakes were the minds of students, the attention of public and government, and above all preferment and patronage in academic appointments. The battle spilled into all British economics, the staffing of other universities, the management of journals. Another personal illustration: I wrote a critique of Kaldor's 'Keynesian' theory of distribution, serious in intent but spoofing in style.[1] It was published in a journal edited by Ursula Hicks, and, by chance, it appeared just before I arrived in Cambridge for a visit. As Harry took me along to a faculty party, he warned me that the local Keynesians did not think it was funny. I was disappointed, but even more let down to find that their anger was directed not at me but at the Hickses, whom they (wrongly) suspected of putting me up to it. [It was hard for an outsider to see why John Hicks, who had done so much to strengthen the logic of the *General Theory*, should be considered an enemy.]

Harry Johnson came to Cambridge favourably predisposed to the political and economic views of the radical Keynesians.

[1] 'Toward a General Kaldorian Theory of Distribution', *Review of Economic Studies* (February, 1960).

Indeed, as an undergraduate at Toronto he had moved left of his family's liberalism, and in his undergraduate year at Cambridge he had studied under the Marxist economist Maurice Dobb. Though it was Robertson who invited Harry back to Cambridge, he had close personal ties to the Keynesians. He became a fellow of King's, and his wife Liz went to work on Keynes's papers. But, as his memoirs relate, he became progressively disillusioned with the group's economics, their influence on government policy, their impact on research and instruction at Cambridge and elsewhere, and their personal treatment of Robertson and of opponents and neutrals in the faculty.

At Manchester Professor Johnson tried to build a serious programme of graduate education, with the help of Ely Devons and Jack Johnston. The time and the setting were not right, and after three years Harry moved on to a chair at Chicago. The contrasts between American and English economics and economics training, and between Chicago and Cambridge, were striking, and all in favour of America and Chicago. In Johnson's view (*Encounter*, August 1976, p. 83) the Chicago economics department was—much more even than Harvard or Yale—the ideal environment for generating published output and for turning neophytes into scientists.

At Chicago Harry ran up against another orthodoxy, with a message quite the opposite of Cambridge Keynesianism: the beneficence of free markets and the evils of government interventions. Chicago was likewise the centre of opposition to the dominant American macroeconomics, a synthesis of Keynesian and neoclassical theory much more moderate than the extreme version of Keynesian economics prevailing in England. On both fronts the formidable Milton Friedman was the central figure, in his way as narrow and ideological as the Cambridge school. So there were struggles at Chicago too, and Harry had troubles when, as in monetary theory, his interests intersected Friedman's. In international economics he was able to carve out a rewarding, independent role. For Harry the saving grace of Chicago, certainly compared to Cambridge, was that it constituted a real community of scholars, teachers, and students committed to serious research and publication. Harry's already extraordinary pace of writing and publication accelerated during his Chicago tenure, the last eighteen years of his life.

Yet his ambition to reform British economics remained alive. The prestigious chair offered him at the London School of

Economics gave him the chance to try a third time; the setting seemed much more promising than either Cambridge or Manchester. From 1966 to 1974 he divided his time between his Chicago and London professorships, with the usual punctuation of visits to other institutions and the customary overload of extramural activity. Once again his hope of building a truly professional graduate programme with a structured curriculum and a strong research orientation was frustrated. At the LSE the trouble was not Oxbridge élitism but bureaucratic inertia, institutional poverty, and the counterpressures of the student revolts of the late 1960s. Once again Harry was discouraged by the general tone of British economics and by the government's economic policies. With a blast that attracted much public attention, he resigned from LSE and from Britain in 1974. Thereafter, he supplemented his two terms a year at Chicago with one in Geneva.

When Harry Johnson joined the Chicago faculty, many of us hoped his example and influence would make that department more moderate and eclectic. Perhaps they did, but not in ways visible to the outsider. The influence of Chicago on Johnson's thought is also hard to assess. The most likely guess is that Chicago was a congenial and supportive environment for trends in Johnson's thought already well established. In England he had moved a long way in conservative directions, mainly from conviction but partly in provocative reaction to the dominant intellectual climate. A similar reaction to the Chicago climate is not evident, but Chicago doctrines were not then as powerful nationally as Cambridge orthodoxy had been in the United Kingdom.

Harry was never an evangelist for free enterprise or any other ideology. Many of his writings have the 'no free lunch' messages so often stressed by Chicago economists, but that is no Midway monopoly. Harry's general preference for market solutions came out most strongly in international contexts. All along he had been impatient with the counterproductive illusions of protectionism, in both advanced and developing countries. He also opposed international commodity agreements and scorned UNCTAD agitation for a 'new economic order'.

On an important issue of scientific methodology Johnson stood squarely against a Chicago dogma, Friedman's 'methodology of positive economics'. The principle is that hypotheses are to be judged by their ultimate implications and tested by comparing those implications with observed facts, not by the plausibility or realism of the assumptions or of the intermediate mechanisms connecting the assumptions to the conclusions. Thus, Friedman's monetarist propositions relied very little on deriving the quantity theory of money from the assumed and observed behaviour of economic agents, but relied a great deal on economy-wide 'reduced-form' correlations of money income or price level with money stocks. Johnson was too committed a theorist to be content with this 'black box' approach, and too sophisticated a scientist to agree that there is just one simple way to test hypotheses.

In macroeconomics and monetary theory Johnson remained eclectic. In 1971 I used my prerogative as President of the American Economic Association to designate Harry Johnson as the Richard T. Ely lecturer at the annual convention. His address 'The Keynesian Revolution and the Monetarist Counter-Revolution' (*American Economic Review*, May 1972) created quite a stir. He predicted—on sociological, methodological, and substantive grounds—that monetarism would subside, with its valid findings absorbed into the Keynesian mainstream. He said, moreover, that the Keynesian concern, Unemployment, was a more serious social problem than the monetarist concern, Inflation:

Yet from the perspective of the 1970s Johnson viewed Keynes's contribution with much less enthusiasm than in his student days and with less favour than in his famous retrospect of 1961, 'The General Theory After Twenty-five Years'. Impressed by the post-war performance of capitalism, Johnson concluded that Keynes and many Keynesians had over-generalized from the Depression, a unique decade in a long history. (Joseph Schumpeter, Harry's Harvard teacher, had said this at the time. In other respects as well, notably his unflattering attention to the sociology of politicians and intellectuals, Johnson became Schumpeterian in his later years.) Moreover, Johnson saw early on that Keynes did not provide a credible theory of inflation. The notion that inflation occurred only when aggregate demand exceeded full employment supply did not accord with experience, and in any case Keynesian theory provided no economic concept of 'full employment'. In the 1950s and 1960s the 'Phillips curve' relating inflation inversely to unemployment appeared to fill the theoretical gap. But, as Johnson acidly observed, it had no firm theoretical base either. The possibility of buying ever fuller employment with limited acceleration of inflation appeared in practice to be short-lived.

Friedman's 'natural rate of unemployment' provided both a concept of full employment and a rationale for the fragility of the Phillips trade-off. But the implied full employment involved a high rate of unemployment, difficult to interpret as wholly voluntary. Johnson noted that neither Keynesian macroeconomics nor monetarism had a satisfactory theory of the short-run division of spending between price and output. He speculated that monetarists would lose influence if they insisted on explaining away high unemployment as natural, and lose their distinctive simplicity of doctrine and policy if they undertook, along with the Keynesians, serious theoretical and empirical study of price and quantity responses to monetary impulses.

In England Johnson seemed to take a more monetarist stance, understandable in the intellectual climate he found there on his return. The dominant English Keynesian tradition, unlike the American, had been as extreme in dismissing the importance of monetary events and policies as the Chicago school was in down-grading all non-monetary factors, including fiscal policies. The British Treasury, even the Bank, followed the line. One of Harry's achievements was to bring money to the centre of the stage in British macroeconomics, organizing an inter-university monetary research group, promoting conferences, editing their proceedings. The trend he supported eventually also restored money to a central role at the Bank of England and in the United Kingdom's economic policy.

Naturally Harry's monetary interests had an important international side. His 'monetary theory of the balance of payments' commanded his attention in his last years and attracted many co-workers. The theory spells out consequences of high mobility of private funds across national currencies. National money stocks are demand-determined rather than supply-determined. If the national central bank provides less or more money than the public desires, the country will import or export money. The resulting surpluses or deficits in international payments are, therefore, monetary rather than real in origin. The system is closed by working out, under various assumptions, the global outcomes of this mechanism. This is an important insight, and Harry regarded the new theory as his most important recent work. Time will tell.

In this memoir I have emphasized Harry Johnson's English and American connections. He also played a commanding role in his native land, described in interesting detail by Reuber and Scott (*Canadian Journal of Economics*, November 1977). He visited Canada frequently, especially between 1959 and 1966 when his only chair was in North America. In 1962 he joined the research staff of the (Porter) Royal Commission on Banking and Finance, where he helped a large group of Canadian academic economists adapt modern macroeconomics and monetary theory to the Canadian setting. Thanks to these and other contacts Johnson knew the Canadian economic scene intimately. There, as in Britain and the US, his repeated message to his colleagues was: be more truly professional in what you do and how you train your successors.

Many honours came Harry's way while he lived, many others were in store for him had he lived. I repeat the list of the former given by Reuber and Scott:

He held seven honorary degrees (five from Canadian universities) and was slated to receive another from his alma mater in the summer of 1977. He was a fellow of the American Academy of Arts and Sciences, the British Academy, the Econometric Society, and the Royal Society of Canada, and an honorary member of the Japan Economic Research Center. He had served as President of the Canadian Political Science Association, Section F of the British Association, the Eastern Economic Association [U.S.], as vice-president of the American Economic Association, and as Chairman of the Association of University Teachers of Economics [U.K.]. In addition he had been awarded the Innis-Gérin medal by the Royal Society of Canada, the Prix Mondial Messim Habif by the University of Geneva, and the Bernhard Harms Prize by the University of Kiel. In 1976 he was named an Officer of the Order of Canada.

Johnson gave Wicksell Lectures, de Vries Lectures, Jahnsson Lectures, the Stamp Lecture, and many more, bringing to such assignments an incomparable blend of wisdom, history, and economic analysis, always beautifully expressed. He soon would have had his turn as President of the American Economic Association. A Nobel Prize? He was the people's choice within the profession. Though selection committees stress quantum innovations, sooner or later they would surely have rewarded the massive incremental and synthetic advancement of knowledge that Johnson achieved.

Harry's main honour, the one that meant the most to him, was the affection and respect of his profession. After his stroke in 1973, worldwide messages of concern and encouragement supported his determined recovery and his brave resumption of accustomed activity. Since his death his fellow scholars have poured out their grief and gratitude not only privately but in an unparalleled volume of tributes and memorials in all the many journals, societies, colleges and universities, and other groups that felt Harry was one of their own. What would please him most are the new research papers his example and memory have inspired.

James Tobin

THE NOBEL MILTON

The happy timing was doubtless inadvertent, but perhaps an invisible hand led the Nobel jury to honour Milton Friedman in 1976, the twin bicentenaries of Adam Smith's "The Wealth of Nations" and Thomas Jefferson's Declaration of Independence. The "system of natural liberty" common to those great documents is the inspiration for the libertarian political economy of which Friedman is the most effective contemporary exponent. The economics profession, the makers of government policy and the general public have been swinging in his direction—thanks partly to events which have made his audience receptive, but also to Friedman's awesome powers of persuasion.

The Nobel award was, of course, for Friedman's contribution to economic science not his formidable ideological and political impact. The prize was certainly merited. Of the many reasons I will mention only four. In his 1945 study of professional incomes, with Simon Kuznets, Friedman was a pioneer in developing and applying the fruitful idea of "human capital." In 1957, Friedman showed how the distinction between permanent and transient income resolved puzzles in consumption and saving statistics for whole economies and for samples of households. His monumental monetary history (in 1963, with Anna Schwartz) is an indispensable treatise packed with theoretic insights and policy analysis as well as historical and statistical narrative. Today nobody can consider trade-offs between unemployment and inflation without confronting the "natural rate of unemployment." Although others had anticipated the idea, Friedman's version, in his brilliant 1967 American Economic Association presidential address, is the classic statement.

The Economist has asked me to comment on Friedman's general impact, rather than on the impressive contributions that earned the Nobel award. The consuming attention he commands from fellow economists

The Nobel prize for economics has been awarded to Chicago University's Professor Milton Friedman. We asked two eminent academic economists to comment on his accomplishments: Professor James Tobin of Yale, one of Friedman's foremost critics, and Professor Harry Johnson, himself now of Chicago University, and broadly sympathetic with Friedmanite economics.

Reprinted by permission from The Economist (23 October 1976):94–95.

and the influence he enjoys worldwide arise from his twin crusades for limited government intervention and for monetarism.

Friedman's over-riding objective is to minimise state compulsion of private individuals—to pay taxes, serve in armies, attend designated schools, sell or buy at prescribed prices, belong to trade unions and in general refrain from mutually agreeable contracts with other citizens. He would minimise both the economic size of the public sector and the scope for government activities. Freedom from state coercion is the ultimate political value, and competitive markets transform the self-interested economic actions of individuals into social benefits.

Friedman, like Adam Smith, has not lacked vulnerable mercantilist targets like tariffs, import quotas, foreign exchange restrictions, farm price supports, rent controls, minimum wages and interest rate ceilings. The notion that governments should intervene to raise the prices of what deserving voters sell, or lower the prices of what they buy, is a durable political fallacy. Friedman is at his best showing—sometimes with exaggerated certainty—that these are inefficient remedies and often even damage the groups whose plights are the rationalisation for the policies. Most economists of all persuasions basically agree.

Nevertheless, many of us are sceptical of Friedman's other claims for the superiority of unfettered market outcomes. There are several reasons.

First, Friedman pays little attention to market imperfections and failures. He is not a notable supporter of government efforts to preserve or promote competition or to improve consumer information. He does not, for example, seem bothered by the possibility that firms will, even from miscalculation of long-run self-interest, market hazardous products or provide unsafe working conditions. He has no solution except voluntary agreement among the parties for the "externalities"—pollution, environmental damage, congestion—that are an increasing feature of economic life. To economists less obsessed with the view that government is the coercive enemy of freedom, government seems the natural agency for arriving at the complex social compacts needed.

Second, Friedman's hard libertarian line is little tempered by egalitarian sentiment. Henry Simons, an early Chicago apostle of laissez-faire, advocated progressive income taxation to accomplish, directly and efficiently, the redistributions which motivate misguided intervention in specific markets. Friedman advocates less progressivity. And though he is rightly credited with the negative income tax device, his proposal was a modest one designed largely to clear the decks of other transfer programmes.

Third, Friedman is unwilling to trust the institutions of representative democracy to determine the size of the public sector and the allocation of resources of public goods. He vigorously suports constitutional limitations on state expenditure and taxes. Somehow the preferences of citizens as voters are not accorded the same respect as their preferences as individual consumers.

Money Matters

The crusade for monetarism began with the slogan "money matters." A healthy corrective to depression scepticism, but not really controversial. Keynes believed in the potency of monetary policy in normal times, and postwar American Keynesians always stressed this importance. In Britain, however, the Radcliffe committee perpetuated the obsolete view that financial flows and interest rates are a sideshow. Over the years monetarism has developed into all-out opposition to Keynesian stabilisation policy, i.e., to discretionary, compensatory use of fiscal and monetary measures. Friedman's alternative is steady growth of the stock of money at a rate that would finance sustainable growth of production with stable prices. Friedman has revived pre-Keynesian faith in the automatic stability of the system. Monetarists claim that an active "stabilisation" policy causes more fluctuations than it cures.

Friedman has never provided a convincing theoretical foundation for his policy prescription. A doctrine which enthrones the stock of money as the sovereign determinant of money, income and prices might be expected to offer a clear conceptual basis for a sharp distinction of "money" from its substitutes and for ignoring systematic and random variation of monetary velocity. Instead Friedman relies on a series of simple empirical correlations between money stocks, variously defined, and money income aggregates or price levels.

These correlations cannot erase significant variations of velocity. In any case causal inferences from such correlations are hazardous. Statistical relations of money and income are based largely on observation when central banks, according to Friedman's own criticism of them, supplied money to accommodate the economy's demands. As recent experience already suggests, past correlations may be unreliable when money stocks are used as controls. Moreover the extraordinary non-policy shocks suffered by the world economies in recent years may be nature's ironical response to the fashionable faith that stable policy means stable economy.

Monetarism converts long-run equilibrium conditions into short-run policy recommendations. Natural rate theory says that no permanent reduction of unemployment can be gained by accepting higher inflation.

Yet anti-inflationary policies entail, as the current travails of the world economy exemplify, severe and protracted social costs in lost output and employment. These "transitional" costs do not weigh heavily in the value scales of monetarists, though Friedman acknowledges them more squarely than many of his evangelical followers. Given their free market ideology, he and they will not entertain wage and price controls or other incomes policies as alternatives or complements to anti-inflationary monetary restrictions. Here the two crusades converge. If they triumph, democratic capitalist economies will suffer high unemployment and slow real growth for some years to come.

Book Reviews

Galbraith Redux

Economics and the Public Purpose. By John Kenneth Galbraith. *Boston: Houghton Mifflin, 1973. Pp. xvi, 334. $10.00.*

Reviewed by James Tobin†

John Kenneth Galbraith is surely the best known economist in the world today and, textbook writers aside, probably the most read economist of all time. *Economics and the Public Purpose*[1] is his mature restatement and extension of the themes of *The New Industrial State* (1967 and 1971)[2] and *The Affluent Society* (1958),[3] both best sellers. The book deserves serious and candid review, and that is what this reviewer, a long-time friend and admirer of the author, is going to give it.

I

As the title says, Galbraith is writing as much about economics as about the American economy. On page after page he contrasts his picture of the economy to that of "neoclassical economics,"[4] and refers derisively to the blindness, obtuseness, and irrelevance of the bulk of his professional colleagues. Worse yet, he finds, economists' sins of omission and commission serve the ruling corporate "technostructure."[5] Although Galbraith does not quite charge conscious venality, he does suggest that economists are protecting "intellectual and pecuniary capital"[6]—this is strong language from the 1972 President of the American Economic Association.

The attack is familiar from Galbraith's earlier books. By now the running battle with neoclassical foes is pretty tiresome. Most of

† Sterling Professor of Economics, Yale University.
1. J. GALBRAITH, ECONOMICS AND THE PUBLIC PURPOSE (1973) [hereinafter cited by page number only].
2. J. GALBRAITH, THE NEW INDUSTRIAL STATE (2d ed. 1971).
3. J. GALBRAITH, THE AFFLUENT SOCIETY (1958).
4. *See* pp. 11-18.
5. *See* p. 82.
6. P. 312.

From *The Yale Law Journal* 83(6) (May 1974):1291–1303. Reprinted by permission of The Yale Law Journal Company and Fred B. Rothman & Company.

Galbraith's readers, of course, know nothing of economics save what he tells them. Even noneconomist readers must wish Galbraith would, for once, make a straightforward argument without foils, straw men, and whipping boys.

There is, goodness knows, plenty of blindness, obtuseness, irrelevance, and parochial scholasticism in the discipline of economics. It is just not true, however, that the profession insists on analyzing the American economy as if it were an ideal type described by Adam Smith. Modern economics does not contend that competitive markets without public intervention do or could achieve maximum satisfaction of the wants of "sovereign" consumers. Anyone who takes a freshman course, reads a textbook, peruses the journals, or scans the titles of new publications can quickly satisfy himself that the profession does not ignore the salient features of the modern economy stressed by Professor Galbraith, including conglomerates, multinationals, monopolies, oligopolies, market failures, environmental "externalities." Most work of economists is highly empirical and closely related to practical issues of policy, such as utility regulation, manpower training, pollution, education, exchange rates, and property taxes.

Galbraith identifies contemporary economics with neoclassical economic theory. Innocent readers have a right to know what "neoclassical" means. Economists have always been looking for a theory of value, a theory which explains the relative prices at which commodities and resources are traded for one another. Classical economists—Adam Smith, David Ricardo, John Stuart Mill, Karl Marx—sought the answer solely in production costs. Neoclassical economists in the late 19th century—William Stanley Jevons, Karl Menger, Leon Walras, Alfred Marshall—showed that relative values are determined by demand as well as supply, tastes as well as technology, subject utility as well as cost.

A great intellectual achievement of the neoclassical tradition has been to spell out what might be called the pure logic of relative scarcity. For given tastes, technologies, and resource availabilities, there is in theory a price for every commodity and every factor of production, a price indicative of its relative scarcity. Corresponding to these prices are determinate outputs and allocations of all resources and all commodities. When elementary students learn that a commodity has an "opportunity cost" both in production and consumption, they encounter a simple version of these ideas. The notion of opportunity cost is indispensable for clear thinking about pollution control, gasoline rationing, university finance, subway fares, supersonic transports, and a host of other practical problems.

The "general equilibrium" solution of the allocation problem could, in principle, be found and implemented by a socialist planning board; under certain conditions it can be achieved by competitive markets. The elegance and power of this insight has attracted the best minds of economics over the years, and the logic of relative scarcity has been clarified, refined, and extended. No one understands its limitations better than its most sophisticated practitioners.[7]

Neoclassical theory itself explains why market results cannot be regarded as socially optimal. First, markets are not competitive. Second, even competitive markets fail to handle the uncertain future, "externalities" like environmental damage, and communally used goods and services. Third, market processes may result in socially unacceptable inequalities of income. Fourth, "consumer sovereignty" must frequently be limited to protect citizens from their own ignorance or shortsightedness and from the irresponsibilities of others. On all these matters a great deal of theoretical and applied work proceeds, unnoticed by Galbraith.

Vulgar apologists for private enterprise do, of course, invoke the "free market" to justify the privileges of the rich and powerful. Galbraith is dead right to object. But it does not follow that every interference with the market proposed by Congressman Wright Patman, Secretary Earl Butz, the Federal Power Commission, the Texas Railroad Commission, or Galbraith himself therefore is justified. We have to choose among imperfect alternatives. One does not have to be a devout disciple of Chicago economic liberalism to prefer market-clearing by price to gas pump queues, rent controls, wheat acreage restrictions and resale price maintenance, or to regard cash transfers as a more efficient and equitable way to redistribute income than farm price supports, minimum wages, and 35-cent subway fares.

There is a big difference between Galbraithian and straight economics, though not the one that Galbraith depicts. He is the leading exemplar of adjectival or denominative economics, creative nomenclature for the phenomenon described by the author. Galbraith's names are suggestive—technostructure, planning system,[8] bureaucratic symbiosis.[9] The names make readers think they understand the institutions. Conventional economists, instead, are obsessed with mechanism.

7. *See, e.g.,* Arrow, *Limited Knowledge and Economic Analysis*, 64 AM. ECON. REV. 1 (1974) (1973 presidential address to the Am. Econ. Ass'n).
8. P. 44.
9. P. 143.

They like to build models that specify the behavior of the various actors in an economic drama and trace the outcomes of their interactions.

For Galbraith the economy is as simple as a bicycle; any intelligent, unbrainwashed observer can see at once how it works. For the straight economist, the economy is more like the human body; a very complex and often baffling network of interlocking systems. Galbraith rarely offers a hypothesis that might be tested and conceivably refuted by observation. New names and colorful adjectives are not testable propositions: Who is to say whether corporate managers and technicians constitute a technostructure? Perhaps because he believes truth is easy to come by (if only vested interests in falsehood are overcome), Galbraith offers little evidence for the propositions he does assert. By contrast, a conventional economist tries to state testable, refutable hypotheses. He is generally impressed with the difficulty of empirical verification, and he goes to great pains to tease information from recalcitrant and ambiguous data.

Consider, for example, Galbraith's description of the United States as a dual economy, split between the "planning" and "market" systems.[10] This distinction is the central theme of the book, and it is important and illuminating. But the observation is only a beginning. Any recent Ph.D. from M.I.T. would embed it in a model which takes account of trade and mobility between the two sectors. Solved or simulated, the model would suggest some observable effects on employment, wages, prices, inflation.[11] With luck the credibility of the model could be statistically checked; it might turn out to be an accurate reflection of reality. No one says Galbraith has to play this game, though one hopes he might have students who would. But does he have to denigrate the serious scientific economists who do engage in this kind of work? The answer is no. It is unbecoming, unwarranted, and unnecessary.

The dismal science is not noted for literary merit. But the style of Galbraith's prose has aroused no inconsiderable admiration. Style and substance are in symbiotic relationship. The style distracts the reader from the substance. For an author this will be perceived as an agreeable circumstance. That sentences are frequently begun with substantive clauses will not escape the attentive reader's notice. Nor

10. *See* pp. 38-51.
11. *See, e.g.,* A. OKUN, UPWARD MOBILITY IN A HIGH PRESSURE ECONOMY 207-52 (Brookings Paper on Economic Activity No. 1, 1973). Of course Okun's Ph.D. is neither recent nor from M.I.T.

is the author a slavish devotee of neoclassical rhetoric. The passive voice is much favored. The double negative is not abhorred. Reviewers' criticisms are explicitly predicted. The reader is invited to regard the fulfillment of those predictions as proof of the author's thesis. The overall tone is one of subtle irony. To sustain subtle irony for 324 pages is a task of no slight sophistication. This technostrategy cannot be too much admired.

II

The argument of the book will be summarized[12] in nine points, each followed by the reviewer's comments.

1. *The Two Systems.* The private enterprise economy of the United States is about evenly divided between the planning system and the market system. The planning system is the world of the thousand largest corporations; the market system contains the smaller corporations, unincorporated businesses, farmers, self-employed professionals and artisans, and merchants of vice. In advanced capitalism the "unequal development"[13] of the two systems has resulted in an "inequality"[14] of power which favors the planning system at the expense of the market system.

Comment. The planning system, as defined by Galbraith, does not comprise as much of the economy as Galbraith says it does. In 1969, private business originated 82 percent of national income; the rest was produced by governments. Of privately produced national income, corporations were the source of 68 percent. There were 1.7 million active corporations, of which the 1,112 largest did 34.5 percent of corporate business. Thus the planning system apparently accounts for about 23 percent of private business activity, or 19 percent of total national income.[15]

---

12. This summary leaves out tangential but topical chapters on women and households, the environment, and the international economy. According to Galbraith, capitalist progress made servants too expensive and became dependent on "converting women to menial personal service" in their own households. P. 31. Galbraith favors liberation and equality. For the environment, Galbraith endorses "explicit and unyielding," p. 290, legal limitations on environmental damage and scornfully dismisses the taxes and prices beloved of neoclassical economists. As for the international economy, Galbraith has no use for monetary tinkering or tinkerers; he rightly says there is no substitute for coordinated planning, p. 322, and most tinkerers would agree.

13. P. 77.

14. *Id.*

15. Of the 1,112 largest corporations, by asset size, 581 were financial companies. Galbraith does not exclude them from his calculations, pp. 42-43, though there is a case for doing so. The 1,079 largest nonfinancial corporations did 40 percent of nonfinancial corporate business, or about 23 percent of national income. If corporations are classified by size of business receipts rather than assets, the 1,137 largest non-

1295

In any event, Galbraith thinks the planning system is too large. Sometimes he gives the impression that ever-increasing disproportion is endemic to our political economy,[16] although he does not flatly say so. Aggregate concentration figures for 1969, however, are much the same as those for 1957. In that year the 1,129 largest of 0.95 million active corporations accounted for 34 percent of corporate business, 23 percent of private business activity, or 19 percent of total national income. Concentration has increased, nevertheless, in the sense that 1,112 companies are a much smaller proportion of the population of enterprises than 1,129 were in 1957.

The concentration of economic activity in the 100 largest corporations has steadily increased since 1945 but at a much slower rate recently. This may be true of the share of the 500 largest manufacturers as well;[17] their sales grew 187 percent from 1955 to 1970, while gross national product grew 145 percent, but the increases between 1965 and 1970, 45 percent and 43 percent respectively, were quite comparable.

Membership in "X largest" lists is not constant. Of the 100 largest industrial corporations, an average of 1.7 are displaced each year.[18]

On trends in concentration in particular markets, there is a lively statistical debate. Thanks to the conglomerate movement, market concentrations have risen less rapidly than aggregate concentration. Some students say that market concentration has not been increasing at all.[19]

None of these subjects is seriously discussed in the book.

2. *The Technostructure's Obsession with Growth.* The business firms of economics textbooks and of the market system seek to maximize the profits of their owner-managers. But the large firms of the planning system are ruled by their managerial technostructures, not by their owners. Individually and jointly, the technostructures' objective is to grow as fast as possible while making decent minimum profits for the shareholders.

Comment. As Galbraith acknowledges, the divorce of ownership and control is an old story, suggested by Thorstein Veblen[20] and

financial corporations did 44 percent of corporate business, or about 25 percent of national income. I cannot reproduce Galbraith's estimate that the planning system accounts for half of private economic activity, which would imply more than 40 percent of national income.

16. *Cf.* p. 105.
17. *See* M. Scherer, Industrial Market Structure and Economic Performance 41-44 (1970).
18. *See id.* at 48-49.
19. *See id.* at 50-63.
20. *See* T. Veblen, The Engineers and the Price System (1921).

documented by Adolph A. Berle and Gardiner Means.[21] William Baumol[22] and Robin Marris[23] argued that corporate management seeks to maximize growth subject to a minimum profit constraint. Galbraith presents no evidence for the truth of this theory. Since growth and profits are usually correlated, the growth hypothesis is not easy to test against profit maximization. Incentive compensation of executives generally is geared to profit performance and share values. But it is also undeniable that managers of large organizations are, other things equal, better paid than those of small organizations.

3. *Planning as a Technological Imperative.* The new industrial state is the inevitable consequence of modern technology. Large corporations—large socialist enterprises, for that matter—generally produce goods (not services) with complex technology requiring large investment commitments long in advance of production and sale. That is why they must plan and why technicians and managers who do the planning have all the power. Failure is an unacceptable risk. So the firm controls its environment. It makes sure that consumers and governments will buy its products. It generates its own investment funds to avoid dependence on financiers. It captures control of needed raw materials and supplies. It arranges a sympathetic political climate. And so on.

Comment. Are the risks and lead times of modern technology exceptional? How about the lead times and risk faced by capitalists who sent sailing ships to the Far East or began laying railroad track across wild prairies?

Are large corporations omnipotent and invulnerable? Young Louis Brandeis made his mark by assailing the corporate octopus that dominated New England financially, politically, and socially: the *New Haven Railroad!* Powerful firms cannot always bend customers to their will. DuPont lost millions on Corfam; the Edsel is only the most striking example of an automobile promotion that failed; and Boeing is only one of many firms to find the Pentagon an inconstant customer. Nor are all large corporations immune from capital markets. (None of them would be if they sacrificed profits to growth in the manner Galbraith describes.) Of the 552 largest nonfinancial corporations, 164 are public utilities, which borrow heavily and constantly.

Galbraith's typical corporation is in manufacturing, a relatively de-

---

21. A. Berle & G. Means, The Modern Corporation and Private Property (1932).
22. *See* W. Baumol, Business Behavior, Value and Growth (1959).
23. *See* R. Marris, The Economic Theory of "Managerial" Capitalism (1964).

1297

clining sector of the economy. The truth, I suspect, is that most of
the time Galbraith is writing about General Motors, a deserving
enough target but hardly typical.

4. *The Public Sector.* The technostructure enjoys a symbiotic relationship with the federal executive and bureaucracy, especially the
Pentagon, and with strategic senior committee chairmen in Congress.[24]
Public expenditure programs which support the planning system prosper. Those which help the market system and the general public
are shortchanged; their only political support comes from powerless
rank and file members of Congress.

Comment. Since the publication of *The Affluent Society* in 1958
—perhaps because of it, who knows?—public civilian use of goods and
services has increased from 10 percent of gross national product
to 19.5 percent. In addition, over the same period governmental
transfer payments to individuals have grown from 6 percent to 10.5
percent of personal income. These trends have not been deflected
by either Vietnam or the Nixon presidency. Civilian government
has grown fast, faster than the economy. Meanwhile defense has declined from 9 percent of gross national product to 6 percent.

Galbraith's readers will not find these figures or any other recognition that the civilian public sector is not as undernourished now
as when the earlier book voiced so eloquently his well merited complaint. Well, aren't many public purposes still shortchanged, relative to the needs? Aren't streets still dirty, parks unsafe, schools ineffective, inner cities blighted, mass transits abysmal, poor people
ill-fed, mental hospitals disgraceful, jails medieval, and the arts—
very important to Galbraith—neglected?

It's all too true, but the morals are not the ones Galbraith leads
the reader to draw. First, the problems are tougher than anyone
imagined or admitted. Schools, neighborhoods, cultures, transportation systems are not that easy to turn around. Money is necessary
but not sufficient. Second, legislators will support the public sector,
but what public sector? The sky's the limit for social security and
agricultural subsidies, not because these programs appeal to the
technostructure but because they, unlike jails and mental hospitals,
have irresistible constituencies.

Nothing in Galbraith's political theory prepares us for these distortions of priority, which are not the will of the corporate establishment but the outcome of pluralistic politics. That same politics

24. *See generally* pp. 134-45, 155-63.

has not reduced defense spending enough to suit Galbraith or me, but cuts in weapons orders have thrown major Pentagon contractors into insolvency.

5. *The Two Systems and Market Power.* Jobs are secure and well paid in the planning system.[25] The technostructure has long since made its peace with the unions, knowing that labor costs can easily be passed on to consumers. But those who cannot gain admission to the planning system are relegated to the market system. Some are self-employed, some are hired workers, but all are overworked, underpaid, and untenured. The market system really operates like the neoclassical model, with competition and flexible prices. The results are disastrous, in part because the planning system imposes severe terms of trade on its powerless suppliers and customers.

Comment. The dual labor market observation rings true and commands widespread agreement. However, by no means all preferred jobs with restricted access are within Galbraith's planning system—consider construction workers, municipal employees, and other well-organized crafts.

The claim that the planning system can with impunity dictate prices to consumers and to the market system is less credible. Here as elsewhere Galbraith artfully dodges the problem of aggregation. The 1,000-firm planning system is not just a single corporation writ large. Galbraith himself gives the various technostructures no credit or blame for coordination; in fact he points out that their individual plans frequently fail to mesh.

The sector as a whole may be able to pass on cost increases, simply because the government, fearing unemployment, inflates demand as needed. But this macroeconomic possibility does *not* mean that a company is assured that its customers will still be there if it individually raises prices. Likewise, large corporations are often competing with each other in buying supplies and services from the market system.

6. *Antitrust and Socialist Alternatives.* Competition can never be enforced in the planning sector. The antitrust myth, kept alive by economists, serves the technostructure by diverting attention and energy from real solutions.[26] Anyway, the problem is not that the planning system is too small, as conventional monopoly theory tells us, but that it is much too large. Galbraith recommends (a) na-

25. *See* pp. 161-62.
26. *See* pp. 215-17.

1299

tionalization of big government contractors and of other "fully mature corporations"[27] (as well as of industries—medical care, transportation, residential construction—where private enterprise has clearly failed),[28] (b) limitation of executive rewards by aggressive unionism (white collar as well as blue), by tax reform, and by government regulation,[29] (c) permanent wage and price controls.[30]

Comment. Certainly it is hard to be optimistic about antitrust policy. Its history is full of decisions which actually impede competition,[31] while blatant concentrations without redeeming economic virtue remain unscathed. Prosecutors and judges are often innocent of economics. Federal administrations are timid. Solutions are genuinely difficult. But fear of antitrust prosecution is a constraint on corporate policy, and we had better not relax it.

The privileges of workers in large parts of the planning system and elsewhere are protected by barriers to entry of other workers, erected by unions with support from employers and governments. This is a topic Galbraith completely avoids. There are no unkind words about trade unions in this book though in the heat of politics Galbraith has been known to speak unfavorably of George Meany.

If some industries in the planning system are too large, as Galbraith alleges, it is because they indulge, not in too much price competition, quite the contrary, but in too much nonprice competition. Galbraith dismisses as "illiberal" any ban on advertising.[32] But, as the present neoclassical liberal reviewer has long advocated, it would be feasible, and not illiberal, to limit the tax deductibility of advertising and sales expenses. As to Galbraith's complaint that top executive salaries and other perquisites are unconscionable and must be brought under control, I can only say Amen. This, too, could be handled in the tax law.

What is to be gained by nationalization of large "mature" corporations if, as Galbraith observes, the technostructure would remain in command? Something would be lost—discipline of management by adverse stock market judgments and possible takeovers.

27. P. 272.
28. Pp. 179-81.
29. Pp. 166-70.
30. Pp. 170-71.
31. *See, e.g.,* Utah Pie Co. v. Continental Baking Co., 386 U.S. 685 (1967). Continental Baking Co. broke into Utah Pie's Salt Lake City market with cheaper frozen apple pies than those offered by Utah Pie. The Court found price discrimination in violation of § 2(a) of the Clayton Act.
32. Pp. 229-30.

Anyway, Galbraith's socialist proposals are too casual to be taken seriously. Galbraith does not tell us how the investment needs of a nationalized automobile company would be determined and financed, how industries would operate half-nationalized and half-private, how collective bargaining would be kept out of Washington politics, or other details. Galbraith is certainly right that government is bound to have a big role in transportation and medicine, but again he does not face the really difficult problems, which will remain whether or not the industries are socialized.

7. *Planning the Market System.* The principal remedy for the unequal development and inequality of the two systems is to equip the market system with countervailing power.[33] Let small businessmen combine to "stabilize prices and output."[34] Let government regulate prices and output when, as in agriculture, producers cannot combine on their own. Encourage unions; universalize and boost the minimum wage. Encourage international commodity agreements; do not on principle deny tariff protection to the market system. Provide government support for the educational, capital, and technological needs of the market system.

This program will reduce output and employment in the market system. Indeed, that is its purpose—to eliminate production which does not yield its producers a decent income. So there must be alternative income guaranteed for those who are unable or unwilling to find jobs. Galbraith evidently has in mind a negative income tax; his illustration is a guarantee of $5000 for a family of five.[35]

Comment. This is the heart of the book. And this is where most of Galbraith's fellow economists will disagree most strongly.

It really is a letdown to go through a supposedly revolutionary book and to learn toward the end that salvation lies in those unlamented inventions of the early New Deal, the NRA and AAA.[36] In brief, Galbraith would have us each in toll booths where we could share in tolls from passers-by, not because they choose to pay for what we can produce but because they have no alternative. Yet there will not be enough toll booths to go around, so the rest of us will live on the dole. It is not just an inefficient prospect; it is unfair and it is terribly dreary.

Today people in the "market system" are excluded from com-

33. *See* pp. 252-63.
34. P. 256.
35. P. 263.
36. *See* pp. 252-63.

1301

petition for the fruits of the "planning system." The solution is not to remake the "market system" with the worst imaginable noncompetitive features. The answer is to break down barriers to equal opportunity throughout the economy.

8. *Macroeconomic Policy.* The planning system is inherently unstable. It is subject to failures of aggregate demand, to excess capacity and unemployment, and to chronic inflation in every kind of economic weather. For stabilizing demand, fiscal policy is the answer. Raise government expenditure when demand is deficient; raise taxes when it is excessive. The asymmetry is a virtue; the policy will gradually raise the share of the public sector in the economy. When the day for a symmetrical policy arrives, "it will be sufficiently noticed and celebrated."[37]

Monetary policy should almost never be used. Keep a permanent level and structure of interest rates, "on the low side."[38] The reason is that monetary policy is socially regressive, hitting the market system, notably home building, but not the planning system.

The aim of demand policy is to avoid all but frictional unemployment in the planning system and to stabilize prices in the market system. But demand policy is not enough. To prevent inflation, beyond a slow drift to accommodate relative price adjustments, permanent controls of wage bargains and of planning system prices are required.

Comment. The chapter on macroeconomic policy is analytically weak. For example, Galbraith confuses marginal and average propensities to save.[39] And, after saying that rich people and corporations do not spend anyway, he tells us that the more we rely on taxing them the more stabilizing the tax system will be.[40] More important, he throws away so many policy instruments that he leaves policymakers with no practical way to stabilize aggregate demand. Fiscal measures, especially expenditures, cannot be adjusted fast enough.

Galbraith does not explain the basic causes of instability and chronic inflation. The consistency of his two criteria for fiscal policy —full employment in the planning system and price stability in the market system—is surely not obvious. But Galbraith does not even regard their possible incompatibility as a problem deserving discus-

---

37. P. 308.
38. P. 309.
39. P. 306.
40. *Id.*

sion. He does not defend his assertion that wage and price controls need apply only to big boys. It needs defense—recent bouts of commodity inflation have made the union-corporation spiral look like price stability. Anyway the author of this chapter evidently forgot that a few pages earlier he was refashioning the market system in the image of the planning system. Once he finishes that job, controls will surely have to be universal. Finally, Galbraith assumes without discussion that inflation is an intolerable evil, just as if he were a Zurich banker.

9. *Irrepressible Liberalism.* How can reform prevail? Belief, politics, government must be emancipated from the planning system and the myths that serve it.[41] Important among those myths is current education in economics and other subjects. Emancipation will be accomplished by "Public Cognizance" of the inherent conflict between the planning purpose and the public purpose.[42]

Comment. In the last pages of every Galbraith book hopeful liberal faith triumphs over the unrelieved cynicism of the earlier chapters. A neoclassical economist or a political philosopher might blush to introduce "public interest" as a principle of obvious, unproblematic content and application. Galbraith is as sure of the public interest, and as dedicated to it, as the most starry-eyed idealistic sophomore.

This confidence has been the foundation of Galbraith's great contributions to the public weal. He awakened the literate public to the undernourishment of the public sector. He challenged the insatiable appetite of the Pentagon and its corporate allies. To any readers of his present book who needed to be convinced that what is best for General Motors or Exxon is not usually best for the country, Galbraith has once again conveyed an important message.

41. *See* pp. 223-32, 241-51.
42. *See* p. 229.

INDEX

Money (cont.)
market, 235
stock of, 20–31
velocity of, 25
wage stickiness, 84
Moore, Geoffrey, employment ratio, 85
Morse, Chandler, 422
Multiplier, 27, 107
long run, 126
for private spending, 309
Mundell, Robert, 464, 465, 468, 473, 485, 490
IS/LM analysis, 108n

Natural rate of growth, 239, 245, 255, 378
Natural rate of unemployment, 41, 75, 86, 117, 183n, 264
Natural resources, role in economic growth, 419
Negative income tax, 510, 518–544, 574, 583, 586, 587, 592, 600, 623
basic allowance, 519
definition of income, 528
income guarantee, 520
methods of payment, 537
offsetting tax, 519
proposals, 521–524
Neoclassical theory
of corporate investment, 53
factors, 423
growth equilibrium, 395
Neo-Keynesianism
models, 92
monetary economists, 115
propositions, 104
Neo-Ricardians, 186
Neutrality of money, 112, 220, 241
New York Stock Exchange, 58
Niehans, Jurg, 455
Nominal interest rate, 204, 467
Nonaccelerating inflation rate of unemployment (NAIRU) 264–265, 269, 273, 279, 281
Nonmarket activities, 397, 405
Nordhaus, William, 38

OASOI, 596, 600, 608
Okun, Arthur, 45
"Okun gap," 77, 91
Okun's law, 20, 109
Old Age, Survivors Disability, and Health Insurance (OASDHI), 533, 542, 562, 563, 571
OPEC, 17, 90, 311
Open economy, IS curve, 252
Open market purchases, 13, 200–202, 470
of bonds, 135–136, 183, 203, 214
Opportunity cost, of time, 450

Orcutt, Guy, and Gail, 284n
OSHA, 297

Permanent income, 92–102, 110, 191
Perry, George, 32, 270n, 282
"The Economic Outlook for 1947," 32
Phelps, Edmund, 183
Phillips curve, 42–43, 76, 201, 229, 251, 264, 270, 272, 275n, 277, 291
long run, 110
short run, 44
Physical capital, 326
Pigou, A. C., 74, 75
effect, 76, 145
Pigou-Keynes-Lerner controversy, 116
Population growth, 377
and sustainable consumption, 429
Porter, Richard C., 356
Portfolio
theory, 50
wealth, 88
Poverty
gap, 572
lines, 588
measurement of, 551
urban, 551
Price index, 14, 492
bonds, 182
consumer, 290, 556
Price level, effect on demand, 76
Prices, downward stickiness, 455
Prime rate, 11
Production function
Cobb-Douglas, 176, 280, 423, 427
constant elasticity of substitution, 287, 423
constant returns to scale, 139, 350, 358, 419, 423, 424
Progressive income tax, 536, 588
Propensity to consume, lifetime, 438
Public debt illusion, 195, 196
Public goods, 374

q (ratio of market value to replacement cost), 4–8, 36, 38, 46, 52, 54
average, 7
effect of inflationary expectations, 7–8
empirical study, 58–73
formulation of IS/LM equation, 56
marginal, 7
Quantity theory of money, 21, 108
long run, 111–114

Rate of price inflation, 14–31
Rational expectations, 492–493
Real assets, 8
Real balance effect, 232
Real investment, 226
Real rate of interest, 36–40